Common Culture

COMMON CULTURE

READING AND WRITING
ABOUT AMERICAN
POPULAR CULTURE

EDITED BY

MICHAEL F. PETRACCA
MADELEINE SORAPURE

University of California, Santa Barbara

A BLAIR PRESS BOOK

Prentice Hall, Englewood Cliffs, NJ 07632

Common culture: reading and writing about American popular culture/
  edited by Michael F. Petracca, Madeleine Sorapure.
      p.   cm.
    "A Blair Press book."
    Includes bibliographical references and index.
    ISBN 0-13-299801-7
      1. Popular culture—United States.   2. United States—Social life
    and customs—1971– .   I. Petracca, Michael F.   II. Sorapure, Madeleine.
    E169.04.C65   1995
    306′.0973—dc20   94-46660
                                                                             CIP

Editorial/production supervision and interior design: Joanne Lowry, Sally Steele
Cover design: Carol Anson
Photo editor: Lorinda Morris-Nantz
Photo researcher: Rona Tuccillo
Cover photos:
  Roller Coaster and Football Game: Tony Stone Images
  Madonna and Spike Lee: Bettmann
  Cheers: Globe Photo
Buyer: Robert Anderson

Acknowledgments appear on pages 645–648, which constitute a
 continuation of the copyright page.

A BLAIR PRESS BOOK

 © 1995 by Prentice-Hall, Inc.
    A Simon & Schuster Company
    Englewood Cliffs, New Jersey 07632

Printed in the United States of America
10 9 8 7 6 5 4 3 2 1

ISBN 0-13-299801-7

Prentice-Hall International (UK) Limited, London
Prentice-Hall of Australia Pty. Limited, Sydney
Prentice-Hall Canada Inc., Toronto
Prentice-Hall of India Private Limited, New Delhi
Prentice-Hall of Japan, Inc., Tokyo
Simon & Schuster Asia Pte. Ltd., Singapore
Editora Prentice-Hall do Brasil, Ltda., Rio de Janeiro

For my sister, brave explorer of nerve pathways,
healer of wounded neckbones, dedicated
connoisseuse *of the half-hour sitcom.*

–M.F.P.

For my mother, whose eclectic tastes I inherited,
and whose grace and courage I admire.

–M.S.

PREFACE

When we started teaching composition courses that examined television, pop music, movies, and other media-generated artifacts, we looked for a text that would cover a full range of topics in the field of popular culture from a variety of theoretical perspectives. We discovered that no satisfactory text existed, and therefore we began putting together assignments and reading materials to meet our needs. From this compilation *Common Culture* emerged.

The more we've taught writing courses based on popular culture, the more convinced we've become that such courses are especially appealing for students and effective in improving their critical thinking, reading, and writing skills. Students come into the writing classroom already immersed in the culture of Beavis and Butthead, Benetton, Beastie Boys, and Barry Bonds. The advantage, then, is that we don't have to "sell" the subject matter of the course and can concentrate on the task at hand—namely, teaching students to think critically and to write clear and effective prose. Obviously, a course that panders to the lowest common denominator of students' taste would be a mindless, unproductive enterprise for all concerned. However, the underlying philosophy of a pop culture–based writing course is this: by reading, thinking, and writing about material they find inherently interesting, students develop their critical and analytical skills—skills which are, of course, crucial to their success in college.

Although students are already familiar with the many aspects of popular culture, few have directed sustained, critical thought to its influence or implications—that is, to what shopping malls might tell them about contemporary culture or to what they've actually learned from

vii

watching "The Cosby Show." Because television shows, advertisements, and music videos, for example, are highly crafted artifacts, they
are particularly susceptible to analysis; and because so much in contemporary culture is open to interpretation and controversy, students
enjoy the opportunity to articulate and argue for their own interpretations of objects and institutions in the world around them.

Although popular culture is undeniably a sexy (or, at least, lively)
subject, it has also, in the past decade, become accepted as a legitimate
object of academic discourse. While some may contend that it's frivolous to write a dissertation on "The Brady Bunch," most scholars recognize the importance of studying the artifacts and institutions of contemporary life. Popular culture is a rich field of study, drawing in
researchers from a variety of disciplines. Because it is also a very inviting field of study for students, a textbook that addresses this subject in
a comprehensive and challenging way will be especially appealing both
to them and to their writing teachers.

Common Culture contains an introductory chapter that walks students through one assignment—in this case, focusing on the Barbie
Doll—with step-by-step instruction in reading carefully and writing effectively. The chapters that follow open with a relevant and catchy cultural artifact (for example, a cartoon, an ad, an album cover) that leads
into a reader-friendly, informative introduction; a selection of engaging
essays on an issue of current interest in the field of pop culture; carefully
constructed reading and discussion questions; and writing assignments
after each reading and at the end of the chapter.

Common Culture approaches the field of popular culture by dividing
it into its constituent parts. The book contains chapters on advertising,
television, music, news, sports, movies, and leisure. Most of the chapters are divided into two parts: the first presents essays that address the
topic generally, while the second offers essays that explore a specific aspect of the topic in depth. For example, in the chapter on advertising,
the essays in the first group discuss theories and strategies of advertising, while later essays explore images of women and men in ads.

We've purposely chosen readings that are accessible and thought-
provoking, while avoiding those that are excessively theoretical or
jargon-ridden. The readings in this book have the added advantage of
serving as good models for students' own writing; they demonstrate a
range of rhetorical approaches, such as exposition, analysis, and argu-
mentation, and they offer varying levels of sophistication and difficulty
in terms of content and style. Similarly, the suggested discussion and
writing topics move from relatively basic concerns to tasks that require

a greater degree of critical skill. Because of this range, instructors using *Common Culture* can easily adapt the book to meet the specific needs of their students.

Acknowledgments

As California instructors and eager participants in the growth-and-awareness movement, we'd like first to thank each other for straying rarely from the path of psychic good will and harmony, and then to thank the universe for raining beneficence and light upon this project. And while on the subject of beneficence and light, we'd like to thank our editor at Blair Press, Nancy Perry, who radiates these qualities and without whose wisdom, largesse, and good humor we would have fallen into deep despair. Thanks, furthermore, to Mark Gallaher, our development editor, who called us at all hours, morning and night, reminding us that we were *slightly* behind schedule and always did so with a cheery and nonjudgmental tone. He contributed much to the continuity and organization of the book. LeeAnn Einert, editorial assistant at Blair Press, made our job easier by attending to countless details of text and layout.

We want to thank Muriel Zimmerman, Director of the Writing Program at UCSB, for lending moral and intellectual support to this project. Johanna Blakely and Bonnie Beedles suggested several of the readings we included here, and Rita Raley assisted in formulating end-of-reading questions. Thanks also to Larry Behrens and Sheridan Blau for lending their expertise in the area of textbook publishing.

Finally, Madeleine would like to thank Tasos Mastroyiannis for his support and good humor during this project. Michael would like to thank his significant other, Jan Ingram, who initiated him into the glories of "The Young and the Restless" along with other pop culture artifacts too numerous to mention.

Michael F. Petracca
Madeleine Sorapure

CONTENTS

CHAPTER 2
Advertising
35

CHAPTER 3
Television
150

CHAPTER 4
Popular Music
255

CHAPTER 5
Sports
348

CHAPTER 6
Journalism
408

CHAPTER 7
Movies
496

CHAPTER 8
Leisure
564

1

READING AND
WRITING ABOUT
AMERICAN
POPULAR CULTURE

If any of these names and phrases sounds familiar—and it would be a great surprise if some didn't—it's because we spend our lives immersed in popular culture. There's no escaping it. Like hydrogen atoms and common-cold viruses, pop culture is everywhere. You absorb it at home watching television, listening to the stereo, or reading a magazine or newspaper; passing billboards or listening to the radio on the street; chatting over coffee at work or having a burger with friends; going out to movies and dance clubs, health spas, fast-food restaurants, shopping malls and sports arenas; even noticing the graffiti that glares out at you on building facades and highway overpasses.

In fact, unless you're isolated in a mountaintop cave, you can hardly avoid the influence of popular culture. Television, radio, newspapers,

1

and magazines shape your ideas and behavior; like family, friends, and school, pop culture is part of your learning environment, supplying ready-made images, ideas, and patterns of behavior that you draw from, consciously or unconsciously, as you live your daily life. Exactly how you learn and just what you learn may not be all that certain, but it is undeniable that popular culture is one of your most powerful teachers.

One reason to study popular culture is that, by paying closer attention to this daily bombardment of information, you can think more critically about how it affects you and others. You may start by asking relatively simple questions—"Do I really need to be 'zestfully clean' today?"—and work your way to far more significant ones—"How can we keep young women from starving themselves in their desire to conform to the images they see in advertisements?" Analyzing pop culture with a critical eye allows you to begin to free yourself from the manipulation of the media; it is an important step toward living an examined life.

What Is Popular Culture?

What do we mean by popular culture? The term may at first seem contradictory. *Popular*, in its broadest sense, means "of the people," while we often associate *culture* with refinement and intellectual superiority, "the best which has been thought and said in the world," as Matthew Arnold put it. We might ask how culture, traditionally reserved for the elite, the educated, and the upper class, can simultaneously belong to the common mass of humanity.

One way to resolve this seeming dilemma is to think of culture in an anthropological sense, as the distinct practices, artifacts, institutions, customs, and values of a particular social group. This is the way, for instance, that we distinguish the culture of the United States in the late twentieth century from the culture of our great-grandparents or from that of societies in other times and places.

We can also define popular culture by distinguishing it from its counterparts: *high culture* and *folk culture.*

High culture consists of the artifacts traditionally considered worthy of study by university academics and other educated people: classical music by composers such as Beethoven and Brahms; "fine" art from the impressionists and expressionists; literature and philosophy written by the likes of Shakespeare and Sartre.

At the other end of the spectrum, folk culture refers to artifacts created by a specific community or ethnic group, usually a relatively isolated nontechnological society such as the pygmies of Africa's Ituri forest or certain communities in our own Appalachian mountains. While high culture is primarily preserved and studied in the academy, folk culture is generally transmitted through oral communication; both, however, place a high value on tradition, on artifacts produced in the past, and on the shared history of the community.

By contrast, popular culture encompasses the most immediate and contemporary elements in our lives—elements which are often subject to rapid changes in a highly technological world in which people are brought closer and closer by the ubiquitous mass media. Pop culture offers a common ground, as the most visible and pervasive level of culture in a given society. If the Metropolitan Opera House represents high culture, then Madison Square Garden represents pop. If the carefully crafted knives used in Asian cooking rely on a folk tradition, then the Veg-O-Matic is their pop counterpart.

Several other terms help us establish a working definition of popular culture. *Mass culture* refers to information we receive through print and electronic media. While mass culture is often denigrated as juvenile or "low," it has to be treated as an important component of popular culture by virtue of the immense size of its audience. The terms *subculture* and *counterculture*, on the other hand, suggest a desire to resist the pressures, implied or explicit, to conform to a common culture. Subcultures are specific segments of society outside the core of dominant culture. Minority groups in the United States might be called subcultures, just as certain groups such as artists, homosexuals, lawyers, or teenagers can be thought of as having cultural markers distinct from the broader culture. A counterculture, on the other hand, is a group or movement which defines itself specifically as opposing or subverting the dominant culture. Hippies of the 1960s and punk-rockers of the 1980s defined themselves as countercultural groups.

Although we may place ourselves in specific folk or high cultures, subcultures or countercultures, we are still aware of, perhaps even immersed in, the broader popular culture simply by virtue of living in society. As Edward Jay Whetmore notes,[1] "Popular culture represents a common denominator, something that cuts across most economic, social, and educational barriers." If the notion of culture reflects a certain degree of social stratification and differentiation, then popular culture represents the elements of everyday life, the artifacts and institutions shared by a society, and a body of common knowledge.

Another distinguishing characteristic of popular culture is its transitory nature. New images appear on our TV screens, replacing the popular images of years or seasons before; new phrases supersede former favorites in our popular lexicon; unknown entertainers become

---

[1] Whetmore, Edward Jay. *Mediamerica: Form, Content, and Consequence of Mass Communication.* Belmont, CA: Wadsworth Pub. Co., 1989.

celebrities overnight, while others fade just as quickly from the spotlight. Madonna takes the place of Gidget; "Studs" replaces "Love Connection," which took over from "The Dating Game"; the expression
"Just do it!" is for the nineties what "Ring around the collar!" was for
the seventies.

Interestingly, if an icon of popular culture survives, it can often make
the leap into high culture. For example, Wilkie Collins's nineteenth-
century horror stories were read as avidly as Stephen King's novels are
today. His works survive among today's elite audiences but are virtually unknown to most popular audiences. We might ask then, what of
contemporary popular culture might survive beyond the immediate
here and now and ultimately speak to future audiences at a higher, more
specialized level.

What, then, is pop culture? Although it's notoriously difficult to define, some elements of a definition emerge from this discussion: pop culture is the shared knowledge and practices of a specific group at a specific time. Because of its commonality, pop culture both reflects and
influences the peoples' way of life; because it is linked to a specific time
and place, pop culture is transitory, subject to change, and often an ini-
tiator of change.

Why Study Popular Culture?

Though pop culture is increasingly accepted as a legitimate object
of academic inquiry, educators still debate whether it should be studied.
Some critics contend that it would be more valuable to study the products of high culture—Shakespeare rather than Spielberg, Eliot rather
than Elvis. Their arguments often center on the issue of *quality*, as they
assert that pop culture, transitory and often trendy, lacks the lasting
value and strong artistic merit of high culture. Further, they argue that,
because pop appeals to a mass audience, rather than an educated elite,
it is necessarily of low quality, no better than average. Although few critics of pop culture deny its pervasive influence, many argue that this influence should be considered negative, and they point to the violence
and sexual explicitness of song lyrics, television programs, and movies,
as well as to the triviality and downright foolishness of many popular
trends. Pop culture debases us, these critics contend, turning us into passive recipients of low-quality goods, distracting us from higher pursuits.

It's important to note that very few proponents of pop culture—pop
cultists, as Marshall Fishwick[2] calls them—take a wholesale, uncritical

---

[2] Browne, Ray B. and Marshall Fishwick. *Symbiosis: Popular Culture and Other Fields*. Bowling
Green, OH: Bowling Green V.P., 1988.

approach and approve all things popular. Many, for example, accept the argument that products with mass appeal are often qualitatively inferior to those intended for an educated, elite audience. However, pop cultists remind us that the gap between the two isn't always so wide; that the same basic activities of creation, refinement, and reception are involved in both popular and high culture; and that, as we've noted, the "popular" works of one era can become the "classics" of another.

Moreover, pop cultists argue for the validity of studying MTV, *The National Enquirer,* video games, and the Miss America Pageant because such mass phenomena serve as a kind of mirror in which we can discern much about ourselves. George Lipsitz,[3] for instance, suggests that "perhaps the most important facts about people have always been encoded within the ordinary and the commonplace." And as Ray Browne,[4] a noted scholar of pop culture, puts it, "Popular culture is a very important segment of our society. The contemporary scene is holding us up to ourselves to see; it can tell us who we are, what we are, and why."

We see reflected in pop culture certain standards and commonly held beliefs about beauty, success, love, or justice. We also see reflected there important social contradictions and conflicts—the tension between races, genders, or generations, for example. To find out about ourselves, then, we can turn to our own popular products and pastimes.

Another argument for studying popular culture focuses on the important influence it exerts on us. The media and other pop culture components are part of the fund of ideas and images that inform our daily activities, sometimes exerting a more compelling influence than family or friends, school or work. When we play sports, we mimic the gestures and movements of professional athletes; we learn to dance from the videos on MTV; we even name our children after popular television characters. More importantly, we discover role models; we learn lessons about villainy and heroism, love and relationships, acceptable and unacceptable behavior; we see interactions with people from other cultures. Even if popular culture is merely low-quality amusement or a means of escaping the demands of the "real" world, it delivers important messages that we may internalize and later act on—for better or for worse. We should examine and analyze pop culture, then, in order to assess—and sometimes resist—its influences.

The readings and assignments in *Common Culture* give you the chance to explore these issues and determine for yourself the role of popular culture in shaping society and in shaping you as an individual. The book includes chapters on important components of popular

---

[3] Lipsitz, George. *Time Passages: Collective Memory and American Popular Culture.* Minneapolis: Univ. of Minnesota Press, 1990.

[4] Browne, Ray B. and Marshall Fishwick. *Symbiosis: Popular Culture and Other Fields.* Bowling Green, OH: Bowling Green V.P., 1988.

culture: advertising, television, music, journalism, sports, movies, leisure activities, and pop culture in the future. You may already know quite a lot about some of these topics, and you may have relatively little interest in or exposure to others. Either way, as disinterested observer or engaged participant, you can bring your critical skills to bear on phenomena of the contemporary world. The readings and assignments encourage you to observe carefully, to question, and to construct and defend your own interpretations of some of the institutions and events, the beliefs and practices, the media and the messages in your everyday life.

Before beginning, we will look at methods of reading and writing that will help you participate fully and critically in reaching the goals of this book.

Active Reading

We've discussed the importance of paying attention to the "common culture" that surrounds you in order to recognize its meanings and influences on your life. In this section, we present specific reading strategies that you can apply both to pop culture and to the essays in this book. Whether you're watching TV or reading an essay about TV, the habit of active, engaged interpretation will make the experience much more worthwhile. While you may have been encouraged to be an active reader of print material, the essays throughout this book also encourage you to be an active reader of the culture around you.

There's a crucial difference between passively receiving and actively reading. Passively ingesting information requires very little effort or interest, and it gives very little in terms of reward or stimulation. Active reading demands more of your time, effort, and thought, but it is ultimately much more useful in helping you develop a better understanding of ideas.

Although reading is generally a solitary activity, it helps to think of active reading as a discussion or dialogue with another person. You listen carefully; you compare what the person tells you to what you already know; you question statements that strike you as complicated, confusing, or incorrect; you identify ideas that are particularly interesting and important to you; you respond with ideas of your own. As a result of your active participation, you come away with new insights and a clearer sense of your own position. You may even be stimulated to seek out more information from other sources in order to clarify your thoughts.

When you read actively—whether printed texts or other products of popular culture—you use very similar strategies, questioning and responding and speculating about what you're reading. You are no longer a disinterested bystander simply "listening in"; rather you are a participant who is energetically engaged with an author's ideas or with the messages underlying a commercial or television program.

Strategies for Active Reading

There are a number of specific stages and strategies involved in active reading. In the **preparatory** stage you develop a general sense of what the essay will be about. In the **reading** stage, begin the actual dialogue with the author by paying close attention to what he or she has written, identifying key points, responding to certain ideas, and asking questions. Next comes the **re-reading** stage, in which you go back through the essay to get a clear and firm understanding of what you've read. Finally, in the **reviewing** stage, you take time to draw conclusions, evaluate the author's position, and develop your own responses; often you'll want to go back to the essay and read certain sections even more carefully or to turn to other sources to help you formulate your response. In the actual practice of active reading, these four stages circle back on one another as well as spiral outward, prompting you to do further reading and exploration.

As you see, active reading is quite different from passively receiving or consuming information. By reading actively, you'll be able to clarify and develop your own ideas and your responses to the influences operating on you in your everyday life. You can become a more proficient and accomplished writer, increasing the range and precision of your vocabulary, using different options for constructing sentences and paragraphs, creating different stylistic effects, and, in general, improving your "feel" for written language.

An Active Reading Casebook: Three Selections about Barbie

This section includes three reading selections—a poem and two essays about the Barbie doll—that demonstrate the strategies of active reading and suggest the kind of reading you'll be doing in later chapters.

We've chosen to begin with a look at Barbie because of her longevity, popularity, and cultural significance. Since her "birth" in 1959, Barbie has achieved celebrity status in United States culture and, indeed, worldwide. More than 775 million Barbies have been sold in the last thirty-five years, and Barbie products continue to bring in hundreds of millions of dollars every year for Mattel Inc., her owner and America's biggest toy company. In 1994 Mattel estimated that 95 percent of girls aged three to eleven own at least one Barbie, while the average is seven.

Barbie lives in nearly every United States and Canadian household that includes children and in more than sixty other countries as well. In addition to her extensive accessories and her many friends (among them, her boyfriend, Ken, and her African-American pal, Shani), Barbie has her own magazine and fan club and her own corps of press agents, advertising executives, and "personal secretaries" to answer her fan mail. Yves St. Laurent and Bill Blass have designed clothes especially for her; Tiffany created a sterling silver version of Barbie; and New York City's Fifth Avenue became "Barbie Boulevard" to mark her twenty-fifth birthday.

For three decades, girls (and boys, too) have been playing with and learning from Barbie, and thus she serves as an important force in conveying cultural values and attitudes. Barbie's influence is undeniable, but opinions vary as to the quality of that influence on the children who play with her and on the adults they become. Barbie's critics argue that her influence has been largely detrimental, that her improbable measurements (36-18-33), her even more improbable hair, and her inexhaustible supply of clothes and accessories help perpetuate an inappropriate model of women's interests and lives. However, defenders argue that her influence has been positive, at least in part. They point out that Barbie has recently had careers such as corporate executive, airline pilot, medical doctor, animal rights activist, and even presidential candidate, offering girls a chance to envision themselves being successful in the working world. Although Barbie's wedding dress is one of her most popular outfits, she's never officially married Ken (or G.I. Joe), and she remains a single, independent career woman, providing, some observers say, an alternative to the view that women's primary roles are wife and mother.

You can see that Barbie has served as a symbolic reference point for broader debates about femininity and masculinity, about beauty and success, about consumerism and lifestyle in our culture. Barbie is a good example of the way elements of popular culture can be interpreted in order to reveal some fundamental aspects of our society.

While reading this background information on Barbie, you may be thinking of your own experience as a child playing with Barbie or with other dolls and toys, and speculating about their formative influence on you. If so, you've begun to prepare for reading, to orient yourself to the topic, explore your own ideas and experiences, and think about the issues at hand.

Preparing to Read   Let's turn now to our first selection, a poem about Barbie written by Hilary Tham. All the readings in this book are accompanied by headnotes, which briefly explain what the reading is about and give some background information on the author. In this sense, headnotes are like the front and back covers of many books, providing an overview of what will follow and serving as the place to begin thinking about the topic. Here is the headnote for the poem "Barbie's Shoes":

> Our first selection is a poem by Hilary Tham. Tham was born in Ke-lang, Malaysia, and currently lives in Virginia with her husband and three daughters. She teaches creative writing in high schools and has published several books of poetry, including *No Gods Today, Paper Boats, Bad Names for Women,* and *Tigerbone Wine.*

You can get an idea of what to expect from the poem both by reading the headnote and by recalling what you know about poetry in general. The headnote tells you that Hilary Tham is originally from Malaysia and now lives in the United States. You might conclude from this information that Tham brings a dual perspective to the Barbie doll and other features of United States pop culture. The headnote also points out that Tham has three daughters and teaches high school students. Before you read the poem, then, you might speculate on how being a mother and a teacher would influence Tham's thoughts about the Barbie doll.

Reading and Annotating   In the reading stage, one of the most useful strategies you can use is *annotating* the text. When you annotate you use a pencil or pen to mark key words and phrases in the text and to write questions and responses in the margins. You underline words that you need to look up in a dictionary and phrases that you find particularly interesting, forceful, important, questionable, or confusing. You also record your reactions, thoughts, questions, and ideas in the margins. By annotating in this way, you keep track of what the author is saying and of what you're thinking as you read.

Here are one student's annotations of Tham's poem, but keep in mind that your annotation would probably identify different elements as particularly important.

• • • • • • • • • • • • •

Barbie's Shoes
HILARY THAM

I'm down in the (basement)   *Why the basement?*
sorting Barbie's shoes:
   sequin pumps, satin courts,   *Different shoes show*
   western boots, Reebok sneakers,   *Barbie's many activities*
   glass slippers, ice-skates, thongs.
All will fit the dainty, forever arched
feet of any one Barbie: Sweet Spring

Glitter-Eyed, Peaches and Cream,
a Brazilian, Russian, Swiss, Hong Kong
Hispanic or a Mexican, Nigerian
or Black Barbie. All are cast
in the (same) mold, (same) rubbery,   *Barbie's are different*
impossible embodiment of male fantasy   *but also the same*
with carefully measured
    doses of melanin to make
    a Caucasian Barbie,
        Polynesian Barbie
        African-American Barbie.
Everyone knows that she is the (same)   *Barbie =*
Barbie and worthy of the American Dream   *American Dream*
House, the Corvette, opera gloves, a
hundred pairs of shoes to step into. If only
the differently colored men and women we know
could be like Barbie, always smiling, eyes
wide with admiration, even when we yank
off an arm with a hard-to-take-off dress.   *Simile: Barbie's shoes*
Barbie's shoes, so easily lost, mismatched,   *are like our prejudices —*
useless; they end up, like our prejudices,   *forgotten, but still there,*
in the basement, forgotten as spiders   *in the basement, like*
sticking webs in our darkest corners,   *spider webs.*
we are amazed we have them still.

• • • • • • • • • • • • • •

Re-reading   After you read and annotate the poem, your task is to fully understand it and formulate your own response to it. Many students close the book after just the first reading without realizing that the next two stages, re-reading and reviewing, are crucial to discovering the significance of what they have read.

In the re-reading stage, you go back through the poem and the annotations in order to develop a good understanding of the writer's ideas. Then you begin to articulate those ideas—in your own words. Here's an example drawn from the earlier annotation of "Barbie Shoes."

> I'm really drawn to the simile in the last few lines: that Barbie's shoes are "like our prejudices, / in the basement, forgotten as spiders / sticking webs in our darkest corners, / we are amazed we have them still." Tham is saying that Barbie's shoes are more than just tiny plastic footwear. They represent prejudices which we think we've thrown away but in fact still have in our "basements" (our subconscious thoughts?). And by comparing these prejudices to spiders' webs "in our darkest corners," perhaps Tham is suggesting that our prejudices still "catch" things; they still operate in our lives even if we've forgotten them or don't see them.

With ideas like these as a starting point, you can go back through the entire poem and begin to formulate a response to other key ideas and phrases: the list of Barbie's shoes; the list of different nationalities and ethnicities of Barbie dolls; the idea that all Barbies are in some ways the same; the suggestion that Barbie represents the American Dream. Re-reading like this will surely provoke further questions about the poem. For instance, why does Tham make a point of mentioning the many different types of Barbies? In what ways are these differences only superficial and unrealistic? And what does Tham mean when she writes, "If only/the differently colored men and women we know/ could be like Barbie, always smiling, even when we yank/off an arm. . . ."? You know that Tham is being ironic (since we don't generally yank arms off other people), but what point is she making in this comparison, and how does it relate to her ideas about prejudice?

These kinds of questions lead you to re-read the poem, clarifying your understanding and finding further meanings in it. After each essay in this book, there are similar sorts of reading questions which help you explore the ideas you've read about. We also encourage you to develop your own questions about what you read to focus your exploration on those points that you find most interesting, important, or controversial.

Reviewing   After re-reading, questioning, and exploring the writer's ideas in detail, you should take time to summarize what you've learned. Here is a student's summary of her analysis of "Barbie's Shoes."

1. Tham suggests that Barbie's shoes are like prejudices (forgotten, seemingly lost, down in the basement, "useless" and "mismatched"); why can't we just throw them out? why are they still in the basement?

2. Why does Barbie have so many shoes?! Perhaps Tham is implying that we have an equal number of seemingly insignificant prejudices, one for every occasion, even.

3. Tham points out that there are many different kinds of Barbie dolls (Caucasian, Polynesian, African-American) but all are "worthy of the American Dream House." In this sense Barbies are all the same. So does Barbie influence us to overlook the real differences in women's lives? We're not dolls, after all, and although we're all worthy of success and accomplishment, we don't all get the same chances.

4. Tham describes Barbie as the "impossible embodiment of male fantasy." How is this observation related to the rest of the poem? Could she be saying that this fantasy is related to prejudice?

Such questions and tentative answers can help you begin to formulate your own interpretation of and complete response to what you've read.

Reading Pop Cultural Criticism   In the previous discussion we used Hilary Tham's poem as our example because poetry can pack so much meaning into the space of relatively few words. In the chapters that follow you'll be reading not poems but rather articles, essays, and chapters of books, most of which fall into one of two categories. The first we might call *pop cultural criticism* and includes the kind of pieces written for general audiences of popular magazines and mass market books. Typically these reflect a particular social perspective, whether traditionalist or cutting edge, conservative or liberal, pro- or anti-capitalist, and often they are written in response to a particular issue or phenomenon reported in the media.

The following piece by John Leo is an example of pop cultural criticism. As you read, practice the strategies that we've discussed. Begin by considering the headnote and what it suggests about Leo's perspective and purpose, then underline important passages in the essay and jot down your thoughts, responses, and questions in the margins.

··············

The Indignation of Barbie
JOHN LEO

John Leo's "The Indignation of Barbie" was first published in U.S. News & World Report *in 1992. Leo, a conservative journalist and social commentator, writes about the controversy surrounding the talking Barbie doll produced by Mattel in the early 1990s. Among Talking Barbie's repertoire of phrases was "Math class is tough," viewed by some feminists and professional women as discouraging girls from pursuing the subject. Here, Leo imagines a dialogue with Barbie, in which the talking doll defends herself against charges that she's a "prefeminist bimbo."*

··············

Barbie will probably survive, but the truth is, she's in a lot of trouble. It seems that the new Teen Talk Barbie, the first talking Barbie in 20 years, has shocked many feminists with a loose-lipped comment about girls and math. Each $25 doll speaks four of 270 programmed one-liners. In one of those messages, Barbie says, "Math class is tough." This was a big error. She should have said, "Math is particularly easy if you're a girl, despite the heavy shackles of proven test bias and male patriarchal oppression."

Because of this lapse from correctness, the head of the American Association of University Women is severely peeved with Barbie, and you can no longer invite both of them to the same party. Other feminists and math teachers have weighed in with their own dudgeon.

Since this is Barbie's darkest hour, I placed a phone call out to Mattel Inc.   3
in California to see how the famous long-haired, long-legged forerunner of
Ivana Trump was holding up. To my astonishment, they put me right
through to Barbie herself.

"Barbie, it's me," I said. As the father of three girls, I have shopped for 35   4
to 40 Barbies over the years, including doctor Barbie, ballerina Barbie, television news reporter Barbie, African-American Barbie, animal-rights Bar-
bie, and Barbie's shower, which takes two days to construct and makes the
average father feel like a bumbling voyeur. So I figured that Barbie would
know me.

Barbie spoke: "Do you want to go for a pizza? Let's go to the mall. Do you   5
have a crush on anyone? Teaching kids is great. Computers make homework fun!"

In a flash I realized that Barbie was stonewalling. These were not sponta-   6
neous comments at all. They were just the prerecorded messages that she
was forced to say, probably under pressure from those heartless, controlling patriarchs at Mattel.

Subtle rebuttal. At the same time, I began to appreciate Barbie's charac-   7
teristic subtlety; by reminding me that she was recommending the educational use of computers to young girls, she was, in effect, stoutly rebutting
the charge of antifeminist backlash among talking toys. I had to admit it
was pretty effective.

So I pleaded with her to speak honestly and clear her name. I heard a tell-   8
tale rustle of satin, and then she spoke. "You're the one who took three days
to put my shower together. That was ugly."

"Two days," I said, gently correcting the world-famous plastic figurine.   9
I asked her about the harsh words of Sharon Schuster, the awfully upset head
of the AAUW. Schuster had said, "The message is a negative one for girls,
telling them they can't do well in math, and that perpetuates a stereotype."

"That's a crock," Barbie replied. "Just because a course is tough or chal-   10
lenging doesn't mean my girls can't do it. Weren't your daughters a little
apprehensive about math?" I admitted that they were. "Well, how did they
do?" "Top of the class," I replied brightly.

"Then tell Sharon Schuster to stop arguing with dolls and go get a life."   11
Her remark was an amazement. This was not roller-skating Barbie or
perfume-wearing Barbie. It was the real thing: in-your-face tough-talking
Barbie.

"The first time I open my mouth after 20 years, and what happens? I get   12
squelched by a bunch of women." At this point, I mentioned that my friend
M. G. Lord, the syndicated columnist who is doing a book on Barbie, is
firmly on her side. M. G. told me: "Math class *is* tough, but it doesn't mean
you have to drop out and go to cosmetology school. These people are projecting a lot of fears onto Barbie."

Barbie was grateful. "Thank M. G. and tell her I look forward to her biog-   13
raphy of me. And tell her that if she ever fails in life, she can always become
head of the AAUW." That remark may have been a trifle sharp, I said.
"Well," said Barbie, "I'm just tired of taking all this guff from women's
groups. They're scapegoating the wrong girl. I'll match feminist credentials
with any of them. I worked my way up from candy striper to doctor. I
was a stewardess in the '60s, and now I'm a pilot. Ken is one of my flight

attendants. You can buy me as Olympic athlete, astronaut and corporate executive."

Barbie was on a roll now. I was writing furiously to keep up. "This summer they put out a presidential candidate Barbie, and two days later, Ross Perot withdrew. Figure it out," she said. "As far back as 1984, my ad slogan was, 'We girls can do anything.' I've done more than any other doll to turn girls into achievers, and still they treat me as a prefeminist bimbo. What's wrong with the women's movement?"   14

I knew enough not to touch that one. Besides, it's a very short column. But I was struck by her comment that Ken was now employed as a flight attendant. "Didn't he used to be a corporate executive?" I asked. "We're not voting for Bush again," she replied bitterly.   15

Then I heard a muffled side comment: "Ken! Be careful with those dishes." I said I felt bad about Ken's comedown, but Barbie brought me back to reality: "Remember," she said, "he's only an accessory." This was tough to take, but the issue was settled. Barbie is indeed a feminist. Over to you, Sharon Schuster.   16

• • • • • • • • • • • • • • •

As you first read Leo's essay, his technique of personifying the doll as an "in-your-face tough-talking Barbie" is most striking and allows him to humorously present a talking Barbie who seemingly speaks up for herself. In re-reading you can see even more clearly Leo's purpose: he uses Barbie's "voice" to offer his own defense of her influence and significance. Moreover, ultimately he is making fun of feminists "projecting a lot of fears onto Barbie," since she herself derisively asks, "What's wrong with the women's movement?" When Leo has Barbie "say" that she's "done more than any other doll to turn girls into achievers," it's clear that Leo himself agrees and feels that Barbie's critics should lighten up.

As a reviewing activity, you might write down your thoughts about the following questions and discuss them with your group or class:

1. Do you agree that Barbie has "done more than any other doll to turn girls into achievers" (paragraph 14)?

2. Do you think Leo's use of humor contributes to the effectiveness of his essay?

3. According to Leo, what is the relationship between Barbie and Ken? Do you agree with Leo's ideas?

4. If you could give speech to Barbie, what would you have her say?

Reading Academic Analyses   In addition to pop cultural criticism, this book provides essays on pop cultural phenomena written not for a general audience, but by academics primarily for other academics. Generally published in academic journals or in collections from scholarly presses, these essays often present the results of extensive research or provide a very close, detailed, and original analysis of the subject at hand. You may find them more difficult than the pieces of pop cultural criticism, but in many ways they are closer to the kind of writing that will be expected of you in many of your college courses.

Note that, while "objective" in tone, academic cultural analysis generally reflects a particular interpretive framework, which may be ideological (e.g. feminist or Marxist) or methodological (e.g. semiotic, structuralist, or quantitative) or some combination of the two. These frameworks will be discussed in more detail in the headnotes to individual readings.

The following excerpt from an essay by Marilyn Ferris Motz is an example of academic cultural analysis, written from a perspective that might be called "feminist-historical." As you read the headnote and the essay itself, apply the strategies we've discussed: familiarize yourself with Motz's view and with the topic as it's presented in the headnote; then read the essay carefully and make your own annotations in the text and in the margins.

•••••••••••••

"Seen Through Rose-Tinted Glasses": The Barbie Doll in American Society
MARILYN FERRIS MOTZ

Originally published in a longer form in The Popular Culture Reader, *Marilyn Motz's "'Seen Through Rose-Tinted Glasses': The Barbie Doll in American Society," takes its title from a 1983 Barbie sticker album marketed by Mattel: "If you stay close to your friend Barbie, life will always be seen through rose-tinted glasses." In her essay, however, Motz suggests that Barbie has other messages for us and that the doll's influence is more problematic, especially for children. Pointing out that several generations of girls have learned cultural values and norms from playing with Barbie, Motz focuses on the fact that, although Barbie has changed through the years to keep up with changes in the "baby boom" generation, the doll and her accessories still convey an outdated image of women's circumstances and interests.*

•••••••••••••

A 1983 Barbie sticker album copyrighted by Mattel describes Barbie: 1

As beautiful as any model, she is also an excellent sportswoman. In fact, Barbie is seen as a typical young lady of the twentieth century, who knows how to appreciate beautiful things and, at the same time, live life to the fullest. To most girls, she appears as the ideal elder sister who manages to do all those wonderful things that they can only dream of. With her fashionable wardrobe and constant journeys to exciting places all over the world, the adventures of Barbie offer a glimpse of what they might achieve one day. If Barbie has a message at all for us, it is to ignore the gloomy outlook of others and concentrate on all those carefree days of youth. Whatever lies in store will come sooner or later. If you stay close to your friend Barbie, life will always be seen through rose-tinted glasses.

Most owners of Barbie dolls are girls between the ages of three and eleven years of age. A Mattel survey shows that by the late 1960s, the median age for Barbie doll play had dropped from age ten to age six (Rakstis 30). Younger children find it difficult to manipulate the relatively small dolls, although Mattel created "My First Barbie," that ostensibly was easier for young children to handle and dress. Although some boys admit to playing with Ken, or even Barbie, Barbie doll play seems to be confined largely to girls.   2

Like all small figures and models, Barbie, at 11½ inches high, has the appeal of the miniature. Most people are fascinated with objects re-recreated on a smaller scale, whether they are model airplanes, electric trains, dollhouse furnishings, or doll clothes. Miniatures give us a sense of control over our environment, a factor that is particularly important for children, to whom the real world is several sizes too large. In playing with a Barbie doll, a girl can control the action, can be omnipotent in a miniature world of her own creation.   3

When a girl plays with a baby doll, she becomes in her fantasy the doll's mother. She talks directly to the doll, entering into the play as an actor in her own right. When playing with a Barbie doll, on the other hand, the girl usually "becomes" Barbie. She manipulates Barbie, Ken and the other dolls, speaking for them and moving them around a miniature environment in which she herself cannot participate. Through the Barbie doll, then, a pre-adolescent can engage in role-playing activities. She can imitate adult female behavior, dress and speech and can participate vicariously in dating and other social activities, thus allaying some of her anxieties by practicing the way she will act in various situations. In consultation with the friends with whom she plays, a girl can establish the limits of acceptable behavior for a young woman and explore the possibilities and consequences of exceeding those limits.   4

The girl playing with a Barbie doll can envision herself with a mature female body. "Growing-Up Skipper," first produced in 1975, grew taller and developed small breasts when her arms were rotated, focusing attention on the bodily changes associated with puberty. Of course, until the end of puberty, girls do not know the ultimate size and shape their bodies will assume, factors they realize will affect the way others will view and treat them. Perhaps Barbie dolls assuage girls' curiosity over the appearance of the adult female body, of which many have only limited knowledge, and allay anxiety over their own impending bodily development.   5

Through Barbie's interaction with Ken, girls also can explore their anxieties about future relationships with men. Even the least attractive and least popular girl can achieve, by "becoming" Barbie, instant popularity in a fantasy world. No matter how clumsy or impoverished she is in real life, she can ride a horse or lounge by the side of the pool in a world undisturbed by the presence of parents or other authority figures. The creator of the Barbie doll, Ruth Handler, claims that "these dolls become an extension of the girls. Through the doll each child dreams of what she would like to be"   6

(Zinsser, "Barbie" 73). If Barbie does enable a girl to dream "of what she would like to be," then what dreams and goals does the doll encourage? With this question, some of the negative aspects of the Barbie doll emerge.

The clothes and other objects in Barbie's world lead the girl playing with Barbie to stress Barbie's leisure activities and emphasize the importance of physical appearance. The shape of the doll, its clothes and the focus on dating activities present sexual attractiveness as a key to popularity and therefore to happiness. Finally, Barbie is a consumer. She demands product after product, and the packaging and advertising imply that Barbie, as well as her owner, can be made happy if only she wears the right clothes and owns the right products. Barbie conveys the message that, as the saying goes, a woman can never be too rich or too thin. The Barbie doll did not create these attitudes. Nor will the doll insidiously instill these values in girls whose total upbringing emphasizes other factors. An individual girl can, of course, create with her own doll any sort of behavior and activities she chooses. Still, the products available for the doll tend to direct play along certain lines. Barbie represents an image, and a rather unflattering one, of American women. It is the extent to which this image fits our existing cultural expectations that explains the popularity of the Barbie doll. . . .

As an icon, Barbie not only reflects traditional, outdated roles for women; she and Ken also represent, in exaggerated form, characteristics of American society as a whole. Through playing with these dolls, children learn to act out in miniature the way they see adults behave in real life and in the media. The dolls themselves and the accessories provided for them direct this play, teaching children to consume and conform, to seek fun and popularity above all else.

Thorstein Veblen wrote in 1899 that America had become a nation of "conspicuous consumers." We buy objects, he wrote, not because we need them but because we want others to know we can afford them. We want our consumption to be conspicuous or obvious to others. The more useless the object, the more it reflects the excess wealth the owner can afford to waste. In the days before designer labels, Veblen wrote that changing fashions represent an opportunity for the affluent to show that they can afford to waste money by disposing of usable clothing and replacing it with new, faddish styles that will in turn be discarded after a few years or even months of wear. (Veblen 60–131)

Sociologist David Riesman wrote in 1950 that Americans have become consumers whose social status is determined not only by what they can afford to buy but also by the degree to which their taste in objects of consumption conforms to that of their peers. Taste, in other words, becomes a matter of assessing the popularity of an item with others rather than judging on the basis of one's personal preference. Children, according to Riesman, undergo a process of "taste socialization," of learning to determine "with skill and sensitivity the probable tastes of the others" and then to adopt these tastes as their own. Riesman writes that "today the future occupation of all moppets is to be skilled consumers" (94, 96, 101). This skill lies not in selecting durable or useful products but in selecting popular, socially acceptable products that indicate the owner's conformity to standards of taste and knowledge of current fashion.

The Barbie doll teaches a child to conform to fashion in her consumption. She learns that each activity requires appropriate attire and that outfits that may at first glance appear to be interchangeable are slightly different from one another. In the real world, what seems to be a vast array of merchandise actually is a large collection of similar products. The consumer must make marginal distinctions between nearly identical products, many of which have different status values. The child playing with a Barbie doll learns to detect these nuances. Barbie's clothes, for instance, come in three lines: a budget line, a medium-priced line, and a designer line. Consumption itself becomes an activity to be practiced. From 1959 to 1964, Mattel produced a "Suburban Shopper" outfit. In 1976 the "Fashion Plaza" appeared on the market. This store consisted of four departments connected by a moving escalator. As mass-produced clothing made fashion accessible to all classes of Americans, the Barbie doll was one of the means by which girls learned to make the subtle fashion distinctions that would guarantee the proper personal appearances.

Barbie must also keep pace with all the newest fashion and leisure trends.   12
Barbie's pony tail of 1959 gave way to a Jackie Kennedy style "Bubble-cut" in the early 1960s and to long straight hair in the 1970s. "Ken-A-Go-Go" of the 1960s had a Beatle wig, guitar and microphone, while the "Now Look Ken" of the 1970s had shoulder-length hair and wore a leisure suit (Leavy 102). In the early 1970s Ken grew a detachable beard. In 1971 Mattel provided Barbie and Ken with a motorized stage on which to dance in their fringed clothes, while Barbie's athletic activities, limited to skiing, skating, fishing, skydiving and tennis in the 1960s, expanded to include backpacking, jogging, bicycling, gymnastics and sailing in the 1970s. On the shelves in the early 1980s were Western outfits, designer jeans, and Rocker Barbie dressed in neon colors and playing an electric guitar. In 1991 a rollerblade Barbie was introduced.

Barbie clearly is, and always has been, a conspicuous consumer. Aside   13
from her lavish wardrobe, Barbie has several houses complete with furnishings, a Ferrari and a '57 Chevy. She has at various times owned a yacht and several other boats as well as a painted van called the "Beach Bus." Through Barbie, families who cannot afford such luxury items in real life can compete in miniature. In her early years, Barbie owned a genuine mink coat. In the ultimate display of uselessness, Barbie's dog once owned a corduroy velvet jacket, net tutu, hat, sunglasses and earmuffs. Barbie's creators deny that Barbie's life is devoted to consumption. "These things shouldn't be thought of as possessions," according to Ruth Handler. "They are props that enable a child to get into play situations" (Zinsser 73). Whether possessions or props, however, the objects furnished with the Barbie doll help create play situations, and those situations focus on consumption and leisure.

A perusal of the shelves of Barbie paraphernalia in the Midwest Toys "R"   14
Us store reveals not a single item of clothing suitable for an executive office. Mattel did produce a doctor's outfit (1973) and astronaut suit (1965 and 1986) for Barbie, but the clothes failed to sell. According to Mattel's marketing manager, "We only kept the doctor's uniform in the line as long as we did because public relations begged us to give them something they could point to as progress" in avoiding stereotyped roles for women (Leavy 102). In the 1960s, Mattel produced "all the elegant accessories" for the patio, including a telephone, television, radio, fashion magazines and a photograph of Barbie and Ken (Zinsser 72). The "Busy Barbie," created in 1972,

had hands that could grasp objects and came equipped with a telephone, television, record player, "soda set" with two glasses and a tray, and a travel case. Apparently Barbie kept busy only with leisure activities; she seems unable to grasp a book or a pen. When Barbie went to college in the 1970s, her "campus" consisted only of a dormitory room, soda shop (with phone booth), football stadium and drive-in movie! (Zinsser 72). In the 1980s, Barbie traveled in her camper, rode her horse, played with her dog and cat, swam in her pool and lounged in her bubble bath (both with real water).

The Barbie doll of the 1980s presents a curiously mixed message. The as-   15
tronaut Barbie wore a pink space suit with puffed sleeves. The executive Barbie wore a hot pink suit and a broad-brimmed straw hat, and she carried a pink briefcase in which to keep her gold credit card. Lest girls think Barbie is all work and no play, the jacket could be removed, the pink and white spectator pumps replaced with high-heeled sandals, and the skirt reversed to form a spangled and frilly evening dress. Barbie may try her hand at high-status occupations, but her appearance does not suggest competence and professionalism. In a story in *Barbie* magazine (Summer 1985) Barbie is a journalist reporting on lost treasure in the Yucatan. She spends her time "catching some rays" and listening to music, however, while her dog discovers the lost treasure. Barbie is appropriately rewarded with a guest spot on a television talk show! Although Barbie is shown in a professional occupation and even has her own computer, her success is attributed to good luck rather than her own (nonexistent) efforts. She reaps the rewards of success without having had to work for it; indeed, it is her passivity and pleasure-seeking (could we even say laziness) that allows her dog to discover the gold. Even at work, Barbie leads a life of leisure.

Veblen wrote that America, unlike Europe, lacked a hereditary aristocracy   16
of families that were able to live on the interest produced by inherited wealth. In America, Veblen wrote, even the wealthiest men were self-made capitalists who earned their own livings. Since these men were too busy to enjoy leisure and spend money themselves, they delegated these tasks to their wives and daughters. By supporting a wife and daughters who earned no money but spent lavishly, a man could prove his financial success to his neighbors. Therefore, according to Veblen, affluent women were forced into the role of consumers, establishing the social status of the family by the clothes and other items they bought and the leisure activities in which they engaged (Veblen 44–131).

Fashions of the time, such as long skirts, immobilized women, making it   17
difficult for them to perform physical labor, while ideals of beauty that included soft pale hands and faces precluded manual work or outdoor activities for upper-class women. To confer status, Veblen writes, clothing "should not only be expensive, but it should also make plain to all observers that the wearer is not engaged in any kind of productive employment." According to Veblen, "the dress of women goes even farther than that of men in the way of demonstrating the wearer's abstinence from productive labor." The high heel, he notes, "makes any, even the simplest and most necessary manual work extremely difficult," and thus is a constant reminder that the woman is "the economic dependent of the man—that, perhaps in a highly idealized sense, she still is the man's chattel" (Veblen 120–21, 129). . . .

Despite changes in the lives and expectations of real women, Barbie   18
remains essentially the woman described by Veblen in the 1890s, excluded

from the world of work with its attendant sense of achievement, forced to live a life based on leisure activities, personal appearance, the accumulation of possessions and the search for popularity. While large numbers of women reject this role, Barbie embraces it. The Barbie doll serves as an icon that symbolically conveys to children and adults the measures of success in modern America: wealth, beauty, popularity and leisure.

Suggestions for Further Reading

Leavy, Jane. "Is There a Barbie Doll in Your Past?" *Ms.* Sept. 1979.

Riesman, David, Nathan Glazer and Reual Denney. *The Lonely Crowd: A Study of the Changing American Character.* Garden City, NY: Doubleday Anchor, 1950.

Rakstis, Ted, "Debate in the Doll House." *Today's Health* Dec. 1970.

Veblen, Thorstein. *The Theory of the Leisure Class.* 1899. New York: Mentor, 1953.

Zinsser, William K. "Barbie is a Million Dollar Doll." *Saturday Evening Post* 12 Dec. 1964: 72–73.

• • • • • • • • • • • • • •

As you can see from Motz's essay, academic cultural analysis can present you with much information and many ideas to digest. A useful re-reading activity is to go through the text and highlight its main points by writing a one- or two-page summary of it. Then in the reviewing stage, you can use your summary to draw your own conclusions and formulate your own responses to the writer's ideas. To do so with Motz's essay, you might use the following questions as starting points:

1. In what ways do you think fashion dolls like Barbie provide a different play experience for children than "baby dolls"? Do you think one type of doll is "healthier" or more appropriate than the other?

2. To what extent do you think Thorstein Veblen's comments on status and consumerism in American society (paragraph 9) still apply today? Do you agree with Motz that Barbie contributes to the promotion of "conspicuous consumption"?

3. If Motz is right that Barbie represents an outdated and potentially detrimental image of women's lives, why do you think the doll continues to sell more and more successfully every year?

4. To what extent do you think that the values represented by Barbie—"wealth, beauty, popularity and leisure" (18)—are still central to success in America?

Ultimately, your goal as a reader in this course will most likely be to prepare yourself to complete specific writing assignments. In the next section, we present the process one writing student went through in composing an essay requested in the following assignment:

> What do you see as the significance of the Barbie doll in contemporary American culture? How are your ideas related to those of Tham, Leo, and Motz in the selections presented here?

The Writing Process

Frequently, when an instructor gives a writing assignment—for example, "Write an essay exploring the significance of the Barbie doll in contemporary American culture"—students experience a type of mini-panic: producing a focused, coherent, informative, and logically developed paper seems a monumental task. Some students may be overwhelmed by the many ideas swirling around in their heads, worrying they won't be able to put them into coherent order. Others may think they won't have enough to say about a given topic and complain, "How long does the paper have to be? How can I come up with four pages!"

However, there's really no reason to panic. Just as there are definable activities in the active process of reading, so the writing process can be broken down into four discrete stages: **prewriting, drafting, distancing,** and **revising.** Taking it a step at a time can make writing an essay a manageable and productive experience.

Prewriting

The first stage of the essay-writing process should be especially invigorating and stress-free, since at this point you don't have to worry about making your prose grammatically sound, logically organized, or convincing to a reader. All you have to do is write whatever comes into your head regarding your topic, so that you can discover the beginnings of ideas and phrasings that may be developed in the drafting stage and ultimately massaged into an acceptable form of academic writing.

There are a number of prewriting strategies writers use to generate ideas and happy turns of phrase. Experiment with all of these, in order to discover which of them "clicks" in terms of how you think and most productively get your ideas down on paper. Most writers rely more heavily on one or two of these prewriting strategies, depending on their own styles and dispositions; it's a matter of individual preference. If you're a spontaneous, organic sort of person, for example, you might spend more time freewriting. On the other hand, if you have a more logical, mathematical mind, you might gravitate naturally to outlining and do very little freewriting. There's no right or wrong way to prewrite; it comes down to whatever works best for you. But what's best usually involves some combination of the three following techniques.

Freewriting   This prewriting strategy lets your mind wander, as minds will, while you record whatever occurs to you. Just write, write, write, with no judgment about the validity, usefulness, grammatical correctness, or literary merit of the words you're putting down. The only requirement is that you write non-stop, either on paper or a word processor, for a manageable period of time: say, fifteen minutes without a break.

Your freewriting can be open—that is, it can be pure, stream-of-consciousness writing in which you "stay in the present moment" and record every thought, sense impression, disturbing sound—or it can be focused on a specific topic, such as Barbie dolls. When freewriting in preparation for writing an essay, it's frequently helpful to keep in mind a central question, either one from your instructor's original topic assignment or one sparked by your own curiosity, so that your freewritten material will be useful when you start composing your actual essay. Here is a typical focused freewrite on the subject of Barbie dolls written by a student in response to the writing assignment quoted earlier:

> *Toys: what did you want as a child vs. what you were given? I don't know, but I wanted cars and ended up with Barbie Corvette. Brother got G.I. Joe, Tonka trucks, I got talking Barbie, Barbie play house, Corvette.*
>
> *B. served as model for ideal female figure, and now that ideal is depicted in magazines. I guess that represents a kind of perpetuation of this image: girls raised on barbie → cycle continues w/ images in the media. The I=ideal image of women in America seems to be let's see: white, flawless, flat nose, wide eyes, that kind of thing. Whatever, it's clear that Barbie creates unreal expectations for women.*
>
> *Yeah! her figure would be inhuman if a real person had it—they would probably die! If she puts on jogging shoes, Barbie stands sloped because she's designed for high heels . . . so it seems as though Barbie is clearly designed for display rather than real activity, let alone profession. Display.*
>
> *literature (written stuff) on Barbie packages—she's not interested in doctoring nurse, etc.; just having money, cars, looking good, taking trips etc. Re: tech—women think computers are "fun." Re: math—women supposedly aren't good at it. Barbie reinforces these stereotypes—and lots more—in girls Changes in society? discuss for concl.?*

Clustering   Clustering is especially useful for discovering relationships between ideas, impressions, and facts. As a prewriting activity, it falls between freewriting and outlining, in that it's usually more focused than freewriting but less logically structured than an outline.

To prewrite by clustering, begin by writing a word or central phrase down in the center of a clean sheet of paper. In the case of the Barbie doll assignment, for example, you would probably start by writing "Barbie" in the middle of the page, and then drawing a circle around it. Having written and circled this central word or phrase, you can then jot down relevant facts, concrete examples, interesting ideas, and so on. Cluster these around the circled word, like this:

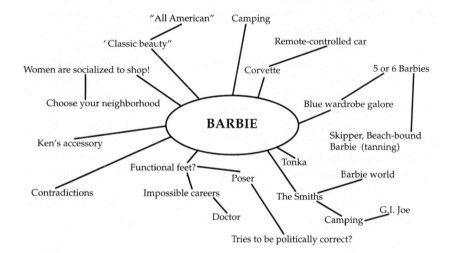

Frequently, one or more of your random jottings will serve as a new central word—as a jumping-off point for a new cluster of ideas. Later on, when you're drafting, you can use these clustered "nodes" as the basis for supporting paragraphs in the body of your essay.

Outlining   If you have a rough idea of what the main points of your paper will be, outlining is an extremely useful prewriting technique, in that it helps you plan the overall structure for your paper and often generates new ideas about your topic. There are several different types of outlines, most notably scratch, sentence and topic outlines.

For a *scratch outline* you list your intended points in a very tentative order, one that may only reflect the fact that you don't yet know in what order you want to put your supporting ideas. A scratch outline might not even suggest which subordinating points are most important to developing your thesis. For this reason, scratch outlines are most useful early in the prewriting phase, as a means of generating ideas as well as beginning to organize your thoughts logically. In fact, if you have not yet arrived at a thesis for your paper, one may emerge in the process of listing all your main and subordinate points and then reviewing that list to discover which of those ideas is the most central and important.

As you think more about your essay and come up with new ideas and supporting evidence, you will almost certainly revise your scratch outline to make it more detailed and conventionally formatted with numbered and lettered headings and subheads. A *topic outline* presents items in key words or brief phrases, rather than sentences, and frequently features no indentation. A *sentence outline* is even more developed than a topic outline, in that it describes the listed items in complete sentences, each of which is essentially a subtopic for a supporting paragraph. In fact, sentence outlines, when fully developed, can contain most of the supporting information you're going to present in your essay, and can therefore be extremely useful tools during the prewriting process.

Developing her freewritten material about Barbie into an outline, our student writer sketched out the following:

I. *Introduction*
   A. *Discuss my own experience with toys while growing up: parents "let" me play with Tonka trucks, but they gave me a Barbie Corvette when I wanted a race car.*
   B. *Discuss social shaping of gender roles generally.*
   C. *Working Thesis: Significance of Barbie in American society is that although people say women have "come a long way" and that there are new expectations, this is not really true. If it were, Barbie, depicted as mere sexual, leisure-seeking consumer, could not be accepted.*
II. *The media see that people—especially young ones—need role models, and manufacture products to fill the following needs.*
   A. *Childhood: Barbie.*
      1. *Barbie presents a totally unrealistic female body as role models for young women.*
      2. *This role-modeling is crucial in young women's psychological development, because little girls role-play with Barbie, taking her actions as their own.*
   B. *Pre-teen: Models in Seventeen magazine.*
   C. *Teen: Vogue and Mademoiselle.*
   D. *Adult: Cosmopolitan, Victoria's Secret lingerie models, advertisements in mainstream magazines.*
III. *The popularity of Barbie depicts the entrenched nature of traditional female roles.*
   A. *The change toward women's equality is not something that is deemed beneficial by everyone, such as the religious ultra-right.*
   B. *People purchasing Barbie either:*
      1. *don't see the image that's being perpetuated; or*
      2. *respect those values and want to pass them on to their children.*
   C. *Significance in popular culture of Barbie is that she illustrates inconsistencies between changing social roles (women and minorities) and the concepts we are teaching youngsters.*
   D. *Although the makers of Barbie make a superficial attempt at updating her, Barbie depicts traditional women absorbed in leisure, consumption, and beauty.*
      1. *Barbie completely reinforces old role expectations.*

2. *Barbie in the '90s can have a career (she has some doctor outfits, I think), but she isn't ever functional in that career. The emphasis is still on leisure.*

IV. *The Racial Issue*
  A. *Barbie illustrates the assimilation of minorities; they lose part of their culture, because Americans are supposed to belong to the "same mold."*
  B. *In the '90s we say that we aren't prejudiced and that everyone should be accepted for who they are, but since the dominant culture is white, white men and women unconsciously (or in some cases consciously, I'm afraid) assume that others must take on white norms.*

V. *Conclusion*
  A. *Bring it back around to my childhood play time and the necessity for parents to think about the sorts of toys they are giving their children, so that they don't reinforce and perpetuate these old patterns.*

You'll discover that this outline, while detailed, doesn't contain some of the points raised in the final essay's supporting paragraphs and that it includes a good deal of material that was not used in the final essay. The reason for this discrepancy is simple and illustrates a key point for you to remember about the writing process. As this writer began her essay, she discovered new points which she thought relevant to her thesis. At the same time, she realized that some of her outlined points were tangential and digressive rather than helpful in supporting her main point. She therefore cut some of those points, even though she thought they were valid and interesting ideas. That's one of the most painful but absolutely necessary tasks of the writer: getting rid of material which took some work to create and seems interesting and well written. If cutting some of your previously written material makes the final result better, then it's worth the sacrifice!

Drafting

Having generated a good amount of prewritten material and perhaps developed it into a detailed outline, your next task is to transform that material into an actual essay. Before proceeding with the drafting of your essay, however, it's a good idea first to consider your audience—your instructor only? Your instructor *and* your classmates? An imaginary editor or publisher? A third-grade student? Consider, too, the point you want to make about your topic to that audience. Unlike freewriting, which is by its nature often rambling and disjointed, essays succeed to the degree that they focus on a specific point and develop that point with illustrations and examples.

Thesis and Thesis Statement   The main point, the central assertion of your essay, is called a *thesis*. It helps to have a clear sense of your thesis before writing a paper. However, keep in mind that this isn't always necessary: some people use writing as a discovery process, and don't arrive at their thesis until they've completed a first draft. Generally, however, the process is easier if you have a thesis in mind—even one that's not yet fully formed or likely to change—before you begin drafting.

While the form of thesis statements may vary considerably, there are some qualities that separate effective thesis statements from vague or weak ones. First of all, your thesis statement should be inclusive but focused: that is, it should be broad enough to encompass your paper's main supporting ideas, but narrow enough to represent a concise explanation of your paper's main point that won't require you to write fifty pages to cover the topic adequately. Furthermore, you want your thesis statement to be a forceful assertion rather than a question or an ambiguous statement of purpose such as, "In this paper I am going to talk about Barbie dolls and their effect on society."

Much more effective, as you will see in the sample student paper that concludes this chapter, is a statement which takes a stand:

> This is certainly one of the more dangerous consequences of Barbie's popularity in our society: a seemingly innocent toy defines for young girls the sorts of career choices, clothing, and relationships that will be "proper" for them as grown-up women.

Notice how this statement gives an excellent sense of the thematic direction the paper will take: clearly, it will examine the relationship between Barbie dolls and gender role identification in contemporary America.

Opening Paragraphs   In most academic writing, you want to arrive at your thesis statement as quickly as possible, so that your reader will have a clear sense of your essay's purpose from the start. Many readers expect to find a thesis statement at the end of the introduction—generally the final sentence of the first or second paragraph. Effective introductions are often structured so as to lead up to the thesis statement: they draw the reader in by opening with an interesting specific point—a question, a quotation, a brief anecdote, a controversial assertion—which serves to introduce the topic generally; a general overview then leads up to the specific statement of the thesis in the last sentence.

In the student essay on page 32, for example, observe how the writer begins with a personal reflection about Barbie. Her anecdote may strike a familiar chord with readers and therefore draw them into the topic. Having made the attempt to arouse her readers' interest in her opening paragraph, the writer moves more pointedly into the general topic, discussing briefly the possible social and psychological implications of her parents' gift choices. This discussion leads into her thesis statement, a focused assertion that concludes her second paragraph.

Keep in mind that many writers wait until they have written a first draft before they worry about an introduction. They simply lead off with a tentative thesis statement, then go back later to look for effective ways to lead up to that statement.

Supporting Paragraphs   As you draft the body of your paper, keep two main goals in mind. First, try to make sure that all your supporting paragraphs are aimed at developing your thesis, so you maintain your focus and don't ramble off the topic. Second, work toward presenting your supporting ideas in logical order, and try to provide smooth transitions between points.

The order in which you choose to present your ideas depends in large part on your topic and purpose. When you are arguing for a particular position, you might begin with less important ideas and work toward a final, crucial point. In this way you can build a case that you "clinch" with your strongest piece of evidence. Other kinds of essays call for different structures. For example, an essay tracing the history of the Barbie doll and its effect on American culture would probably be structured chronologically, from the introduction of the toy to its present-day incarnations, since that would be the most natural way to develop the discussion.

The student essay at the end of this chapter moves from a personal reflection on the topic of Barbie (1); to a thesis statement that asserts the point of the paper (2); to a transitional paragraph moving from the writer's childhood experiences to a more general discussion of Barbie's role in reinforcing of gender-role stereotypes in other young girls (3); to an overview of how sociologists and historians critique the Barbie phenomenon (4); to an examination of whether Barbie has changed in response to evolving attitudes regarding women in society (5–7), the heart of the writer's argument; to a conclusion that frames the essay by returning to the original, personal example (8). Each new discussion seems to flow naturally into the next because the writer uses a transitional phrase or parallel language to link the first sentence in each paragraph to the end of the preceding paragraph.

Evidence   Using evidence effectively is the critical task in composing body paragraphs, because your essay will be convincing only to the degree that you make your arguments credible. Evidence can take many forms, from facts and figures you collect from library research to experiences you learn about in conversations with friends. While library research isn't necessary for every paper, it helps to include at least some "hard" facts and figures gathered from outside sources—journals, newspapers, textbooks—even if you're not writing a full-blown research paper. Frequently, gathering your evidence doesn't require scrolling through computer screens in your school's library; it could be accomplished by watching the six o'clock newscast or while reading the paper over breakfast.

Quotations from secondary sources are another common way of developing and supporting a point in a paragraph. Using another person's spoken or written words will lend your arguments a note of authenticity, especially when your source is a recognized authority in the field about which you're writing. A few points to remember when using quotations:

1. Generally, don't begin or end a supporting paragraph with a quotation. Articulate your point *in your own words* in the first sentence or two of the paragraph; *then* provide the quotation as a way of supporting your point. After the quotation, you might include another focusing sentence or two that analyzes the quotation and suggests how it relates to your point.

2. Keep your quotations brief. Overly lengthy quotations can make a paper difficult to read. You've probably read texts that nearly put you to sleep because of their overuse of quotations. As a general rule, quote source material only when the precise phrasing is necessary to support your abstract points. Be careful not to allow cited passages to overpower your own assertions.

3. Remember that all of your secondary material—whether quoted or paraphrased—needs to be accurately attributed. Make sure to mention the source's name and include other information (such as the publication date or page number) as required by your instructor.

While quotations, facts, and figures are the most common ways of developing your supporting paragraphs with evidence, you can also use your imagination to come up with other means of substantiating your points. Design a questionnaire, hand it out to your friends, and compile the resulting data as evidence. Interview a local authority on your topic, make notes about the conversation, and draw upon these as evidence. Finally, be your own authority: use your own powers of reasoning to come up with logical arguments that convince your readers of the validity of your assertions.

This body paragraph from the student essay on Barbie provides a good example of a writer using evidence to support her points:

> As Motz observes later in her article, Barbie has changed to adjust to the transforming attitudes of society over time. Both her facial expressions and wardrobe have undergone subtle alterations: "The newer Barbie has a more friendly, open expression, with a hint of a smile, and her lip and eye make-up is muted" (226), and in recent years Barbie's wardrobe has expanded to include some career clothing in addition to her massive volume of recreational attire. This transition appears to represent a conscious effort on the part of Barbie's manufacturers to integrate the concept of women as important members of the work force, with traditional ideals already depicted by Barbie.

The paragraph begins with an assertion of the general point that Barbie has changed in some ways over the years to reflect changes in societal attitudes toward women. This point is then supported with a quotation from an expert, and the page number of the original source is noted parenthetically. (Note that page references in this student essay are from the complete original essay by Motz, published in *The Popular Culture Reader*, not from the excerpt of the Motz essay earlier in this chapter.) The point is further developed with evidence presented in the writer's own words. The paragraph concludes with a final sentence that summarizes the main point of the evidence presented in the previous sentences, keeps the paragraph focused on the essay's thesis that Barbie perpetuates gender stereotypes, and sets the reader up for a transition into the next subtopic.

Obviously, all supporting paragraphs won't take this exact form; essays would be deadly boring if every paragraph looked the same. You'll encounter body paragraphs in professional essays that begin with quotations or end with quotations, for example. Just keep in mind that you want to *support* whatever general point you're making, so each paragraph should include a good balance of specific, concrete evidence. The more you practice writing the more ways you'll discover to develop body paragraphs with illustrations, examples, and evidence.

Conclusions You may have learned in high school English courses that an essay's conclusion should restate the main points made in the paper, so that the reader is left with a concise summary that leaves no doubt as to the paper's intention. This was an excellent suggestion for high school students, as it reinforced the notion of focusing an essay on a specific, concrete point. In college, however, you'll want to start developing a more sophisticated academic style. Conclusions to college-level essays should do more than merely repeat the paper's main points; they should leave the reader with something to think about.

Of course, what that *something* is, depends on your topic, your audiences, and your purpose in writing. Sometimes it may be appropriate to move from an objective discussion of a topic to a more subjective reflection on it. For instance, in analyzing the social effects of Barbie dolls, you might end by reflecting on the doll's significance in your own life or by commenting ironically on feminist critics who in your view make too much of Barbie's influence. Other ways to conclude are: providing a provocative quotation, offering a challenge for the future; asserting a forceful opinion; creating a striking image or memorable turn of phrase; or referring back to an image or idea in your introduction.

What you want to avoid is a bland and overly general conclusion along the lines of, "Thus, in conclusion, it would seem to this author that Barbie has had great and wide-reaching impact on today's contemporary society." Note how the writer of the Barbie essay created a strong conclusion by first returning to the subject of her opening paragraph—her own childhood toys—and then leaving the reader with a relatively memorable final sentence offering a challenge for the future:

> Looking back at my childhood, I see my parents engaged in this same struggle. By surrounding me with toys that perpetuated both feminine and masculine roles, they achieved a kind of balance among the conflicting images in society. However, they also seemed to succumb to traditional social pressures by giving me that Barbie Corvette, when all I wanted was a radio-controlled formula-one racer, like the one Emerson Fittipaldi drives. In a time when most parents agree that young girls should be encouraged to pursue their goals regardless of gender boundaries, their actions do not always reflect these ideals. Only when we demand that toys like Barbie no longer perpetuate stereotypes will this reform be complete.

Distancing

Distancing is the easiest part of the writing process because it involves doing nothing more than putting your first draft aside and giving yourself some emotional and intellectual distance from it. Pursue your daily activities, go to work or complete assignments for other classes, take a hike, throw a frisbee, polish your shoes, do anything but read over your draft . . . ideally for a day or two.

The reason to take the time to distance yourself is simple: you've been working hard on your essay and therefore have a strong personal investment in it. In order to revise effectively, you need to be able to see your essay dispassionately, almost as though someone else had written it. Stepping away from it for a day or two gives you the opportunity to approach your essay as an editor who has no compunction about changing, reordering, or completely cutting passages that don't work.

Also, the process of distancing allows your mind to work on the essay subconsciously even while you're going about your other non-writing activities. Frequently, during this distancing period, you'll find yourself coming up with new ideas that you can use to supplement your thesis as you revise.

Finally, factoring the process of distancing into the writing process will help you avoid the dread disease of all students: procrastination. Since you have to allot yourself enough time to write a draft *and* let it sit for a couple of days, you'll avoid a last-minute scramble for ideas and supporting material, and you'll have time to do a thorough revision.

One note of warning: Don't get so distanced from your draft that you forget to come back to it. If you do forget, all your prewritings and drafting will have gone to waste.

Revising

Many professional writers believe that revision is the most important stage in the writing process. Writers view the revision stage as an opportunity to clarify their ideas, to rearrange text so that the logical flow of their work is enhanced, to add new phrases or delete ones that don't work, to modify their thesis and change editorial direction . . . or, in some extreme cases, to throw the whole thing out and start over!

Just as with prewriting and drafting, many students dread revision because all the different issues that need to be considered make it appear to be a forbidding task. Most find it helpful to have a clear set of criteria with which to approach their first drafts. Following is such a checklist of questions, addressing specific issues of content, organization, and stylistics/mechanics. If you find that your answer is "no" to any one of these questions, then you need to rework your essay for improvement in that specific area.

Revision Checklist

Introduction
✓ Does the paper begin in a way that draws the reader into the paper while introducing the topic?
✓ Does the introduction provide some general overview that leads up to the thesis?
✓ Does the introduction end with a focused, assertive thesis in the form of a statement (not a question)?

Supporting Paragraphs and Conclusion
✓ Do your supporting paragraphs relate back to your thesis, so that the paper has a clear focus?

✓ Do your body paragraphs connect logically, with smooth transitions between them?
✓ Do your supporting paragraphs have a good balance between general points and specific, concrete evidence?
✓ If you've used secondary sources for your evidence, do you attribute them adequately to avoid any suspicion of plagiarism?
✓ If you've used quotations extensively, have you avoided having quoted material overpower your own writing?
✓ Does your last paragraph give your readers something to think about rather than merely restate what you've already said elsewhere in the essay?

Style and Mechanics
✓ Have you chosen your words aptly and sometimes inventively, avoiding clichés and overused phrases?
✓ Have you varied your sentence lengths effectively, thus helping create a pleasing prose rhythm?
✓ Have you proofread carefully, to catch any grammatical problems or spelling errors?

Make the minor changes or major overhauls required in your first draft. Then type or print out a second draft, and read *out loud* to yourself, to catch any awkward or unnatural sounding passages, wordy sentences, grammatical glitches and so on. Reading your prose out loud may seem weird—especially to your roommates who can't help overhearing—but doing so helps you gain some new perspective on the piece of writing you have been so close to, and frequently highlights minor, sentence-level problems that you might otherwise overlook.

Sample Student Essay

The following essay demonstrates one way of approaching the assignment we presented earlier. As you read, note the essay's introductory paragraphs and thesis statement, the way body paragraphs are developed with illustrations and examples, the way it concludes without simply restating the writer's points, the writer's effective use of words, and sentence structure.

• • • • • • • • • • • • • •

Role-Model Barbie: Now and Forever?
CAROLYN MUHLSTEIN

During my early childhood, my parents avoided placing gender bound-   1
aries on my play time. My brother and I both had Tonka trucks, and these

were driven by Barbie, Strawberry Shortcake, and GI Joe to my doll house, or to condos built with my brother's Erector Set. However, as I got older, the boundaries became more defined, and certain forms of play became "inappropriate." For example, I remember asking for a remote controlled car one Christmas, anticipating a powerful race car like the ones driven at De Anza Days, the local community fair. Christmas morning waiting for me under the tree was a bright yellow Barbie Corvette. It seemed as though my parents had decided that if I had to have a remote controlled car, at least it could be a feminine Barbie one!

Although I was too young to realize it at the time, this gift represented a   2
subtle shift in my parent's attitudes toward my gender-role choices. Where before my folks seemed content to let me assume either traditional "boy" or traditional "girl" roles in play, now they appeared to be subtly directing me toward traditional female role-playing. This is certainly one of the more dangerous consequences of Barbie's popularity in our society: a seemingly innocent toy defines for young girls the sorts of career choices, clothing, and relationships that will be "proper" for them as grown-up women.

Perhaps the Barbie Corvette was my parents' attempt to steer me back to-   3
ward more traditional feminine pursuits. Since her birth thirty-five years ago, Barbie has been used by many parents to illustrate the "appropriate" role of a woman in society. During earlier decades, when women were expected to remain at home, Barbie's lifestyle was extremely fitting. Marilyn Ferris Motz writes that Barbie "represents so well the widespread values of modern American society, devoting herself to the pursuit of happiness through leisure and material goods . . . teaching them [female children] the skills by which their future success will be measured." (212). Barbie, then serves as a symbol of the woman's traditional role in our society, and she serves to reinforce those stereotypes in young girls.

Motz' opinion isn't an isolated one. In fact, the consensus among sociolo-   4
gists, historians, and consumers is that Barbie represents a life of lazy leisure and wealth. Her "forever arched feet" and face "always smiling, eyes wide with admiration" (Tham 180) allow for little more than evenings on the town and strolls in the park. In addition, the accessories Barbie is equipped with are almost all related to pursuits of mere pleasure. According to a Barbie sticker album created by Mattel:

> Barbie is seen as a typical young lady of the twentieth century, who knows how to appreciate beautiful things and, at the same time, live life to the fullest . . . with her fashionable wardrobe and constant journeys to exciting places all over the world, the adventures of Barbie offer a glimpse of what they [girls] might achieve one day. (qtd. in Motz 218)

In this packaging "literature"—and in the countless other advertisements and packaging materials that have emerged since Barbie's invention some thirty years ago—the manufacturers exalt Barbie's materialism, her appreciation of "beautiful things," fine clothing, and expensive trips as positive personality traits: qualities which all normal, healthy girls in this society should try to emulate, according to the traditional view.

As Motz observes later in her article, Barbie has changed to adjust to the   5
transforming attitudes of society over time. Both her facial expressions and wardrobe have undergone subtle alterations: "The newer Barbie has a more friendly, open expression, with a hint of a smile, and her lip and eye make-up is muted" (226), and in recent years Barbie's wardrobe has expanded to include some career clothing in addition to her massive volume of

recreational attire. This transition appears to represent a conscious effort on the part of Barbie's manufacturers to integrate the concept of women as important members of the work force, with traditional ideals already depicted by Barbie.

Unfortunately, a critical examination of today's Barbie doll reveals that   6
this so-called integration is actually a cynical, half-hearted attempt to satisfy the concerns of some people—especially those concerned with feminist issues. Sure, Barbie now has office attire, a doctor outfit, a nurse outfit, and a few other pieces of "career" clothing, but her image continues to center on leisure. As Motz observes, "Barbie may try her hand at high-status occupations, but her appearance does not suggest competence and professionalism" (230). Quite the opposite, in fact: there are few, and in some cases, no accessories with which a young girl might imagine a world of professional competence for Barbie. There are no Barbie hospitals and no Barbie doctor offices; instead, she has only mansions, boats, and fast cars. Furthermore, Barbie's arched feet make it impossible for her to stand in anything but heels, so a career as a doctor, an astronaut—or anything else that requires standing up for more than twenty minutes on a fashion runway—would be nearly impossible!

From these examples, it's clear that Barbie's manufacturers have failed to   7
reconcile the traditional image of women as sexual, leisure-seeking consumers with the view that women are assertive, career-oriented individuals, because their "revision" of the Barbie image is at best a token one. This failure to reconcile two opposing roles for Barbie parallels the same contradiction in contemporary society. By choice and necessity women are in the work force in large numbers, seeking equal pay and equal opportunities with men; yet the more traditional voices in our culture continue to perpetuate stereotyped images of women. If we believe that we are at a transitional point in the evolution toward real equality for women, then Barbie exemplifies this transitional stage perfectly.

Looking back at my childhood, I see my parents engaged in this same   8
struggle. By surrounding me with toys that perpetuated both feminine and masculine roles, they achieved a kind of balance among the conflicting images in society. However, they also seemed to succumb to traditional social pressures by giving me that Barbie Corvette, when all I wanted was a radio-controlled formula-one racer, like the one Emerson Fittipaldi drives. In a time when most parents agree that young girls should be encouraged to pursue their goals regardless of gender boundaries, their actions do not always reflect these ideals. Only when we demand that toys like Barbie no longer perpetuate stereotypes will this reform be complete.

References

Motz, Marilyn Ferris. "Through Rose-Tinted Glasses," in *Popular Culture: An Introductory Text*, eds. Jack Trachbar and Kevin Lause. Bowling Green: Bowling Green V.P., 1992.

Tham, Hilary, "Barbie's Shoes," in *Mondo Barbie*, eds. Lucinda Ebersole and Richard Peabody. New York: St. Martin's Press, 1993.

2
ADVERTISING

You may be shocked by the accompanying advertisement for Benetton clothes, which features a dying AIDS patient surrounded by grieving friends and family. Along with other Benetton ads, it has raised a storm of controversy both within the professional advertising community and among the broader public. Some people argue that such advertisements succeed in raising public consciousness about AIDS (and Benetton clothes), while others insist the ads are in poor taste and should be banned. As one consumer put it, "I personally won't buy clothes from a company that has bloody corpses in their advertising." Whether the creators of the Benetton campaign were motivated by true sympathy for the plight of AIDS patients, or whether they merely wanted to draw attention to themselves and their product by shocking the public, we cannot know. One thing is certain, however: the ad and a host of others offering surprising or controversial images have been phenomenally successful in bringing recognition to the Benetton brand name.

Because the images they present are so often politically charged, Benetton ads are radically different from most of the advertising we see in magazines and on TV. Rarely do we think of advertising as topical or even socially relevant. In fact, most advertisers seem to play it safe, preferring to focus on such innocuous issues as "ring around the collar" or "the heartbreak of psoriasis." Even at their blandest and most inoffensive, however, advertisements still carry subtly powerful messages—about appropriate modes of behavior, standards of beauty and success,

35

gender roles, and a variety of other markers for normalcy. In fact, advertisers spend a great deal of time and money trying to understand the complex psychodynamics of their target audiences. In tailoring ads to appeal both to basic human impulses and to more culturally conditioned attitudes, they also ultimately reinforce and even engender such impulses and attitudes.

In previous courses you may have encountered the concept of "subliminal advertising," in which, for example, a skull is subtly drawn into the ice cube in a whiskey ad as a way of frightening readers subconsciously so they want to numb themselves with a stiff drink. And you may have been skeptical that such techniques could work. After all, the notion that advertisers somehow hypnotize us and turn us into walking zombies craving their products flies in the face of most of our experience. Yet there's no denying that we are manipulated by advertising in any number of ways, as the readings in this chapter suggest. Jib Fowles, for example, points out a variety of ways in which advertisements appeal to our emotions even though we may think we are making product choices using our intellect. Taking a similar approach, Berkeley Rice describes a technique called "psychographics" that advertisers use to plumb the inner workings and motivations of their target audiences. The readings in the second section of the chapter look at how advertising works to manipulate our notions of masculinity and femininity.

Whatever your view of advertising, keep in mind as you read the following selections that everything in advertisements—from ice cubes to sexy models to terminally ill patients and their families—exist solely for three well-calculated reasons: to sell, sell, and sell.

Approaches to Advertising

In the Shadow of the Image

Stuart and Elizabeth Ewen

*W*e begin *this chapter with a selection from Stuart and Elizabeth Ewen's book* Channels of Desire *(1982), in which they point out the impact of mass produced images on our lives and on our sense of identity. As the title suggests, the Ewens see us as existing in the shadow of these mass produced images, confronting them, puzzling over them, responding to them, judging ourselves in terms of them—in short, being influenced by images, especially advertising images, in ways about which we may not be fully aware.*

In this introduction to their book, the Ewens present a number of different scenes—"Meaningless moments. Random incidents. Memory traces"—in which people respond to the mass media images that surround them. Although each incident is seemingly insignificant, the Ewens suggest that, viewed together as "an ensemble, an integrated panorama of social life, human activity, hope and despair, images and information, another tale unfolds from these vignettes." As you'll see, this is a tale about contemporary American culture, about how we understand ourselves and relate to one another, and about the subtle yet profound influence of advertising and the mass media on our lives.

To begin your reading, think of some familiar images from television, magazine, and billboard advertisements. Consider the effect these images have on you as you read the Ewens' description of the effect of such images on other people. How much of yourself do you see in the Ewens' scenes?

•••••••••••••••••••

Maria Aguilar was born twenty-seven years ago near Mayagüez, on the island of Puerto Rico. Her family had lived off the land for generations. Today she sits in a rattling IRT subway car, speeding through the iron-and-rock guts of Manhattan. She sits on the train, her ears dazed by the loud outcry of wheels against tracks. Surrounded by a galaxy of unknown fellow strangers, she looks up at a long strip of colorful signboards placed high above the bobbing heads of the others. All the posters call for her attention.

Looking down at her, a blond-haired lady cabdriver leans out of her driver's side window. Here is the famed philosopher of this strange urban world, and a woman she can talk to. The tough-wise eyes of

1

2

the cabby combined with a youthful beauty, speaking to Maria Aguilar directly:

> *Estoy sentada 12 horas al dia.*
> *Lo último que necesito son hemorroides.*
>
> *(I sit for twelve hours a day. The last thing I need are hemorrhoids.)*

Under this candid testimonial lies a package of Preparation H ointment, and the promise "Alivia dolores y picasonas. Y ayuda a reducir la hinchazón." (Relieves pain and itching. And helps reduce swelling.) As her mind's eye takes it all in, the train sweeps into Maria's stop. She gets out; climbs the stairs to the street; walks to work where she will spend her day sitting on a stool in a small garment factory, sewing hems on pretty dresses.   3

Every day, while Benny Doyle drives his Mustang to work along State Road Number 20, he passes a giant billboard along the shoulder. The billboard is selling whiskey and features a woman in a black velvet dress stretching across its brilliant canvas.   4

As Benny Doyle downshifts by, the lounging beauty looks out to him. Day after day he sees her here. The first time he wasn't sure, but now he's convinced that her eyes are following him.   5

The morning sun shines on the red-tan forehead of Bill O'Conner as he drinks espresso on his sun deck, alongside the ocean cliffs of La Jolla, California. Turning through the daily paper, he reads a story about Zimbabwe.   6

"Rhodesia," he thinks to himself.   7

The story argues that a large number of Africans in Zimbabwe are fearful about black majority rule, and are concerned over a white exodus. Two black hotel workers are quoted by the article. Bill puts this, as a fact, into his mind.   8

Later that day, over a business lunch, he repeats the story to five white business associates, sitting at the restaurant table. They share a superior laugh over the ineptitude of black African political rule. Three more tellings, children of the first, take place over the next four days. These are spoken by two of Bill O'Conner's luncheon companions; passed on to still others in the supposed voice of political wisdom.   9

Barbara and John Marsh get into their seven-year-old Dodge pickup and drive twenty-three miles to the nearest Sears in Cedar Rapids. After years of breakdowns and months of hesitation they've decided to buy a new washing machine. They come to Sears because it is there,   10 and because they believe that their new Sears machine will be steady and reliable. The Marshes will pay for their purchase for the next year or so.

Barbara's great-grandfather, Elijah Simmons, had purchased a cream-separator from Sears, Roebuck in 1897 and he swore by it.   11

When the clock-radio sprang the morning affront upon him, Archie Bishop rolled resentfully out of his crumpled bed and trudged slowly to the john. A few moments later he was unconsciously squeezing toothpaste out of a mess of red and white Colgate packaging. A dozen scrubs of the mouth and he expectorated a white, minty glob into the basin.   12

Still groggy, he turned on the hot water, slapping occasional palmfuls onto his gray face.   13

A can of Noxzema shave cream sat on the edge of the sink, a film of crud and whiskers across its once neat label. Archie reached for the bomb and filled his left hand with a white creamy mound, then spread it over his beard. He shaved, then looked with resignation at the regular collection of cuts on his neck.   14

Stepping into a shower, he soaped up with a soap that promised to wake him up. Groggily, he then grabbed a bottle of Clairol Herbal Essence Shampoo. He turned the tablet-shaped bottle to its back label, carefully reading the "Directions."   15

"Wet hair."   16

He wet his hair.   17

"Lather."   18

He lathered.   19

"Rinse."   20

He rinsed.   21

"Repeat if necessary."   22

Not sure whether it was altogether necessary, he repeated the process according to directions.   23

Late in the evening, Maria Aguilar stepped back in the subway train, heading home to the Bronx after a long and tiring day. This time, a poster told her that "The Pain Stops Here!"   24

She barely noticed, but later she would swallow two New Extra Strength Bufferin tablets with a glass of water from a rusty tap.   25

Two cockroaches in cartoon form leer out onto the street from a wall advertisement. The man cockroach is drawn like a hipster, wearing shades and a cockroach zoot-suit. He strolls hand-in-hand with a lady cockroach, who is dressed like a floozy and blushing beet-red. Caught   26 in the midst of their cockroach-rendezvous, they step sinfully into a Black Flag Roach Motel. Beneath them, in Spanish, the words:

Las Cucarachas entran . . . pero non pueden salir.
(In the English version: Cockroaches check in . . but they don't check out.)

The roaches are trapped; sin is punished. Salvation is gauged by one's ability to live roach-free. The sinners of the earth shall be inundated by ɪoaches. Moral tales and insects encourage passersby to rid their houses of sin. In their homes, sometimes, people wonder whether God has forsaken them.

Beverly Jackson sits at a metal and tan Formica table and looks through the *New York Post*. She is bombarded by a catalog of horror. Children are mutilated . . . subway riders attacked. . . . Fanatics are marauding and noble despots lie in bloody heaps. Occasionally someone steps off the crime-infested streets to claim a million dollars in lottery winnings. 28

Beverly Jackson's skin crawls; she feels a knot encircling her lungs. She is beset by immobility, hopelessness, depression. 29

Slowly she walks over to her sixth-floor window, gazing out into the sooty afternoon. From the empty street below, Beverly Jackson imagines a crowd yelling "Jump! . . . Jump!" 30

Between 1957 and 1966 Frank Miller saw a dozen John Wayne movies, countless other westerns and war dramas. In 1969 he led a charge up a hill without a name in Southeast Asia. No one followed; he took a bullet in the chest. 31

Today he sits in a chair and doesn't get up. He feels that images betrayed him, and now he camps out across from the White House while another movie star cuts benefits for veterans. In the morning newspaper he reads of a massive weapons buildup taking place. 32

Gina Concepcion now comes to school wearing the Jordache look. All this has been made possible by weeks and weeks of afterschool employment at a supermarket checkout counter. Now, each morning, she tugs the decorative denim over her young legs, sucking in her lean belly to close the snaps. 33

These pants are expensive compared to the "no-name" brands, but they're worth it, she reasons. They fit better, and she fits better. 34

The theater marquee, stretching out over a crumbling, garbage-strewn sidewalk, announced "The Decline of Western Civilization." At the ticket window a smaller sign read "All seats $5.00." 35

It was ten in the morning and Joyce Hopkins stood before a mirror next to her bed. Her interview at General Public Utilities, Nuclear Divi- 36 sion, was only four hours away and all she could think was "What to wear?"

A half hour later Joyce stood again before the mirror, wearing a slip 37 and stockings. On the bed, next to her, lay a two-foot-high mountain of discarded options. Mocking the title of a recent bestseller, which she hadn't read, she said aloud to herself, "Dress for Success. . . . What *do* they like?"

At one o'clock she walked out the door wearing a brownish tweed 38 jacket; a cream-colored Qiana blouse, full-cut with a tied collar; a dark beige skirt, fairly straight and hemmed (by Maria Aguilar) two inches below the knee; shear fawn stockings, and simple but elegant reddish-brown pumps on her feet. Her hair was to the shoulder, her look tawny.

When she got the job she thanked her friend Millie, a middle man- 39 ager, for the tip not to wear pants.

Joe Davis stood at the endless conveyor, placing caps on a round- 40 the-clock parade of automobile radiators. His nose and eyes burned. His ears buzzed in the din. In a furtive moment he looked up and to the right. On the plant wall was a large yellow sign with THINK! printed on it in bold type. Joe turned back quickly to the radiator caps.

Fifty years earlier in another factory, in another state, Joe's grand- 41 father, Nat Davis, had looked up and seen another sign:

A Clean Machine Runs Better.
Your Body Is a Machine.
KEEP IT CLEAN.

Though he tried and tried, Joe Davis' grandfather was never able to 42 get the dirt out from under his nails. Neither could his great-grand-father, who couldn't read.

In 1952 Mary Bird left her family in Charleston to earn money as a 43 maid in a Philadelphia suburb. She earned thirty-five dollars a week, plus room and board, in a dingy retreat of a ranch-style tract house.

Twenty-eight years later she sits on a bus, heading toward her small 44 room in north Philly. Across from her, on an advertising poster, a sump-tuous meal is displayed. Golden fried chicken, green beans glistening with butter and flecked by pimento, and a fluffy cloud of rice fill the greater part of a calico-patterned dinner plate. Next to the plate sit a steaming boat of gravy, and an icy drink in an amber tumbler. The plate is on a quilted blue placemat, flanked by a thick linen napkin and colo-nial silverware.

As Mary Bird's hungers are aroused, the wording on the placard in- 45 structs her: *"Come home to Carolina."*

Shopping List   46

> paper towels
> milk
> eggs
> rice crispies
> chicken
> snacks for kids (twinkies, chips, etc.)
> potatoes
> coke, ginger ale, plain soda
> cheer
> brillo
> peanut butter
> bread
> ragu (2 jars)
> spaghetti
> saran wrap
> salad
> get cleaning, bank, *must pay electric!!!*

On his way to Nina's house, Sidney passed an ad for Smirnoff   47
vodka. A sultry beauty with wet hair and beads of moisture on her
smooth, tanned face looked out at him. *"Try a Main Squeeze."* For a
teenage boy the invitation transcended the arena of drink; he felt a quick
throb-pulse at the base of his belly and his step quickened.

In October of 1957, at the age of two and a half, Aaron Stone was   48
watching television. Suddenly, from the black screen, there leaped a circus clown, selling children's vitamins, and yelling "Hi! boys and girls!"
He ran, terrified, from the room, screaming.

For years after, Aaron watched television in perpetual fear that the   49
vitamin clown would reappear. Slowly his family assured him that the
television was just a mechanical box and couldn't really hurt him, that
the vitamin clown was harmless.

Today, as an adult, Aaron Stone takes vitamins, is ambivalent about   50
clowns, and watches television, although there are occasional moments
of anxiety.

These are some of the facts of our lives; disparate moments, discon-   51
nected, dissociated. Meaningless moments. Random incidents. Memory
traces. Each is an unplanned encounter, part of day-to-day existence.
Viewed alone, each by itself, such spaces of our lives seem insignificant,
trivial. They are the decisions and reveries of survival; the stuff of small

talk; the chance preoccupations of our eyes and minds in a world of images—soon forgotten.

Viewed together, however, as an ensemble, an integrated panorama   52
of social life, human activity, hope and despair, images and information, another tale unfolds from these vignettes. They reveal a pattern of life, the structures of perception.

As familiar moments in American life, all of these events bear the   53
footprints of a history that weighs upon us, but is largely untold. We live and breathe an atmosphere where mass images are everywhere in evidence; mass produced, mass distributed. In the streets, in our homes, among a crowd, or alone, they speak to us, overwhelm our vision. Their presence, their messages are given; unavoidable. Though their history is still relatively short, their prehistory is, for the most part, forgotten, unimaginable.

The history that unites the seemingly random routines of daily life   54
is one that embraces the rise of an industrial consumer society. It involves explosive interactions between modernity and old ways of life. It includes the proliferation, over days and decades, of a wide, repeatable vernacular of commercial images and ideas. This history spells new patterns of social, productive, and political life.

. . . .

Examining the Text

1. What is the effect of the Ewens' strategy in this essay of presenting a number of brief, disconnected episodes in the lives of different people? Do you think it would have been more effective to include more commentary connecting the scenes? Why or why not?

2. What connections do you see among the episodes presented here? What thematic unities are there among the stories?

3. In their conclusion, the Ewens suggest that the moments they describe portray "explosive interactions between modernity and old ways of life" and spell "new patterns of social, productive, and political life" (paragraph 54). In your own words, what do you think the authors are suggesting here? Do you find their point persuasive?

For Group Discussion

Choose one of the scenes presented and, after rereading and reflecting on your understanding, discuss as a group the similarities and differences in your responses to this scene.

Writing Suggestion

Add to the Ewens' essay an experience of your own in which you or someone you know is "in the shadow of an image." You might consider influential images in advertisements, TV shows, music videos, or movies.

Masters of Desire

Jack Solomon

*T*his selection is taken from the book The Signs of Our Time *(1988), in which Jack Solomon uses semiology, the study of signs, in analyzing contemporary American culture. In this excerpt, Solomon interprets advertising from a semiological perspective, noting the signs and symbols at work in specific ads and suggesting what they mean and why they appeal to the American consumer.*

Solomon asserts that "the American dream breeds desire, a longing for a greater share of the pie," and that in order to sell us products advertisements exploit this and other desires, fears, and guilts we share. Specifically, ads present signs that encourage us to think that particular products can satisfy our desires (for social status, or belonging, or sexual attractiveness), alleviate our fears, and calm our guilt. On a conscious level, we know that most products can't do these things and that we shouldn't be swayed by such promises of beauty, popularity, and success. But the companies that spend millions of dollars on advertising are obviously betting that subconsciously we're more susceptible than we like to admit.

As you read, pay attention to the way Solomon interprets specific ads, identifying the signs they contain and the reasons these signs are effective. After you finish the essay, you'll have a chance to develop your own semiotic interpretation of an ad of your choice.

• • • • • • • • • • • • • • • • •

> Amongst democratic nations, men easily attain a certain equality
> of condition; but they can never attain as much as they desire.
> ALEXIS DE TOCQUEVILLE

On May 10, 1831, a young French aristocrat named Alexis de Tocqueville arrived in New York City at the start of what would become one of the most famous visits to America in our history. He had come to observe firsthand the institutions of the freest, most egalitarian society of the age, but what he found was a paradox. For behind America's mythic promise of equal opportunity, Tocqueville discovered a desire for *un-*

1

equal social rewards, a ferocious competition for privilege and distinction. As he wrote in his monumental study, *Democracy in America:*

> When all privilege of birth and fortune are abolished, when all profes-
> sions are accessible to all, and a man's own energies may place him at
> the top of any one of them, an easy and unbounded career seems open
> to his ambition. . . . But this is an erroneous notion, which is corrected
> by daily experience. [For when] men are nearly alike, and all follow the
> same track, it is very difficult for any one individual to walk quick and
> cleave a way through the same throng which surrounds and presses
> him.

Yet walking quick and cleaving a way is precisely what Americans   2
dream of. We Americans dream of rising above the crowd, of attaining
a social summit beyond the reach of ordinary citizens. And therein lies
the paradox.

The American dream, in other words, has two faces: the one com-   3
munally egalitarian and the other competitively elitist. This contradiction is no accident; it is fundamental to the structure of American society. Even as America's great myth of equality celebrates the virtues of
mom, apple pie, and the girl or boy next door, it also lures us to achieve
social distinction, to rise above the crowd and bask alone in the glory.
This land is your land and this land is my land, Woody Guthrie's populist anthem tells us, but we keep trying to increase the "my" at the expense of the "your." Rather than fostering contentment, the American
dream breeds desire, a longing for a greater share of the pie. It is as if
our society were a vast high-school football game, with the bulk of the
participants noisily rooting in the stands while, deep down, each of
them is wishing he or she could be the star quarterback or head cheerleader.

For the semiotician, the contradictory nature of the American myth   4
of equality is nowhere written so clearly as in the signs that American
advertisers use to manipulate us into buying their wares. "Manipulate"
is the word here, not "persuade"; for advertising campaigns are not
sources of product information, they are exercises in behavior modification. Appealing to our subconscious emotions rather than to our conscious intellects, advertisements are designed to exploit the discontent-
ments fostered by the American dream, the constant desire for social
success and the material rewards that accompany it. America's consumer economy runs on desire, and advertising stokes the engines by
transforming common objects—from peanut butter to political candidates—into signs of all the things that Americans covet most.

But by semiotically reading the signs that advertising agencies man-   5
ufacture to stimulate consumption, we can plot the precise state of desire in the audiences to which they are addressed. In this [essay], we'll

look at a representative sample of ads and what they say about the emotional climate of the country and the fast-changing trends of American life. Because ours is a highly diverse, pluralistic society, various advertisements may say different things depending on their intended audiences, but in every case they say something about America, about the status of our hopes, fears, desires, and beliefs.

Let's begin with two ad campaigns conducted by the same company that bear out Alexis de Tocqueville's observations about the contradictory nature of American society: General Motors' campaigns for its Cadillac and Chevrolet lines. First, consider an early magazine ad for the Cadillac Allanté. Appearing as a full-color, four-page insert in *Time*, the ad seems to say "I'm special—and so is this car" even before we've begun to read it. Rather than being printed on the ordinary, flimsy pages of the magazine, the Allanté spread appears on glossy coated stock. The unwritten message here is that an extraordinary car deserves an extraordinary advertisement, and that both car and ad are aimed at an extraordinary consumer, or at least one who wishes to appear extraordinary compared to his more ordinary fellow citizens.

Ads of this kind work by creating symbolic associations between their product and what is most coveted by the consumers to whom they are addressed. It is significant, then, that this ad insists that the Allanté is virtually an Italian rather than an American car, an automobile, as its copy runs, "Conceived and Commissioned by America's Luxury Car Leader—Cadillac" but "Designed and Handcrafted by Europe's Renowned Design Leader—Pininfarina, SpA, of Turin, Italy." This is not simply a piece of product information, it's a sign of the prestige that European luxury cars enjoy in today's automotive marketplace. Once the luxury car of choice for America's status drivers, Cadillac has fallen far behind its European competitors in the race for the prestige market. So the Allanté essentially represents Cadillac's decision, after years of resisting the trend toward European cars, to introduce its own European import—whose high cost is clearly printed on the last page of the ad. Although $54,700 is a lot of money to pay for a Cadillac, it's about what you'd expect to pay for a top-of-the-line Mercedes-Benz. That's precisely the point the ad is trying to make: the Allanté is no mere car. It's a potent status symbol you can associate with the other major status symbols of the 1980s.

American companies manufacture status symbols because American consumers want them. As Alexis de Tocqueville recognized a century and a half ago, the competitive nature of democratic societies breeds a desire for social distinction, a yearning to rise above the crowd. But given the fact that those who do make it to the top in socially mobile societies have often risen from the lower ranks, they still look like everyone else. In the socially immobile societies of aristocratic Europe, generations of fixed social conditions produced subtle class signals. The accent of one's voice, the shape of one's nose, or even the set of one's chin, immediately communicated social status. Aside from the nasal bray and uptilted head of the Boston Brahmin, Americans do not have any native sets of personal status signals. If it weren't for his Mercedes-Benz and Manhattan townhouse, the parvenu Wall Street millionaire often couldn't be distinguished from the man who tailors his suits. Hence, the demand for status symbols, for the objects that mark one off as a social success, is particularly strong in democratic nations—stronger even than in aristocratic societies, where the aristocrat so often looks and sounds different from everyone else.

Status symbols, then, are signs that identify their possessors' place 9
in a social hierarchy, markers of rank and prestige. We can all think of any number of status symbols—Rolls-Royces, Beverly Hills mansions, even Shar Pei puppies (whose rareness and expense has rocketed them beyond Russian wolfhounds as status pets and has even inspired whole lines of wrinkle-faced stuffed toys)—but how do we know that something *is* status symbol? The explanation is quite simple: when an object (or puppy!) either costs a lot of money or requires influential connections to possess, anyone who possesses it must also possess the necessary mean and influence to acquire it. The object itself really doesn't matter, since it ultimately disappears behind the presumed social potency of its owner. Semiotically, what matters is the signal it sends, its value as a sign of power. One traditional sign of social distinction is owning a country estate and enjoying the peace and privacy that attend it. Advertisements for Mercedes-Benz, Jaguar, and Audi automobiles thus frequently feature drivers motoring quietly along a country road, presumably on their way to or from their country houses.

Advertisers have been quick to exploit the status signals that belong 10
to body language as well. As Hegel observed in the early nineteenth century, it is an ancient aristocratic prerogative to be seen by the lower orders without having to look at them in return. Tilting his chin high in the air and gazing down at the world under hooded eyelids, the aristocrat invites observation while refusing to look back. We can find such a pose exploited in an advertisement for Cadillac Seville in which we see an elegantly dressed woman out for a drive with her husband in their new Cadillac. If we look closely at the woman's body language, we can see her glance inwardly with a satisfied smile on her face but not outward toward the camera that represents our gaze. She is glad to be seen by us in her Seville, but she isn't interested in looking at *us*!

Ads that are aimed at a broader market take the opposite approach. 11
If the American dream encourage the desire to "arrive," to vault above

the mass, it also fosters a desire to be popular, to "belong." Populist commercials accordingly transform products into signs of belonging, utilizing such common icons as country music, small-town life, family picnics, and farmyards. All of these icons are incorporated in GM's "Heartbeat of America" campaign for its Chevrolet line. Unlike the Seville commercial, the faces in the Chevy ads look straight at us and smile. Dress is casual; the mood upbeat. Quick camera cuts take us from rustic to suburban to urban scenes, creating an American montage filmed from sea to shining sea. We all "belong" in a Chevy.

Where price alone doesn't determine the market for a product, ad-   12
vertisers can go either way. Both Johnnie Walker and Jack Daniel's are better-grade whiskies, but where a Johnnie Walker ad appeals to the buyer who wants a mark of aristocratic distinction in his liquor, a Jack Daniel's ad emphasizes the down-home, egalitarian folksiness of its product. Johnnie Walker associates itself with such conventional status symbols as sable coats, Rolls-Royces, and black gold; Jack Daniel's gives us a Good Ol' Boy in overalls. In fact, Jack Daniel's Good Ol' Boy is an icon of backwoods independence, recalling the days of the moonshiner and the Whisky Rebellion of 1794. Evoking emotions quite at odds with those stimulated in Johnnie Walker ads, the advertisers of Jack Daniel's have chosen to transform their product into a sign of America's populist tradition. The fact that both ads successfully sell whisky is itself a sign of the dual nature of the American dream.

Beer is also pitched on two levels. Consider the difference between   13
the ways Budweiser and Michelob market their light beers. Bud Light and Michelob Light cost and taste about the same, but Budweiser tends to target the working class while Michelob has gone after the upscale market. Bud commercials are set in working-class bars that contrast with the sophisticated nightclubs and yuppie watering holes of the Michelob campaign. "You're one of the guys," Budweiser assures the assembly-line worker and the truck driver, "this Bud's for you." Michelob, on the other hand, makes no such appeal to the democratic instinct of sharing and belonging. You don't share, you take, grabbing what you can in a competitive dash to "have it all."

Populist advertising is particularly effective in the face of foreign   14
competition. When Americans feel threatened from the outside, they tend to circle the wagons and temporarily forget their class differences. In the face of the Japanese automotive "invasion," Chrysler runs populist commercials in which Lee Iacocca joins the simple folk who buy his cars as the jingle "Born in America" blares in the background. Seeking to capitalize on the popularity of Bruce Springsteen's *Born in the USA* album, these ads gloss over Springsteen's ironic lyrics in a vast display of flag-waving. Chevrolet's "Heartbeat of America" campaign similarly

attempts to woo American motorists away from Japanese automobiles by appealing to their patriotic sentiments.

The patriotic iconography of these campaigns also reflects the general cultural mood of the early- to mid-1980s. After a period of national anguish in the wake of the Vietnam War and the Iran hostage crisis, America went on a patriotic binge. American athletic triumphs in the Lake Placid and Los Angeles Olympics introduced a sporting tone into the national celebration, often making international affairs appear like one great Olympiad in which America was always going for the gold. In response, advertisers began to do their own flag-waving. 15

The mood of advertising during this period was definitely upbeat. Even deodorant commercials, which traditionally work on our self-doubts and fears of social rejection, jumped on the bandwagon. In the guilty sixties, we had ads like the "Ice Blue Secret" campaign with its connotations of guilt and shame. In the feel-good Reagan eighties, "Sure" deodorant commercials featured images of triumphant Americans throwing up their arms in victory to reveal—no wet marks! Deodorant commercials once had the moral echo of Nathaniel Hawthorne's guilt-ridden *The Scarlet Letter;* in the early eighties they had all the moral subtlety of *Rocky IV,* reflecting the emotions of a Vietnam-weary nation eager to embrace the imagery of America Triumphant. 16

The commercials for Worlds of Wonder's Lazer Tag game featured the futuristic finals of some Soviet-American Lazer Tag shootout ("Practice hard, America!") and carried the emotions of patriotism into an even more aggressive arena. Exploiting the hoopla that surrounded the victory over the Soviets in the hockey finals of the 1980 Olympics, the Lazer Tag ads pandered to an American desire for the sort of clear-cut nationalistic triumphs that the nuclear age has rendered almost impossible. Creating a fantasy setting where patriotic dreams are substituted for complicated realities, the Lazer Tag commercials sought to capture the imaginations of children caught up in the patriotic fervor of the early 1980s. 17

Live the Fantasy

By reading the signs of American advertising, we can conclude that America is a nation of fantasizers, often preferring the sign to the substance and easily enthralled by a veritable Fantasy Island of commercial illusions. Critics of Madison Avenue often complain that advertisers create consumer desire, but semioticians don't think the situation is that simple. Advertisers may give shape to consumer fantasies, but they need raw material to work with, the subconscious dreams and desires of the marketplace. As long as these desires remain unconscious, 18 advertisers will be able to exploit them. But by bringing the fantasies to the surface, you can free yourself from advertising's often hypnotic grasp.

I can think of no company that has more successfully seized upon   19
the subconscious fantasies of the American marketplace—indeed the world marketplace—than McDonald's. By no means the first nor the only hamburger chain in the United States, McDonald's emerged victorious in the "burger wars" by transforming hamburgers into signs of all that was desirable in American life. Other chains like Wendy's, Burger King, and Jack-In-The-Box continue to advertise and sell widely, but no company approaches McDonald's transformation of itself into a symbol of American culture.

McDonald's success can be traced to the precision of its advertising.   20
Instead of broadcasting a single "one-size-fits-all" campaign at a time, McDonald's pitches its burgers simultaneously at different age groups, different classes, even different races (Budweiser beer, incidentally, has succeeded in the same way). For children, there is the Ronald McDonald campaign, which presents a fantasy world that has little to do with hamburgers in any rational sense but a great deal to do with the emotional desires of kids. Ronald McDonald and his friends are signs that recall the Muppets, *Sesame Street*, the circus, toys, storybook illustrations, even *Alice in Wonderland*. Such signs do not signify hamburgers. Rather, they are displayed in order to prompt in the child's mind an automatic association of fantasy, fun, and McDonald's.

The same approach is taken in ads aimed at older audiences—teens,   21
adults, and senior citizens. In the teen-oriented ads we may catch a fleeting glimpse of a hamburger or two, but what we are really shown is a teenage fantasy: groups of hip and happy adolescents singing, dancing, and cavorting together. Fearing loneliness more than anything else, adolescents quickly respond to the group appeal of such commercials. "Eat a Big Mac," these ads say, "and you won't be stuck home alone on Saturday night."

To appeal to an older and more sophisticated audience no longer so   22
afraid of not belonging and more concerned with finding a place to go out to at night, McDonald's has designed the elaborate "Mac Tonight" commercials, which have for their backdrop a nightlit urban skyline and at their center a cabaret pianist with a moon-shaped head, a glad manner, and Blues Brothers shades. Such signs prompt an association of McDonald's with nightclubs and urban sophistication, persuading us that McDonald's is a place not only for breakfast or lunch but for dinner too, as if it were a popular off-Broadway nightspot, a place to see and be seen. Even the parody of Kurt Weill's "Mack the Knife" theme song that Mac the Pianist performs is a sign, a subtle signal to the sophisticated

hamburger eater able to recognize the origin of the tune in Bertolt Brecht's *Threepenny Opera*.

For yet older customers, McDonald's has designed a commercial 23 around the fact that it employs a large number of retirees and seniors. In one such ad, we see an elderly man leaving his pretty little cottage early in the morning to start work as "the new kid" at McDonald's, and then we watch him during his first day on the job. Of course he is a great success, outdoing everyone else with his energy and efficiency, and he returns home in the evening to a loving wife and happy home. One would almost think that the ad was a kind of moving "help wanted" sign (indeed, McDonald's *was* hiring elderly employees at the time), but it's really just directed at consumers. Older viewers can see themselves wanted and appreciated in the ad—and perhaps be distracted from the rationally uncomfortable fact that many senior citizens take such jobs because of financial need and thus may be unlikely to own the sort of home that one sees in the commercial. But realism isn't the point here. This is fantasyland, a dream world promising instant gratification no matter what the facts of the matter may be.

Practically the only fantasy that McDonald's doesn't exploit is the 24 fantasy of sex. This is understandable, given McDonald's desire to present itself as a family restaurant. But everywhere else, sexual fantasies, which have always had an important place in American advertising, are beginning to dominate the advertising scene. You expect sexual come-ons in ads for perfume or cosmetics or jewelry—after all, that's what they're selling—but for room deodorizers? In a magazine ad for Claire Burke home fragrances, for example, we see a well-dressed couple cavorting about their bedroom in what looks like a cheery preparation for sadomasochistic exercises. Jordache and Calvin Klein pitch blue jeans as props for teenage sexuality. The phallic appeal of automobiles, traditionally an implicit feature in automotive advertising, becomes quite explicit in a Dodge commercial that shifts back and forth from shots of a young man in an automobile to teasing glimpses of a woman—his date—as she dresses in her apartment.

The very language of today's advertisements is charged with sexu- 25 ality. Products in the more innocent fifties were "new and improved," but everything in the eighties is "hot!"—as in "hot woman," or sexual heat. Cars are "hot." Movies are "hot." An ad for Valvoline pulses to the rhythm of a "heat wave, burning in my car." Sneakers get red hot in a magazine ad for Travel Fox athletic shoes in which we see male and female figures, clad only in Travel Fox shoes, apparently in the act of copulation—an ad that earned one of *Adweek*'s annual "badvertising" awards for shoddy advertising.

The sexual explicitness of contemporary advertising is a sign not so 26 much of American sexual fantasies as of the lengths to which advertisers will go to get attention. Sex never fails as an attention-getter, and in a particularly competitive, and expensive, era for American marketing, advertisers like to bet on a sure thing. Ad people refer to the proliferation of TV, radio, newspaper, magazine, and billboard ads as "clutter," and nothing cuts through the clutter like sex.

By showing the flesh, advertisers work on the deepest, most coercive human emotions of all. Much sexual coercion in advertising, however, is a sign of a desperate need to make certain that clients are getting their money's worth. The appearance of advertisements that refer directly to the prefabricated fantasies of Hollywood is a sign of a different sort of desperation: a desperation for ideas. With the rapid turnover of advertising campaigns mandated by the need to cut through the "clutter," advertisers may be hard pressed for new ad concepts, and so they are more and more frequently turning to already-established models. In the early 1980s, for instance, Pepsi-Cola ran a series of ads broadly alluding to Steven Spielberg's *E.T.* In one such ad, we see a young boy who, like the hero of *E.T.*, witnesses an extraterrestrial visit. The boy is led to a soft-drink machine where he pauses to drink a can of Pepsi as the spaceship he's spotted flies off into the universe. The relationship between the ad and the movie, accordingly, is a parasitical one, with the ad taking its life from the creative body of the film.   27

Pepsi did something similar in 1987 when it arranged with the producers of the movie *Top Gun* to promote the film's video release in Pepsi ad to the video itself. This time, however, the parasitical relationship between ad and film was made explicit. Pepsi sales benefited from the video, and the video's sales benefited from Pepsi. It was a marriage made in corporate heaven.   28

The fact that Pepsi believed that it could stimulate consumption by appealing to the militaristic fantasies dramatized in *Top Gun* reflects similar fantasies in the "Pepsi generation." Earlier generations saw Pepsi associated with high-school courtship rituals, with couples sipping sodas together at the corner drugstore. When the draft was on, young men fantasized about Peggy Sue, not Air Force Flight School. Military service was all too real a possibility to fantasize about. But in an era when military service is not a reality for most young Americans, Pepsi commercials featuring hotshot fly-boys drinking Pepsi while streaking about in their Air Force jets contribute to a youth culture that has forgotten what military service means. It all looks like such fun in the Pepsi ads, but what they conceal is the fact that military jets are weapons, not high-tech recreational vehicles.   29

For less militaristic dreamers, Madison Avenue has framed ad campaigns around the cultural prestige of high-tech machinery in its own   30

right. This is especially the case with sports cars, whose high-tech appeal is so powerful that some people apparently fantasize about *being*
sports cars. At least, this is the conclusion one might draw from a
Porsche commercial that asked its audience, "If you were a car, what
kind of car would you be?" As a candy-red Porsche speeds along a rain-
slick forest road, the ad's voice-over describes all the specifications
you'd want to have if you *were* a sports car. "If you were a car," the commercial concludes, "you'd be a Porsche."

In his essay "Car Commercials and *Miami Vice*," Todd Gitlin ex-   31
plains the semiotic appeal of such ads as those in the Porsche campaign.
Aired at the height of what may be called America's "myth of the entrepreneur," these commercials were aimed at young corporate managers who imaginatively identified with the "lone wolf" image of a
Porsche speeding through the woods. Gitlin points out that such images
cater to the fantasies of faceless corporate men who dream of entrepreneurial glory, of striking out on their own like John DeLorean and telling
the boss to take his job and shove it. But as DeLorean's spectacular failure demonstrates, the life of the entrepreneur can be extremely risky. So
rather than having to go it alone and take the risks that accompany entrepreneurial independence, the young executive can substitute fantasy
for reality by climbing into his Porsche—or at least that's what Porsche's
advertisers wanted him to believe.

But there is more at work in the Porsche ads than the fantasies of   32
corporate America. Ever since Arthur C. Clarke and Stanley Kubrick
teamed up to present us with HAL 9000, the demented computer of
2001: A Space Odyssey, the American imagination has been obsessed
with the melding of man and machine. First there was television's *Six
Million Dollar Man,* and then movieland's *Star Wars, Blade Runner,* and
Robocop, fantasy visions of a future dominated by machines. Androids
haunt our imaginations as machines seize the initiative. *Time* magazine's "Man of the Year" for 1982 was a computer. Robot-built automobiles appeal to drivers who spend their days in front of computer
screens—perhaps designing robots. When so much power and prestige
is being given to high-tech machines, wouldn't you rather be a Porsche?

In short, the Porsche campaign is a sign of a new mythology that is   33
emerging before our eyes, a myth of the machine, which is replacing the
myth of the human. The iconic figure of the little tramp caught up in the
cogs of industrial production in Charlie Chaplin's *Modern Times* signified a humanistic revulsion to the age of the machine. Human beings,
such icons said, were superior to machines. Human values should come
first in the moral order of things. But as Edith Milton suggests in her essay, "The Track of the Mutant," we are now coming to believe that machines are superior to human beings, that mechanical nature is superior

to human nature. Rather than being threatened by machines, we long to merge with them. *The Six Million Dollar Man* is one iconic figure in the new mythology; Harrison Ford's sexual coupling with an android is another. In such an age it should come as little wonder that computer-synthesized Max Headroom should be a commercial spokesman for Coca-Cola, or that Federal Express should design a series of TV ads featuring mechanical-looking human beings revolving around strange and powerful machines.

Fear and Trembling in the Marketplace

While advertisers play on and reflect back at us our fantasies about everything from fighter pilots to robots, they also play on darker imaginings. If dream and desire can be exploited in the quest for sales, so can nightmare and fear. 34

The nightmare equivalent of America's populist desire to "belong," for example, is the fear of not belonging, of social rejection, of being different. Advertisements for dandruff shampoos, mouthwashes, deodorants, and laundry detergents ("Ring Around the Collar!") accordingly exploit such fears, bullying us into consumption. Although ads of this type are still around in the 1980s, they were particularly common in the fifties and early sixties, reflecting a society still reeling from the witch-hunts of the McCarthy years. When any sort of social eccentricity or difference could result in a public denunciation and the loss of one's job or even liberty, Americans were keen to conform and be like everyone else. No one wanted to be "guilty" of smelling bad or of having a dirty collar. 35

"Guilt" ads characteristically work by creating narrative situations in which someone is "accused" of some social "transgression," pronounced guilty, and then offered the sponsor's product as a means of returning to "innocence." Such ads, in essence, are parodies of ancient religious rituals of guilt and atonement, whereby sinning humanity is offered salvation through the agency of priest and church. In the world of advertising, a product takes the place of the priest, but the logic of the situation is quite similar. 36

In commercials for Wisk detergent, for example, we witness the drama of a hapless housewife and her husband as they are mocked by the jeering voices of children shouting "Ring Around the Collar!" "Oh, those dirty rings!" the housewife groans in despair. It's as if she and her husband were being stoned by an angry crowd. But there's hope, there's help, there's Wisk. Cleansing her soul of sin as well as her husband's, the housewife launders his shirts with Wisk, and behold, his collars are clean. Product salvation is only as far as the supermarket. 37

The recent appearance of advertisements for hospitals treating drug   38
and alcohol addiction have raised the old genre of the guilt ad to new
heights (or lows, depending on your perspective). In such ads, we see
wives on the verge of leaving their husbands if they don't do something
about their drinking, and salesmen about to lose their jobs. The man is
guilty; he has sinned; but he upholds the ritual of guilt and atonement
by "confessing" to his wife or boss and agreeing to go to the hospital the
ad is pitching.

If guilt looks backward in time to past transgressions, fear, like de-   39
sire, faces forward, trembling before the future. In the late 1980s, a new
kind of fear commercial appeared, one whose narrative played on the
worries of young corporate managers struggling up the ladder of success. Representing the nightmare equivalent of the elitist desire to "arrive," ads of this sort created images of failure, storylines of corporate
defeat. In one ad for Apple computers, for example, a group of junior
executives sits around a table with the boss as he asks each executive
how long it will take his or her department to complete some publishing jobs. "Two or three days," answers one nervous executive. "A week,
on overtime," a tight-lipped woman responds. But one young up-and-
comer can have everything ready tomorrow, today, or yesterday, because his department uses a Macintosh desktop publishing system.
Guess who'll get the next promotion?

Fear stalks an ad for AT&T computer systems too. A boss and four   40
junior executives are dining in a posh restaurant. Icons of corporate
power and prestige flood the screen—from the executives' formal
evening wear to the fancy table setting—but there's tension in the air. It
seems that the junior managers have chosen a computer system that's
incompatible with the firm's sales and marketing departments. A whole
new system will have to be purchased, but the tone of the meeting suggests that it will be handled by a new group of managers. These guys
are on the way out. They no longer "belong." Indeed, it's probably no
accident that the ad takes place in a restaurant, given the joke that went
around in the aftermath of the 1987 market crash, "What do you call a
yuppie stockbroker?" the joke ran. "Hey, waiter!" Is the ad trying subtly to suggest that junior executives who choose the wrong computer
systems are doomed to suffer the same fate?

For other markets, there are other fears. If McDonald's presents se-   41
nior citizens with bright fantasies of being useful and appreciated beyond retirement, companies like Secure Horizons dramatize senior citizens' fears of being caught short by a major illness. Running its ads in
the wake of budgetary cuts in the Medicare system, Secure Horizons designed a series of commercials featuring a pleasant old man named
Harry—who looks and sounds rather like Carroll O'Connor—who tells

us the story of the scare he got during his wife's recent illness. Fearing that next time Medicare won't cover the bills, he has purchased supplemental health insurance from Secure Horizons and now securely tends his rooftop garden.

Among all the fears advertisers have exploited over the years, I find 42 the fear of not having a posh enough burial site the most arresting. Advertisers usually avoid any mention of death—who wants to associate a product with the grave?—but mortuary advertisers haven't much choice. Generally, they solve their problem by framing cemeteries as timeless parks presided over by priestly morticians, appealing to our desires for dignity and comfort in the face of bereavement. But in one television commercial for Forest Lawn we find a different approach. In this ad we are presented with the ghost of an old man telling us how he might have found a much nicer resting place than the run-down cemetery in which we find him had his wife only known that Forest Lawn was so "affordable." I presume the ad was supposed to be funny, but it's been pulled off the air. There are some fears that just won't bear joking about, some nightmares too dark to dramatize.

The Future of an Illusion

There are some signs in the advertising world that Americans are 43 getting fed up with fantasy advertisements and want to hear some straight talk. Weary of extravagant product claims and irrelevant associations, consumers trained by years of advertising to distrust what they hear seem to be developing an immunity to commercials. At least, this is the semiotic message I read in the "new realism" advertisements of the eighties, ads that attempt to convince you that what you're seeing is the real thing, that the ad is giving you the straight dope, not advertising hype.

You can recognize the "new realism" by its camera techniques. The 44 lighting is usually subdued to give the ad the effect of being filmed blinds were drawn. The camera shots are jerky and off-angle, often zooming in for sudden unflattering close-ups, as if the cameraman was an amateur with a home video recorder. In a "realistic" ad for AT&T, for example, we are treated to a monologue by a plump stockbroker—his plumpness intended as a sign that he's for real and not just another actor—who tells us about the problems he's had with his phone system (not AT&T's) as the camera jerks around, generally filming him from below as if the cameraman couldn't quite fit his equipment into the crammed office and had to film the scene on his knees. "This is no fancy advertisement," the ad tries to convince us, "this is sincere."

An ad for Miller draft beer tries the same approach, recreating the   45
effect of an amateur videotape of a wedding celebration. Camera shots
shift suddenly from group to group. The picture jumps. Bodies are
poorly framed. The color is washed out. Like the beer it is pushing, the
ad is supposed to strike us as being "as real as it gets."

Such ads reflect a desire for reality in the marketplace, a weariness   46
with Madison Avenue illusions. But there's no illusion like the illusion
of reality. Every special technique that advertisers use to create their "reality effects" is, in fact, more unrealistic than the techniques of "illusory"
ads. The world, in reality, doesn't jump around when you look at it. It
doesn't appear in subdued gray tones. Our eyes don't have zoom lenses,
and we don't look at things with our heads cocked to one side. The irony
of the "new realism" is that it is more unrealistic, more artificial, than
the ordinary run of television advertising.

But don't expect any truly realistic ads in the future, because a real-   47
istic advertisement is a contradiction in terms. The logic of advertising
is entirely semiotic: it substitutes signs for things, framed visions of consumer desire for the thing itself. The success of modern advertising, its
penetration into every corner of American life, reflects a culture that has
itself chosen illusion over reality. At a time when political candidates all
have professional image-makers attached to their staffs, and the President of the United States is an actor who once sold shirt collars, all the
cultural signs are pointing to more illusions in our lives rather than
fewer—a fecund breeding ground for the world of the advertiser.

••••••••••••••••••••

Examining the Text

1. What does Solomon see as the basic contradiction or conflict inherent in the American Dream? How does advertising exploit this contradiction? Think of specific ads you've seen recently that are manipulative or exploitative in the way that Solomon describes.

2. Solomon points out that advertisers manipulate consumers, using
our dreams and desires as the "raw material" (paragraph 18). How does
he propose we defend ourselves against this manipulation? What do
you think of his solution?

3. Solomon offers short interpretations of some specific advertising
campaigns—Pepsi, Porsche, McDonald's, and Cadillac, among others.
For one example that you found particularly interesting, restate Solomon's interpretation. What would you add to make this interpretation
stronger?

For Group Discussion

According to Solomon, advertisers usually appeal either to our dreams and desires or to our guilt and fear. Recall some ads that you think are particularly effective. Were they manipulating our fantasies or our nightmares or did they use other strategies discussed by Solomon? Discuss which strategies you think work best, and why.

Writing Suggestion

In this essay, Solomon takes a semiotic approach to advertising, because, as he explains, "The logic of advertising is entirely semiotic: it substitutes signs for things, framed visions of consumer desire for the thing itself" (47). List the signs you find in a recent magazine ad that interests you and explore in writing the meaning and the appeal of each of them. What overall conclusions about the ad can you draw from your own semiological analysis?

Advertising's Fifteen Basic Appeals
Jib Fowles

*I*n *the following essay, Jib Fowles looks at how advertisements work by examining the emotional, subrational appeals that they employ. We are confronted daily by hundreds of ads, only a few of which actually attract our attention. These few do so, according to Fowles, through "something primary and primitive, an emotional appeal, that in effect is the thin edge of the wedge, trying to find its way into a mind." Drawing on research done by the psychologist Henry A. Murray, Fowles describes fifteen emotional appeals or wedges that advertisements exploit.*

Underlying Fowles's psychological analysis of advertising is the assumption that advertisers try to circumvent the logical, cautious, skeptical powers we develop as consumers, to reach, instead, the "unfulfilled urges and motives swirling in the bottom half of [our] minds." In Fowles's view, consumers are well advised to pay attention to these underlying appeals in order to avoid responding unthinkingly.

As you read, note which of Fowles's fifteen appeals seem most familiar to you. Do you recognize these appeals in ads you can recall? How have you responded?

....

Emotional Appeals

The nature of effective advertisements was recognized full well by   1
the late media philosopher Marshall McLuhan. In his *Understanding Media*, the first sentence of the section on advertising reads, "The continuous pressure is to create ads more and more in the image of audience motives and desires."

By giving form to people's deep-lying desires, and picturing states   2
of being that individuals privately yearn for, advertisers have the best chance of arresting attention and affecting communication. And that is the immediate goal of advertising: to tug at our psychological shirt sleeves and slow us down long enough for a word or two about whatever is being sold. We glance at a picture of a solitary rancher at work, and "Marlboro" slips into our minds.

Advertisers (I'm using the term as a shorthand for both the prod-   3
ucts' manufacturers, who bring the ambition and money to the process, and the advertising agencies, who supply the know-how) are ever more compelled to invoke consumers' drives and longings; this is the "continuous pressure" McLuhan refers to. Over the past century, the American marketplace has grown increasingly congested as more and more products have entered into the frenzied competition after the public's dollars. The economies of other nations are quieter than ours since the volume of goods being hawked does not so greatly exceed demand. In some economies, consumer wares are scarce enough that no advertising at all is necessary. But in the United States, we go to the other extreme. In order to stay in business, an advertiser must strive to cut through the considerable commercial hub-bub by any means available—including the emotional appeals that some observers have held to be abhorrent and underhanded.

The use of subconscious appeals is a comment not only on conditions   4
among sellers. As time has gone by, buyers have become stoutly resistant to advertisements. We live in a blizzard of these messages and have learned to turn up our collars and ward off most of them. A study done a few years ago at Harvard University's Graduate School of Business Administration ventured that the average American is exposed to some 500 ads daily from television, newspapers, magazines, radio, billboards, direct mail, and so on. If for no other reason than to preserve one's sanity, a filter must be developed in every mind to lower the number of ads a person is actually aware of—a number this particular study estimated at about seventy-five ads per day. (Of these, only twelve typically produced a reaction—nine positive and three negative, on the average.) To be among the few messages that do manage to gain access to minds, advertisers must be strategic, perhaps even a little underhanded at times.

There are assumptions about personality underlying advertisers' ef-   5
forts to communicate via emotional appeals, and while these assumptions have stood the test of time, they still deserve to be aired. Human
beings, it is presumed, walk around with a variety of unfulfilled urges
and motives swirling in the bottom half of their minds. Lusts, ambitions,
tendernesses, vulnerabilities—they are constantly bubbling up, seeking
resolution. These mental forces energize people, but they are too crude
and irregular to be given excessive play in the real world. They must be
capped with the competent, sensible behavior that permits individuals
to get along well in society. However, this upper layer of mental activity, shot through with caution and rationality, is not receptive to advertising's pitches. Advertisers want to circumvent this shell of consciousness if they can, and latch on to one of the lurching, subconscious drives.

In effect, advertisers over the years have blindly felt their way   6
around the underside of the American psyche, and by trial and error
have discovered the softest points of entree, the places where their messages have the greatest likelihood of getting by consumers' defenses. As
McLuhan says elsewhere, "Gouging away at the surface of public sales
resistance, the ad men are constantly breaking through into the *Alice in
Wonderland* territory behind the looking glass, which is the world of subrational impulses and appetites."

An advertisement communicates by making use of a specially se-   7
lected image (of a supine female, say, or a curly-headed child, or a
celebrity) which is designed to stimulate "subrational impulses and desires" even when they are at ebb, even if they are unacknowledged by
their possessor. Some few ads have their emotional appeal in the text,
but for the greater number by far the appeal is contained in the artwork.
This makes sense, since visual communication better suits more primal
levels of the brain. If the viewer of an advertisement actually has the im-
portuned motive, and if the appeal is sufficiently well-fashioned to call
it up, then the person can be hooked. The product in the ad may then
appeal to take on the semblance of gratification for the summoned motive. Many ads seem to be saying, "If you have this need, then this product will help satisfy it." It is a primitive equation, but not an ineffective
one for selling.

Thus, most advertisements appearing in national media can be un-   8
derstood as having two orders of content. The first is the appeal to deep-
running drives in the minds of consumers. The second is information
regarding the good[s] or service being sold: its name, its manufacturer,
its picture, its packaging, its objective attributes, its functions. For example, the reader of a brassiere advertisement sees a partially undraped
but blandly unperturbed woman standing in an otherwise commonplace public setting, and may experience certain sensations; the reader

also sees the name "Maidenform," a particular brassiere style, and, in tiny print, words about the material, colors, price. Or, the viewer of a television commercial sees a demonstration with four small boxes labelled 650, 650, 650, and 800; something in the viewer's mind catches hold of this, as trivial as thoughtful consideration might reveal it to be. The viewer is also exposed to the name "Anacin," its bottle, and its purpose.

Sometimes there is an apparently logical link between an ad's emotional appeal and its product information. It does not violate common sense that Cadillac automobiles be photographed at country clubs, or that Japan Air Lines be associated with Orientalia. But there is no real need for the linkage to have a bit of reason behind it. Is there anything inherent to the connection between Salem cigarettes and mountains, Coke and a smile, Miller Beer and comradeship? The link being forged in minds between product and appeal is a pre-logical one.

People involved in the advertising industry do not necessarily talk in the terms being used here. They are stationed at the sending end of this communications channel, and may think they are up to any number of things—Unique Selling Propositions, explosive copywriting, the optimal use of demographics or psychographics, ideal media buys, high recall ratings, or whatever. But when attention shifts to the receiving end of the channel, and focuses on the instant of reception, then commentary becomes much more elemental: an advertising message contains something primary and primitive, an emotional appeal, that in effect is the thin end of the wedge, trying to find its way into a mind. Should this occur, the product information comes along behind.

When enough advertisements are examined in this light, it becomes clear that the emotional appeals fall into several distinguishable categories, and that every ad is a variation on one of a limited number of basic appeals. While there may be several ways of classifying these appeals, one particular list of fifteen has proven to be especially valuable.

Advertisements can appeal to:
1. The need for sex
2. The need for affiliation
3. The need to nurture
4. The need for guidance
5. The need to aggress
6. The need to achieve
7. The need to dominate
8. The need for prominence

9. The need for attention
10. The need for autonomy
11. The need to escape
12. The need to feel safe
13. The need for aesthetic sensations
14. The need to satisfy curiosity
15. Physiological needs: food, drink, sleep, etc.

Murray's List

Where does this list of advertising's fifteen basic appeals come   12
from? Several years ago, I was involved in a research project which was
to have as one segment an objective analysis of the changing appeals
made in post-World War II American advertising. A sample of magazine ads would have their appeals coded into the categories of psychological needs they seemed aimed at. For this content analysis to happen,
a complete roster of human motives would have to be found.

The first thing that came to mind was Abraham Maslow's famous   13
four-part hierarchy of needs. But the briefest look at the range of appeals
made in advertising was enough to reveal that they are more varied, and
more profane, than Maslow had cared to account for. The search led on
to the work of psychologist Henry A. Murray, who together with his colleagues at the Harvard Psychological Clinic has constructed a full taxonomy of needs. As described in *Explorations in Personality*, Murray's
team had conducted a lengthy series of depth interviews with a number of subjects in order to derive from scratch what they felt to be the essential variables of personality. Forty-four variables were distinguished
by the Harvard group, of which twenty were motives. The need for
achievement ("to overcome obstacles and obtain a high standard") was
one, for instance; the need to defer was another; the need to aggress was
a third; and so forth.

Murray's list had served as the groundwork for a number of subse-   14
quent projects. Perhaps the best-known of these was David C. McClelland's extensive study of the need for achievement, reported in his *The
Achieving Society*. In the process of demonstrating that a people's high
need for achievement is predictive of later economic growth, McClelland coded achievement imagery and references out of a nation's folk-
lore, songs, legends, and children's tales.

Following McClelland, I too wanted to cull the motivational appeals   15
from a culture's imaginative product—in this case, advertising. To de-

velop categories expressly for this purpose, I took Murray's twenty motives and added to them others he had mentioned in passing in *Explorations in Personality* but not included on the final list. The extended list
was tried out on a sample of advertisements, and motives which never
seemed to be invoked were dropped. I ended up with eighteen of Mur-
rays' motives, into which 770 print ads were coded. The resulting distribution is included in the 1976 book *Mass Advertising as Social Forecast*.

Since that time, the list of appeals has undergone refinements as a   16
result of using it to analyze television commercials. A few more adjust-
ments stemmed from the efforts of students in my advertising classes
to decode appeals; tens of term papers surveying thousands of advertisements have caused some inconsistencies in the list to be hammered
out. Fundamentally, though, the list remains the creation of Henry Murray. In developing a comprehensive, parsimonious inventory of human
motives, he pinpointed the subsurface mental forces that are the least
quiescent and most susceptible to advertising's entreaties.

Fifteen Appeals

1. *Need for sex.* Let's start with sex, because this is the appeal   17
which seems to pop up first whenever the topic of advertising is raised.
Whole books have been written about this one alone, to find a large audience of mildly titillated readers. Lately, due to campaigns to sell blue
jeans, concern with sex in ads has redoubled.

The fascinating thing is not how much sex there is in advertising,   18
but how little. Contrary to impressions, unambiguous sex is rare in these
messages. Some of this surprising observation may be a matter of definition: the Jordache ads with the lithe, blouse-less female astride a similarly clad male is clearly an appeal to the audience's sexual drives, but
the same cannot be said about Brooke Shields in the Calvin Klein commercials. Directed at young women and their credit-card carrying
mothers, the image of Miss Shields instead invokes the need to be
looked at. Buy Calvins and you'll be the center of much attention, just
as Brooke is, the ads imply; they do not primarily inveigle their target
audience's need for sexual intercourse.

In the content analysis reported in *Mass Advertising as Social Forecast*,   19
only two percent of ads were found to pander to this motive. Even *Playboy* ads shy away from sexual appeals: a recent issue contained eighty-
three full-page ads, and just four of them (or less than five percent) could
be said to have sex on their minds.

The reason this appeal is so little used is that it is too blaring and   20
tends to obliterate the product information. Nudity in advertising has

the effect of reducing brand recall. The people who do remember the product may do so because they have been made indignant by the ad; this is not the response most advertisers seek.

To the extent that sexual imagery is used, it conventionally works   21
better on men than women; typically a female figure is offered up to the male reader. A Black Velvet liquor advertisement displays an attractive woman wearing a tight black outfit, recumbent under the legend, "Feel the Velvet." The figure does not have to be horizontal, however, for the appeal to be present as National Airlines revealed in its "Fly me" campaign. Indeed, there does not even have to be a female in the ad; "Flick my Bic" was sufficient to convey the idea to many.

As a rule, though, advertisers have found sex to be a tricky appeal,   22
to be used sparingly. Less controversial and equally fetching are the appeals to our need for affectionate human contact.

2. *Need for affiliation.*   American mythology upholds autonomous   23
individuals, and social statistics suggest that people are ever more going it alone in their lives, yet the high frequency of affiliative appeals in ads belies this. Or maybe it does not: maybe all the images of companionship are compensation for what Americans privately lack. In any case, the need to associate with others is widely invoked in advertising and is probably the most prevalent appeal. All sorts of goods and services are sold by linking them to our unfulfilled desires to be in good company.

According to Henry Murray, the need for affiliation consists of de-   24
sires "to draw near and enjoyably cooperate or reciprocate with another; to please and win affection of another; to adhere and remain loyal to a friend." The manifestations of this motive can be segmented into several different types of affiliation, beginning with romance.

Courtship may be swifter nowadays, but the desire for pair-bond-   25
ing is far from satiated. Ads reaching for this need commonly depict a youngish male and female engrossed in each other. The head of the male is usually higher than the female's, even at this late date; she may be sitting or leaning while he is standing. They are not touching in the Smirnoff vodka ads, but obviously there is an intimacy, sometimes frolicsome, between them. The couple does touch for Martell Cognac when "The moment was Martell." For Wind Song perfume they have touched, and "Your Wing Song stays on his mind."

Depending on the audience, the pair does not absolutely have to be   26
young—just together. He gives her a DeBeers diamond, and there is a tear in her laugh lines. She takes Geritol and preserves herself for him. And numbers of consumers, wanting affection too, follow suit.

Warm family feelings are fanned in ads when another generation is   27
added to the pair. Hallmark Cards brings grandparents into the picture,

and Johnson and Johnson Baby Powder has Dad, Mom, and baby, all fresh from the bath, encircled in arms and emblazoned with "Share the Feeling." A talc has been fused to familial love.

Friendship is yet another form of affiliation pursued by advertisers.   28 Two women confide and drink Maxwell House coffee together; two men walk through the woods smoking Salem cigarettes. Miller Beer promises that afternoon "Miller Time" will be staffed with three or four good buddies. Drink Dr. Pepper, as Mickey Rooney is coaxed to do, and join in with all the other Peppers. Coca-Cola does not even need to portray the friendliness; it has reduced this appeal to "a Coke and a smile."

The warmth can be toned down and disguised, but it is the same af-   29 filiative need that is being fished for. The blonde has a direct gaze and her friends are firm businessmen in appearance, but with a glass of Old Bushmill you can sit down and fit right in. Or, for something more up-beat, sing along with the Pontiac choirboys.

As well as presenting positive images, advertisers can play to the   30 need for affiliation in negative ways, by invoking the fear of rejection. If we don't use Scope, we'll have the "Ugh! Morning Breath" that causes the male and female models to avert their faces. Unless we apply Ultra-Brite or Close-Up to our teeth, it's good-bye romance. Our family will be cursed with "House-a-tosis" if we don't take care. Without Dr. Scholl's anti-perspirant foot spray, the bowling team will keel over. There go all the guests when the supply of Dorito's nacho cheese chips is exhausted. Still more rejection if our shirts have ring-around-the-collar, if our car needs to be Midasized. But make a few purchases, and we are back in the bosom of human contact.

As self-directed as Americans pretend to be, in the last analysis we   31 remain social animals, hungering for the positive, endorsing feelings that only those around us can supply. Advertisers respond, urging us to "Reach out and touch someone," in the hopes our monthly bills will rise.

3. *Need to nurture.*   Akin to affiliative needs is the need to take care   32 of small, defenseless creatures—children and pets, largely. Reciprocity is of less consequence here, though; it is the giving that counts. Murray uses synonyms like "to feed, help, support, console, protect, comfort, nurse, heal." A strong need it is, woven deep into our genetic fabric, for if it did not exist we could not successfully raise up our replacements. When advertisers put forth the image of something diminutive and furry, something that elicits the word "cute" or "precious," then they are trying to trigger this motive. We listen to the childish voice singing the Oscar Mayer weiner song, and our next hot-dog purchase is prescribed. Aren't those darling kittens something, and how did this Meow Mix get into our shopping cart?

This pitch is often directed at women, as Mother Nature's chief nur- 33
turers. "Make me some Kraft macaroni and cheese, please," says the
elfin preschooler just in from the snowstorm, and mothers' hearts go
out, and Kraft's sales go up. "We're cold, wet, and hungry," whine the
husband and kids, and the little woman gets the Manwiches ready. A
facsimile of this need can be hit without children or pets: the husband is
ill and sleepless in the television commercial, and the wife grudgingly
fetches the NyQuil.

But it is not women alone who can be touched by this appeal. The 34
father nurses his son Eddie through adolescence while the John Deere
lawn tractor survives the years. Another father counts pennies with his
young son as the subject of New York Life Insurance comes up. And all
over America are businessmen who don't know why they dial Qantas
Airlines when they have to take a trans-Pacific trip; the koala bear
knows.

4. *Need for guidance.* The opposite of the need to nurture is the need 35
to be nurtured: to be protected, shielded, guided. We may be loath to
admit it, but the child lingers on inside every adult—and a good thing
it does, or we would not be instructable in our advancing years. Who
wants a nation of nothing but flinty personalities?

Parent-like figures can successfully call up this need. Robert Young 36
recommends Sanka coffee, and since we have experienced him for
twenty-five years as television father and doctor, we take his word for
it. Florence Henderson as the expert mom knows a lot about the advantages of Wesson oil.

The parent-ness of the spokesperson need not be so salient; some- 37
times pure authoritativeness is better. When Orson Welles scowls and
intones, "Paul Masson will sell no wine before its time," we may not
know exactly what he means, but we still take direction from him. There
is little maternal about Brenda Vaccaro when she speaks up for Tampax,
but there is a certainty to her that many accept.

A celebrity is not a necessity in making a pitch to the need for guid- 38
ance, since a fantasy figure can serve just as well. People accede to the
Green Giant, or Betty Crocker, or Mr. Goodwrench. Some advertisers
can get by with no figure at all: "When E.F. Hutton talks, people listen."

Often it is tradition or custom that advertisers point to and con- 39
sumers take guidance from. Bits and pieces of American history are
used to sell whiskeys like Old Crow, Southern Comfort, Jack Daniel's.
We conform to traditional male/female roles and age-old social norms
when we purchase Barclay cigarettes, which informs us "The pleasure
is back."

The product itself, if it has been around for a long time, can consti- 40
tute a tradition. All those old labels in the ad for Morton salt convince

us that we should continue to buy it. Kool-Aid says, "You loved it as a kid. You trust it as a mother," hoping to get yet more consumers to go along.

Even when the product has no history at all, our need to conform to 41 tradition and to be guided are strong enough that they can be invoked through bogus nostalgia and older actors. Country-Time lemonade sells because consumers want to believe it has a past they can defer to.

So far the needs and the ways they can be invoked which have been 42 looked at are largely warm and affiliative; they stand in contrast to the next set of needs, which are much more egoistic and assertive.

5. *Need to aggress.* The pressures of the real world create strong re- 43 taliatory feelings in every functioning human being. Since these impulses can come forth as bursts of anger and violence, their display is normally tabooed. Existing as harbored energy, aggressive drives present a large, tempting target for advertisers. It is not a target to be aimed at thoughtlessly, though, for few manufacturers want their products associated with destructive motives. There is always the danger that, as in the case of sex, if the appeal is too blatant, public opinion will turn against what is being sold.

Jack-in-the-Box sought to abruptly alter its marketing by going af- 44 ter older customers and forgetting the younger ones. Their television commercials had a seventy-ish lady command, "Waste him," and the Jack-in-the-Box clown exploded before our eyes. So did public reaction, until the commercials were toned down. Print ads for Club cocktails carried the faces of octogenarians under the headline, "Hit me with a Club"; response was contrary enough to bring the campaign to a stop.

Better disguised aggressive appeals are less likely to backfire: Tri- 45 umph cigarettes has models making a lewd gesture with their uplifted cigarettes, but the individuals are often laughing and usually in the close company of others. When Exxon said, "There's a Tiger in your tank," the implausibility of it concealed the invocation of aggressive feelings.

Depicted arguments are a common way for advertisers to tap the 46 audience's needs to aggress. Don Rickles and Lynda Carter trade gibes, and consumers take sides as the name of Seven-Up is stitched on minds. The Parkay tub has a difference of opinion with the user; who can forget it, or who (or what) got the last word in?

6. *Need to achieve.* This is the drive that energizes people, causing 47 them to strive in their lives and careers. According to Murray, the need for achievement is signalled by the desires "to accomplish something difficult. To overcome obstacles and attain a high standard. To excel one's self. To rival and surpass others." A prominent American trait, it is one that advertisers like to hook on to because it identifies their product with winning and success.

The Cutty Sark ad does not disclose that Ted Turner failed at his lat-   48
est attempt at yachting's America Cup; here he is represented as a champion on the water as well as off in his television enterprises. If we drink
this whiskey, we will be victorious alongside Turner. We can also succeed with O.J. Simpson by renting Hertz cars, or with Reggie Jackson by
bringing home some Panasonic equipment. Cathy Rigby and Stayfree
Maxipads will put people out front.

Sports heroes are the most convenient means to snare consumers'   49
needs to achieve, but they are not the only one. Role models can be established, ones which invite emulation, as with the profiles put forth by
Dewar's scotch. Successful, tweedy individuals relate they have "grad-
uated to the flavor of Myer's rum." Or the advertiser can establish a
prize: two neighbors play one-on-one basketball for a Michelob beer in
a television commercial, while in a print ad a bottle of Johnnie Walker
Black Label has been gilded like a trophy.

Any product that advertises itself in superlatives—the best, the first,   50
the finest—is trying to make contact with our needs to succeed. For
many consumers, sales and bargains belong in this category of appeals,
too; the person who manages to buy something at fifty percent off is
seizing an opportunity and coming out ahead of others.

7. *Need to dominate.*   This fundamental need is the craving to be   51
powerful—perhaps omnipotent, as in the Xerox ad where Brother Do-
minic exhibits heavenly powers and creates miraculous copies. Most of
us will settle for being just a regular potentate, though. We drink Budweiser because it is the King of Beers, and here comes the powerful
Clydesdales to prove it. A taste of Wolfschmidt vodka and "The spirit
of the Czar lives on."

The need to dominate and control one's environment is often   52
thought of as being masculine, but as close students of human nature
advertisers know, it is not so circumscribed. Women's aspirations for
control are suggested in the campaign theme, "I like my men in English
Leather, or nothing at all." The females in the Chanel No. 19 ads are
"outspoken" and wrestle their men around.

Male and female, what we long for is clout; what we get in its place   53
is Mastercard.

8. *Need for prominence.*   Here comes the need to be admired and re-   54
spected, to enjoy prestige and high social status. These times, it appears,
are not so egalitarian after all. Many ads picture the trappings of high
position; the Oldsmobile stands before a manorial doorway, the Volvo
is parked beside a steeplechase. A book-lined study is the setting for Dewar's 12, and Lenox China is displayed in a dining room chock full of
antiques.

Beefeater gin represents itself as "The Crown Jewel of England" and   55

uses no illustrations of jewels or things British, for the words are sufficient indicators of distinction. Buy that gin and you will rise up the prestige hierarchy, or achieve the same effect on yourself with Seagram's 7
Crown, which ambiguously describes itself as "classy."

Being respected does not have to entail the usual accoutrements of   56
wealth: "Do you know who I am?" the commercials ask, and we learn
that the prominent person is not so prominent without his American Express card.

9. *Need for attention.* The previous need involved being *looked up*   57
to, while this is the need to be *looked at.* The desire to exhibit ourselves
in such a way as to make others look at us is a primitive, insuppressible
instinct. The clothing and cosmetic industries exist just to serve this
need, and this is the way they pitch their wares. Some of this effort is
aimed at males, as the ads for Hathaway shirts and Jockey underclothes.
But the greater bulk of such appeals is targeted singlemindedly at
women.

To come back to Brooke Shields: this is where she fits into American   58
marketing. If I buy Calvin Klein jeans, consumers infer, I'll be the object
of fascination. The desire for exhibition has been most strikingly played
to in a print campaign of many years duration, that of Maidenform lingerie. The woman exposes herself, and sales surge. "Gentlemen prefer
Hanes" the ads dissemble, and women who want eyes upon them know
what they should do. Peggy Fleming flutters her legs for L'eggs, encouraging females who want to be the star in their own lives to purchase
this product.

The same appeal works for cosmetics and lotions. For years, the lit-   59
tle girl with the exposed backside sold gobs of Coppertone, but now the
company has picked up the pace a little: as a female, you are supposed
to "Flash 'em a Coppertone tan." Food can be sold the same way, especially to the diet-conscious; Angie Dickinson poses for California avocados and says, "Would this body lie to you?" Our eyes are too fixed on
her for us to think to ask if she got that way by eating mounds of gua-
comole.

10. *Need for autonomy.* There are several ways to sell credit card   60
services, as has been noted: Mastercard appeals to the need to dominate,
and American Express to the need for prominence. When Visa claims,
"You can have it the way you want it," yet another primary motive is
being beckoned forward—the need to endorse the self. The focus here
is upon the independence and integrity of the individual; this need is
the antithesis of the need for guidance and is unlike any of the social
needs. "If running with the herd isn't your style, try ours," says Rotan-
Mosle, and many Americans feel they have finally found the right bro-
kerage firm.

The photo is of a red-coated Mountie on his horse, posed on a snow-   61
covered ledge; the copy reads, "Windsor—One Canadian stands alone."
This epitome of the solitary and proud individual may work best with
male customers, as may Winston's man in the red cap. But one-figure advertisements also strike the strong need for autonomy among American
women. As Shelly Hack strides for Charlie perfume, females respond to
her obvious pride and flair; she is her own person. The Virginia Slims'
tale is of people who have come a long way from subservience to independence. Cachet perfume feels it does not need a solo figure to work
this appeal, and uses three different faces in its ads; it insists, though,
"It's different on every woman who wears it."

Like many psychological needs, this one can also be appealed to in
a negative fashion, by invoking the loss of independence or self-regard.
Guilt and regrets can be stimulated: "Gee, I could have had a V-8." Next
time, get one and be good to yourself.

11. *Need to escape.*   An appeal to the need for autonomy often co-   63
occurs with one for the need to escape, since the desire to duck out of
our social obligations, to seek rest or adventure, frequently takes the
form of one-person flight. The dashing image of a pilot, in fact, is a standard way of quickening this need to get away from it all.

Freedom is the pitch here, the freedom that every individual yearns   64
for whenever life becomes too oppressive. Many advertisers like appealing to the need for escape because the sensation of pleasure often
accompanies escape, and what nicer emotional nimbus could there be
for a product? "You deserve a break today," says McDonald's, and
Stouffer's frozen foods chime in, "Set yourself free."

For decades men have imaginatively bonded themselves to the   65
Marlboro cowboy who dwells untarnished and unencumbered in Marlboro Country some distance from modern life; smokers' aching needs
for autonomy and escape are personified by that cowpoke. Many
women can identify with the lady ambling through the woods behind
the words, "Benson and Hedges and mornings and me."

But escape does not have to be solitary. Other Benson and Hedges   66
ads, part of the same campaign, contain two strolling figures. In Salem
cigarette advertisements, it can be several people who escape together
into the mountaintops. A commercial for Levi's pictured a cloudbank
above a city through which ran a whole chain of young people.

There are varieties of escape, some wistful like the Boeing "Some-   67
day" campaign of dream vacations, some kinetic like the play and parties in soft drink ads. But in every instance, the consumer exposed to the
advertisement is invited to momentarily depart his everyday life for a
more carefree experience, preferably with the product in hand.

12. *Need to feel safe.*   Nobody in their right mind wants to be in-   68

timidated, menaced, battered, poisoned. We naturally want to do whatever it takes to stave off threats to our well-being, and to our families'. It is the instinct of self-preservation that makes us responsive to the ad of the St. Bernard with the keg of Chivas Regal. We pay attention to the stern talk of Karl Malden and the plight of the vacationing couples who have lost all their funds in the American Express travelers cheques commercials. We want the omnipresent stag from Hartford Insurance to watch over us too.

In the interest of keeping failure and calamity from our lives, we like   69
to see the durability of products demonstrated. Can we ever forget that Timex takes a licking and keeps on ticking? When the American Tourister suitcase bounces all over the highway and the egg inside doesn't break, the need to feel safe has been adroitly plucked.

We take precautions to diminish future threats. We buy Volkswagen   70
Rabbits for the extraordinary mileage, and MONY insurance policies to avoid the tragedies depicted in their black-and-white ads of widows and orphans.

We are careful about our health. We consume Mazola margarine be-   71
cause it has "corn goodness" backed by the natural food traditions of the American Indians. In the medicine cabinet is Alka-Seltzer, the "home remedy"; having it, we are snug in our little cottage.

We want to be safe and secure; buy these products, advertisers are   72
saying, and you'll be safer than you are without them.

13. *Need for aesthetic sensations.*   There is an undeniable aesthetic   73
component to virtually every ad run in the national media: the photography or filming or drawing is near-perfect, the type style is well chosen, the layout could scarcely be improved upon. Advertisers know there is little chance of good communication occurring if an ad is not visually pleasing. Consumers may not be aware of the extent of their own sensitivity to artwork, but it is undeniably large.

Sometimes the aesthetic element is expanded and made into an ad's   74
primary appeal. Charles Jordan shoes may or may not appear in the accompanying avant-grade photographs; Kohler plumbing fixtures catch attention through the high style of their desert settings. Beneath the slightly out of focus photograph, languid and sensuous in tone, General Electric feels called upon to explain, "This is an ad for the hair dryer."

This appeal is not limited to female consumers: J&B scotch says "It   75
whispers" and shows a bucolic scene of lake and castle.

14. *Need to satisfy curiosity.*   It may seem odd to list a need for in-   76
formation among basic motives, but this need can be as primal and compelling as any of the others. Human beings are curious by nature, interested in the world around them, and intrigued by tidbits of knowledge and new developments. Trivia, percentages, observations counter to

conventional wisdom—these items all help sell products. Any advertisement in a question-and-answer format is strumming this need.

A dog groomer has a question about long distance rates, and Bell   77
Telephone has a chart with all the figures. An ad for Porsche 911 is replete with diagrams and schematics, numbers and arrows. Lo and behold, Anacin pills have 150 more milligrams than its competitors; should we wonder if this is better or worse for us?

15. *Physiological needs.*   To the extent that sex is solely a biological   78
need, we are now coming around full circle, back toward the start of the list. In this final category are clustered appeals to sleeping, eating, drinking. The art of photographing food and drink is so advanced, sometimes these temptations are wondrously caught in the camera's lens: the crab meat in the Red Lobster restaurant ads can start us salivating, the Quarterpounder can almost be smelled, the liquor in the glass glows invitingly. Imbibe, these ads scream.

Styles

Some common ingredients of advertisements were not singled out   79
for separate mention in the list of fifteen because they are not appeals in and of themselves. They are stylistic features, influencing the way a basic appeal is presented. The use of humor is one, and the use of celebrities is another. A third is time imagery, past and future, which goes to several purposes.

For all of its employment in advertising, humor can be treacherous,   80
because it can get out of hand and smother the product information. Supposedly, this is what Alka-Seltzer discovered with its comic commercials of the late sixties; "I can't believe I ate the whole thing," the sad-faced husband lamented, and the audience cackled so much it forgot the antacid. Or, did not take it seriously.

But used carefully, humor can punctuate some of the softer appeals   81
and soften some of the harsher ones. When Emma says to the Fruit-of-the-Loom fruits, "Hi, cuties. Whatcha doing in my laundry basket?" we smile as our curiosity is assuaged along with hers. Bill Cosby gets consumers tickled about the children in his Jell-O commercials, and strokes the need to nurture.

An insurance company wants to invoke the need to feel safe, but   82
does not want to leave readers with an unpleasant aftertaste; cartoonist Rowland Wilson creates an avalanche about to crush a gentleman who is saying to another, "My insurance company? New England Life, of course. Why?" The same tactic of humor undercutting threat is used in the cartoon commercials for Safeco when the Pink Panther wanders

from one disaster to another. Often humor masks aggression: comedian Bob Hope in the outfit of a boxer promises to knock out the knock-knocks with Texaco; Rodney Dangerfield, who "can't get no respect," invites aggression as the comic relief in Miller Lite commercials.

Roughly fifteen percent of all advertisements incorporate a celeb-   83
rity, almost always from the fields of entertainment or sports. This approach can also prove troublesome for advertisers, for celebrities are human beings too, and fully capable of the most remarkable behavior; if anything distasteful about them emerges, it is likely to reflect on the product. The advertisers making use of Anita Bryant and Billy Jean King suffered several anxious moments. An untimely death can also reflect poorly on a product. But advertisers are willing to take risks because celebrities can be such a good link between producers and consumers, performing the social role of introducer.

There are several psychological needs these middlemen can play   84
upon. Let's take the product class of cameras and see how different celebrities can hit different needs. The need for guidance can be invoked by Michael Landon, who plays such a wonderful dad on "Little House on the Prairie"; when he says to buy Kodak equipment, many people listen. James Garner for Polaroid cameras is put in a similar authoritative role, so defined by a mocking spouse. The need to achieve is summoned up by Tracy Austin and other tennis stars for Canon AE-1; the advertiser first makes sure we set these athletes playing to win. When Cheryl Tiegs speaks up for Olympus cameras, it is the need for attention that is being targeted.

The past and future, being outside our grasp, are exploited by ad-   85
vertisers as locales for the projection of needs. History can offer up heroes (and call up the need to achieve) or traditions (need for guidance) as well as art objects (need for aesthetic sensations). Nostalgia is a kindly version of personal history and is deployed by advertisers to rouse needs for affiliation and for guidance; the need to escape can come in here, too. The same need to escape is sometimes the point of futuristic appeals, but picturing the avant-garde can also be a way to get at the need to achieve.

Analyzing Advertisements

When analyzing ads yourself for their emotional appeals, it takes a   86
bit of practice to learn to ignore the product information (as well as one's own experience and feelings about the product). But that skill comes soon enough, as does the ability to quickly sort out from all the non-product aspects of an ad the chief element which is the most striking, the most likely to snag attention first and penetrate brains farthest. The

key to the appeal, this element usually presents itself centrally and for-
wardly to the reader or viewer.

Another clue: the viewing angle which the audience has on the ad's   87
subjects is informative. If the subjects are photographed or filmed from
below and thus are looking down at you much as the Green Giant does,
then the need to be guided is a good candidate for the ad's emotional
appeal. If, on the other hand, the subjects are shot from above and appear deferential, as is often the case with children or female models, then
other needs are being appealed to.

To figure out an ad's emotional appeal, it is wise to know (or have   88
a good hunch about) who the targeted consumers are; this can often be
inferred from the magazine or television show it appears in. This piece
of information is a great help in determining the appeal and in deciding
between two different interpretations. For example, if an ad features a
partially undressed female, this would typically signal one appeal for
readers of *Penthouse* (need for sex) and another for readers of *Cosmopolitan* (need for attention).

It would be convenient if every ad made just one appeal, were   89
aimed at just one need. Unfortunately, things are often not that simple.
A cigarette ad with a couple at the edge of a polo field is trying to hit
both the need for affiliation and the need for prominence; depending on
the attitude of the male, dominance could also be an ingredient in this.
An ad for Chimere perfume incorporates two photos: in the top one the
lady is being commanding at a business luncheon (need to dominate),
but in the lower one she is being bussed (need for affiliation). Better ads,
however, seem to avoid being too diffused; in the study of post-World
War II advertising described earlier, appeals grew more focused as the
decades passed. As a rule of thumb, about sixty percent have two conspicuous appeals; the last twenty percent have three or more. Rather
than looking for the greatest number of appeals, decoding ads is most
productive when the loudest one or two appeals are discerned, since
those are the appeals with the best chance of grabbing people's attention.

Finally, analyzing ads does not have to be a solo activity and prob-   90
ably should not be. The greater number of people there are involved, the
better chance there is of transcending individual biases and discovering
the essential emotional lure built into an advertisement.

Do They or Don't They?

Do the emotional appeals made in advertisements add up to the sin-   91
ister manipulation of consumers?

It is clear that these ads work. Attention is caught, communication   92 occurs between producers and consumers, and sales result. It turns out to be difficult to detail the exact relationship between a specific ad and a specific purchase, or even between a campaign and subsequent sales figures, because advertising is only one of a host of influences upon consumption. Yet no one is fooled by this lack of perfect proof; everyone knows that advertising sells. If this were not the case, then tight-fisted American businesses would not spend a total of fifty billion dollars annually on these messages.

But before anyone despairs that advertisers have our number to the extent that they can marshall us at will and march us like automatons to the check-out counters, we should recall the resiliency and obduracy of the American consumer. Advertisers may have uncovered the softest spots in minds, but that does not mean they have found truly gaping apertures. There is no evidence that advertising can get people to do things contrary to their self-interests. Despite all the finesse of advertisements, and all the subtle emotional tugs, the public resists the vast majority of the petitions. According to the marketing division of the A.C. Nielsen Company, a whopping seventy-five percent of all new products die within a year in the marketplace, the victims of consumer disinterest which no amount of advertising could overcome. The appeals in advertising may be the most captivating there are to be had, but they are not enough to entrap the wiley consumer.   93

The key to understanding the discrepancy between, on the one hand, the fact that advertising truly works, and, on the other, the fact that it hardly works, is to take into account the enormous numbers of people exposed to an ad. Modern-day communications permit an ad to be displayed to millions upon millions of individuals; if the smallest fraction of that audience can be moved to buy the product, then the ad has been successful. When one percent of the people exposed to a television advertising campaign reach for their wallets, that could be one million sales, which may be enough to keep the product in production and the advertisements coming.   94

In arriving at an evenhanded judgment about advertisements and their emotional appeals, it is good to keep in mind that many of the purchases which might be credited to these ads are experienced as genuinely gratifying to the consumer. We sincerely like the goods or service we have bought, and we may even like some of the emotional drapery that an ad suggests comes with it. It has sometimes been noted that the most avid students of advertisements are the people who have just bought the product; they want to steep themselves in the associated imagery. This may be the reason that Americans, when polled, are not negative about advertising and do not disclose any sense of being misused. The volume of advertising may be an irritant, but the product   95 information as well as the imaginative material in ads are partial compensation.

A productive understanding is that advertising messages involve costs and benefits at both ends of the communications channel. For those few ads which do make contact, the consumer surrenders a moment of time, has the lower brain curried, and receives notice of a product; the advertiser has given up money and has increased the chance of sales. In this sort of communications activity, neither party can be said to be the loser.

96

· · · · · · · · · · · · · · · · · · · ·

Examining the Text

1. Fowles's basic claim in this essay is that advertisers try to tap into basic human needs and emotions, rather than consumers' intellect. How does he go about proving this claim? What examples or other proof strike you as particularly persuasive? Where do you see weaknesses in Fowles's argument?

2. What do advertisers assume about the personality of the consumer, according to Fowles? How do these assumptions contribute to the way they sell products? Do you think that these assumptions about personality are correct? Why or why not?

3. Fowles's list of advertising's fifteen basic appeals is, as he explains, derived from Henry Murray's inventory of human motives. Which of these motives strike you as the most significant or powerful? What other motives would you add to the list?

For Group Discussion

In his discussion of the way advertising uses "the need for sex" and "the need to aggress," Fowles debunks the persistent complaints about the use of sex and violence in the mass media. What current examples support Fowles's point? Discuss your responses to his explanations.

Writing Suggestion

Working with Fowles's list of the fifteen appeals of advertising, survey a recent magazine, looking at all the ads and categorizing them based on their predominant appeal. In an essay, describe what your results tell you about the magazine and its readership. Based on your survey, would you amend Fowles's list? What additions or deletions would you make?

The Selling of Lifestyles

Berkeley Rice

To persuade others to do what we want them to do, we need to know as much as we can about our audience so we can choose techniques that will work with them and discard those that won't. Advertisers—who are, of course, trying to persuade us to buy certain products—operate under the same principle: the more they know about us, the more effectively they can tailor their ads to appeal to our desires and needs.

In the following article, which originally appeared in Psychology Today, *Berkeley Rice describes "psychographics," a technique which many advertisers use to delve into not only the "beliefs, motivations and attitudes," but the whole lifestyles of consumers. According to Rice, psychographics has largely replaced demographics, which divided people up according to quantifiable items such as salary, age, and number of children. Psychographics instead tries to measure basic character traits and lifestyles and group consumers together according to these traits.*

Rice details a particular psychographic market research program called VALS, which divides the American public into nine categories based on their "values and lifestyles." Advertisers use VALS and psychographics to determine their consumer base and to tailor the ads to that particular group. However, some early enthusiasts have become disenchanted with the psychographic approach, charging that it puts people into "boxes" that are superficial and that its accuracy is debatable.

***Before you read,** recall four or five advertisements that have really worked with you, appealed to you, sold you on trying a product. What features do these ads have in common? What conclusions can you draw about yourself as a consumer and potential target for advertisers? To what extent do you find yourself agreeing with the critics of psychographics?*

• • • • • • • • • • • • • • • • • • •

You may not care about psychographics, but psychographics cares about you. It cares about what you think, what you feel, what you believe, the way you live and, most of all, the products and services that you use.

Ever since the snake convinced Eve to sample an apple in the Garden of Eden, advertisers and marketers have been trying to discover why consumers buy what they do. A few years ago, marketers thought the reason was demographics, and that buying was governed by consumers' age, sex, income, education, occupation and other characteristics.

They also tried to divide the purchasing world up according to social class.

These mass-marketing strategies, however, are now considered crude and overly general. Marketing researchers today want to get into the individual consumer's head, so that companies can aim their products at more specific segments of the population. Some think that psychographics is their ticket inside.

Psychographic analyses for Schlitz beer, for example, revealed that heavy beer drinkers were real macho men who feel that pleasures in their lives are few and far between, and they want something more, according to Joseph Plummer, the researcher who conducted the study. This insight led to Schlitz commercials that told people "You only go around once," so you might as well "reach for all the gusto you can."

When the current walking-shoe boom began, the athletic-shoe industry assumed that most walkers were simply burned-out joggers. Psychographic research, however, has shown that there are really several different groups of walkers: Some walk for fun, some walk with religious dedication, others walk to work and still others walk the dog. Some really want to exercise, and some want the illusion of exercise. As a result, there are now walking shoes aimed at several groups, ranging from Nike Healthwalkers to Footjoy Joy-Walkers.

When Merrill Lynch learned through psychographics that the bulk of its clients saw themselves as independent-minded, upwardly mobile achievers, the investment firm changed the image in its commercials. Instead of the familiar thundering herd of bulls from the 1970s, Merrill Lynch ads portrayed scenes of a solitary bull: "a breed apart."

The term psychographics first began to pop up in the business community during the late 1960s, referring to attempts to classify consumers by their beliefs, motivations and attitudes. In 1970, psychologist Daniel Yankelovich, who headed his own social-research firm, launched an annual survey of changing values and attitudes called the Yankelovich Monitor. It tracks more than 50 trends in people's attitudes toward time, money, the future, family, self, institutions and many other aspects of their life-style. By measuring these shifts in attitudes, Monitor researchers claim to have spotted or predicted trends such as the shift to white wine and light alcoholic beverages, and the rising sales of supermarket-chain brands and generic drugs. About 100 companies now pay $28,500 a year to subscribe to the Monitor survey.

By the mid 1970s, "life-style" had become a popular buzzword in advertising and marketing circles. Many advertising agencies began to do their own psychographic research: Needham, Harper and Steers (now DDB Needham), for example, divided consumers into 10 life-style categories typified by characters such as Thelma, the old-fashion traditionalist; Candice, the chic suburbanite; and Fred, the frustrated factory worker. A flurry of ads tried—often blatantly—to pitch products by appealing to the life-style of people commonly referred to as the "upscale market." An ad for Chrysler's 1979 LeBaron, for example, featured an attractive young couple engaged in typically active, upscale pursuits such as tennis and sailing. The ad copy gushed: "It's got style. It's got life. Put some life in your style."

While all of this was going on, a researcher named Arnold Mitchell   9 wrote a series of reports analyzing the way people's basic needs and values influenced their attitudes and behavior, particularly as consumers. Working at what is now SRI International in Menlo Park, California, he had administered a lengthy questionnaire to nearly 2,000 people. Using the results, Mitchell divided consumers into categories based in part on the theories of the late psychologist Abraham Maslow and his hierarchy of "needs growth."

Maslow believed that most human behavior is based on certain in-   10 ternal drives or needs, and that personal development consists of stages of maturity marked by fulfillment of these needs. Until the needs of one stage are satisfied, an individual cannot progress to the next level of maturity. At the lowest level are basic bodily needs such as hunger and sleep, followed by needs for safety, shelter and comfort. The next levels consist of psychological needs: to belong, to have self-esteem and to be respected by others. Near the top comes the need for self-actualization: fully developing one's potential. People who reach this level are likely to be more creative, successful and influential than people who haven't attained it. Finally, Maslow said, the needs for spirituality and sensitivity lead to the highest level of consciousness.

Mitchell also claimed that each stage of an individual's develop-   11 ment is marked by a "particular pattern of priorities. . . a unique set of dominating values and needs." He used his survey findings to create nine psychologically graphic portraits of consumers, one for each pattern he identified. By 1983, when Mitchell published a book called *The Nine American Lifestyles,* his work had attracted considerable interest from marketers and advertisers. Based on his work, SRI had formed a commercial marketing-research program called VALS, an acronym for Values and Lifestyles. Before he died in 1985, Mitchell saw VALS become the country's most widely used system of psychographic research.

The VALS typology begins with two life-styles, the Survivors and   12 the Sustainers, both small groups with limited financial resources. Survivors are typically elderly and poor: Most feel trapped in their poverty, with no hope of escape. Sustainers, only slightly better off, are struggling at the edge of poverty. Although they often bitterly blame "the system" for their troubles, Sustainers have not quite given up.

VALS then divides into two pathways, Inner-Directed and Outer-   13
Directed, terms drawn from the work of sociologist David Riesman.
There are three Outer-Directed types: Belongers, Emulators and Achievers. Belongers are the largest VALS group of all, making up 38 percent
of the country's population. These stable, hard-working blue-collar or
service-industry workers are conservative and conforming; they know
what's right and what's wrong, and they stick to the rules because they
want to fit in.

Emulators are more ambitious, more competitive and more status   14
conscious than Belongers. They also make more money, but they envy
the life-style of the Achievers, one level above them. Emulators would
like to feel they're "on the way up," but most will never make it. They
wonder if they're getting a fair shake from the system.

Achievers, who make up 20 percent of the population, are the suc-   15
cessful business managers and professional people. Competent and
self-reliant, "they know what they want and they make it happen." They
want the trappings of success—expensive homes, cars and vacations—and most expect to get them. Having achieved the American
Dream, they are generally staunch defenders of the society that rewarded them.

Parallel to but quite different from the Outer-Directed types are the   16
three Inner-Directed VALS categories. The first, the I-Am-Me's, is a tiny
group: generally young, highly individualistic, very egocentric and often confused about their goals in life. As their outlook broadens and they
become more sure of themselves, they tend to mature into Experientials.
If they then extend their view to include society as a whole, they become
the Societally Conscious. This is the largest of the Inner-Directed groups;
its members tend to be knowledgeable and concerned about social
causes such as conservation. Many earn a good deal of money, but their
life-styles emphasize simplicity and involvement.

At the pinnacle of VALS is the tiny group of psychologically mature   17
Integrateds, the lucky few who have put it all together. They combine
the best of Inner and Outer Direction: the power and drive of the
Achievers and the sensitivity of the Societally Conscious. They have a
sense of balance in their lives and confidence in their place in the world.

SRI has produced a half-hour video that provides brief looks at peo-   18
ple in different VALS categories. Estelle, an elderly Survivor in the film,
lives alone, scraping by on a tight budget. Moe is a Hispanic Sustainer
who spends his afternoons at the racetrack hoping for a big win. Dave
and Donna, a young Belonger couple who believe in God, family and
country, live in a small house in a development of similar homes. Art,
the Emulator, is a door-to-door salesman who drives through a fancy
neighborhood and wonders, "What did they do right?" Steve, a lawyer-

entrepreneur Achiever who's pictured soaking in his hot tub with his attractive wife, insists that money's "just a way of keeping score."

Mitchell's idea that basic psychological needs or drives affect con-   19 sumer behavior makes a good deal of sense, and few researchers would quarrel with it. It's less clear, however, that VALS survey methods really tap into the things that Maslow was talking about. VALS "does not measure basic psychological characteristics, but social values which are purported reflections of those characteristics," says psychologist Joseph Smith, president of the market-research firm Oxtoby-Smith. Those values, Smith contents, don't predict consumer behavior very well: "Maslow was working in the world of clinical and developmental psychology. To try to adapt his theories and language from that world, as VALS has done, is an engaging idea but bound to be fruitless."

But bear fruit VALS has. Since SRI began marketing psychographic   20 research, 250 corporate clients or "members," as SRI calls them, have used VALS data. Most VALS clients sell consumer products and services: packaged goods, automobiles, insurance, television, publishing and advertising. Depending on how much customized service they want, 150 current VALS members pay from $20,000 to more than $150,000 per year, producing reported annual revenues of more than $2 million for Mitchell's brainchild.

Member companies can combine VALS profiles with much larger   21 marketing systems that provide information on specific product brands and media use. Or they can link VALS to several "geodemographic" marketing services that group people by ZIP codes or neighborhood, according to the demographic features of typical households.

Advertising agencies such as Young & Rubicam, Ogilvy and Mather   22 and J. Walter Thompson have used VALS information to place ads on TV shows and in magazines that draw the right psychographic segments for their clients' products or to design commercials and print ads that target specific consumer groups. They have learned, for example, that TV's daytime soap operas draw heavily among Survivors, Sustainers and Belongers, because they're often home alone. Achievers watch a lot of sports and news shows, while the Societally Conscious prefer dramas and documentaries.

Magazines such as *Time* and *The New Yorker* have a lot of Achiever   23 readers, while *Reader's Digest* has more Belongers (*Psychology Today*, which uses a different psychographic system, has readers who are broad-minded, style conscious and experimenters—probably more Inner-than Outer-Directed).

VALS has attracted many clients from the auto industry, including   24 GM, Ford, Nissan, Honda and Mercedes-Benz. VALS studies show what you might expect: that Belongers tend to buy family-sized domestic cars, while Emulators and I-Am-Me's prefer "muscle" cars like the Chevy Camaro. Achievers usually buy luxury cars, often foreign models like Mercedes or BMW, not so much because of their superior quality but because they represent achievement and status. Societally Conscious types might also buy a Mercedes, but more for its technical excellence than what it "says" about them.

To complicate matters for advertisers, nearly half of all couples are "mixed" marriages of two different VALS types. Ads for mini-vans, therefore, may need to carry a double message: one to appeal to an Achiever husband who might use it for golfing or fishing expeditions with his buddies and another to appeal to his Belonger wife, who sees it primarily as a vehicle for ferrying the children.   25

Corporate clients can use a 30-item VALS questionnaire to survey their own markets and have SRI classify the results into VALS types. The questionnaire asks people to indicate their agreement or disagreement with statements such as "What I do at work is more important to me than the money I earn" or "I would rather spend a quiet evening at home than go out to a party" or "I like to be outrageous."   26

By using such research methods, client companies can construct VALS profiles for their own markets or those of their competitors; position products or design packaging to appeal to particular groups; or spot trends in product use and consumer needs.   27

Ray Ellison Homes, a big real estate developer and builder in San Antonio, Texas, took advantage of this type of VALS research. The company began by mailing a VALS questionnaire to 5,000 home buyers in the area and also asked them how much they valued items such as wallpaper or landscaping. "We needed to find out their values," says Jim Tilton, vice president of merchandising and advertising, "so we could really build to their needs and desires."   28

The company then conducted in-depth group interviews with the three VALS types most likely to buy its homes—Belongers, Achievers and Societally Conscious—to probe for further insights. When a group of Achiever women saw pictures of a big country kitchen, one of them exclaimed, "There's no way I'd clean all that tile!" A similar display of tile in the luxurious master bathroom, however, did not put her off. Apparently, the kitchen make her think of work, but she viewed the bathroom as a place of relaxation.   29

On the basis of these interviews and the survey results, Tilton says, "we took our standard houses apart and started from scratch, putting them back together piece by piece." To attract Achievers, for instance, the company added impressive facades, luxury carpeting and elaborate security systems. For the Societally Conscious, they designed energy-efficient homes. "What we've done," executive vice president Jack   30

Robinson explains, "is really get inside the consumer's head, into what his perceived values are, and give them back to him—in land, in financing and in the features of a home."

While VALS is the best-known and most successful psychographic 31 research program around, it is hardly the only one doing this kind of work. Yankelovich's Monitor is still going strong, and many smaller firms do custom-tailored research for individual clients or specific markets. Some large consumer-goods companies and TV networks now do their own psychographic studies.

Despite this popularity, psychographics has plenty of doubters. 32 Some critics, like Smith, question its utility: "We can't really measure the important personal attributes based on surveys," he says. "Psychographic research gives you a lot of superficial, inconsequential and titillating material but very little of pointed use to the guy who is designing products or trying to advertise and sell them." Because psychographic research firms guard their methods very carefully, as trade secrets, outsiders have been unable to test the data's validity and reliability (most firms claim they do their own validity testing).

Russell Haley, a professor of marketing at the University of New 33 Hampshire, who heads a market-research firm, points out that decisions to buy some products are simply not closely related to personal values. "If you're dealing with paper towels," he says, "personal values are not likely to be that relevant. On the other hand, if you're selling cosmetics or insurance, VALS may be quite useful because people's attitudes toward beauty or money are very relevant." He concludes: "I have some clients who like it, and some who don't."

Some companies that have used VALS and other psychographic re- 34 search in the past no longer do so, having decided it's not worth the extra cost. Some claim that psychographics merely reveals the obvious or that it duplicates what demographic data show more clearly. In demographic language, Belongers are 57 years old on average, and the majority earn less than $20,000 per year; 72 percent of them are married, and only 3 percent have graduated from college. Experientials are 28 years old and earn $32,000 per year, on average; only 31 percent of them are married, and 40 percent attended college.

"When VALS first came out," says Bob Hoffman, president of Mojo 35 MDA, a San Francisco advertising agency, "it enlightened us and described behavior in certain ways that some people hadn't thought of before. But now it makes people think in boxes." Hoffman and others argue that psychographics tries too hard to categorize everyone into discrete types, ignoring the fact that most people have traits and behavior common to several types. People also don't always think and behave consistently in every context. Some individuals may vote as

Belongers but think like Achievers when they walk into the automobile showroom. Some Achievers may act like Belongers when pushing a baby's stroller through a supermarket.

In response to such critics, VALS marketing director Jack Tyler insists that "We've never claimed that all individuals fit neatly into one category, like cookie-cutter types, or that they have a stereotypical response to every situation. We provide our clients with secondary VALS scores that indicate these other characteristics." VALS simply claims that people's general behavior fits the profile of a given category, Tyler says, and that these categories offer valuable insights into the consumer.   36

What VALS and other life-style studies have done is provide vivid portraits of American consumers; while the accuracy of the pictures is debatable, psychographics still has many believers. Says Jerry Hamilton of Ketchum Advertising in San Francisco, "VALS makes it possible to personalize marketing and to understand the target we're trying to reach better than any other piece of research. Sure, it may oversimplify. No matter what classification system you use you're distorting everybody's individuality. But the alternative is to tailor advertising to 80 million individual households."   37

. . . .

Examining the Text

1. Briefly define "psychographics" in your own words. How is it different from demographics? Why do you think it has replaced demographics?

2. According to Rice, how is VALS related to Maslow's hierarchy of "needs growth"? Does this fact give VALS legitimacy for you?

3. Rice quotes Jack Robinson, an executive vice president of a large real estate development firm: "What we've done," Robinson says, "is really get inside the consumer's head, into what his perceived values are, and give them back to him—in land, in financing and in the features of the home" (paragraph 30). What, if any, problems do you see with advertisers or salespeople "getting inside the consumer's head"?

4. Do you agree with any or all of the criticisms of those who question the validity of approaches like VALS?

For Group Discussion

Re-read the section describing the nine VALS groups: Survivors, Sustainers, Belongers, Emulators, Achievers, I-Am-Me's, Experientials, Societally-Conscious, and Integrateds. Then look through a variety

of magazines to find an ad which seems designed to appeal to each of
these groups. (Group members might be assigned several specific VALS
groups and each bring representative ads to class.) For each ad, discuss
the specific features intended to appeal to the targeted consumers.

Writing Suggestion

Make a list of product brands that you buy regularly, everything
from beverages, breakfast foods, and fast foods, to cosmetics, cleaning
products, and clothing. Next list any products and brands that you "desire": cars, stereo equipment, and any other major ticket items that come
to mind, and survey the advertising for these specific brands. To what
VALS categories do these ads seem designed to appeal? In what ways
do they appeal to you? In an essay, use these examples to explore your
own relation to the VALS approach. Do any of the categories adequately
describe you? To what extent are your "brand loyalties" determined by
VALS targeting?

Buy Hip

T. C. Frank

*I*n *"Buy Hip," T. C. Frank offers a detailed explanation of the motivations
of one particular group of consumers: the nonconformists or rebels. These consumers fit most neatly into the "I-Am-Me" category in the VALS typology described in the previous essay: they are generally young and individualistic, and
as Frank points out, they disdain the establishment and its "traditional values."
The irony, however, is that these nonconformists are, in fact, model consumers.
In buying clothing, jewelry, music, and other products to express their individuality, these nonconformists consume heavily and discard rapidly, fueling
the economy of the system they claim to disdain.*

*This phenomenon has not been lost on the advertisers. Frank cites the ex-
ample of Spike Lee and Andre Agassi ("Image Is Everything") and suggests
that "consumer culture has used images of rebellion to encourage a mind-set of
endless dissatisfaction with the old and a never-ending compulsion to buy, buy,
buy the new."*

Before you read, *consider the extent to which the desire to be a noncon-
formist influences the choices you make in the clothing, music, and other items
that you purchase.*

Thirty-five years ago, Norman Mailer first gave voice to the idea   1
that the "hipster"—the young, art-appreciating free spirit alienated
from an increasingly repressive society—was the existential hero of the
day. In an America terrified by the bomb, stagnating from over-organi-
zation, and cowed into conformity by red scares, the "hipster" was supposed to represent liberty and the affirmation of life. "The only life-giving answer" to the deadly drag of American civilization, Mailer wrote,
was to embrace rebellion, particularly the rebellion associated with the
black American subculture of jazz and drugs. The distinction between
those who resisted mass society and those who collaborated was a clear
and obvious one. Mailer insisted: "One is Hip or one is Square . . . , one
is a rebel or one conforms."

Today the opposite is true. In advertising, television, and all the   2
other organs of culture, hipsters are figures to be revered. They have
been turned into a central symbol of the system they are supposed to be
subverting.

Spike Lee has made his reputation as a film innovator by posturing   3
as a free-floating radical, as a spokesman for the nation's oppressed, as
a fulminator against convention and bourgeois morality. He is also a
spokesman for the Nike corporation, and you can regularly see this daring and revolutionary young filmmaker on prime-time TV, selling an ex-
traordinarily expensive athletic show.

On another channel the Burger King corporation confides that   4
"Sometimes You Gotta Break the Rules." A brand of perfume called
"Tribe" calls upon consumers to "Join the Uprising." Mazda tells us if
"You're not John Doe, why drive his car?"

For some time now, consumer culture has used images of rebellion   5
to encourage a mind-set of endless dissatisfaction with the old and a
never-ending compulsion to buy, buy, buy the new. The commercialization of deviance is fast becoming the universal motif of our age. The
beautiful hipsters depicted in ads are always celebrating their liberation,
because it is rebellion that makes them into model consumers. Modern
American rebels exhibit an automatic scorn for anything even vaguely
established or permanent, which reinforces the identification of individuality with products. This is the attitude we all must adopt if we are
to do our part in keeping the great American economic machine racing
at fever pitch.

Our young pseudo-radicals buy, eat, and discard freely and unre-   6
strainedly, unencumbered by the repressive moral baggage of their
square, tightwad elders, who didn't buy a lot of things they didn't need,
who saved money and didn't buy on credit, whose dull, unliberated
lives centered on producing goods rather than consuming them.

So American youth and its young-thinking parents fall over one an-   7 other rushing to patronize the latest consumer expression of rebellion, whether it's acid-washed jeans, leather motorcycle jackets, or multiple-pierced ears. We let our hair grow, cut it short, tie it in a ponytail, dye it, cut lines and words into it. We wear all black. We purchase every new product, visit every new nightclub we think will set us apart from the crowd, and exemplify our daring disdain for tradition. And then a few months later we do it all over again, with other products and other places.

What is it about celebrity rebel hipsters such as Spike Lee that makes   8 them such effective corporate symbols? It's not just their fame but also the marketability of their poses—the alienation, the hipness, the shock of the new.

The commodification of dissent is the great ideological innovation   9 of our time, the central theme of most all our mass culture. Multimillionaire singer and Pepsi pusher Michael Jackson opens a video with classic images of youthful rebellion against adult authority. Zubaz markets garish trousers for thicklegged men by admonishing us to "Dare to Be Different." Irritating tennis champion Andre Agassi, who routinely dresses up like a rock star, endorses a camera called "The Rebel" with the line "Image Is Everything." Insincere insurgency is now standard in advertising for beer, fast food, cigarettes, radio stations, and cars.

Like the hipster (who in Mailer's essay was supposed to be a sort of   10 "White Negro"), the African-American is exploited as a standard element of the ad world's visual vocabulary, used not merely to appeal to the black community but also to symbolize the noble outsider as consumer. Thus the "United Colors of Benetton" campaign reinforces that company's desire for us to resist convention and buy a very great number of distinctive outfits, to reject the Square, to embrace the Other, and to do it again and again and again as long as our credit holds out. To avoid traditionally sanctioned norms, Americans must buy 20 products where just one or two would have sufficed in the conformist age of the gray flannel suit.

In the 1950s consumerism was a pathetic and clumsy thing, appeal-   11 ing openly to people's status fears and terror of standing out. Sometime between now and then the whole direction of consumerism changed, and it is not difficult to pinpoint when: the '60s. While challenging bigotry, autocracy, and hierarchy on all fronts, the youth movement of that era can also be understood as a consumer revolution. Anyone who has noticed the number of expensive cars bearing Grateful Dead stickers can understand how the '60s people's hedonist, anti-establishmentarian obsession with doing their own thing could be easily transformed into '80s people's hedonist, anti-establishmentarian obsession with owning things.

The '60s was above all a time of lifestyle experimentation. As es- 12
tablished models of understanding the world were discarded, young
rebels were free to adopt any identity they chose. With identities no
more stable than songs on the Top 40 charts, the '60s became a retailers'
dream—because each identity, each new phase of rebellion, necessitated
an extensive shopping expedition. Yes, the baby boomers railed against
the establishment and its "traditional" values, but mainly because they
didn't want to be bound to any single identity or image: They would
be rockers, mods, flower children, Easy Riders, meditators, revolution-
aries, back-to-the-landers, and young urban pioneers in quick succes-
sion.

And the '60s live on today in suburban malls across the republic as 13
youngsters and their young-thinking parents live out the rebel dream,
breaking away from the rat race, from the lonely crowd, spending
unrestrainedly and staying always one step ahead of that demon
conformity.

••••••••••••••••••

Examining the Text

1. In your own words, define the phenomenon Frank refers to as "the
commercialization of deviance" (paragraph 5). Can you offer other examples of its existence, or does Frank exaggerate its effects?

2. Frank's article was originally subtitled "Why nonconformists make
model consumers." How does Frank explain that statement? What do
you think of his explanation?

3. What point does Frank make about the exploitation of African-American culture in advertising and other aspects of popular culture? To
what extent are other minority cultures similarly exploited?

4. Frank uses many brief examples of advertisements and celebrities to
help prove his point. In your opinion, which of these examples is most
persuasive in supporting his main ideas?

For Group Discussion

Assume for the moment that everything Frank says in this essay is
true, that "the commodification of dissent is the great ideological innovation of our time, the central theme of most all our mass culture" (9).
As a group, list some problems or concerns arising from this current attribute of mass culture. If Frank is right, what do his observations suggest about the direction in which contemporary American culture is
moving?

Writing Suggestions

Frank's essay was written in 1992. Since then, there are probably even more advertisements, TV shows, movies, and songs that appeal to the desire to rebel and the fear of conformity. Update Frank's essay by exploring some new examples. Briefly describe how each supports or alters Frank's thesis. When you are finished, draw your own conclusion about whether nonconformists still make model consumers.

IMAGES OF WOMEN AND MEN IN ADVERTISING

Media Mirrors

Carol Moog

*T**he following selection comes from Carol Moog's book "Are They Sell-*
ing Her Lips?": Advertising and Identity (1990), in which she examines ad-
vertising from two quite distinct perspectives: that of a psychologist interested
in how ads influence our sense of who we are and who we want to be; and that
of a consultant to ad agencies, who sees the decisions, sometimes illogical and
arbitrary, made in designing an ad campaign.

In "Media Mirrors," Moog studies the evolution of Maidenform bra ad
campaigns from the 1950s to the late 1980s, an era marked both by unprece-
dented success and unexpected controversy. Moog concludes that Maidenform,
like most other companies, both reflects and responds to broader social changes
in its attempt to touch the conscious and subconscious wishes of consumers.
Because it sells to women, Maidenform, like other companies, has been com-
pelled to stay current with the changes in women's lives and in their images of
themselves, although they have not always been successful in this.

Moog focuses on lingerie advertising and so her essay raises questions
about images of women in advertising. **Before you read**, *take a moment to re-*
flect on some current ads for both women's products and men's products. How
well do these ads reflect the lives and interests of men and women in the 1990s?

• • • • • • • • • • • • • • • • •

Breasts.
Philip Roth yearned for them.
Hef built an empire on them.
But Maidenform made the fortune from them.

Sharon, the forty-seven-year-old wife of a dentist with two grown   1
children, is telling me about the dream she had three nights before:

> Richard and I were in a restaurant. I think it was the Citadel, where we
> ate about a month ago—I don't know. But it was different. There were
> all these men around, and I felt uncomfortable. But they weren't alone.
> They were there with some old women—like their mothers or grand-
> mothers or something. And I was very angry at Richard. I remember
> fighting with him there before too. He kept telling me to shut up, that
> I was drinking too much. Suddenly, I realized I didn't have anything

on and he was mad at me because everyone was staring. I thought, I've got to get out of here. I panicked. But I couldn't move. No one at the other tables seemed to pay any attention. And here's where it got really strange. I started to relax. I felt beautiful. And Richard smiled.

Sharon's dream has triggered a thought in my mind that starts to   2
crystallize into an image that helps me understand what she's thinking about. I'm imagining Bea Coleman and her mother, Ida Rosenthal, and the brilliant campaign they launched more than thirty years ago. A campaign so brilliant that it touched the most potent fantasies of a woman's dreams.

It was the Maidenform fantasy. The "I dreamed I was . . . in my   3
Maidenform bra" campaign ran for twenty years and made Bea Coleman and Ida Rosenthal rich beyond their wildest dreams.

The original Maidenform ads were created by the agency of Nor-   4
man, Craig and Kummel Advertising, and showed women acting out fantasies (frequently controversial fantasies), that fully displayed their Maidenform bras. Ads like the lady lawyer who "dreamed I swayed the jury in my Maidenform bra" unleashed and exposed the secret fantasies of traditional women of the fifties and invited them to step brazenly into dreams of power and influence. What the ads had women "dream" was that they could go ahead and be exhibitionistic, but not just about their bodies; about their capabilities. Clearly, a psychological chord was struck with this campaign. Women sent scores of unsolicited photos of themselves in endless scenes of "I dreamed I was . . . in my Maidenform bra." In terms of how the campaign portrayed women, it was a real set-breaker. The campaign put the company on the map and gave cultural approval to powerful wishes women certainly harbored but rarely advertised.

What was going on in the women who responded so positively to   5
the Maidenform campaign? This was pre-women's lib, when gender roles were still plainly spelled out: Females were Devoted Housewives and males were Preoccupied Breadwinners. Then along comes Maidenform with full-color photos of poised, clear-eyed, confident women unabashedly exposing their fantasies along with their chests. They're not in the least self-conscious. They're relaxed and composed. The campaign offered a sensational subconscious release for the duty-bound women of that period. It was enormously gratifying to identify with the courage of the Maidenform woman daring to show herself as fully developed to anyone interested in looking. Interested persons included parents, husbands, clergymen, and teachers. The fifties woman got to vicariously thumb her nose at all the right people. She got to break out of the socially appropriate straitjacket she'd willingly donned—

ostensibly for the good of family and cultural stability—and try on a new identity.

Psychologically, that's what dreams are about anyway. They're what the unconscious produces, busily fulfilling wishes that our rational selves have deemed too outrageous to express in real life. There's something else about dreams. They show us images of ourselves that we've already accepted internally but that we haven't risked trying out yet. 6

I see the "I dreamed . . ." campaign as a kind of emotional road map for the women's lib activities that came to the surface in the seventies. Phyllis is the only woman I know who actually, ceremoniously, *burned* a bra—and if I told her that she could thank Maidenform for helping her get a picture of herself as an independent person, she'd have been furious. But like it or not, the campaign set the stage for Phyllis and the other women of her generation. Women interacted with the ads in spite of themselves because they were already gearing up for the kind of real-life dreams they made happen when the feminist movement took hold. 7

The "I dreamed I took the cue in my Maidenform bra" ad is a prime example of the kind of ad that could get to Phyllis, regardless of her conscious protests. When a woman already fantasizing about being less inhibited reads the line "I dreamed I took the cue . . . ," she's already projecting herself into the picture. She's already hooked into seeing herself taking charge in what was traditionally a male-dominated situation. Not only does she take the cue stick, but she proceeds to handle it in a deft behind-the-back maneuver, all without losing a trace of her sultry femininity. The fantasy was powerful but safe. Although Phyllis would never admit it, it was perfectly congruent with women's needs at that time to stay feminine while getting strong. At the same time, the campaign helped women picture having power and control far outside the domestic domain. 8

Here was a landmark campaign that came at precisely the right time to rivet women's attention. A piece of anatomical support empowered their dreams, permitting them to become "Maidenform women," in control of themselves, their circumstances, and their future. The Maidenform campaign was a strong one, largely because it reflected one advertiser's personal convictions. Bea Coleman, Maidenform's dynamic CEO, always admired her entrepreneurial mother, Ida Rosenthal, who founded the company with her physician-husband, William. Ida was a powerhouse. Mother and daughter both dared to dream big and do more. The "I dreamed . . ." concept was turned down by another lingerie company but embraced by Maidenform, perhaps because it was consistent with both Bea's and Ida's perceptions of women. Bea seemed to use her mother as a positive role model, and Ida may have unintentionally modeled aspects of herself through the endless permutations of 9 the dream campaign. She persuaded women not just to buy $100 million worth of underwear, but to see themselves as more capable people.

But the dream campaign hit social forces beyond its control—and   10
turned with the tide of change. By the late sixties, the younger women who should have been buying Maidenform bras had begun to associate "I dreamed . . ." images with their mothers—and bras themselves with the constraints of traditional female roles and functions. When young women started ditching their bras along with their mothers' ideas as they reached for autonomy, the advertiser responded to the psychological climate by ditching the "I dreamed . . ." campaign. (Interestingly, Bea Coleman's own story runs a close parallel to the course of the campaign—this was just about the time that she shocked the male-dominated intimate-apparel industry in 1968 by taking over the company as president after her husband's death.)

What happened? Like Bea Coleman herself, women weren't just ac-   11
knowledging their dreams of power, they were out there making them happen. The dream campaign symbolized the exciting but frustrated longings of the past. These were fantasy ads meant for the women they were trying to escape in their mothers and in themselves. The ads no longer had their initial freeing effect. Instead, they waved a red flag. Women like my old friend Phyllis were burning their bras, not dreaming about showing them off.

The Maidenform woman was mothballed for eleven years. When   12
she reappeared, she launched the greatest controversy in bra history. In a reincarnation created by the Daniel & Charles advertising agency, she was still depicted doing active, even aggressive things, like commuting to work, reading *The Wall Street Journal,* going to the theater, or being a lawyer. She was daringly clad in her matching bra and panties. But now *there were men in the picture!* They appeared disinterested, oblivious to the delectable spectacle of "The Maidenform Woman. You never know where she'll turn up." The men were shot slightly out of focus. They were deeply absorbed, eyes discreetly everywhere else but you-know-where.

Here was a real twist, and the campaign ended up generating the   13
kind of hot attention that left feminists seething and Maidenform sales soaring. Completely unanticipated! Maidenform didn't intend (as many advertisers do) to create a potentially explosive campaign. The agency just thought it had a great new approach for a new age. Advertiser and agency were equally surprised when the campaign got scorching reviews from angered members of women's movements. It also put Maidenform in the painful position of having to reevaluate the "success" of a campaign that, without question, was a success in terms of sales.

What ticked off women when Maidenform tried to turn them on?   14

As the advertiser sees it, the campaign was inadvertently suggesting that the Maidenform woman had achieved her enviable position, such as tiger tamer, strictly on the basis of her sexuality rather than her actual competence. The most noteworthy clunker, the one that finally deep-sixed the "You never know where she'll turn up" campaign, was the white-coated lady doctor piece. Everyone (male or female) who had ever worn a white coat—nurses, lab technicians, beauticians, the American Medical Association—bombarded Maidenform with calls and letters of protest.

As the mail indicated, there were some obvious reasons why this 15 campaign caused the uproar it did. With a female doctor exposing herself in a patient's hospital room, women's lib took a giant step backward. "Strip off the professional cover," these ads seemed to be saying, "and what you'll find is just another sex object."

At the time this campaign got started, however, I thought it would 16 have upset people for an entirely different unconscious reason. I showed the ad to some of my colleagues and just asked their opinions of it. Mark, a Ph.D. psychologist who's been practicing about as long as I have, came up with what turned out to be the consensus:

"That's going to be one angry lady!"   17

"Okay," I asked, "why?"   18

Mark pointed to the two samples I'd shown him—the woman in the 19 tiger cage and the doctor ad—and noted, "Look at the men in the pictures. Here's a woman with her clothes off, and they aren't paying any attention to her at all."

Mark and the others confirmed my own sense of the underlying 20 problem. The most insulting thing about the ads was not that the woman had exposed herself—even in a professional role. That might have been intellectually offensive—yes, it could be demeaning to women who were rising in their professions—but it didn't explain the strength of the emotional reactions women had to the ads.

What was really most offensive were the self-indulgent, narcissistic 21 posturings of the *men* in the picture. For the woman wearing a Maidenform bra, the experience was no longer a good dream. It was a bad dream. It is humiliating on the deepest levels, where our feelings of self-worth are most fragile, for any of us to expose ourselves at our most naked and vulnerable . . . and make no impact whatsoever. Women can easily identify with the Maidenform image in the ads, put themselves in her position and feel the angry confusion of someone who dolls herself up but still gets ignored.

There's more. Despite being pictured in the trappings of power, this 22 Maidenform woman ended up looking weak and vulnerable. Look at the contrast between the unblinking confidence and forward-thrusting body posture of the lady pool-shark and check out the demure, downcast glance and tight-kneed toe-tipped stance of the tiger tamer. Maidenform tried to tell women that it was listening, that it respected their hard-won accomplishments, but it sent some subtle messages that undercut the communication. Women bought the bras but were left with images of themselves as "sweet nothings"—ironically the name of one of Maidenform's best-selling lines.

After four years of profitable (although sometimes uncomfort- 23 able) campaigning, Maidenform pulled back from its big-strong-pretty young-things-turning-up-half-naked-in-front-of-self-involved-men approach. Romance, Maidenform perceived, was coming back. It was time to turn from power to syrup. Women were beginning to gag on advertisers' endless portraits of them as superhuman jugglers of kids, career, hubby, and housework.

Stripped of any power cues, the next Maidenform Woman was one 24 who "Dares to Dream." And what are her daring dreams about now? Sitting around wearing underwear and a wistful, vacant expression, she boldly fantasizes about going out on a date. Here is a woman with no pretensions of being anything other than the lovely, compliant, and ever-so-feminine creature her mother modeled in the fifties. She's straight out of the whistle-clean Harlequin Romance series, right down to the quasi-book-jacket logo in the corner. And like these little stories, Maidenform declares that its "Delectables" will "make your life as soft and smooth as your dreams."

At this stage of the game, all of us, women especially, have gotten 25 to be fairly sophisticated cynics. We know that advertisers run various images of us to see whether they can stir a ripple of salesworthy responses. The "Dares to Dream" campaign reached out to women who had been feeling like miserable failures for fantasizing about guys. While everybody else was out there self-actualizing into steel-plated CEOs, Maidenform gave the "new romantics" permission to go ahead and dream the dreams of adolescent girls if they wanted.

Sales proved that many women wanted just that. Enough battling 26 against male indifference and resistance. Maidenform was tired of trying to tickle the fancies of feminists; the campaign regressed to the lowest-risk imagery for the masses—woman as a glowworm for love.

While it clearly qualifies as a fluff piece, Wyse Advertising's "Dares 27 to Dream" campaign is surpassed in regressiveness by its next series of "lifestyle" ads. "The Maidenform Woman. Today she's playful," whisks our heroine backward in time until she's a prepubescent who gets kind of emotional, but that's okay, because Maidenform will "fit" her "every move and mood" so she can stay just as cute as she is now. She's not even old enough to think about guys—"frisky as a kitten," "Today she's playful."

Now, no angry letters spewed forth on the heels of "Today she's 28 playful." Whom *did* this appeal to? Well, there's Liz. She's very bright and possesses an MBA, which she sometimes waves over a conversation like a silk scarf—something to be admired but not used. She's surrounded by working friends, but she's filled her life with tennis and shopping and lunches. I like Liz, and it's over one of these lunches that she says to me, "I feel like having a temper tantrum."

I can't help thinking about how Liz creates herself in the image of   29
the "Today she's playful" ad—defining herself not in terms of what she's accomplishing, but by her moods. Does Liz know what she's doing? I don't think so. Did the agency know what it was doing? I don't think so. Both are just creating what they hope are pretty pictures.

Where do you go with this? Unfortunately, Liz will probably just   30
continue to be the subject of her moods. Maidenform wasn't quite so stuck—it changed agencies.

Following this purely saccharine retreat from Maidenform's gutsy   31
heritage, the sixty-five-year-old lingerie company set out in pursuit of the Holy Grail of advertising—a new image. After a grueling selection process, Levine, Huntley, Schmidt & Beaver won the account—and the opportunity to sweat its way toward a singularly brilliant advertising idea.

What Levine, Huntley, Schmidt & Beaver created, and what the ad-   32
vertiser had the courage to appreciate, is a radical departure for lingerie ads.

No women, no product—just male movie-star-types like Omar   33
Sharif, Michael York, and Corbin Bernsen. The campaign has been noticed by the media, by competitors, and apparently by women, who've written comments to the advertiser like "I don't normally watch commercials—however, your Michael York commercial is fantastic! So much so I've switched to Maidenform." "Your commercial will be shown at our annual meeting . . . as a prime example of excellent advertising. It appeals to women as adults, not children . . . keep up the good work." And "This is the type of commercial that instills a need in me to purchase your product."

Now just what is driving these ads? What happens when women   34
see someone like Omar Sharif shot in deep shadows, murmuring, "Lingerie says a lot about a woman. I listen as often as possible"? There's an edge of the forbidden, the dangerous, to Sharif's exotic, rakish seductiveness that is a psychological turn-on to the dainty dreamers of Maidenform's recent past. They can rebel against the sweet-young-thing image, and run away (in their fantasies) with a sexy devil. No one has to take the modesty of a woman publicly displayed in her underwear. Sharif's appeal is also clearly to a mature market; he's not exactly the current heartthrob of younger women. So the advertiser moved away

from charming vignettes of moody little models and is effectively hooking grown-ups with male bait.

With Corbin Bernsen of *L.A. Law,* the psychological lure isn't just   35
juicy evil. Here's a recognizably competent lady-killer, who enters the mysterious realm of a lingerie department and finds it "a little embarrassing. A little intimidating." What a gift to the female ego! If Maidenform can give women a way to embarrass and intimidate the likes of Mr. Bernsen, even "a little," it's not just underwear anymore—it's personal power.

The story of women's relationship with Maidenform's images re-   36
flects the complex interactions we all have with advertising. Advertisers have to communicate with as large a group of us consumers as possible, but in reality, the communication is always one-to-one. Maidenform's first "I dreamed I . . ." campaign was a success because the fantasy it promoted matched the underlying aspirations of enough individuals to make up a mass market. The advertiser gave a big push to a hoop already rolling out the kitchen door of convention, but things changed when the fantasy of sexual power turned to the reality of political and social power

Then Maidenform held up concrete images of strong women to try   37
to keep up with all the changes. The trouble came when the advertiser unwittingly introduced doubts and insecurities with its "You never know where she'll turn up" series and women felt a bit as though they'd bought a measure of male indifference along with Maidenform's dream images. The advertiser responded by attempting to soothe its buyers with pictures of romantic security. And finally it courts its market with its latest put-yourself-in-the-picture invitations offered by dashing male sex objects.

The promise is still largely romance. But a woman isn't just faced   38
with relating to an image of herself; now, she's asked to relate to her idea of a man's image of her. For this to work for Maidenform, a woman has to have enough self-confidence to imagine that she is the object of these lingerie lovers' underwear fantasies. It would work for Liz, but not for Ann. Ann's a nice woman who feels fat and unattractive and prefers to undress in the dark. These ads make her feel worse because she *can't* imagine herself in them. She flunks the fantasy test.

Maidenform's current strategy works for one other important rea-   39
son—it sidesteps the question faced by all lingerie advertisers: How can you show a woman in her underwear without making her look either like an idiot or a slut. Most answers bomb. . . .

Advertisers don't deliberately insult the people they are trying to   40
seduce; they're basically family-oriented, intelligent, profit-minded sorts who often take really lousy pictures that they think are great shots

of their subject. Even more interesting is that we may like how we look in a picture at one point in our lives, and later on feel disgusted or embarrassed by the same photo. What we identified with in an ad five years ago may be completely out of sync with who we are now. And we form these conclusions almost immediately—not from logical deliberation, but by unconsciously weighing all the subtle verbal and nonverbal cues that make up an advertising message. If some of the pieces don't fit, don't ring true—if we don't like how we see ourselves now or how we'd like to see ourselves in the future—we can end up feeling insulted, misunderstood, or confused. . . .

The trouble with the advertising mirror is that we never really see   41
ourselves reflected; we only see reflections of what advertisers want us to think their products will do for us. If the image of who we might be if we used the advertiser's product resonates with where we secretly, or not so secretly, wish we were—then there we are, consciously or unconsciously, measuring up to Madison Avenue. Sometimes that's not such a bad thing, but sometimes whatever insecurities we have get exacerbated by advertisers' image-making and by our own intense desires to make it—to win first prize in Madison Avenue's perpetual lookalike contest.

●●●●●●●●●●●●●●●●●●●●

Examining the Text

1. Briefly summarize Moog's descriptions of how the various Maidenform advertising campaigns appealed to several decades of consumers. Why does she think some campaigns were more successful than others? Does her analyses seem reasonable?

2. As a psychologist, Moog incorporates several references in this essay to the psychological effects of advertisements on specific people. What point do you think she is making with these references to the psychological impact of advertising? Can you think of any psychological impact that specific ads have had on you?

3. According to Moog, what role do consumers play in influencing advertising campaigns? How is Moog's view of consumer influence different from the view of other writers in this chapter? How do you account for this difference?

For Group Discussion

Moog concludes her essay by suggesting that "If the image of who we might be if we used the advertiser's product resonates with where we secretly, or not so secretly wish we were—then there we are, consciously or unconsciously, measuring up to Madison Avenue" (paragraph 41). In your group, identify ad campaigns that "resonate" with where contemporary college students wish they were. Identify some characteristics these advertisements share that make them particularly appealing.

Writing Suggestion

Underlying Moog's essay is the presumption that advertisements reflect and respond to the social context in which they exist, and that they change with the times. Follow Moog's model and trace the development of advertising campaigns for a specific product, looking through magazines from the 1950s, 1960s, 1970s, 1980s and 1990s and studying the changes in that product's ads. What conclusions can you draw about how the ads respond to and reflect broader social changes?

Skin Deep

Wendy Chapkis

*T*he following essay by Wendy Chapkis, which is excerpted from her book Beauty Secrets: Women and the Politics of Appearance *(1986), moves our theme of women's images in advertising to the international level. As Chapkis points out, the worldwide proliferation of American-made advertisements, television, and movies promotes an image of ideal female beauty that is distinctly "white, Western, and wealthy." Global advertising campaigns and the Americanization of world media largely ignore national, ethnic, and economic differences and "contribute to the belief that success and beauty are brand names with a distinctly white American look to them. . . ." Women throughout the world, then, are given a standard of beauty that, for many, is inappropriate.*

In addition to examining American images abroad, Chapkis discusses the way non-Western women are portrayed in American-made advertisements. These ads present women of color as exotic and subservient, and picture Third World countries as "holiday fantasylands." In all cases, Chapkis suggests, advertising and other media relay a culturally biased image of the world that is inaccurate, even harmful.

Before you read, *think of what the term "beauty" means to you, particularly your notion of "ideal female beauty." To what extent to you think advertising and mass media in general have influenced the formation of your idea of beauty?*

. . . .

"Mirror, mirror on the wall, who is the fairest of them all?" As children we accept that "the fairest" is the same sort of measure as the fastest, the tallest or the richest. Later, in the growing sophistication of adulthood, we determine that the most beautiful is more like the bravest, the most popular or the most powerful. It becomes a judgment about which one might have an *opinion* but remains a quality that ultimately can be established by an independent and attentive authority. "Ladies and Gentlemen, the judges have reached a decision. The new Miss World is. . . ." 1

Adults thus continue to pose the question "who is the fairest" as thought it were meaningful, even when the category of "them all" includes women of diverse races and nationalities. Indeed female beauty is becoming an increasingly standardized quality throughout the world. A standard so strikingly white, Western, and wealthy it is tempting to conclude there must be a conscious conspiracy afoot. 2

But in fact no hidden plot is needed to explain the pervasiveness of this image. The fantasy of the Good Life populated by Beautiful People wearing The Look has seized the imagination of much of the world. This Western model of beauty represents a mandate for a way of life for women throughout the world regardless of how unrelated to each of our ethnic or economic possibilities it is. We invest a great deal in the fantasy, perhaps all the more, the further we are from being able to attain it. This international fantasy becomes the basis of our myths of eroticism, success and adventure. 3

It is "Charlie's Angels" (stars of a 1970s U.S. TV show) who appear to have a good time in the world, not women who are fat or small or dark-skinned. As the center of a world economic system, the U.S. owns the biggest share of the global culture machine. By entering that world in imagination, each woman aims to be whiter, more Western, more upper class. This goes beyond simple manipulation. 4

While the Hearst Corporation is trying to maximize profits on a global scale, that does not fully explain *Cosmopolitan's* popularity in seventeen languages around the world. The Cosmo package seems to offer everything: sexuality, success, independence and beauty. It is powerful and compelling. A woman working all day making microchips who buys lipstick or cigarettes is buying some tiny sense of dignity and self-esteem along with the glamour. 5

In large part, the content of the global image is determined by the mechanics of the sell: who creates the images for what products to be marketed through which media controlled by whom? The beauty trade (cosmetics, toiletries, fragrance and fashion) is expanding its market worldwide. And a world market means global marketing. For instance, during the Christmas season of 1982, the same commercials for Antaeus 6 and Chanel No. 5 perfumes were being used throughout Europe, the U.S. and Latin America. And in 1985, *Business Week* reported that Playtex had kicked off:

> . . . a one ad fits all campaign . . . betting that a single marketing effort can sell a new bra around the world . . . At one point several years ago, Playtex had 43 versions of ads running throughout the world with local managers in charge . . . This year Playtex gave all its world wide business to New York's Grey Advertising.

Tony Bodinetz, vice-chair of KMP in London (a division of the huge   7 international advertising corporation Saatchi and Saatchi) believes this kind of advertising campaign arises in part from cultural chauvinism:

> The use of the same ad in various countries is in part based on a calculation of cost effectiveness, but partly it is simply a reflection of an attitude of mind. Some company executive in Pittsburg or Los Angeles or somewhere thinks "if it works in Pittsburg it'll work in London . . . why the hell would they be any different?" One of the things we fight against here is the fact that American solutions are often imposed on us.

Bodinetz appears to be a minority voice in a company committed to   8 just such a global advertising strategy: "They are committed to it because they need to be. They are looking to get those huge world clients and the way to get the clients is to sell this concept, so they have to believe it," says Bodinetz. The competition among the advertising giants for the large corporate accounts is intense. And the world of multinational product and image is very small indeed.

About a dozen advertising agencies worldwide represent the ma-   9 jority of major multinational corporations and themselves operate across national boundaries. The number three advertising agency in the U.S., J. Walter Thompson, for example, is also the most important agency in Argentina, Chile and Venezuela, number two in Brazil and ABC—the American Broadcasting Corporation—a private television these global image makers are American advertising agencies. The products they hype are also overwhelmingly American. U.S. companies alone account for nearly half of global expenditures on advertising, outspending the closest rival, Japan, by five to one. Small wonder then that advertising images tend to be recognizably North American.

These global advertising campaigns increasingly ignore national   10 differences in determining the products to be marketed and the images used to sell them. The ads contribute to the belief that success and beauty are brand names with a distinctly white American look to them. Trade journals *Advertising Age* and *Business Abroad* note the trend:

"Rubinstein Ads not Altered for Señoras;" "World Wide Beauty Hints:
How Clairol Markets Glamour in Any Language."

The advertising agency Saatchi and Saatchi is enthusiastic about   11
"world branding" and global culture:

> Market research will be conducted to look for similarities not seek
> out differences. Similarities will be exploited positively and effi-
> ciently . . . developing advertising for an entire region of the world,
> and not simply for one market to find a real advertising idea so deep
> in its appeal that it can transcend national borders previously thought
> inviolate.

Western corporations are not alone in pursuing this transcendent ad-   12
vertising ideal. Shiseido, the Japanese giant in cosmetics, has recently re-
vamped its advertising to present a "determinedly international thrust."
"It is easy to create an ordinary, nice picture with a nice model and a nice
presentation for the product," explains a company executive, "but we
wanted to be memorable without being too realistic. Realism would
have too closely defined our market." Shiseido hints at its Asian origin—"intrigue from the Orient"—but its models are white and its targeted market is "the international affluent elite." Saatchi and Saatchi
agrees that this is the strategy of the future:

> Are social developments making outmoded the idea that the differ-
> ences between nations with regard to this or that durable, cosmetic
> or coffee were crucial for marketing strategy? Consumer convergence
> in demography, habits and culture are increasingly leading manufac-
> turers to a consumer-driven rather than a geography-driven view of
> their marketing territory . . . Marketers will be less likely to tailor
> product positioning to the differing needs of the country next door
> and more likely to operate on the basis of the common needs for their
> products.

A "consumer-driven" view of marketing means focusing on that   13
segment of any society likely to purchase a given product. For many
products, in particular luxury items, the potential market in large parts
of the world remains extremely limited. It is certainly true that members
of these national elites often more closely resemble their counterparts in
other countries than they do their own less affluent compatriots.

In turn, the upper class serves as the model of success and glamour   14
for the rest of the nation. All the pieces of the picture begin to fit neatly
together, confirming that there is but one vision of beauty. The woman
on the imported American television program resembles the woman in
the Clairol ad resembles the wife of the Prime Minister or industrial
magnate who dresses in the latest French fashion as faithfully reported
in the local version of *Cosmopolitan*.

Corporate advertising is not, then, uniquely responsible for the   15 homogenization of culture around the world. But it is an important team player. Tony Bodinetz explains:

> I don't think you can just point the finger and blame advertising, because advertising never leads. But admittedly it is very quick to sense what is happening on the streets or around the world and to jump on a bandwagon. Of course while it is true that advertising never sets the pace, it cannot escape its share of the responsibility for confirming the view that to "join the club" you've got to look like this, smell like this, speak like this and dress like this.

This vision of beauty and success has been made familiar around   16
the world not only through ads but via the American media of magazines, television and motion pictures. In much of the world, a large portion of television programming is composed of American imports. Foreign programs make up well over half of television fare in such countries as Ecuador, Chile and Malaysia. In Western Europe, the Middle East and parts of Asia more than 20 percent of all television programs are made in the U.S. One popular American program, "Bonanza," was once seen in 60 countries with an estimated audience of 350 million. The contemporary equivalent, "Dallas," is watched by millions from Malaysia to South Africa.

The Americanization of the world media has had useful spinoffs for   17
marketing. Saatchi and Saatchi again:

> . . . television and motion pictures are creating elements of shared culture. And this cultural convergence is facilitating the establishment of multinational brand characters. The worldwide proliferation of the Marlboro brand would not have been possible without TV and motion picture education about the virile rugged character of the American West and the American cowboy, helped by increasing colour TV penetration.

That American television should be so omnipresent is not entirely   18
due to chance or to the excellence of the U.S. "sitcom." In the 1950s, ABC—the American Broadcasting Corporation, a private television company, received U.S. government AID funding to create the first television stations in Educador, Colombia and Peru. They also provided technical assistance for the development of many others. By the early 1970s, ninety countries throughout the world were buying ABC programs and business agreements between ABC and its Latin American affiliates allow the corporation to choose both programs and sponsors for peak viewing hours. Even without such direct control, foreign imports are often the programming of choice because small local networks find it much cheaper to buy American programs than to produce their own.

Television, and the related Hollywood film industry, are not the   19
only media plying their wares around the world. Many of the top

twenty American magazine corporations also produce for a world market. Hearst Corporation, the third largest magazine corporation in the U.S., produces a Latin American version of "Good Housekeeping"—*Buenhogar*—and *Vanidades* (the women's magazine with the largest circulation in Latin America). Hearst also publishes the internationally popular *Cosmopolitan.* Conde Nast, number six on the U.S. list, publishes and distributes adapted versions of *Vogue* magazine in many countries.

Researchers in Latin America studied the content of these transna- 20 tional women's magazines and found striking similarities from country to country. The majority of articles focused on beauty, fashion or products for use in the home. Perhaps even more telling, almost a third of the total space was devoted to advertising and 60 percent of all advertisements were for the products of transnational corporations.

Of course, the media have always relied heavily on advertising. 21 Now, though, the relationship is so intimate that one corporation may own both the magazine advertising a product and the company producing it. Media authority Ben Bagdikian puts it bluntly: "The major media and giant corporations have always been allies; they are now a single entity."

Four of the fifty largest U.S. media corporations are among the fifty 22 largest advertisers. All three of the major American television networks and three of the four leading movie studios are part of companies so large that they appear on the list of the 500 largest corporations in the United States. Thus, not only does one country determine the jingle much of the world will hum, but a very few, large corporations own the piper.

While it would be wrong to suggest that this is the result of a con- 23 scious conspiracy among the various parts of the global culture machine (U.S.-based multinational corporations. U.S.-dominated international advertising and the U.S. entertainment and media industries), it is safe to say that they all benefit from a collective global fantasy of success and beauty defined by white skin, Western culture and imported products.

> Elaborate make-up is part of the electronics image in Malaysia, and the factories even provide classes in how to apply it. This allows the workers to feel they are part of a global culture which includes the choice between Avon and Mary Quant products.
>
> There just seems to be a great desire to aspire to Western values and Western culture . . . Often an ad will be written in English because that is one way of flattering the audience: "You are smart, sophisticated and educated." I suppose that is also why the models tend to be white . . .
>
> . . . Dr. Fu Nong Yu [a plastic surgeon in Peking] performs "eye jobs" to create folded or "double" eyelids, considered a mark of wide-eyed beauty. . . . Most northern Chinese are born without double eyelids and

Fu takes a few stitches to remove the epicanthal fold in the upper eyelid that is typical of Asians . . .

Japanese television commercials are a paean to the American way of
life, full of glamorous movie stars and famous sports heroes . . . Despite
a growing pride in things Japanese, the United States remains a cultural pacesetter for Japan . . . If a Japanese company cannot find an
American celebrity to endorse its product, it may opt for displaying the
product in a recognizably U.S. setting or placing a blue-eyed, blond
model alongside it.

Naturally, this trend toward global cultural homogenization has not   24
gone unchallenged. Indigenous culture remains a powerful alternative
to the white Western model of success and beauty. In some countries,
traditional images are officially promoted as a response to the flood of
imported Western culture. In other countries, local culture acts subver-
sively as the bearer of otherwise illegal messages of political, economic
and cultural resistance.

Following the Sandinista victory over the Somoza dictatorship in   25
Nicaragua, sexist advertising was banned. If a woman now appears in
an advertisement, there must be a reason other than providing a sexual
come-on to the potential buyer. While *Vanidades* and *Cosmopolitan*, with
their transnational advertising, can still be purchased in Managua, the
local billboards do not offer images of the wealthy white glamour girl.

Another, although very different reaction to Western sexualized im-   26
agery of women, is evidenced in the Islamic countries of North Africa
and the Middle East. A dramatic symbol of religious, national and patriarchal culture, the veil, is increasingly being adopted by women in
these countries. The use of the veil to reclaim (and in some cases to re-
invent) indigenous culture is clearly problematic but hardly inexplicable. Shortly before the overthrow of the Shah in Iran, the most popular
women's magazine in that country was *Zan-e Ruz (Woman of Today)* with
a circulation of over 100,000. The periodical was filled with love stories
starring blonde, blue-eyed heroines lifted directly from Western magazines. Of the 35 percent of the periodical taken up with ads, much focused on beauty and cosmetic products again often featuring blonde
models. One researcher observed "the great stress on physical appearance in a situation of acute sexual repression is . . . somehow ironic."
More than ironic, the resulting tensions may have helped encourage
both the Islamic revival and the subsequent return to the veil.

Significantly, while the veil may be an important and visible sym-   27
bol of resistance to Western culture and values, it is worn by women
only. Women throughout the world tend to be designated as culture
bearers and given the burdensome responsibility of preserving traditional values and aesthetics. In recent studies in several African

countries, researchers discovered that women were seen both as repositories of traditional culture and those most likely to succumb to Western influences. Women in Uganda, for example, were seen as:

> . . . scapegoats not only for male confusion and conflict over what the contemporary roles of women should be, but for the dilemmas produced by adjusting to rapid social change. Where men have given up traditional customs and restraints on dress, but feel traitors to their own culture, they yearn for the security and compensation of a least knowing that women are loyal to it.

In much the same way, women in Zambia have been held responsi-   28
ble "when the state of morality was chaotic . . ." and when cultural traditions became "contaminated by Western influence." Unfortunately, women of the Third World singlehandedly can no more turn back Western cultural domination than they can be held responsible for its powerful and enduring influence. And while women certainly *are* at the forefront of many forms of resistance including the cultural, "tradition" may not be the only element women will choose to draw on in creating a culture that speaks of and to their lives.

At the international festival of women's culture, Black women fill   29
the stage night after night with their presence. To watch them is not simply to admire but to feel pride. They allow for no less. Their self-respect is utterly contagious and offers a vision of power beyond the borders of white commercial culture.

These women using music, language and movement different from   30
my own, still speak directly me. "This is a heart beat. This is all of our heart beats. And it is beating for you. And for you. And for you." (Edwina Lee Tyler playing her African drum.)

The destructive effect of racism on the self-image of people of color   31
is well-documented and much bemoaned—especially among anti-racist whites. Isn't it terrible that Blacks have felt a need to "relax" their curly hair to appear more attractive? Isn't it shocking that eye jobs creating a Western eyelid were popular among certain Vietnamese women during the war? Isn't it distressing that the model for female beauty sold to developing nations is the same White Woman sold to the West?

Yes. But at some level it is also profoundly reassuring to white   32
women; we are, after all, the model. We do embody at least one element of the beauty formula. Our white Western lives are the stuff of global fantasy and demonstrably enviable.

This international commercial trend can easily be misrepresented as   33
evidence of a unanimous esthetic judgment. But people of color are not alone in buying fantasies packaged in a distant ethnic reality. For the Western white, "paradise is tropical, and passion, rhythmic movement

and sensuality all wear dark skin. Just as the white Western world serves as the repository for certain elements of a global myth of success and beauty, so too does the world of color represent related myths of sensuality, adventure and exoticism.

The fantasy of the Western Good Life is grounded in the reality of 34 the economic privilege of the industrialized West. Perhaps the fantasy of sensuality and passion ascribed to the Third World reflects something similar about the realities of privilege and oppression. It is certainly true that to maintain a position of privilege in a world of tremendous poverty requires some measure of emotional shutting down, a distancing of the self from the unentitled other. Puerto Rican poet Aurora Levins Morales suggests that this has consequences for white culture:

> There is a kind of aliveness that has been obtained in oppressed cultures that gets shut down in dominant culture. There is a lot of fear that comes with privilege. Fear that others want to take your stuff away from you. It means an incredible locking down. Also you have to be in control all the time. Being always in control is not conducive to sensuality.

Power is the arbiter determining which characteristics will be as- 35 cribed to the self and which will be projected onto the other. These complimentary images are the basis of myths of white and black, male and female, the self and Other. . . .

The world of advertising is a rich source of imagery of women of 36 color, often combining racist and sexist stereotypes in one picture. Advertisements using Asian women, for example, are evocative not only of the sexual mystery but also the docility and subservience supposedly "natural to the oriental female." This is true whether the product is the woman herself (as an assembly line worker or a "hospitality girl" in a holiday "sex tour") or another good or service enhanced by the female touch. A Malaysian electronics firm advertising brochure reads:

> The manual dexterity of the oriental female is famous the world over. Her hands are small and she works fast with extreme care. Who, therefore, could be better qualified by nature and inheritance to contribute to the efficiency of the bench assembly line than the oriental girl?

And this from Thai International Airlines:

> Gentle people . . . caring for you comes naturally to the girls of Thai. The gentle art of service and courtesy is one they learn from childhood . . . Beautiful Thai.

As the advertising technique of "world branding" helps spread 37 white Western culture to developing nations, Third World women increasingly appear in advertisements in the West promising entry to that vanishing world of the exotic. These women thus become metaphors for adventure, cultural difference and sexual subservience; items apparently increasingly hard to come by in the industrialized West.

Especially interesting are those ads selling travel and tourism. Their 38 invitation is to escape to paradise on earth—in itself fascinating given the way Third World countries are represented in the other media. The split images are quite remarkable: the exotic is marketed as a holiday fantasyland while "the underdeveloped world" is used in the West as shorthand for poverty, hunger, political corruption and religious fanaticism.

Of course, airlines and other branches of the tourist industry, are in 39 the business of selling fantasy not theories of underdevelopment. "A taste of Paradise to Sri Lanka . . . Discover the infinite beaches with the people of Paradise" whispers the Air Lanka ad. The text is set against a picture of a deserted white sandy beach with a small inserted photo of a smiling Asian flight hostess.

The use of foreign locales and peoples to enhance the magic prop- 40 erties of a product is an effective marketing technique. It is easier to suspend judgment and accept the promise of the fantastic if it is set far from familiar soil. Just as we doubt that the truly romantic can happen to people who look too ordinary, it is harder to believe that the truly fantastic can happen too close to home.

In the past, travel belonged to a small, very privileged elite. We saw 41 pictures of Brigitte Bardot in St. Tropez and knew both were the stuff of dreams. Now we can choose to visit the Côte d'Azur on a holiday, taking advantage of bargain flights or package tours. But when we walk the streets of our collective dreams, we don't look like Bardot. And the romantic adventures that befell her seem to pass us by. Perhaps we are not beautiful enough, or rich enough, to bring out the true magic of St. Tropez?

Rather than concluding that the fantasy was never a full and true 42 reflection of reality, we simply set our sights on ever more distant shores. The more inaccessible the better. Travel brochures almost always suggest that this spot is still "unspoiled"; perhaps the compulsive clicking of cameras is an attempt to recapture the quiet, frozen images of the dream we thought we bought. Back home, looking through the carefully composed shots, the exotic again resembles the airline ads that fed our fantasies.

Ironically, travel to exotic lands actually robs us of their exoticism; 43 the exotic must remain unfamiliar in order to retain its mystery. Experience creates familiarity, something our culture teaches us is the antithesis of romance. So while travel ads promise access to the exotic, they must also emphasize its unknowable Otherness. A Singapore Airlines ad reads: "Across four continents of the earth . . . you are an unsolved mystery in a *sarong kebaya.* Who are you Singapore Girl?"

A serenely beautiful Asian woman stares directly into the camera, an intimate look, steady and deep: "The airline with the most modern fleet in the world still believes in the romance of travel." And, as Singapore Airlines reminds us, there is nothing more romantic than the mysterious Asian woman. Nothing else appears in their ads. Exotic cloth is wrapped around undemanding oriental gentleness: "Enjoy the kind of inflight service even other airlines talk about, with gentle hostesses in sarong kebayas caring for you as only they know how." Yes, their girls have a reputation, but they don't mind. 44

Hilton International promotes their hotels in Hong Kong, Jakarta, Kuala Lumpur, Manila, Singapore, Taipei and Tokyo with the picture of five Asian women (some dressed in traditional outfits, others in Western service uniforms): "Life oriental style . . . A carefully melded crossroads of East and West. You've focused on Hilton International. A unique blend of Oriental hospitality and international service." 45

The ad speaks to the fantasy and the *fear* of travel in exotic lands. Hilton will help smooth out the cultural confusions by carefully melding East and West. A safe way to enjoy exoticism. You can "enter a world where a myriad of surrounding sights and sensations tantalize your imagination, and let the Hilton International world of thoughtful services *put your mind at ease."* The hotel is no simple place to sleep, no more than an airline is simply a means of transportation. It is a fantasy, indeed A Way of Life, or at least the safe imitation of one. "Specializing in the unexpected—a lobby in exact replica of a sultan's palace. Our own cruising replica of a pirate chasing brigantine . . ." 46

Perfumes, cosmetics and certain fashion lines promise the look of the exotic for those unable or unwilling to actually travel to distant countries. The Ultima II cosmetic line by Revlon is marketed as a way for East to meet West. "The collection is Ultima's lyrical translation of the loveliest colors the Orient has to offer." Note the use of the word orient in so many of these ads. Orient is a realm of fantasy; Asia is a real life place. Orient brings to mind the mystery of the exotic region of the East; Asia says Vietnam, Red China, Toyota car competition. The most striking thing about the Ultima II "East Meets West" advertisement is the photograph accompanying it. Lauren Hutton sits on a cushion wearing something reminiscent of a kimono (but showing too much flesh). She looks down with a slightly amused smile at her hands folded in her lap. Across from her, an Asian woman dressed in a real kimono bows to this symbol of daring Western womanhood. This is apparently the proper attitude for East when meeting West. 47

Perfume ads are particularly fond of the exotic motif. And here 48
again the racial stereotypes and the promise of exotic fantasy reign: "Island Gardenia by Jovan: Delicate. Exotic. Above all . . . Sensuous. Only
in the islands do the most delicate flowers grow a little wilder." "Fidji
by Guy Laroche: Fidji, le parfum des paradis retrouvés." "Mitsouko by
Guerlain: Serenely mysterious . . ."

Even such a mundane product as panty hose can be sold with a 49
touch of the exotic: "The look . . . the feel . . . of the Orient. Now yours
in a pantyhose. Sheer Elegance, Silky smooth, radiant . . ." This ad
points out one of the stereotypes that may help make the Asian woman
the model of acceptable exotic sexuality. Like an idealized child, she is
described as small, docile, available and never demanding. Her body
is as "smooth and silky" as the hairless body of a sexually innocent
child.

High fashion, too, often makes use of exotica. *Vogue* magazine is es- 50
pecially fond of setting its white models, dressed in "native inspired"
fashions, against such backdrops as the Tunesian Oasis of Nefta. Magazines for working class women, on the other hand, only rarely show
such exotic fashions or locales. In part this may reflect the fact that the
Hilton International Way of Life is a much more familiar fantasy to
Vogue readers. And while *Vogue* suggests that, for the wealthy, fashion
is artful play, the *Cosmopolitan* reader knows that in the realm of Dress
for Success, clothing is serious business.

For working women, the exotic is, at best, an *after hours* image cre- 51
ated through cosmetics, perfumes and daring sexual practices—all important elements of the "Sex and the Single Girl" success package. Apparently only those who are beyond any doubt white, Western and
wealthy can afford to look Third World.

· · · · · · · · · · · · · · · · · · · ·

Examining the Text

1. What does Chapkis mean by "global cultural homogenization"
(paragraph 24)? What evidence of its existence does she offer? Who or
what is responsible for this homogenization, according to Chapkis? Are
you convinced by her argument?

2. In Chapkis's opinion, how are women "culture bearers" (paragraph
27)? What are the burdens and benefits of this responsibility?

3. According to Chapkis, how do travel and cosmetic advertisements
present Asian women? What does Chapkis think is wrong with these
images? To what extent do you agree with her?

4. What do you think is Chapkis's purpose in writing this essay? What sort of reforms do you think she would like to see in the way beauty is defined in America and internationally? Do you think any changes have taken place since 1986, when this essay was written?

For Group Discussion

Chapkis asserts that the standard of feminine beauty in American culture is "white, Western, and wealthy." Reflect as a group on other dimensions of popular culture (television, music, movies, sports, and so on), and list further evidence that supports this assertion. Also list any evidence that contradicts this assertion. Use your lists to evaluate Chapkis's central argument.

Writing Suggestion

Look through the ads in a recent women's magazine, and note any images of women of color in the advertisements. What generalizations or conclusions can you can draw about the portrayal of women of color in these ads? In an essay, explain to what extent these images correspond to what Chapkis describes as "the exotic."

A Gentleman and a Consumer

Diane Barthel

*D*iana Barthel's essay, taken from her book Putting On Appearances: Gender and Advertising *(1988), focuses on what ads have to say about men. As Barthel points out, advertising, like the culture in general, proposes certain notions of what it means to be masculine and what it means to be feminine. Whereas the feminine is stereotypically passive, narcissistic, and noncompetitive, masculinity is presented in terms of action, competitiveness, and power.*

In examining a number of ads designed for men—ads for cars as well as ads for what are typically considered "women's products" like moisturizers, haircare products, and cologne—Barthel focuses on the appeal to "power, performance, and precision" in images in which the male is in charge, decisive, and desirable. Barthel also points out a number of "homilies" or short sermons that we often see in advertising directed to a male audience. Like women, male consumers can be influenced by advertisements to accept certain standards of masculinity to which they must measure up. The question, as Barthel and others in this chapter have suggested, is whether we want to accept these conventional standards of masculinity and femininity.

Before you read, think about what the term "masculinity" means to you. What qualities are associated with being "masculine"? And how many of these qualities are also associated with the term "feminine"?

. . . .

There are no men's beauty and glamour magazines with circula-   1
tions even approaching those of the women's magazines we have been examining here. The very idea of men's beauty magazines may strike one as odd. In our society men traditionally were supposed to make the right appearance, to be well groomed and neatly tailored. What they were *not* supposed to do was to be overly concerned with their appearance, much less vain about their beauty. That was to be effeminate, and not a "real man." Male beauty was associated with homosexuals, and "real men" had to show how red-blooded they were by maintaining a certain distance from fashion.

Perhaps the best-known male fashion magazine is *GQ* founded in   2
1957 and with a circulation of 446,000 in 1986. More recently, we have seen the launching of *YMF* and *Young Black Male,* which in 1987 still have few advertising pages. *M* magazine, founded in 1983, attracts an audience "a cut above" that of *GQ.*

Esquire magazine, more venerable (founded in 1933), is classified as   3
a general interest magazine. Although it does attract many women readers, many of the columns and features and much of the advertising are definitely directed toward attracting the attention of the male readers, who still make up the overwhelming majority of the readership.

As mentioned in the introduction, the highest circulations for men's   4
magazines are for magazines specializing either in sex (*Playboy,* circulation 4.1 million; *Penthouse,* circulation nearly 3.8 million; and *Hustler,* circulation 1.5 million) or sports (*Sports Illustrated,* circulation 2.7 million). That these magazines share an emphasis on power—either power over women or over other men on the playing field—should not surprise. In fact, sociologist John Gagnon would argue that sex and sports now represent the major fields in which the male role, as defined by power, is played out, with physical power in work, and even in warfare, being less important than it was before industrialization and technological advance.

If we are looking for comparative evidence as to how advertise-   5
ments define gender roles for men and women, we should not then see the male role as defined primarily through beauty and fashion. This seems an obvious point, but it is important to emphasize how different cultural attitudes toward both the social person and the physical body shape the gender roles of men and women. These cultural attitudes are changing, and advertisements are helping to legitimate the use of beauty

products and an interest in fashion for men, as we shall see. As advertisements directed toward women are beginning to use male imagery,
so too advertisements for men occasionally use imagery resembling that
found in advertisements directed toward women. We are speaking of
two *modes*, then. As Baudrillard writes, these modes "do not result from
the differentiated nature of the two sexes, but from the differential logic
of the system. The relationship of the Masculine and the Feminine to real
men and women is relatively arbitrary." Increasingly today, men and
women use both modes. The two great terms of opposition (Masculine
and Feminine) still, however, structure the forms that consumption
takes; they provide identities for products and consumers.

Baudrillard agrees that the feminine model encourages a woman to   6
please herself, to encourage a certain complacency and even narcissistic solicitude. But by pleasing herself, it is understood that she will also
please others, and that she will be chosen. "She never enters into direct
competition. . . . If she is beautiful, that is to say, if this woman is a
woman, she will be chosen. If the man is a man, he will choose his
woman as he would other objects/signs (HIS car, HIS woman, HIS eau
de toilette).

Whereas the feminine model is based on passivity, complacency, and   7
narcissism, the masculine model is based on exactingness and choice.

> All of masculine advertising insists on rule, on choice, in terms of rigor
> and inflexible minutiae. He does not neglect a detail . . . It is not a ques-
> tion of just letting things go, or of taking pleasure in something, but
> rather of distinguishing himself. To know how to choose, and not to
> fail at it, is here the equivalent of the military and puritanical virtues:
> intransigence, decision, "virtus."

This masculine model, these masculine virtues, are best reflected in   8
the many car advertisements. There, the keywords are masculine terms:
power, performance, precision. Sometimes the car is a woman, responding
to the touch and will of her male driver, after attracting him with her
sexy body. "Pure shape, pure power, pure Z. It turns you on." But, as the
juxtaposition of shape and power in this advertisement suggest, the car
is not simply other; it is also an extension of the owner. As he turns it
on, he turns himself on. Its power is his power; through it, he will be
able to overpower other men and impress and seduce women.

> How well does it perform?
> How well can you drive? (Merkur XR4Ti)

> The 1987 Celica GT-S has the sweeping lines and aggressive stance
> that promise performance. And Celica keeps its word.

> Renault GTA:
> Zero to sixty to zero in 13.9 sec.

> It's the result of a performance philosophy where acceleration and braking are equally important.
> There's a new Renault sports sedan called GTA. Under its slick monochromatic skin is a road car with a total performance attitude. . . . It's our hot new pocket rocket.

In this last example, the car, like the driver, has a total performance   9
attitude. That is what works. The slick monochromatic skin, like the Bond Street suit, makes a good first impression. But car, like owner, must have what it takes, must be able to go the distance faster and better than the competition. This point is explicitly made in advertisements in which the car becomes a means through which this masculine competition at work is extended in leisure. Some refer directly to the manly sport of auto-racing: "The Mitsubishi Starion ESI-R. Patiently crafted to ignite your imagination. Leaving little else to say except . . . gentlemen, start your engines." Others refer to competition in the business world: "To move ahead fast in this world, you've got to have connections. The totally new Cordolla FX 16 GT-S has the right ones." Or in life in general. "It doesn't take any [Japanese characters] from anyone. It won't stand for any guff from 300ZX. Or RX-7. Introducing Conquest Tsi, the new turbo sport coupe designed and built by Mitsubishi in Japan." Or Ferrari, which says simply, "We are the competition." In this competition between products, the owners become almost superfluous. But the advertisements, of course, suggest that the qualities of the car will reflect the qualities of the owner, as opposed to the purely abstract, apersonal quality of money needed for purchase. Thus, like the would-be owner, the BMW also demonstrates a "relentless refusal to compromise." It is for "those who thrive on a maximum daily requirement of high performance." While the BMW has the business attitude of the old school ("aggression has never been expressed with such dignity"), a Beretta suggests what it takes to survive today in the shark-infested waters of Wall Street. In a glossy three-page cover foldout, a photograph of a shark's fin cutting through indigo waters is accompanied by the legend "Discover a new species from today's Chevrolet." The following two pages show a sleek black Beretta similarly cutting through water and, presumably, through the competition: "Not just a new car, but a new species . . . with a natural instinct for the road . . . Aggressive stance. And a bold tail lamp. See it on the road and you won't soon forget. Drive it, and you never will."

And as with men, so with cars. "Power corrupts. Absolute power cor-   10
rupts; absolutely" (Maserati). Not having the money to pay for a Maserati, to corrupt and be corrupted, is a source of embarrassment. Advertisements reassure the consumer that he need not lose face in this manly battle. Hyundai promises, "It's affordable. (But you'd never know it.)"

On first impression, the new Hyundai Excel GLS Sedan might seem a
trifle beyond most people's means. But that's entirely by design. Sleek
European design, to be exact.

Many advertisements suggest sexual pleasure and escape, as in   11
"Pure shape, pure power, pure Z. It turns you on." Or "The all-new
Chrysler Le Baron. Beauty . . . with a passion for driving." The Le Baron
may initially suggest a beautiful female, with its "image of arresting
beauty" and its passion "to drive. And drive it does!" But it *is* "Le
Baron," not "La Baronness." And the advertisement continues to emphasize how it *attacks* [emphasis mine] the road with a high torque, 2.5
fuel-injected engine. And its turbo option can blur the surface of any
passing lane." Thus the object of the pleasure hardly has to be female if
it is beautiful or sleek. The car is an extension of the male that conquers
and tames the (female) road: "Positive-response suspension will calm
the most demanding roads." The car becomes the ultimate lover when,
like the Honda Prelude, it promises to combine power, "muscle," with
finesse. Automobile advertisements thus play with androgyny and
sexuality; the pleasure is in the union and confusion of form and movement, sex and speed. As in any sexual union, there is ultimately a merg-
ing of identities, rather than rigid maintenance of their separation.
Polymorphous perverse? Perhaps. But it sells.

Though power, performance, precision as a complex of traits find   12
their strongest emphasis in automobile advertisements, they also appear as selling points for products as diverse as shoes, stereos, and sunglasses. The car performs on the road, the driver performs for women,
even in the parking lot, as Michelin suggests in its two-page spread
showing a male from waist down resting on his car and chatting up a
curvaceous female: "It performs great. And looks great. So, it not only
stands out on the road. But in the parking lot. Which is one more place
you're likely to discover how beautifully it can handle the curves" (!).

As media analyst Todd Gitlin points out, most of the drivers shown   13
in advertisements are young white males, loners who become empowered by the car that makes possible their escape from the everyday.
Gitlin stresses the advertisements' "emphasis on surface, the blankness
of the protagonist; his striving toward self-sufficiency, to the point of
displacement from the recognizable world." Even the Chrysler advertisements that coopt Bruce Springsteen's "Born in the USA" for their
"Born in America" campaign lose in the process the original political
message, "ripping off Springsteen's angry anthem, smoothing it into a
Chamber of Commerce ditty as shots of just plain productive-looking
folks, black and white . . . whiz by in a montage-made community." As
Gitlin comments, "None of Springsteen's losers need apply—or rather,

if only they would roll up their sleeves and see what good company they're in, they wouldn't feel like losers any longer."

This is a world of patriarchal order in which the individual male can   14
and must challenge the father. He achieves identity by breaking loose of the structure and breaking free of the pack. In the process he recreates the order and reaffirms the myth of masculine independence. Above all, he demonstrates that he knows what he wants; he is critical, demanding, and free from the constraints of others. What he definitely does not want, and goes to some measure to avoid, is to appear less than masculine, in any way weak, frilly, feminine.

Avoiding the Feminine

Advertisers trying to develop male markets for products previously   15
associated primarily with women must overcome the taboo that only women wear moisturizer, face cream, hair spray, or perfume. They do this by overt reference to masculine symbols, language, and imagery, and sometimes by confronting the problem head-on.

There is not so much of a problem in selling products to counteract   16
balding—that traditionally has been recognized as a male problem (a bald woman is a sexual joke that is not particularly amusing to the elderly). But other hair products are another story, as the March 1987 *GQ* cover asks, "Are you man enough for mousse?" So the advertisements must make their products seem manly, as with S-Curl's "wave and curl kit" offering "The Manly Look" on its manly model dressed in business suit and carrying a hard hat (a nifty social class compromise), and as in college basketball sportscaster Al McGuire's testimonial for Consort hair spray:

> "Year's ago, if someone had said to me, 'Hey Al, do you use hair spray?' I would have said, 'No way, baby!'"
> "That was before I tried Consort Pump."
> "Consort adds extra control to my hair without looking stiff or phony. Control that lasts clean into overtime and post-game interviews . . ."
> Grooming Gear for Real Guys. *Consort.*

Beside such "grooming gear" as perms and hair sprays, Real Guys   17
use "skin supplies" and "shaving resources." They adopt a "survival strategy" to fight balding, and the "Fila philosophy"—"products with a singular purpose: performance"—for effective "bodycare." If they wear scent, it smells of anything *but* flowers: musk, woods, spices, citrus, and surf are all acceptable. And the names must be manly, whether symbolizing physical power ("Brut") or financial power ("Giorgio VIP Special

Reserve," "The Baron. A distinctive fragrance for men," "Halston—For the privileged few").

As power/precision/performance runs as a theme throughout ad- 18 vertising to men, so too do references to the business world. Cars, as we have seen, promise to share their owner's professional attitude and aggressive drive to beat out the competition. Other products similarly reflect the centrality of business competition to the male gender role. And at the center of this competition itself, the business suit.

> At the onset of your business day, you choose the suit or sportcoat that will position you front and center . . .

> The Right Suit can't guarantee he'll see it your way. The wrong suit could mean not seeing him at all.

Along with the Right Suit, the right shirt, "You want it every time 19 you reach across the conference table, or trade on the floor, or just move about. You want a shirt that truly fits, that is long enough to stay put through the most active day, even for the taller gentleman." The businessman chooses the right cologne—Grey Flannel, or perhaps Quorum. He wears a Gucci "timepiece" as he conducts business on a cordless telephone from his poolside—or prefers the "dignity in styling" promised by Raymond Weil watches, "a beautiful way to dress for success."

Men's products connect status and success; the right products show 20 that you have the right stuff, that you're one of them. In the 1950s C. Wright Mills described what it took to get ahead, to become part of the "power elite":

> The fit survive, and fitness means, not formal competence . . . but conformity with the criteria of those who have already succeeded. To be compatible with the top men is to act like them, to look like them, to think like them: to be of and for them—or at least to display oneself to them in such a way as to create that impression. This, in fact, is what is meant by "creating"—a well-chosen word—"a good impression." This is what is meant—and nothing else—by being a "sound man," as sound as a dollar.

Today, having what it takes includes knowing "the difference be- 21 tween dressed, and well dressed" (Bally shoes). It is knowing that "what you carry says as much about you as what you put inside it" (Hartmann luggage). It is knowing enough to imitate Doug Fout, "member of one of the foremost equestrian families in the country."

> Because of our adherence to quality and the natural shoulder tradition, Southwick clothing was adopted by the Fout family years ago. Clearly, they have as much appreciation for good lines in a jacket as they do in a thoroughbred.

There it is, old money. There is no substitute for it, really, in business   22
or in advertising, where appeals to tradition form one of the mainstays
guaranteeing men that their choices are not overly fashionable or feminine, not working class or cheap, but, rather, correct, in good form,
above criticism. If, when, they achieve this status of gentlemanly perfection, then, the advertisement suggests, they may be invited to join the
club.

When only the best of associations will do

Recognizing style as the requisite for membership, discerning men
prefer the natural shoulder styling of Racquet Club. Meticulously tailored in pure wool, each suit and sportcoat is the ultimate expression
of the clubman's classic good taste.

Ralph Lauren has his Polo University Club, and Rolex picks up on   23
the polo theme by sponsoring the Rolex Gold Cup held at the Palm
Beach Polo and Country Club, where sixteen teams and sixty-four players competed for "the pure honor of winning, the true glory of victory":

It has added new lustre to a game so ancient, its history is lost in legend. Tamerlane is said to have been its patriarch. Darius's Persian cav-
alry, we're told, played it. It was the national sport of 16th-century India, Egypt, China, and Japan. The British rediscovered and named it in
1857.
     The linking of polo and Rolex is uniquely appropriate. Both spon-
sor and sport personify rugged grace. Each is an arbiter of the art of
thinking.

In the spring of 1987, there was another interesting club event—or   24
nonevent. The prestigious New York University Club was ordered to
open its doors to women. This brought the expected protests about freedom of association—and of sanctuary. For that has been one of the
points of the men's club. It wasn't open to women. Members knew
women had their place, and everyone knew it was not there. In the advertisements, as in the world of reality, there is a place for women in
men's lives, one that revolves around:

Sex and Seduction

As suggested earlier, the growing fascination with appearances, en-   25
couraged by advertising, has led to a "feminization" of culture. We are
all put in the classic role of the female: manipulable, submissive, seeing
ourselves as objects. This "feminization of sexuality" is clearly seen in
men's advertisements, where many of the promises made to women are
now made to men. If women's advertisements cry, "Buy (this product)

and he will notice you," men's advertisements similarly promise that female attention will follow immediately upon purchase, or shortly thereafter. "They can't stay away from Mr. J." "Master the Art of Attracting Attention." She says, "He's wearing my favorite Corbin again." Much as in the advertisements directed at women, the advertisements of men's products promise that they will do the talking for you. "For the look that says come closer." "All the French you'll ever need to know."

Although many advertisements show an admiring and/or depen- 26 dent female, others depict women in a more active role. "I love him— but life in the fast lane starts at 6 A.M.," says the attractive blonde tying on her jogging shoes, with the "him" in question very handsome and very asleep on the bed in the background. (Does this mean he's in the slow lane?) In another, the man slouches silhouetted against a wall; the woman leans aggressively toward him. He: "Do you always serve Tia Maria . . . or am I special? She: "Darling, if you weren't special . . . you wouldn't be here."

The masculine role of always being in charge is a tough one. The 27 blunt new honesty about sexually transmitted diseases such as AIDS appears in men's magazines as in women's, in the same "I enjoy sex, but I'm not ready to die for it" condom advertisement. But this new fear is accompanied by old fears of sexual embarrassment and/or rejection. The cartoon shows a man cringing with embarrassment in a pharmacy as the pharmacist yells out, "Hey, there's a guy here wants some information on Trojans." ("Most men would like to know more about Trojan brand condoms. But they're seriously afraid of suffering a spectacular and terminal attack of embarrassment right in the middle of a well-lighted drugstore.") Compared with such agony and responsibility, advertisements promising that women will *want* whatever is on offer, and will even meet the male halfway, must come as blessed relief. Men can finally relax, leaving the courting to the product and seduction to the beguiled woman, which, surely, must seem nice for a change.

Masculine Homilies

A homily is a short sermon, discourse, or informal lecture, often on 28 a moral topic and suggesting a course of conduct. Some of the most intriguing advertisements offer just that, short statements and bits of advice on what masculinity is and on how real men should conduct themselves. As with many short sermons, many of the advertising homilies have a self-congratulatory air about them; after all, you do not want the consumer to feel bad about himself.

What is it, then, to be a man? It is to be *independent*. "There are some 29

things a man will not relinquish." Among them, says the advertisement,
his Tretorn tennis shoes.

It is to *savor freedom*. "Dress easy, get away from it all and let Tom   30
Sawyer paint the fence," advises Alexander Julian, the men's designer.
"Because man was meant to fly, we gave him wings" (even if only on
his sunglasses).

It is to live a life of *adventure*. KL Homme cologne is "for the man   31
who lives on the edge." Prudential Life Insurance preaches, "If you can
dream it, you can do it." New Man sportswear tells the reader, "Life is
more adventurous when you feel like a New Man."

It is to *keep one's cool*. "J&B Scotch. A few individuals know how to   32
keep their heads, even when their necks are on the line."

And it is to stay one step *ahead of the competition*. "Altec Lansing.   33
Hear what others only imagine." Alexander Julian again: "Dress up a bit
when you dress down. They'll think you know something they don't."

What is it, then, to be a woman? It is to be *dependent*. "A woman   34
needs a man," reads the copy in the Rigolletto advertisement showing
a young man changing a tire for a grateful young woman.

The American cowboy as cultural model was not supposed to care   35
for or about appearances. He was what he was, hard-working, straightforward, and honest. He was authentic. Men who cared "too much"
about how they looked did not fit this model; the dandy was effete, a
European invention, insufficient in masculinity and not red-blooded
enough to be a real American. The other cultural model, imported from
England, was the gentleman. A gentleman did care about his appearance, in the proper measure and manifestation, attention to tailoring
and to quality, understatement rather than exaggeration.

From the gray flannel suit of the 1950s to the "power look" of the   36
1980s, clothes made the man fit in with his company's image. Sex appeal and corporate correctness merged in a look that spelled success,
that exuded confidence.

Whether or not a man presumed to care about his appearance, he   37
did care about having "the right stuff," as Tom Wolfe and *Esquire* call it,
or "men's toys," as in a recent special issue of *M* magazine. Cars, mo-
torcycles, stereos, sports equipment: these are part of the masculine appearance. They allow the man to demonstrate his taste, his special
knowledge, his affluence: to extend his control. He can be and is demanding, for only the best will do.

He also wants to be loved, but he does not want to appear needy.   38
Advertisements suggest the magic ability of products ranging from cars
to hair creams to attract female attention. With the right products a man
can have it all, with no strings attached: no boring marital ties, hefty
mortgages, corporate compromises.

According to sociologist Barbara Ehrenreich, *Playboy* magazine did   39
much to legitimate this image of male freedom. The old male ethos, up
to the postwar period, required exchanging bachelor irresponsibility
for married responsibility, which also symbolized entrance into social
adulthood. The perennial bachelor, with his flashy cars and interchangeable women, was the object of both envy and derision; he had
fun, but and because he was not fully grown up. There was something
frivolous in his lack of purpose and application.

This old ethos has lost much of its legitimacy. Today's male can, as   40
Baudrillard suggests, operate in both modes: the feminine mode of in-
dulging oneself and being indulged and the masculine mode of exi-
gency and competition. With the right look and the right stuff, he can
feel confident and manly in boardroom or suburban backyard. Consumer society thus invites both men and women to live in a world of appearances and to devote ever more attention to them.

·····················

Examining the Text
1. In your own words, restate Baudrillard's definition of the Masculine
and Feminine modes in our culture (paragraphs 5–8). What do you
think of Barthel's conclusion that men today can operate in both modes?
Do you think that women can also operate in both modes?

2. According to Barthel, what strategies do advertisers use in their
efforts to sell men products that are associated primarily with women?
Do you see evidence of this in contemporary advertising?

3. What do you think is the significance of the title of this essay? How,
according to Barthel, is being a gentleman related to being a consumer?

For Group Discussion
Barthel's essay was written in 1988. Consider some of the more recent images of men in advertising—in ads for Obsession cologne or
Guess clothing, for example. What new trends or strategies do they indicate in advertising to male consumers? What do you think lies behind
these trends?

Writing Suggestion
Go through the ads in a men's magazine like *Esquire* or *Sports Illus-
trated*. Drawing on the list of "masculine homilies" (28–33) presented in
Barthel's essay, write an explanation of ways in which the ads use these

homilies. Create your own list of "short sermons" that the ads deliver to their male audience.

Getting Dirty

Mark Crispin Miller

Mark Crispin Miller's essay comes from his 1988 book Boxed In, *a study of the meaning and influence of television and advertising in contemporary American culture. In "Getting Dirty," Miller analyzes a television ad for Shield soap, paying close attention to seemingly neutral details and finding meanings that may surprise us. For instance, Miller suggests that the ad woos female viewers with a "fantasy of dominance," offering "a subtle and meticulous endorsement of castration," playing on certain "guilts and insecurities" of men and women. The way the commercial reverses stereotypical gender roles makes it an interesting and complex example of the ways images of men and women are used in advertising.*

To those who think he is "reading too much into the ad," Miller counters that it is through the details, often unnoticed by viewers, that ads convey some of their most powerful—and questionable—messages.

In this essay Miller is analytical but also is trying to persuade readers that his analysis of the advertisement is correct. **As you read,** *note the strategies that Miller uses to construct a persuasive, well-supported analysis, and note as well those moments where Miller does not persuade you of his interpretation.*

••••••••••••••••••

We are outside a house, looking in the window, and this is what we   1
see: a young man, apparently nude and half-crazed with anxiety, lunging toward the glass. "Gail!" he screams, as he throws the window open and leans outside, over a flowerbox full of geraniums: "The most important shower of my life, and you switch deodorant soap!" He is, we now see, only half-naked, wearing a towel around his waist; and he shakes a packaged bar of soap—"Shield"—in one accusing hand. Gail, wearing a blue man-tailored shirt, stands outside, below the window, clipping a hedge. She handles this reproach with an ease that suggests years of contempt. "Shield is better," she explains patiently, in a voice somewhat deeper than her husband's. "It's extra strength." (Close-up of the package in the husband's hand. Gail's efficient finger gliding along beneath the legend. THE EXTRA STRENGTH DEODORANT SOAP.) "Yeah," whimpers Mr. Gail, "but my first call on J. J. Siss [sic], the company's *toughest customer,* and *now this!*" Gail nods with broad mock-

sympathy, and stands firm: "Shield fights odor better, so you'll feel *cleaner*," she assures her husband, who darts away with a jerk of panic, as Gail rolls her eyes heavenward and gently shakes her head, as if to say, "What a half-wit!"

Cut to our hero, as he takes his important shower. No longer frantic, he now grins down at himself, apparently delighted to be caked with Shield, which, in its detergent state, has the consistency of wet cement. He then goes out of focus, as if glimpsed through a shower door. "Clinical tests prove," proclaims an eager baritone. "Shield fights odor better than the *leading* deodorant soap!" A bar of Shield (green) and a bar of that other soap (yellow) zip up the screen with a festive toot, forming a sort of graph which demonstrates that Shield does, indeed, "fight odor better, so you'll feel *cleaner!*"

This particular contest having been settled, we return to the major one, which has yet to be resolved. Our hero reappears, almost transformed: calmed down, dressed up, his voice at least an octave lower. "I *do* feel cleaner!" he announces cheerily, leaning into the doorway of a room where Gail is arranging flowers. She pretends to be ecstatic at this news, and he comes toward her, setting himself up for a profound humiliation by putting on a playful air of suave command. Adjusting his tie like a real man of the world, he saunters over to his wife and her flower bowl, where he plucks a dainty purple flower and lifts it to his lapel: "And," he boasts throughout all this, trying to make his voice sound even deeper, "with old J. J.'s business and my brains—" "—you'll . . . *clean up again?*" Gail asks with suggestive irony, subverting his authoritative pose by leaning against him, draping one hand over his shoulder to dangle a big yellow daisy down his chest. Taken aback, he shoots her a distrustful look, and she titters at him.

Finally, the word SHIELD appears in extreme close-up and the camera pulls back, showing two bars of the soap, one packaged and one not, on display amidst an array of steely bubbles. "Shield fights odor better, so you'll feel *cleaner!* the baritone reminds us, and then our hero's face appears once more, in a little square over the unpackaged bar of soap: "I feel *cleaner* than *ever before!*" he insists, sounding faintly unconvinced.

Is all this as stupid as it seems at first? Or is there, just beneath the surface of this moronic narrative, some noteworthy design, intended to appeal to (and to worsen) some of the anxieties of modern life? A serious look at this particular trifle might lead us to some strange discoveries.

We are struck, first of all, by the commercials' pseudofeminism, an advertising ploy with a long history, and one ubiquitous on television nowadays. Although the whole subject deserves more extended treatment, this commercial offers us an especially rich example of the strategy. Typically, it woos its female viewers—i.e., those who choose the soap in most households—with a fantasy of dominance; and it does so by inverting the actualities of woman's lot through a number of imperceptible details. For instance, in this marriage it is the wife, and not the husband, who gets to keep her name; and Gail's name, moreover, is a potent one, because of its brevity and its homonymic connotation. (If this housewife were more delicately named, called "Lillian" or "Cecilia," it would lessen her illusory strength.) She is also equipped in more noticeable ways; she's the one who wears the button-down shirt in this family, she's the one who's competent both outdoors and in the house, and it is she, and only she, who wields the tool.

These visual details imply that Gail is quite a powerful housewife, 7 whereas her nameless mate is a figure of embarrassing impotence. This "man," in fact, is actually Gail's *wife;* he is utterly feminized, striking a posture and displaying attributes which men have long deplored in women. In other words, this commercial, which apparently takes the woman's side, is really the expression (and reflection) of misogyny. Gail's husband is dependent and hysterical, entirely without that self-possession which we expect from solid, manly types, like Gail. This is partly the result of his demeanor: in the opening scene, his voice sometimes cracks ludicrously, and he otherwise betrays the shrill desperation of a man who can't remember where he left his scrotum. The comic effect of this frenzy, moreover, is subtly enhanced by the mise-en-scène, which puts the man in a conventionally feminine position—in dishabille, looking down from a window. Thus we infer that he is sheltered and housebound, a modern Juliet calling for his/her Romeo; or—more appropriately—the image suggests a scene in some suburban red-light district, presenting this husband as an item on display, like the flowers just below his stomach, available for anyone's enjoyment, at a certain price. Although in one way contradictory, these implications are actually quite congruous, for they both serve to emasculate the husband, so that the wife might take his place, or play his part.

Such details, some might argue, need not have been the conscious 8 work of this commercial's markers. The authors, that is, might have worked by instinct rather than design, and so would have been no more aware of their work's psychosocial import than we ourselves: they just wanted to make the guy look like a wimp, merely for the purposes of domestic comedy. While such an argument certainly does apply to many ads, in this case it is unlikely. Advertising agencies do plenty of research, by which we can assume that they don't select their tactics arbitrarily. They take pains to analyze the culture which they help to sicken, and then, with much wit and cynicism, use their insights in devising their small dramas. This commercial is a subtle and meticulous endorsement of castration, meant to play on certain widespread guilts and insecurities; and all we need to do to demonstrate this fact is to subject the two main scenes to the kind of visual analysis which commercials, so brief and broad, tend to resist (understandably). The ad's visual implications are too carefully achieved to have been merely accidental or unconscious.

The crucial object in the opening shot is that flower box with its 9 bright geraniums, which is placed directly in front of the husband's groin. This clever stroke of composition has the immediate effect of equating our hero's manhood with a bunch of flowers. This is an exquisitely perverse suggestion, rather like using a cigar to represent the Eternal Feminine: flowers are frail, sweet, and largely ornamental, hardly an appropriate phallic symbol, but (of course) a venerable symbol of *maidenhood*. The geraniums stand, then, not for the husband's virility, but for its absence.

More than a clever instance of inversion, furthermore, these phallic 10 blossoms tell us something odd about this marital relationship. As Gail, clippers in hand, turns from the hedge to calm her agitated man, she appears entirely capable of calming him quite drastically, if she hasn't done so already (which might explain his hairless chest and high-pitched voice). She has the power, that is, to take away whatever slender potency he may possess, and uses the power repeatedly, trimming her husband (we infer) as diligently as she prunes her foliage. And, as she can snip his manhood, so too can she restore it, which is what the second scene implies. Now the flower bowl has replaced the flower box as the visual crux, dominating the bottom center of the frame with a crowd of blooms. As the husband, cleaned and dressed, comes to stand beside his wife, straining to affect a new authority, the flower bowl too appears directly at his lower center; so that Gail, briskly adding flowers to the bouquet, appears to be replenishing his vacant groin with extra stalks. He has a lot to thank her for, it seems: she is his helpmate, confidante, adviser, she keeps his house and grounds in order, and she is clearly the custodian of the family jewels.

Of course, her restoration of his potency cannot be complete, or he 11 might shatter her mastery by growing a bit too masterful himself. He could start choosing his own soap, or take her shears away, or—worst of all—walk out for good. Therefore, she punctures his momentary confidence by taunting him with that big limp daisy, countering his lordly gesture with the boutonniere by flaunting that symbol of his floral status. He can put on whatever airs he likes, but she still has his fragile vigor firmly in her hand.

Now what, precisely, motivates this sexless battle of the sexes? That 12 is, what really underlies this tense and hateful marriage, making the man so weak, the woman so contemptuously helpful? The script, seemingly nothing more than a series of inanities, contains the answer to these questions, conveying, as it does, a concern with cleanliness that amounts to an obsession: "Shield fights odor better, so you'll feel cleaner!" "I *do* feel cleaner!" "Shield fights odor better, so you'll feel *cleaner!*" "I feel *cleaner* than *ever before!*" Indeed, the commercial emphasizes the feeling of cleanliness even more pointedly than the name of the product, implying, by its very insistence, a feeling of dirtiness, an apprehension of deep filth.

And yet there is not a trace of dirt in the vivid world of this commercial. Unlike many ads for other soaps, this one shows no sloppy children, no sweatsoaked workingmen with blackened hands, not even a bleary housewife in need of her morning shower. We never even glimpse the ground in Gail's world, nor is her husband even faintly smudged. In fact, the filth which Shield supposedly "fights" is not physical but psychological besmirchment: Gail's husband feels soiled because of what he has to do for a living, in order to keep Gail in that nice big house, happily supplied with shirts and shears.

"My first call on J. J. Siss, the company's *toughest customer*, and now *this!*" The man's anxiety is yet another feminizing trait, for it is generally women, and not men, who are consumed by doubts about the sweetness of their bodies, which must never be offensive to the guys who run the world. (This real anxiety is itself aggravated by commercials.) Gail's husband must play the female to the mighty J. J. Siss, a name whose oxymoronic character implies perversion: "J. J." is a stereotypic nickname for the potent boss, while "Sis" is a term of endearment, short for "sister" (and perhaps implying "sissy," too, in this case). Gail's husband must do his boyish best to please the voracious J. J. Siss, just as a prostitute must satisfy a demanding trick, or "tough customer." It is therefore perfectly fitting that this employee refer to the encounter, not as a "meeting" or "appointment," but as a "call"; and his demeaning posture in the window—half dressed and bent over—conveys, we now see, a definitive implication.

Gail's job as the "understanding wife" is not to rescue her husband from these sordid obligations, but to help him meet them successfully. She may seem coolly self-sufficient, but she actually depends on her husband's attractiveness, just as a pimp relies on the charm of his whore. And, also like a pimp, she has to keep her girl in line with occasional reminders of who's boss. When her husband starts getting uppity *après la douche,* she jars him from the very self-assurance which she had helped him to discover, piercing that "shield" which was her gift.

"And, with old J. J.'s business and my brains—" "—you'll . . . *clean up again?*" He means, of course, that he'll work fiscal wonders with old

J. J.'s account, but his fragmentary boast contains a deeper significance, upon which Gail plays with sadistic cleverness. "Old J. J.'s business and my brains" implies a feminine self-description, since it suggests a variation on the old commonplace of "brains vs. brawn": J. J's money, in the world of this commercial (as in ours), amounts to brute strength, which the flexible husband intends to complement with his mother wit. Gail's retort broadens this unconscious hint of homosexuality: "—you'll . . . *clean up again?*" Given the monetary nature of her husband's truncated remark, the retort must mean primarily, "You'll make a lot of money." If this were all it meant, however, it would not be a joke, nor would the husband find it so upsetting. Moreover, we have no evidence that Gail's husband ever "cleaned up"—i.e., made a sudden fortune—in the past. Rather, the ad's milieu and *dramatis personae* suggest upward mobility, gradual savings and a yearly raise, rather than one prior killing. What Gail is referring to, in fact, with the "again," is her husband's shower: she implies that what he'll have to do, after his "call" on J. J. Siss, is, quite literally, wash himself off. Like any other tidy hooker, this man will have to clean up after taking on a tough customer, so that he might be ready to take on someone else.

These suggestions of pederasty are intended, not as a literal char- 17
acterization of the husband's job, but as a metaphor for what it takes to get ahead: Gail's husband, like most white-collar workers, must debase himself to make a good impression, toadying to his superiors, offering himself, body and soul, to the corporation. Maybe, therefore, it isn't really Gail who has neutered him; it may be his way of life that has wrought the ugly change. How, then, are women represented here? The commercial does deliberately appeal to women, offering them a sad fantasy of control; but it also, perhaps inadvertently, illuminates the unhappiness which makes that fantasy attractive.

The husband's status, it would seem, should make Gail happy, since it makes her physically comfortable, and yet Gail can't help loathing her husband for the degradations which she helps him undergo. For her part of the bargain is, ultimately, no less painful than his. She has to do more than put up with him; she has to prepare him for his world of affairs, and then must help him to conceal the shame. Of course, it's all quite hopeless. She clearly despises the man whom she would bolster; and the thing which she provides to help him "feel cleaner than ever before" is precisely what has helped him do the job that's always made him feel so dirty. "A little water clears us of this deed" is her promise, which is false, for she is just as soiled as her doomed husband, however fresh and well-ironed she may look.

Of course, the ad not only illuminates this mess, but helps perpetu- 18
ate it, by obliquely gratifying the guilts, terrors, and resentments that
underlie it and arise from it. The strategy is not meant to be noticed, but
works through the apparent comedy, which must therefore be studied
carefully, not passively received. Thus, thirty seconds of ingenious advertising, which we can barely stand to watch, tell us something more
than we might want to know about the souls of men and women under
corporate capitalism.

Afterword

Advertising Age came back at this essay with an edifying two- 1
pronged put-down. In the issue for 7 June 1982, Fred Danzig (now the
magazine's editor) devoted his weekly column to the Shield analysis:
"The professor prunes a television trifle," ran the headline. After a ge-
nial paraphrase of my argument, Danzig reported a few of the things I'd
told him in a telephone conversation, and then finally got down to the
necessary business of dismissive cluckling: "[Miller's] confession that
he had watched the Shield spot more than 15 times quickly enabled me
to diagnose his problem: Self-inflicted acute soap storyboard sickness.
This condition inevitably leads to a mind spasm, to hallucination." The
column featured the ad's crucial frames, over a caption quoting an un-
named "Lever executive": "We can hardly wait for Mr. Miller to get his
hands on the Old Testament. His comments merit no comment from us;
the Shield commercial speaks for itself."

Leaving aside (with difficulty) that naive crack about the Bible, 2
I point here to the exemplary suppressiveness of his seeming "trifle"
in *Advertising Age*. Indeed, "the Shield commercial speaks for itself,"
but the guardians of the spectacle try to talk over it, permitting it no
significance beyond the superficial pitch:"—so you'll feel *cleaner!*"
Through managerial scorn ("no comment") and journalistic ridicule
("mind spasm . . . hallucination"), they would shut down all discussion.
(J. Walter Thompson later refused to send anyone to debate the matter
with me on a radio program.) Thus was a divergent reading written off
as the perversity of yet another cracked "professor"—when in fact it was
the ad itself that was perverse.

Although that campaign did not appeal to its TV audience (J. Wal- 3
ter Thompson ultimately lost the Shield account), such belligerent
"common sense" does have a most receptive public. While the admakers—and others—insist that "people today are adwise" in fact most
Americans still perceive the media image as transparent, a sign that

simply says what it means and means what it says. They therefore tend to dismiss any intensi ve explication as a case of "reading too much into it"—an objection that is philosophically dubious, albeit useful to the admakers and their allies. It is now, perhaps, one obligation of the academic humanists, empowered, as they are, by critical theory, to demonstrate at large the faultiness—and the dangers—of that objection.

A historical note on the shield commercial's pseudofeminism. Since 4
1982, the contemptuous housewife has all but vanished from the anti-septic scene of advertising; Gail was among the last of an endangered species. By now, the housewife/mother is a despised figure—most de-spised by actual housewife/mothers, who make up 60% of the prime-time audience. Since these viewers now prefer to see themselves repre-sented as executives, or at least as mothers with beepers and attaché cases, the *hausfrau* of the past, whether beaming or sneering, has largely been obliterated by the advertisers. In 1985, Advertising to Women Inc., a New York advertising agency, found that, out of 250 current TV ads, only nine showed recognizable Moms.

This is a triumph not for women's liberation, but for advertising; for, 5
now that Mom is missing from the ads, presumably off knocking heads together in the boardroom, it is the commodity that seems to warm her home and tuck her children in at night.

In any case, the Shield strategy itself has certainly outlasted the wry 6
and/or perky Mommy-imagoes of yesteryear. Indeed, because the sexes are now at war within the scene of advertising (and elsewhere), the nasty visual metaphors have become ubiquitous.

● ● ● ● ● ● ● ● ● ● ● ● ● ● ● ● ● ● ●

Examining the Text

1. Briefly define the term "pseudofeminism" (paragraph 6) in your own words. How, according to Miller, does the Shield advertisement display "pseudofeminism"? Is Miller justified in criticizing the ad in these terms?

2. Recalling that the title of this essay is "Getting Dirty," summarize Miller's points about cleanliness and dirt in the Shield advertisement. What do you think of Miller's statement that "the filth which Shield supposedly 'fights' is not physical but psychological besmirchment" (paragraph 13)?

3. Describe the strategic importance of Miller's eighth paragraph. What is Miller doing in this paragraph, and why does he place it here in the essay rather than earlier or later? Do you agree with Miller's ultimate conclusion that "the ad's visual implications are too carefully achieved to have been merely accidental or unconscious"?

4. How would you describe the tone of Miller's essay, particularly in the opening section in which he describes the Shield commercial? Why do you think Miller adopts this tone? Do you find it helps him convey his points? Why or why not?

5. What is Miller's main point in the Afterword? To what extent does the Afterword help make the essay itself more persuasive?

Group Discussion

Miller comments in the Afterword that "In fact most Americans still perceive the media image as transparent, a sign that simply says what it means and means what it says. They therefore tend to dismiss any intensive explication as a case of 'reading too much into it'" (3). How does this quote relate to your own response to Miller's essay? If you think Miller "reads too much into" the Shield ad, where in the essay does this occur? What could he do to make these parts of the essay more persuasive?

Writing Suggestion

Miller's analysis of the Shield advertisement focuses on its hidden misogyny. Reflect on other advertisements that you're familiar with that also show some degree of misogyny, and write a description about how this works in one specific ad. How does this ad, like the one for Shield, manage to appeal to female consumers where its message is essentially derogatory toward women?

Sex, Lies and Advertising

Gloria Steinem

This chapter concludes with an essay by one of the most important and influential figures in the American feminist movement, Gloria Steinem. Steinem's essay, originally published in Ms. *magazine (which she cofounded), addresses some of the broader issues involving advertising and gender. As she demonstrates, we need to be aware of more than just the* content *of advertisements, but also how advertising agencies and their clients make demands that affect the entire content of magazines, women's magazines in particular.*

Steinem describes the difficulties Ms. faced when soliciting advertisements for their new magazine in the 1970s. As a magazine with an entirely female readership, Ms. had first to convince advertisers that women were intelligent, active consumers. Then, the editors had to placate advertisers who demanded editorials and articles to promote their products. Steinem offers numerous examples of how companies try to influence the magazines they advertise in.

Before you read, *look at a recent issue of a woman's magazine, such as* Ms. *or* Working Woman *or* Vogue *to notice what sort of advertisements and articles you find there. To what extent do you think these magazines represent the interests and needs of their female readership?*

••••••••••••••••••

About three years ago, as *glasnost* was beginning and *Ms.* seemed to be ending, I was invited to a press lunch for a Soviet official. He entertained us with anecdotes about new problems of democracy in his country. Local Communist leaders were being criticized in their media for the first time, he explained, and they were angry. 1

"So I'll have to ask my American friends," he finished pointedly, "how more *subtly* to control the press." In the silence that followed. I said, "Advertising." 2

The reporters laughed, but later, one of them took me aside: How *dare* I suggest that freedom of the press was limited? How dare I imply that his newsweekly could be influenced by ads? 3

I explained that I was thinking of advertising's media-wide influence on most of what we read. Even newsmagazines use "soft" cover stories to sell ads, confuse readers with "advertorials,"[1] and occasionally self-censor on subjects known to be a problem with big advertisers. 4

But, I also explained, I was thinking especially of women's magazines. There, it isn't just a little content that's devoted to attracting ads, it's almost all of it. That's why advertisers—not readers—have always been the problem for *Ms.* As the only women's magazine that didn't supply what the ad world euphemistically describes as "supportive editorial atmosphere" or "complementary copy" (for instance, articles that praise food/fashion/beauty subjects to "support" and "complement" food/fashion/beauty ads), *Ms.* could never attract enough advertising to break even. 5

"Oh, *women's* magazines," the journalist said with contempt. "Everybody knows they're catalogs—but who cares? They have nothing to do with journalism." 6

---

[1] **advertorial** Advertisement designed to mimic the appearance of a feature article.—Eds.

I can't tell you how many times I've had this argument in 25 years   7
of working for many kinds of publications. Except as moneymaking machines—"cash cows" as they are so elegantly called in the trade—wom-
en's magazines are rarely taken seriously. Though changes being made
by women have been called more far-reaching than the industrial revolution—and though many editors try hard to reflect some of them in the
few pages left to them after all the ad-related subjects have been covered—the magazines serving the female half of this country are still far
below the journalistic and ethical standards of news and general interest publications. Most depressing of all, this doesn't even rate an exposé.

If *Time* and *Newsweek* had to lavish praise on cars in general and   8
credit General Motors in particular to get GM ads, there would be a
scandal—maybe a criminal investigation. When women's magazines
from *Seventeen* to *Lear's* praise beauty products in general and credit
Revlon in particular to get ads, it's just business as usual.

When *Ms.* began, we didn't consider *not* taking ads. The most im-   9
portant reason was keeping the price of a feminist magazine low
enough for most women to afford. But the second and almost equal reason was providing a forum where women and advertisers could talk to
each other and improve advertising itself. After all, it was (and still is)
as potent a source of information in this country as news or TV and
movie dramas.

We decided to proceed in two stages. First, we would convince mak-   10
ers of "people products" used by both men and women but advertised
mostly to men—cars, credit cards, insurance, sound equipment, financial services, and the like—that their ads should be placed in a women's
magazine. Since they were accustomed to the division between editorial[2] and advertising in news and general interest magazines, this would
allow our editorial content to be free and diverse. Second, we would add
the best ads for whatever traditional "women's products" (clothes,
shampoo, fragrance, food, and so on) that surveys showed *Ms.* readers
used. But we would ask them to come in *without* the usual quid pro quo
of "complementary copy."

We knew the second step might be harder. Food advertisers have al-   11
ways demanded that women's magazines publish recipes and articles
on entertaining (preferably ones that name their products) in return
for their ads; clothing advertisers expect to be surrounded by fashion
spreads (especially ones that credit their designers); and shampoo, fragrance, and beauty products in general usually insist on positive edito-

---

[2] **editorial** In the magazine industry, all nonadvertising content in a magazine, including
regular columns and feature articles.—Eds.

rial coverage of beauty subjects, plus photo credits besides. That's why women's magazines look the way they do. But if we could break this link between ads and editorial content, then we wanted good ads for "women's products," too.

By playing their part in this unprecedented mix of *all* the things our   12
readers need and use, advertisers also would be rewarded: Ads for products like cars and mutual funds would find a new growth market; the best ads for women's products would no longer be lost in oceans of ads for the same category; and both would have access to a laboratory of smart and caring readers whose response would help create effective ads for other media as well.

I thought then that our main problem would be the imagery in ads   13
themselves. Car makers were still draping blondes in evening gowns over the hoods like ornaments. Authority figures were almost always male, even in ads for products that only women used. Sadistic, he-man campaigns even won industry praise. (For instance, *Advertising Age* had hailed the infamous Silva Thin cigarette theme, "How to Get a Woman's Attention: Ignore Her," as "brilliant.") Even in medical journals, tranquilizer ads showed depressed housewives standing beside piles of dirty dishes and promised to get them back to work.

Obviously, *Ms.* would have to avoid such ads and seek out the best   14
ones—but this didn't seem impossible. *The New Yorker* had been selecting ads for aesthetic reasons for years, a practice that only seemed to make advertisers more eager to be in its pages. *Ebony* and *Essence* were asking for ads with positive black images, and though their struggle was hard, they weren't being called unreasonable.

Clearly, what *Ms.* needed was a very special publisher and ad sales   15
staff. I could think of only one woman with experience on the business side of magazines—Patricia Carbine, who recently had become a vice president of *McCall's* as well as its editor in chief—and the reason I knew her name was a good omen. She had been managing editor at *Look* (really *the* editor, but its owner refused to put a female name at the top of his masthead) when I was writing a column there. After I did an early interview with Cesar Chavez, then just emerging as a leader of migrant labor, and the publisher turned it down because he was worried about ads from Sunkist, Pat was the one who intervened. As I learned later, she had told the publisher she would resign if the interview wasn't published. Mainly because *Look* couldn't afford to lose Pat, it *was* published (and the ads from Sunkist never arrived).

Though I barely knew this woman, she had done two things I al-   16
ways remembered; put her job on the line in a way that editors often talk about but rarely do, and been so loyal to her colleagues that she never told me or anyone outside *Look* that she had done so.

Fortunately, Pat did agree to leave *McCall's* and take a huge cut in   17
salary to become publisher of *Ms.* She became responsible for training
and inspiring generations of young women who joined the *Ms.* ad sales
force, many of whom went on to become "firsts" at the top of publishing. When *Ms.* first started, however, there were so few women with experience selling space that Pat and I made the rounds of ad agencies ourselves. Later, the fact that *Ms.* was asking companies to do business in a
different way meant our saleswomen had to make many times the usual
number of calls—first to convince agencies and then client companies
besides—and to present endless amounts of research. I was often asked
to do a final ad presentation, or see some higher decision-maker, or speak
to women employees so executives could see the interest of women they
worked with. That's why I spent more time persuading advertisers than
editing or writing for *Ms.* and why I ended up with an unsentimental
education in the seamy underside of publishing that few writers see
(and even fewer magazines can publish).

Let me take you with us through some experiences, just as they hap-   18
pened:

• Cheered on by early support from Volkswagen and one or two other
car companies, we scrape together time and money to put on a major reception in Detroit. We know U.S. car-makers firmly believe that women
choose the upholstery, not the car, but we are armed with statistics and
reader mail to prove the contrary: A car is an important purchase for
women, one that symbolizes mobility and freedom.

But almost nobody comes. We are left with many pounds of shrimp   19
on the table, and quite a lot of egg on our face. We blame ourselves for
not guessing that there would be a baseball pennant play-off on the
same day, but executives go out of their way to explain they wouldn't
have come anyway. Thus begins ten years of knocking on hostile doors,
presenting endless documentation, and hiring a full-time saleswoman
in Detroit; all necessary before *Ms.* gets any real results.

This long saga has a semihappy ending: foreign and, later, domes-   20
tic car-makers eventually provided *Ms.* with enough advertising to
make cars one of our top sources of ad revenue. Slowly, Detroit began
to take the women's market seriously enough to put car ads in other
women's magazines, too, thus freeing a few pages from the hothouse of
fashion-beauty-food ads.

But long after figures showed a third, even a half, of many car mod-   21
els being bought by women, U.S. makers continued to be uncomfortable addressing women. Unlike foreign car-makers, Detroit never quite
learned the secret of creating intelligent ads that exclude no one, and
then placing them in women's magazines to overcome past exclusion.
(*Ms.* readers were so grateful for a routine Honda ad featuring rack and

pinion steering, for instance, that they sent fan mail.) Even now, Detroit continues to ask, "Should we make special ads for women?" Perhaps that's why some foreign cars still have a disproportionate share of the U.S. women's market.

• In the *Ms.* Gazette, we do a brief report on a congressional hearing 22 into chemicals used in hair dyes that are absorbed through the skin and may be carcinogenic. Newspapers report this too, but Clairol, a Bristol-Myers subsidiary that makes dozens of products—a few of which have just begun to advertise in *Ms.*—is outraged. Not as newspapers or news magazines, just at us. It's bad enough that *Ms.* is the only women's magazine refusing to provide the usual "complementary" articles and beauty photos, but to criticize one of their categories—*that* is going too far.

We offer to publish a letter from Clairol telling its side of the story. 23 In an excess of solicitousness, we even put this letter in the Gazette, not in Letters to the Editors where it belongs. Nonetheless—and in spite of surveys that show *Ms.* readers are active women who use more of almost everything Clairol makes than do the readers of any other women's magazine—*Ms.* gets almost none of these ads for the rest of its natural life.

Meanwhile, Clairol changes its hair-coloring formula, apparently in 24 response to the hearings we reported.

• Our saleswomen set out early to attract ads for consumer electron- 25 ics: sound equipment, calculators, computers, VCRs, and the like. We know that our readers are determined to be included in the technological revolution. We know from reader surveys that *Ms.* readers are buying this stuff in numbers as high as those of magazines like *Playboy,* or "men 18 to 34," the prime targets of the consumer electronics industry. Moreover, unlike traditional women's products that our readers buy but don't need to read articles about, these are subjects they want covered in our pages. There actually *is* a supportive editorial atmosphere.

"But women don't understand technology," say executives at the 26 end of ad presentations. "Maybe now," we respond, "but neither do men—and we all buy it."

"If women *do* buy it," say the decision-makers, "they're asking their 27 husbands and boyfriends what to buy first." We produce letters from *Ms.* readers saying how turned off they are when salesmen say things like "Let me know when your husband can come in."

After several years of this, we get a few ads for compact sound sys- 28 tems. Some of them come from JVC, whose vice president, Harry Elias, is trying to convince his Japanese bosses that there is something called a women's market. At his invitation, I find myself speaking at huge trade shows in Chicago and Las Vegas, trying to persuade JVC dealers that showrooms don't have to be locker rooms where women are made to feel unwelcome. But as it turns out, the shows themselves are part of the problem. In Las Vegas, the only women around the technology displays are seminude models serving champagne. In Chicago, the big attraction is Marilyn Chambers, who followed Linda Lovelace of *Deep Throat* fame as Chuck Traynor's captive and/or employee. VCRs are being demonstrated with her porn videos.

In the end, we get ads for a car stereo now and then, but no VCRs;   29
some IBM personal computers, but no Apple or Japanese ones. We notice that office magazines like *Working Woman* and *Savvy* don't benefit as much as they should from office equipment ads either. In the electronics world, women and technology seem mutually exclusive. It remains a decade behind even Detroit.

• Because we get letters from little girls who love toy trains, and who   30
ask our help in changing ads and box-top photos that feature little boys only, we try to get toy-train ads from Lionel. It turns out that Lionel executives *have* been concerned about little girls. They made a pink train, and were surprised when it didn't sell.

Lionel bows to consumer pressure with a photograph of a boy *and*   31
a girl—but only on some of their boxes. They fear that, if trains are associated with girls, they will be devalued in the minds of boys. Needless to say, *Ms.* gets no train ads, and little girls remain a mostly unexplored market. By 1986, Lionel is put up for sale.

But for different reasons, we haven't had much luck with other   32
kinds of toys either. In spite of many articles on child-rearing; an annual listing of nonsexist, multiracial toys by Letty Cottin Pogrebin; Stories for Free Children, a regular feature also edited by Letty; and other prizewinning features for or about children, we get virtually no toy ads. Generations of *Ms.* saleswomen explain to toy manufacturers that a larger proportion of *Ms.* readers have preschool children than do the readers of other women's magazines, but this industry can't believe feminists have or care about children.

• When *Ms.* begins, the staff decides not to accept ads for feminine hy-   33
giene sprays or cigarettes: they are damaging and carry no appropriate health warnings. Though we don't think we should tell our readers what to do, we do think we should provide facts so they can decide for themselves. Since the antismoking lobby has been pressing for health warnings on cigarette ads, we decide to take them only as they comply.

Philip Morris is among the first to do so. One of its brands, Virginia   34
Slims, is also sponsoring women's tennis and the first national polls of women's opinions. On the other hand, the Virginia Slims theme, "You've come a long way, baby," has more than a "baby" problem. It makes smoking a symbol of progress for women.

We explain to Philip Morris that this slogan won't do well in our   35 pages, but they are convinced its success with some women means it will work with *all* women. Finally, we agree to publish an ad for a Virginia Slims calendar as a test. The letters from readers are critical—and smart. For instance: Would you show a black man picking cotton, the same man in a Cardin suit, and symbolize the antislavery and civil rights movements by smoking? Of course not. But instead of honoring the test results, the Philip Morris people seem angry to be proven wrong. They take away ads for *all* their many brands.

This costs *Ms.* about $250,000 the first year. After five years, we can   36
no longer keep track. Occasionally, a new set of executives listens to *Ms.* saleswomen, but because we won't take Virginia Slims, not one Philip Morris product returns to our pages for the next 16 years.

Gradually, we also realize our naiveté in thinking we *could* decide   37
against taking cigarette ads. They became a disproportionate support of magazines the moment they were banned on television, and few magazines could compete and survive without them; certainly not *Ms.*, which lacks so many other categories. By the time statistics in the 1980s showed that women's rate of lung cancer was approaching men's, the necessity of taking cigarette ads has become a kind of prison.

• General Mills, Pillsbury, Carnation, DelMonte, Dole, Draft, Stouffer,   38
Hormel, Nabisco: You name the food giant, we try it. But no matter how desirable the *Ms.* readership, our lack of recipes is lethal.

We explain to them that placing food ads *only* next to recipes asso-   39
ciates food with work. For many women, it is a negative that works *against* the ads. Why not place food ads in diverse media without recipes (thus reaching more men, who are now a third of the shoppers in supermarkets anyway), and leave the recipes to specialty magazines like *Gourmet* (a third of whose readers are also men)?

These arguments elicit interest, but except for an occasional ad for   40
a convenience food, instant coffee, diet drinks, yogurt, or such extras as avocados and almonds, this mainstay of the publishing industry stays closed to us. Period.

• Traditionally, wines and liquors didn't advertise to women: Men   41
were thought to make the brand decisions, even if women did the buying. But after endless presentations, we begin to make a dent in this category. Thanks to the unconventional Michel Roux of Carillon Importers (distributors of Grand Marnier, Absolute Vodka, and others), who assumes that food and drink have no gender, some ads are leaving their men's club.

Beermakers are still selling masculinity. It takes *Ms.* fully eight years   42
to get its first beer ad (Michelob). In general, however, liquor ads are less stereotyped in their imagery—and far less controlling of the editorial content around them—than are women's products. But given the

underrepresentation of other categories, these very facts tend to create a disproportionate number of alcohol ads in the pages of *Ms.* This in turn dismays readers worried about women and alcoholism.

• We hear in 1980 that women in the Soviet Union have been pro-   43
ducing feminist *samizdat* (underground, self-published books) and circulating them throughout the country. As punishment, four of the leaders have been exiled. Though we are operating on our usual shoestring, we solicit individual contributions to send Robin Morgan to interview these women in Vienna.

The result is an exclusive cover story that includes the first news of   44
a populist peace movement against the Afghanistan occupation, a prediction of *glasnost* to come, and a grassroots, intimate view of Soviet women's lives. From the popular press to women's studies courses, the response is great. The story wins a Front Page award.

Nonetheless, this journalistic coup undoes years of efforts to get an   45
ad schedule from Revlon. Why? Because the Soviet women on our cover *are not wearing make-up.*

• Four years of research and presentations go into convincing airlines   46
that women now make travel choices and business trips. United, the first airline to advertise in *Ms.* is so impressed with the response from our readers that one of its executives appears in a film for our ad presentations. As usual, good ads get great results.

But we have problems unrelated to such results. For instance: Be-   47
cause American Airlines flight attendants include among their labor demands the stipulation that they could choose to have their last names preceded by "Ms."on their name tags—in a long-delayed revolt against the standard. "I am your pilot, Captain Rothgart, and this is your flight attendant, Cindy Sue"—American officials seem to hold the magazine responsible. We get no ads.

There is still a different problem at Eastern. A vice president cancels   48
subscriptions for thousands of copies on Eastern flights. Why? Because he is offended by ads for lesbian poetry journals in the *Ms.* Classified. A "family airline," as he explains to me coldly on the phone, has to "draw the line somewhere."

It's obvious that *Ms.* can't exclude lesbians and serve women. We've   49
been trying to make that point ever since our first issue included an article by and about lesbians, and both Suzanne Levine, our managing editor, and I were lectured by such heavy hitters as Ed Kosner, then editor of *Newsweek* (and now of *New York Magazine*), who insisted that *Ms.* should "position" itself *against* lesbians. But our advertisers have paid to reach a guaranteed number of readers, and soliciting new subscriptions to compensate for Eastern would cost $150,000, plus rebating money in the meantime.

Like almost everything ad-related, this presents an elaborate orga-   50
nizing problem. After days of searching for sympathetic members of the
Eastern board, Frank Thomas, president of the Ford Foundation, kindly
offers to call Roswell Gilpatrick, a director of Eastern. I talk with Mr.
Gilpatrick, who calls Frank Borman, then the president of Eastern. Frank
Borman calls me to say that his airline is not in the business of censoring magazines: *Ms.* will be returned to Eastern flights.

• Women's access to insurance and credit is vital, but with the excep-   51
tion of Equitable and a few other ad pioneers, such financial services address men. For almost a decade after the Equal Credit Opportunity Act
passes in 1974, we try to convince American Express that women are a
growth market—but nothing works.

Finally, a former professor of Russian named Jerry Welsh becomes   52
head of marketing. He assumes that women should be cardholders, and
persuades his colleagues to feature women in a campaign. Thanks to
this 1980s series, the growth rate for female cardholders surpass that for
men.

For this article, I asked Jerry Welsh if he would explain why Amer-   53
ican Express waited so long. "Sure," he said, "they were afraid of having a 'pink' card."

• Women of color read *Ms.* in disproportionate numbers. This is a   54
source of pride to *Ms.* staffers, who are also more racially representative
than the editors of other women's magazines. But this reality is obscured
by ads filled with enough white women to make a reader snowblind.

Pat Carbine remembers mostly "astonishment" when she requested   55
African American, Hispanic, Asian, and other diverse images. Marcia
Ann Gillespie, a *Ms.* editor who was previously the editor in chief of
Essence, witnesses ad bias a second time: Having tried for *Essence* to get
white advertisers to use black images (Revlon did so eventually, but
L'Oréal, Lauder, Chanel, and other companies never did), she sees sim-
ilar problems getting integrated ads for an integrated magazine. Indeed,
the ad world often creates black and Hispanic ads only for black and
Hispanic media. In an exact parallel of the fear that marketing a product to women will endanger its appeal to men, the response is usually,
"But your [white] readers won't identify."

In fact, those we are able to get—for instance, a Max Factor ad made   56
for *Essence* that Linda Wachner gives us after she becomes president—
are praised by white readers, too. But there are pathetically few such images.

• By the end of 1986, production and mailing costs have risen astro-   57
nomically, ad income is flat, and competition for ads is stiffer than ever.
The 60/40 preponderance of edit over ads that we promised to readers
becomes 50/50; children's stories, most poetry, and some fiction are

casualties of less space; in order to get variety into limited pages, the length (and sometimes the depth) of articles suffers; and, though we do refuse most of the ads that would look like a parody in our pages, we get so worn down that some slip through. Still, readers perform miracles. Though we haven't been able to afford a subscription mailing in two years, they maintain our guaranteed circulation of 450,000.

Nonetheless, media reports on *Ms.* often insist that our unprofitability must be due to reader disinterest. The myth that advertisers simply follow readers is very strong. Not one reporter notes that other comparable magazines our size (say, *Vanity Fair* or *The Atlantic)* have been losing more money in one year than *Ms.* has lost in 16 years. No matter how much never-to-be-recovered cash is poured into starting a magazine or keeping one going, appearances seem to be all that matter. (Which is why we haven't been able to explain our fragile state in public. Nothing causes ad flight like the smell of nonsuccess.)   58

My healthy response is anger. My not-so-healthy response is constant worry. Also an obsession with finding one more rescue. There is hardly a night when I don't wake up with sweaty palms and pounding heart, scared that we won't be able to pay the printer or the post office; scared most of all that closing our doors will hurt the women's movement.   59

Out of chutzpah and desperation, I arrange a lunch with Leonard Lauder, president of Estée Lauder. With the exception of Clinique (the brainchild of Carol Philllips), none of Lauder's hundreds of products has been advertised in *Ms.* A year's schedule of ads for just three or four of them could save us. Indeed, as the scion of a family-owned company whose ad practices are followed by the beauty industry, he is one of the few men who could liberate many pages in all women's magazines just by changing his mind about "complementary copy."   60

Over a lunch that costs more than we can pay for some articles, I explain the need for his leadership. I also lay out the record of *Ms.:* more literary and journalistic prizes won, more new issues introduced into the mainstream, new writers discovered, and impact on society than any other magazine; more articles that became books, stories that became movies, ideas that became television series, and newly advertised products that became profitable; and, most important for him, a place for his ads to reach women who aren't reachable through any other women's magazine. Indeed, if there is one constant characteristic of the everchanging *Ms.* readership, it is their impact as leaders. Whether it's waiting until later to have first babies, or pioneering PABA as sun protection in cosmetics, *whatever* they are doing today, a third to a half of American women will be doing three to five years from now. It's never failed.   61

But, he *says, Ms.* readers are not *our* women. They're not interested   62
in things like fragrance and blush-on. If they were, *Ms.* would write articles about them.

On the contrary, I explain, surveys show they are more likely to buy   63
such things than the readers of, say, *Cosmopolitan* or *Vogue.* They're good
customers because they're out in the world enough to need several sets
of everything: home, work, purse, travel, gym, and so on. They just
don't need to read articles about these things. Would he ask a men's
magazine to publish monthly columns on how to shave before he advertised Aramis products (his line for men)?

He concedes that beauty features are often concocted more for   64
advertisers than readers. But *Ms.* isn't appropriate for his ads anyway,
he explains. Why? Because Estée Lauder is selling "a kept-woman mentality."

I can't quite believe this. Sixty percent of the users of his products   65
are salaried, and generally resemble *Ms.* readers. Besides, his company
has the appeal of having been started by a creative and hardworking
woman, his mother, Estée Lauder.

That doesn't matter, he says. He knows his customers, and they   66
would *like* to be kept women. That's why he will never advertise in *Ms.*

In November 1987, by vote of the Ms. Foundation for Education and   67
Communication (*Ms.*'s owner and publisher, the media subsidiary of
the Ms. Foundation for Women), *Ms.* was sold to a company whose officers, Australian feminists Sandra Yates and Anne Summers, raised the
investment money in their country that *Ms.* couldn't find in its own.
They also started *Sassy* for teenage women.

In their two-year tenure, circulation was raised to 550,000 by in-   68
vestment in circulation mailings, and, to the dismay of some readers, editorial features on clothes and new products made a more traditional bid
for ads. Nonetheless, ad pages fell below previous levels. In addition,
Sassy, whose fresh voice and sexual frankness were an unprecedented
success with young readers, was targeted by two mothers from Indiana
who began, as one of them put it, "calling every Christian organization
I could think of." In response to this controversy, several crucial advertisers pulled out.

Such links between ads and editorial content was a problem in Aus-   69
tralia, too, but to a lesser degree. "Our readers pay two times more for
their magazines," Anne explained, "so advertisers have less power to
threaten a magazine's viability."

"I was shocked," said Sandra Yates with characteristic directness.   70
"In Australia, we think you have freedom of the press—but you don't."

Since Anne and Sandra had not met their budget's projections for   71 ad revenue, their investors forced a sale. In October 1989, *Ms.* and *Sassy* were bought by Dale Lang, owner of *Working Mother, Working Woman,* and one of the few independent publishing companies left among the conglomerates. In response to a request from the original *Ms.* staff—as well as to reader letters urging that *Ms.* continue, plus his own belief that *Ms.* would benefit his other magazines by blazing a trail—he agreed to try the ad-free, reader-supported *Ms.* . . . and to give us complete editorial control.

In response to the workplace revolution of the 1970s, traditional   72
women's magazines—that is, "trade books" for women working at home—were joined by *Savvy, Working Woman,* and other trade books for women working in offices. But by keeping the fashion/beauty/entertaining articles necessary to get traditional ads and then adding career articles besides, they inadvertently produced the antifeminist stereotype of Super Woman. The male-initiative, dress-for-success woman carrying a briefcase became the media image of a woman worker, even though a blue-collar woman's salary was often higher than her glorified secretarial sister's, and though women at a real briefcase level are statistically rare. Needless to say, these dress-for-success women were also thin, white, and beautiful.

In recent years, advertisers' control over the editorial content of   73
women's magazines has become so institutionalized that it is written into "insertion orders" or dictated to ad salespeople as official policy. The following are recent typical orders to women's magazines:

• Dow's Cleaning Products stipulates that ads for its Vivid and Spray   74
'n Wash products should be adjacent to "children or fashion editorial"; ads for Bathroom Cleaner should be next to "home furnishing/family" features; and so on for other brands. "If a magazine fails for the brands or more," the Dow order warns, "it will be omitted from further consideration."

• Bristol-Myers, the parent of Clairol, Windex, Drano, Bufferin, and   75
much more, stipulates that ads be placed next to a "full page of compatible editorial."

• S.C. Johnson & Son, makers of Johnson Wax, lawn and laundry   76
products, insect sprays, hair sprays, and so on, orders that its ads *"should not be opposite extremely controversial features or material antithetical to the nature/copy of the advertised product."* (Italics theirs.)

• Maidenform, manufacturer of bras and other apparel, leaves a blank   77
for the particular product and states: "The creative concept of the _____ campaign, and the very nature of the product itself appeal to the positive emotions of the reader/consumer. Therefore, it is imperative that all editorial adjacencies reflect that same positive tone. The editorial

must not be negative in content or lend itself contrary to the _____
product imagery/message (e.g., *editorial relating to illness, disillusion-
ment, large size fashion, etc.*)." (Italics mine.)

• The De Beers diamond company, a big seller of engagement rings,   78
prohibits magazines from placing its ads with "adjacencies to hard news
or anti/love-romance themed editorial."

• Procter & Gamble, one of this country's most powerful and diver-   79
sified advertisers, stands out in the memory of Anne Summers and Sandra Yates (no mean feat in this context): Its products were not to be
placed in *any* issue that included *any* material on gun control, abortion,
the occult, cults, or the disparagement of religion. Caution was also demanded in any issue covering sex or drugs, even for educational purposes.

Those are the most obvious chains around women's magazines.   80
There are also rules so clear they needn't be written down: for instance,
an overall "look" compatible with beauty and fashion ads. Even "real"
nonmodel women photographed for a woman's magazine are usually
made up, dressed in credited clothes, and retouched out of all reality.
When editors do include articles on less-than-cheerful subjects (for instance, domestic violence), they tend to keep them short and unillus-
trated. The point is to be "upbeat." Just as women in the street are asked,
"Why don't you smile, honey?" women's magazines acquire an institu-
tional smile.

Within the text itself, praise for advertisers' products has become so   81
ritualized that fields like "beauty writing" have been invented. One of
its frequent practitioners explained seriously that "It's a difficult art.
How many new adjectives can you find? How much greater can you
make a lipstick sound? The FDA restricts what companies can say on labels, but we create illusion. And ad agencies are on the phone all the
time pushing you to get their product in. A lot of them keep the business based on how many editorial clippings they produce every month.
The worst are products," Like Lauder's as the writer confirmed, "with
their own name involved. It's all ego."

Often, editorial becomes one giant ad. Last November, for instance,   82
Lear's featured an elegant woman executive on the cover. On the contents page, we learned she was wearing Guerlain makeup and Samsara,
a new fragrance by Guerlain. Inside were full-page ads for Samsara and
Guerlain antiwrinkle cream. In the cover profile, we learned that this executive was responsible for launching Samsara and is Guerlain's director of public relations. When the *Columbia Journalism Review* did one of
the few articles to include women's magazines in coverage of the influence of ads, editor Frances Lear was quoted as defending her magazine
because "this kind of thing is done all the time."

Often, advertisers also plunge odd-shaped ads into the text, no mat-   83
ter what the cost to the readers. At *Woman's Day,* a magazine originally
founded by a supermarket chain, editor in chief Ellen Levine said, "The
day the copy had to rag around a chicken leg was not a happy one."

Advertisers are also adamant about where in a magazine their ads   84
appear. When Revlon was not placed as the first beauty ad in one Hearst
magazine, for instance, Revlon pulled its ads from *all* Hearst magazines.
Ruth Whitney, editor in chief of *Glamour,* attributes some of these demands to "ad agencies wanting to prove to a client that they've squeezed
the last drop of blood out of a magazine." She also is, she says, "sick and
tired of hearing that women's magazines are controlled by cigarette
ads." Relatively speaking, she's right. To be as censoring as are many
advertisers for women's products, tobacco companies would have to
demand articles in praise of smoking and expect glamorous photos of
beautiful women smoking their brands.

I don't mean to imply that the editors I quote here share my objec-   85
tions to ads: Most assume that women's magazines have to be the way
they are. But it's also true that only former editors can be completely
honest. "Most of the pressure came in the form of direct product mentions," explains Sey Chassler, who was editor in chief of *Redbook* from
the sixties to the eighties. "We got threats from the big guys, the Revlons,
blackmail threats. They wouldn't run ads unless we credited them.

"But it's not fair to single out the beauty advertisers because these   86
pressures came from everybody. Advertisers want to know two things:
What are you going to charge me? What *else* are you going to do for me?
It's a holdup. For instance, management felt that fiction took up too
much space. They couldn't put any advertising in that. For the last ten
years, the number of fiction entries into the National Magazine Awards
has declined.

"And pressures are getting worse. More magazines are more bottom-   87
line oriented because they have been taken over by companies with no
interest in publishing.

"I also think advertisers do this to women's magazines especially,"   88
he concluded, "because of the general disrespect they have for women."

Even media experts who don't give a damn about women's maga-   89
zines are alarmed by the spread of this ad-edit linkage. In a climate *The
Wall Street Journal* describes as an unacknowledged Depression for media, women's products are increasingly able to take their low standards
wherever they go. For instance: Newsweeklies publish uncritical stories
on fashion and fitness. *The New York Times Magazine* recently ran an article on "firming creams," complete with mentions of advertisers. *Vanity Fair* published a profile of one major advertiser, Ralph Lauren, illustrated by the same photographer who does his ads, and turned the

lifestyle of another, Calvin Klein, into a cover story. Even the outrageous *Spy* has toned down since it began to go after fashion ads.

And just to make us really worry, films and books, the last media 90 that go directly to the public without having to attract ads first, are in danger, too. Producers are beginning to depend on payments for displaying products in movies, and books are now being commissioned by companies like Federal Express.

But the truth is that women's products—like women's magazines— 91 have never been the subjects of much serious reporting anyway. News and general interest publications, including the "style" or "living" sections of newspapers, write about food and clothing as cooking and fashion, and almost never evaluate such products by brand name. Though chemical additives, pesticides, and animal fats are major health risks in the United States, and clothes, shoddy or not, absorb more consumer dollars than cars, this lack of information is serious. So is ignoring the contents of beauty products that are absorbed into our bodies through our skins, and that have profit margins so big they would make a loan shark blush.

What could women's magazines be like if they were as free as 92 books? as realistic as newspapers? as creative as films? as diverse as women's lives? We don't know.

But we'll only find out if we take women's magazines seriously. If 93 readers were to act in a concerted way to change traditional practices of *all* women's magazines and the marketing of *all* women's products, we could do it. After all, they are operating on our consumer dollars: money that we now control. You and I could:

• write to editors and publishers (with copies to advertisers) that we're willing to pay *more* for magazines with editorial independence, but will *not* continue to pay for those that are just editorial extensions of ads;

• write to advertisers (with copies to editors and publishers) that we want fiction, political reporting, consumer reporting—whatever is, or is not, supported by their ads;

• put as much energy into breaking advertising's control over content as into changing the images in ads, or protesting ads for harmful products like cigarettes;

• support only those women's magazines and products that take *us* seriously as readers and consumers.

• Those of us in the magazine world can also use the carrot-and-stick technique. For instance: Pointing out that, if magazines were a regulated medium like television, the demands of advertisers would be against FCC rules. Payola and extortion could be punished. As it is, there are probably illegalities. A magazine's postal rates are determined by the ratio of ad to edit pages, and the former costs more than the latter. So much for the stick.

The carrot means appealing to enlightened self-interest. For in-   94
stance: There are many studies showing that the greatest factor in determining an ad's effectiveness is the credibility of its surroundings. The
"higher the rating of editorial believability," concluded a 1987 survey
by the *Journal of Advertising Research,* "the higher the rating of the advertising." Thus, an impenetrable wall between edit and ads would also
be in the best interest of advertisers.

Unfortunately, few agencies or clients hear such arguments. Editors   95
often maintain the false purity of refusing to talk to them at all. Instead,
they see ad salespeople who know little about editorial, are trained in
business as usual, and are usually paid by commission. Editors might
also band together to take on controversy. That happened once when all
the major women's magazines did articles in the same month on the
Equal Rights Amendment. It could happen again.

It's almost three years away from life between the grindstones of ad-   96
vertising pressures and readers' needs. I'm just beginning to realize how
edges got smoothed down—in spite of all our resistance.

I remember feeling put upon when I changed "Porsche" to "car"   97
in a piece about Nazi imagery in German pornography by Andrea
Dworkin—feeling sure Andrea would understand that Volkswagen, the
distributor of Porsche and one of our few supportive advertisers, asked
only to be far away from Nazi subjects. It's taken me all this time to realize that Andrea was the one with a right to feel put upon.

Even as I write this, I get a call from a writer for *Elle,* who is doing   98
a whole article on where women part their hair. Why, she wants to
know, do I part mine in the middle?

It's all so familiar. A writer trying to make something of a nothing   99
assignment; an editor laboring to think of new ways to attract ads; readers assuming that other women must want this ridiculous stuff; more
women suffering for lack of information, insight, creativity, and laughter that could be on these same pages.

I ask you: Can't we do better than this?   100

· · · · · · · · · · · · · · · · · · · ·

Examining the Text

1. What do you think of the anecdote at the beginning of the essay, in
which Steinem remarks to a Soviet official that advertising is a way to
limit freedom of the press? Do you think that her essay supports this assertion? Why or why not?

2. According to Steinem, what is the relationship between advertising and editorial content in magazines? Does your own reading of magazines support the assertion that advertising affects content?

3. In what ways do women's magazines have a different relationship to advertising than other magazines? What are some of the significant problems that *Ms.* encountered in dealing with advertisements and advertisers?

4. How would you describe the structure of this essay? What effect do the numerous specific examples Steinem cites in the first and second parts of the essay have on you as a reader?

For Group Discussion

Steinem asks, "What could women's magazines be like if they were as free as books? as realistic as newspapers? as creative as films? as diverse as women's lives?" (paragraph 92). How would you answer these questions? What would be the content of an "ideal" women's magazine? Would it be different from an "ideal" men's magazine? In what ways? Do any magazines read by group members approach these "ideals"?

Writing Suggestion

Look at recent issues of several women's magazines and test Steinem's assertions about the relationship between advertising and editorial content. Take note of any "complementary copy" in the magazine and any other ways editorial decisions might have been influenced by advertising. In an essay, explore your conclusions about the extent to which advertising affects the content and organization of women's magazines.

ADDITIONAL SUGGESTIONS
FOR WRITING ABOUT ADVERTISING

1. Choose a magazine, television, or radio advertisement that you find particularly interesting, appealing, or puzzling, and write a narrative essay describing your response to the ad.

Begin by recording your initial impressions of the ad. What do you notice first, and why are you drawn to that element of the ad? What emotions or thoughts strike you as you first look at the ad? Then describe your step-by-step progress through the ad. Where does your eye go next? How do your thoughts or emotions change as you notice more of the ad? Finally, record your impressions after you've taken all the ad in. How does this final impression differ from your first impression?

You might conclude your narrative by commenting on whether, based on your response, the ad achieves its objectives of selling the product. In other words, do you think you responded as the designers of the ad intended?

2. Devise your own ad campaign for a product with which you're familiar, including several different ads, each appealing to a different audience.

After deciding on the product, briefly describe each audience group. You might want to use Berkeley Rice's essay on psychographics as a basis for your descriptions. Choose the form in which you want your advertisements to appear (magazine ads, TV segments, audio presentations, billboards, or other forms and venues) and then decide on the persuasive methods that you want to use. Do you want to appeal to emotion or intellect or both? What motives will you try to reach? You might refer to Fowles's list of advertising's basic appeals.

Finally, design the ads and write briefly explaining the reasoning behind each design.

3. Write a detailed analysis of a magazine or television advertisement, based on Solomon's semiological approach in "Masters of Desire" or on Miller's unorthodox reading of a Shield ad in "Getting Dirty."

After choosing an advertisement with sufficient complexity and interest, take notes on the signs in the ad, such as clothing, setting, colors, body positioning, words (spoken or written), and any other elements that the ad incorporates. Draw conclusions about what those signs stand for, what sort of appeals they make to the consumer, and how they potentially manipulate the consumer. Develop these notes into an essay interpreting the ad's strategies, techniques, and underlying meanings.

4. Choose recent issues of a women's magazine and a men's magazine, and compare and contrast the ads in each.

How many advertisements are there? What products are being advertised? What techniques are used in the ads and how do these techniques differ significantly between men's and women's magazines? What are the differences in the appeals the ads make? What are the differences in the images of men and women?

From your findings, draw conclusions about how advertisers envision and represent differences in gender. What (if any) stereotypes of men and women do the ads present?

5. Imagine that you are a member of a citizens' group working to improve the quality of advertising. What specific recommendations would you make and what standards would you want to see enforced? Illustrate your ideas with ads you can find that either meet or fall below these standards.

3

Television

THE BOYS ALWAYS FOUND SUNSET ON
THE PRAIRIE A PARTICULARLY
MOVING EXPERIENCE

Drawing by Glen Baxter; © 1991 The New Yorker Magazine, Inc.

We may laugh at these "boys" who stand in the middle of a barren Southwest desert watching a sunset on TV as the real sun sets behind them. Yet the joke is also on us because—like the boys—we might often find ourselves more engaged, more entertained, and even more emotionally touched by what we watch on television than by our own experiences in real life.

Some critics even suggest that people regard what they see on television as more real than what goes on around them and thus virtually narrow their world to what comes to them on "the tube." Paradoxically, television's greatest benefit is its potential to broaden our experience, to bring us to places we could never visit, to people we could never meet, and to a range of ideas otherwise unavailable to many people.

This complex relationship between television and people as individuals and as a society leads thoughtful people to examine closely the way television diverts our attention from what could be our own rich, nonmediated experiences; the way it entertains and informs us through otherwise inaccessible experiences; the way it shapes our perceptions of the world around us.

The readings in the first part of this chapter address some of the important questions raised in regard to this ubiquitous medium: Why do Americans spend so much time watching television? What essential needs and desires does television satisfy? How accurately does television represent reality? How strongly do its distortions of reality affect our ideas and behavior? To what extent does television intervene in our everyday lives, influencing families and communities, domestic space, and leisure time?

The readings in the second part of the chapter expand on these questions and focus on three popular television genres—game shows, soap operas, and situation comedies. The writers use a variety of critical methods to uncover meanings beneath the surface that passive observers (as most of us often are) internalize with little awareness.

As you read these essays, remember the television-entranced cowboys at the opening of the chapter. As you hone your own critical abilities you will go beyond the passive observer to become an active, critically-engaged viewer.

THE CULTURAL INFLUENCES
OF TELEVISION

Spudding Out

Barbara Ehrenreich

*D*o *you head straight for the TV when you arrive home after work or school, flicking on the set before you talk to your roommate or feed the cat? If so, you may be exhibiting symptoms of "couch potato" syndrome—a condition cultural critic Barbara Ehrenreich laments in the following essay. Referring to a more active and gregarious America in days past, Ehrenreich observes an onset of a "mass agoraphobia," which she argues has been directly caused by television. This TV-induced phobia—an irrational fear of being away from the tube—has led to a significant loss in human contact and activity, according to Ehrenreich: no longer do people look outside the little box for relaxation or entertainment; instead, Americans have retreated to their living rooms, kitchens, bedrooms or wherever they lounge comfortably in front of a TV and, in fact, are isolating themselves there.*

Cocooned in chairs, couches, beds, and blankets, and armed with that indispensible accessory of modern life—the remote control keypad—today's Americans are tuned in to the artificial images of TV land and tuned out from the rest of the world. Moreover, Ehrenreich points to a paradox in our relationship to television: "We love TV because TV brings us a world in which TV does not exist."

***As you read** this essay, observe Ehrenreich's tone, which succeeds in being both funny and biting. Notice also how she uses irony and exaggeration to make her critique simultaneously understated and incisive.*

••••••••••••••••••••

Someone has to speak for them, because they have, to a person, lost   1
the power to speak for themselves. I am referring to that great mass of
Americans who were once known as the "salt of the earth," then as
"the silent majority," more recently as "the viewing public," and now,
alas, as "couch potatoes." What drives them—or rather, leaves them
sapped and spineless on their reclining chairs? What are they seeking—
beyond such obvious goals as a tastefully colorized version of *The
Maltese Falcon?*

My husband was the first in the family to "spud out," as the ex-   2
pression now goes. Soon everyone wanted one of those zip-up "Couch

Potato Bags," to keep warm in during David Letterman. The youngest, and most thoroughly immobilized, member of the family relies on a remote that controls his TV, stereo, and VCR, and can also shut down the neighbor's pacemaker at fifteen yards.

But we never see the neighbors anymore, nor they us. This saddens   3
me, because Americans used to be a great and restless people, fond of the outdoors in all of its manifestations, from Disney World to miniature golf. Some experts say there are virtues in mass agoraphobia, that it strengthens the family and reduces highway deaths. But I would point out that there are still a few things that cannot be done in the den, especially by someone zipped into a body bag. These include racquetball, voting, and meeting strange people in bars.

Most psychologists interpret the couch potato trend as a negative   4
reaction to the outside world. Indeed, the list of reasons to stay safely tucked indoors lengthens yearly. First there was crime, then AIDS, then side-stream smoke. To this list should be added "fear of the infrastructure," for we all know someone who rashly stepped outside only to be buried in a pothole, hurled from a collapsing bridge, or struck by a falling airplane.

But it is not just the outside world that has let us down. Let's face it,   5
despite a decade-long campaign by the "profamily" movement, the family has been a disappointment. The reason lies in an odd circular dynamic: we watch television to escape from our families because television shows us how dull our families really are.

Compare your own family to, for example, the Huxtables, the Kea-   6
tons, or the peppy young people on *Thirtysomething*. In those families, even the three-year-olds are stand-up comics, and the most insipid remark is hailed with heartening outbursts of canned laughter. When television families aren't gathered around the kitchen table exchanging wisecracks, they are experiencing brief but moving dilemmas, which are handily solved by the youngest child or by some cute extraterrestrial house-guest. Emerging from *Family Ties* or *My Two Dads*, we are forced to acknowledge that our own families are made up of slow-witted, emotionally crippled people who would be lucky to qualify for seats in the studio audience of *Jeopardy!*

But gradually I have come to see that there is something besides fear   7
of the outside and disgust with our families that drives us to spudhood—some positive attraction, some deep cathexis to television itself. For a long time it eluded me. When I watched television, mainly as a way of getting to know my husband and children, I found that my mind wandered to more interesting things, like whether to get up and make ice cubes.

Only after many months of viewing did I begin to understand the   8
force that has transformed the American people into root vegetables. If

you watch TV for a very long time, day in, day out, you will begin to notice something eerie and unnatural about the world portrayed therein.
I don't mean that it is two-dimensional or lacks a well-developed critique of the capitalist consumer culture or something superficial like
that. I mean something so deeply obvious that it's almost scary: when
you watch television, you will see people doing many things—chasing
fast cars, drinking lite beer, shooting each other at close range, etc. But
you will never see people *watching television*. Well, maybe for a second,
before the phone rings or a brand-new, multiracial adopted child walks
into the house. But never *really watching*, hour after hour, the way *real*
people do.

Way back in the beginning of the television era, this was not so   9
strange, because real people actually did many of the things people do
on TV, even if it was only bickering with their mothers-in-law about
which toilet paper to buy. But modern people, i.e., couch potatoes, do
nothing that is ever shown on television (because it is either dangerous
or would involve getting up from the couch). And what they do do—
watch television—is far too boring to be televised for more than a fraction of a second, not even by Andy Warhol, bless his boredom-proof little heart.

So why do we keep on watching? The answer, by now, should be   10
perfectly obvious: we love television because television brings us a
world in which television does not exist. In fact, deep in their hearts, this
is what the spuds crave most: a rich, new, participatory life, in which
family members look each other in the eye, in which people walk outside and banter with the neighbors, where there is adventure, possibility, danger, feeling, all in natural color, stereophonic sound, and three
dimensions, without commercial interruptions, and starring . . . us.

"You mean some new kind of computerized interactive medium?"   11
the children asked hopefully, pert as the progeny on a Tuesday night sitcom. But before I could expand on this concept—known to our ancestors as "real life"—they were back at the box, which may be, after all,
the only place left to find it.

....

Examining the Text

1. Ehrenreich's tone in this essay is basically satirical. Point out several
examples of this approach and consider why she adopts this tone. Does
she only intend to be amusing or would you say she is making a serious
point? If so, what is it?

2. What differences does Ehrenreich note between what we see on television and "real life"? Could these differences be viewed as criticism of television and/or of how we live our lives? Should television reflect the way most people live?

3. "Couch potato" was widely quoted in the media during the middle and late eighties when Ehrenreich wrote this essay, but the term is not as common today. Has the "couch potato" phenomenon been a significant aspect of U.S. culture over the last decade or so? How does the way you answer these questions color your responses to Ehrenreich's essay?

For Group Discussion

Working in a group, choose several currently popular programs that focus on family life and list the characteristics of the families they portray—the relationships among family members, the way they behave, the problems they face and how they solve them. (For balance, choose at least one situation comedy and one hour-long dramatic series.) How well do these characteristics correspond to those that Ehrenreich notes? As a class, consider how accurately these television families reflect the "average" American family and, in fact, whether there is any such thing as an "average" American family.

Writing Suggestion

Based on your own experiences and your observations of your own family and friends, how would you characterize the television viewing habits of most people? In an essay, analyze the different reasons people have for watching television. In doing so, you may wish to expand upon or counter Ehrenreich's observations.

Television and Cultural Behavior
Conrad P. Kottak

*I*n the following essay Conrad Kottak, a professor of cultural anthropology, chooses an unusual subject for study: the students in his own large Introductory Anthropology course. Treating his classroom as a microcosm that can reveal important information about our society, he extends this comparison even to the point of half jokingly calling his students "natives."

Implicitly arguing with other scholars who might see television as trivial—and against distinctions between "high" and "low" forms of culture—Kottak takes television as his cultural artifact and object of study. The crux of his argument is that years of television watching have fundamentally conditioned the *behavior of post-1955 generations of Americans, and that this "teleconditioning" has caused them to adopt behavior styles learned while watching TV. To develop his somewhat unorthodox thesis, Kottak connects his role as a teacher to the role of the television set in modern life. According to Kottak, these behavior patterns manifest themselves in his classroom, where his students react to the "live" instructor—namely, himself—as they would a TV screen.*

For Kottak, television is as powerful as our other societal and cultural institutions—such as family, church, and state—and his attempt to subject it to traditional anthropological study includes the use of academic language and the creation of new terminology such as "teleconditioning."

As you read, consider what you may know of anthropology from your own studies, and notice how Kottak is trying to "modernize" his discipline by treating technology as a contemporary cultural artifact. Consider also the validity of his thesis in your life: Have you been "teleconditioned" into treating a lecturer the same way you would your television set?

• • • • • • • • • • • • • • • • • • • •

Why should a cultural anthropologist, trained to study primitive societies, be interested in television, which is the creation of a complex, industrial society? My interest in television's impact on human social behavior arose mainly through contacts with young Americans. These include my children, their friends, and particularly the college students at the University of Michigan to whom I have been teaching introductory anthropology since 1968.   1

Most of the freshmen I have taught during the past decade were born after 1955. They belong to the first generation raised after the almost total diffusion of television into the American home. Most of these young Americans have never known a world without TV. The tube has been as much a fixture in their homes as mom or dad. Considering how common divorce has become, the TV set even outlasts the father in many homes. American kids now devote 22–30 hours to television each week. By the end of high school, they will have spent 22,000 hours in front of the set, versus only 11,000 in the classroom (*Ann Arbor News* 1985b). Such prolonged exposure must modify Americans' behavior in several ways.   2

I have discussed the behavior modification I see in my classroom with university colleagues, and many say they have observed similar changes in students' conduct. The thesis to be defended in this book is somewhat different from those of other studies about television's effects on behavior. Previous researchers have found links between exposure to media content (for example, violence) and individual behavior (hyperactivity, aggression, "acting out"). I also believe that content affects   3 behavior. However, I make a more basic claim: The very habit of watching television has modified the behavior of Americans who have grown up with the tube.

Anyone who has been to a movie house recently has seen examples 4 of TV conditioned behavior—**teleconditioning.** People talk, babies cry, members of the audience file in and out getting snacks and going to the bathroom. Students act similarly in college courses. A decade ago, there was always an isolated student who did these kinds of things. What is new is a behavior pattern, characteristic of a group rather than an individual. This cultural pattern is becoming more and more pronounced, and I link it directly to televiewing. Stated simply, the pattern is this: *Televiewing causes people to duplicate inappropriately, in other areas of their lives, behavior styles developed while watching television.*

Some examples are in order. Almost nothing bothers professors 5 more than having someone read a newspaper in class. If lecturers take their message and teaching responsibilities seriously, they are understandably perturbed when a student shows more interest in a sports column or "Doonesbury." I don't often get newspapers in class, but one day I noticed a student sitting in the front row reading a paperback novel. Irritated by her audacity, I stopped lecturing and asked "Why are you reading a book in my class?" Her answer: "Oh, I'm not in your class. I just came in here to read my book."

How is this improbable response explained? Why would someone 6 take the trouble to come into a classroom in order to read? The answer, I think, is this: Because of televiewing, many young Americans have trouble reading unless they have background noise. Research confirms that most Americans do something else while watching television. Often they read. Even I do it. When I get home from work I often turn on the television set, sit down in a comfortable chair, and go through the mail or read the newspaper.

Research on television's impact in other countries confirms that tele- 7 viewing evolves through certain stages. The first stage, when sets are introduced, is rapt attention, gazes glued to the screen. Some of us can remember from the late 1940s and 1950s sitting in front of our first TV, dumbly watching even test patterns. Later, as the novelty diminishes, viewers become progressively less attentive. Televiewers in Brazil, whom I began studying systematically in 1983, had already moved past the first stage, but they were still much more attentive than Americans.

A study done in Brazil's largest city, São Paulo, illustrates the con- 8 trast. The study shocked Rede Globo, Brazil's dominant network (and the most watched commercial TV network in the world). It revealed that half the viewers were not paying full attention when commercials were shown. Afraid of losing advertising revenues, Rede Globo attacked the accuracy of the research. American sponsors are so accustomed to inattention and, nowadays, to remote control tune-outs, that it would probably delight them if even half the audience stayed put.

The student who came to my class to read her novel was simply an extreme example of a culture pattern derived from television. Because of her lifelong TV dependency, she had trouble reading without background noise. It didn't matter to her whether the background hum came from a stereo, a TV set, or a live professor. Accustomed to machines that don't talk back, she probably was amazed that I noticed her at all. Perhaps my questioning even prompted her to check her set that night to see if someone real was lurking inside.   9

Another example of a televiewing effect is students' increasing tendency to enter and leave classrooms at will. Of course, individual students do occasionally get sick or have a dentist's appointment. But here again I'm describing a group pattern rather than individual idiosyncrasies. Only during the past few years have I regularly observed students getting up in mid-lecture, leaving the room for a few minutes, then returning. Sometimes they bring back a canned soft drink.   10

These students intend no disrespect. They are simply transferring a home-grown pattern of snack-and-bathroom break from family room to classroom. They perceive nothing unusual in acting the same way in front of a live speaker and fellow students as they do when they watch television. (A few students manage to remain seated for only 10–15 minutes. Then they get up and leave the classroom. They are exhibiting a less flattering pattern. Either they have diarrhea, as one student told me he did, or they have decided to shut off the "set" or "change channels.")   11

Today, almost all Americans talk while watching television. Talking is becoming more common in the classroom, as in the movie house, and this also illustrates television's effects on our collective behavior. Not only do my students bring food and drink to class, some lie down on the floor if they arrive too late to get a seat. I have even seen couples kissing and caressing just a few rows away.   12

New examples of teleconditioning pop up all the time. In each of the past two semesters I've taught introductory anthropology, at least one student has requested that I say publicly "Happy Birthday" to a friend in the class. These students seem to perceive me as a professorial analog of Willard Scott, NBC's *Today* show weatherman, who offers birthday greetings (to people 100 and over). Long ago I put into my syllabus injunctions against reading newspapers and eating crunchy foods in class. Last semester I felt compelled to announce that I "don't do birthdays."   13

All these are examples of effects of televiewing on social behavior   14 of young Americans. They are not individual idiosyncrasies (the subject matter of psychology) but new *culture patterns* that have emerged since the 1950s. As such they are appropriate objects for anthropological analysis. **Culture,** as defined by anthropologists, consists of knowledge, beliefs, perceptions, attitudes, expectations, values, and patterns of behavior that people learn by growing up in a given society. Above all else, culture consists of *shared* learning. In contrast to education, it extends well beyond what we learn in school, to encompass everything we learn in life. Much of the information that contemporary Americans share comes from their common exposure to the mass media, particularly television.

TV Content's Cultural Impact

TV *content's* impact on American culture enters the story when we   15
consider that contemporary Americans share common information and experiences because of the programs they have seen. Again, I learn from my students. The subject matter of introductory anthropology includes the kinship systems of the United States and other societies. One habit I acquired about five years ago takes advantage of my students' familiarity with television. My practice is to illustrate changes in American family structure and household organization by contrasting television programs of the 1950s with more recent examples.

Three decades ago, the usual TV family was a nuclear family con-   16
sisting of employed father (who often knew best), homemaker mother, and children. Examples include *Father Knows Best, Ozzie and Harriet,* and *Leave It to Beaver.* These programs, which were appropriate for the 1950s, are out of sync with the social and economic realities of the late 1980s. Only 16 million American women worked outside the home in 1950, compared with three times that number today. By the mid-1980s, fewer than 10 percent of American households had the composition that was once considered normal: breadwinner father, homemaker mother, and two children. Still, today's college students remain knowledgeable about these 1950s shows through syndicated reruns. Afternoon television is a pop culture museum that familiarizes kids with many of the same images, characters, and tales that their parents saw in recent days of yore.

Virtually all my students have seen reruns of the series *The Brady*   17
Bunch. Its family organization provides an interesting contrast with earlier programs. It illustrates what anthropologists call "blended family organization." A new (blended) family forms when a widow with three daughters marries a widower with three sons. Blended families have

been increasing in American society because of more frequent divorce and remarriage. However, a first spouse's death may also lead to a blended family, as in *The Brady Bunch*. During *The Brady Bunch*'s first run, divorce remained controversial and thus could not give rise to the Brady household.

The occupation of Mike, the Brady husband-father, a successful ar-   18 chitect, illustrates a trend toward upper-middle-class jobs and life-styles that continues on American television today. TV families tend to be more professional, more successful, and richer than the average real-life family. More recent examples include the Huxtables (*The Cosby Show*) and the Keatons (*Family Ties*). There are also ultra-rich night-time soap families such as the Carringtons of *Dynasty* and the Ewings of *Dallas*. Mike and Carol Brady were wealthy enough to employ a housekeeper, Alice. Mirroring American culture when the program was made, the career of the wife-mother was part time and subsidiary, if it existed at all. Back then, women like Carol Brady who had been lucky enough to find a wealthy husband didn't compete with other women—even professional housekeepers—in the work force.

I use familiar examples like *The Brady Bunch* to teach students how   19 to draw the genealogies and kinship diagrams that anthropologists use routinely in fieldwork and in making cross-cultural comparisons. TV family relationships may be represented with the same symbols and genealogical charts used for the Bushmen of the Kalahari Desert of southern Africa, or any other society. In particular, I chart changes in American family organization, showing how real-life changes have been reflected in television content, with which students tend to be familiar. *The Brady Bunch*, for example, illustrates a trend toward showing non-traditional families and households. We also see this trend in day-time soaps and in prime time, with the marital breakups, reconciliations, and extended family relationships of *Dallas, Dynasty, Falcon Crest,* and *Knot's Landing*. The trend toward newer household types is also obvious in *Kate & Allie* and *The Golden Girls*.

Students enjoy learning about anthropological techniques with cul-   20 turally familiar examples. Each time I begin my kinship lecture, a few people in the class immediately recognize (from reruns) the nuclear families of the 1950s. They know the names of all the Cleavers—Ward, June, Wally, and Beaver. However, when I begin diagramming the Bradys, my students can't contain themselves. They start shouting out "Jan," "Bobby," "Greg," "Cindy," "Marsha," "Peter," "Mike," "Carol," "Alice." The response mounts. By the time we get to Carol and Alice, almost everyone is taking part in my blackboard kinship chart. Whenever I give my Brady Bunch lecture, Anthropology 101 resembles a revival meeting. Hundreds of young natives shout out in unison names made almost as familiar as their parents' through television reruns.

As the natives take up this chant—learned by growing up in post- 21 1950s America—there is an enthusiasm, a warm glow, that my course will not recapture until next semester's rerun of my Brady Bunch lecture. It is as though my students find nirvana, religious ecstasy, through their collective remembrance of the Bradys, in the rituallike incantation of their names.

Given my own classroom experiences, I was hardly surprised to 22 read that in a 1986 survey of 1550 American adults, more people said they got pleasure from TV than from sex, food, liquor, money, or religion. In that survey, people indicated which of the following "give you a great deal of pleasure and satisfaction." The percentages were as follows:

watching TV	68
friends	61
helping others	59
vacations	58
hobbies	56
reading	55
marriage	45
sexual relationships	42
food	41
money	40
sports	32
religion	32

Furthermore, when people were asked what they liked to do for relaxation, watching TV again topped the list, followed by just relaxing and doing nothing, vacationing, music, reading and going out to eat. Sex and religion were each chosen by a mere one percent.

The Cultural Dimension

I often wonder how my more traditional colleagues in anthropol- 23 ogy have managed to avoid becoming interested in television—so striking are the behavioral modifications it has wrought in the natives we see and talk to most frequently: our fellow citizens in modern society. Nationwide and ubiquitous, television cuts across demographic boundaries. It presents to diverse groups a set of common symbols, vocabularies, information, and shared experiences. Televiewing encompasses men and women of different ages, colors, classes, ethnic groups, and levels of educational achievement. Television is seen in cities, suburbs, towns, and country—by farmers, factory workers, and philosophers (although the last may be loath to admit it).

Television is stigmatized as trivial by many people (particularly orthodox intellectuals). However, it is hardly trivial that the average American household has more television sets (2.2 per home) than bathrooms. Given the level of television's penetration of the modern home, we should hardly ignore its effects on socialization and enculturation. The common information that members of a mass society come to share as a result of watching the same thing is indisputably *culture* as anthropologists use the term. This anthropological definition of culture encompasses a much broader spectrum of human life than the definition that focuses on "high culture"—refinement, cultivation, taste, sophistication, education, and appreciation of the fine arts. From the anthropological perspective, not just university graduates, but all people are cultured.

Anthropology's subject matter must include features of modern culture that some regard as too trivial to be worthy of serious study, such as commercial television. As a cultural product and manifestation, a rock star may be as interesting as a symphony conductor, a comic book as significant as a book-award winner. It is axiomatic in anthropology that the most significant cultural forces are those that affect us every day of our lives. Particularly important are those features influencing children during **enculturation**—the process whereby one grows up in a particular society and absorbs its culture.

Culture is collective, shared, meaningful. It is transmitted by conscious and unconscious learning experiences. People acquire it not through their genes, but as a result of growing up in a particular society. Hundreds of culture-bearers have passed through the Anthropology 101 classroom over the past decade. Many have been unable to recall the full names of their parents' first cousins. Some have forgotten a grandmother's maiden name, and few contemporary students know many Biblical or Shakespearean characters. Most, however, have no trouble identifying names and relationships in mythical families that exist only in televisionland.

As the Bible, Shakespeare, and classical mythology did in the past, television influences the names we bestow on our children and answer to all our lives. For example, "Jaime" rose from 70th to 10th most popular girl's name within two years of the debut of *The Bionic Woman*, whose title character was Jaime Sommers. The first name of the program's star, Lindsay Wagner, also became popular. *Charlie's Angels* boosted "Tiffany" and "Sabrina." Younger kids are named "Blake," "Alexis," "Fallon," and "Krystle" (spellings vary) after *Dynasty*'s Carringtons. In other cultures children still receive names of gods (Jesus, Mohammed) and heroes (Ulysses). The comparably honored Olympians of contemporary America lead their glamorous, superhuman lives not on a mountaintop, but in a small square box. We don't even have to go to church to worship them, because we can count on them to come to us in weekly visitations.

Psychologists are still debating the precise effects of television on *individual* behavior and psychopathology; TV murders and car chases may indeed influence kids toward aggressive or destructive behavior. However, television's *cultural* effects are indubitable. Examples of the medium's impact on U.S. culture—on the collective behavior and knowledge of contemporary Americans—are everywhere.   28

My conclusions about television can be summarized as follows: New culture patterns related to television's penetration of the American home have emerged since the 1950s. As *technology*, television affects collective behavior, as people duplicate, in many areas of their lives, habits developed while watching TV. Television *content* also influences mass culture because it provides widely shared common knowledge, beliefs, and expectations.   29

I became interested in television because I saw that its effects are comparable to those of humanity's most powerful traditional institutions—family, church, state, and education. Television is creating new cultural experiences and meanings. It is capable of producing intense, often irrationally based, feelings of solidarity and *communitas* ("community feeling") shared widely by people who have grown up within the same cultural tradition. Nothing so important to natives could long escape the eye of the anthropologist.   30

••••••••••••••••••••

Examining the Text

1. Kottak coins a term "teleconditioning" to refer to certain television-induced patterns of behavior and provides several examples drawn from movie audiences and students in his classes. What other sorts of behavior have you observed recently that might be the result of teleconditioning?

2. Given that students in large lectures do exhibit the behavior Kottak describes—reading newspapers and drifting in and out of class, for example—are there other ways to account for this behavior other than teleconditioning? Does Kottak's assertion that such behavior has increased since the 1960s support his analysis or are there other conditions that could have contributed to this change?

3. Kottak suggests that television is as powerful an institution in influencing culture as "family, church, state, and education" (paragraph 30). What examples does he give of this influence? Can you think of others? Do you think Kottak's assessment is accurate or does he exaggerate his case?

For Group Discussion

How closely does Kottak's list of pleasurable activities (22) correspond to your own and those of other college students? Reorder his list to reflect your own observations, adding and deleting as you wish. Then compare your group members' lists and try to reach some consensus on an accurate list. Finally, discuss each group's lists as a class.

Writing Suggestion

Kottak discusses the significance of *The Brady Bunch* in his anthropology classes. In an essay, consider other family-based series from the 1970s and 1980s that are current reruns. What significance do they have both as representations of family structure and as widely shared points of cultural reference?

Television Viewing as Ritual

Michael T. Marsden

Combining elements of psychoanalysis and structuralism, this essay by critic Michael T. Marsden investigates television viewing as a quintessential ritual of American culture. Marsden sees TV viewing as not just a habit but rather as a "way of life" and likens it to religious rituals, noting that the right side of the brain—the so-called "creative" or "intuitive" side—is activated both during religious rituals and during sessions of watching TV. Furthermore, Marsden observes that television appeals to human emotions, as opposed to linear and logical thought processes. Instead of offering an escape from the problems of contemporary life—the function which many critics see for television viewing—the "ritual" of watching television is an entrance into a rich dream world. By tapping into and portraying society's "deepest needs and desires," in a sense television helps viewers tap into a collective unconscious of "common, shared experiences and images."

Marsden makes two closely related points about the ritual of TV viewing: first, that the particular programs being watched are not as important as the viewing process itself; and, second, that "viewing" might be redefined as "receiving," thus implying that the viewer has a certain measure of choice and action. By emphasizing the possible "uses" of TV, Marsden implicitly argues against the per-

vasive and popular depiction of the TV viewer as a passive nonparticipant. He even suggests that the ritual has become increasingly governed by choice with technological developments: the proliferation of sets, the creation of video games, and the introduction of videotaping, for example, have all made it possible for individual viewers to tailor the ritual to suit their own needs and desires.

As you read *this essay, then, explore the notion of myth and religious ritual—and the way you have previously considered these concepts and practices—in light of this central question: how does Marsden's conception of television as viewing ritual fit into your own beliefs about religious rituals and practices?*

• • • • • • • • • • • • • • • • • • •

One of the classic scholastic attributes of God was omnipresence, a   1
quality which in turn became an operative definition. Given the penetration level of television receivers in the Western world, it would seem to be quite logical to extend the argument and suggest that television has taken on some god-like qualities, not the least of which is omnipresence. In addition, the television receiver has quietly and smoothly assumed the role of household god, becoming the focal point for interior designer and homeowner alike. Television viewing is not an activity; it is a way of life, a contemporary, electronic creed. True, we are not always "watching" our television receivers when they have "power on," but they most assuredly are a part of our environment at that moment. In fact, television occupies a larger part of our waking consciousness as a society than does eating, and it is rivaling sleeping in the amount of our time it consumes.

Television viewing is too often examined in terms of content, which   2
while an extremely important focus for the cultural analyst, is not the only valid or viable perspective. Equally important is the perspective of "flow" so effectively presented and exemplified by Raymond Williams in his book *Television: Technology and Cultural Form.* People do not watch programs, they watch television. And they read about television, not about programs in *TV Guide* or in their local newspapers. (Reading about television provides an interesting sub-ritual which exists to balance the non-linear bias of television viewing.) It is not by accident that prime-time television runs three hours per evening; Americans have regularly and systematically enjoyed a three-hour block of entertainment for an evening from 19th century popular theater (a five act play plus a one act farce), to vaudeville (10 to 15 distinct acts averaging a total of three hours of programming), to a double-bill movie (two features plus a newsreel plus a cartoon), etc. The pattern was well established for a complete evening's entertainment long before the first experimental

images of Felix the Cat disturbed the airways in and around New York City in the late 1920s.

But behind the patterned and timed entertainment forms were the cultural needs that these various entertainment forms so effectively fulfilled. Popular culture in general, and the popular arts in particular, do not provide the audience with an opportunity for escape *from* anything. To the contrary what they provide is the option of escaping *into* a restructured, reformulated world in which the senseless makes sense, where the logic of feeling rules, and where resolution is not only possible but demanded. It is a world which some call fantasy but which the wiser call dreaming. It is a conscious state of unconsciousness in which the human mind can deal with issues which in the "normal," destructured world would prove intolerable or unacceptable. The function of the popular arts is basically the same function served by all of art through the ages; only the aesthetic codes are different. Television as, in the words of Horace Newcomb, "the most popular art" has a most special function in our contemporary culture, serving to focus our cultural needs and wishes through programming into an extended block of time in which we can reorder our world until it is psychologically acceptable. It is time that we took television producers at their word; they are truly trying to give us what we want, and we are not always as clear as they would like us to be on what it is we want. That is why we devise rating systems and various feedback mechanisms. That is why the relationship between television producer/television audience/television programming is a highly dynamic, organic one which can and does flex to meet the deep-felt needs and desires of all parties. When the American audience did not get the trial of a President on PBS through the Watergate Hearings they turned to commercial television and *Washington Behind Closed Doors* for their sense of justice and satisfaction. But it is television viewing as a whole, not the viewing of particular programs or even programming forms, which is the major ritual in our society.

Rituals, whether religious or secular, exist as paradigms of order for the purpose of placing the immediate environment into perspective. Television programming, whether it be a highly creative 60 second commercial, a half-hour newscast, or a 90 minute made-for-television movie, exists to provide the viewer with a mediated experience which is highly emotional in nature. It has been suggested that television, unlike the print medium, emphasizes the right side of the brain. While the left side of the brain controls sequential, linear thought processes, the right side of the brain involves itself in simultaneous, non-sequential processes. We thus become emotional scanners, tuning in and out of melodramatic and dramatic scenes of restructured reality for the purposes of preparing ourselves to more effectively and efficiently deal with the nontelevised world once the "power is off." The parallels to a religious liturgical service are many and obvious.

While the left side of the brain promotes the intellect, the right side 5 is busy processing feelings. The ritual of television viewing is most heavily involved with activating the feelings of the viewers, with involving them in restructured experiences. It may well be argued that the ritual of television viewing is the most powerful secular ritual in contemporary society because of its pervasiveness. A number of separate experiments in the United States and Europe involving deprivation of television viewing (several of which actually paid the volunteers not to watch television) have resulted in notable failures.

One of the most misinformed generalizations to spring from World 6 War II media research was that of a monolithic mass audience, the creation of the researcher's imagination but hardly a reflection of reality. Perhaps in times of world paranoia such evasions of reason are understandable; perhaps we even did have "an enemy" and needed to believe that all Germans were Nazis and all Japanese kamikazes. But in post-World War II America there should have been a return to reason within research circles, a claim on rationality, clear thinking when it came to research studies on the mass media.

Television was born full-commercial into a cultural climate of mono- 7 lithic media thought in which there was an enemy who could change media forms easily and quickly: before World War II the movies were at fault, but in the early 1950s comic books received the researchers' glare. There was more than enough laser-like thinking left over for television when it began to be clearly seen as *the* major threat to American culture in the 1950s and 1960s. Intellectuals who would under almost any other circumstances question the exception to the exception to the rule found themselves quite comfortably, at times even cozily, living with and embellishing generalizations about the "mass media" and their clear-cut effects upon a poor, misguided, image-hungry audience who were simply waiting for media-generated signals to react to, whether they be signals for role behavior or purchasing habits.

Out of this intellectual clay was created the "mass viewer," who was 8 described as passive, mindless, soulless, consumption-oriented and certainly without any normal discriminatory powers. This viewer became the "they" of countless, condescending conversations, which became so rote that they themselves were ritualized. We even created an archetypal chair for this "mass viewer," personified it as "Archie's chair," and then enshrined it in the Smithsonian. It was widely assumed that "mass viewers" could be sold anything if only they could be manipulated properly, for they were without the intellectual equipage to protect themselves. In short, advertising empires were built upon the non-logic of the monolithic audience. These ways of life, and reactions to them, were, like the conversations about them, made subconscious and the action toward and reaction to them ritualized.

In the 1970s media research began quite properly to question some   9
of the sacred assumptions about the "mass viewers" and their habits. It became clear that the audience was not an audience at all, but an assemblage of many distinct audiences who were united only under special circumstances and for very special needs and purposes, such as the coverage of the moon landing or the broadcast of Super Bowl games. Demographics became crucial to the television industry, and to support industries to a greater extent in the 1970s than had been the case in the earlier decades, psychographics became a further refined tool for marketing research and the development of advertising strategies.

Despite the obvious and significant rise in multiple-set ownership,   10
researchers kept working out of the pre-transistor radio listening paradigm of a "typical" family sitting in front of their radio receiver tuned into the popular culture of the airwaves *sans* interruptions. Yet the evidence was there in force in the 1960s that people were viewing television in increasing numbers in private, personal ways; they were not communally consuming the culture via this new medium as they had done with previous media. Television sets found their ways into bedrooms, bathrooms, garages, workshops, offices, etc. And programming types followed: Johnny Carson certainly knew his audience was in the bedroom in significant numbers. Television sets further merged into and began in turn to shape lifestyles.

The shift in audience utilization of hardware was further demarked   11
in the 1970s by the advent of home videotaping equipment which moved television into new time frames and into the more private, personal realms of human behavior. Video games were but one illustration of our need to develop additional ways of manipulating and thus further utilizing the television medium.

During the 1970s researchers finally began to examine how people   12
used the medium. We became wise enough to realize that while the average American household may have had the television set *on* for better than six hours a day, that did not mean that the set(s) was being *watched* for that length of time by any combination of viewers. What it did mean is that television programming has become a regularized part of our everyday environment for large portions of our waking days. And it also meant that people have learned to use the medium in creative ways, as background sound, as a "buffer" against other "realities" of the household, as a babysitter, a companion, another member of the family. Television "viewing" then may well not be viewing at all—it may be more properly referred to as "receiving."

Researchers are just now beginning to carefully examine the condi-   13
tions under which the ritual of television viewing is occurring. Certainly
the audience is not exclusively comprised of compulsively passive
viewers who exercise little or no choice in programming taste. To the
contrary, evidence would seem to suggest that viewers are diverse in
their uses of the medium and often are quite active in their interactions
with the television viewing ritual.

Virtually every member of Western civilization is involved directly   14
or indirectly in the ritual of television viewing. The television receiver is
not unlike the medieval cathedral which served as a focal point for the
culture and a window to rituals which were culturally significant. Television provides a series of common, shared experiences and images
which have become part of the collective, shared traditions of our society. Viewers ritualistically enter into televisionland which is not as much
a world of fantasized fact as it is of fact fantasized. Television is clearly
a dream world, a state of mind in which resolution and closure occur
with a satisfying regularity. It is also a dream world in which the deepest needs and desires of the society are depicted in living color eighteen
broadcast hours a day, seven days a week. And through reruns we share
in a kind of living history of the medium and the concerns it shared with
the society. Television viewing is quite simply *the* American ritual.

And it will remain the American ritual—universal, omnipresent,   15
and apparently satisfying—until it is replaced by an equally satisfactory
cultural experience. Most rituals are accompanied by considerable manifest liturgy, but the television viewing ritual has been largely internal-
ized, thus reducing the visibility of its liturgy for the non-serious cultural analyst. The ritual of television viewing involves the mind, not the
body, and in the words of Marshall McLuhan, the viewer is "trans-
ported" into a different world of mediated events whose purpose is to
reassure, to reaffirm and to reestablish harmony in an essentially dishar-
monious world. This household god may be largely taken for granted,
but that does not diminish its awesome cultural power.

•••••••••••••••••••

Examining the Text

1. Marsden examines television viewing as "ritual," and he says that
"rituals, whether religious or secular, exist as paradigms of order for the
purpose of placing the immediate environment into perspective" (paragraph 4). What does he mean by "paradigms of order"? How does this
definition correspond to your own definition of "ritual"? In what ways
do you think television serves as a ritual?

2. According to Marsden, "people do not watch programs, they watch television" (2). What distinction is he making between the two activities? Does his point seem valid to you? How does it relate to his central thesis about television viewing as ritual?

3. According to Marsden, how did the notion of the "mass viewer" evolve, and why has the term fallen into disfavor in recent years? In your experience, are television viewers, as Marsden says, "diverse in their uses of the medium" (13)? If so, provide several examples.

For Group Discussion

Marsden says that "television has taken on some god-like qualities, not the least of which is omnipresence" (1). As a group, brainstorm a list of qualities and functions that people generally associate with a deity. Then, as a class, discuss the extent to which television embodies these god-like attributes.

Writing Suggestion

Marsden says that television is "a dream world in which the deepest needs and desires of the society are depicted" (14). In an essay evaluate this assertion, citing specific programs or kinds of programs to support or criticize his point.

Life According to TV

Harry Waters

The world of television directly influences how people see the "real" world around them. So says George Gerbner, a noted cultural critic and communications scholar. Gerbner and his staff spent over fifteen years studying the televised programs America watches. Their results paint a damning picture of the TV industry. In the following essay Harry Waters summarizes Gerbner's research about how the televised world matches up to "reality" and to people's perception of reality. To that end, Gerbner breaks the television-viewing audience into a number of different representative categories—gender, age, race, and lifestyle, just to name a few—and he observes how people in each category are portrayed in different television shows.

Frequently, Gerbner's results, as detailed by Waters, are surprising. For example, contrary to most studies of the relationship between TV and crime which suggest that television causes people to become more violent, Gerbner argues that the prevalence of crime on TV creates a "fear of victimization" in the viewer. This fear ultimately leads to a "mean-world syndrome" in which view-

ers come to see their social surroundings as hostile and threatening. Waters balances Gerbner's conclusions with comments from network officials who, not surprisingly, often take Gerbner to task.

As you read this selection, pay particular attention to the way Waters maintains his objectivity by attributing most of the opinions and conclusions to Gerbner and his assistants. Notice, too, how Waters's opinions about Gerbner's research can be detected in phrasing such as "the gospel of Gerbner," "tidy explanation," and "comforting."

Since this is an article originally published in Newsweek—a magazine which claims to report the news without bias, you might ask just how objective actually so-called "objective" reporting is.

•••••••••••••••••••

The late Paddy Chayefsky, who created Howard Beale, would have 1 loved George Gerbner. In "Network," Chayefsky marshaled a scathing, fictional assault on the values and methods of the people who control the world's most potent communications instrument. In real life, Gerbner, perhaps the nation's foremost authority on the social impact of television, is quietly using the disciplines of behavioral research to construct an equally devastating indictment of the medium's images and messages. More than any spokesman for a pressure group, Gerbner has become the man that television watches. From his cramped, book-lined office at the University of Pennsylvania springs a steady flow of studies that are raising executive blood pressures at the networks' sleek Manhattan command posts.

George Gerbner's work is uniquely important because it transports 2 the scientific examination of television far beyond familiar children-and-violence arguments. Rather than simply studying the link between violence on the tube and crime in the streets, Gerbner is exploring wider and deeper terrain. He has turned his lens on TV's hidden victims— women, the elderly, blacks, blue-collar workers and other groups—to document the ways in which video-entertainment portrayals subliminally condition how we perceive ourselves and how we view those around us. Gerbner's subjects are not merely the impressionable young; they include all the rest of us. And it is his ominous conclusion that heavy watchers of the prime-time mirror are receiving a grossly distorted picture of the real world that they tend to accept more readily than reality itself.

The 63-year-old Gerbner, who is dean of Penn's Annenberg School 3 of Communications, employs a methodology that meshes scholarly observation with mundane legwork. Over the past 15 years, he and a tireless trio of assistants (Larry Gross, Nancy Signorielli and Michael

Morgan) videotaped and exhaustively analyzed 1,600 prime-time programs involving more than 15,000 characters. They then drew up multiple-choice questionnaires that offered correct answers about the world at large along with answers that reflected what Gerbner perceived to be the misrepresentations and biases of the world according to TV. Finally, these questions were posed to large samples of citizens from all socioeconomic strata. In every survey, the Annenberg team discovered that heavy viewers of television (those watching more than four hours a day), who account for more than 30 percent of the population, almost invariably chose the TV-influenced answers, while light viewers (less than two hours a day), selected the answers corresponding more closely to actual life. Some of the dimensions of television's reality warp:

Sex

Male prime-time characters outnumber females by 3 to 1 and, with   4
a few star-turn exceptions, women are portrayed as weak, passive satellites to powerful, effective men. TV's male population also plays a vast variety of roles, while females generally get typecast as either lovers or mothers. Less than 20 percent of TV's married women with children work outside the home—as compared with more than 50 percent in real life. The tube's distorted depictions of women, concludes Gerbner, reinforce stereotypical attitudes and increase sexism. In one Annenberg survey, heavy viewers were far more likely than light ones to agree with the proposition: "Women should take care of running their homes and leave running the country to men."

Age

People over 65, too, are grossly underrepresented on television.   5
Correspondingly, heavy-viewing Annenberg respondents believe that the elderly are a vanishing breed, that they make up a smaller proportion of the population today than they did 20 years ago. In fact, they form the nation's most rapidly expanding age group. Heavy viewers also believe that old people are less healthy today than they were two decades ago, when quite the opposite is true. As with women, the portrayals of old people transmit negative impressions. In general, they are cast as silly, stubborn, sexually inactive and eccentric." They're often shown as feeble grandparents bearing cookies," says Gerbner. "You never see the power that real old people often have. The best and

possibly only time to learn about growing old with decency and grace is in youth. And young people are the most susceptible to TV's messages."

Race

The problem with the medium's treatment of blacks is more one of   6
image than of visibility. Though a tiny percentage of black characters come across as "unrealistically romanticized," reports Gerbner, the overwhelming majority of them are employed in subservient, supporting roles—such as the white hero's comic sidekick. "When a black child looks at prime time," he says, "most of the people he sees doing interesting and important things are white." That imbalance, he goes on, tends to teach young blacks to accept minority status as naturally inevitable and even deserved. To access the impact of such portrayals on the general audience, the Annenberg survey forms included questions like "Should white people have the right to keep blacks out of their neighborhoods?" and "Should there be laws against marriages between blacks and whites?" The more that viewers watched, the more they answered "yes" to each question.

Work

Heavy viewers greatly overestimated the proportion of Americans   7
employed as physicians, lawyers, athletes and entertainers, all of whom inhabit prime-time in hordes. A mere 6 to 10 percent of television characters hold blue-collar or service jobs vs. about 60 percent in the real work force. Gerbner sees two dangers in TV's skewed division of labor. On the one hand, the tube so overrepresents and glamorizes the elite occupations that it sets up unrealistic expectations among those who must deal with them in actuality. At the same time, TV largely neglects portraying the occupations that most youngsters will have to enter. "You almost never see the farmer, the factory worker or the small businessman," he notes. "Thus not only do lawyers and other professionals find they cannot measure up to the image TV projects of them, but children's occupational aspirations are channeled in unrealistic directions." The Gerbner team feels this emphasis on high-powered jobs poses problems for adolescent girls, who are also presented with views of women as homebodies. The two conflicting views, Gerbner says, add to the frustration over choices they have to make as adults.

Health

Although video characters exist almost entirely on junk food and   8
quaff alcohol 15 times more often than water, they manage to remain
slim, healthy and beautiful. Frequent TV watchers, the Annenberg in-
vestigators found, eat more, drink more, exercise less and possess an almost mystical faith in the curative powers of medical science. Concludes
Gerbner: "Television may well be the single most pervasive source of
health information. And its overidealized images of medical people,
coupled with its complacency about unhealthy life-styles, leaves both
patients and doctors vulnerable to disappointment, frustration and
even litigation."

Crime

On the small screen, crime rages about 10 times more often than in   9
real life. But while other researchers concentrate on the propensity of TV
mayhem to incite aggression, the Annenberg team has studied the hidden side of its imprint: fear of victimization. On television, 55 percent of
prime-time characters are involved in violent confrontations once a
week; in reality, the figure is less than 1 percent. In all demographic
groups in every class of neighborhood, heavy viewers overestimated
the statistical chance of violence in their own lives and harbored an exaggerated mistrust of strangers—creating what Gerbner calls a "mean-
world syndrome." Forty-six percent of heavy viewers who live in cities
rated their fear of crime "very serious" as opposed to 26 percent for light
viewers. Such paranoia is especially acute among TV entertainment's
most common victims: women, the elderly, nonwhites, foreigners and
lower-class citizens.

Video violence, proposes Gerbner, is primarily responsible for im-   10
parting lessons in social power: it demonstrates who can do what to
whom and get away with it. "Television is saying that those at the bottom of the power scale cannot get away with the same things that a
white, middle-class American male can," he says. "It potentially conditions people to think of themselves as victims."

At a quick glance, Gerbner's findings seem to contain a cause-and-   11
effect, chicken-or-the-egg question. Does television make heavy viewers view the world the way they do or do heavy viewers come from the
poorer, less experienced segment of the populace that regards the world
that way to begin with? In other words, does the tube create or simply
confirm the unenlightened attitudes of its most loyal audience? Gerbner, however, was savvy enough to construct a methodology largely

immune to such criticism. His samples of heavy viewers cut across all ages, incomes, education levels and ethnic backgrounds—and every category displayed the same tube-induced misconceptions of the world outside.

Needless to say, the networks accept all this as enthusiastically as they would a list of news-coverage complaints from the Ayatollah Khomeini. Even so, their responses tend to be tinged with a singular respect for Gerbner's personal and professional credentials. The man is no ivory-tower recluse. During World War II, the Budapest-born Gerbner parachuted into the mountains of Yugoslavia to join the partisans fighting the Germans. After the war, he hunted down and personally arrested scores of high Nazi officials. Nor is Gerbner some videophobic vigilante. A Ph.D. in communications, he readily acknowledges TV's beneficial effects, noting that it has abolished parochialism, reduced isolation and loneliness and provided the poorest members of society with cheap, plug-in exposure to experiences they otherwise would not have. Funding for his research is supported by such prestigious bodies as the National Institute of Mental Health, the surgeon general's office and the American Medical Association, and he is called to testify before congressional committees nearly as often as David Stockman.

Mass Entertainment

When challenging Gerbner, network officials focus less on his findings and methods than on what they regard as his own misconceptions of their industry's function. "He's looking at television from the perspective of a social scientist rather than considering what is mass entertainment," says Alfred Schneider, vice president of standards and practices at ABC. "We strive to balance TV's social effects with what will capture an audience's interests. If you showed strong men being victimized as much as women or the elderly, what would comprise the dramatic conflict? If you did a show truly representative of society's total reality, and nobody watched because it wasn't interesting, what have you achieved?"

CBS senior vice president Gene Mater also believes that Gerbner is implicitly asking for the theoretically impossible. "TV is unique in its problems," says Mater. "Everyone wants a piece of the action. Everyone feels that their racial or ethnic group is underrepresented or should be portrayed as they would like the world to perceive them. No popular entertainment form, including this one, can or should be an accurate reflection of society."

On that point, at least, Gerbner is first to agree; he hardly expects   15
television entertainment to serve as a mirror image of absolute truth. But
what fascinates him about this communications medium is its marked
difference from all others. In other media, customers carefully choose
what they want to hear or read: a movie, a magazine, a best seller. In
television, notes Gerbner, viewers rarely tune in for a particular program. Instead, most just habitually turn on the set—and watch by the
clock rather than for a specific show. "Television viewing fulfills the criteria of a ritual," he says. "It is the only medium that can bring to people things they otherwise would not select." With such unique power,
believes Gerbner, comes unique responsibility: "No other medium
reaches into every home or has a comparable, cradle-to-grave influence
over what a society learns about itself."

Match

In Gerbner's view, virtually all of TV's distortions of reality can be   16
attributed to its obsession with demographics. The viewers that prime-
time sponsors most want to reach are white, middle-class, female and between 18 and 49—in short, the audience that purchases most of the consumer products advertised on the tube. Accordingly, notes Gerbner, the
demographic portrait of TV's fictional characters largely matches that of
its prime commercial targets and largely ignores everyone else. "Television," he concludes, "reproduces a world for its own best customers."

Among TV's more candid executives, that theory draws consider-   17
able support. Yet by pointing a finger at the power of demographics,
Gerbner appears to contradict one of his major findings. If female viewers are so dear to the hearts of sponsors, why are female characters cast
in such unflattering light? "In a basically male-oriented power structure," replies Gerbner, "you can't alienate the male viewer. But you can
get away with offending women because most women are pretty well
brainwashed to accept it." The Annenberg dean has an equally tidy explanation for another curious fact. Since the corporate world provides
network television with all of its financial support, one would expect
businessmen on TV to be portrayed primarily as good guys. Quite the
contrary. As any fan of "Dallas," "Dynasty" or "Falcon Crest" well
knows, the image of the company man is usually that of a mendacious,
dirty-dealing rapscallion. Why would TV snap at the hand that feeds it?
"Credibility is the way to ratings," proposes Gerbner. "This country has
a populist tradition of bias against anything big, including big business.
So to retain credibility, TV entertainment shows businessmen in relatively derogatory ways."

In the medium's Hollywood-based creative community, the gospel   18
of Gerbner finds some passionate adherents. Rarely have TV's best and
brightest talents viewed their industry with so much frustration and
anger. The most sweeping indictment emanates from David Rintels, a
two-time Emmy-winning writer and former president of the Writers
Guild of America, West. "Gerbner is absolutely correct and it is the people who run the networks who are to blame," says Rintels. "The networks get bombarded with thoughtful, reality-oriented scripts. They
simply won't do them. They slam the door on them. They believe that
the only way to get ratings is to feed viewers what conforms to their biases or what has limited resemblance to reality. From 8 to 11 o'clock each
night, television is one long lie."

Innovative thinkers such as Norman Lear, whose work has been prac-   19
tically driven off the tube, don't fault the networks so much as the climate
in which they operate. Says Lear: "All of this country's institutions have
become totally fixated on short-term bottom-line thinking. Everyone
grabs for what might succeed today and the hell with tomorrow. Television just catches more of the heat because it's more visible." Perhaps the
most perceptive assessment of Gerbner's conclusions is offered by one
who has worked both sides of the industry street. Deanne Barkley, a former NBC vice president who now helps run an independent production
house, reports that the negative depictions of women on TV have made it
"nerve-racking" to function as a woman within TV. "No one takes responsibility for the social impact of their shows," says Barkley. "But then
how do you decide where it all begins? Do the networks give viewers what
they want? Or are the networks conditioning them to think that way?"

Gerbner himself has no simple answer to that conundrum. Neither   20
a McLuhanesque shaman nor a Naderesque crusader, he hesitates to
suggest solutions until pressed. Then out pops a pair of provocative notions. Commercial television will never democratize its treatments of
daily life, he believes, until it finds a way to broaden its financial base.
Coincidentally, Federal Communications Commission chairman Mark
Fowler seems to have arrived at much the same conclusion. In exchange
for lifting such government restrictions on TV as the fairness doctrine
and the equal-time rule, Fowler would impose a modest levy on station
owners called a spectrum-use fee. Funds from the fees would be set
aside to finance programs aimed at specialized tastes rather than the
mass appetite. Gerbner enthusiastically endorses that proposal: "Let the
ratings system dominate most of prime time but not every hour of every
day. Let some programs carry advisories that warn: 'This is not for all
of you. This is for nonwhites, or for religious people or for the aged and
the handicapped. Turn it off unless you'd like to eavesdrop.' That would
be a very refreshing thing."

Role

In addition, Gerbner would like to see viewers given an active role   21
in steering the overall direction of television instead of being obliged to
passively accept whatever the networks offer. In Britain, he points out,
political candidates debate the problems of TV as routinely as the issue
of crime. In this country, proposes Gerbner, "every political campaign
should put television on the public agenda. Candidates talk about
schools, they talk about jobs, they talk about social welfare. They're going to have to start discussing this all-pervasive force."

There are no outright villains in this docudrama. Even Gerbner rec-   22
ognizes that network potentates don't set out to proselytize a point of
view; they are simply businessmen selling a mass-market product. At
the same time, their 90 million nightly customers deserve to know the
side effects of the ingredients. By the time the typical American child
reaches the age of reason, calculates Gerbner, he or she will have absorbed more than 30,000 electronic "stories." These stories, he suggests,
have replaced the socializing role of the preindustrial church: they create a "cultural mythology" that establishes the norms of approved behavior and belief. And all Gerbner's research indicates that this new
mythological world, with its warped picture of a sizable portion of society, may soon become the one most of us think we live in.

Who else is telling us that? Howard Beale and his eloquent alarms   23
have faded into offnetwork reruns. At the very least, it is comforting to
know that a real-life Beale is very much with us . . . and *really* watching.

•••••••••••••••••••

Examining the Text

1. Waters reports extensive studies by George Gerbner and his associates which show that heavy television viewers have a generally
"warped" view of reality, influenced by television's own "reality warp"
(paragraph 3). Which viewers do you think would be affected most negatively by these "warped" viewpoints, and why?

2. Gerbner's studies show that "55 percent of prime-time characters are
involved in violent confrontations once a week; in reality, the figure
is less than 1 percent" (9). While violent crime is known to rank as
middle-class America's primary concern most violent crime occurs in
neighborhoods far removed from most middle-class people. How do
you explain these discrepancies? Why is "violent confrontation" so
common on television? How does the violence you see on television affect you?

3. Waters interviewed a number of different people when he wrote this article for *Newsweek*. Collectively, they offer a variety of explanations for and solutions to the limited images television provides. Look closely at these suggested causes and solutions. Which seem most reasonable to you? In general, is Waters's coverage of the issue balanced? Why or why not?

For Group Discussion

This article was first published more than ten years ago. With your group, look again at Gerbner's categories and discuss what significant recent examples suggest about the way current television programming represents reality. Do today's shows seem more accurate than those of ten years ago? As a class, discuss whether or not most viewers want more "reality" on television.

Writing Suggestion

Starting with Gerbner's six categories, analyze any ways you have come to realize that television distorts your views of reality. In an essay, consider the source of these distortions, how it is that you can perceive reality more accurately, and what you think the relationship between television images and "real life" could be.

INTERPRETING TELEVISION

1. TWO GAME SHOWS

The following two pieces are examples of cultural criticism written for a popular audience. Essentially journalistic, both are "reports" that draw heavily on the writers' own particular viewpoints.

Family Feud

Mark Crispin Miller

*W*ho *would have predicted the overwhelming popularity of a show on which two families laugh and cheer and bounce around the set, vying to come up with the most popular response to such earth-shaking topics as "things you can't do when it's raining" and "the items most commonly found at a barbecue"? In the following analysis of* Family Feud, *Mark Crispin Miller attempts to tease out the sources of the show's popularity, and in the process, reveals some of its more insidious aspects.*

As Miller observes, the family bond mentioned in the show's title is illusory: in fact, the structure of the game itself requires that each family member/contestant shed his or her claim to a distinct and unique identity since the game rewards the most common, least creative answers. What results from this process is a plurality of age and race, but not of personality or temper. In other words, despite physical differences, all of the families are "indistinguishably blithe and peppy."

Miller goes on to argue that the show's original host, Richard Dawson, embodies the medium of television itself, and that the show's symbols are a parody of the fictionality of the American family: the opening music, the simulated Victorian portrait, and the needlepoint logo.

As you read, notice how Miller uses humor and a meticulous attention to detail to lighten and soften his fundamentally political argument. Notice also how his use of narrative to retell the "story" of a typical game show masks his critique in such a way that his scathing analysis actually seems subtle rather than bold.

∙∙∙∙∙∙∙∙∙∙∙∙∙∙∙∙∙∙∙∙

"Family Feud" may well be the cleverest game show on TV. It's certainly the most absorbing. "Family Feud" has been on the air since 1975, 1 it comes on (in most cities) twice a day, and yet it hasn't lost its fascination, and probably never will, as long as millions stare at millions of TV sets. When Mark Goodson and his associates first cooked this trifle up, they created one of TV's few abiding things, a spectacle as durable and bright as Johnny Carson, or a no-wax floor.

If you aren't a regular viewer of "Family Feud," you might enjoy a 2 leisurely description. Of course, trying to describe a game show is a bit like trying to describe the kind of dreams you have when half-asleep with fever. Even the weirdest of fantasies, however, has its own implicit structure, and so does "Family Feud," whose generic craziness conceals a form as rigid and significant as the plan of any other public ritual.

The show starts with the usual sudden uproar. "It's time for—'*Fam-* 3 *ily Feud*'!!" someone yells, backed by a screechy din that sounds like bluegrass music played by speed freaks. We see the title, its dark red letters rendered in mock needlepoint across a yellow oval, like an enormous sampler, and then the title turns into some surname—PFISTER, say—also lettered in mock needlepoint. The studio audience goes nuts, the music yelps and twangs, as the oval zips leftward like a sliding door, revealing a sort of mock-Victorian parlor, where the five immobile Pfisters pose in wacky imitation of some old-fashioned family portrait. After the announcer shouts their names, the Pfisters break out of this *tableau vivant* and line up, five abreast, applauding back at the applauding crowd. This rapid process then repeats itself, showing us the Pfisters' rival house—say, GRUBB—and then both little clans come bounding out onto the stage, a hectic edifice of lurid hues and tiny winking lights, and face off gaily, five abreast, each standing in a happy row behind a sort of elongated podium.

Now the music turns to brass, hiccuping and blaring in the Vegas 4 mode, and everybody's clapping. Then, ". . . the *star* of 'Family Feud,'" whoops the announcer, "—*Richard Dawson!!*" The place goes crazier, and out strolls this aging, deeply suntanned figure, resplendent in a roomy three-piece suit of glossy brown or gray, a huge carnation shining on his left lapel. He meanders downstage between the cheering Grubbs and Pfisters, as a much-loved drunk might join a raucous party thrown in his honor, and halts to do a spot of mellow shtick. We see at once that Dawson is no typical M.C., not an unctuous, chortling "host," beaming like a salesman, but rather comes on with the boozy self-possession of a weathered libertine. He seems pure show biz, a veteran of unnumbered poolside hangovers. As he glistens on the screen, his asides a little slurred, his shirt cuffs vast and blinding, you start to feel a little groggy, and your Sony starts to smell of aftershave. And yet, while Dawson thus evinces the authority of smooth decay, he also wears, incongruously, the uniform of high-paid middle management—

the ample suit, the boutonniere, a glittering watch chain. He is, in short, an ingenious combination of intimidating traits. With his gray Neronian bangs, his puffy, umbered face, and his obtrusive vest, he looks like some old Roman debauchee now working as a district manager for Burger King.

The families on "Family Feud" clearly regard this wry and shiny 5 boss, not just with something like affection, but with deep respect. At first, this seems a little strange, given the glaring contrast between him and them. For, whether the Grubbs and Pfisters claim to hail from L.A., the Bronx, or Salt Lake City, they really represent our fabled heartland. Invariably bright-eyed, cheery, vigorous, and neat, these folks all look as stolid and clean-cut as Dawson seems unwholesome. Although he's clearly not their type, however, Dawson counteracts his daunting aura with intense displays of flattering concern. He falls all over them from start to finish, with an oleaginous noblesse oblige perhaps unrivaled on TV.

After his moment downstage, he turns to do some quick prelimi- 6 nary schmoozing with each team's captain, usually the Dad or elder brother. Leaning forward chummily, with a familiar drawl, Dawson orders Mr. Pfister to identify the family, and the eager patriarch booms back at him, with strained heartiness: "Well, Richard," Pfister thunders, "this is my beautiful wife Adele—my lovely daughter Gina—my good lookin' son Todd," and so on, as the camera pans across this taut ménage, each Pfister greeting "Richard" with a bellow or a chirp, according to gender. There's some talk about how Pfister earns his livelihood, and then, at the chat's conclusion, the team formally presents the star of "Family Feud" with some homely offering, usually handmade, such as a bag of cookies, a necklace made of chestnuts, or an inscribed hat.

After a similar brief visit with the Grubbs, Dawson shouts, "Let's 7 play the feud!" and swaggers over to his central place behind a smaller podium, beneath a big bright board comprised of numbered slats. A Pfister and a Grubb stand ready at his left and right, as Dawson reads a question, which he always introduces with the same revealing formula: "One hundred people surveyed, top six answers on The Board, here's the question: Name an appliance that's always plugged in." Grubb and Pfister each lunge forward, and the first to smack a massive button on Dawson's podium gets to answer first: "A vacuum cleaner!" hollers Grubb, who is not, perhaps, as quick as his right hand. Chuckling, Dawson looks up at The Board: "*Vacuum cleaner?*" he calls out, but The Board is still, and there flashes over it a coarse red "X," emphasized by a derisive honk. Dawson turns to Pfister, who, knowing her appliances, shrieks out, "A *toaster!*" Dawson addresses The Board with this wiser answer, whereupon one of the slats turns over with a ping, revealing the word "toaster" and a certain number, representing points.

The Pfisters exult, because they've won the chance to play this question out. Dawson proceeds down the line along their podium, asking each of them to name another ever-plugged-in thing. Until the schedule starts to tighten, Dawson will conduct each brief interrogation with an efficient stream of cagey banter; and he always greets each female panelist with a loud kiss on the lips, as the menfolk stand there, grinning tightly. (The kiss is Dawson's trademark.) The Pfisters keep it up until they win or lose the round. That is, they either guess every answer on The Board, thereby winning all the points available, or they come up with three "wrong" answers, whereupon the Grubbs jump in and try to guess one answer yet unchosen, stealing the round if they succeed. 8

The game goes on through several rounds, each devoted to another mundane question—one that refers either to the world of goods ("Name something you have two of in your bathroom"), the teachings of TV ("Name the wealthiest man in show business"), or the routines of daily life ("Name the first thing you do when you wake up in the morning"). Finally, whichever family earns three hundred points gets to play the "Lightning Round." After a show of deft commiseration with the losing Grubbs, who, no less upbeat, promptly disappear, Dawson moves down front and center, as one quivering Pfister comes to stand beside him and another prances off stage left. All is quiet; the Pfister's head, inclined, eyes closed, as if in prayer, appears in closeup—and then Dawson reads off five quick questions, the Pfister blurting out an answer to each one, as fifteen seconds tick away. When time's up, both turn around to hot applause, and face a sort of scoreboard at the rear of the stage. With one familiar arm around the Pfister's neck, Dawson repeats each question and reply, pausing as each answer shows up on the scoreboard with some number next to it. Once we get the grand subtotal, Pfister No. 2 sprints back to undergo the same ordeal. The suspense is captivating, as we wait to find out if the Pfisters have racked up two hundred points, which will win them $10,000. 9

If the family succeeds, the crowd once again goes berserk, and the winning Pfisters grab each other, bouncing up and down as if attempting a collective levitation. As Dawson wanders offstage, many further Pfisters, hitherto unknown, come bolting down the aisles to join their kin. We cut to a commercial. When the show comes back, the much-augmented house of Pfister stands spread out, euphorically, across the stage, and Dawson hands one of them (usually a tot or oldster) a big sheet of white cardboard, with the amount they've won inscribed in Magic Marker, in a childish scrawl. Sometimes, if there are any kids onstage, he hands out lollipops. Finally, we see the credits, and, under 10 them, the Pfisters frolicking and clapping to the rhythm of the grating theme.

What is this all about? Why is this show so popular, why so engrossing? Unlike other game shows, "Family Feud" is never heatedly competitive, nor does the cash prize ultimately matter. Dawson tends to discourage the grim desire to score, turning faintly chilly when confronted with impatient avarice. Usually, however, he doesn't need to convey such scorn, since the players are nearly always buoyant, either good winners or good losers. In fact, both families have more or less cleaned up before the game begins, since the show pays for their trips west, puts them up in a hotel for two nights, and provides them with a car and a comfortable per diem.

If the point of "Family Feud" is not the prize, then maybe it's the emphasis on kinship. "Family Feud" would seem the most straightforward *family* show on television. Its "stars" appear to be just plain folks, exemplars of the old domestic virtues. For one thing, each household sticks together with amazing loyalty. No matter how stupid someone's answer, even if Dawson gets the giggles, the others show maniacal support, clapping hard and roaring out, "Good answer! Good answer!" Such clannishness seems out of place on television, whose impulse is to shatter families, not unite them, ceaselessly exhorting each and every "individual" to go his/her "own way," i.e., to live a "life" of nonstop buying. "Family Feud" appears a broad exception to the TV rule, from its opening title, with "family" proclaimed in scarlet letters, through its closing video portrait of the Pfisters/Grubbs/O'Rourkes/Barzinis/ Goldbergs/Jeffersons/Wongs/Romeros, each group rewarded, seemingly, for its intense togetherness.

And yet, in fact, it isn't the familial bond that wins the prize on "Family Feud," but the family's successful self-erasure. Each of Dawson's questions is a test of sameness, its answers based on tallies of "one hundred people surveyed," well ahead of time, by the show's producers. A "correct" reply is therefore not the smartest, but the *least* inventive answer, matching an alleged "consensus" expertly defined and validated by the show itself. Thus the irresistible appeal of "Family Feud" is also the attraction of TV, which tells us endlessly what "we" believe, thereby using our supposed group sentiments to reconfirm its own authority. "Family Feud" is basically a festive variant of those other forms of modern tabulation, the marketing survey and the opinion poll. And so it is precisely like TV itself—a pseudopopulist diversion based on crude statistics.

For all its seeming family pride, then, each group that plays on "Family Feud" does not come on to manifest its own discrete identity, but rather struggles to get rid of it. Victory demands the absolute suppression of any wayward thought or preference, any eccentricity that might define the family apart from TV's bland reconstruction of ourselves. If they want to win, the players must respond with ready minds of total emptiness, letting the mythic mass speak through them. Thus "Family Feud" is actually a high-speed ritual of absorption, which has its consummation only when five beings demonstrate their own ecstatic averageness. In visual terms, the real reward is not the money, which we never glimpse, nor even Dawson's cardboard token, but the climactic moment when those nameless others pour from the audience onto the stage, creating the illusion of an oceanic merger, as the separated clan now happily dissolves into the gathering flood of erstwhile watchers.

Once we recall its proper meaning, the title too suggests this termi- 15 nal absorption. A "family feud" is not, in fact, a dispute between two separate houses, but one that divides a *single* family into warring factions. The show's real purpose is to celebrate, not specific households, but the encroaching, all-inclusive tribe of viewers, that unseen mass into which those households long to be reintegrated, nervously competing for acceptance like extruded siblings. In other words, all the families on "Family Feud" appear to be related to each other, seeming fundamentally alike, however various their surnames, hue, or points of origin.

These superficial differences mean quite a lot to the show's creators, 16 who consider "Family Feud" a tremendous example of progressive toleration. As the show's producer, Howard Felsher, told me, it is "the only game show to use interracial families," and the only one that features handicapped players (other shows preferring to exclude them, since viewers turn nasty when they see afflicted persons lose). Dawson, furthermore, meticulously kisses every female, "irrespective of age, color, or religion," a practice that inspires "a lot of hate mail."

Even if it does offend a few thousand crackpots, however, all the os- 17 tensible diversity on "Family Feud" actually amounts to nothing, because the program's many families are, in fact, impossible to tell apart. Some may be multicolored, another may include a paraplegic, but nearly all are indistinguishably blithe and peppy, displaying exactly the same "good attitude." This is the only quality that counts on "Family Feud," whose process of selection is, therefore, exquisitely exclusive, since it is intended to screen out, not any patent traits, but subtler deficiencies of mood or temper.

Of course, the show's custodians are unconscious of its real exclu- 18 siveness. Felsher's paean to the show's warmhearted liberalism was immediately followed, and subverted, by his account of just how few would-be contestants finally ever make it onto "Family Feud." "Within two or three years," he recalled, "we had milked L.A. of the cream of

L.A. families," and so they set out to the north and east, in search of further families no less fresh and thick than that original Californian product. By now the producers have extracted players from every state of the union, and continue to maintain their stores with frequent and expensive junkets all around, inspecting, on each stop, about eight hundred families in four days. All in all, it costs roughly $500,000 per annum "just to keep the show good," that is, to make sure that everyone we watch will seem to certify the program's image of the ideal family. A player might sometimes play a little too intently, but there is never any bickering, no livid disappointment, no angry blame on "Family Feud," whose teams all bounce and clap alike, all cheer each other's errors and successes equally.

The families' apparent sameness must, in part, reflect an actual similarity. For instance, many of the families represent the same vague social stratum. Although we sometimes see a team whose captain is a cabby, say, or an ophthalmologist, most of the father figures seem to inhabit that gray realm of low-to-middle management wherein Richard Dawson's vest appears to symbolize the highest power. However, the players' sameness may have less to do with any prior class identity than with the implicit pressures of the show itself, which will reward with its exposure only those contestants who can and will behave like grateful employees, or overstimulated children. And yet the presentation is more complicated still, because this TV show does not just fabricate a certain image of the happy norm, but at the same time undercuts that image, in order to enhance the dominance of TV. 19

For it is basically TV which Dawson stands for, TV that lends him his charisma, charging his outlandish image with its cool power. Although his suit and suntan each evince a different kind of potency, it is TV that makes him seem unassailably superior to his dim, childlike wards. Whereas these indistinct contestants just flash by, tense and squealing, Dawson is a finished man of television, having mastered its style completely in the course of his imperceptible career: after an apprenticeship in British show biz, he became a regular on "Hogan's Heroes," and then a "permanent panelist" on "The Match Game," a frequent guest host on "The Tonight Show," and is now a quintessential TV entity, as smart, detached, and self-contradictory as the medium containing it. 20

Dawson approaches his provincial visitors exactly as TV regards its viewers. On the face of it, he seems to think the world of his players. He beams and coos all over each bright guest, as if, beneath his smarmy surface, there beats the doting heart of some old grandma. And yet this deft solicitude is not maternal, but commercial, the factitious "caring" of the corporate ad. Like McDonald's, Sears, American Airlines, IBM, etc., 21

Dawson feigns a tender admiration for his subjects that actually belittles them. He always makes a beeline for the youngest or the oldest or the one on crutches, singling out, for his most ardent flatteries, those players who are most helpless. And when the captain describes his dismal job ("Well, Richard, I'm the assistant comptroller of a major hospital supply corporation!"), Dawson marvels politely, as you might treat a nine-year-old who tells you his career plans. Thus, through his pretense of esteem for these figures, Dawson genially exacts their full compliance, getting them to jump around and squeak like tots assaulting some department store Santa. Praising Dawson's fulsome tact, Howard Felsher put his finger squarely (if, again, unwittingly) on the crucial contradiction: "Dawson goes to each person, and *talks* to them, and gets to *know* them, and pats them on the *head*, and gives them a *lollipop*. He treats them like *human beings!*"

And Dawson dominates these human beings, not just by patronizing them, but also through the constant threat of his incisive ridicule. His is that televisual sangfroid that we also note in such comedians as, for instance, Johnny Carson, David Letterman, or Martin Mull, and in (again) most TV commercials—that air of laidback irony against which all enthusiasm seems contemptible. Underlying his displays of maudlin warmth, in other words, there is in Richard Dawson a relentless impulse to deride, with true aplomb, whatever is uncool or idiosyncratic, i.e., whatever is outside of, or less cool than, television. Whenever someone gives an odd or idiotic answer, Dawson devastates it swiftly with a murmured gag; and he often breaks into sudden fits of mimicry, putting on a redneck's twang when talking to the Arbs of Arkansas, doing Sessue Hayakawa in his exchanges with the Nakamuras of New York, and so on. Despite his able clucking, we always sense the abler parodist that lurks within; and so, we gather, do the families, who perceive that Dawson could, if he felt like it, utterly humiliate them, and who therefore seek to mollify this witty manager through those ritual gestures of propitiation: they let him kiss their women, and they try to impress their innocence upon him with pathetic tokens of their wholesomeness.   22

Thus they attempt to win his, and TV's, acceptance, but the attempt   23
must fail, because that joyful norm which they've been made to represent does not exist. The image of community on "Family Feud," and in the sunny worlds of numberless commercials, is merely a device whose function is to make TV seem like our happy home; whereas TV, in fact, only keeps us dispossessed, an extended mob of orphans with our noses pressed against the glass. The families on the screen may seem to have arrived in that bright place which we can only gape at, they may seem to have embodied that ideal which TV disingenuously proffers; and yet all they're really doing is what we do when we sit and watch: trying

desperately to keep up with that low "reality" which TV and its sponsors have arranged for us. Although Dawson's questions seem simply to refer, objectively, to our bleak status quo, in fact they reinforce it. Implicitly ruling out the possibility of other ways of life, they require each player to know perfectly the consumer's trivial daily world, and nothing else. The show rewards those who, through their "right" answers, manifest a dumb acceptance of "the way it is"—the daily grind, the flood of products, the names and faces on TV.

Within this exhausting system, it becomes impossible to cling for 24 long to any close community, although we are repeatedly enticed with images of that elusive closeness. It is therefore fitting that this apparent tribute to the family should turn out to be a shattering burlesque, as we discover once we take another look at the explosive opening of "Family Feud." The mock sampler, the mock bluegrass, the mock-Victorian mock portrait each suggest TV's familiar attitude of up-to-date contempt for the archaic family, an institution that once seemed to resist the blandishments of TV and its clientele. The opening, moreover, not only jeers at those dated symbols, but visibly subverts them, showing that TV has now replaced those emblems of familial fixity with its own endless, pointless, self-advancing change. The "sampler" slides away, the figures in the "portrait" jump into motion, the "bluegrass music," suggestive of the settled clan, turns into Richard Dawson's cue. Paradoxically, this spectacle itself has now become familiar, although it never can replace that real community which it applauds and cancels out. Absorbed by this off-putting introduction, we watch until the family that cheers together disappears together, and then we stare at something else.

Afterword

In 1988, LBS communications produced a new version of "Family 1 Feud" for prime-time broadcast in the fall. Dawson "was never considered for the job," claimed LBS's chairman. "It's not that he didn't do an effective job, but you've got to move on." Dawson was replaced by a comedian named Ray Combs, who started his career doing warm-up routines for sitcom audiences. "Richard Dawson was great," Combs told *Advertising Age* in February 1988, "but his time for that show has passed. There are going to be people who love him, and people who love me. That's show business."

Certainly there is nothing new or interesting about such pitiless re- 2 placement—an essential feature of the market system generally, "show business" included. It is worth noting, however, that the second "Family Feud" was immediately touted as a show better than the first— better because more ironic. Thus *Advertising Age:* "Remember the osculating Richard Dawson who planted his lips on every female contestant on the old 'Family Feud'? Forget him. This new version dispenses with blandishments in favor of gibes. Host Ray Combs is a stand-up comic who trades jokes with the contestants. And it works."

The implication here is that Dawson was not also an ironist, not full   3
of "gibes," but an old-fashioned suitor, quaintly serious with his "blandishments" and "osculations," and therefore laughable himself, in our cool eyes. Thus does the culture of TV continually sell the flattering myth of both "our" recent graduation into irony, and the comic earnestness of everyone who came before.

....

Examining the Text

1. In paragraphs 2–10 Miller gives a detailed, if satirical, description of the game show *Family Feud* and its original host, Richard Dawson. In the rest of the essay, Miller analyzes the show. How does the long opening description help prepare readers for the subsequent analysis? Do you think Miller assumes his readers have never seen *Family Feud,* or does he want them to see it through his eyes?

2. Miller rejects the idea that *Family Feud* promotes family togetherness, arguing instead that it presents "the family's successful self-erasure" (paragraph 13). What reasons does he give for this? Is this a legitimate assertion? Why, or why not?

3. *Family Feud* continues to be a popular syndicated game show, although with a third new host and a somewhat revised format that often uses, rather than real families, celebrity "families" (such as cast members from a soap opera) who play for "their favorite charities." How does substituting celebrity "families" for real families tie in with Miller's analysis?

For Group Discussion

Miller contends that *Family Feud* rewards "averageness." As a group choose two or three other game shows with which all members are familiar, and list the kinds of contestants they attract and the skills (or lack of skills) these shows reward. As a class try to reach some consensus about what the average television game show today values.

Writing Suggestion

Miller argues that *Family Feud* both fabricates an image of the "happy norm" and undercuts that image "in order to enhance the dominance of TV." In an essay consider what Miller means by this, and apply the idea to two or three other kinds of television programs, such as situation comedies or made-for-television movies.

Triumph of the Wheel
Lewis Grossberger

*W*ritten *with the cynicism and humor characteristic of* Rolling Stone *magazine, Lewis Grossberger's article may be loosely characterized as "cultural materialist," meaning that it studies a cultural product in its historical, political, and economic contexts. Grossberger sets out to investigate the immense and wide-spread popularity of the TV game show* Wheel of Fortune. *It's not difficult, he discovers, to identify the material manifestations of the show's success—forty-two million viewers, a $250 million selling price, and a parking space near Johnny Carson's for* Wheel of Fortune *host Pat Sajak. However, finding the reasons behind this success is not quite as easy.*

Ultimately, Grossberger argues, Wheel of Fortune *is the quintessential, "state-of-the-art eighties game show" because it plays out the "average" American's fantasies of instant wealth; it exploits desperate responses to desperate economic times in the Reagan-Bush era. Like a lottery or Vegas slot machine,* Wheel of Fortune *is a "wish-fulfillment machine," and the contestants are virtually invisible—allowing you, the viewer, to participate in your own little fantasy of economic well-being.*

As you read, *notice how Grossberger's use of irony and puns and his chatty tone draw you in while also suggesting his opinions of the show, its contestants, and its viewers. In the way that he writes himself into his own text—mentioning his sleeping patterns, his interaction with the show's stars and producers, and so forth—Grossberger in fact seems to be writing not only about game shows, but also about the act of writing itself, and his participation in that act.*

• • • • • • • • • • • • • • • • • • •

The first time I saw "Wheel of Fortune," I thought it was a vapid piece of fluff that could appeal only to brain-dead TV zombies. Five minutes of this tedious dreck was all it took to waft me sleepward.   1

But the second time my reaction was different. The second time I realized—having been assigned meantime to write an article on the show that would bring a much-needed fee—that "Wheel of Fortune" was, in fact, a fascinating, deeply significant national phenomenon, the comprehension of which was essential to any proper understanding of our era.   2

Thank God I'm open-minded.   3

Soon I was wafting westward on an urgent sociophilosophical in-   4
quiry, clutching an envelope fat with press clippings that further impressed upon me the importance of my subject. *The Washington Post's*
TV critic said, "Wheel" is watched by 42 million people a day. *Time* said
"Wheel" is the highest-rated syndicated series in television history. *The
New York Times* said "Wheel" is so popular it has become a dominant
factor in TV scheduling, sometimes wreaking havoc with local and network news. *People* said that Vanna White has blond hair, weighs 107,
measures thirty-six-twenty-three-thirty-three, and adores greasy hamburgers from White Castle.

Vanna White is the hostess on "Wheel of Fortune," which should   5
not be confused with the master of ceremonies, who is Pat Sajak, although he is not called the MC but the host. Despite the fact that
Vanna's function is mainly decorative and that she is rarely permitted
to utter more than a parting "bye," she has become, *People* assured me,
a bigger cult sensation than Paul Shaffer, Max Headroom, or even
Willard Scott.

The only thing the press failed to tell me was *why*.   6

Why a silly game show based on a simple children's spelling game   7
and a cheesy carnival wheel so captivates the mightiest nation on earth.
Now here was a journalistic challenge worthy of Murrow, of Woodward
and Bernstein, perhaps even of the great Geraldo Rivera. Immune to the
show's mysterious allure, I could operate with scientific detachment. By
God, I would take up the gauntlet. I would find out why—or doze off
trying.

"I swear on the grave of every game-show host who ever lived that   8
I have no idea," said Pat Sajak.

Pat Sajak is overqualified for his job in that he is capable of wit. A for- 9
mer TV weatherman, he sounds a little like Bob Newhart and looks
like . . . well, if Dick Clark went through that teleportation gizmo from
The Fly and this time a chipmunk sneaked in, out would come Pat Sajak.

I talked with Pat Sajak in his dressing room and found him a per-   10
sonable and modest man who readily admits that game-show hosting
"is kind of a dopey way to make a living." I talked as rapidly as possible. When I arrived at the NBC studios in fabled Burbank, the publicity
lady who collected me said that the staff would be taping five half-hour
shows that night and that I could examine Pat and Vanna only during
the fifteen-to-twenty-minute breaks between shows. She was very
apologetic, but, you know, everyone wants them, it's so exhausting, we
have to protect them. I groused a bit—journalistic reflex—but, in truth,
it didn't matter. Both host and hostess had been asked to explain the *why*
before. They never could.

"I mean, I know why it's successful," said Pat. "It's an easy game to   11
play—you know, the people at home, unless you're a total moron, can
generally solve the puzzles ahead of the people in the studio, so you feel
kind of superior. It's a compelling game. You walk by the set and the
puzzle's on and you tend to play along. But that just explains why it's a
successful game show. Why it has gone beyond success to become—I
don't know—part of the pop culture, I haven't the foggiest idea. I don't
think anyone knows."

I assured him that I would know. Soon. For that was my quest. My   12
Grail. He responded politely enough, but I could see he was skeptical.
It seemed like we'd been talking only a few minutes when a pounding
on the door commenced, and a voice demanded Pat's presence, and he
went forth to hostify.

The "Wheel of Fortune" set looks like that of most eighties game   13
shows, decorated in feel-good Vegas. Gaudy with bright splashes of
color, flashing lights, and revolving mounds of, as the announcer
usually describes them, "fantastic prizes, fabulous and exciting merchandise." The studio audience of close to two hundred well-behaved
androids was stashed safely out of the way behind a sideline array of
cameras, electronic gear, crew, and staff. As the taping began, I noticed that the rousing "Wheel . . . of . . . Fortune!" chant that kicks off
each show is canned, and that the gold curtain Vanna White waltzes
through so fetchingly when introduced has no other function whatever.
It drops magically from the ceiling for her big entrance, then quickly
reascends.

The actual gaming consists of a word puzzle and, naturally, a wheel.   14
Large, multicolored, divided into slim wedges, each marked with a different dollar amount, the wheel is set horizontally in front of the three
contestants, so they can lean forward and spin it. By going so, they may
accumulate a dollar account to be later spent on prizes.

Between twirls, they take whacks at the word puzzle, which is ba-   15
sically that old childhood chestnut, hangman. The puzzle is mounted on
a big vertical display board on a platform that's hauled on and off the
set by crewmen at alarming speeds, usually with the courageous Vanna
aboard. A display of blank tiles tells the contestants how many words
and letters there are in a mystery phrase. As the contestants guess at
the letters and Vanna rushes purposefully about, uncovering those correctly called out, the mystery phrase (usually something as banal as
"walking on air" or "curiosity killed the cat") gradually emerges until
someone identifies it. The winner then may go shopping among the
price-tagged prizes until his or her account is exhausted. At the end of
the proceedings, the champion tackles a bonus-round puzzle for a grand
prize.

Viewed at home, the whole ephemeral affair slips by in a smooth, 16
slick, seamless blur, leaving no shadow or aftertaste. Conditioned as I
was to somnolence, it was all I could do to stay alert. Fortunately, I was
allowed to roam.

I watched one show from the control room, where the personnel de- 17
bated whether a contestant on an earlier show got a fair shake when he
correctly guessed "the patience of Job" but was disqualified for mispro-
nouncing "Job." Then I spied on the letter lighters, two staffers who sit
backstage and illuminate the tiles that show Vanna what to flip. A serene
crewman named Vern pressed buttons, and a serious young research
coordinator named Cheryl indicated which buttons. Over Vern's control board were crayoned the words WHEEL OF TORTURE.

"They all use the same letters," said Vern, indicating a contestant. 18
"Watch, she'll say *t.*" He was right.

During one break I was taken to meet the hostess. Vanna was in her 19
dressing room, snacking from a take-out dish and wearing a snappy off-
the-shoulder number. (She changes costume and hairdo for each show.)
She was very energetic and cheerful and was able to maintain, under
close interrogation, not only that Vanna White was her real name but
also that she had known four other Vannas while growing up in South
Carolina.

A small-town girl, Vanna, who is now twenty-nine, drove to Holly- 20
wood in a U-Haul truck six years ago, because it was a childhood dream.
Hollywood, not trucks. After landing some bit parts in movies, she
heard that "Wheel of Fortune" needed a new hostess, and she beat out
two hundred other young women, even though in her final on-air au-
dition she was so nervous her knees shook and she couldn't talk. Fortunately, speech was not a job qualification.

Laboring under the cloud of bimbosity imposed by the alternately 21
fawning and smirking media, Vanna told me what she always tells in-
terviewers: "It's a lot harder than it looks. It really is."

It seemed to me the wrong tactic. Were I her media adviser, I'd coun- 22
sel this approach: "Hey, I look great, I walk sexy. For this they pay me
a hundred big ones and put me on the cover of *People*. I should turn
them down? Is it my fault I live in a society that accentuates superficial
values?"

Too soon came the inevitable pounding, and Vanna vanished, leav- 23
ing me back on the set, watching a woman named Ruth win a Toyota by
guessing "League of Women Voters." I talked to a contestant from
Fresno named Bill. Bill told me that his family watches "Wheel of Fortune" all the time and that he was so good at it his wife got after him to
become a contestant. He did. But he hadn't won a Toyota, and he
seemed a little tense.

I was not to meet "Wheel's" biggest winner. Who is that? Why,   24
Merv Griffin. Yes, the same Merv Griffin who has spent the last twenty-
three years demonstrating what Johnny Carson would be like without
jokes. Merv always did seem a bit dazed, as though his mind were on
something else. Now we know what. Puzzles. It was Merv who invented "Wheel of Fortune," hired Pat Sajak and Vanna White, and still
approves every single puzzle. It was Merv who recently sold Merv Griffin Enterprises, which produces "Wheel" (not to mention "Jeopardy"
and "Dance Fever") to Coca-Cola for—my fingers go numb as I type
this—a reported $250 million. According to Tom Shales, TV critic for
The Washington Post, Merv was rumored to have run around his office
waving his quarter-of-a-billion-dollar check in the air, joking that he
couldn't find anyone to cash it.

Puzzles. All this from puzzles. The man is a lifelong puzzle junkie.   25
"You would think," said Sajak, "that a man who's worth $84 billion, or
whatever he is, would have better things to do than make up puzzles—
but he does. If you have lunch with Merv, the waiter comes over and
says, 'May I take your order?' and Merv goes, 'Ooo! "May I take your
order?" What a great puzzle!' And he writes it down."

People, we underestimated Merv Griffin. We dismissed him as   26
some kind of welfare agency for the Gabor sisters. But Merv figured out
what America wanted, and he provided it. And became very, very rich.
Much too rich to talk to the likes of me. But Nancy Jones, "Wheel's" producer, a woman who actually has puzzle meetings with Merv, did. Her
take on *why* was family. "It's a show the whole family can enjoy. Anybody from six to a hundred can watch 'Wheel of Fortune.' They're gonna
understand what's going on. You know, there are kids in college now
that learned their A B Cs by watching 'Wheel.'" Interesting, I thought,
but not convincing. Not incisively all-encompassing. After all, there are
plenty of family shows that don't have 42 million viewers.

If stats like 42 million or quarter of a billion haven't sufficiently de-   27
fined the scope of "Wheel's" triumph for you, surely Pat Sajak's parking spot will. It was one away from Johnny Carson's. Now *that's* success. I discovered this when Pat gave me a lift back to my hotel, a nice
gesture. But he voiced a depressing vision. "This could literally be a
show that is never canceled," he said. "You know, my grandkid will be
up there, spinning the wheel, saying silly things and putting on hair
spray."

Considerably sobered, I retired and the next morning flew away. I'd   28
already spent an evening on this investigation—in my view more than
enough. En route to the airport, a chatty cabby pointed out an evocative
sight: a new, exclusive real-estate development on a hill where, he said,
the houses start at $1 million. The hill had previously served as a

garbage dump, and the driver indicated a pumping station built to clear away the methane gas constantly seeping forth. So scarce is land in L.A. there had been no problem finding wealthy people to reside on top of Old Stinky.

Soon afterward I was on the plane thinking about "Wheel of Fortune," which, as always, acted as a soporific. I dreamed of the lovely Vanna. She's in a terrific gold lamé jump suit, and she's starring in a big-budget disaster movie (a silent, oddly) about a gassy mountain threatening to explode and bury a nervous populace neck deep in putrid lava. Desperately trying to avert panic, Mayor Merv announces that the mountain, with its shining edifices concealing a rotten nether world, is merely a metaphor for an overly materialistic society, but then he whispers to me that only I can save the day—if I can complete this common, everyday phrase: 29

V-C-R---S THR-LLS

Then Pat Sajak's grandkid spins the wheel. The pointer falls on BANKRUPT, and Swill Hill erupts, burying me neck deep in lethal sludge. I woke high over the Jersey swamps, and I had the answer. I knew *why*.

Start with the game show revival. Game shows have been with us since the days of old-time radio. When TV arrived in the late forties, they proved easily adaptable to the new medium, taking various forms. There were celebrity-panel shows like "What's My Line" and "I've Got a Secret!'" humiliation shows like "Truth or Consequences," and oddities like "You Bet Your Life," on which Groucho Marx posed the classic consolation-prize question "Who's buried in Grant's Tomb?" 30

Then arose the big-money quiz show, a world unto itself. Programs like "The $64,000 Question" and "Twenty-One" became phenomenal hits, and contestants like Charles Van Doren, a handsome young Columbia University professor, became national heroes. Even before the scandal broke, it was one of the strangest episodes in TV history. Imagine millions of Americans riveted by the spectacle of brain athletes struggling with impossible multipart questions whose answers not one viewer in a million had a clue to. (A student then, I always suspected that the secret appeal was the joy of watching someone else sweat out a vicious final exam from which you were exempt.) 31

When the news came in 1958 that some of the winners had been fed answers, a gullible nation reeled. Careers were destroyed, innocence was lost, legislation was passed to ensure that such a tragedy could never again be visited upon our land. And game shows disappeared. 32

Temporarily. In television, nothing successful ever dies. Producers like game shows because they're cheap. There's one set and few performers; you can tape a week's worth of shows in a day; and many of the prizes are donated by manufacturers. Sponsors have to love game shows, too. Their products in the commercials blend right into the endless parade of prizes.

By the sixties, game shows were back, though largely confined to 33 the nine-to-twelve morning ghetto, with more modest prizes and a party atmosphere of easygoing fun. And now it's the eighties and the game show is king. Why? Just look to your politico-economic Big Picture.

As in the fifties, a conservative Republican is ensconced in the White 34 House, and the nation prospers. But it's a nervous prosperity. The economy is stagnant, and there's a whiff of trouble ahead with our national debt ballooning, farms in crisis, banks at the mercy of tottering banana republics, our industry looking anemic and backward compared to Japan's, and droves of nomads roaming the streets. Lots of families are doing well (with two people working), but many middle classers and blue collars are having trouble making ends meet. Those who have wealth are encouraged to flaunt it. Consuming runs amok. Yuppies graze. The media fling the rich and famous in your face. The unrelenting message is that if you haven't made it big, you're a schmuck. Increasingly, the American dream seems to coalesce into a narrow vision of mere wealth. And people seem willing to do anything for it: wheel and deal, rig stocks, sell national secrets, peddle crack, anything to score. So what's a poor would-be entrepreneur to do who hasn't the guts or opportunity for any of that? Well, he can turn to the little man's last resorts—lotteries and sweepstakes (bigger than ever), the track, the numbers, Vegas, Atlantic City, and . . . on a fantasy level, game shows.

Game shows are part of the wish-fulfillment machine that helps left- 35 out Americans maintain the hope that anyone can hit it big, even if he has no navy codes to sell the Russians. But of all the game shows, why "Wheel of Fortune"? It gives away no cash. Its prizes are no more opulent than those of other shows. It lacks gunshots and nudity.

"Wheel of Fortune" has been on the air since 1975. With Chuck 36 Woolery (whom Sajak replaced in 1981) as host, "Wheel" became a fixture of NBC's morning schedule and eventually television's highest-rated syndicated game show. It was the only one at the network to escape the ax when the legendary Fred Silverman became convinced that game shows were dead.

In the fall of eighty-three, "Wheel's" producers decided to spin off 37 a syndicated nighttime version. It was a momentous decision. Syndicated shows are sold directly to local stations by independent distributors. This is attractive to station owners, who get to keep a bigger chunk of advertising revenue than they do from network shows. The new "Wheel" was aimed at the so-called prime-access slot. That's the hour before prime time, which the FCC requires to be set aside for nonnetwork programming, believing, in its charmingly idiotic way, that this will stimulate diversity.

When the nighttime "Wheel of Fortune" debuted, the slot was occupied by magazine shows like "Entertainment Tonight" and "PM Magazine." The conventional wisdom was that only older women—not the bigger-spending eighteen-to-forty-five mixed audience advertisers drool for—watched gamers. But "Wheel" took off. Soon it was on 163 stations, in many cities twice a day. It was huge. 38

Obviously, night gave "Wheel" bigger audience potential than day had. More sets are on at night. (Daytime "Wheel" pulls a measly 8 million faces.) But night alone doesn't explain the show's hegemony. What does explain it is the subtle but powerful wonder ingredient all successful game shows have, but none so purely as "Wheel of Fortune." It starts with a V, like Vanna. It's called Vicariousness. 39

Vicariousness. "Wheel of Fortune" creates the illusion for the hardworking treadmill trotting Middle American yearner (the show's greatest strength is outside the major media markets) that he or she is in the big game. Viewers don't exactly identify with the contestants; they *become* the contestants. 40

Look at the elements of the show. 41

The Players: Unlike the dramatized big domes of the fifties, "Wheel" contestants are ordinary folk who serve as the viewers' surrogates. In the whoopee-cushion seventies, game-show contestants screamed, bounced, and wet themselves, but in the we-mean-business eighties, Americans are cooler and less likely to appear in public dressed as yams. "Wheel" subtly de-emphasizes its contestants, who seem interchangeable. Pat introduces these undemonstrative, low-profile types with the briefest possible questioning, then the camera quickly moves off them and zooms in on the game. With the contestants relegated to the background, the viewer can put himself in their place and play. And when a winner goes prize picking, we see only a small head shot in a corner of the screen; the main focus is on the merchandise. Even if undefeated, a contestant is booted out after three days. No stars are born here. (Which is why there's no chance "Wheel of Fortune" is rigged—the producers don't care who wins.) In your fantasy, you are the star. 42

The Game: Both games promise easy success, one through luck, the other skill. The wheel—hypnotic, alluring, symbolic of nearly everything—is luckier than a roulette wheel, since it can yield only two bad outcomes: BANKRUPT or LOSE A TURN. Any other spin wins. Nice odds. 43

The word puzzle is simple but compelling—it gets easier as you play, because more letters fill in. (No Gloomy Gus, Merv discarded the morbid scoring system of the original hangman, which utilizes a stick figure dangling from a gallows. Like casino owners, game-show proprietors want you to be cheery.) As Pat Sajak noted, viewers often solve the puzzle before contestants. With the whole family watching, someone at home is almost bound to. The result: You feel happy, excited, superior. You're chalking up wins. You're on a roll.

The Payoff: During play, the wheel-whirling contestants (and, by extension, the viewers) are given credit. A nice touch. Who doesn't love credit? It's like betting on someone else's tab. And when you win, you don't win mere cash or some preordained prize. You go *shopping!* A brilliant touch. Shopping may be the ultimate thrill in this commodity-crazed era, an actual addiction for some. And it doesn't hurt "Wheel," in the yuppie department, either. Merv himself once said, "It's like being let loose on Rodeo Drive." As the winner shops, the camera lovingly roves around the prize showcase, as though the viewers' own eyeballs have been let loose amid the VCRs, Isuzu pickups, Tahitian vacations, and ceramic Dalmatians. "Wheel's" ambiance blends the organized excitement of the casino with the primal pull of the department store.

The Cast: Game-show hosts are permitters and forgivers. Their benign presence signals that it's okay to indulge your greed, just in case some shred of conscience or old-fashioned values intrudes to make you feel guilty for craving wealth without work. Pat Sajak is today's kind of authority figure: casual, low-key, jocular, even a bit irreverent. Dignified and well dressed, he could be a yuppie cleric, lawyer, or doctor. He could switch jobs with Ronald Reagan and little would change. Merv has said Pat is like everyone's son-in-law. He must have meant everyone's fantasy son-in-law.

And Vanna? Pat Sajak likes to say that Vanna's silence gives her a mysterious air. But there isn't any mystery. Her personality shines through without benefit of speech. She's a *cheerleader.* Your own personal cheerleader. Her most vital function is not really her letter turning (artistic though it is) but her clapping! She is forever clapping for the contestants (all of them—Vanna is impartial). Despite her glitzy outfits, which sophisticates find tacky but most Americans probably find glamorous, she's a throwback to the kind of simple, sunny, apple-pie-sexy, all-American girl next door who'd be content to stay on the sidelines cheering for someone else. Vanna knows what she's doing, sort of. When I asked if she'd been a cheerleader in high school, she said, "Of course. Who would have ever thought I'd still be a cheerleader?"

And that's *why.* Now you know. Let me just add, before taking a well-deserved nap, that I doubt that Merv and his minions set out to design "Wheel of Fortune" around the Big V Principle or analyzed the economy. I think they just happened, by instinct, experience—and good luck—to hit on a formula that would make it the state-of-the-art eighties game show. A formula that sucks the viewer through the screen and into that dazzling dreamscape—Vanna's Nirvana—where he is transformed from a nullity, a hapless anonymous bozo, a nobody from nowhere, to the only being now worth being: a Winner. Someone possessed of wealth, luck, and, maybe more important, television exposure. Someone, in short, who finally exists. You know, a big wheel.

••••••••••••••••••••

Examining the Text

1. When Grossberger refers to *Wheel of Fortune* as "a fascinating, deeply significant national phenomenon, the comprehension of which was essential to any proper understanding of our era" (paragraph 2), what is he implying about himself, about his writing task, and about the serious study of popular culture?

2. How does the puzzle "V-C-R---S THR-LLS" in Grossberger's "dream" (29) embody what he sees as *Wheel of Fortune*'s appeal to mass audiences?

3. Grossberger suggests that Vanna White stays "on the sidelines cheering for someone else" (46) and labors "under the cloud of bimbosity imposed by the alternatively fawning and smirking media" (21). What is his point? Would you say that many women on television and in the United States generally serve a similar function and labor under the same cloud?

For Group Discussion

Grossberger says that in inventing *Wheel of Fortune* "Merv [Griffin] figured out what America wanted and he provided it" (26). First, try to determine why you and the people you know watch the shows that you do. Then, as a group, determine four or five specific things that Americans want from game shows—or any type of television programming. Finally, as a class, consider what accounts for the similarities and differences in your group lists.

Writing Suggestion

Grossberger suggests that game shows mirror the country's prevailing social and political climate. Can you name any 1990s game shows that are notably popular? If so, what do these shows suggest about life and attitudes in the United States today? If not, why do you think that is the case? Has another genre of programming emerged that more clearly mirrors contemporary popular culture? If so, what is it?

2. THE SOAP OPERA

The following two essays are more academic in presentation than the previous two. The writers, for example, cite a number of previously published critical works to substantiate their own views. However, both can be read easily by an educated popular audience because neither writer relies heavily on technical concepts and language.

Soaps Day and Night

Ronald Berman

"*And as sands through the hourglass, so are the days of our lives."
Even the most ardent critic of soap operas will likely recognize this tag line from one of daytime television's most popular series, and whether we hate or love them, we have to acknowledge widespread popularity of the soaps and the hold they exert over the hearts and minds of millions of Americans.*

In this chapter from his book How Television Sees Its Audience, *Ronald Berman argues that modern day soap operas are a form of the serial fiction of an earlier time, available and accessible to the masses. Still there are differences, and Berman points out many of the characteristics that make soap opera a unique genre. For example, despite its emphasis upon sex and the physical aspects of relationships, at the center of the soap opera is the family unit; it is the family that holds the episodes together and provides a cohesive structure. Further, the plots tend to be nonlinear and the dialogue tends toward stream-of-consciousness narration used less to move the plot forward or direct the action than simply to express states of mind.*

Berman contrasts nighttime and daytime soaps and finds marked class differences between the two. Nighttime characters tend to be more glamorous and have more money, so there is more fantasy involved, while daytime characters cut across a wider socio-economic stratum and are therefore more "realistic." Both types of soap, however, enact a kind of "middle-class fantasy," where wealth is "the good" and it is this preoccupation with money and the self, Berman suggests, that places the genre within its contemporary cultural and social context.

As you read this piece, think about Berman's analysis of the role of wealth in terms of our possibilities for expression and action in a material world. How can money (and preoccupation with financial conditions) either free or limit our consciousness? Notice, too, that Berman draws comparisons between soap characters and the characters of Shakespeare. Shakespeare was a producer of the popular culture in his day, but are his works and soap operas of equal value?

....

Stories and Selves

Serial fiction isn't new; it began when publication caught up with 1
demand. In the early part of the nineteenth century, books were expensive and writers like Dickens and Thackeray could not reach all their potential customers. Literacy had in effect become a commodity. For the Victorians the problem was solved by printing novels in monthly or even weekly installments. For a shilling the customer could get the latest chapter of *Pickwick Papers*. He or she could join a sympathetic group of equals gathered around a London newsstand (or, for that matter, a newsstand in Bombay), anxious to know the fate of Little Nell. Serial publication, like soap opera on television, brought together fiction and a mass public.

Emotions once reserved for high tragedy were drawn out of every- 2
day life. Here is an excerpt from a letter to Dickens about the death of Paul Dombey in *Dombey and Son:* "Oh my dear dear Dickens! . . . I have so cried and sobbed over it last night, and again this morning: and felt my heart purified by those tears." Judging from other responses, this is, I think, pretty much representative. One's deepest feelings were affected by stories about one's own time, place, and social condition. Horror and pity, once the subjects of Shakespeare or Sophocles, became feelings attached to life and death in the middle class.

Now the novel has been supplanted, and the work it used to do, 3
telling us about daily life, has been taken on by other forms. They don't do it as well, but that matters little to their audience, who demand from our own kind of serial fiction a limited number of effects. The soap opera audience, although much less literate than the audience for the novel, wants also to know about self and social class, about money, about rising and falling in the world, and about love.

I suppose you could say that the soap opera has risen a notch or two 4
in social class since the novel established caste and class as interests of fiction. The romance once associated with love is now attached to

money. Although the broad range of daytime soaps concern themselves with jobs and careers, the nighttime programs are about big money. Like a historical novel, the soap of the eighties is about the various generations of a family. During the day this family tends to be organized around business or professions. At night, in a more fantastic world, it is gathered around oil wells or ranches—the struggle is not for survival but for control. Like so many little King Lears, the fathers of nighttime soap are surrounded by the ungrateful young. This may be either a convenient literary strategy or a sign of the times. At any rate, the family of either day or nighttime soap opera is split around opposed interests. Parents and children disapprove of each other's business tactics or consultants or, now and then, lovers. But the essential fact in the structure of any soap is the family caught up in various ways with some kind of enterprise.

During the day we see more of communities than simply of Colbys   5
or Carringtons. There will be a greater variety of character, more minorities, more of a sense of necessity in choosing careers, mates, or opportunities. Daytime soaps are on a much smaller economic scale, and will show us dramas about the fate of housemaids or police officers. Social class really means something on daytime soaps—it is not just a fantasy of wealth but something you can climb into or fall out of.

On either kind of soap love is probably less interesting than its after-   6
effects. People are unquestionably drawn to each other, and acts of passion naturally result, but they are characterized by social self-consciousness. Men and women on soaps, before and after bed, ask themselves and each other if this has been "right" for them; if it suggests a break in their social lives; if it betrays their wives or husbands; what effect it has on their friends, acquaintances, former lovers, or spouses; and how it will affect business.

This is all natural to domestic fiction. The real issues always have   7
been the social effects of personal actions. And of course in an age such as our own, when both men and women work, one's real interest is reserved for the long haul, not for happy interludes. So that soaps, which may get steamy now and then, and which feature altogether wonderful characters like Susan Lucci or Joan Collins, nevertheless concentrate far more on lives, money, and careers than they do on love. A great American critic, Lionel Trilling, once wrote that we learned from the novel "most of what we know about modern society, about class and its strange rituals, about power and influence and about money." With very little transposition the same could now be said about soaps. They don't teach as well, but they do show us what we know—and they show us ourselves.

How does a soap proceed? Not like a movie, which has a beginning,   8
a middle, and an end. Nor like a novel, which defines and develops

characters. A soap is new every time we see it, even from Monday to Tuesday. This tends to be confusing to those of us educated under the old dispensation. If you cannot instantly disengage your expectations, to say nothing of your memory, you will not be able to watch a soap comfortably. It is a chronicle, not a history.

In soap opera it is perfectly possible to mislay a character. You   9
can be born into or die out of the show—and there are probably more deaths on soaps due to accountants than to mortality. The obverse can also be true: It is easy to be resurrected. If one of the cast should happen to die in a car crash, it will be no surprise months later to find him flourishing although amnesiac. One of the reasons for this is that the crash is rarely portrayed in detail on film—it is simply said to have happened.

This has real implications for the rest of the soap story. Like the car   10
crash that may or may not have happened as reported, the soap is built around ambiguities. One hardly knows who is alive or dead, who is an imposter or the real thing. Soaps are full of long-lost brothers who are as genuine as the script allows them to be. The key to the soap is nôt the action, but the script. Again, this is something hard to grasp for those brought up on different kinds of fiction. Reality is not what the plot suggests—nor even what the camera observes. Reality is what the script says it is.

Over the short term this doesn't matter much. Over the long term,   11
however, the soap is basically incomprehensible. If a show has had a run of a few years its plot will look like a particularly ingeniously confused Turkish carpet. Its action spreads out laterally instead of developing in a progressive line.

Drama or Monologue?

The soap *looks* like a drama, and it involves adversarial figures and   12
answering dialogue, but it does not really depend on interaction. The one great essential about soaps is that they are literally all talk. There really is very little action in proportion to production time.

In any drama the dialogue has some special meaning. It is shot   13
through with particular themes and ideas, articulated through significant images. It corresponds to, is tailored for, individual characters. In a drama, everyone has his or her own vocabulary. Very little of this is true for soaps. In fact, it can be said with little exaggeration that on a soap the dialogue doesn't have dramatic meaning. It may not have *any* meaning. That is because soap dialogue is not meant to further the action. It is a series of *statements* or expressions that show us not what people are thinking but what is on their minds, which is different. The soap script

is designed to allow characters to empty themselves out, to cleanse themselves emotionally. Think not of the drama or the novel when looking at soap opera, but of the diary or journal.

Soap dialogue allows one to listen to oneself. It is almost purely ex-   14
pressive and subjective. Of course its subject will always be the self measuring its own claims to happiness, or stating its own consciousness, or simply letting off steam.

Soap dialogue has an odd resemblance to the talk of a patient to an   15
analyst. The most common moment in soap conversation involves two people, one with personal emotional anguish that must be stated, and the other with no business but to witness that. Unhappiness does not really require a necessary cause—the characters of soapland are unhappy from the beginning. They have been or are insufficiently loved; perhaps they have been wounded in their self-conception. Or they have been emotionally traumatized in the past. They seem to be constructs of some common psychological needs now popular. We all evidently need far more emotional gratification than we get. Even if we *succeed* in life we may be deeply deprived. Our own self-worth is rarely visible to others. Born with this attitude, soap opera people do not really need what have been called the "blocking characters" of drama or the novel. Regardless of the opposition of villains, life on soaps would be psychologically unhappy. If Dickens had written a soap instead of a novel, David Copperfield would not have needed Uriah Heep to complicate his life. He would have needed only to let us know that he was unhappy with himself, or uncertain about his career or sexual choices. Soaps have many villains, but most people make their own troubles for themselves.

What is the first rule of soap opera? No one should suffer in silence.   16
Not to express all of one's anxiety would be an unthinkable deviation. There may be secrets suppressed in order to advance the plot, but no one ever hides the sources of his or her own discontent. They are all talked out. This is pretty much the opposite of real life, which may constitute one of the principal attractions of the soap opera. Few of us ever get to let the world know exactly how we feel. Clearly, the audience of soap opera is smitten not so much with melodrama as with psychodrama.

Since a soap is literally all talk, it becomes necessary to institution-   17
alize the role of listener or confidante. The confidante, long a part of sentimental drama, becomes the most obvious fixture of soaps and their stories. Every character has a friend who listens to his or her story. A social illusion is necessarily created that no one is solitary. In the world of soaps, not only do we express our deepest feelings, but the social world listens and responds to them. We are *visible* in the world of soap opera,

far more visible than in reality. And the most visible thing about us is our psychology. The main characters (and many of the minor ones) reveal themselves in bursts of emotional rhetoric: in apology or declaration or demand or revelation of some kind. Common to most kinds of dialogue (or, frequently, monologue shared by two people) is the theme of subjectivity. The soaps are the product of an era fascinated by the self-evident topics of magazines like *People* or *Self*, which is to say that they cash in on the democratic tendency to reduce all things to a certain size. On soaps, what matters is not the state of the world but how you feel about it.

There is one large problem that soaps have not been able to solve: 18 Their language is dreary, imprecise, not really capable of expressing much meaning. This really hurts because self-awareness, self-pity, and self-consciousness are, after all, interesting things. But, as the following collection of samples, from a single episode of *General Hospital* indicates, the characters don't often get the tools they need from the writers:

> And that means trouble.
> I'd better get to her before . . .
> I've got an idea.
> I'll get to the bottom of it.
> I'm going to lose him.
> I know how you feel.
> We must look to the future.
> All our troubles are over.

These clichés can't really express the emotional depth of suffering. 19 Pitched to the general illiteracy of the audience, the soap tries to find a language that everyone will understand. It is not surprising that soap language, which needs help so badly, gets it from spectacle and music. Deep emotion is suggested not by adequate statement but by the universal heavy sigh repeated every few minutes every day, from *The Young and the Restless* through *One Life to Live*. Everyone on soap opera has that sign, followed by a little wince. And there is music all the time. Music serves the same purpose for the soap that the laugh track serves for comedy. It is heavy, portentous, and sentimental. And it is there all the time, covering stretches between dialogue, instructing us how to feel, trying to do what language has already failed to do.

The soap is full of nonverbal clues to character and feeling. To sigh 20 is to have feelings. To wear a hat or especially a turban is (for women) the infallible sign of great wealth. To respond to animals or infants is to indicate moral value. To listen earnestly is to suggest moral purpose.

Even when tempered, as it is now, by fantasy, the soap is about hus- 21 bands and wives. Its central institution is the family. One of the basic soap plots is about the formation of a family, from the first attraction

between two individuals to the social resonance caused by their eventual connection.

In the good old days of radio, where soaps originated, family prob-   22
lems tended to be simple and solutions tended to be moral. Domestic
uncertainty and unhappiness were the great subjects, and they were
looked at from a woman's point of view. Today we are much more likely
to hear about issues, many of them involving social change. Soap characters are involved in running corporations and vineyards and oil wells.
They brush up against politics (although most of the ideas are carefully
washed out). They are threatened by technology; for example, on one of
the nighttime soaps, the ongoing pollution of inherited property. We
hear now in the soaps about abortion and computers, about working
women and market trends.

Clearly the biggest issue of social change is the liberation of women.   23
Since the soap is designed for a female audience, the issue is a natural.
The news of the day tells us that more women are now in the work
force—and the soap responds by mixing career women in among
housewives. Statistics indicate that many of these women are now executives—and the soap shows us women in skyscraper offices running
financial empires. The news reveals the new sexual morality—and the
soap is now about women attracted to (or suffering from) sexual freedom. The old standard problem of the soap opera, getting married, has
been joined by the new one of extracting a "commitment" and maintaining a "relationship."

But for every social action there is bound to be a reaction. Not every-   24
one in the audience is liberated. So the soaps keep men on in positions
of authority—as physicians and lawyers and heads of households.
Mothers continue to be best sources of love, sympathy, and advice. And,
according to one survey, the soap is in some ways antifeminist:

> Conservative, nurturing women tended to be good characters, while
> evil women were career-oriented and nontraditional in their behavior.
> *All My Children's* Erica Kane Martin, who informed her mother that she
> was a feminist (November 1, 1982, episode, and others), is the classic
> example of a selfish, ambitious, "bad" woman. This example suggests
> that soaps equate "good" with traditional, sex-typed behavior; that is,
> a "good" woman is not career-oriented and ambitious.

The information is interesting, but I'm not sure about the interpre-   25
tation. The passage cited above seems to confuse character with occupation. Erica (or Alexis on *Dynasty*) would be what they are whether
they had careers or were locked in a closet. And "badness" is relative—
the audience is I think quite pleased to see Joan Collins sexually and
financially triumphant. In fiction, *good* and *bad* are tricky terms—
remember that Shylock and Iago take all the curtain calls.

Character and Social Values

The soap opera is never funny about anything. It would be as out of   26
place to be witty on this kind of show as in a campaign for state assem-
blyman. It might even be said that the soap has less of a sense of humor
than almost any other fictional genre. In a way this is understandable:
Some of the roles are already like cartoons and might lose their credibility if they were questioned. A sense of humor questions everything.
But why are soaps so relentlessly *serious?* Serious especially about character and social values? There are comic characters even in *Hamlet* and
King Lear. Is it the case that middle-class values or aspirations are too
important for laughter? Or that the soap avoids any modality that might
allow the viewer to look at the show in more than one designated way?

In soap opera, no social institution is ever satirized. The hospital   27
and the ranch and the corporation all seem to be good by definition. The
life they encourage, if lived rightly, seems to be just fine. This has several consequences for character. No one is ever allowed to be ambivalent about "basic" values. Characters may from time to time not know
what they want, or make the wrong choice of bed, board, or career, but
their philosophy is never in doubt. To see a soap requires more than one
kind of suspension of disbelief. We have to accept that all its troubles occur in a social universe that really hasn't been responsible for causing
them.

One of the big values on soap opera is money. The "bad" characters   28
are corrupt in pursuit of it, but the money itself is okay. In fact, the
"good" characters seem innocent enough in its pursuit. On certain soap
operas what money does is fiercely admired by the cast and, one imagines, by the audience. Money and what it can buy are always on display
and we are invited to pant over its power and uses. The set and costumes have come to matter increasingly, and soaps have become visual
displays for *haute couture.* Current nighttime soaps are very nearly
pornographic about wealth. One doesn't know what matters most to the
producers, Joan Collins's body or her wardrobe—probably the wardrobe. Her clothes are calculated to be the last word not in style or beauty
but in the appearance of expense. As in the commercials she now does
for *Time* and other magazines, they are "statements" about acquisition.
Although Joan Collins is often viewed as a middle-aged sex goddess,
she may be much more like Imelda Marcos than *Venus Geriatrix.*

In the mid-1980s, the soaps seem to have moved away from middle-   29
class actuality and toward middle-class fantasy. They are now about
conspicuous consumption. In some ways the soaps are fictional versions
of *Lifestyles of the Rich and Famous.* But there is a real difference between
interest in wealth and the depiction of wealth as a value in itself. Possi-

bly the writers of *Dallas* and *Dynasty* are saying with a straight face what F. Scott Fitzgerald once wrote satirically: "The richer a fella is, the better I like him."

In more traditional fiction wealth is an object of suspicion, and its 30 acquisition is part of a tension between ambition and surrender to its values. Especially in the last two centuries, the centuries both of the modern novel and the modern experience of "rising" into the "upper" middle class, getting money has been a major theme of both life and art. And serious literature has used the theme well. If one looks over Fitzgerald and Hemingway—or Balzac and Dickens—it's fairly plain that wealth has a Faustian effect on character. It frees us from the ordinary human fate. We are no longer compelled by necessity. Which means that *we are free to act out what we really are.* Wealth allows character to reveal itself, finally, because there is no need any longer to subscribe to the hypocrisies of manners and morals. The rich, like Tom Buchanan in *The Great Gatsby*, are free to be themselves. Or, like the inimitable Joan Collins, to show the world actual human desires unmediated by conscience or other social inhibitions. In great literature—and now and then on soaps—wealth really does free character and express nature. It certainly disposes of the merely social obstacles to self-expression.

For the most part, however, soaps do not rise to the occasion. To be 31 rich, like the Colbys or the Carringtons, means to be very much like the audience. To have money is to be lucky rather than different. The character of Blake Carrington is passive to the extent of being dimwitted. Wealth has done nothing for him psychologically except allow him to pay his bills.

I've suggested that there is a kind of pornography of wealth on soap 32 opera—the audience is invited to lust after houses and jewels and stock-market options. The women of soap are not undressed, as moralists might fear, but overdressed. Again, there are some interesting differences between the fiction of high culture and this offshoot of mass culture. In Fitzgerald's short story "The Diamond as Big as the Ritz," there are some great lines describing the reaction of the middle class to the real thing, big money. The hero of the story, John T. Ungar, from the small and superrespectable town of Hades on the Mississippi, has just gotten into a preposterous automobile owned by the Washington family. It is lavish beyond belief: The upholstery is made of tapestry and embroidery, covered with woven gold and even with the supererogatory "ends of ostrich feathers." It is This Year's Model in spades. But the appropriate reaction to the display of buying power is very far from laughter:

> If the car was any indication of what John would see, he was prepared to be astonished indeed. The simple piety prevalent in Hades has the earnest worship of and respect for riches as the first article of its

creed—had John felt otherwise than radiantly humble before them, his parents would have turned away in horror at his blasphemy.

And so, one imagines, would the producer turn away in horror if it had occurred to him or her that the world of wealth on soaps was not a proper world at all. Or that characters could become caricatures if they were defined entirely by having money and acting out our dreams of consumption.

Dualities

There are some characters on soaps, brilliantly acted, who escape   33
the general fate. They are not reductive because money is for them a means to power—so is sex. Everything refers itself to a motive, and not merely the generalized desire for "happiness." J.R. Ewing of *Dallas,* Alexis of *Dynasty,* and Erica of *All My Children* are motivated by genuine self-interest and because of this are morally isolated from other characters on their shows. Those others, who serve as foils for Alexis and Erica and J.R., are radically innocent. They are convinced of two things in general: One is that the happiness of others is implied by their own, and the second is that the pursuit (and even capture) of happiness is a natural right. The burden of the many monologues and dialogues of soap opera is that there must be a solution to human problems. Since nothing is wrong with the world as it is, and since the pursuit of wealth, power, love and, "happiness" is normative, the failure to get what you want is only a failure of means.

This philosophy underlies soap-opera motivation and discourse.   34
The typical argument unfolded in a moment of truth on screen will be that if something had been done in the past, if some opportunity had been taken or some temptation resisted, then things in the present would have been uncritically good. If only the right advice had been listened to, or the rules observed more closely. This view, pretty much by definition, is the opposite of tragic—and there will be some who call it the opposite of realistic. Nothing in the nature of things except for decisions accounts for happiness or unhappiness. No "star-crossed" lovers for the soaps.

In his recent book *The Culture of Narcissism,* Christopher Lasch has   35
described a change in cultural definition: "The pursuit of self-interest, formerly identified with the rational pursuit of gain and the accumulation of wealth, has become a search for pleasure and psychic survival." The observation seems especially accurate for soap opera, which is in its own way a mirror of the times, except that on soaps, characters are liable to practice both kinds of self-interest at once. It is altogether fascinating to see how J.R., Erica, and Alexis link the two kinds of pleasure,

money and sex. Most of their encounters in the bedroom lead to changes in stock options. And there is a kind of cross-fertilization, as attitudes conventional for business are transposed in love. It is no wonder that, at a time when the mass media's other forms ceaselessly exhort us to see ourselves as upwardly mobile consumers of every kind of property or pleasure, that these characters should have become cultural heroes. Joan Collins finds her natural metier, the advertisement; Larry Hagman comes to symbolize American manners and mores on the television sets of Namibia, Chad, and Tongo; and Susan Lucci is a conglomerate of her own:

> Television's greatest villainess isn't really Alexis (Joan Collins) on "Dynasty." The real vixen in TV is Erica Kane (Susan Lucci) on the popular ABC soap opera "All My Children." The network has been literally holding its corporate breath waiting to see what Lucci might do once her contract ended. . . . She was entertaining offers from all the networks and lots of other organizations too.

What do these great consumers of love and money bring to their 36 shows? Unlike their foils, they are self-aware. They are capable of being jealous without cause, of bringing down destruction for a whim, like the ancient gods. Like Alexis, they do what they want. Like Erica, they do what is easiest. But whatever they do is conceived as an extension of ordinary human possibility: They take the logic of the situation past the point that most of us dare to.

Their victims believe that happiness for one person means happi- 37 ness for someone else as well. But Erica and company have given a certain amount of thought to the subject, and have concluded that their own happiness does not depend on that of anyone else. Nor need it make anyone else happy. They are perfectly subjective, images of psychological change in our national self-conception. The majority of innocent, striving characters of soap opera seem not to realize that there are those to whom the happiness of others is offensive.

This heightened sense of character, and of its intensely subjective 38 values, makes it difficult to agree that the soap opera is confined to domestic themes. One recent summary of studies on the subject concludes that the soap is "a world dominated by interpersonal relationships, where characters discuss romantic, marital, and family problems, and where health and work are major concerns within these contexts." Within limits this is true enough. But the soap does other kinds of work as well. In trying to keep up with the present it alters the old form. Right now, in the middle of the eighties, the major characters of the soaps are not very domestic. They display all the signs that we have come to associate with the personal liberation that marks this decade. They are alone, very much self-concerned, and interested in the various kinds of power, both material and emotional. They are not romantic—even though deep sexuality is hinted at, it turns out that sexual relationships are rarely ends in themselves. The major characters—those most enthusiastically accepted by the American (and even the world) audience—may live in family circumstances, but they go through sequential marriages and "relationships." If art imitates life, then these kinds of characters show the decade to itself.

My own guess, then, is that two kinds of social change are the underlying subjects of soap opera. One is fairly visible: These programs now translate news events into fiction. They show us the use and abuse of controlled substances. They have the latest attitudes toward alcoholism or sexual deviation. They are definitively about the new status of women—and, consequently, of men. They suggest the high incidence of crime in actual life and of terrorism. They contain characters far from the small town that was the origin of the genre, characters who step in from the vagueness of outer geography to the *mise-en-scène* of Texas or Colorado. The "interpersonal relationships" of soap opera now are incredibly complicated because of the current history they are meant to represent. In this respect, then, the soap is almost literally a form of "news of the day." 39

But it is in a second respect that the soap displays social change more tellingly. It has two sets of characters, the simple and the complex, who tell us not about the news but about ourselves. The simple—who are often victims of the complex—represent in their innocent way all the hopes and desires of their audience. And their attitude is certainly representative: Without any sense of hubris at all they demand from life every natural right that has been drafted since 1789. They want happiness—and in order to get it they construe the social, political, and psychological world as if it existed only to respond to human desires. These characters worry us even when they are blameless. Always talking of themselves, always invoking happy moments of their past, always demanding that the world listen to them, they seem to have sprung up from the shelves of self-help and self-fulfillment. The complex characters are, paradoxically, more comfortable to understand. They hover on the edge of drama because they demand real "interaction." And in their powerful self-awareness and emotional selfishness they too help delineate the portrait of an age. Both kinds of characters unite to show some new social values, and we draw from their depiction an uneasy recognition of individualism concerned not with political freedom but with emotional indulgence. Are the soaps an art form? Not to me. Are they meaningful? Very much so. Better than most other forms of fiction in 40 our time, they show us the passionate concern with the self that has been made possible by a new kind of cultural economy.

•••••••••••••••••••••

Examining the Text

1. How would you describe Berman's attitude toward soap operas? What does he see as the similarities and differences between serial fiction of the nineteenth century and the soap operas of today? Why does he make this comparison?

2. Soaps, says Berman, are "literally all talk" (paragraph 12), but the language consists of "clichés . . . pitched to the general illiteracy of the audience" (19). Analyze Berman's criticism of the dialogue in soap operas (12–19). From your experiences watching soap operas, do you find his criticisms valid?

3. According to Berman, "nothing in the nature of things except for decisions accounts for happiness or unhappiness" in soap operas (34). What does he mean by this statement, and what are its broader social and economic implications? Do you agree that, in general, soap opera characters are "happy" or "unhappy" based exclusively on the decisions they've made in the past?

For Group Discussion

Writing about prime-time soap operas popular during the early 1980s, such as *Dallas* and *Dynasty*, Berman suggests that "a kind of pornography of wealth" was fundamental to their appeal (32). As a group, discuss two or three more recent prime-time soap operas, such as *Melrose Place* and *Beverly Hills 90210*; if possible, you might also consider a prime-time soap opera from an earlier decade, such as *Family* or *Peyton Place*. In what ways do these other shows reflect the values Berman describes? In what ways do they rely on different values for their appeal? As a class, consider the extent to which the appeal of prime-time soap operas reflects the mood of the country.

Writing Suggestion

In an essay, evaluate Berman's statement that "the soap opera is never funny about anything" (26). According to his interpretation, why are soap operas so serious in regard to character and social values? Can you use his point to distinguish "soap operas" from other serial-like programs that are often funny, such as *LA Law* and *Northern Exposure*?

Soap Opera, Melodrama, and Women's Anger

Tania Modleski

*T*he following selection, excerpted from Tania Modleski's Loving with a Vengeance: Mass-Produced Fantasies for Women, *is more scholarly than previous essays in this chapter. Modleski weaves together elements of psychoanalytic theory, film criticism, and statistical research. Her strategy is to use the texts of "high" critical theory to raise the status of popular art and then to argue that the soap opera itself is "in the vanguard" of popular aesthetic forms.*

Frequently dismissed by critics as the worst of television—and possibly the "nadir of art forms"—the soap opera is instead, Modleski argues, a central and primary female narrative form. Given the data (she notes that of approximately twenty million daily viewers, 90 percent are women), Modleski sets out to account for the widespread appeal of the soaps, which initially she pinpoints to be the pleasure women find in the narrative. Modleski draws constant parallels between the narrative structure of the soap opera and the structure of a woman's life in late twentieth century America. For example, she compares the suspended conclusion, the delay of gratification, to what she sees as the essential condition of a woman's life: waiting. Further, in linking morality and goodness with the category of motherhood, the soaps "affirm the primacy of the family." Yet despite the benevolence of the heroines, true power resides in the villainesses. Viewers, Modleski suggests, can thus identify with both, simultaneously playing out their fantasies of domesticity and of power.

As you read, *notice how Modleski reads the soap opera as a "text" and how she analyzes it in terms of its "codes" and structure. Despite her insistent focus upon popular art forms, Modleski's work is formulated with an academic audience in mind; she cites other scholars to lend credibility to her own points. You might think of each of her sources as threads she weaves together to support her own argument, a strategy you may want to use in your own academic writing.*

••••••••••••••••••

Approximately twelve soap operas are shown daily, each half an   1
hour to an hour and a half long. The first of them goes on the air at about 10:00 A.M., and they run almost continuously until about 3:30 P.M. (of course, the times vary according to local programming schedules). In 1975 the *New York Times Magazine* reported that 20 million people watch soap operas daily, the average program attracting 6.7 million viewers, almost 90 percent of them female. Further:

The households break down economically and educationally in proportions similar to the population as a whole—51.3 percent with
household incomes under $10,000, for instance, and 23.9 percent with
incomes over $15,000. About 24.8 percent of household heads have
only an elementary school education, while 56.2 percent have a high
school education or better. . . . The programs gross more than $300 mil-
lion a year from the makers of soaps, deodorants, cake mixes and other
household products, providing a disproportionate share of network
profits though nighttime budgets are much larger.[1]

With the exception of "Ryan's Hope," which takes place in a big city,   2
the soap operas are set in small towns and involve two or three families
intimately connected with one another. Families are often composed of
several generations, and the proliferation of generations is accelerated
by the propensity of soap opera characters to mature at an incredibly
rapid rate; thus, the matriarch on "Days of Our Lives," who looks to be
about 65, has managed over the years to become a great-great-grand-
mother. Sometimes on a soap opera one of the families will be fairly well
to do, and another somewhat lower on the social scale though still, as a
rule, identifiably middle-class. In any case, since there is so much inter-
mingling and intermarrying, class distinctions quickly become hopelessly blurred. Children figure largely in many of the plots, but they
don't appear on the screen all that often; nor do the very old. Blacks and
other minorities are almost completely excluded.

Women as well as men frequently work outside the home, usually   3
in professions such as law and medicine, and women are generally on
a professional par with men. But most of everyone's time is spent experiencing and discussing personal and domestic crises. Kathryn Weibel
lists "some of the most frequent themes":

> the evil woman
> the great sacrifice
> the winning back of an estranged lover/spouse
> marrying her for her money, respectability, etc.
> the unwed mother
> deceptions about the paternity of children
> career vs. housewife
> the alcoholic woman (and occasionally man).[2]

Controversial social problems are introduced from time to time: 4
rape was recently an issue on several soap operas and was, for the most
part, handled in a sensitive manner. In spite of the fact that soap operas
contain more references to social problems than do most other forms of

---

[1] Anthony Astrachan, quoted in Dan Wakefield, *All Her Children*, p. 149.
[2] Weibel, p. 56.

mass entertainment, critics tend to fault them heavily for their lack of social realism.

If television is considered by some to be a vast wasteland, soap operas are thought to be the least nourishing spot in the desert. The surest way to damn a film, a television program, or even a situation in real life is to invoke an analogy to soap operas. In the same way that men are often concerned to show that what they are, above all, is not women, not "feminine," so television programs and movies will, surprisingly often, tell us that they are not soap operas. On a recent "Phil Donahue Show," a group of handicapped Vietnam War Veterans were bitterly relating their experiences; at one point Donahue interrupted the conversation to assure his audience (comprised almost entirely of women) that he was not giving them soap opera, but he thought it important to "personalize" the war experience. An afternoon "Money Movie," *Middle of the Night*, an interminable Paddy Chayevsky affair starring Frederick March, dealt with one man's life-crisis as, on the brink of old age, he falls in love with a very young Kim Novak and struggles against the petty and destructive jealousy of his sister and daughter. "This is *not* a soap opera," he reprimands the sister at one point. Since to me it had all the ingredients of one, I could only conclude that men's soap operas are not to be thought of as soap operas only because they are *for men* (or about men).

It is refreshing, therefore, to read Horace Newcomb's book, *T.V.: The Most Popular Art*, in which he suggests that far from being the nadir of art forms, as most people take them to be, soap operas represent in some ways the furthest advance of T.V. art. In other words, for all their stereotypical qualities, they combine to the highest degree two of the most important elements of the television aesthetic: "intimacy" and "continuity." Television, says Newcomb, is uniquely suited to deal with character and interpersonal relations rather than with action and setting. Soap operas, of course, play exclusively on the intimate properties of the medium. Newcomb also points out that because of the serial nature of the programs television can offer us depictions of people in situations which grow and change over time, allowing for a greater "audience involvement, a sense of becoming a part of the lives and actions of the characters they see."[3] Thus far it is mainly soap opera which has taken advantage of these possibilities for continuity, nighttime programs, by and large, tending to "forget" from week to week all of the conflicts and lessons which have gone before.

---

[3] Horace Newcomb, *T.V.: The Most Popular Art*, p. 253.

Newcomb's book is important in that, by refusing to indulge in an   7
antifeminine bias against soap operas, it reveals a new way of seeing
these programs which allows them to be placed in the vanguard of T.V.
aesthetics (dubious as this distinction may seem to many people). My
approach is different from, though in no sense opposed to Newcomb's.
I propose not to ignore what is "feminine" about soap operas but to focus on it, to show how they provide a unique narrative pleasure which,
while it has become thoroughly adapted to the rhymths of women's
lives in the home, provides an alternative to the dominant "pleasures of
the text" analyzed by Roland Barthes and others. Soap operas may be
in the vanguard not just of T.V. art but of all popular narrative art.

Whereas the meaning of Harlequin Romances depends almost en-   8
tirely on the sense of an ending, soap operas are important to their viewers in part because they never end. Whereas Harlequins encourage
our identification with one character, soap operas invite identification
with numerous personalities. And whereas Harlequins are structured
around two basic enigmas, in soap operas, the enigmas proliferate:
"Will Bill find out that his wife's sister's baby is really his by artificial in-
semination? Will his wife submit to her sister's blackmail attempts, or
will she finally let Bill know the truth? If he discovers the truth, will this
lead to another nervous breakdown, causing him to go back to Spring
General where his ex-wife and his illegitimate daughter are both doctors and sworn enemies?" Tune in tomorrow, not in order to find out the
answers, but to see what further complications will defer the resolutions
and introduce new questions. Thus the narrative, by placing ever more
complex obstacles between desire and fulfillment, makes anticipation of
an end an end in itself. Soap operas invest exquisite pleasure in the central condition of a woman's life: waiting—whether for her phone to ring,
for the baby to take its nap, or for the family to be reunited shortly after
the day's final soap opera has left *its* family still struggling against dissolution.

According to Roland Barthes, the hermeneutic code,[4] which pro-   9
pounds the enigmas, functions by making "expectation . . . the basic
condition for truth: truth, these narratives tell us, is what is *at the end* of
expectation. This design implies a return to order, for expectation is a

---

[4] Hermeneutic code: In Roland Barthes's theory of fiction, everything in a story is understood in terms of one or more of five codes. One of these, the hermeneutic code, organizes the
reader's desire to find out the truth about the characters and events in any story. This code is
very active in detective stories, of course, but it is present in every kind of narrative. Modleski's point, in the present case, is that soap operas are different from most kinds of narrative,
in that they will never reach that conclusion in which everything is revealed. If there is truth in
them, it cannot be the kind of truth we learn only at the end of the tale. [Eds.]

disorder."[5] But, of course, soap operas do not end. Consequently, truth for women is seen to lie not "at the end of expectation," but *in* expectation, not in the "return to order," but in (familial) disorder.

Many critics have considered endings to be crucial to narratives.   10
Frank Kermode speculates that fictive ends are probably "figures" for death.[6] In his essay on "The Storyteller," Walter Benjamin comes to a similar conclusion:

> The novel is significant . . . not because it presents someone else's fate to us, perhaps didactically, but because this stranger's fate by virtue of the flame which consumes it yields us the warmth which we never draw from our own fate. What draws the reader to the novel is the hope of warming his shivering life with a death he reads about.[7]

But soap operas offer the promise of immortality and eternal re-   11
turn—same time tomorrow. Although at first glance, soap opera seems in this respect to be diametrically opposed to the female domestic novels of the nineteenth century, which were preoccupied with death, especially the deaths of infants and small children, a second look tells us that the fantasy of immortality embodied in modern melodrama is not so very different from the fantasies expressed in the older works. In the latter, it is not the case that, in Benjamin's words, "the 'meaning' of a character's life is revealed only in his death";[8] rather, for women writers and readers, forced to endure repeatedly the premature loss of their children, it was the meaning of the character's death that had to be ascertained, and this meaning was revealed only in the afterlife, only in projections of eternity.

"[T]racts of time unpunctuated by meaning derived from the end   12
are not to be borne," says Frank Kermode, confidently.[9] But perhaps for women (no doubt for men too) certain kinds of endings are attended by a sense of meaninglessness even less capable of being borne than limitless expanses of time which at least hold open the possibility that something may sometime happen to confer sense upon the present. The loss of a child was, for nineteenth century women, an example of such an unbearable ending: it was, as Helen Papashvily has called it, "a double tragedy—the loss of a precious individual and the negation of her creativity,"[10] and it threatened, perhaps more than any other experience, to give the lie to the belief in a benevolent God and the ultimate right-

---

[5] Barthes, *S/Z*, p. 76.
[6] Frank Kermode, *The Sense of an Ending*, p. 7.
[7] Walter Benjamin, "The Storyteller," in his *Illuminations*, p. 101.
[8] Benjamin, "The Storyteller," pp. 100–101.
[9] Kermode, p. 162.
[10] Papashvily, p. 194.

ness of the world order. And so, it was necessary to believe that the child would join a heavenly family for all eternity.

For twentieth-century woman, the loss of her family, not through   13 death, but through abandonment (children growing up and leaving home) is perhaps another "ending" which is feared because it leaves women lonely and isolated and without significant purpose in life. The fear, as Barbara Easton persuasively argues, is not without foundation:

> With the geographical mobility and breakdown of communities of the twentieth century, women's support networks outside the family have weakened, and they are likely to turn to their husbands for intimacy that earlier generations would have found elsewhere.[11]

The family is, for many women, their only support, and soap operas   14 offer the assurance of its immortality.[12] They present the viewer with a picture of a family which, though it is always in the process of breaking down, stays together no matter how intolerable its situation may get. Or, perhaps more accurately, the family remains close precisely because it is perpetually in a chaotic state. The unhappiness generated by the family can only be solved in the family. Misery becomes not, as in many nineteenth-century women's novels, the consequence and sign of the family's breakdown, but the very means of its functioning and perpetuation. As long as the children are unhappy, as long as things *don't* come to a satisfying conclusion, the mother will be needed as confidante and adviser, and her function will never end.

One critic of soap opera remarks, "If . . . as Aristotle so reasonably   15 claimed, drama is the imitation of a human action that has a beginning, a middle, and an end, soap opera belongs to a separate genus that is entirely composed of an indefinitely expandable middle."[13] It is not only that successful soap operas do not end, it is also that they cannot end. In *The Complete Soap Opera Book*, an interesting and lively work on the subject, the authors show how a radio serial forced off the air by television tried to wrap up its story.[14] It was an impossible task. Most of the storyline had to be discarded and only one element could be followed through to its end—an important example of a situation in which what Barthes calls the "discourse's instinct for preservation" has virtually tri-

---

[11] Barbara Easton, "Feminism and the Contemporary Family," p. 30.

[12] Not only can women count on a never ending story line, they can also, to a great extent, rely upon the fact that their favorite characters will never desert them. To take a rather extreme example: when, on one soap opera, the writers killed off a popular female character and viewers were unhappy, the actress was brought back to portray the character's twin sister. See Madeleine Edmondson and David Rounds, *From Mary Noble to Mary Hartman: The Complete Soap Opera Book*, p. 208.

[13] Dennis Porter, "Soap Time: Thoughts on a Commodity Art Form," p. 783.

[14] Edmondson and Rounds, *The Complete Soap Opera Book*, pp. 104–110.

umphed over authorial control.[15] Furthermore, it is not simply that the story's completion would have taken too long for the amount of time allotted by the producers. More importantly, I believe it would have been impossible to resolve the contradiction between the imperatives of melodrama—the good must be rewarded and the wicked punished—and the latent message of soap operas—everyone cannot be happy at the same time, no matter how deserving they are. The claims of any two people, especially in love matters, are often mutually exclusive.

John Cawelti defines melodrama as having   16

> at its center the moral fantasy of showing forth the essential 'rightness' of the world order. . . . Because of this, melodramas are usually rather complicated in plot and character; instead of identifying with a single protagonist through his line of action, the melodrama typically makes us intersect imaginatively with many lives. Subplots multiply, and the point of view continually shifts in order to involve us in a complex of destinies. Through this complex of characters and plots we see not so much the working of individual fates but the underlying moral process of the world.[16]

It is scarcely an accident that this essentially nineteenth-century   17
form continues to appeal strongly to women, whereas the classic (male) narrative film is, as Laura Mulvey points out, structured "around a main controlling figure with whom the spectator can identify."[17] Soap operas continually insist on the insignificance of the individual life. A viewer might at one moment be asked to identify with a woman finally reunited with her love, only to have that identification broken in a moment of intensity and attention focused on the sufferings of the woman's rival.

If, as Mulvey claims, the identification of the spectator with "a main   18
male protagonist" results in the spectator's becoming "the representative of power,"[18] the multiple identification which occurs in soap opera results in the spectator's being divested of power. For the spectator is never permitted to identify with a character completing an entire action. Instead of giving us one "powerful ideal ego . . . who can make things happen and control events better than the subject/spectator can,"[19] soap operas present us with numerous limited egos, each in conflict with the others, and continually thwarted in its attempts to control events because of inadequate knowledge of other peoples' plans, motivations, and schemes. Sometimes, indeed, the spectator, frustrated by

---

[15] Barthes, *S/Z*, p. 135.
[16] John G. Cawelti, *Adventure, Mystery and Romance*, pp. 45–46.
[17] Laura Mulvey, "Visual Pleasure and Narrative Cinema," p. 420.
[18] Mulvey, p. 420.
[19] Mulvey, p. 420.

the sense of powerlessness induced by soap operas, will, like an inter-
fering mother, try to control events directly:

> Thousands and thousands of letters [from soap fans to actors] give ad-
> vice, warn the heroine of impending doom, caution the innocent to be-
> ware of the nasties ("Can't you see that your brother-in-law is up to no
> good?"), inform one character of another's doings, or reprimand a
> character for unseemly behavior.[20]

Presumably, this intervention is ineffectual, and feminine power-   19
lessness is reinforced on yet another level.

The subject/spectator of soap operas, it could be said, is constituted   20
as a sort of ideal mother: a person who possesses greater wisdom than
all her children, whose sympathy is large enough to encompass the conflicting claims of her family (she identifies with them all), and who has
no demands or claims of her own (she identifies with no one character
exclusively). The connection between melodrama and mothers is an old
one. Harriet Beecher Stowe, of course, made it explicit in *Uncle Tom's
Cabin,* believing that if her book could bring its female readers to see the
world as one extended family, the world would be vastly improved. But
in Stowe's novel, the frequent shifting of perspective identifies the
reader with a variety of characters in order ultimately to ally her with
the mother/author and with God who, in their higher wisdom and understanding, can make all the hurts of the world go away, thus insuring
the "essential 'rightness' of the world order." Soap opera, however, denies the "mother" this extremely flattering illusion of her power. On the
one hand, it plays upon the spectator's expectation of the melodramatic
form, continually stimulating (by means of the hermeneutic code) the
desire for a just conclusion to the story, and, on the other hand, it constantly presents the desire as unrealizable, by showing that conclusions
only lead to further tension and suffering. Thus soap operas convince
women that their highest goal is to see their families united and happy,
while consoling them for their inability to realize this ideal and bring
about familial harmony.

This is reinforced by the character of the good mother on soap op-   21
eras. In contrast to the manipulating mother who tries to interfere with
her children's lives, the good mother must sit helplessly by as her children's lives disintegrate; her advice, which she gives only when asked,
is temporarily soothing, but usually ineffectual. Her primary function is to be sympathetic, to tolerate the foibles and errors of others.
Maeve Ryan, the mother on "Ryan's Hope," is a perfect example.
"Ryan's Hope," a soap opera centered around an Irish-Catholic, bar-

---

[20] Edmondson and Rounds, p. 193.

owning family which, unlike the majority of soap families, lives in a large city, was originally intended to be more "realistic," more socially oriented than the majority of soap operas.[21] Nevertheless, the function of the mother is unchanged: she is there to console her children and try to understand them as they have illegitimate babies, separate from their spouses (miraculously obtaining annulments instead of divorces), and dispense birth control information in the poor neighborhoods.

It is important to recognize that soap operas serve to affirm the primacy of the family not by presenting an ideal family, but by portraying a family in constant turmoil and appealing to the spectator to be understanding and tolerant of the many evils which go on within that family. The spectator/mother, identifying with each character in turn, is made to see "the larger picture" and extend her sympathy to both the sinner and the victim. She is thus in a position to forgive all. As a rule, only those issues which can be tolerated and ultimately pardoned are introduced on soap operas. The list includes careers for women, abortions, premarital and extramarital sex, alcoholism, divorce, mental and even physical cruelty. An issue like homosexuality, which could explode the family structure rather than temporarily disrupt it, is simply ignored. Soap operas, contrary to many people's conception of them, are not conservative but liberal, and the mother is the liberal par excellence. By constantly presenting her with the many-sidedness of any question, by never reaching a permanent conclusion, soap operas undermine her capacity to form unambiguous judgments.

In this respect, soap opera melodrama can be said to create in the spectator a divisiveness of feeling totally different from the "monopathic" feeling Robert Heilman sees as constituting the appeal of traditional melodrama. There, he writes, "one enjoys the wholeness of a practical competence that leads to swift and sure action; one is untroubled by psychic fumbling, by indecisiveness, by awareness of alternate courses, by weak muscles or strong counterimperatives."[22] But in soap operas, we are constantly troubled by "psychic fumbling" and by "strong counterimperatives." To take one example, Trish, on "Days of Our Lives," takes her small son and runs away from her husband David in order to advance her singing career. When she gets an opportunity to go to London to star in a show, she leaves the child with her mother. When the show folds, she becomes desperate to get back home to see her child, but since she has no money, she has to prostitute herself. Finally she is able to return, and after experiencing a series of difficulties, she locates her son, who is now staying with his father. Once she is in

21 See Paul Mayer, "Creating 'Ryan's Hope.'"
22 Robert B. Heilman, *Tragedy and Melodrama*, p. 85.

town, a number of people, angry at the suffering she has caused David, are hostile and cruel towards her. Thus far, the story seems to bear out the contention of the critics who claim that soap opera characters who leave the protection of the family are unequivocally punished. But the matter is not so simple. For the unforgiving people are shown to have limited perspectives. The larger view is summed up by Margo, a woman who has a mysterious and perhaps fatal disease and who, moreover, has every reason to be jealous of Trish since Trish was the first love of Margo's husband. Margo claims that no one can ever fully know what private motives drove Trish to abandon her family; besides, she says, life is too short to bear grudges and inflict pain. The spectator, who sees the extremity of Trish's sorrow, assents. And at the same time, the spectator is made to forgive and understand the unforgiving characters, for she is intimately drawn into their anguish and suffering as well.

These remarks must be qualified. If soap operas keep us caring about everyone; if they refuse to allow us to condemn most characters and actions until all the evidence is in (and, of course, it never is), there is one character whom we are allowed to hate unreservedly; the villainess, the negative image of the spectator's ideal self.[23] Although much of the suffering on soap opera is presented as unavoidable, the surplus suffering is often the fault of the villainess who tries to "make things happen and control events better than the subject/spectator can." The villainess might very possibly be a mother trying to manipulate her children's lives or ruin their marriages. Or perhaps she is a woman avenging herself on her husband's family because it has never fully accepted her.

This character cannot be dismissed as easily as many critics seem to think.[24] The extreme delight viewers apparently take in despising the villainess testifies to the enormous amount of energy involved in the spectator's repression and to her (albeit unconscious) resentment at being constituted as an egoless receptacle for the suffering of others.[25] The villainess embodies the "split-off fury" which in the words of Dorothy Dinnerstein, is "the underside of the 'truly feminine' woman's mon-

24

25

---

[23] There are still villains on soap operas, but their numbers have declined considerably since radio days—to the point where they are no longer indispensable to the formula. "The Young and the Restless," for example, does without them.

[24] According to Weibel, we quite simply "deplore" the victimizers and totally identify with the victim (p. 62).

[25] "A soap opera without a bitch is a soap opera that doesn't get watched. The more hateful the bitch the better. Erica of 'All My Children' is a classic. If you want to hear some hairy rap, just listen to a bunch of women discussing Erica.
'Girl, that Erica needs her tail whipped.'
'I wish she'd try to steal my man and plant some marijuana in my purse. I'd be mopping up the street with her new hairdo.'" Bebe Moore Campbell, "Hooked on Soaps," p. 103.

strously overdeveloped talent for unreciprocated empathy."[26] This aspect of melodrama can be traced back to the middle of the nineteenth century when *Lady Audley's Secret,* a drama based on Mary Elizabeth Braddon's novel about a governess turned bigamist and murderess, became one of the most popular stage melodramas of all time.[27] In her discussion of the novel, Elaine Showalter shows how the author, while paying lipservice to conventional notions about the feminine role, managed to appeal to "thwarted female energy":

> The brilliance of *Lady Audley's Secret* is that Braddon makes her would-be murderess the fragile blond angel of domestic realism. . . . The dangerous woman is not the rebel or the bluestocking, but the "pretty little girl" whose indoctrination in the female role has taught her secrecy and deceitfulness, almost as secondary sex characteristics.[28]

Thus the villainess is able to transform traditional feminine weaknesses into the sources of her strength.   26

Similarly, on soap operas, the villainess seizes those aspects of a   27
woman's life which normally render her most helpless and tries to turn them into weapons for manipulating other characters. She is, for instance, especially good at manipulating pregnancy, unlike most women, who, as Mary Ellmann wittily points out, tend to feel manipulated by it:

> At the same time, women cannot help observing that conception (their highest virtue, by all reports) simply happens or doesn't. It lacks the style of enterprise. It can be prevented by foresight and device (though success here, as abortion rates show, is exaggerated), but it is accomplished by luck (good or bad). Purpose often seems if anything, a deterrent. A devious business benefitting by indirection, by pretending not to care, as though the self must trick the body. In the regrettable conception, the body instead tricks the self—much as it does in illness or death.[29]

In contrast to the numerous women on soap operas who are either   28
trying unsuccessfully to become pregnant or who have become pregnant as a consequence of a single unguarded moment in their lives, the villainess manages, for a time at least, to make pregnancy work for her. She gives it the "style of enterprise." If she decides she wants to marry a man, she will take advantage of him one night when he is feeling especially vulnerable and seduce him. And if she doesn't achieve the hoped-for pregnancy, undaunted, she simply lies to her lover about

[26] Dorothy Dinnerstein, *The Mermaid and The Minotaur,* p. 236.

[27] "The author, Mary Elizabeth Braddon, belonged to that class of writers called by Charles Reade 'obstacles to domestic industry.'" Frank Rahill, *The World of Melodrama,* p. 204.

[28] Elaine Showalter, *A Literature of Their Own,* p. 204.

[29] Mary Ellmann, *Thinking About Women,* p. 181. Molly Haskell makes a similar point in her discussion of "The Woman's Film," in *From Reverence to Rape,* pp. 172–73.

being pregnant. The villainess thus reverses male/female roles: anxiety about conception is transferred to the male. He is the one who had better watch his step and curb his promiscuous desires or he will find himself burdened with an unwanted child.

Some episodes on "The Young and the Restless" perfectly illustrate   29 the point. Lori's sister Leslie engages in a one night sexual encounter with Lori's husband, Lance. Of course, she becomes pregnant as a result. Meanwhile Lori and Lance have been having marital difficulties, and Lori tries to conceive a child, hoping this will bring her closer to her husband. When she finds out about her sister and Lance, she becomes frantic about her inability to conceive, realizing that if Lance ever finds out he is the father of Leslie's child, he will be drawn to Leslie and reject her. Vanessa, Lance's mother and a classic villainess, uses her knowledge of the situation to play on Lori's insecurities and drive a wedge between her and Lance. At the same time, Lori's father has been seduced by Jill Foster, another villainess, who immediately becomes pregnant, thus forcing him to marry her.

Furthermore, the villainess, far from allowing her children to rule   30 her life, often uses them in order to further her own selfish ambitions. One of her typical ploys is to threaten the father or the woman possessing custody of the child with the deprivation of that child. She is the opposite of the woman at home, who at first is forced to have her children constantly with her, and later is forced to let them go—for a time on a daily recurring basis and then permanently. The villainess enacts for the spectator a kind of reverse *fort-da* game, in which the mother is the one who attempts to send the child away and bring it back at will, striving to overcome feminine passivity in the process of the child's appearance and loss.[30] Into the bargain, she also tries to manipulate the man's disappearance and return by keeping the fate of his child always hanging in the balance. And again, male and female roles tend to get reversed: the male suffers the typically feminine anxiety over the threatened absence of his children. On "Ryan's Hope," for example, Delia continually uses her son to control her husband and his family. At one point she clashes with another villainess, Raye Woodward, over the child and the

---

[30] The game, observed by Freud, in which the child plays "disappearance and return" with a wooden reel tied to a string. "What he did was to hold the reel by the string and very skilfully throw it over the edge of his curtained cot, so that it disappeared into it, at the same time uttering his expressive 'O-O-O-O'. [Freud speculates that this represents the German word *'fort'* or *'gone.'*] He then pulled the reel out of the cot again by the string and hailed its reappearance with a joyful *'da'* ['there']." According to Freud, "Throwing away the object so that it was 'gone' might satisfy an impulse of the child's, which was suppressed in his actual life, to revenge himself on his mother for going away from him. In that case it would have a defiant meaning: 'All right then, go away! I don't need you. I'm sending you away myself.'" Sigmund Freud, *Beyond the Pleasure Principle,* pp. 10–11.

child's father, Frank Ryan, from whom Delia is divorced. Raye realizes that the best way to get Frank interested in her is by taking a maternal interest in his child. When Delia uncovers Raye's scheme, she becomes determined to foil it by regaining custody of the boy. On "The Young and the Restless," to take another example, Derek is on his way out of the house to try to intercept Jill Foster on her way to the altar and persuade her to marry him instead of Stuart Brooks. Derek's ex-wife Suzanne thwarts the attempt by choosing that moment to inform him that their son is in a mental hospital.

The villainess thus continually works to make the most out of events   31 which render other characters totally helpless. Literal paralysis turns out, for one villainess, to be an active blessing, since it prevents her husband from carrying out his plans to leave her; when she gets back the use of her legs, therefore, she doesn't tell anyone. And even death doesn't stop another villainess from wreaking havoc; she returns to haunt her husband and convince him to try to kill his new wife.

The popularity of the villainess would seem to be explained in part   32 by the theory of repetition compulsion, which Freud saw as resulting from the individual's attempt to become an active manipulator of her/ his own powerlessness.[31] The spectator, it might be thought, continually tunes into soap operas to watch the villainess as she tries to gain control over her feminine passivity, thereby acting out the spectator's fantasies of power. Of course, most formula stories (like the Western) appeal to the spectator/reader's compulsion to repeat: the spectator constantly returns to the same story in order to identify with the main character and achieve, temporarily, the illusion of mastery denied him or her in real life. But soap operas refuse the spectator even this temporary illusion of mastery. The villainess's painstaking attempts to turn her powerlessness to her own advantage are always thwarted just when victory seems most assured, and she must begin her machinations all over again. Moreover, the spectator does not comfortably identify with the villainess. Since the spectator despises the villainess as the negative image of her ideal self, she not only watches the villainess act out her own hidden wishes, but simultaneously sides with the forces conspiring against fulfillment of those wishes. As a result of this "internal contestation,"[32] the spectator comes to enjoy repetition for its own sake and

---

[31] Speaking of the child's *fort-da* game, Freud notes, "At the outset he was in a passive situation—he was overpowered by experience; but by repeating it, unpleasurable though it was, as a game, he took on an *active* part. These efforts might be put down to an instinct for mastery that was acting independently of whether the memory was in itself pleasurable or not." In *Beyond the Pleasure Principle*, p. 10.

[32] Jean-Paul Sartre's phrase for the tension surrealism's created object sets up in the spectator is remarkably appropriate here. See *What Is Literature?*, p. 133n.

takes her adequate pleasure in the building up and tearing down of the plot. In this way, perhaps, soap operas help reconcile her to the meaningless, repetitive nature of much of her life and work within the home.

Soap operas, then, while constituting the spectator as a "good 33 mother," provide in the person of the villainess an outlet for feminine anger: in particular, as we have seen, the spectator has the satisfaction of seeing men suffer the same anxieties and guilt that women usually experience and seeing them receive similar kinds of punishment for their transgressions. But that anger is neutralized at every moment in that it is the special object of the spectator's hatred. The spectator, encouraged to sympathize with almost everyone, can vent her frustration on the one character who refuses to accept her own powerlessness, who is unashamedly self-seeking. Woman's anger is directed at woman's anger, and an eternal cycle is created.

And yet, if the villainess never succeeds, if, in accordance with the 34 spectator's conflicting desires, she is doomed to eternal repetition, then she obviously never permanently fails either. When, as occasionally happens, a villainess reforms, a new one immediately supplants her. Generally, however, a popular villainess will remain true to her character for most or all of the soap opera's duration. And if the villainess constantly suffers because she is always foiled, we should remember that she suffers no more than the good characters, who don't even try to interfere with their fates. Again, this may be contrasted to the usual imperatives of melodrama, which demand an ending to justify the suffering of the good and punish the wicked. While soap operas thrive they present a continual reminder that women's anger is alive, if not exactly well.

Works Cited

Barthes, Roland. S/Z. Translated by Richard Miller. New York: Hill and Wang, 1974.

Benjamin, Walter. *Illuminations.* Translated by Harry Zohn, Edited by Hannah Arendt. New York: Schocken Books, 1969.

Campbell, Bebe Moore. "Hooked on Soaps." *Essence,* November 1978, pp. 100–103.

Cawelti, John G. *Adventure, Mystery, and Romance.* Chicago: University of Chicago Press, 1976.

Dinnerstein, Dorothy. *The Mermaid and the Minotaur: Sexual Arrangements and Human Malaise.* New York: Harper & Row, 1976.

Easton, Barbara. "Feminism and the Contemporary Family." *Socialist Review* 8, no. 3 (1978), pp. 11–36.

Edmondson, Madeleine, and Rounds, David. *From Mary Noble to Mary*

Hartmann: *The Complete Soap Opera Book*. New York: Stein and Day, 1976.

Ellmann, Mary. *Thinking about Women*. New York: Harvest Books, 1968.

Freud, Sigmund. *Beyond the Pleasure Principle*. Translated by James Strachey. New York: W. W. Norton Co., 1961.

Haskell, Molly. *From Reverence to Rape: The Treatment of Women in the Movies*. New York: Penguin, 1974.

Heilman, Robert B. *Tragedy and Melodrama: Versions of Experience*. Seattle: University of Washington Press, 1968.

Kermode, Frank. *The Sense of an Ending: Studies in the Theory of Fiction*. New York: Oxford University Press, 1967.

Mayer, Paul. "Creating 'Ryan's Hope.'" In *T.V. Book*. Edited by Judy Fireman. New York: Workman Publishing Co., 1977.

Mulvey, Laura. "Visual Pleasure and Narrative Cinema." In *Women and the Cinema*. Edited by Karyn Kay and Gerald Peary. New York: E. P. Dutton, 1977.

Newcome, Horace. *T.V.: The Most Popular Art*. New York: Anchor Books, 1974.

Papashvily, Helen Waite. *All the Happy Endings, A Study of the Domestic Novel in America, the Women Who Wrote It, the Women Who Read It, in the Nineteenth Century*. New York: Harper & Brothers, 1956.

Porter, Dennis. "Soap Time: Thoughts on a Commodity Art Form." *College English* 38 (1977): 782–88.

Rahill, Frank. *The World of Melodrama*. University Park: Pennsylvania State University Press, 1967.

Sartre, Jean-Paul. *What Is Literature?* Translated by Bernard Frechtman. New York: Washington Square Press, 1966.

Showalter, Elaine. *A Literature of Their Own*. Princeton: Princeton University Press, 1977.

Wakefield, Dan. *All Her Children*. Garden City, N.Y.: Doubleday & Co., 1976.

Weibel, Kathryn. *Mirror, Mirror: Images of Women Reflected in Popular Culture*. Garden City, N.Y.: Anchor Books, 1977.

•••••••••••••••••

Examining the Text

1. Modleski's attitude toward soap operas seems much more positive than Berman's. Point to some instances of her praise. How does her focus on "intimacy" and "continuity" (paragraph 6) and on the "feminine" in soap operas (7) color her attitude?

2. In soap operas, Modleski says, "the enigmas proliferate . . . the narrative, by placing ever more complex obstacles between desire and fulfillment, makes anticipation of an end an end in itself" (8). What does she mean? How does the fact that soap operas "cannot end" (15) contribute to her comparison of this genre and traditional melodrama? Do Modleski's observations correspond to your own experience of soap operas?

3. Modleski focuses on the image of women in soap operas and their relationship to the spectator (the "ideal" but "ineffectual" spectator/mother, able "to forgive both the sinner and the victim," and "the villainess, the negative image of the spectator's ideal self"). How does she relate these opposing images to feminine powerlessness? How do they contribute to the dynamics and appeal of soap operas?

For Group Discussion

Modleski argues that soap operas "are not conservative but liberal" (22). As a group, determine what she means by "liberal" in this context and how you think soap operas do or do not fit this definition. As a class, evaluate Modleski's analysis of soap operas. Do you agree or disagree with her basic assertions?

Writing Suggestion

Modleski notes that in 1982, when she was writing about daytime soap operas, approximately twelve were on the air. Almost as many are broadcast today, mostly the same ones. In an essay consider the extent to which Modleski's observations hold true today and the extent to which there may be changes. Are soap operas still marked by "intimacy" and "continuity"? Are the plot dynamics similar and the basic roles of "good mother" and "villainess" still prominent? Have there been changes in the representation of minorities (2) and the presentation of controversial issues, such as abortion and homosexuality (22)? What can you conclude about soap operas' essential appeal and the extent to which they adapt to changing audiences.

3. TWO SITUATION COMEDIES

The following two analyses are the most technical and abstract in this section, each relying on some fairly complex terminology unique to the writer's field and interpretative approach. Both writers gear their essays for an academic rather than a popular audience.

"He's Everything You're Not . . . ":
A Semiological Analysis of *Cheers*
Arthur Asa Berger

*I*s *it symbolic that Diane Chambers, one of the original leads in the sit-com* Cheers, *has blond hair? Why does Carla the waitress have a temper and kid around so frankly about sex? What is signified by the name Norm? These are just a few of the questions that Arthur Asa Berger sets out to answer in his semiological analysis of one of the most popular situation comedies of all time. Taking his critical position from the structuralists Ferdinand Saussure and Umberto Eco, Berger "reads" the text of* Cheers *through the lens of semiotics. For Berger, this reading is a process of decoding a text and of interpreting the sign systems it contains. He defines a sign as a unit made up of a sound image and a concept—or, in the terminology of the structuralists, of a signifier and a signified.*

Berger is careful to point out that the sign is not natural; *in other words, blond hair means something to us not because there is a natural connection between blond hair and its so-called "meaning," but because of the cultural and historical values that we have invested it with. The rules for establishing a relationship between the signifier and the signified, then, are called "codes," and these codes tells us what signs mean. When this type of semiotic study is applied to a situation comedy, some interesting subtexts, or concealed meanings, come to light. For example, the bar itself may signify more than just a building in which the characters can buy alcohol. Its geographical location (Boston) and its interior decorating suggest that it is "classier" than a college or working class bar. For Berger, both of these signifiers give the* Cheers *bar a meaning beyond its dictionary definition.*

Not only does Berger provide a critical apparatus—semiotics—with which to "read" Cheers, *but he also provides a model for reading and interpreting "texts" you come across in your daily lives. For example, you might easily apply these same critical methods to the vast number of signifying systems in commercials on television and in the advertisements in magazines, looking at signs, codes, and "binary oppositions" in those everyday pop-cultural artifacts to determine the meanings those "texts" impart.*

• • • • • • • • • • • • • • • • • • • •

The basic question that semiology (or semiotics or structuralism) asks of a television program or film or advertisement—or any "text"—is this: How do people understand what's going on? How do people derive meaning from a text? How do they know how to interpret facial expressions, body movements, clothes the characters wear, kinds of shots, the scenery, correctly? How is meaning generated and conveyed?   1

A hint comes from Jonathan Culler, who writes in *Structuralist* 2
Poetics:

> The notion that linguistics might be useful in studying other cultural
> phenomena is based on two fundamental insights: first, that social and
> cultural phenomena are not simply material objects or events but ob-
> jects and events with meaning, and hence signs; and second, that they
> do not have essences but are defined by a network of relations.[1]

Meaning, Culler tells us, stems from considering phenomena as 3
signs and from looking at the relationships among these signs. These
two notions are at the heart of the semiological enterprise. In this semiological analysis of the pilot episode of "Cheers,"[2] we will be considering the text as a collection or system of signs. We will define signs in the
Saussurean manner as a combination of a sound and an image (signifier) and a concept or understanding (signified).

The problem of meaning arises from the fact that the relation be- 4
tween the signifier and the signified is arbitrary and conventional, so
signs can mean anything. And, as Umberto Eco points out, they can lie.
A signifier (such as a gesture) can mean different things to different people, depending upon their social class, cultural level, location, and other
factors. Since the relation between signifier and signified is arbitrary, we
must discover the codes that explain the signs, that help us interpret the
signifiers. In addition, we must look for important relationships (other
than that of signifier and signified) found in texts that help us understand cultural phenomena.

Here again Saussure is useful. He writes in his *Course in General Lin-* 5
guistics, "[C]oncepts are purely differential and defined not by their positive content but negatively by their relations with the other terms of the
system. Their most precise characteristic is in being what the others are
not."[3] Nothing means anything in itself, and everything (as far as concepts are concerned) is dependent on relationships. The most important
relationship is that of polar or binary opposition; binary oppositions are
the fundamental way in which the human mind finds meaning. This notion has been adapted by Claude Lévi-Strauss[4] into a means of looking
at texts such as myths and Greek tragedies—and, by extension here,
"Cheers." In essence we search for the hidden set of oppositions that in-

---

[1] Jonathan Culler, *Structuralist Poetics: Structuralism, Linguistics and the Study of Literature* (Ithaca, NY: Cornell University Press, 1975), 4.

[2] The first episode of "Cheers" aired on September 30, 1982, on NBC and was 30 minutes in length. The cast was Shelley Long as Diane Chambers, Ted Danson as Sam Malone, Rhea Perlman as Carla Tortelli, John Retzenberg as Cliff, George Wendt as Norm, and Nicholas Colosante as Coach.

[3] Ferdinand de Saussure, *Course in General Linguistics* (New York: McGraw-Hill, 1966), 117.

[4] Claude Lévi-Strauss, *Structural Anthropology* (Garden City, NY: Doubleday, 1967).

form a text and thus generate meaning. This meaning is not necessarily recognized by people but is there nevertheless, and can be elicited by the semiologist.

Signs

The title of the series, "Cheers," tells us something. It suggests happiness, good spirits (in this case literally as well as figuratively), and companionship. "Cheers" is a toast we make when drinking with others, so there is an element of conviviality and sociability involved. In this series, which takes place in a bar named Cheers, we thus find ourselves with expectations about what might transpire. We expect something pleasant . . . and we are not disappointed.

Boston

The bar itself is a sign system. It is not drab or shabby, like a working-class bar, nor is it a fancy, trendy bar. It seems to be a neighborhood bar that caters mainly to middle-class people. The bar and the row of liquor bottles are primary signifiers of what might be called "barness." And the bar is in Boston, which gives it a certain flavor and gives us certain understandings because of the way Boston is perceived. Boston has an identity due, in part, to its being on the east coast and closely identified with English culture, the revolutionary period, and Harvard University. Bostonians are perceived as somewhat effete and a bit snobbish—though this is reserved for upper-class, aristocratic (Protestant) types and certainly not for the Irish working-class types one finds there. The fact that this series takes place in Boston, I would suggest, prepares us for all kinds of characters—eccentrics, snobs, weirdos, con artists.

Blondness

One of the most important signs in the text is the color of Diane Chambers's hair. She's a blond, and blondness is a sign of considerable richness and meaning. America is a country where "gentlemen prefer blonds," and blond hair coloring is the most popular color sold. But what does blondness signify?

For some women blond hair color is a means of escaping (or attempting to escape) their ethnic identity, or, in some cases, their age. It is used to cover gray hair. But there are other aspects that are much more important. Some of these are pointed out by Charles Winick in his book *The New People:*

> [F]or a substantial number of women, the attraction of blondeness is less an opportunity to have more fun than the communication of a withdrawal of emotion, a lack of passion. One reason for Marilyn Monroe's enormous popularity was that she was less a tempestuous temptress than a non-threatening child. The innocence conveyed by blonde hair is also suggested by the 70 percent of baby dolls whose hair is blonde.
>
> D. H. Lawrence pointed out that blonde women in American novels are often cool and unobtainable, while the dark woman represents passion. Fictional blondes also tend to be vindictive and frigid.[5]

This innocence of the blond is appealing to men because blonds, not being experienced, could not be very judgmental about men's sexual performances—if, that is, things ever get to that stage. Thus, when Sumner calls Diane a "child," there is more significance to the term than we might imagine. 10

The book that Diane attempts to read and her numerous allusions to and quotations from great literary figures are signs of her (and Sumner's) status as intellectuals. And the lack of a "proper" response (awe, respect) by Sam and his friends is an indication of their status as nonintellectuals. They are more interested in the Boston Patriots than in John Donne, in linebackers than in literature. 11

Names

Let us move on to something a bit more speculative—an examination of the names of the characters to see whether we can find anything of interest and significance. Another name for Diane (Diana) in mythology is Artemis, a virgin huntress associated with the moon. Thus she is well named, for her basic role in the series is that of an object of sexual desire, a "child"/woman who becomes embroiled in a battle of the sexes with the hero, Sam Malone. (I will not comment on the fact that her last name, Chambers, suggests a room—especially a bedroom, my dictionary tells me.) 12

Sam's name does not tell us much, though we might make something of the fact that we can find an "alone" in Malone and it is his status as a male with no ties that facilitates the battle with Diane. Carla Tortelli is another matter; in her name we find "tort," which is a description of her argumentative personality. She is an injured party (her husband left her with four children) and bitter about it. Even Sumner Sloane's name is interesting, for he is, in effect, "on loan" to Diane from 13

---

[5] Charles Winick, *The New People: Desexualization in American Life* (New York: Pegasus, 1968), 169.

his ex-wife Barbara. She takes him back when the time is appropriate. Norm, the fat beer drinker, is a perfect everyman figure and well named; he is a representation of the typical American bar patron, drinking the beverage of the common man. "Coach" is a different matter; his name is used ironically. He is not a guide and teacher but, instead, an absent-minded and somewhat daffy character who cannot remember his own name and is always confused.

I cannot argue that the names of the characters were deliberately 14 chosen for their semiological significance, but it is interesting (and maybe more than purely coincidental) that the characters have the names they do. The writers of the series are educated and bring in many names from "elite culture," such as Kierkegaard and Nietzsche[6] (to show that Diane is an intellectual). It wouldn't be too much of a stretch of the imagination to assume that there was some conscious thought about the names of the characters.

Codes

If the relationship between signifier and signified is arbitrary, we 15 must have rules for interpreting things, and these rules are what we call codes. Codes tell us what signs mean. What complicates matters, as I suggested earlier, is that different groups and subgroups have different codes in certain cases and there is, at times, code confusion between a creator or user of a sign and an interpreter or receiver of a sign. Thus we have the problem of what Umberto Eco calls "aberrant decoding." He writes in his essay "Towards a Semiotic Inquiry into the Television Message": "Codes and subcodes are applied to the message in the light of a general framework of cultural references, which constitutes the receiver's patrimony of knowledge; his ideological, ethical, religious standpoints, his psychological attitudes, his tastes, his value systems, etc."[7] Codes are connected to culture and social class to a great degree, which means that people who watch "Cheers" may not always "get" everything the writers have put into the show. Or some people, at least.

In the same light, the characters themselves do not understand one 16 another all the time; this is a source of the humor in numerous cases. Let me suggest that humor, in general, is connected to code confusion and violation. The difference between what one expects (knowing the code) and what one gets (due to code confusion and violation) generates

---

[6] Mentioned in later episodes.
[7] Umberto Eco, "Towards a Semiotic Inquiry into the Television Message," *Working Papers in Cultural Studies* 3 (Autumn 1972):115.

laughter. We are dealing with a form of incongruity or perhaps, to be more accurate, an explanation of incongruity. The situation is very complicated, for we find the characters in "Cheers" do not understand one another and the audience of "Cheers" does not understand everything that goes on in the episode. Nevertheless, the audience probably gets a lot of the humor—or large enough audiences do—for the series to be successful.

Let's consider the codes of "Cheers" in some detail. First, we know   17
we are watching a comedy and thus are prepared to laugh, to give everything a nonserious, humorous interpretation. Therefore we watch the program with certain expectations that color the way we interpret the events in the episode and relate to the characters. Since it is a comedy, we also expect to see eccentric types who play off against one another; we are prepared for the zanies, weirdos, and others who are found in comedies and who often represent "types" rather than being three-dimensional characters.

In this episode of "Cheers" much of the humor comes from misun-   18
derstandings and misinterpretations made by the various characters, though there are also some "nonresponses." These two forms of code violation or aberrant decoding come from the different social and cultural backgrounds of the characters. Diane and Sumner are highly educated, middle-class types, whereas the rest of the characters are working class and presumably less educated.

Thus, when Carla talks about putting her husband through school,   19
Diane assumes "school" means a university, not a television repair academy. And when Coach talks about "working six years on his novel," Diane asks, increduously, whether he's writing a novel. She discovers, instead, that he's reading one. Cultural and class differences are at the root of these misunderstandings. The same can be said of the scene where Diane has answered the phone and is talking to a woman with whom Sam has presumably spent the night. He doesn't want to talk to the woman and his mouth is full of food, so he tries to indicate to Diane that she should tell the woman he's gone for a haircut. Instead Diane says, "He's taking a mime class." She may be intelligent, but she doesn't have much common sense. The same thing can be said about Sumner, who leaves his young fiancé in order to retrieve a ring from his ex-wife.

We find a case of "nonresponse" in the scene where Sumner Sloane   20
has just introduced himself and informed Sam that he is "professor of world literature at Boston University." Instead of being awed, Sam says nothing; he refuses to "validate" Sumner, a response that university professors and students to whom I have shown the program find hilarious. Sam's nonresponse is viewed as a proper one because Sumner is so pompous and deserves, we feel, to be deflated. Sumner has violated the

egalitarian code that is so important in American culture and has set himself up for his punishment.

Below I list some codes and violations found in the episode so we 21 can see how important this phenomenon is.

Code	Violation
Common sense	Diane and the "mime" scene
Propriety	Diane, as waitress, sits with patrons
Egalitarianism	Sam's nonresponse to Sumner's identification of himself
Loyalty	Sumner jilts Diane
Law	Kid tries to get a drink with false identification
Self-awareness	Coach doesn't know his own name
Logic	Alcoholic owns a bar
Normalcy	Eccentric types found in "Cheers"

This list indicates the importance of code confusion and violation in 22 the text. In order for viewers to understand this text fully, they must be able to recognize the violations of the codes, which means they must be able to interpret facial expressions and other signs, understand motivations, and assess characters. That is, viewers must bring a great deal of knowledge to the text; and the more they know, the more they will understand. "Cheers" must be seen as a figure to be interpreted against the ground of American culture and society; and culture, from our perspective, is a collection of codes and subcodes. When we watch "Cheers," we are, semiologically speaking, decoding a text . . . whether we know it or not.

Oppositions

Bipolar oppositions, we have learned, are a basic means by which 23 we find meaning; this is because nothing has meaning in itself. It is the network of relationships that is crucial to the generation of meaning. What I have written deals with concepts, but it also may be used to understand characters in a text. Let's look at some oppositions between various characters in "Cheers": Diane and Carla, Sam Malone and Sumner Sloane, and Diane and Sam.

Diane	Carla
Tall	Short
Blond	Dark hair

Single (to be married)	Was married (now single)
Cool/reserved	Hot/bitchy
Middle class	Working class
WASP	Ethnic
Innocent	Experienced
(Schoolmarm)	(Bargirl)

We can see that these two characters are opposites in many im- 24
portant respects. The same can be said for Sam Malone and Sumner
Sloane.

Sam Malone	**Sumner Sloane**
Tall	Short
Young	Old
Jock	Egghead
Modest	Pompous
Regular guy	Goof
Common sense	Intelligence
The world	The academy
Hires Diane	Abandons Diane

Sumner's character is, in a sense, defined by how different he is from   25
Sam. Diane has said, in an important line spoken to Sam, that Sumner
is "everything you're not." And this is quite true. Sumner is an intellectual, but he lacks common sense and morality—he abandons Diane after being "mesmerized" by his former wife, Barbara. He is a highly
stereotyped figure: academics are conventionally seen as intelligent but
unworldly, lacking common sense and often lacking decency. Sam has
no problem in immediately sizing Sumner up as a "goof." This polarity
between the intelligent but impractical and unworldly scholar and the
uneducated but naturally "wise" common man has deep roots in American culture, and can be found in the early 1800s in our idealization of
the various "nature's noblemen" we identified with. It is connected to
ideas we had about ourselves and the way we contrasted ourselves with
Europeans.

In essence, we saw ourselves as innocent, wise, egalitarian, indi- 26
vidualistic characters living in a classless society in a state of nature,
and contrasted this with Europeans, whom we saw as guilt-ridden,
trained conformists living in a hierarchically organized society dominated by institutions such as the church and nobility. Sam is shown as
a classic American "regular guy" figure, and Sumner is portrayed as a
European-like character. The fact that he is a professor of world literature suggests his lack of Americanness and that he has, somehow, been
tainted.

Finally, let us move to the central opposition between characters in   27
this text and the opposition that is to be crucial in the series—the differences between Diane Chambers and Sam Malone.

Diane Chambers	Sam Malone
Female	Male
Blond	Dark hair
Middle class	Working class
Education	Common sense
Vulnerable	Worldly
Beauty	Beast (magnificent pagan)
Worker	Boss
Useless	Handy

One of the common themes in the series is to be the "battle" (of the   28
sexes) between Sam and Diane. They are attracted to each other but
refuse to admit it; they cannot fall in love and get married lest the series
become a "domestic comedy," so they spend their time flirting, becoming involved in ridiculous situations from which they extricate themselves with great difficulty. That obviously is their fate. We do not know
this when we see the pilot, but we can presume this will be the case from
our knowledge of the genre and the logic of the situation.

In addition to the oppositions that exist among characters, there is   29
a central set of oppositions in the text that is worth considering. These
oppositions involve characters but have broader implications.

Youth	Adulthood
Kid who can't drink	Grown-ups who can drink
Young teaching assistant	Old(er) professor
Working Class	**Middle Class**
Workers, patrons	Sumner Sloane, Diane Chambers
The Future	**The Past**
The marriage	Ex-baseball player
Grad student	Ex-wife of Sumner
Con Artists	**Marks**
The kid	Sam
Sumner's ex-wife	Sumner
Inside	**Outside**
The bar	The outside world
Regulars	Strangers, aliens
The Beauty	**The Beast**
Diane	Sam

These oppositions are of central importance in the episode—and in   30
the whole series. It is the "battle of the sexes," "the battle of the classes,"
and a whole series of other confrontations that generate not only dra-

matic interest and tension, but also humor, because the possibilities for misunderstanding and misinterpretation, are enormous.

There is another kind of opposition worth mentioning here: that be-   31 tween the main characters, who will appear in each episode, and the various characters, such as Sumner Sloane, who will be seen in only one episode. As we watch the series, we will get to know the main characters, and the series will function as a kind of "ground" that will help us interpret what these characters do and understand them better. They will have a different "status" than the characters who appear for an episode and then disappear. These characters will remain more stereotyped and one-dimensional; we will understand them because they will be "types," with conventional signs and codes. With each episode the main characters, even though they may be stereotyped, will become more real because we will know more of their history.

Thus the characters in a television program/series that lasts a long   32 time become, so to speak, a part of us; their history merges with our lives. And the situations in which they become involved take on a significance for the regular viewer that they do not have for the casual viewer. This leads, I suggest, to an inevitable humanization and rounding of the characters, especially in a medium like television, where facial expressions and other signifying systems reveal character tellingly. It might be argued that regular viewers of a series like "Cheers" see more in a given episode than casual viewers do, though in the pilot episode I'm discussing, all viewers start on an equal footing.

From a semiological perspective, stereotyping involves the use of   33 conventional and easily understood signifiers and codes . . . and easily perceived oppositions. This instant decoding is necessary because television programs don't have a great deal of time to develop characters, and must rely on commonly understood attitudes about types of people and their motivations. Stereotyping may also be connected to the inability of some audiences to decode more complex characterizations.

Conclusion

A semiotic analysis of a text such as "Cheers" focuses on how mean-   34 ing is generated and conveyed, and thus on such matters as signs and codes, polar oppositions, and sequential structures. The text functions as a figure against the ground of culture, and the figure reflects (though not always in perfectly accurate ways) the ground, just as the ground helps interpret the figure. A text such as "Cheers" is extremely complex and could yield a semiological analysis of great length. The lighting, the pacing, the dialogue, the costuming, the blocking, the facial expressions of the characters, the music, the sound—all lend themselves to semio-logical analysis because they all function as signs (and, in particular, sig-nifiers).

I have offered a semiological quick study of "Cheers" in an attempt 35 to show how a semiological or semiotic analysis of this text might be done. There's plenty of room at the bar for others.

• • • • • • • • • • • • • • • • • • • •

Examining the Text

1. Explain the "semiological approach" as described by Berger. How do semiologists determine meanings within any text? What are "binary op-positions" (paragraph 5) and "signifiers" (3–4), and what role do they play in semiotic interpretation?

2. Define "codes" (15) as Berger discusses them. In what ways, accord-ing to Berger, do these codes play a role in any kind of humor? Do you agree with Berger's analysis?

3. Berger deals specifically with the pilot episode of *Cheers.* The series, of course, continued for many years and during that time underwent a number of changes; new rivals for Sam and Diane were introduced, blond Shelly Long left to be replaced by dark-haired Kirstie Alley, and so forth. List as many major changes in *Cheers* over the years as you can. How do these changes, new characters' names, for example, and their bipolar relation to other characters fit in with Berger's analysis of the show's first episode?

For Group Discussion

Choose another situation comedy with which all group members are familiar and subject it to the same kind of general semiological anal-ysis that Berger uses. Consider multiple significations of the title, signi-fiers of the setting, physical traits of the characters, and their names. Also draw up a list of bipolar oppositions for two of the central charac-ters. As a class, discuss the extent to which such an analysis is instruc-tive in looking at a television program.

Writing Suggestions

Using Berger's essay as a model, analyze one episode of a popular situation comedy from a semiological perspective. Ideally, you should be familiar with the show and be able to tape the episode you're analyzing so you can watch it several times (or, alternatively, take detailed notes). Look for particularly meaningful signs in the setting, the characters' clothing, their physical traits, and their names; for implicit codes and violations of those codes; and for binary oppositions. Develop a thesis that suggests the show's underlying meanings and accounts for its comedic appeal.

Golden Girls: Feminine Archetypal Patterns of the Complete Woman

Anne K. Kaler

The following essay by Anne Kaler "reads" a television sitcom from the perspective of myth, illuminating a text of popular culture by evoking texts of the "high" culture of world mythology. Here, Kaler takes a psychoanalytic (specifically Jungian) approach to interpreting the popular situation comedy, Golden Girls. *Kaler argues that the show's success is predicated upon its embodiment of the four phases of a woman's life—virgin, spouse, mother, and wise woman—as represented in countless myths throughout the world.*

Kaler's four phases are based upon a Jungian theory of archetypes. Psychologist Carl Jung (1875–1961) believed that human beings share certain primal representations and dream-symbols in common, whatever their level of technological achievement, social organization, or place in history. For example, one finds the symbol of the cross in many cultures, Christian and non-Christian, "civilized" or "primitive." In this essay, Kaler explains that the "ancient, hidden, unconscious archetypal images" of women—images that we see, today, in contemporary media representations of women—have their origins in Greco-Roman myth and the western metaphysical divisions between life/death and spirit/matter. Following these mythical lines, Kaler reads the character of Dorothy in Golden Girls *as the Athena/Amazon warrior figure, Rose as the virginal Artemis/Diana figure, Blanche as the seductress/Venus figure, and Sophia as the wise woman and Sybil/Hecate figure. In looking for these archetypes, Kaler pays close attention to the title of the show, the women's clothing, the set and staging of the production, and the textual and etymological roots of the characters' names; her analysis extends even to specific items on a kitchen table!*

As you can see from her terminology, Kaler is concerned with issues of femininity and cultural archetypes, or "models" for the human personality. This method falls squarely in the tradition of psychoanalytic criticism in which scholars apply Freud's or Jung's theories to different texts (as Kaler does with the TV sitcom) in order to discover the ways in which those texts reach people on a deep, psychological level. **As you read,** *then, think about how this essay was written with certain ideas of order, myth, structures, archetypes, and the* *unconscious in mind. Consider this central question: How closely does Kaler's four-sided model of the human personality, or the four-phase model of a woman's life, coincide with the ways in which you perceive people's personalities and behaviors?*

••••••••••••••••••

Any work of popular culture is successful as long as it replicates a   1
familiar psychological pattern of completeness. Until recently, no television show approached this healing pattern of the complete woman— the autonomous androgynous blend of the four dominant stages of a woman's life—as virgin, spouse, mother, and wise woman. No show, that is, until CBS's *Golden Girls.*

Ever since George Lucas constructed the fantasy universe of *Star*   2
Wars, which splintered the complete human personality into individual characters, archetypal patterns have become fashionably *de rigueur* for popular entertainment. Television is no exception: the success of a show is often based on the right mix of archetypal patterns which the viewers may recognize only subconsciously but which the producers have consciously planned. Just as viewers may identify with the hero of a drama because of his or her outstanding characteristic, so also do viewers like a show because of the image of completeness which the synergy of the archetypal patterns presents.

Patterns of the complete personality have been identified by psy-   3
chologists like Carl Jung. Expanding his concept that the human personality is an androgynous entity containing masculine and feminine aspects, Jung suggested that the human personality can be divided into a trinity or triad of the *animus* (male reasoning), and *anima* (female intuitive force), and the shadow (primitive generative force). But, when he found that the human symbol system seems to repeat the mandala-like "quaternity (or element of 'fourness')," Jung included a fourth aspect of the male trinity as a weaker female force, squaring the Jungian triad to bring it into the perfect balance of a four-sided mandala symbol, a four-sided division of the human personality, the "quaternity."

Early television shows constantly reinforced only the Jung's mas-   4
culine quaternity of the "four gods, coming from the 'four corners'" in their use of the archetypal pattern of the triad-plus-one formula of three men and one woman for action series like *Houston* or *Gunsmoke.* While the successful thirteen-year run of *M*A*S*H* stressed the masculine Jungian quaternity of Colonel Potter as the father figure or *animus,* BJ as the feminine or compassionate side or *anima,* Hawkeye as the shadow or trickster, the show still needed "Hot Lips" Margaret O'Houlihan as the weaker feminine, the fourth corner of the quaternity. However, as

M*A*S*H evolved, the original blend of characters fragmented into the more complex aspects of human nature—Radar as the virginal child, the priest as the religious aspect, Major Burns as the weak whining child, Klinger as the androgyne, Charles as the intellectual snob, etc. Although these secondary characters often possessed feminine aspects, they were still males; no other strong consistent feminine character ever developed to challenge Margaret because she contained her own quaternity in being all four phases of women simultaneously—daughter, seductress, mother, wise woman. She was daughter to Colonel Potter, temptress to Hawkeye and Burns, mother to Radar and her patients, wise woman to her nurses and to BJ. As a nurse, she preserved life and aided in death; as an army nurse, she restored life to send the same man back to their death by war. She was all the woman *M*A*S*H* needed. She was a completed personality and the success of the show can be attributed to her multi-faceted femininity in the face of a masculine quaternity in that most masculine enterprise of war.

For the masculine quaternity flourishes. When the western hero in   5
Gunsmoke, the space adventurer in *Star Trek,* and the private eye in *Magnum* and *Houston* developed, they gave only a nominal nod to the feminine component in their personalities. Granted an occasional doctor show permitted men to display feminine aspects such as compassion but only in the context of science; granted that *Gunsmoke* permitted Matt Dillon to show uncertainty but only in his relationship to Miss Kitty. Even when the complex story lines of *Hill Street Blues* and *St. Elsewhere* demanded the more emotional commitment for rounded characters, the feminine took only a small part in the female characters each series used. In these action-packed shows, the masculine component forced women into traditional roles as helpmates and nurses, despite the fact that women were performing tasks usually associated with men. Only one episode of *St. Elsewhere* showed the quaternity present in the nursing staff; predictably, the scene was played in front of mirrors in the rest room, a commentary on the worth of the feminine component. Similarly, the characters on *Cagney and Lacey* used the unpainted rest room as their "conference room," the one place they could be fully feminine without masculine interruption.

In situation comedies, the feminine fell too easily into stereotypes—   6
the sacrificing mother, the housewife, the career woman, the prostitute—none of which offered a satisfactory archetypal pattern of the feminine. Situation comedies were, after all, just that—half-hour comedies to entertain, not to instruct or inform; they saw no need to provide archetypal patterns beyond the masculine ones already suggested.

As viewers grew more sophisticated, however, more shows sought   7
to present deeper patterns of femininity. While the *Mary Tyler Moore*

show eventually included three friends (the unpredictable Rhoda, the eccentric Cloris, and the overwrought and ever-pregnant housewife), the feminine quaternity worked only within the heroine's private life and never within her professional life. As the single working woman, she was pitted against the masculine triad (her boss, her colleague, and her eccentric newscaster) and she was forced into becoming the feminine and necessary fourth corner of their quaternity. The popularity of such quaternities is proven by the number of spin-offs which they developed.

This is not to say that shows about women were not popular but rather that they did not present a completed Jungian quaternity as the major framework. While the show *Cagney and Lacey*, for example, has its female characters complete as professionals in their policework, Lacey's husband Harvey is often assigned feminine attributes—his compassion, his nurturing of the children, his concern with the home. The divorced women on *Kate and Allie* embody the dichotomous split of career versus homemaking with both sharing the duties. Lately, however, a steady suitor has appeared for Allie while Kate's beaus fluctuate in the same way that Cagney's beaus do. When such a four-fold division is present, the show possesses a sense of psychic completeness which is satisfying to its viewers; the completed personality is bodied forth in the Jungian quaternity of the feminine which Erich Neumann sees as "the Great Mother as goddess, the Archetypal Feminine [which] suddenly bursts forth upon the world of men in overwhelming wholeness and perfection."

Only the producers of NBC's *Golden Girls* have supplied this familiar pattern of completeness of the Jungian quaternity by restoring the ancient, hidden, unconscious archetypal images in their four heroines. To do this, they extended the classical triad of goddesses into the more satisfying quaternity of the four phases of a woman's life.

These four phases evolved from the essential dichotomy of life and death, spirit and matter (the classic Demeter-Kore dyad), which then divided into the familiar Greco-Roman goddesses of life (Juno/Hera, Athena/Minerva, and Aphrodite/Venus) opposing the goddess of death and wisdom (Hecate/Sybil). Using Erich Neumann's schema of the Great Mother, Andrew Greeley in his work on Mary, *The Mary Myth*, differentiates the quaternity into "(1) woman as source of life, (2) woman as inspiration, (3) woman as source of sexual satisfaction, and (4) woman as absorbing in ego-destroying death"—life against death, inspiration or spirituality against sensuality or materialism. Greeley further categorizes Neumann's types as the Madonna, the Virgo, the Sponsa, and the Pieta.

As Leonardo Boff in his *Maternal Face of God* suggests "all of the symbolism of the . . . feminine archetypes are, like all others, ambivalent . . .

a potentiality, a predisposition, a psychic category [which] has no content of its own, no meaning. It is the mold." *Golden Girls* fits the mold or, to be more correct, it was made to fit the mold. In seeking the correct mix of characters, the producers felt that the original story line of *Golden Girls*, which had only three middle-aged women living together, did not provide enough comedy situations; they added the character of Sophia, Dorothy's mother, to balance the mix. She became the fourth corner of the quaternity.

The mold is a familiar one because it is complete. The show is a suc-   12
cess because of its essential recognition of the complex four-fold nature of human personality, typified by each of the characters—virgin, spouse, mother, and wise woman. These are their most general terms, although the names Greeley uses for these four aspects demonstrate the international blend of the goddesses: "Demeter and Isis, goddesses of fertility; Kali and Gorgon, goddesses of Death; the platonic Sophia, the Greek Muse, the Christian Mary (in Neumann's model) as the source of positive spiritual ecstasy, and Astarte (and I might add Venus) as the symbols of physical ecstasy." While all these aspects fluctuate among the characters of the Golden Girls, the easiest way to categorize them is through the Greco-Roman triad of Dorothy as the Athena/Minerva figure, Rose as the virginal Kore/Artemis/Diana, Blanche as the Aphrodite/Venus, and Sophia as the dual Sybil/Hecate figure. From episode to episode, the triad shifts slightly to allow the Hera/Juno aspect of the mother of the gods to be subsumed by Dorothy as the strongest person and by Sophia as the wisest. In the same manner, Rose occasionally subsumes the mother's role with her caring attitude and her maintenance of the household; it is she who bakes or brings food home.

The most immediate use of the triad is in the show's title of "Golden   13
Girls"; when the Trojan prince Paris awarded the prize as the most beautiful to Aphrodite/Venus over her sister goddesses, he was given Helen as his reward, an act which triggered the Trojan war. The triad of goddesses are the "golden girls" since the prize was the golden fruit— a pomegranate, orange, or apple; in the television show, the women are "golden" because, being over fifty, they allegedly are living the "golden" or mature years in the "golden" sunlight of Florida where tans or "golden skins" and "golden fruits" are common.

The term "girls" is less flattering since, while it is a euphemism for   14
women of an indeterminate age, it is also a pejorative term, indicating their inability to function as adult women. And, as the triad of goddesses, the three women lack the final element—that of the death-dealing hag, Hecate. To emphasize their basic dual nature as life-giving (virgin, spouse, and mother) and as death-dealing, Jung attempts to ex-

plain such archetypal images by pushing back past the Greco-Roman myth into this darker realm of Campbell, Fraser, Neumann, and even Boff, who explains this phenomenon of the Great Mother as "the basic feminine archetype [which] can be aggressive and attacking, or inspiring, sustaining."

In contradiction to the feuding classical triad, the four women are 15 made to share a companionship for economic necessity. In finding it necessary to live in one house, albeit with separate bedrooms, they imitate those ancient communities of women, like the Beguines, who have long banded together for mutual support, companionship, and economic necessity. But what the producers have seen fit to slide over is the economic reality that older women often cannot afford to live alone. Three of the women are working sporadically at low income jobs which also help to characterize them—Dorothy as a teacher or tutor, Rose as a counselor, Blanche as a volunteer museum curator or party organizer, a job which emphasizes her "society woman" status. To offset this possible problem, the producers have constructed a growing friendship between the women which somehow obliterates the economic reality.

The women, like their archetypes, are independent of men for eco- 16 nomic and for emotional support. At best, the men in their lives are peripheral, remembered fondly or humorously over the cheesecake at the kitchen table. Occasionally one man will surface—a long-lost son or brother or nephew or date—but few men stay. Only Stanley, Dorothy's ex-husband, is a steady character, dredged up to engender poignancy for the least feminine of the goddesses, Athena.

Specifically how is the quaternity represented by the four women? 17 Representing the masculine reasoning faculty in Jung's quaternity, Dorothy is the Athena/Minerva portion of the triad, the intelligent warrior goddess. As a teacher, she demonstrates her Athenian wisdom which enables her to find a satisfying life in her teaching: her "wisdom" also implies an anti-intellectualist prejudice that smart women are not beautiful or sexy enough. Much reference is made to her inability to attract men as her mother Sophia reminds her of her philandering husband and Blanche reminds her of her current lack of beaus.

As a warrior, she is an Amazon who cannot get along with her hus- 18 band because she is morally and probably physically stronger than he; she can exist without men, needing them only to fertilize her, as did the Amazons. Tallest of the four actresses, her dark voice and dramatic stature are emphasized by the flamboyant clothes she wears. She looks as draped as any statue of Athena; her clothes feature long intricate folds, which de-emphasize her sexuality by disguising her waist and hips. Attention is often drawn to her breast area by a lapel or flap of discordant material rather like a shield; both the design and the earth colors of her clothes act as a camouflage befitting her as a warrior. Like Minerva, she wages verbal warfare with her ex-husband Stanley over his infidelity which caused their divorce. If her remarks are sometimes coarse, they reflect the soldier's view of life as brutal reality.

Significantly her name Dorothy echoes back to the *Wizard of Oz.* The 19 Dorothy of *Golden Girls,* however, is no naive twelve-year-old seeking the Emerald city; rather, she is a too tall, too masculine, too intelligent, too self-conscious Amazon who longs for the safety of Kansas but who ends up with Toto. Like Chaucer's Wyf whose fairy-tale like story belies her robust personality, Dorothy's name betrays her sharp-tongued wit and vulnerable personality.

As the aging southern belle, Blanche is the one most like Aphrodite/ 20 Venus. Her name comes from two sources: Tennessee Williams' Blanche Dubois of *A Streetcar Named Desire* and Bianca of Shakespeare's *The Taming of the Shrew.* In both cases, the name is ironic for she is not "white" or virginal in her approach to life or to men. She is overly conscious of her looks and weight, concerned with her loss of sex appeal through menopause, and a poor communicant with her children. There is little mention of her husband(s) just as there is little known about Aphrodite's husband(s); lovers there are plenty, money there is plenty, but affection she finds only in her relationship with the other three women. And this puzzles her, for women were always rivals and never her friends before, as befits her archetype as the goddess of sensuality. In living up to her quintessential role as the southern belle, she abjures women as a group.

Her promiscuity (or the appearance of it) fits the Aphrodite arche- 21 type; her sultry voice and walk speak of seduction while her fleeting beauty and coy ways portray the decay of the American south. In her role of Venus, she is a disturber of the civil order; as Helen's beauty brought ruin to Troy at Venus' instigation, so also does Blanche's concept of her own beauty often bring disharmony among the women. Because the show is a comedy, the dissension is resolved before the show ends but often at the expense of civil unity. Her social *faux pas* bring her embarrassment and little learning; she is often malicious, conceited, and inconsiderate but her earthy vitality offsets these traits.

As fits her role, Blanche dresses in the extreme of fashion. Where 22 Dorothy is dramatic and Rose is conservative, Blanche is seductive; her clothes emphasize her breast and pelvic areas with flashy textures and slinky drapes. Her nightclothes especially are intended for seduction with their see-through fabrics and daringly low cuts designs.

Rose, the final member of the triad, is aptly named. She is the Rose 23 of Snow White and Rose Red, the blonde fairy-tale heroine who wins all hearts, the virgin goddess Artemis/Diana, the innocent daughter, Kore or Persephone before Pluto. While she is not a physical virgin because she was married, she embodies the essence of modern virginity in her integrity and her apparent unworldliness. Her view of the world may be limited, but it is self-limited; if she does not participate in evil, she acknowledges it occasionally by succumbing to temptation. In one episode, where a manipulating little girl blackmails her out of her teddy bear, Rose outmaneuvers the child, much to the surprise and delight of the other women.

While Sophia uses her tales of Sicily as parables of old world wisdom, Rose uses tales of her Norwegian roots as a gentle gibe at the innocence of American wisdom. The name of the town from which she comes—St. Olaf and its neighboring towns with the names of obscure Scandinavian saints—show her almost holy innocence. The tales of St. Olaf are charming recitations of innocence meant to offset Sophia's parables and Blanche's southern tales of passion. In her role as peacemaker, her tales of St. Olaf string together such mind-boggling *non sequiturs* that, by the time the other women stop to figure out what happened in the story, they have forgotten what they were fighting about. For example, when she tries to settle a problem by telling of the great herring war, it evolves into the ludicrous image of a herring in a circus volunteering to be shot from a canon. She is a peacemaker also by her gentleness; when she writes the Russian president to stop nuclear war because children are being scared by nuclear war threats, she sees nothing wrong in forging a child's name. While she is naive and simple, she is not totally a fool.

Her clothing differs from the other three. Her dresses are usually shirtwaists with trim bodices and full skirts to emphasize her all-American housewife image; their pastel colors enhance her innocence and her blond fairness.

Even with this classical triad, the picture of humanity is not complete until the opposite is incorporated into the quaternity in the Sybil/Hecate figure of death-dealing mother and the wise woman. The need for this counterbalance is best expressed by Leonardo Boff's definition of this figure: "the bountiful mother is Sophia, Wisdom, while the terrible, fearsome mother is the Gorgon who throttles her own children. The great, all-engendering mother is Isis—the androgynous goddess who procreates the whole universe alone, representing as she does, in her sole person, both the masculine and the feminine originating principles."

Such "feminine originating principles" are lodged in the relatively minor character of Sophia, Dorothy's mother. A compromise by the producers who thought that three single women could not provide enough interaction for contrast. Sophia serendipitously introduces another minority—the elderly—as a source for mother-daughter jokes: instead of being a compromise, she becomes the necessary fourth and lesser corner of the Jungian quaternity, the Sybil/Hecate, the woman wise in years and experience, the hag goddess of death and decay, the irreverent one who fears neither life nor death.

Her name alone suggests her role—Sophia is Lady Wisdom of the Old Testament, the Sybil/Cybele of Sicily and the volcanoes, the wise woman of myth. As the agent of death in the quaternity, she often refers to being old (she admits to being eighty or eighty-one) and enjoys the freedom which age gives her: "I'm old. I'm supposed to be colorful." Because her age brings her so near to death, she can get away with comments and actions that would be objectionable in younger characters. As the gateway to death, she is fittingly gaunt and smaller in stature than the other characters, as if the Florida sun has mummified her. Sal, her husband, is an echo of the young boy Tripolemus, Demeter's son; he is the Dummaz to Inanna's goddess, the expendable son-husband, the "Salvatore" or savior sun-god. Even in the name of the retirement home, "Shady Pines," which she abandoned after it burned down, Sophia's mythic background is shown. The word "shady" is verbally reminiscent of the land of the shades that all men become after death in Hades; the word "pines" recalls the wood used for coffins as in the expression, a "pine box"; and finally the fact that the home burned down fits Sophia who, as the death goddess Hecate, rules over the fires of Hades. 28

In her role as wise woman, Sophia counterbalances the relatively easy life of the three women with her stories of Sicily, of her marriage, and of the Depression. Like many old people, she revels in her life history, turning it into a therapeutic life review which often precedes death. She forces the others to listen to her advice—when it turns sours, she twits them for believing an old woman; when it works, she takes the glory. In her parables of Sicily, she adapts a fairy-tale opening, "picture this, Sicily 1920, a young girl . . . ," to heighten attention. Action stops while teaching goes on; action resumes when she as storyteller comments that "every story has a natural build"; whether the story applies or not does not matter. In her role as Wisdom, she is essentially the oral historian of the group, the caretaker of memory and the recorder of deeds, the death-dealing goddess of judgment, the medieval Justice or Law who weighs men's and women's deeds on her golden scales. 29

As such, she becomes one with her name, Sophia or Wisdom of experience, to balance the flighty and incomplete triad. In the first episode featuring her, she arrives fully developed—proper jersey print housedress, acrylic sweater, cameo at her lace collar, plastic straw bag and disrespectful tongue which belies her grandmotherly image. In the subsequent episodes, her physical appearance has changed subtly from a 30 dowdy rest-home inhabitant to a fashionable Gray Panther—her suits are conservative Chanel or boxy. Her pantsuits may be of pastel polyester but the length of the slacks is fashionably longer than older women wear them. Her figure is trim, her shoes low-heeled but not orthopedic. Her hair is white and curled, her Medusa locks controlled by hair spray.

Of all her physical attributes, her handbag typifies her best; it is 31
molded straw covered with plastic, rigid in its form and uncompromising in its clasp. She carries it everywhere—jogging, sleeping, visiting—always over her arm, always ready for action. It is her dramatic metaphor because it is the womb she represents—rigid now and stiff with age but easily opened to dispense necessary nurturing. Sophia is the darker side of the *Magna Mater*.

Television's technical details also support the quaternity. Given the 32
blocking difficulties of four people in one frame, the directors wisely confine their sets to two main ones—the living room and the kitchen. As a drawing room comedy based on verbal interaction, the living room is a conventional room for television—a three-seat couch dead center with flanking arm chairs and compulsory coffee table. Here the scenes usually involve the women's social life in Florida—polite, controlled, outgoing.

Only the patio scenes seem awkward and contradictory. Even 33
though the show is filmed in California whose vegetation is similar to Miami, there is no attempt to go outdoors for activity. The women do not garden, they don't mow the lawn, they don't play sports, they don't barbecue, and they don't swim. Rather, the story is set in Miami because of the preponderance of elderly who flock to the south for a warmer climate; demographic studies show that a disproportionately large number of them are women since women tend to live longer than men. Why do the producers not use California which has a similar climate? The answer is their ages. Whereas California is a young person's state, one connected with the beach and outdoor activities, Florida possesses a quieter lifestyle, more suited to women over fifty. So, whenever the patio scenes are shown, there is a restlessness and uncertainty, as if women over fifty do not belong outdoors, because these are young people's activities, unbecoming in older and wiser adults who fear skin cancer.

The physical distances between chairs in the living room and patio 34
prevents the television blocking from achieving the intimacy needed for the close work of the four characters. Accordingly, the kitchen is the main set, not because a kitchen is the traditional domain of women, but because it provides a central arena for interaction—the table with three chairs facing the camera and the broader view of the kitchen behind it.

Notice that when the three major women are seated at the table, the 35
fourth corner of the quaternity, Sophia, appears on a stool at a work table

behind and to the viewer's right. This is significant because of the theatrical blocking tradition which replicates the movement of the eyes in Western reading habits, namely from left to right. Thus, when a person enters from the left of the screen, such action seems natural and nonthreatening whereas, if action stems from the right, the person presents an unnatural or more threatening side. By putting Sophia there to the viewer's right, her role as adversarial authority is maintained because from there she can snipe at the other women. As such, she is in a sybil-like position, raised above the rest but smaller because her role is relatively smaller, like that of the Egyptian lesser gods in the hieroglyphics. A mother goddess of Sophia's stature does not need much exposure to be effective in the same way as the feminine principle or Muse needs only a dash to initiate growth in the quaternity of males.

Occasionally a stove to the viewer's right obtrudes into the action but only as Sophia's domain; no one else uses it as much as she does since her cure for her problems is to cook exotic Sicilian dishes and to dish out advice. As the reigning mother goddess who incorporates all roles, Sophia's use of the kitchen and cooking establish her as Hestia, the mother-hearth goddess who nurtures by nourishment. 36

The practicality of the roundness of the kitchen table for camera angles does not obliterate its use as a symbol of the equality of the three women and its archetypally feminine shape. As its tablecloths serve as a modesty shield, its round draperies offset and complement the oblong wooden table of male reason behind it, the table always softened by a bowl of feminine fruit. 37

On the table, cruets continually stress the feminine archetypes. They vary in size and shape but are always rounded, in pairs, and earthenware. They are not the salt and pepper shakers one would expect but the large cruets for milk and sugar or oil and vinegar; both sets of condiments are symbolic since the oil of Rose's good-nature does not obliterate the acidity of Dorothy's tongue nor does the sugar of Blanche's endearments sweeten the milk of motherhood of Sophia. The last cruets used were particularly noticeable; squat, highly figured in blue, white and yellow, more Mexican or Russian than American, they stress the universal complexity of the female in society. 38

While the kitchen table provides a ready-made arena for the interaction of differing values and attributes of the three major women, what unites them most at the table is their love for (and their devouring of) cheesecake. As a fairly late arrival among American popular foods, this rich dessert fits the *Golden Girls* archetype as mothers; basically milk and cheese, products intimately connected with women's nurturing nature, the cheesecake presents the forbidden oppositional concepts of being 39 caloric but creamy, sweet but cold, tempting but harmful. The women's preference is for chocolate, now known for the chemical which induces love. The combination of chocolate and cheesecake makes an unbeatable combination, especially when the second meaning of cheesecake is considered. As an euphemism for lurid photography of women, exposing their legs, the three women seem unlikely candidates for cheesecake yet in one episode Blanche and Rose do a creditable soft-shoe routine in high-cut tap pants and tuxedos.

Details of one episode may serve to show the importance of the table 40 as a meeting ground for the women as they talk about sex. Someone complains that they only talk about sex late at night while eating cheesecake. During the episode, each woman reveals her attitudes toward sex. Blanche fondly recalls her first sexual experience with Billy "or was it Bobby, no Billy, or was it Ben?" As Aphrodite, her memory may fail with menopause but her sexual interest does not lessen. As the virginal persona, Rose discloses that her first experience "the first time she ever saw a man," as she puts it, was on her wedding night when it "all seemed so ridiculous." It took five years for her to find out what made "her eyes go back into her head." As the asexual intellectual Athena, Dorothy relates that her first experience was over so fast that she had no proof until the baby came nine months later. She complains that her marriage with Stanley often had sex happening "before I got into the room." As Wisdom and Hecate, Sophia listens and contributes only that Salvatore's demands were only a duty; whatever physical pleasure there was existed in the past; survival is what matters now to Sophia—survival of herself and her three goddess-daughters.

While the story of four older women living in Florida would seem 41 to run against the modern youth-oriented trend, the geriatric American dream—retirement to the Sunbelt—draws a viewing audience of its own. Since Saturday night is the choicest dating time for young people, that time-honored prime time Saturday night slot has long been considered sacred for older people, the Lawrence Welk show being a case in point. The time slot *Golden Girls* inhabits contributes to its success but does not cause it. There is little madcap humor such as in the *I Love Lucy* show, little dependence on children such as in *Cosby* or *Family Ties,* little physical action such as in *Miami Vice,* little soap opera glitz as in *Dynasty* or *Dallas.* What you see is what you get—three women and a mother in Miami, a classical quaternity of the geriatric set. Perhaps the success of *Golden Girls* is due to its strict adherence, whether conscious or unconscious, to the archetypal image of the Jungian quaternity of goddesses—the four phases of the moon, the four seasons of the year, the four phases of a woman's life—virgin, spouse, mother, and wise woman—all weaving the satisfying pattern of the complete woman.

....

Examining the Text

1. Kaler suggests that since George Lucas' *Star Wars* series "splintered the complete human personality into individual characters, archetypal patterns have become fashionably *de rigueur* for popular entertainment" (paragraph 2). What are some archetypal patterns, and how have they been identified and defined? What is a "quaternity," and why is the concept important to Kaler's analysis?

2. Kaler argues that the four characters in the situation comedy *Golden Girls* offer a symbolic or archetypal representation of "the complete woman." What are the four aspects of this "feminine quaternity," and how are they different from the "triad-plus-one formula" of the "masculine quaternity"?

3. Review all the evidence Kaler offers to support her thesis regarding the four women on *Golden Girls*, beginning in paragraph 17: the actresses' physical traits, their clothes, their names, their relationships with men, the roles they play with one another, even the kitchen setting and the cruets on the table. Does it seem to you that Kaler is reading too much into *Golden Girls*, or do you find her analysis enlightening? Why, or why not?

For Group Discussion

Consider the various archetypes Kaler mentions: the rational father figure representing power, the intuitive feminine figure representing motherhood and compassion, the trickster, the priest, the warrior goddess, the Aphrodite/Venus, the virgin, the wise woman, the whining child, and so forth. As a group, apply such archetypes to a television show with a large cast, such as *Northern Exposure,* or to another situation comedy, such as *Murphy Brown.* Keep in mind that male characters may represent female archetypes and female characters represent male archetypes. As a class, consider whether such archetypes actually seem to be embodied in much popular culture.

Writing Suggestions

In an essay apply Kaler's concepts of triads and quaternities to several television shows that you watch frequently. What insights to these shows does this approach yield?

ADDITIONAL SUGGESTIONS
FOR WRITING ABOUT TELEVISION

1. This chapter includes essays about three genres of television: game shows, soap operas, and situation comedies. Choose another genre (such as talk shows, dating-game shows, tabloid news shows, detective shows, cartoons, or live police dramas) and analyze the underlying presuppositions of this genre. What specific beliefs, actions, and relationships do these shows encourage? How and why do these shows appeal to the audience? If everything that you knew were based on your exposure to this genre of show, what kind of world would you expect to encounter, how would you expect people to behave toward each other, and what sort of values would you expect them to have? To support your analysis of the genre, use examples from specific shows, but keep in mind that your essay should address the genre or category of shows in general.

2. According to sociologists and psychologists, human beings are driven by certain basic needs and desires. All of the essays in this chapter attempt to account for the powerful appeal of television in our culture, and several suggest that we rely on television to fulfill needs that aren't met elsewhere. Consider some of the following basic needs and desires that television might satisfy for you or for the broader viewing public:

> to be amused
> to gain information about the world
> to have shared experiences
> to find models to imitate
> to see authority figures exalted or deflated
> to experience, in a controlled and guilt-free situation, extreme
>   emotions
> to see order imposed on the world
> to reinforce our belief in justice
> to experience thrilling or frightening situations
> to believe in romantic love
> to believe in magic, the marvelous and the miraculous
> to avoid the harsh realities of life
> to see others make mistakes

Referring to items on this list, or formulating your own of needs and desires, compose an essay in which you argue that television succeeds or fails in meeting our basic needs and desires. Use specific television programs that you're familiar with as concrete evidence for your assertions.

3. Modleski and Berman disagree on whether soap operas should be considered "art." Relying on the essays in this chapter along with outside reading, devise your own definition of "art" and apply this to three or four specific shows that you know relatively well. To what degree do these meet your criteria of "art"?

4. Design a research project based on the Jungian analysis offered by Anne Kaler in her essay, "*Golden Girls*: Feminine Archetypal Patterns of the Complete Woman," and apply Kaler's method to a television program with which you're familiar. In order to write your essay you will need to synthesize a variety of sources, including journals, books, and your first-hand evidence derived from a television show or shows. You might want to use this rough outline or adapt it for yourself: (1) overview Carl Jung's basic ideas, specifically his notion of archetypes and the collective unconscious; (2) move into a discussion of the programs you're analyzing (for the purposes of this essay you can assume that your audience has seen it a few times but didn't pay much attention to it); (3) apply the Jungian analytical model to relevant details in the show, such as characters, setting, typical plots, and dialogue; (4) draw some conclusions from your analysis about whether the appeal of the program you have chosen is based on some essential subconscious identification.

4
Popular Music

A naked man, arms outstretched suggestive of Christ on the cross or an Olympian swimmer about to take the plunge, stands atop a cassette deck. Electric pulses from the tape player reach his brain through headphones as he gazes heavenward as if in a trace. The phrase "Be the music" scrolls about his midsection, concealing—perhaps replacing—his maleness, as the music fills his every cell. Such is the power music has over us, this TDK ad suggests, that it can take us over completely—mentally, physically, emotionally.

With its driving rhythms, insistent melodies, and sheer volume, contemporary popular music does indeed have the capacity to take us out of our ordinary reality and profoundly affect our moods, our thoughts, our level of energy and sexual responses. Combined with music's powerful aural appeals, lyrics become all the more potent and suggestive, influencing our feelings of belonging, our relationships, our notions of love and romance, our attitudes toward authority, our views of class, gender, and race.

The writers in this chapter consider how peoples' beliefs, values, attitudes, and morals may be shaped by the music they listen to. In the first essay, Allan Bloom sees this influence of music as potentially dangerous, particularly because he believes that rock music encourages young people to transgress long-established boundaries of "civilized" societies. Other critics, however, contend that rock and other forms of popular music play highly positive roles in contemporary society, giving voice to feelings and ideas that would not otherwise be disseminated widely. Rap and hip hop, for example, have spread far beyond the inner city where they had their genesis, giving disenfranchised urban youth a more pervasive presence in popular culture. Yet two of the writers criticize these musical forms for potentially perpetuating negative stereotypes.

The second half of this chapter looks closely at what the music we choose to listen to reveals about ourselves and how it in turn influences our attitudes and personalities. This section begins with two academic reports that survey, first, how college students "use" music and, second, how their beliefs can be predicted according to the music they prefer. Then the final readings in the section consider several genres of popular music in terms listeners' lifestyles.

As you read this chapter—perhaps as your favorite recording artist blasts through your stereo or Walkman—consider the implications of music in your own life. Why do you listen to the music that you do? What messages are you responding to in the rhythms, the melodies, and the lyrics? What pleasures—and dangers—do we encounter when we seek to "be the music"?

ROCK AND RAP: MUSICAL CONTROVERSIES

....

Music

Allan Bloom

*T*hroughout *its forty-odd year history, rock music has been criticized variously as wicked, immoral, and depraved. But in the late 1980s rock and its proponents found themselves the object of a new criticism.*

In his controversial and widely-read study of American culture, The Closing of the American Mind *(1987), Allan Bloom contends that rock music is worthless "junk food for the soul" and focuses on rock's antithetical relationship to "high" learning, civilization, and the classical tradition. Bloom, for many years a professor at the University of Chicago, argues that rock music debilitates listeners' capacity to reason, and he charges that its effects on the imagination of today's youth are crippling and drug-like. Bloom believes that music, in its ideal form, should cultivate a sense of harmony and unity that uplifts the human subject to a higher good, and he laments the fact that crucial moral and spiritual values have been lost as rock has supplemented other, classically-oriented forms of music in the second half of the twentieth century. More than anything, perhaps, Bloom is concerned with the passionate drives that rock music taps and releases in listeners. For Bloom, rock turns life into a "masturbational fantasy," and as such poses a threat to the psychological and sociological balance of human rationality. In its "barbaric appeal to sexual desire," rock plugs into an unconscious and untamed passion, one which leads humanity away from the order of civilization: Bloom argues that this escape into an irrational and primitive fantasy world has contributed to the deterioration of the great Western cultural tradition.*

As you read, *note how Bloom calls on a long tradition of "high" culture and his own experience as a teacher to bolster his authority. Where do you find his argument most persuasive? Least convincing?*

....

Though students do not have books, they most emphatically do   1
have music. Nothing is more singular about this generation than its addiction to music. This is the age of music and the states of soul that accompany it. To find a rival to this enthusiasm, one would have to go back at least a century to Germany and the passion for Wagner's operas. They had the religious sense that Wagner was creating the meaning of life and

257

that they were not merely listening to his works but experiencing that meaning. Today, a very large proportion of young people between the ages of ten and twenty live for music. It is their passion; nothing else excites them as it does; they cannot take seriously anything alien to music. When they are in school and with their families, they are longing to plug themselves back into their music. Nothing surrounding them—school, family, church—has anything to do with their musical world. At best that ordinary life is neutral, but mostly it is an impediment, drained of vital content, even a thing to be rebelled against. Of course, the enthusiasm for Wagner was limited to a small class, could be indulged only rarely and only in a few places, and had to wait on the composer's slow output. The music of the new votaries, on the other hand, knows neither class nor nation. It is available twenty-four hours a day, everywhere. There is the stereo in the home, in the car; there are concerts; there are music videos, with special channels exclusively devoted to them, on the air nonstop; there are the Walkmans so that no place—not public transportation, not the library—prevents students from communing with the Muse, even while studying. And, above all, the musical soil has become tropically rich. No need to wait for unpredictable genius. Now there are many geniuses, producing all the time, two new ones rising to take the place of every fallen hero. There is no dearth of the new and the startling.

The power of music in the soul—described to Jessica marvelously by Lorenzo in the *Merchant of Venice*—has been recovered after a long period of desuetude. And it is rock music alone that has effected this restoration. Classical music is dead among the young. This assertion will, I know, be hotly disputed by many who, unwilling to admit tidal changes, can point to the proliferation on campuses of classes in classical music appreciation and practice, as well as performance groups of all kinds. Their presence is undeniable, but they involve not more than 5 to 10 percent of the students. Classical music is now a special taste, like Greek language or pre-Columbian archeology, not a common culture of reciprocal communication and psychological shorthand. Thirty years ago, most middle-class families made some of the old European music a part of the home, partly because they liked it, partly because they thought it was good for the kids. University students usually had some early emotive association with Beethoven, Chopin, and Brahms, which was a permanent part of their makeup and to which they were likely to respond throughout their lives. This was probably the only regularly recognizable class distinction between educated and uneducated in America. Many, or even most, of the young people of that generation also swung with Benny Goodman, but with an element of self-consciousness—to be hip, to prove they weren't snobs, to show solidarity with the democratic ideal of a pop culture out of which would grow a new high culture. So there remained a class distinction between high and low, although private taste was beginning to create doubts about whether one really liked the high very much. But all that has changed. Rock music is as unquestioned and unproblematic as the air the students breathe, and very few have any acquaintance at all with classical music. This is a constant surprise to me. And one of the strange aspects of my relations with good students I come to know well is that I frequently introduce them to Mozart. This is a pleasure to me, inasmuch as it is always pleasant to give people gifts that please them. It is interesting to see whether and in what ways their studies are complemented by such music. But this is something utterly new to me as a teacher; formerly my students usually knew much more classical music than I did.

Music was not all that important for the generation of students preceding the current one. The romanticism that had dominated serious music since Beethoven appealed to refinements—perhaps overrefinements—of sentiments that are hardly to be found in the contemporary world. The lives people lead or wish to lead and their prevailing passions are of a different sort than those of the highly educated German and French bourgeoisie, who were avidly reading Rousseau and Baudelaire, Goethe and Heine, for their spiritual satisfaction. The music that had been designed to produce, as well as to please, such exquisite sensibilities had a very tenuous relation to American lives of any kind. So romantic musical culture in America had had for a long time the character of a veneer, as easily susceptible to ridicule as were Margaret Dumont's displays of coquettish chasteness, so aptly exploited by Groucho Marx in *A Night at the Opera*. I noticed this when I first started teaching and lived in a house for gifted students. The "good" ones studied their physics and then listened to classical music. The students who did not fit so easily into the groove, some of them just vulgar and restive under the cultural tyranny, but some of them also serious, were looking for things that really responded to their needs. Almost always they responded to the beat of the newly emerging rock music. They were a bit ashamed of their taste, for it was not respectable. But I instinctively sided with the second group, with real, if coarse, feelings as opposed to artificial and dead ones. Then their musical sans-culotteism won the revolution and reigns unabashed today. No classical music has been produced that can speak of this generation.

Symptomatic of this change is how seriously students now take the famous passages on musical education in Plato's *Republic*. In the past, students, good liberals that they always are, were indignant at the censorship of poetry, as a threat to free inquiry. But they were really thinking of science and politics. They hardly paid attention to the discussion of music itself and, to the extent that they even thought about it, were really puzzled by Plato's devoting time to rhythm and melody in a serious treatise on political philosophy. Their experience of music was as an entertainment, a matter of indifference to political and moral life. Students today, on the contrary, know exactly why Plato takes music so seriously. They know it affects life very profoundly and are indignant because Plato seems to want to rob them of their most intimate pleasure. They are drawn into argument with Plato about the experience of music, and the dispute centers on how to evaluate it and deal with it. This encounter not only helps to illuminate the phenomenon of contemporary music, but also provides a model of how contemporary students can profitably engage with a classic text. The very fact of their fury shows how much Plato threatens what is dear and intimate to them. They are little able to defend their experience, which has seemed unquestionable until questioned, and it is most resistant to cool analysis. Yet if a student can—and this is most difficult and unusual—draw back, get a critical distance on what he clings to, come to doubt the ultimate value of what he loves, he has taken the first and most difficult step toward the philosophic conversion. Indignation is the soul's defense against the wound of doubt about its own; it reorders the cosmos to support the justice of its cause. It justifies putting Socrates to death. Recognizing indignation for what it is constitutes knowledge of the soul, and is thus an experience more philosophic than the study of mathematics. It is Plato's teaching that music, by its nature, encompasses all that is today most resistant to philosophy. So it may well be that through the thicket of our greatest corruption runs the path to awareness of the oldest truths.

Plato's teaching about music is, put simply, that rhythm and melody, accompanied by dance, are the barbarous expression of the soul. Barbarous, not animal. Music is the medium of the *human* soul in its most ecstatic condition of wonder and terror. Nietzsche, who in large measure agrees with Plato's analysis, says in *The Birth of Tragedy* (not to be forgotten is the rest of the title, *Out of the Spirit of Music*) that a mixture of cruelty and coarse sensuality characterized this state, which of course was religious, in the service of gods. Music is the soul's primitive and primary speech and it is *alogon*, without articulate speech or reason. It is not only not reasonable, it is hostile to reason. Even when articulate speech is added, it is utterly subordinate to and determined by the music and the passions it expresses.

Civilization or, to say the same thing, education is the taming or domestication of the soul's raw passions—not suppressing or excising them, which would deprive the soul of its energy—but forming and informing them as art. The goal of harmonizing the enthusiastic part of the soul with what develops later, the rational part, is perhaps impossible to attain. But without it, man can never be whole. Music, or poetry, which is what music becomes as reason emerges, always involves a delicate balance between passion and reason, and, even in its highest and most developed forms—religious, warlike, and erotic—that balance is always tipped, if ever so slightly, toward the passionate. Music, as everyone experiences, provides an unquestionable justification and a fulfilling pleasure for the activities it accompanies: the soldier who hears the marching band is enthralled and reassured; the religious man is exalted in his prayer by the sound of the organ in the church; and the lover is carried away and his conscience stilled by the romantic guitar. Armed with music, man can damn rational doubt. Out of the music emerge the gods that suit it, and they educate men by their example and their commandments.

Plato's Socrates disciplines the ecstasies and thereby provides little consolation or hope to men. According to the Socratic formula, the lyrics—speech and, hence, reason—must determine the music—harmony and rhythm. Pure music can never endure this constraint. Students are not in a position to know the pleasures of reason; they can only see it as a disciplinary and repressive parent. But they do see, in the case of Plato, that that parent has figured out what they are up to. Plato teaches that, in order to take the spiritual temperature of an individual or a society, one must "mark the music." To Plato and Nietzsche, the history of music is a series of attempts to give form and beauty to the dark, chaotic, premonitory forces in the soul—to make them serve a higher purpose, an ideal, to give man's duties a fullness. Bach's religious intentions and Beethoven's revolutionary and humane ones are clear enough examples. Such cultivation of the soul uses the passions and satisfies them while sublimating them and giving them an artistic unity. A man whose noblest activities are accompanied by a music that expresses them while providing a pleasure extending from the lowest bodily to the highest spiritual, is whole, and there is no tension in him between the pleasant and the good. By contrast a man whose business life is prosaic and unmusical and whose leisure is made up of coarse, intense entertainments, is divided, and each side of his existence is undermined by the other.

Hence, for those who are interested in psychological health, music is at the center of education, both for giving the passions their due and for preparing the soul for the unhampered use of reason. The centrality of such education was recognized by all the ancient educators. It is hardly noticed today that in Aristotle's *Politics* the most important passages about the best regime concern musical education, or that the *Poetics* is an appendix to the *Politics*. Classical philosophy did not censor the singers. It persuaded them. And it gave them a goal, one that was understood by them, until only yesterday. But those who do not notice the role of music in Aristotle and despise Plato went to school with Hobbes, Locke, and Smith, where such considerations have become unnecessary. The triumphant Enlightenment rationalism thought that it had discovered other ways to deal with the irrational part of the soul, and that reason needed less support from it. Only in those great critics of Enlightenment and rationalism, Rousseau and Nietzsche, does music return, and they were the most musical of philosophers. Both thought that the passions—and along with them their ministerial arts—had become thin under the rule of reason and that, therefore, man *himself* and what he sees in the world have become correspondingly thin. They wanted to cultivate the enthusiastic states of the soul and to re-experience the Corybantic possession deemed a pathology by Plato. Nietzsche, particularly, sought to tap again the irrational sources of vitality, to replenish our dried-up stream from barbaric sources, and thus encouraged the Dionysian and the music derivative from it.

This is the significance of rock music. I do not suggest that it has any 9 high intellectual sources. But it has risen to its current heights in the education of the young on the ashes of classical music, and in an atmosphere in which there is no intellectual resistance to attempts to tap the rawest passions. Modern-day rationalists, such as economists, are indifferent to it and what it represents. The irrationalists are all for it. There is no need to fear that "the blond beasts" are going to come forth from the bland souls of our adolescents. But rock music has one appeal only, a barbaric appeal, to sexual desire—not love, not *eros,* but sexual desire undeveloped and untutored. It acknowledges the first emanations of children's emerging sensuality and addresses them seriously, eliciting them and legitimating them, not as little sprouts that must be carefully tended in order to grow into gorgeous flowers, but as the real thing. Rock gives children, on a silver platter, with all the public authority of the entertainment industry, everything their parents always used to tell them they had to wait for until they grew up and would understand later.

Young people know that rock has the beat of sexual intercourse. 10 That is why Ravel's *Bolero* is the one piece of classical music that is commonly known and liked by them. In alliance with some real art and a lot of pseudo-art, an enormous industry cultivates the taste for the orgiastic state of feeling connected with sex, providing a constant flood of fresh material for voracious appetites. Never was there an art form directed so exclusively to children.

Ministering to and according with the arousing and cathartic mu- 11 sic, the lyrics celebrate puppy love as well as polymorphous attractions, and fortify them against traditional ridicule and shame. The words implicitly and explicitly describe bodily acts that satisfy sexual desire and treat them as its only natural and routine culmination for children who do not yet have the slightest imagination of love, marriage, or family. This has a much more powerful effect than does pornography on youngsters, who have no need to watch others do grossly what they can so easily do themselves. Voyeurism is for old perverts; active sexual relations are for the young. All they need is encouragement.

The inevitable corollary of such sexual interest is rebellion against   12 the parental authority that represses it. Selfishness thus becomes indignation and then transforms itself into morality. The sexual revolution must overthrow all the forces of domination, the enemies of nature and happiness. From love comes hate, masquerading as social reform. A worldview is balanced on the sexual fulcrum. What were once unconscious or half-conscious childish resentments become the new Scripture. And then comes the longing for the classless, prejudice-free, conflictless, universal society that necessarily results from liberated consciousness—"We Are the World," a pubescent version of *Alle Menschen werden Brüder,* the fulfillment of which has been inhibited by the political equivalents of Mom and Dad. These are the three great lyrical themes: sex, hate, and a smarmy, hypocritical version of brotherly love. Such polluted sources issue in a muddy stream where only monsters can swim. A glance at the videos that project images on the wall of Plato's cave since MTV took it over suffices to prove this. Hitler's image recurs frequently enough in exciting contexts to give one pause. Nothing noble, sublime, profound, delicate, tasteful, or even decent can find a place in such tableaux. There is room only for the intense, changing, crude, and immediate, which Tocqueville warned us would be the character of democratic art, combined with a pervasiveness, importance, and content beyond Tocqueville's wildest imagination.

Picture a thirteen-year-old boy sitting in the living room of his fam-   13 ily home doing his math assignment while wearing his Walkman headphones or watching MTV. He enjoys the liberties hard won over centuries by the alliance of philosophic genius and political heroism, consecrated by the blood of martyrs; he is provided with comfort and leisure by the most productive economy ever known to mankind; science has penetrated the secrets of nature in order to provide him with the marvelous, lifelike electronic sound and image reproduction he is enjoying. And in what does progress culminate? A pubescent child whose body throbs with orgasmic rhythms; whose feelings are made articulate in hymns to the joys of onanism or the killing of parents; whose ambition is to win fame and wealth in imitating the drag-queen who makes the music. In short, life is made into a nonstop, commercially prepackaged masturbational fantasy.

This description may seem exaggerated, but only because some   14
would prefer to regard it as such. The continuing exposure to rock music is a reality, not one confined to a particular class or type of child. One
need only ask first-year university students what music they listen to,
how much of it, and what it means to them, in order to discover that the
phenomenon is universal in America, that it begins in adolescence or a
bit before and continues through the college years. It is *the* youth culture
and, as I have so often insisted, there is now no other countervailing
nourishment for the spirit. Some of this culture's power comes from the
fact that it is so loud. It makes conversation impossible, so that much of
friendship must be without the shared speech that Aristotle asserts is
the essence of friendship and the only true common ground. With rock,
illusions of shared feelings, bodily contact and grunted formulas, which
are supposed to contain so much meaning beyond speech, are the basis
of association. None of this contradicts going about the business of life,
attending classes, and doing the assignments for them. But the meaningful inner life is with the music.

This phenomenon is both astounding and indigestible, and is   15
hardly noticed, routine and habitual. But it is of historic proportions that
a society's best young and their best energies should be so occupied.
People of future civilizations will wonder at this and find it as incomprehensible as we do the caste system, witch-burning, harems, cannibalism, and gladiatorial combats. It may well be that a society's greatest
madness seems normal to itself. The child described has parents who
have sacrificed to provide him with a good life and who have a great
stake in his future happiness. They cannot believe that the musical vo-
cation will contribute very much to that happiness. But there is nothing
they can do about it. The family spiritual void has left the field open to
rock music, and they cannot possibly forbid their children to listen to it.
It is everywhere; all children listen to it; forbidding it would simply
cause them to lose their children's affection and obedience. When they
turn on the television, they will see President Reagan warmly grasping
the daintily proffered gloved hand of Michael Jackson and praising him
enthusiastically. Better to set the faculty of denial in motion—avoid
noticing what the words say, assume the kid will get over it. If he has
early sex, that won't get in the way of his having stable relationships
later. His drug use will certainly stop at pot. School is providing real values. And popular historicism provides the final salvation; there are new
lifestyles for new situations, and the older generation is there not to impose its values but to help the younger one to find its own. TV, which
compared to music plays a comparatively small role in the formation of
young people's character and taste, is a consensus monster—the Right
monitors its content for sex, the Left for violence, and many other in-

terested sects for many other things. But the music has hardly been touched, and what efforts have been made are both ineffectual and misguided about the nature and extent of the problem.

The result is nothing less than parents' loss of control over their children's moral education at a time when no one else is seriously concerned with it. This has been achieved by an alliance between the strange young males who have the gift of divining the mob's emergent wishes—our versions of Thrasymachus, Socrates' rhetorical adversary—and the record-company executives, the new robber barons, who mine gold out of rock. They discovered a few years back that children are one of the few groups in the country with considerable disposable income, in the form of allowances. Their parents spend all they have providing for the kids. Appealing to them over their parents' heads, creating a world of delight for them, constitutes one of the richest markets in the postwar world. The rock business is perfect capitalism, supplying to demand and helping to create it. It has all the moral dignity of drug trafficking, but it was so totally new and unexpected that nobody thought to control it, and now it is too late. Progress may be made against cigarette smoking because our absence of standards or our relativism does not extend to matters of bodily health. In all other things the market determines the value. (Yoko Ono is among America's small group of billionaires, along with oil and computer magnates, her late husband having produced and sold a commodity of worth comparable to theirs.) Rock is a vary big business, bigger than the movies, bigger than professional sports, bigger than television, and this accounts for much of the respectability of the music business. It is difficult to adjust our vision to the changes in the economy and to see what is really important. McDonald's now has more employees than U.S. Steel, and likewise the purveyors of junk food for the soul have supplanted what still seems to be more basic callings.

This change has been happening for some time. In the late fifties, DeGaulle gave Brigitte Bardot one of France's highest honors. I could not understand this, but it turned out that she, along with Peugeot, was France's biggest export item. As Western nations became more prosperous, leisure, which had been put off for several centuries in favor of the pursuit of property, the means to leisure, finally began to be of primary concern. But, in the meantime, any notion of the serious life of leisure, as well as men's taste and capacity to live it, had disappeared. Leisure became entertainment. The end for which they had labored for so long has turned out to be amusement, a justified conclusion if the means justify the ends. The music business is peculiar only in that it caters almost exclusively to children, treating legally and naturally imperfect human beings as though they were ready to enjoy the final or complete satisfaction. It perhaps thus reveals the nature of all our entertainment and our loss of a clear view of what adulthood or maturity is, and our incapacity to conceive ends. The emptiness of *values* results in the acceptance of the natural *facts* as the ends. In this case infantile sexuality is the end, and I suspect that, in absence of other ends, many adults have to agree that it is.

It is interesting to note that the Left, which prides itself on its critical approach to "late capitalism" and is unrelenting and unsparing in its analysis of our other cultural phenomena, has in general given rock music a free ride. Abstracting from the capitalist element in which it flourishes, they regard it as a people's art, coming from beneath the bourgeoisie's layers of cultural repression. Its antinomianism and its longing for a world without constraint might seem to be the clarion of the proletarian revolution, and Marxists certainly do see that rock music dissolves the beliefs and morals necessary for liberal society and would approve of it for that alone. But the harmony between the young intellectual Left and rock is probably profounder than that. Herbert Marcuse appealed to university students in the sixties with a combination of Marx and Freud. In *Eros and Civilization* and *One Dimensional Man* he promised that the overcoming of capitalism and its false consciousness will result in a society where the greatest satisfactions are sexual, of a sort that the bourgeois moralist Freud called polymorphous and infantile. Rock music touches the same chord in the young. Free sexual expression, anarchism, mining of the irrational unconscious and giving it free rein are what they have in common. The high intellectual life . . . and the low rock world are partners in the same entertainment enterprise. They must both be interpreted as parts of the cultural fabric of late capitalism. Their success comes from the bourgeois's need to feel that he is not bourgeois, to have undangerous experiments with the unlimited. He is willing to pay dearly for them. The Left is better interpreted by Nietzsche than by Marx. The critical theory of late capitalism is at once late capitalism's subtlest and crudest expression. Antibourgeois ire is the opiate of the Last Man.

This strong stimulant, which Nietzsche called Nihiline, was for a very long time, almost fifteen years, epitomized in a single figure, Mick Jagger. A shrewd, middle-class boy, he played the possessed lower-class demon and teen-aged satyr up until he was forty, with one eye on the mobs of children of both sexes whom he stimulated to a sensual frenzy and the other eye winking at the unerotic, commercially motivated adults who handled the money. In his act he was male and female, heterosexual and homosexual; unencumbered by modesty, he could enter everyone's dreams, promising to do everything with everyone; and, above all, he legitimated drugs, which were the real thrill that parents and policemen conspired to deny his youthful audience. He was beyond the law, moral and political, and thumbed his nose at it. Along with all this, there were nasty little appeals to the suppressed inclinations toward sexism, racism, and violence, indulgence in which is not now publicly respectable. Nevertheless, he managed not to appear to contradict the rock ideal of a universal classless society founded on love, with the distinction between brotherly and bodily blurred. He was the hero and the model for countless young persons in universities, as well as elsewhere. I discovered that students who boasted of having no heroes secretly had a passion to be like Mick Jagger, to live his life, have his fame. They were ashamed to admit this in a university, although I am not certain that the reason has anything to do with a higher standard of taste. It is probably that they are not supposed to have heroes. Rock music itself and talking about it with infinite seriousness are perfectly respectable. It has proved to be the ultimate leveler of intellectual snobbism. But it is not respectable to think of it as providing weak and ordinary persons with a fashionable behavior, the imitation of which will make others esteem them and boost their own self-esteem. Unaware and unwillingly, however, Mick Jagger played the role in their lives that Napoleon played in the lives of ordinary young Frenchmen throughout the nineteenth century. Everyone else was so boring and unable to charm youthful passions. Jagger caught on.

In the last couple of years, Jagger has begun to fade. Whether Michael 20 Jackson, Prince, or Boy George can take his place is uncertain. They are even weirder than he is, and one wonders what new strata of taste they have discovered. Although each differs from the others, the essential character of musical entertainment is not changing. There is only a constant search for variations on the theme. And this gutter phenomenon is apparently the fulfillment of the promise made by so much psychology and literature that our weak and exhausted Western civilization would find refreshment in the true source, the unconscious, which appeared to the late romantic imagination to be identical to Africa, the dark and unexplored continent. Now all has been explored; light has been cast everywhere; the unconscious has been made conscious, the repressed expressed. And what have we found? Not creative devils, but show business glitz. Mick Jagger tarting it up on the stage is all we brought back from the voyage to the underworld.

My concern here is not with the moral effects of this music— 21 whether it leads to sex, violence, or drugs. The issue here is its effect on education, and I believe it ruins the imagination of young people and makes it very difficult for them to have a passionate relationship to the art and thought that are the substance of liberal education. The first sensuous experiences are decisive in determining the taste for the whole of life, and they are the link between the animal and spiritual in us. The period of nascent sensuality has always been used for sublimation, in the sense of making sublime, for attaching youthful inclinations and longings to music, pictures, and stories that provide the transition to the fulfillment of the human duties and the enjoyment of the human pleasures. Lessing, speaking of Greek sculpture, said "beautiful men made beautiful statues, and the city had beautiful statues in part to thank for beautiful citizens." This formula encapsulates the fundamental principle of the esthetic education of man. Young men and women were attracted by the beauty of heroes whose very bodies expressed their nobility. The deeper understanding of the meaning of nobility comes later, but is prepared for by the sensuous experience and is actually contained in it. What the senses long for as well as what reason later sees as good are thereby not at tension with one another. Education is not sermonizing to children against their instincts and pleasures, but providing a natural continuity between what they feel and what they can and should be. But this is a lost art. Now we have come to exactly the opposite point. Rock music encourages passions and provides models that have no relation to any life the young people who go to universities can possibly lead, or to the kinds of admiration encouraged by liberal studies. Without the cooperation of the sentiments, anything other than technical education is a dead letter.

Rock music provides premature ecstasy and, in this respect, is like the drugs with which it is allied. It artificially induces the exaltation naturally attached to the completion of the greatest endeavors—victory in a just war, consummated love, artistic creation, religious devotion, and discovery of the truth. Without effort, without talent, without virtue, without exercise of the faculties, anyone and everyone is accorded the equal right to the enjoyment of their fruits. In my experience, students who have had a serious fling with drugs—and gotten over it—find it difficult to have enthusiasms or great expectations. It is as though the color has been drained out of their lives and they see everything in black and white. The pleasure they experienced in the beginning was so intense that they no longer look for it at the end, or as the end. They may function perfectly well, but dryly, routinely. Their energy has been sapped, and they do not expect their life's activity to produce anything but a living, whereas liberal education is supposed to encourage the belief that the good life is the pleasant life and that the best life is the most pleasant life. I suspect that the rock addiction, particularly in the absence of strong counterattractions, has an effect similar to that of drugs. The students will get over this music, or at least the exclusive passion for it. But they will do so in the same way Freud says that men accept the reality principle—as something harsh, grim, and essentially unattractive, a mere necessity. These students will assiduously study economics or the professions and the Michael Jackson costume will slip off to reveal a Brooks Brothers suit beneath. They will want to get ahead and live comfortably. But this life is as empty and false as the one they left behind. The choice is not between quick fixes and dull calculation. This is what liberal education is meant to show them. But as long as they have the Walkman on, they cannot hear what the great tradition has to say. And, after its prolonged use, when they take it off, they find they are deaf.

....

Examining the Text

1. Why did Bloom "instinctively" side with rock-listening students when he was young (paragraph 3)? What drew him to this group of listeners, or to the music itself? What would he say led him to change his opinion? Do you think anything else might have contributed to this change?

2. What does Bloom mean by the statement, "Indignation is the soul's defense against the wound of doubt about its own; it reorders the cosmos to support the justice of its cause" (4)? Does anything in Bloom's argument make you "indignant"? Why does Bloom want students to recognize such indignations "for what it is"?

3. Explain the statement "Antibourgeois ire is the opiate of the Last Man" (18), in light of Bloom's discussion of the relationship among capitalism, the Left, Marxism, and rock music. Do you agree that rock music today embodies this superficial antibourgeous ire?

For Group Discussion

What, according to Bloom, is the singular appeal of rock music to young people? As a group, use Jib Fowles' catalog (p. 61) of advertising's psychological appeals—sex, affiliation, nurturing, and so forth—to list and explore possible additional appeals that rock music may have to its listeners.

Writing Suggestion

Consider Bloom's assertion that when students are "in school and with their families, they are longing to plug themselves back into their music." In an essay, explain the broad social point Bloom is making about the role of popular music in young people's lives, and then go on to discuss the role of popular music in your own life, citing examples from your experience and that of your friends and peers.

Rock and Sexuality

Simon Frith

The expression of explicit sexuality has become increasingly prevalent in rock lyrics and musical performances, a phenomenon described by many critics as radical—even subversive. However, while many believe that rock music and musicians are becoming more and more liberated, other critics argue that contemporary popular music may in fact be expressing conservative ideologies in a new, different—and frequently disguised—form.

In the following historical analysis of the relationship between rock and sexuality, Simon Frith carefully distinguishes between sexual practice and sexual ideology as he argues that rock music often contributes to ordering and normalizing certain codes of gender and sexual behavior. For example, he argues that gender hierarchies and a "sexual double standard" are absolutely bound up with the sexual ideology of rock 'n' roll in the 1950s and 1960s. It wasn't until the advent of the punk and disco movements, Frith argues, that women finally found an aesthetic and erotic niche of their own within the narrow sexual confines of rock music. An interesting sidebar to Frith's argument is his discussion of the "gay aesthetic" of the disco movement: dedicated to eroticism and intensity, disco dancing created a new arena for physical pleasure, even ecstasy.

A well-known rock journalist and university professor in England, Frith has written for The Village Voice, Creem, *and* In These Times. *His books include* Art into Pop, Music for Pleasure, Facing the Music, *and* Sound Effects: Youth, Leisure, and the Politics of Rock 'n' Roll, *from which the following selection is taken.* **As you read,** *notice that he incorporates ideology, economics, and social behavior into the analysis. Look for examples of each means of study.*

• • • • • • • • • • • • • • • • • • •

The girl culture . . . is teenage culture, essentially working-class, but   1
such leisure constraints also apply to student culture, even if the sexual differentiation of economic opportunity is less blatant for middle-class youth. Indeed it was on college campuses in the 1920s that many of the conventions of postwar teenage sexual behavior were first established: it was college girls who first decided which sex acts a respectable girl could enjoy, which were illicit; it was college boys who first organized sex as a collective male activity, turned seductions into "scores"; it was at college that petting (an extraordinary American sexual institution) was first turned into a routine. College youth culture was interpreted at the time as "liberating," particularly for the girls, but they weren't liberated from the double standard.

If girls' leisure is limited by its use as the setting for courtship, 2 courtship itself has to be understood in the context of a particular sort of ideology of marriage, an ideology that does give girls a freedom—the freedom to choose partners. Historians have argued that boys had a youth, a time of transition from childhood to adulthood as they moved from home to work, long before girls. Adolescence as a social status is predicated on a degree of independence, and as long as girls were protected through puberty, confined to one household until they were given away in marriage to another, they had no youth. Girls could only become teenagers when free marital choice became the norm, when marriage was expected to be preceded by love. Only then did a transitional period become necessary for women too, a period when they could play the marriage field for themselves. This ideology only began to be a general norm at the beginning of this century, as ragtime and the dance craze began. Rudi Blesh and Harriet Janis quote the *Sedalia Times* from 1900:

> When the girls walk out evenings with the sole purpose of picking up a young man and continuing the walk, it is time to have a curfew law that will include children over sixteen. The restlessness that comes upon girls upon summer evenings results in lasting trouble unless it is speedily controlled. The right kind of man does not look for a wife on the streets, and the right kind of girl waits till the man comes to her home for her.[1]

Lawrence Stone, in his history *The Family, Sex and Marriage in Eng-* 3 *land,* argues that the ideology of sentimental love and "well-tried personal affection" as the basis of marriage spread from the aristocracy to the bourgeoisie in Europe in the latter part of the eighteenth century (the move was marked by the rise of the romantic novel) and moved gradually down the social scale during the nineteenth century. But this was neither a natural nor an uncomplicated change of ideas. Youthful courtship carried dangers—the threat of sexual disorder, a challenge to parental authority.

These dangers seemed to be multiplied by the emergence of 4 working-class adolescents. From early in the nineteenth century, the feature of the industrial revolution that most concerned middle-class moralists was its apparent effect on the working-class family, as girls worked in the new factories alongside boys, achieving with them an "unnatural" independence from their parents. The bourgeoisie themselves were slowly adopting the ideology of romantic love as a way of regulating adolescent sexuality and guaranteeing their children's

---

[1] Rudi Blesh and Harriet Janis, *They All Played Ragtime* (New York, 1950), p. 33.

orderly transition to adult respectability. Romantic love was idealized in bourgeois fiction, in love songs, stories, and poetry, and routinized in the suburbs, in middle-class clubs and sports and dances where girls could meet boys who would be guaranteed to be suitable partners for love and marriage. Peer groups began to take over from parents as the arbiters of correct sexual behavior.

By the end of the nineteenth century middle-class reformers were beginning to apply the romantic approach to the problem of working-class adolescence too—in England and France, for example, romance was promoted as a replacement for community control of working-class sexuality, and young workers were encouraged to join their own "rational" peer-group leisure associations—youth clubs, cycle clubs, sports clubs, and so forth. In the USA the most important institution for the control of adolescent sexuality was, at least after 1918, the high school. Paula Fass suggests that the 1920s, in particular, were crucial for the development of American youth culture, because it was then that the ideology of sentimental love was fused with a new kind of advocacy of sexual pleasure. It was, in her words, the "dual process of the sexualization of love and the glorification of sex that helped to anchor the twentieth-century American marriage pattern, the horse-and-carriage ideal."

The "sexualization of love" was made possible by the spread of relatively efficient contraception. Delayed small families encouraged companionate marriages; sex itself, freed from conception, was reinterpreted as a form of emotional expression, a source of mutual pleasure—from the 1920s, middle-class marriage manuals recognized female sexuality. But the other side of this process was the domestication of sex. If sexual expression, for its own sake, became one of the pleasures and purposes of marriage, so marriage itself was defined as the necessary setting for the most pleasurable sex—necessary now not in terms of traditional morality but in terms of romance: love had become the reason for sex, and true love involved a commitment to marriage. First an engagement, later going steady, became the moment in youth culture when it was morally permissible to go all the way; and from the 1920s, middle-class girls, as prospective wives, could express their "sexual personalities" publicly, could use sexual devices, like makeup, that had previously been confined to prostitutes, to "loose women."

What made this ideology initially shocking was that it legitimated youthful sexual activity as an aspect of efficient mate selection; parents lost control not only over their children's marriage choices but also over their sexual behavior. Their place was taken, once more, by peer groups, which elaborated new rules of sexuality according to which some premarital pleasure was permissible, for girls and boys alike, but not such pleasure as would disrupt the romantic transition to marriage. Paula

Fass quotes a female student from Ohio State University writing in 1922 in defense of her physical enjoyment of "smoking, dancing like voodoo devotees, dressing décolleté, petting and drinking." Her point was that although

> our tastes may appear riotous and unrestrained, the aspect of the situation is not alarming. The college girl—particularly the girl in the co-educational institution—is a plucky, coolheaded individual who thinks naturally. She doesn't lose her head—she knows her game and can play it dexterously. She is armed with sexual knowledge. . . . She is secure in the most critical situations—she knows the limits, and because of her safety in such knowledge she is able to run almost the complete gamut of experience.[2]

By the 1950s, knowledge of "the limits" was an aspect of teenage   8
culture generally, but if the task of teenage peer groups was to control teenage sexuality, the issue was, really, girls' sexual behavior. It was female morality that was defined as chastity, female "trouble" that meant pregnancy. Adults worried about boys in terms of violence, the threat to order; they only worried about girls in terms of sex, the threat to the family. And they worried about all girls in these terms, their fears weren't confined to "delinquents."

Nineteen-fifties rock 'n' roll is usually described as a particularly   9
sexual form of expression, a source of physical "liberation," but teenage culture was already sexualized by the time it appeared. The question we really have to examine concerns the use of music not in the general expression of sexuality but in its ordering. Sexuality is not a single phenomenon that is either expressed or repressed; the term refers, rather, to a range of pleasures and experiences, a range of ways in which people make sense of themselves as sexed subjects. Sexual discourses determine prohibitions as well as possibilities, what can't be expressed as well as what can. But the most important function of 1950s teenage culture wasn't to "repress" sexuality but to articulate it in a setting of love and marriage such that male and female sexuality were organized in quite different ways. And rock 'n' roll didn't change that sexual order. Elvis Presley's sexuality, for example, meant different things to his male and female fans. There was an obvious tension between his male appropriation as cock-rocker and his female appropriation as a teeny-bop idol. Rock 'n' roll was, say its historians significantly, "emasculated," but its "decline" (from crude, wild dance music to crafted romantic ballads and spruce idols) marked not a defused rebellion but a shift of sex-

---

[2] Paula S. Fass, *The Damned and the Beautiful: American Youth in the 1920s* (New York: Oxford University Press, 1977), p. 307.

ual discourse as the music moved from the street to the bedroom. In neither place did it challenge the conventions of peer-group sex.

The youth culture that developed in the 1960s was, in sexual terms, 10 more rebellious: the family was part of the system under attack. Domestic ideology was subverted, sexuality separated from marriage, romantic love intercut with fleeting hedonism. In Tom Hayden's words, there was "a generation of young whites with a new, less repressed attitude toward sex and pleasure, and music has been the means of their liberation."

Rock was experienced as a new sort of sexual articulation by women 11 as well as men. The music was, in Sheila Rowbotham's words, "like a great release after all those super-consolation ballads." Rock, writes Karen Durbin, "provided me and a lot of women with a channel for saying 'want,' and for asserting our sexuality without apologies and without having to pretty up every passion with the traditionally 'feminine' desire for true love and marriage, and that was a useful step towards liberation." At a time when girls were still being encouraged from all directions to interpret their sexuality in terms of romance, to give priority to notions of love and commitment, rock performers like the Rolling Stones were exhilarating because of their antiromanticism, their concern for "the dark side of passion," their interest in sex as power and feeling. But the problem quickly became a different one: not whether rock stars were sexist, but whether women could enter their discourse, appropriate their music, without having to become "one of the boys."

Rock and Sexual Liberation

Male sexuality is no more "naturally" aggressive, assertive, and ur- 12 gent than female sexuality is "naturally" passive, meek, and sensitive. But the issue is not the nature of sex and its representations, and they work not by describing feelings, but by constructing them. The sexual content of rock can't be read off its texts unambiguously—lyrics are the sign of a voice, instrumental sounds don't have fixed connotations. The sexuality of music is usually referred to in terms of its rhythm—it is the beat that commands a directly physical response—but rock sexuality has other components too. The rock experience is a social experience, involves relationships among the listeners, refers to people's appreciation of other genres, other sound associations; and in sexual terms our musical response is, perhaps above all, to the grain of a voice, the "touch" someone has on an instrument, the sense of personality at play. The "pleasure of the text" is the pleasure of music production itself, and one reason for the dissolution of rock's liberating promises to the male routines of the 1970s was simply the inevitable translation of an open text into a closed formula: cock-rock, by definition, rules out the possibilities of surprise and delight. But the question remains: Why this formula? Nineteen-sixties rock was expressly opposed to the love and marriage ideology of traditional teenage culture; how then did it come to articulate an even more rigid sexual double standard?

The concept of youth developed in the 1960s by rock (among other media) involved the assumption that good sex meant spontaneity, free expression, an "honesty" that could only be judged in terms of immediate feelings. Sex was thus best experienced *outside* the restrictive sphere of marriage, with its distracting deceits of love and long-term commitment. This was, in principle, an ideology of sexual equality—men and women alike were entitled to set their own limits on their sexual experiences.   13

Such permissiveness reflected a number of shifts in the material situation of middle-class youth: an increasing number of them were at college for an increasing length of time (by the end of the 1960s more than a quarter of *all* twenty-one- to twenty-four-year-olds in the USA were in school), and they were enjoying new levels of affluence (a reflection of rising parental income), mobility, and independence. It was, therefore, increasingly possible to enjoy sex without any reference to marriage; and the pill, in particular, enabled women to manage their sex lives without reference to family, community, or peer group. Sex became just another form of leisure, and the ideology of leisure itself began to change. Free time was used increasingly impulsively, irrationally, unproductively, with reference to immediate gratification rather than to usefulness or respectability or sense of consequence. The expansion of sexual opportunity, in other words, occurred in the context of a new leisure stress on hedonism, and the result was that sex became an experience to be consumed, used up in the moment, like any other leisure good. Sex was now defined without reference to domestic ideology or romantic love, but it was still gender-bound: men were, by and large, the sexual consumers; women were, by and large, the sexual commodities, their charms laid out for customer approval in a never-ending supply of magazines and films and "spreads."   14

Rock sexuality developed in this permissive context, but defined itself (initially, at least) against such "plastic" consumer sex. Rock sex was bohemian sex—earthy, real, "free." The woman's place, though, remained subordinate.   15

Bohemian freedom, particularly in its young rebel version, is defined primarily against the family. It is from their families that the young must escape, it is through their family quarrels that they first recognize themselves as rebels, and it is their refusal to settle down to a respectable   16 domestic life that makes their rebellion permanent. Youthful bohemia begins, then, as a revolt against women, who are identified with the home as mothers, sisters, potential domesticators. The young rebel has to be a loner, to move on, and female sexuality becomes, in itself, something repressive, confining, enveloping. In the Hollywood version of the young rebel's story (a story repeated in numerous films over the last thirty years, although James Dean remains the model for rock 'n' roll's rebellious style), the message is plain enough: the boy must get out, the girl tries to hold him back. The original middle-class youth rebels in America, the bohemians drawn to big-city life and leisure at the turn of the century, were fascinated precisely by those proletarian institutions—gambling, drinking, sports like pool—which were, in Ned Polsky's words, aspects of a "bachelor subculture": they were institutions for men without women, and the only intimate relationships bohemians can have are with each other, as friends.

Even rebels need sexual and domestic female services, though (one   17
1960s result was the symbolic hippie woman, the fleet-footed earth mother), and, traditionally, the ideal bohemian woman is the "innocent" prostitute—antidomestic and a symbol of sex as transitory pleasure. The prostitute can be treated (as rock stars treat groupies) with a mixture of condescension and contempt, as someone without an autonomous sexuality. Sex as self-expression remains the prerogative of the man; the woman is the object of *his* needs and fantasies, admired, in a way, for her lack of romantic hypocrisy but despised for her anonymity.

Sexual relationships involve a number of necessary oppositions.   18
These oppositions don't have to be divided between sexual partners, aren't gender defined, but mean constant negotiation, exploration, struggle, and experiment. These negotiations are the source of sexual pleasure as well as pain, and the issues at stake—independence/dependence, risk/security, activity/passivity, movement/stability, incident/routine, creation/consumption—inform the best rock music, which deals with the sexual *frisson* of relationships, the fact that all interesting affairs are alive. But, in general (and whatever the concerns of individual musicians like Neil Young or Van Morrison or Joni Mitchell), rock performers lay claim to sexual values—movement, independence, creativity, action, risk—in such a way that female sexuality is defined (just as in working-class street culture) by the opposite values—stability, dependence, inaction, security. Women are excluded from this "rebellion" by definition; rock's antidomestic ideology doesn't move women out of the home, but leaves them in it, as inadequates.

The issue here is sexual ideology, not sexual practice. The actual be-   19
havior of men and women is far more complicated than the ideology

implies. . . . But there is one more practical point to be made. Nineteen-sixties youth culture opposed impulse to calculation, irrationality to rationality, the present to the future; but these values posed quite different problems for boys than for girls. Girls have to keep control. They can't get drunk or drugged with the same abandon as boys because to lose control *is* to face consequences—pregnancy most obviously ("I got drunk at a party . . ."), a bad reputation more generally ("She'll do *anything* . . ."). As long as female attraction is defined by the male gaze, girls are under constant pressure too to keep control of their appearance; they can't afford to let their performance go. A drunken, "raddled" woman remains a potent image of ugliness; a haggard Keith Richards retains a far more *glamorous* appeal than a haggard Janis Joplin or Grace Slick. The irrational elements of the counterculture—in other words, the sex and drugs and rock 'n' roll—could not be appropriated by girls as they were by boys without affecting their self-definitions, their relationships, their lives.

By the 1970s women were giving their own answers to the counter- 20 cultural questions about sex and domesticity and love—the terms of male domination were challenged. One effect of the feminist rewriting of the sexual rule book has been a male movement to more irrational forms of sexual power—rape, violent fantasy, a neurotic inability to sustain any sexual relationship. As one male property right (as husband) is denied, another (as purchaser) is asserted; sex, and therefore women, have been commoditized. "I think," writes Lester Bangs about Debbie Harry at the end of the decade, "that if most guys in America could somehow get their fave-rave poster girl in bed and have total license to do whatever they wanted with this legendary body for one afternoon, at least 75 percent of the guys in the country would elect to beat her up." It is in this context that we have to analyze the musical forms of 1970s sexuality—punk and disco.

Punk Sex and Disco Pleasure

Punks rejected both romantic and permissive conventions, and re- 21 fused, in particular, to allow sexuality to be constructed as a commodity. They flaunted sex-shop goods in public, exposing the mass production of porno fantasy, dissolving its dehumanizing effects through shock—"Oh bondage! Up yours!" (not that this stopped the media from running numerous pictures of "punkettes" in corsets and fishnet tights). Punks denied that their sexuality had any significance at all—"My love lies limp," boasted Mark Perry of Alternative TV; "What is sex anyway?" asked Johnny Rotten. "Just thirty seconds of squelching noises."

Punk was the first form of youth music not to rest on love songs (ro-   22
mance remained the staple of rock lyrics throughout the countercultural
1960s), and one consequence of this was that new female voices were
heard on record, stage, and radio—shrill, assertive, impure, individual
voices, singer as subject not object. Punk's female musicians had a stri-
dent insistence that was far removed from the appeal of most postwar
glamour girls (the only sexual surprise of a self-conscious siren like
Debbie Harry, for example, was that she became a teeny-bop idol for a
generation of young girls).

Punk interrupted the long-standing rock equation of sex and plea-   23
sure, though the implications of this interruption still remain unclear.
British punk subculture itself hardly differed, in sexual terms, from
any other working-class street movement—the boys led, the girls (fewer
of them) hung on; and in the end it was probably punk's sexual effect
on performers rather than on audiences that mattered—women were
brought into a musical community from which they'd previously been
excluded, and they brought with them new questions about sound and
convention and image, about the sexuality of performance and the performance of sexuality. Whether these questions get answered we have
yet to see, but at least punks opened the possibility that rock could be
against sexism.

Disco, which between 1974 and 1978 became the dominant sound   24
of mass music across the world, had different origins and different effects. The success of *Saturday Night Fever* simply confirmed the resonance of a genre that was already an $8-billion-per-year industry in the
USA, already accounted for half the albums and singles in *Billboard's* hot
hundreds. Disco had changed the sound of radio, the organization of
record companies, the status of club deejays, the meaning of a good
night out, and all this has to be understood in the context of the 1970s'
sexual mores. Disco was not a response (like punk) to rock itself, but
challenged it indirectly, by the questions it asked about music and *dance.*

The dance floor is the most public setting for music as sexual ex-   25
pression and has been an important arena for youth culture since the
dance crazes of the beginning of the century when Afro-American
rhythms began to structure white middle-class leisure, to set new norms
for physical display, contact, and movement. Dance has been, ever since,
central to the meaning of popular music. Girls, in particular, have always flocked to dance halls, concerned not just about finding a husband,
but also about pursuing their own pleasure. They may be attracting the
lurking boys through their clothes, makeup, and appearance, but on
the dance floor their energy and agility is their own affair. The most
dedicated dancers in Britain, for example, the Northern soul fans, are

completely self-absorbed, and even in *Saturday Night Fever* (in which dancing power was diluted by pop interests) John Travolta transcended Hollywood's clumsy choreography with the sheer quality of his commitment—from the opening shots of his strut through the streets, his gaze on himself never falters; the essence of dance floor sex is physical control, and, whatever happens, John Travolta is never going to let himself go.

Dancing as a way of life, an obsession, has a long American history. Shorty Snowden, the John Travolta of the Savoy Ballroom in the 1920s, suffered from "Sunday Night Fever": "We started getting ready for Sunday on Saturday. The ideal was to get our one sharp suit to the tailor to be pressed on Saturday afternoon. Then we'd meet at the poolroom and brag about what we were going to do on the dance floor the next night. . . . "[3]

The 1920s dance cult spread quickly to "hep" white teenagers who tried to dress, dance, move like these sharp black "dudes," and the Depression stimulated dancing among the nonhep too. Thousands of small, cheap bars with dance floors, used pianos, record players, radios, and jukeboxes to fill the weekends with noise. Such working-class dance halls were crucial to the culture of courtship, but dancing meant something else even more important: it was an escape, a suspension of real time, a way in which even the unemployed could enjoy their bodies, their physical skills, the sense of human power their lives otherwise denied. Such power does not need to be rooted in sexual competition (though it often enough is); parties, Friday and Saturday night bursts of physical pleasure, sex or no sex, have always been the most intense setting for working-class musics, from ragtime to punk.

A party matters most, of course, to those people who most need to party, and, whatever else happened to mass music in the 1950s and 1960s, there were many people (black working-class Americans, British working-class teenagers, using much the same music) who never stopped dancing—1970s disco itself emerged musically from black clubs, depended commercially on its continuing white youth appeal. But, sexually, disco was most important as a gay aesthetic, and what was surprising, socially, was the appropriation of this aesthetic by the mass middle class.

Disco is dance music in the abstract, its content determined by its form. Middle-class dance music in the past, even in the 1930s, was a form determined by its content—there were still influential dance hall

26

27

28

29

---

[3] Marshall and Jean Stearns, p. 322.

instructors, sheet music salesmen, and band leaders who laid down rules of partnership, decorum, uplift, and grace. There are no such rules in disco, but, on the other hand, individual expression means nothing when there is nothing individual to express. Disco is not, despite its critics, anything like Muzak. Muzak's effect is subliminal; its purpose is to encourage its hearers to do anything but listen to it. Disco's effect is material; its purpose is to encourage its hearers to do nothing but listen to it.

What do they hear? An erotic appeal, most obviously—what Richard Dyer calls "whole body eroticism." All dancing means a commitment to physical sensation, but disco expanded the possibilities of sensation. Disco pleasure is not closed off, bound by the song structures, musical beginnings and ends, but is expressed, rather, through an open-ended series of repetitions, a shifting *intensity* of involvement. And disco, as Dyer suggests, shares rock's rhythmic pulse, while avoiding rock's phallocentrism: disco is committed to the 4:4 beat in all its implications. Disco dancing is sinuous, it avoids the jerk and grind and thrust of rock; disco dancers hustle and slide, they use all their bodies' erotic possibilities. 30

Dancing has always been a physical pleasure sufficiently intense to block out, for the moment, all other concerns, but disco pushed such enjoyment to new extremes: the disco experience is an overwhelming experience of *now-ness*, an experience intensified still further by drugs like amyl nitrite, an experience in which the dancer is, simultaneously, completely self-centered and quite selfless, completely sexualized and, in gender terms, quite sexless. On the disco floor there is no overt competition for partners, no isolation; and disco (unlike bohemia) signifies nothing, makes no expressive claims—if bohemia suggests a different way of life, disco simply offers a different experience of it. 31

The disco version of eroticism and ecstasy is not, in itself, homosexual, but the aesthetic uses of these experiences did reflect gay consciousness. They were imbued, for example, with gay romanticism: disco sensations were associated with the fleeting emotional contacts, the passing relationships of a culture in which everything in a love affair can happen in a night. Disco eroticism became, too, the sign of a sexuality that was always being constructed. It was the process of construction, the very artificiality of the disco experience, that made it erotic. Disco was a version of camp: the best disco records were those made with a sense of irony, an aggressive self-consciousness, a concern for appearances. There was an obvious link between the vocal styles of disco and 1930s torch songs: Billie Holiday and Donna Summer alike stylized feelings, distanced pain, opened up the texts of sexuality (and for this reason, disco, despised by punk-rockers on principle, had an immense appeal to the postpunk avant-garde). 32

Mainstream disco, the Saturday night fever of the teenage working   33
class, continued to operate according to the traditional street party line;
teenagers danced in different ways, to different sounds than gays.But it
was the gay disco aesthetic that middle-class dancers began to appropriate from 1974 on. If 1960s "permissive" sexual ideology had reflected
new leisure and sexual opportunities, then 1970s disco culture reflected
their emotional consequences. Disco was music for singles bars, sexual
mobility, heterosexual cruising, weekend flings, and transitory fantasies.
Gay culture reflected, in its own way, the problems and possibilities of
sex without domesticity, love without the conventional distinctions of
male and female. These problems and possibilities had become important now for heterosexuals too.

Disco was about eroticism and ecstasy as material goods, produced   34
not by spiritual or emotional work, God or love, but by technology,
chemistry, wealth. The disco experience (the music and the mood, the
poppers and the lights) revealed the artificiality and transience of sexual feelings—they were produced to be consumed; and disco pleasure,
as it moved into the commercial mainstream, became the pleasure of
consumption itself. This was obvious enough in the chic appeal of Studio 54, but was just as important for the strut of the factory girls, equally
chic, up the steps of Tiffany's in provincial Britain. Disco made no claims
to folk status; there was no creative disco community. The music was,
rather, the new international symbol of American consumer society.
Chic discos sprang up around the world, each offering the secret of eternal American youth; the pleasures of consumption and the pleasures of
sex became, in such settings, the same thing.

The problem with escapism is not the escape itself, but what's still   35
there when it's over—the rain still falls when Monday morning dawns.
Once something's been consumed it's gone; new goods are necessary,
new experiences, new highs, new sex. As many observers commented, by
the end of the 1970s disco had become a drug, but it was leisure itself that
had a new desperation. In Andrew Holleran's disco novel, *Dancer from the
Dance,* the most dedicated disco-goers are the most eager to escape:

> They seldom looked happy. They passed one another without a word
> in the elevator, like silent shades in hell, hell-bent on their next look
> from a handsome stranger. Their next rush from a popper. The next
> song that turned their bones to jelly and left them all on the dance floor
> with heads back, eyes nearly closed, in the ecstasy of saints receiving
> the stigmata. They pursued these things with such devotion that they
> acquired, after a few seasons, a haggard look, a look of deadly seri-
> ousness. Some wiped everything they could off their faces and reduced
> themselves to blanks. Yet even these, when you entered the hallway
> where they stood waiting to go in, would turn toward you all at once
> in that one unpremeditated moment (as when we see ourselves in a

mirror we didn't know was there), the same look on their faces: Take me away from this.[4]

....

Examining the Text

1. In what ways, by Frith's account, did rock music in the 1960s provide women a "useful step toward liberation" (paragraph 11)? What problems grew out of this "useful step"? Do you agree with Frith that there is no "natural" male or female sexuality?

2. Frith says that "rock's antidomestic ideology doesn't move women out of the home, but leaves them in it, as inadequates" (18). How, according to Frith, does rock music exclude women from rebellion against such qualities as dependence and passivity? What are your responses to these observations?

3. How does disco music reflect gay consciousness, according to Frith (28–33)? What caused the "demise" of disco, at the end of the 1970s, and what do you think accounts for its fairly consistent rebursts of popularity in the years since?

For Group Discussion

Frith states, "Nineteen-sixties rock was expressly opposed to the love and marriage ideology of traditional teenage culture" (12), but he also suggests that rock "articulated" a more rigid sexual double standard. In a group discussion, explain and comment on this apparent paradox, based upon Frith's discussion of the evolution of contemporary youth culture. List some specific ways in which rock and rap in the 1990s differ from (or are similar to) this earlier music in its messages about sexuality.

Writing Suggestion

Toward the end of this piece, Frith comments that, with punk rock, "women were brought into a musical community from which they'd previously been excluded, and they brought with them new questions about sound and convention and image, about the sexuality of performance and the performance of sexuality. Whether these questions get answered we have yet to see . . ." (23). In an essay explain and respond to this comment: how has popular music in recent years contributed to reducing or perpetuating sexism among young people? Use specific examples from rock and rap songs to substantiate your assertions.

---

[4] Andrew Holleran, *Dancer from the Dance* (New York: Morrow, 1978), pp. 38–39.

The Rap on Rap

David Samuels

*I*n 1989, with the success of Public Enemy's "Fight the Power," the birth of Yo! MTV Raps, and the controversial first album of N.W.A., rap music began a meteoric rise to national attention. After computerized reporting of record sales went into effect in 1991, the widespread popularity of rap became even clearer; surprised industry observers discovered rap's largest audience to be white, suburban males.

In this article written for **The New Republic,** *a monthly magazine with a moderate to conservative editorial slant, David Samuels argues that these white consumers have come to largely dictate rap's form and content. Rap's appeal to white male teenagers, Samuels believes, lies in its representation of a "foreign, sexually charged, and criminal underworld." Rap music offers middle-class white listeners their exotic "other" in a prepackaged, easily consumable form, providing the vicarious thrills of transgression (drugs, guns, and sex) without the risk. Moreover, Samuels maintains, in order to appeal to these white fans, rap musicians and producers have created an increasingly violent and antisocial image of black males, an image that has important—and in many ways negative—repercussions.*

As you read *this selection, think about whether you agree with Samuels's basic premise that the images presented in much of rap music are dictated more by the demands of white consumers than by black culture. You might also be reflecting on whether it is possible for any musical form to achieve widespread popularity without falling under the influence of bourgeois white America.*

·····················

This summer Soundscan, a computerized scanning system, changed *Billboard* magazine's method of counting record sales in the United States. Replacing a haphazard system that relied on big-city record stores, Soundscan measured the number of records sold nationally by scanning the bar codes at chain store cash registers. Within weeks the number of computed record sales leapt, as demographics shifted from minority-focused urban centers to white, suburban, middle-class malls. So it was that America awoke on June 22, 1991, to find that its favorite record was not *Out of Time,* by aging college-boy rockers R.E.M., but *Niggaz4life,* a musical celebration of gang rape and other violence by N.W.A., or Niggers With Attitude, a rap group from the Los Angeles ghetto of Compton whose records had never before risen above No. 27 on the Billboard charts.

From *Niggaz4life* to *Boyz N the Hood*, young black men committing   2
acts of violence were available this summer in a wide variety of entertainment formats. Of these none is more popular than rap. And none
has received quite the level of critical attention and concern. Writers on
the left have long viewed rap as the heartbeat of urban America, its authors, in Arthur Kempton's words, "the pre-eminent young dramatur-
gists in the clamorous theater of the street." On the right, this assumption has been shared, but greeted with predictable disdain.

Neither side of the debate has been prepared, however, to confront   3
what the entertainment industry's receipts from this summer prove beyond doubt: although rap is still proportionally more popular among
blacks, its primary audience is white and lives in the suburbs. And the
history of rap's degeneration from insurgent black street music to mainstream pop points to another dispiriting conclusion: the more rappers
were packaged as violent black criminals, the bigger their white audiences became.

If the racial makeup of rap's audience has been largely misunder-   4
stood, so have the origins of its authors. Since the early 1980s a tightly
knit group of mostly young, middle-class, black New Yorkers, in close
concert with white record producers, executives, and publicists, has
been making rap music for an audience that industry executives con-
cede is primarily composed of white suburban males. Building upon a
form pioneered by lower-class black artists in New York between 1975
and 1983, despite an effective boycott of the music by both black and
white radio that continues to this day, they created the most influential
pop music of the 1980s. Rap's appeal to whites rested in its evocation of
an age-old image of blackness: a foreign, sexually charged, and criminal
underworld against which the norms of white society are defined, and,
by extension, through which they may be defied. It was the truth of this
latter proposition that rap would test in its journey into the mainstream.

"Hip-hop," the music behind the lyrics, which are "rapped," is a   5
form of sonic bricolage with roots in "toasting," a style of making music by speaking over records. (For simplicity, I'll use the term "rap" interchangeably with "hip-hop" throughout this article.) Toasting first
took hold in Jamaica in the mid-1960s, a response, legend has it, to the
limited availability of expensive Western instruments and the concur-
rent proliferation of cheap R&B instrumental singles on Memphis-based
labels such as Stax-Volt. Cool DJ Herc, a Jamaican who settled in the
South Bronx, is widely credited with having brought toasting to New
York City. Rap spread quickly through New York's poor black neighborhoods in the mid- and late 1970s. Jams were held in local playgrounds, parks, and community centers, in the South and North Bronx,
Brooklyn, and Harlem.

Although much is made of rap as a kind of urban streetgeist, early   6
rap had a more basic function: dance music. Bill Stephney, considered
by many to be the smartest man in the rap business, recalls the first time
he heard hip-hop: "The point wasn't rapping, it was rhythm, DJs cutting
records left and right, taking the big drum break from Led Zeppelin's
'When the Levee Breaks,' mixing it together with 'Ring My Bell,' then
with a Bob James Mardi Gras jazz record and some James Brown. You'd
have 2,000 kids in any community center in New York, moving back and
forth, back and forth, like some kind of tribal war dance, you might say.
It was the rapper's role to match this intensity rhythmically. No one
knew what he was saying. He was just rocking the mike."

Rap quickly spread from New York to Philadelphia, Chicago, Bos-   7
ton, and other cities with substantial black populations. Its popularity
was sustained by the ease with which it could be made. The music on
early rap records sounded like the black music of the day: funk or, more
often, disco. Performers were unsophisticated about image and presentation, tending toward gold lamé jumpsuits and Jericurls, a second-rate
appropriation of the stylings of funk musicians like George Clinton and
Bootsy Collins.

The first rap record to make it big was "Rapper's Delight," released   8
in 1979 by the Sugar Hill Gang, an ad hoc all-star team drawn from three
New York groups on Sylvia and Joey Robinson's Sugar Hill label. Thanks
to Sylvia Robinson's soul music and background, the first thirty seconds
of "Rapper's Delight" were indistinguishable from the disco records of
the day: light guitars, high-hat drumming, and hand-claps over a deep
funk bass line. What followed will be immediately familiar to anyone
who was young in New York City that summer:

> I said, hip-hop, de-hibby, de-hibby-dibby,
> Hip-hip-hop you don't stop.
> Rock it out, Baby Bubba to the boogie de-bang-bang,
> Boogie to the boogie to be.
> Now what you hear is not a test,
> I'm rapping to the beat . . .
> I said, "By the way, baby, what's your name?"
> She said, "I go by the name Lois Lane
> And you can be my boyfriend, you surely can
> Just let me quit my boyfriend, he's called Superman."
> I said, "he's a fairy, I do suppose
> Flying through the air in pantyhose . . .
> You need a man who's got finesse
> And his whole name across his chest" . . .

Like disco music and jumpsuits, the social commentaries of early   9
rappers like Grandmaster Flash and Mellie Mel were for the most part

transparent attempts to sell records to whites by any means necessary. Songs like "White Lines" (with its anti-drug theme) and "The Message" (about ghetto life) had the desired effect, drawing fulsome praise from white rock critics, raised on the protest ballads of Bob Dylan and Phil Ochs. The reaction on the street was somewhat less favorable. "The Message" is a case in point. "People hated that record," recalls Russell Simmons, president of Def Jam Records. "I remember the Junebug, a famous DJ of the time, was playing it up at the Fever, and Ronnie DJ put a pistol to his head and said, 'Take that record off and break it or I'll blow your fucking head off.' The whole club stopped until he broke that record and put it in the garbage."

It was not until 1984 that rap broke through to a mass white audi- 10
ence. The first group to do so was Run-DMC, with the release of its debut album, *Run-DMC*, and with *King of Rock* one year later. These albums blazed the trail that rap would travel into the musical mainstream. Bill Adler, a former rock critic and rap's best-known publicist, explains: "They were the first group that came on stage as if they had just come off the street corner. But unlike the first generation of rappers, they were solidly middle class. Both of Run's parents were college-educated. DMC was a good Catholic schoolkid, a mama's boy. Neither of them was deprived and neither of them ever ran with a gang, but on stage they became the biggest, baddest, streetest guys in the world." When Run-DMC covered the Aerosmith classic "Walk This Way," the resulting video made it onto MTV, and the record went gold.

Rap's new mass audience was in large part the brainchild of Rick 11
Rubin, a Jewish punk rocker from suburban Long Island who produced the music behind many of rap's biggest acts. Like many New Yorkers his age, Rick grew up listening to Mr. Magic's Rap Attack, a rap radio show on WHBI. In 1983, at the age of 19, Rubin founded Def Jam Records in his NYU dorm room. (Simmons bought part of Def Jam in 1984 and took full control of the company in 1989.) Rubin's next group, the Beastie Boys, was a white punk rock band whose transformation into a rap group pointed rap's way into the future. The Beasties' first album, *Licensed to Ill*, backed by airplay of its authentic frat-party single "You've Got to Fight for Your Right to Party," became the first rap record to sell a million copies.

The appearance of white groups in a black musical form has histor- 12
ically prefigured the mainstreaming of the form, the growth of the white audience, and the resulting dominance of white performers. With rap, however, this process took an unexpected turn: white demand indeed began to determine the direction of the genre, but what it wanted was music more defiantly black. The result was Public Enemy, produced and

marketed by Rubin, the next group significantly to broaden rap's appeal to young whites.

Public Enemy's now familiar mélange of polemic and dance music   13
was formed not on inner-city streets but in the suburban Long Island towns in which the group's members grew up. The children of successful black middle-class professionals, they gave voice to the feeling that, despite progress toward equality, blacks still did not quite belong in white America. They complained of unequal treatment by the police, of never quite overcoming the color of their skin: "We were suburban college kids doing what we were supposed to do, but we were always made to feel like something else," explains Stephney, the group's executive producer.

Public Enemy's abrasive and highly politicized style made it a fast   14
favorite of the white avant-garde, much like the English punk rock band The Clash ten years before. Public Enemy's music, produced by the Shocklee brothers Hank and Keith, was faster, harder, and more abrasive than the rap of the day, music that moved behind the vocals like a full-scale band. But the root of Public Enemy's success was a highly charged theater of race in which white listeners became guilty eavesdroppers on the putative private conversation of the inner city. Chuck D denounced his enemies (the media, some radio stations), proclaimed himself "Public Enemy #1," and praised Louis Farrakhan in stentorian tones, flanked onstage by black-clad security guards from the Nation of Islam, the SIWs, led by Chuck's political mentor, Professor Griff. Flavor Flav, Chuck's homeboy sidekick, parodied street style: oversize sunglasses, baseball cap cocked to one side, a clock the size of a silver plate draped around his neck, going off on wild verbal riffs that often meant nothing at all.

The closer rap moved to the white mainstream, the more it became   15
like rock 'n' roll, a celebration of posturing over rhythm. The back catalogs of artists like James Brown and George Clinton were relentlessly plundered for catchy hooks, then overlaid with dance beats and social commentary. Public Enemy's single "Fight the Power" was the biggest college hit of 1989:

> Elvis was a hero to most
> But he never meant shit to me, you see
> Straight-up racist that sucker was simple and plain
> Motherfuck him and John Wayne
> 'Cause I'm black and I'm proud
> I'm ready and hyped, plus I'm amped
> Most of my heroes don't appear on no stamps
> Sample a look back, you look and find
> Nothing but rednecks for 400 years if you check.

After the release of "Fight the Power," Professor Griff made a series of anti-Semitic remarks in an interview with *The Washington Times*. Griff was subsequently asked to leave the group, for what Chuck D termed errors in judgment. Although these errors were lambasted in editorials across the country, they do not seem to have affected Public Enemy's credibility with its young white fans.

Public Enemy's theatrical black nationalism and sophisticated noise ushered in what is fast coming to be seen as rap's golden age, a heady mix of art, music, and politics. Between 1988 and 1989 a host of innovative acts broke into the mainstream. KRS-One, now a regular on the Ivy League lecture circuit, grew up poor, living on the streets of the South Bronx until he met a New York City social worker, Scott La Rock, later murdered in a drive-by shooting. Together they formed BDP, Boogie Down Productions, recording for the Jive label on RCA. Although songs like "My Philosophy" and "Love's Gonna Get 'Cha (Material Love)" were clever and self-critical, BDP's roots remained firmly planted in the guns-and-posturing of the mainstream rap ghetto.   16

The ease with which rap can create such aural cartoons, says Hank Shocklee, lies at the very heart of its appeal as entertainment: "Whites have always liked black music," he explains. "That part is hardly new. The difference with rap was that the imagery of black artists, for the first time, reached the level of black music. The sheer number of words in a rap song allows for the creation of full characters impossible in R&B. Rappers become like superheroes. Captain America or the Fantastic Four."   17

By 1988 the conscious manipulation of racial stereotypes had become rap's leading edge, a trend best exemplified by the rise to stardom of Schoolly D, a Philadelphia rapper on the Jive label who sold more than half a million records with little mainstream notice. It was not that the media had never heard of Schoolly D: white critics and fans, for the first time, were simply at a loss for words. His voice, fierce and deeply textured, could alone frighten listeners. He used it as a rhythmic device that made no concessions to pop-song form, talking evenly about smoking crack and using women for sex, proclaiming his blackness, accusing other rappers of not being black enough. What Schoolly D meant by blackness was abundantly clear. Schoolly D was a misogynist and a thug. If listening to Public Enemy was like eavesdropping on a conversation, Schoolly D was like getting mugged. This, aficionados agreed, was what they had been waiting for: a rapper from whom you would flee in abject terror if you saw him walking toward you late at night.   18

It remained for N.W.A., a more conventional group of rappers from Los Angeles, to adapt Schoolly D's stylistic advance for the mass white   19 market with its first album-length release, *Straight Out of Compton*, in 1989. The much-quoted rap from that album, "Fuck the Police," was the target of an FBI warning to police departments across the country, and a constant presence at certain college parties, white and black:

> "Fuck the Police" coming straight out the underground
> A young nigger got it bad 'cause I'm brown
> And not the other color. Some police think
> They have the authority to kill the minority . . .
> A young nigger on the warpath
> And when I'm finished, it's gonna be a bloodbath
> Of cops, dying in L.A.
> Yo, Dre I've got something to say: Fuck the Police.

Other songs spoke of trading oral sex for crack and shooting strangers for fun. After the release of *Straight Out of Compton*, N.W.A.'s lead rapper and chief lyricist, Ice Cube, left the group. Billing himself as "the nigger you love to hate," Ice Cube released a solo album, *Amerikkka's Most Wanted*, which gleefully pushed the limits of rap's ability to give offense. One verse ran: 20

> I'm thinking to myself, "why did I bang her?"
> Now I'm in the closet, looking for the hanger.

But what made *Amerikkka's Most Wanted* so shocking to so many record buyers was the title track's violation of rap's most iron-clad taboo—black on white violence: 21

> Word, yo, but who the fuck is heard:
> It's time you take a trip to the suburbs.
> Let 'em see a nigger invasion
> Point blank, on a Caucasian.
> Cock the hammer and crack a smile:
> "Take me to your house, pal . . ."

Ice Cube took his act to the big screen this summer in *Boyz N the Hood*, drawing rave reviews for his portrayal of a young black drug dealer whose life of crime leads him to an untimely end. The crime-doesn't-pay message, an inheritance from the grade-B gangster film is the stock-in-trade of another L.A. rapper-turned-actor. Ice-T of *New Jack City* fame, a favorite of socially conscious rock critics. Taking unhappy endings onto glorifications of drug dealing and gang warfare, Ice-T offers all the thrills of the form while alleviating any guilt listeners may have felt about consuming drive-by shootings along with their popcorn. 22

It was in this spirit that "Yo! MTV Raps" debuted in 1989 as the first national broadcast forum for rap music. The videos were often poorly produced, but the music and visual presence of stars like KRS-One, LL Cool J, and Chuck D proved enormously compelling, rocketing "Yo!" to the top of the MTV ratings. On weekends bands were interviewed and 23 videos introduced by Fab Five Freddie; hip young white professionals watched his shows to keep up with urban black slang and fashion. Younger viewers rushed home from school on weekdays to catch ex-Beastie Boys DJ Dr. Dre, a sweatsuit-clad mountain of a man, well over 300 pounds, and Ed Lover, who evolved a unique brand of homeboy Laurel and Hardy mixed with occasional social comment.

With "Yo! MTV Raps," rap became for the first time the music of   24 choice in the white suburbs of middle America. From the beginning, says Doug Herzog, MTV's vice president for programming, the show's audience was primarily white, male, suburban, and between the ages of 16 and 24, a demographic profile that "Yo!"'s success helped set in stone. For its daytime audience, MTV spawned an ethnic rainbow of well-scrubbed pop rappers from MC Hammer to Vanilla Ice to Gerardo, a Hispanic actor turned rap star. For "Yo" itself, rap became more overtly politicized as it expanded its audience. Sound bites from the speeches of Malcolm X and Martin Luther King became de rigueur introductions to formulaic assaults on white America mixed with hymns to gang violence and crude sexual caricature.

Holding such polyglot records together is what *Village Voice* critic   25 Nelson George has labeled "ghettocentrism," a style-driven cult of blackness defined by crude stereotypes. P.R. releases, like a recent one for Los Angeles rapper DJ Quik, take special care to mention artists' police records, often enhanced to provide extra street credibility. When Def Jam star Slick Rick was arrested for attempted homicide, Def Jam incorporated the arrest into its publicity campaign for Rick's new album, bartering exclusive rights to the story to *Vanity Fair* in exchange for the promise of a lengthy profile. Muslim groups such as Brand Nubian proclaim their hatred for white devils, especially those who plot to poison black babies. That Brand Nubian believes the things said on its records is unlikely: the group seems to get along quite well with its white Jewish publicist, Beth Jacobson of Electra Records. Anti-white, and, in this case, anti-Semitic, rhymes are a shorthand way of defining one's opposition to the mainstream. Racism is reduced to fashion, by the rappers who use it and by the white audiences to whom such images appeal. What's significant here are not so much the intentions of artist and audience as a dynamic in which anti-Semitic slurs and black criminality correspond to "authenticity," and "authenticity" sells records.

The selling of this kind of authenticity to a young white audience is   26 the stock-in-trade of *The Source*, a full-color monthly magazine devoted exclusively to rap music, founded by Jon Shecter while still an undergraduate at Harvard. Shecter is what is known in the rap business as a Young Black Teenager. He wears a Brooklyn Dodgers baseball cap, like

Spike Lee, and a Source T-shirt. As editor of *The Source,* Shecter has become a necessary quote for stories about rap in *Time* and other national
magazines.

An upper-middle-class white, Shecter has come in for his share of   27
criticism, the most recent of which appeared as a diatribe by the sometime critic and tinpot racist Harry Allen in a black community newspaper, *The City Sun,* which pointed out that Shecter is Jewish. "There's no
place for me to say anything," Shecter responds. "Given what I'm doing, my viewpoint has to be that whatever comes of the black community, the hip-hop community which is the black community, is the right
thing. I know my place. The only way in which criticism can be raised
is on a personal level, because the way that things are set up, with the
white-controlled media, prevents sincere back-and-forth discussion
from taking place." The latest venture in hip-hop marketing, a magazine
planned by Time Warner, will also be edited by a young white, Jonathan
van Meter, a former Condé Nast editor.

In part because of young whites like Shecter and van Meter, rap's in-   28
fluence on the street continues to decline. "You put out a record by Big
Daddy Kane," Rubin says, "and then put out the same record by a pop
performer like Janet Jackson. Not only will the Janet Jackson record sell
ten times more copies, it will also be the cool record to play in clubs."
Stephney agrees: "Kids in my neighborhood pump dance hall reggae on
their systems all night long, because that's where the rhythm is. . . . People complain about how white kids stole black culture. The truth of the
matter is that no one can steal a culture." Whatever its continuing significance in the realm of racial politics, rap's hour as innovative popular music has come and gone. Rap forfeited whatever claim it may have had to
particularity by acquiring a mainstream white audience whose tastes increasingly determined the nature of the form. What whites wanted was
not music, but black music, which as a result stopped really being either.

White fascination with rap sprang from a particular kind of cultural   29
tourism pioneered by the Jazz Age novelist Carl Van Vechten. Van
Vechten's 1926 best seller *Nigger Heaven* imagined a masculine, criminal, yet friendly black ghetto world that functioned, for Van Vechten
and for his readers, as a refuge from white middle-class boredom. In *Really the Blues,* the white jazzman Mezz Mezzrow went one step further,
claiming that his own life among black people in Harlem had physically
transformed him into a member of the Negro race, whose unique sensibility he had now come to share. By inverting the moral values attached
to contemporary racial stereotypes, Van Vechten and Mezzrow at once
appealed to and sought to undermine the prevailing racial order. Both
men, it should be stressed, conducted their tours in person.

The moral inversion of racist stereotypes as entertainment has lost   30
whatever transformative power it may arguably have had fifty years

ago. MC Serch of 3rd Bass, a white rap traditionalist, with short-cropped hair and thick-rimmed Buddy Holly glasses, formed his style in the uptown hip-hop clubs like the L.Q. in the early 1980s. "Ten or eleven years ago," he remarks, "when I was wearing my permanent-press Lee's with a beige campus shirt and matching Adidas sneakers, kids I went to school with were calling me a 'wigger,' 'black wanna-be,' all kinds of racist names. Now those same kids are driving Jeeps with MCM leather interiors and pumping Public Enemy."

The ways in which rap has been consumed and popularized speak   31
not of cross-cultural understanding, musical or otherwise, but of a voyeurism and tolerance of racism in which black and white are both complicit. "Both the rappers and their white fans affect and commodify their own visions of street culture," argues Henry Louis Gates, Jr., of Harvard University, "like buying Navajo blankets at a reservation roadstop. A lot of what you see in rap is the guilt of the black middle class about its economic success, its inability to put forth a culture of its own. Instead they do the worst possible thing, falling back on fantasies of street life. In turn, white college students with impeccable gender credentials buy nasty sex lyrics under the cover of getting at some kind of authentic black experience."

Gates goes on to make the more worrying point: "What is poten-   32
tially very dangerous about this is the feeling that by buying records they have made some kind of valid social commitment." Where the assimilation of black street culture by whites once required a degree of human contact between the races, the street is now available at the flick of a cable channel—to black and white middle class alike. "People want to consume and they want to consume easy," Hank Shocklee says. "If you're a suburban white kid and you want to find out what life is like for a black city teenager, you buy a record by N.W.A. It's like going to an amusement park and getting on a roller coaster ride—records are safe, they're controlled fear, and you always have the choice of turning it off. That's why nobody ever takes a train up to 125th Street and gets out and starts walking around. Because then you're not in control anymore: it's a whole other ball game." This kind of consumption—of racist stereotypes, of brutality toward women, or even of uplifting tributes to Dr. Martin Luther King—is of a particularly corrupting kind. The values it instills find their ultimate expression in the ease with which we watch young black men killing each other: in movies, on records, and on the streets of cities and towns across the country.

．．．．．．．．．．．．．．．．．．．．

Examining the Text

1. According to Samuels why did "white suburban males" begin listening to rap in such large numbers during the 1980s? What black stereotypes does rap perpetuate? Does Samuels's causal analysis correspond to your experience?

2. How, by Samuels's account, did Run-DMC contribute to moving rap into the "musical mainstream" of young American society? How persuasive do you find Samuel's reasoning here?

3. What does *Village Voice* critic Nelson George mean by his term "ghettocentrism" (paragraph 25)? How might this phenomenon encourage the tolerance of racism, as Samuels suggests it does? What forces in our culture do you see as bearing the greatest responsibility for the "crude stereotype" promulgated in much rap music?

For Group Discussion

In this selection, Samuels describes a historical phenomenon: "The appearance of white groups in a black musical form has historically prefigured the mainstreaming of the form, the growth of the white audience, and the resulting dominance of white performers" (12). As a group activity, paraphrase this statement to derive its central meaning, and then discuss the validity of Samuels's views on "mainstreaming," listing several examples that prove or disprove his central point.

Writing Suggestion

Samuels sees rap as a musical form on the decline: "Whatever its continuing significance in the realm of racial politics, rap's hour as innovative popular music has come and gone" (28). In an essay, explain what Samuels means by this statement, state whether or not you agree with him, and cite examples of rap music that either support or disprove his claim.

2 Live Crew, Decoded

Henry Louis Gates, Jr.

*A*dding another voice to the ongoing debate about rap music's content *and effect on young listeners, Henry Louis Gates, Jr.—a Harvard professor who is well-known as one of the country's foremost proponents of the African-American tradition—adds a cultural perspective on the controversy. In this piece, which appeared on the Op-Ed page of the* New York Times, *Gates attempts to* *explain (and even apologize for) the music and lyrics of 2 Live Crew. One of the witnesses for the defense in 2 Live Crew's 1990 obscenity trial in Florida, Gates suggests that those listening to the music of this and other rap groups within the context of the black experience in America find messages that those outside African-American culture would probably miss.*

By insisting that 2 Live Crew be interpreted within the context of the black community and its traditions, Gates maintains that many of the media's criticisms of the group, specifically of the blatantly sexist and "obscene" lyrical content, are unfair and may in fact stem from racial bias. The sexism of the group's music, he says, may be so purposely exaggerated that nobody within the black community would ever take the lyrics seriously. Likewise, the allegedly pornographic words should be regarded as "sexual carnivalesque"—that is, as parody of real sexual beliefs and practices.

As you read *this article, then, consider the validity of Gates's main premise: that only those who "become literate in the vernacular traditions of African-Americans" can fairly judge the products of that culture. Is it, in fact, possible for persons who are outside that rich cultural tradition to become literate enough to judge its products? If so, how could someone acquire that kind of literacy?*

• • • • • • • • • • • • • • • • • • • •

1   The rap group 2 Live Crew and their controversial hit recording, "As Nasty as They Wanna Be," may well earn a signal place in the history of First Amendment rights. But just as important is how these lyrics will be interpreted and by whom.

2   For centuries, African-Americans have been forced to develop coded ways of communicating to protect them from danger. Allegories and double meanings, words redefined to mean their opposites ("bad" meaning "good," for instance), even neologisms ("bodacious") have enabled blacks to share messages only the initiated understand.

3   Many blacks were amused by the transcripts of Marion Barry's sting operation which reveals that he used the traditional black expression about one's "nose being opened." This referred to a love affair and not, as Mr. Barry's prosecutors have suggested, to the inhalation of drugs. Understanding this phrase could very well spell the difference (for the Mayor) between prison and freedom.

4   2 Live Crew is engaged in heavy-handed parody, turning the stereotypes of black and white American culture on their heads. These young artists are acting out, to lively dance music, a parodic exaggeration of the age-old stereotypes of the oversexed black female and male. Their exuberant use of hyperbole (phantasmagoric sexual organs, for ex-

ample) undermines—for anyone fluent in black cultural codes—a too literal-minded hearing of the lyrics.

This is the street tradition called "signifying" or "playing the dozens," which has generally been risqué, and where the best signifier or "rapper" is the one who invents the most extravagant images, the biggest "lies," as the culture says. (H. "Rap" Brown earned his nickname in just this way.) In the face of racist stereotypes about black sexuality, you can do one of two things: you can disavow them or explode them with exaggeration.

2 Live Crew, like many "hip-hop" groups, is engaged in sexual carnivalesque. Parody reigns supreme, from a take-off of standard blues to a spoof of the black power movement, their off-color nursery rhymes are part of a venerable Western tradition. The group even satirizes the culture of commerce when it appropriates popular advertising slogans ("Tastes great!" "Less filling!") and puts them in a bawdy context.

2 Live Crew must be interpreted within the context of black culture generally and of signifying specifically. Their novelty, and that of other adventuresome rap groups, is that their defiant rejection of euphemism now voices for the mainstream what before existed largely in the "race record" market—where the records of Redd Foxx and Rudy Ray Moore once were forced to reside.

Rock songs have always been about sex but have used elaborate subterfuges to convey that fact. 2 Live Crew uses Anglo-Saxon words and is self-conscious about it: a parody of a white voice in one song refers to "private personal parts," as a coy counterpart to the group's bluntness.

Much more troubling than its so-called obscenity is the group's overt sexism. Their sexism is so flagrant, however, that it almost cancels itself out in a hyperbolic war between the sexes. In this, it recalls the inter-sexual jousting in Zora Neale Hurston's novels. Still, many of us look toward the emergence of more female rappers to redress sexual stereotypes. And we must not allow ourselves to sentimentalize street culture: the appreciation of verbal virtuosity does not lessen one's obligation to critique bigotry in all of its pernicious forms.

Is 2 Live Crew more "obscene" than, say, the comic Andrew Dice Clay? Clearly, this rap group is seen as more threatening than others that are just as sexually explicit. Can this be completely unrelated to the specter of the young black male as a figure of sexual and social disruption, the very stereotypes 2 Live Crew seem determined to undermine?

This question—and the very large question of obscenity and the First Amendment—cannot even be addressed until those who would answer them become literate in the vernacular traditions of African

Americans. To do less is to censor through the equivalent of intellectual prior restraint—and censorship is to art what lynching is to justice.

•••••••••••••••••••••

Examining the Text

1. Gates says that "in the face of racist stereotypes about black sexuality, you can do one of two things: you can disavow them or explode them with exaggeration" (paragraph 5). According to Gates, how do many hip-hop groups—and 2 Live Crew specifically—overturn these age-old stereotypes? Do you agree that this is the effect of the sexual content, of much rap and hip-hop?

2. Gates believes the novelty of 2 Live Crew and other rap groups "is that their defiant rejection of euphemism now voices for the mainstream what before existed largely in the 'race record' market" (7). What does he mean by "defiant rejection of euphemism?" Do you think that other popular forms of music deal essentially in euphemism?

3. Gates's discussion of language construction in rap music suggests that rappers' word choices have changed audiences' perception of what is acceptable in "mainstream" music. Do you find any further evidence to support this idea? If so, do you find this basically a positive change?

For Group Discussion

Gates contends that for centuries "African-Americans have been forced to develop coded ways of communicating to protect them from danger" (2). What specific "dangers" is he referring to? As a group, brainstorm five specific examples of "coded ways of communicating" within other communities, such as interest groups (sports fans, for example) and even academic departments at your school.

Writing Suggestion

Gates admits that 2 Live Crew's "overt sexism" is troubling (9). In an essay, discuss how Gates responds to the accusations of sexism frequently leveled at rap groups. Evaluate Gates's response from your own perspective: does his argument convince you, and why (or why not)? Use specific examples from rap hits past and present to develop your supporting arguments. If you have little or no experience with rap music, then substitute rock music, or some other popular form with which you are more familiar, to formulate your thesis for this paper.

When Black Feminism Faces the Music, and the Music Is Rap

Michele Wallace

If you've ever been torn between championing the free speech of rappers, yet feeling discomfort at the content of their free expression, then you'll empathize with Michele Wallace's dilemma about contemporary rap and hip-hop. Writing within a black feminist academic tradition that includes Alice Walker, bell hooks, and Ntozake Shange, Wallace concerns herself specifically with how black feminists can reconcile the conflicting interests of gender and race when they critique representations of women in most rap lyrics and videos.

As many critics have noted, male rap artists generally portray women solely as sex objects—manipulative or powerless, willing or unresponsive— and describe sexual activity in blunt, violent terms. Videos fetishize and eroticize women's bodies as they gyrate in tight and revealing clothing, while men's bodies remain covered. Arguing that such representations dismiss and deny the "humanity of the black woman," Wallace faults the implicit message of many of the lyrics that "women should be silent and prone."

Yet Wallace also values rap as an art form fundamental to black culture. She carefully positions herself between two extremes: the one which wholeheartedly condemns rap (and can be construed as condemning or devaluing black culture in general) and the other which endorses misogyny in rap as a legitimate expression of black manhood. While she links anti-sexist rap music with ethics, morality, and emotional maturity, she also proclaims that "sexism in rap is a necessary evil."

As you read, *think about this last statement and ask yourself whether gender and race can or should be mutually exclusive concerns.*

· · · · · · · · · · · · · · · · · ·

Like many black feminists, I look on sexism in rap as a necessary 1
evil. In a society plagued by poverty and illiteracy, where young black
men are as likely to be in prison as in college, rap is a welcome articulation of the economic and social frustrations of black youth.

In response to disappointments faced by poor urban blacks negoti- 2
ating their future, rap offers the release of creative expression and historical continuity: it draws on precedents as diverse as jazz, reggae, calypso, Afro-Cuban, African and heavy-metal, and its lyrics include
rudimentary forms of political, economic and social analysis.

But with the failure of our urban public schools, rappers have taken   3
education into their own hands; these are oral lessons (reading and writing being low priorities). And it should come as no surprise that the end
result emphasizes innovations in style and rhythm over ethics and
morality. Although there are exceptions, like raps advocating world
peace (the W.I.S.E. Guyz's "Time for Peace") and opposing drug use
(Ice-T's "Im Your Pusher"), rap lyrics can be brutal, raw and, where
women are the subject, glaringly sexist.

Given the genre's current cross-over popularity and success in the   4
marketplace, including television commercials, rap's impact on young
people is growing. A large part of the appeal of pop culture is that it can
offer symbolic resolutions to life's contradictions. But when it comes to
gender, rap has not resolved a thing.

Though styles vary—from that of the X-rated Ice-T to the sybaritic   5
Kwaneé to the hyperpolitics of Public Enemy—what seems universal is
how little male rappers respect sexual intimacy and how little regard
they have for the humanity of the black woman. Witness the striking
contrast within rap videos: for men, standard attire is baggy outsize
pants; for women, spike heels and short skirts. Videos often feature the
ostentatious and fetishistic display of women's bodies. In Kool Moe
Dee's "How Ya Like Me Now," women gyrate in tight leather with large
revealing holes. In Digital Underground's video "Doowutchyalike," set
poolside at what looks like a fraternity house party, a rapper in a clown
costume pretends to bite the backside of a woman in a bikini.

As Trisha Rose, a black feminist studying rap, puts it, "Rap is basi-   6
cally a locker room with a beat."

The recent banning of the sale of 2 Live Crew's album "As Nasty as   7
They Wanna Be" by local governments in Florida and elsewhere has
publicized rap's treatment of women as sex objects, but it also made a
hit of a record that contains some of the bawdiest lyrics in rap. Though
such sexual explicitness in lyrics is rare, the assumptions about women—
that they manipulate men with their bodies—are typical.

In an era when the idea that women want to be raped should be ob-   8
solete, rap lyrics and videos presuppose that women always desire sex,
whether they know it or not. In Bell Biv De-Voe's rap-influenced pop hit
single "Poison," for instance, a beautiful girl is considered poison because she does not respond affirmatively and automatically to a sexual
proposition.

In "Yearning: Race, Gender, Cultural Politics" (Southend, 1990), bell   9
hooks sees the roots of rap as a youth rebellion against all attempts to
control black masculinity, both in the streets and in the home. "That rap
would be anti-domesticity and in the process anti-female should come
as no surprise," Ms. Hooks says.

At present there is only a small platform for black women to address   10
the problems of sexism in rap and in their community. Feminist criticism, like many other forms of social analysis, is widely considered part
of a hostile white culture. For a black feminist to chastise misogyny in
rap publicly would be viewed as divisive and counterproductive. There
is a widespread perception in the black community that public criticism
of black men constitutes collaborating with a racist society.

The charge is hardly new. Such a reaction greeted Ntozake Shange's   11
play "For Colored Girls Who Have Considered Suicide When the Rainbow Is Enuf," my own essays, "Black Macho and the Myth of the Su-
perwoman," and Alice Walker's novel "The Color Purple," all of which
were perceived as critical of black men. After the release of the film version of "The Color Purple," feminists were lambasted in the press for
their supposed lack of support for black men; such critical analysis by
black women has all but disappeared. In its place is "A Black Man's
Guide to the Black Woman," a vanity-press book by Shahrazad Ali,
which has sold more than 80,000 copies by insisting that black women
are neurotic, insecure and competitive with black men.

Though misogynist lyrics seem to represent the opposite of Ms.   12
Ali's world view, these are, in fact, just two extremes on the same theme:
Ms. Ali's prescription for what ails the black community is that women
should not question men about their sexual philandering, and should
be firmly slapped across the mouth when they do. Rap lyrics suggest
just about the same: women should be silent and prone.

There are those who have wrongly advocated censorship of rap's   13
more sexually explicit lyrics, and those who have excused the misogyny
because of its basis in black oral traditions.

Rap is rooted not only in the blaxploitation films of the '60s but also   14
in an equally sexist tradition of black comedy. In the use of four-letter
words and explicit sexual references, both Richard Pryor and Eddie
Murphy, who themselves drew upon the earlier examples of Redd Foxx,
Pigmeat Markham and Moms Mabley, are conscious reference points
for the 2 Live Crew. Black comedy, in turn, draws on an oral tradition in
which black men trade "toasts," stories in which dangerous bagmen and
trickster figures like Stackolee and Dolomite sexually exploit women
and promote violence among men. The popular rapper Ice Cube, in the
album "Amerikkka's Most Wanted," is Stackolee come to life. In "The
Nigga Ya Love to Hate," he projects an image of himself as a criminal as
dangerous to women as to the straight white world.

Rap remains almost completely dominated by black males and this   15
mind-set. Although women have been involved in rap since at least the
mid-80s, record companies have only recently begun to promote them.
And as women rappers like Salt-n-Pepa, Monie Love, M. C. Lyte, L. A.

Star and Queen Latifah slowly gain more visibility, rap's sexism may emerge as a subject for scrutiny. Indeed, the answer may lie with women, expressing in lyrics and videos the tensions between the sexes in the black community.

Today's women rappers range from a high ground that doesn't 16 challenge male rap on its own level (Queen Latifah) to those who subscribe to the same sexual high jinks as male rappers (Oaktown's 3.5.7). M. C. Hammer launched Oaktown's 3.5.7., made up of his former backup dancers. These female rappers manifest the worst-case scenario: their skimpy, skintight leopard costumes in the video of "Wild and Loose (We Like It)" suggest an exotic animalistic sexuality. Their clothes fall to their ankles. They take bubble baths. Clearly, their bodies are more important than rapping. And in a field in which writing one's own rap is crucial, their lyrics are written by their former boss, M. C. Hammer.

Most women rappers constitute the middle ground: they talk of ro- 17 mance, narcissism and parties. On the other hand, Salt-n-Pepa on "Shake Your Thang" uses the structure of the 1969 Isley Brothers song "It's Your Thing" to insert a protofeminist rap response: "Don't try to tell me how to party. It's my dance and it's my body." M. C. Lyte, in a dialogue with Positive K on "I'm Not Havin' It," comes down hard on the notion that women can't say no and criticizes the shallowness of the male rap.

Queen Latifah introduces her video, "Ladies First," performed with 18 the English rapper Monie Love, with photographs of black political heroines like Winnie Mandela, Sojourner Truth, Harriet Tubman and Angela Davis. With a sound that resembles scat as much as rap, Queen Latifah chants "Stereotypes they got to go" against a backdrop of newsreel footage of the apartheid struggle in South Africa. The politically sophisticated Queen Latifah seems worlds apart from the adolescent, buffoonish sex orientation of most rap. In general, women rappers seem so much more grown up.

Can they inspire a more beneficent attitude toward sex in rap? 19

What won't subvert rap's sexism is the actions of men; what will is 20 women speaking in their own voice, not just in artificial female ghettos, but with and to men.

•••••••••••••••••••••

Examining the Text

1. Wallace—a feminist herself—looks on sexism in rap music "as a necessary evil." How does she resolve the seeming inconsistency of this statement? Do you find her position convincing? Why or why not?

2. Wallace takes a basically positive critical stance with regard to rap: "Rap is a welcome articulation of the economic and social frustrations of black youth" (paragraph 1). In her view does rap "articulate" these frustrations, and why is it "welcome"? How would David Samuels ("The Rap on Rap") respond? With whom do you agree?

3. Toward the end of her article, Wallace wonders whether women rappers can inspire a "more beneficent attitude toward sex in rap" (19). How, in Wallace's view, might women rappers be able to effect such a change? Do you think this is possible? Do you see any evidence that such a change is occurring?

For Group Discussion

Wallace asserts, "A large part of the appeal of pop culture is that it can offer symbolic resolutions to life's contradictions" (4). As a group, consider one of the central contradictions of contemporary life: that we value the concept of the "family" highly but increasingly find little time for true family life. Then arrive at a list of pop culture "artifacts"—advertisements, television shows, and so forth—that might offer symbolic resolution to this contradiction.

Writing Suggestion

In Wallace's eyes, rap favors "innovations in style and rhythm over ethics and morality" (3). Citing examples of popular music in general—and rap in particular—as evidence for the points you make in your supporting paragraphs, write a paper agreeing with or disproving the claim that contemporary popular music emphasizes stylistic and rhythmic features over moral values.

POPULAR MUSIC'S INFLUENCE ON LIFESTYLE
....

Popular Music: Emotional Use and Management

Alan Wells

If you've ever used a particular song or album to alter your state of mind—to relax, to stimulate feelings of nostalgia, or to "pump up" for a party, then you're a typical pop music listener, according to Alan Wells. In this 1987 qualitative study of youth's relationship to popular music, Wells suggests that young people use music to manipulate their moods and behaviors, finding "deep emotional meaning" in the rhythm, melody and lyrics of popular tunes.

In surveying his respondents' favorite music for listening and dancing, Wells found slight but significant gender differences in young people's uses of and responses to pop music. For example, female respondents listed "happiness" and "love" as predominant themes and emotions elicited by popular music, while "excitement" above those two was on the top of the list for males. Although "proving" that men and women respond differently to similar musical stimuli, Wells still believes both genders use music as a form of "self-administered psychotherapy" to create and control their emotional responses.

As you read this essay, observe how heavily Wells, a sociologist by profession, relies on percentile norms and other numerical values as his data, a research strategy which writers in the social and "hard" sciences use to lend validity to their conclusions. However, you may also test his conclusions against your own musical experience. How closely do you conform to the conclusions which Wells draws in this article? Do you rely on your favorite music in ways that Wells's survey suggests?

....

The study of popular music is a relatively new field in communica- 1
tion (Chaffee, 1985). Recent book length treatments of the topic (Frith, 1981; Lull, 1987), the continuation of the scholarly journal *Popular Music and Society,* and articles published in other journals, are adding to existing knowledge. (Curtis 1987:2) has noted that technology and the audience are the least studied aspects of popular music. Similarly, Lewis (1981, 1983) urges the desirability of the "uses and gratifications" approach to fill gaps in our knowledge of popular music. The study re-

ported here is in this tradition, and also employs ideas from the sociology of emotions that has recently emerged from symbolic interaction theory.

A survey of college students was conducted to gauge their consumption and use of popular music. The focus was on dance and emotions, and gender is the single independent variable. They were asked to select their favorite type of music, and indicate their dance activity and favorite dance music. Subjects were then asked to list their three favorite songs and identify emotions that they associated with them. Finally, they were asked what effect they thought music had on them and whether they ever use music to change their mood.

Three previous studies have a bearing on the research reported here. Gantz *et al* (1978) studied the gratification of popular music claimed by a sample of secondary and college students. The listeners, they found, used music primarily to relieve boredom, ease tensions, manipulate their moods, and fight loneliness. The researchers, however, did not examine emotional uses or identify music preferences.

Rosenbaum and Prinsky (1987) asked a junior and senior high school sample to choose their favorite three songs and select one of seven reasons for liking them. Except for dance, differences between the genders were small. In order of preference, the reasons the songs were chosen were (1987:85): "It helps me to relax and stop thinking about things" (30% Male, 34% Female); "Helps get me into the right mood" (25% Male, 29% Female); "It's good to dance to" (16% Male, 35% Female); "Words express how I feel" (17% Male, 24% Female); "It creates a good atmosphere when I'm with others" (16% Male, 13% Female); "It helps pass the time" (13% Male, 10% Female); and "I want to listen to the words" (11% Male, 7% Female). Dance or emotional impact are highly represented.

In a survey of college students similar to that employed here, Melton and Galician consciously employ a uses and gratification model. They found that "Respondents felt that both radio and music videos provided need satisfaction in passing time, relieving tension, relaxation, mood shifting, and forgetting about problems" (1987:41).

Sample

Self-administered questionnaires were completed by two groups of college students, 105 from a sociology class at a medium-size rural campus in New England, and 119 in a communication class at a large East Coast University. Both colleges are state supported and serve a broad range of social classes. Although the sample cannot be claimed to be representative of college youth, high agreement exists between the two groups, and with a Midwestern sample of 141 (predominantly middle class) students in a similar study (Wells, 1985). The results may be suggestive for a larger universe.

The mean age of the subject was 19.6 years. Approximately 32 percent were 18 years old or less; 30% were 19 or 20; 22% were 21 or 22; and 7% were 23 years or older. There were 115 males and 119 females, of whom 19 identified themselves as minorities (Black 16, Hispanic 3, all in East Coast group). Because of the similarities between the two groups the findings report for the entire sample. Any large discrepancies are noted in the discussion. 7

Findings: Music Choice, Dance, Emotions and Meanings

(1) **Favorite music.** Respondents were asked to indicate their favorite type of music from the following list: Classical, Easy listening, Heavy metal, Jazz, R & B/Soul, Country, Pop, Rock, and Other (which they were encouraged to specify. (Only one respondent questioned these terms, asking "What the hell is pop!") 8

Table I shows the respondents' favorite type of music. Rock and pop are clearly the dominant forms of music. The popularity of R & B/Soul can be attributed largely to Black respondents: 9 of the 16 made it their top choice. Country music had less than a one percent following, and classical and jazz had miniscule followings. The musics that are grouped under the heading "new wave" were the only significant addition to the list provided. The response to heavy metal is perhaps the least expected. 9

Table I: Favorite Popular Music, by Gender Percent Choosing Music Type

	Males (n = 115)	Females (n = 119)	Total (n = 234)
Rock	53	40	47
Pop	14	29	22
R & B/Soul	7	11	9
New wave[*1]	7	8	7
Heavy metal	3	3	3
Easy listening	1	3	2
Jazz	1	1	1
Classical	0	2	1
Reggae	2	1	1
Multiple/All	5	1	3
Other/NR	6	1	3

*Includes progressive, punk, hardcore, underground, and new music.

The music is usually thought to appeal to young males, while women prefer softer, romantic rock (Frith, 1981; Weinstein, 1983). While the latter may be true (women's higher preference for pop), male respondents had a low approval of heavy metal, the same as that for females. Perhaps the male respondents are already beyond the "metal" age.

The variety available in popular music is indicated by the respondents' choices of popular songs. Most were able to identify three favorites, and selected from an approximately 20-year pool of popular songs. Many were first heard by the respondents in their early teens. While current hits are represented, the bulk of the choices indicate a broad variety of musical preference. Nor can music be seen as a purely youth phenomenon, since respondents are now selecting music from their parents' generation. While younger listeners may only know current hits (Stipp, 1985), tastes of college-age people are much more varied. 10

In all, 277 artists or groups were mentioned as favorites (out of a total of 702 possible choices), which indicates a wide variety of popular music. The top choice, the contemporary Irish group U2, received 26 mentions. The next eight most popular choices have been performing for more than a decade: Pink Floyd (18), Bruce Springsteen (17), Led Zeppelin (11), Genesis and Bob Marley (12), Billy Joel (11), Elton John and the Beatles (10). Contemporary "star" George Michael completes the top ten artists with 9 mentions. There were twenty-two other artists receiving four or more mentions. Only two were women—Whitney Houston and Madonna. Only a few were relatively new groups (The Cure, R.E.M. Prince, The Smiths (Morrissey), the remainder veterans of pop music (Eagles, Rolling Stones, Journey, Peter Gabriel, the Police, Boston, Van Halen, Stevie Wonder, Lynyrd Skynyrd, Phil Collins, Sting, the Who, Queen, Steve Winwood, Elvis Presley, and Vivaldi). 11

The favorite song artists were identified by gender and the choices of male and female respondents are shown in Table II. As expected, females were more likely than men to choose female artists or mixed gender groups. But like male respondents, women still usually choose 12

Table II: Gender and Favorite Songs, Artists by Respondent's Gender, Respondent Gender

Gender of Artists	Female	Male	Total
Male	91 (83%)	99 (93%)	190
Female	16 (15%)	7 (7%)	23
Males and females	3 (3%)	1 (1%)	4
	110 (100%)	107 (100%)	217

*17 choices could not be identified by artists gender and are omitted.

Table III: Dance Frequency by Gender

Frequency	Females (%)	Males (%)
Everyday	15 (13)	13 (11)
Twice or more/week	39 (33)	17 (15)
Once per week	32 (27)	15 (13)
Once per month	17 (14)	36 (31)
Seldom/never	11 (9)	29 (25)
No response	5 (4)	5 (1)
Total	119 (100)	115 (99)

songs by male artists. During the Madonna, Cyndi Lauper, Tina Turner peak (Wells 1985), 30% of a similar sample of women chose female or mixed groups.

(2) **Music for Dancing.**   The survey provides information on how   13 often respondents dance, and what type of music they dance to. Table III shows dance frequency by gender. Women clearly dance more often than men, in part, perhaps, because it is socially acceptable for women to dance together. Both males and females in the New England sample danced more than the East Coast respondents (except in the "everyday" category, inflated for the East by 6 of 11 Black females). Seventy-three percent of the women dance at least once per week, compared to 39 percent of the men.

If popular music is primarily for dancing, the choice of dance mu-   14 sic should be similar to the favorite music shown in Table I. Since women apparently dance the most, it should be especially true for them. Table IV shows to what degree this holds. While it is true that Rock, Pop and R & B/Soul are the most popular types of music, pop is used more for dancing, rock for listening. While new wave is about equally valued, the other types of music (all "write-ins") are chosen specifically for dancing. Thus dance/club and disco/funk are represented in Table IV, but not Table I. The relatively high no response category represents primarily non-dancers. Clearly dancing is one use of popular music, but it is not the most important use for the most popular (overall) type of music, rock. Dance, however, does popularize types of music that capitalize on dancability over other qualities.

(3) **Music and Emotions.**   Christenson and Lindlof have summa-   15 rized what is known from the scarce studies of the effects of music on children. It may ". . . have a significant *emotional* or *affective* impact . . . there is evidence that two of the prime determinants of children's mu-

Table IV: Favorite Dance Music by Gender Percent Choosing Music Type

	Males (n = 115)	Females (n = 119)	Total (n = 234)
Pop/Top 40	22	33	28
Rock	18	13	16
R & B/Soul	12	11	12
Dance/Club	9	7	8
New wave	7	9	8
Disco funk	5	7	6
Reggae	1	1	2
Other	6	9	8
No response	18	7	12
	98*	98*	99*

*Less than 100 due to rounding and omitting Jazz, Country, Easy Listening, and Heavy Metal which each had less than 1% response.

sical preferences are the mood and sentiment of the music . . . Most rock music is by its very nature an excitatory stimulus and can arouse the listener" (1983:36). The same effects can be expected in young adults.

Hochschild (1981) has analyzed some of the complexities of a single emotion, love, and the differing ways that males and females deal with it. Hochschild (1983) has also persuasively argued that the genders manage their emotions in different ways. We can therefore hypothesize gender differences in the emotional use of music.

Love, in its many varieties, is widely acknowledged to be the most common component of western popular music, a claim supported by the findings reported below. Denisoff and Bridges (1983) have cited the numerous studies on the love component of American popular music and the differing uses of music by males and females. Similarly, Frith (1981) discusses at length the meaning of pop music to British teenagers. He describes the features of female youth culture (1981:225–234) which produces the "dream lover" phenomenon while males gravitate to "macho" music. While he notes that rock has been a force in liberating sexuality (1981:235–48) there is neither sexual equality among performing artists nor a unisex homogenization of musical tastes. Of course, the expression of a range of emotions in popular music is complex. The music itself may imply emotions and the artist's interpretation of lyrics can convey other than their surface meaning. A recent song by John Waite, for example, used the repeated line "I ain't missing you." Rather than a simple declaration of fact, the artist's intonation implied alternatively anger, hate, sadness and remorse. The analysis here suspends such considerations and deals only with emotional content of a song perceived by the listener-respondent.

Respondents were presented the list of emotions and asked to iden- 18
tify those (if any) which they thought were expressed in their chosen
songs. The emotions were chosen from the most frequently cited terms
in the Dictionary of Emotional Meaning (Davitz, 1969:11). They were:

Fear	Anger	Hate	Relief
Hope	Confidence	Passion	Shame
Love	Delight	Pity	Grief
Surprise	Happiness	Pride	Excitement

Respondents were also encouraged to add the emotions not on the list.
The results are shown in Table V.

Very few respondents had any difficulty in their selection. None 19
claimed that songs do not express emotions. As Table V shows, women
selected slightly less emotions on average than males. Contrary to the
pernicious "non-emotional" stereotype of males, they do in fact exhibit
strong emotional use of music. Overall, there is a striking congruence of
the frequency of male and female selections of emotions.

As would be expected, love is high on the list. It is often claimed to 20
be the overwhelming theme of popular music. Happiness, however is a
more frequent choice for both males and females, and the males' top

Table V: Emotions Identified in Favorite Songs, by Gender

	Female (n = 119)		Males (n = 115)		Total (n = 234)
Emotion	No. of Mentions	Per Respondent	No. of Mentions	Per Respondent	No. of Mentions
Happiness	131	1.10	88	.77	219
Excitement	86	.72	121	1.05	207
Love	109	.92	71	.61	183
Hope	79	.66	55	.48	134
Confidence	59	.50	73	.63	132
Delight	49	.11	81	.70	130
Passion	66	.55	18	.42	114
Pride	19	.16	36	.31	55
Grief	33	.28	17	.15	50
Anger	7	.06	35	.30	42
Relief	13	.11	24	.21	37
Fear	12	.10	19	.17	31
Pity	11	.09	12	.10	23
Hate	1	.01	9	.08	10
Surprise	5	.01	5	.01	10
Shame	2	.02	4	.03	6
Total	701	5.89	733	6.36	1134

choice was excitement. While popular music exposes the listener to a broad range of emotional feelings, the top seven in Table V appear to be the most common. The same emotions were also the most chosen in Wells (1985).

Gender differences do not appear to be great. Women chose songs   21 that express hope, happiness, passion and grief slightly more than men. Men are a little more swayed by excitement, delight, anger and hate.

The tendency for women to be a little more positive than men was   22 indicated by comments explaining their choices in Wells (1985): "It's a love song; it talks about the importance and feeling of a relationship." "I like soft music usually, words about love or lost love," or "I want to know what love is." All is not optimism, however. "The songs are all about hope and love but there is also anger at times." Another writes "loneliness, despair—small doses of unhappiness are good for a person."

Men are perhaps less tranquil. A few are pessimistic, alienated and   23 angry: One male describing a song that expresses fear, anger and grief says that ". . . irregardless of what happens, what you do, who you are—is of no consequence, it's all bigger than us and we have no control over it." Another selects a song that expresses fear, trouble, anger and recounts ". . . how the U.S. is facing bad times with unemployment, murders, and misguided youth." No songs of this genre were chosen by women.

(4) Effects of Music.   Qualitative comments indicate that there   24 may be differences between male and female uses of music as Frith (1981) has suggested. In an earlier study (Wells, 1985) a minority of the men liked "head-banger," so called "heavy metal" music, which they claimed energizes them, sometimes within a sexual context: "The songs

Table VI: Music Effects. Responses to the question:
"What effect does listening to music have on you?"
Percentage of responses falling in category.

	Male	Female
Mellows out, relaxes	18	14
Excites or relaxes	13	21
Makes me happy	4	8
Memories	3	7
Uplifts	4	2

can get you up and make you wild with your girlfriends." Others commented that it gets them in the mood "to party": "It's a kick-ass song when you're stoned." Women were more likely to comment that their favorite music relaxes them: "It makes me feel as if the world is just so beautiful and there are no troubles to worry about." another claimed her favorite choices were "good to put you in a relaxed state." Overall, then, men may use music to "wind up," women to "wind down."

Many of the comments on effects indicate the intensity that music 25 inspires. Only two people said music had no effect on them, and most express an emotional, personal impact that is probably far more important to them than, for example, watching a TV soap opera or reading a textbook. A female claims "music to me is the difference between merely existing and living." Males add "music has more effect on me than anything else," "sometimes I feel as if I'm addicted to music," and "music is the essence of life, as important as food. It helps free my mind." A male musician attests "It's the ultimate thing in my life" and another male claims "I often lose myself in the music. I have been known to listen for as much as 6 hours at a time, never leaving my room."

Both males and females commonly associate songs with current or 26 past loves. Respondents in the Midwest (Wells, 1985) claim "Me and my girlfriend's song" (male); and (female) "I like the . . . songs because they remind me of my boyfriend and our love." Songs can also evoke other memories, sometimes tragic ones: "It has sentimental value because it was a favorite song of a good friend who died in a car accident" (female respondent). Similar comments were made in this study. A male says "music is like a time machine and when I want to return to certain past experiences I listen to the music that was present at that time." A female adds "It makes me feel love and brings back memories of the past that I cherish." The results, however, are not always positive. A male notes, "when I hear certain songs, it makes me think about girls I used to go out with and gets me a little depressed." Music, then, appears to be a major link of biography and nostalgia.

(5) Emotional Management.   The respondents were asked if they 27 ever use music to change their mood. Their answers often showed an unanticipated passion. A female replies "Yes, most definitely. All I need to do is to put on the radio and after a long day of being cranky and irritable it completely changes my mood." Another says "Yes! Whenever I'm angry or upset I use music to calm me, sometimes I use it to pep me up." A third is even more emphatic: "Yes!! I find that music is a large contributor to my emotional standing." A similarly enthusiastic male adds "Yes!! If I am bored or down I listen to my favorite music and it usually picks me up."

Table VII: Emotional Management, by Gender. Responses to the question: "Do you ever use music to change your mood?"

	Percent of Females (n = 118)	Percent of Males (n = 107)
Yes	85	71
Lift spirits	(44)	(30)
Pick up and calm down	(16)	(13)
Mellow out, relax	(10)	(10)
Get pumped up	(1)	(11)
Multiple uses	(7)	(3)
Enhance mood	7	10
Both (change and enhance)	3	3
No	6	13

Table VII shows the grouping of responses to the open ended ques- 28
tion on mood management. A high percentage of both females and
males claim to use music in this way. A minority of each gender say that
they use music to enhance an existing mood. One replies "Yes. To accent
the mood, like getting ready for a party." Another says "I usually use it
to enhance a mood—Dance music when I'm happy, the Carpenters
when I'm suicidal." A higher proportion of men than women replied
that they do not use music in this way.

Many of the "yes" responses fell into the broad categories shown in 29
the table. The most common for both genders was combating depression or being upset. Music, they claimed, could lift their spirits. Thus a
male says "If I am depressed I will play some of my favorite music to
cheer me up." Others claim that music helps them calm down, to "mellow out," or relax. For example a female says "If I'm ever mad at someone I use music to relax, calm down." A few respondents claimed both
uses, to pick themselves up or calm themselves: "When I'm depressed,
angry or bored, music can either calm me down or cheer me up" (female). "I can listen to an AC/DC album and get really rowdy yet if I listen to a soft Elton John song I turn melancholy" (male). A few respondents, more females than males, report multiple changes in moods.

The most noticeable gender difference was in reporting that music 30
could enervate the listener. Males said they use music to "pump themselves up" for parties or sports competition. One says that ". . . before
every [hockey] game I listen to some Rock psych songs to get myself
pumped up." Others claim "music . . . psyches me up when I play
sports," and "before I go to parties I listen to some Elvis Costello to get
me pumped up." Parties are perhaps the equivalent to sports events for
males, and both demand vigorous physical performance.

All "yes" responses could not be subsumed in the sub-categories 31
listed in Table VII. Individual replies point to the diversity of mood management uses. For one male music counters alcohol abuse: "If I'm hung
over, I listen to mellow Zeppelin or Hendrix blues to get me going
again." Another reports "It makes me feel as though I'm not experiencing something alone—I know someone else went through it before." A
female adds "listening to music is a very inner and personal thing to me.
It makes me more confident and more caring about myself and others."

Conclusions

While the subjects in the study were not a representative sample of 32
either college students or young American adults, the similarities between the East Coast and New England groups may indicate that the
findings may at least be suggestive for these populations. Music, clearly,
is important in the lives of many young adults. The most popular music genres are pop and rock, but there is a broad diversity of favorite
choices within them. Favorite music is not predominantly current hits,
but chosen from a two decades or more catalogue of music. Dance is one
popular use of music, but subjects discriminate between dancability and
deeper musical values.

Gender differences in the use of music are present, but as Melton 33
and Galician (1987) found, often less significant than expected. Women
dance more than men, prefer softer music, and derive somewhat different gratifications. But music also represents something that is shared
and has meaning across genders. Males and females not only dance and
listen to music together, they may also judge one another on the basis
of musical preference.

Music has deep emotional meaning, both in its sound and lyrics. It 34
can also have meaning by its association with personal experiences.
Both genders report that they use music to change their moods and
manipulate emotions. It is not just noise or entertainment, but a self-
administered psychotherapy that works.

Suggestions for Further Reading

Chaffee, Steven 1985 "Popular music and communication research: an
    editorial epilogue" *Communication Research,* 12:413–424.
Christenson, Peter G. and Lindlof, Thomas R. 1983 "The Role of Audio
    Media in the Lives of Children," *Popular Music and Society,* ix:3, pp.
    25–40.
Curtis, Jim 1987 Rock Eras: Interpretations of Music and Society, 1954–
    1984. Bowling Green, Ohio: Bowling Green State University Press.

Davitz, Joel R. 1969 *The Language of Emotion.* New York: Academic Press.

Frith, Simon. 1981 *Sound Effects: Youth, Leisure and the Politics of Rock 'n' Roll.* New York: Pantheon.

Gantz, Walter; Gattenberg, Howard M.; Pearson, Martin I., & Schiller, Seth O. 1978 "Gratifications and Expectations Associated with Pop Music Among Adolescents," *Popular Music and Society,* 6:81–89.

Hochschild, Arlie Russell. 1981 "Attending to Codifying and Managing Feelings: Sex Differences in Love." In Laurel Walum-Richardson & Verta Taylor (eds.) *Sex and Gender.* New York: Heath. 1983 *The Managed Heart.* Berkeley and Los Angeles University of California Press.

Lewis, George I. 1983 "The meaning's in the music and the music's in me: popular music as symbolic communication," *Theory, Culture and Society* I (3):133–141.

_____ 1981 "Towards a Uses and Gratification Approach: An Examination of Commitment and Involvement in Popular Music." *Popular Music and Society,* 8 (1):10–18.

Lull, James (editor). 1987 *Popular Music and Communication,* Beverly Hills: Sage.

Melton, Gary W. and Mary-Lou Galician. 1987 "A Sociological Approach to the Pop Music Phenomenon: Radio and Music Video Utilization for Expectation, Motivation and Satisfaction," *Popular Music and Society,* Vol. 11, No. 3 (Fall), pp. 35–46.

Stipp, Horst. 1985 "Children's Knowledge Of and Taste in Popular Music," *Popular Music and Society,* 10:2, pp. 1–17.

Weinstein, Deena. 1983 "Rock: Youth and Its Music," *Popular Music and Society,* ix:3, pp. 2–16.

Wells, Alan. 1985 "Gender, Emotions and Popular Music: Paper presented at the Midwest Sociological Society Annual Meeting, St. Louis.

·················

Examining the Text

1. What does Wells mean by the term "uses and gratifications" as it applies to the study of popular music? What are your own "uses and gratifications" in regard to popular music? In what other fields of study might such a focus be useful?

2. The author contends, "Nor can music be seen as a purely youth phenomenon, since respondents are now selecting music from their parents' generation" (paragraph 10). What point is he making about the musical tastes of the current generation? In your experience, are his observations apt?

3. As a class, complete Wells's survey, totaling up responses and breaking them down by gender. Do your class results support Wells's? How do you account for similarities or differences?

For Group Discussion

In assessing his sample research population, Wells found that "approximately 32 percent were 18 years or less; 30% were 19 or 20; 22% were 21 or 22; and 7% were 23 years or older. There were 115 males and 119 females, of whom 19 identified themselves as minorities (Black 16, Hispanic 3, all in East coast group)" (7). Consider your class as a sample research population. How might the ethnic/gender makeup of your class make your results different from Wells's?

Writing Suggestion

Wells conducted this study in 1987. Write an essay in which you examine the changes that have taken place in popular music since then. How would you suggest the results of Wells's study would be modified by current trends in music? Be as specific as you can considering contemporary movements in popular music.

Popular Music and Individual Differences

Christine Hall Hansen and Ronald D. Hansen

If you've ever wondered why certain fanatic pop-music devotees, such as heavy metal fans, act as they do, then this psychological study by Christine Hall Hansen and Ronald D. Hansen might give you some answers.

Hall and Hansen, psychology professors at Oakland University, conducted a consensus survey of undergraduates between the ages of 18 and 25, in order to establish connections between rock music preferences and behavior patterns. The two researchers argue that the dominant personality characteristics of heavy metal fans (that is, hypersexuality, satanism, and sexism) and of punk rock fans (disregard for authority) both lead these fans to prefer the music they do and are strengthened by exposure to that music. Their survey focuses particularly on the role of the music media in the development of these "negative" personality characteristics. Finally, the Hansens claim that "music preferences are meaningful markers of social attitudes and personality characteristics." Thus, the CD you choose to listen to might indicate something significant about your personality and your view of the world.

As you read, notice also that this essay is different in tone and style than others in this chapter. Because it is a psychological research essay, it is more concerned with scientific method, research results, data, evidence, and numer-

ical conclusions than most other kinds of writing. Scientific essays have a style all their own; you may need to adopt this style and format for certain research essays during your college career.

••••••••••••••••••••

The study examined the relationship of popular music preferences to individual differences in social judgments and to personality characteristics. Individuals who expressed liking for heavy metal music were higher in machiavellianism and machismo and lower in need for cognition than nonfans. Heavy metal fans also made higher estimates than nonfans of consensus among young people for sexual, drug-related, occult, and antisocial behaviors and attitudes. Punk rock fans were less accepting of authority than those who disliked this music. Punk fans also estimated higher frequencies than nonfans of antiauthority behaviors such as owning weapons, committing a crime, shoplifting, and going to jail. The results are discussed using interactive and social-cognitive models for the acquisition of stable attitudes and personality characteristics.

By virtue of their growing presence in the lives of young people,   1
electronic media play an increasingly important role in socialization, which is the acquisition, maintenance, and modification of the social beliefs, attitudes, and values that form the core of an individual's understanding of social reality. Past research indicates that adolescents are likely to find an important niche in the vast electronic environment of popular music. The decline in general television viewing that occurs in adolescence is accompanied by an increase in the rate of exposure to popular music in all its electronic forms: radio, recorded music, and, more recently, MTV and music videos (cf. Avery, 1979; Larson & Kubey, 1983). It is not surprising, then, that previous researchers have discovered that popular music plays a major rule in adolescent socialization (Gantz, Gartenberg, Pearson, & Schiller, 1978; Lull, 1985; Sun & Lull, 1986). Apparently, adolescents realize this as well; one of the most important reasons cited by adolescents for seeking exposure to popular music is to learn about their social world (Sun & Lull, 1986).

The importance of popular music in the lives of young people sug-   2
gests that their music preferences are related to social perceptions and personality. This study explored these relationships for two commonly recognized subcategories of music popular with young audiences: punk rock and heavy metal.

Common elements are present in most popular music (i.e., the ex-   3
pression of nontraditional values [Lull, 1985]), but there are distinct

differences between subcategories. Punk rock and heavy metal, for example, may seem indistinguishable to the nonfan, but are actually characterized by distinctive musical elements and themes. Heavy metal music typically is loud, fast, and discordant, and its performers are aggressive (often sexually aggressive), macho, antisocial, and occasionally violent (Bashe, 1985). The prevalent themes in heavy metal might be characterized as sexual, violent, antisocial, and callous toward women (Bashe, 1985). Further, heavy metal music has been strongly criticized for its sexual, violent, occult, drug-related, and antisocial lyrics (Bashe, 1985; Gore, 1987).

In contrast, punk rock has other salient characteristics. Punk rock   4
originated out of dissatisfaction with mainstream rock 'n' roll, which "carried no meaningful [social] message" (Henry, 1984, p. 31), and the prevalent themes in punk are characterized by antiestablishment messages, alienation from society, rebelliousness against authority, and anomie (Bodinger-deUriarte, 1985; Gold, 1987; Henry, 1984). The music itself is "performed at a jarring decibel level [with] an incredibly fast, repetitive rhythm rather than a melody . . ." (Henry, 1984, p. 31), which further distinguishes punk rock from heavy metal.

Are individuals' popular music preferences associated with social   5
perceptions and behaviors, or perhaps a social perspective that is consistent with the themes prevalent in the music of their choice? There is limited empirical evidence to support this assumption, at least for heavy metal music. Yee, Britton, and Thompson (1988) found that positive attitudes toward premarital sex, drug and alcohol use, and satanism were significantly associated with a liking for heavy metal music. Trostle (1986) found a significant link between liking for heavy metal and increased belief in witchcraft and the occult. There has been little empirical research investigating the relationship between preference for punk rock and attitudes, social perceptions, or personality variables. Gold (1987), however, found evidence suggestive of differences between delinquent punk rock fans and nonfans in family dynamics believed to be related to the development of personality; many more fans than nonfans reported feeling misunderstood by their parents and fans were more likely to feel that their families were not close while they were growing up.

Three theoretical perspectives explain how a liking for each of these   6
types of music may be related to differences in social perceptions and personality characteristics: a) media preferences may be determined largely by extant personality differences; b) frequent exposure to media portrayals alters social perceptions and personality to conform to the portrayals; and c) causation may be interactive between media exposure and social perceptions and personality.

If media preferences are guided largely by existing personality dif-   7
ferences, then young people might gravitate toward heavy metal music
because some aspect of its content is congruent with their perceptions
of social reality. Certainly there is ample research supporting the contention that people seek exposure to stimuli that are consistent with
their attitudes and are attracted to portrayals and interpretations of
events that confirm their view of social reality. This, of course, provides
a theoretical underpinning for the often articulated opinion that media
reflect the desires of their consumers, giving people what they want.

An approach grounded in contemporary theories of social cognition   8
specifies an opposite causal direction—one in which media shape consumers. According to this perspective, the more often one is exposed to
a category of social information (e.g., sexism, antisocial behavior, violence), the more established the category becomes in long-term memory
and the more likely it is to be used to interpret social reality. For example, frequent exposure to heavy metal music that contains antisocial
content renders antisocial thoughts and events highly accessible in memory; through frequent use of these information categories, the attitudes
and personality of the heavy metal fan might become more antisocial.
Additionally, this pattern of exposure and cognition will influence the
individual's perceptions of the prevalence of antisocial behavior in the
population at large (Bargh, 1984; Tversky & Kahneman, 1982), often
leading to overestimates of its prevalence. In this way, the fan's social
perceptions and personality conforms with the music's content.

A third perspective asserts an interactive process of socialization   9
more akin to cultivation theory (Gerbner et al., 1986) within which the
pervasive media environment is seen to be neither a mindless reflection
of social reality nor ignorant of it; instead, its content both reflects and
shapes social reality. To thrive, media must be sensitive to and satisfy
the wishes, needs, and values of consumers. But consumers, in turn,
conform to the social reality depicted in media content. The interactive
socialization process is marked by gradual shifts in social values toward
those supported in media content. These influences will be enhanced to
the extent that a particular social reality extant in media content dominates the individual's cultural commerce. For example, young people
may gravitate toward heavy metal music because they possess attributes that attract them to some aspect of the content, and these attributes are strengthened through frequent exposure to heavy metal.

This investigation focuses on personality dimensions related to sex-   10
ism, acceptance of antisocial behavior, and rejection of authority. Given
the themes that dominate heavy metal music, an interactive perspective
would anticipate heavy metal fans to be both more antisocial and more
sexist. The dominant themes of punk music yield the prediction that

punk rock fans would not be as accepting of the traditional values of authority.

A model of interactive causation predicts that these effects also   11
would be evident in individuals' perceptions of social reality. Given the
content of heavy metal music, we anticipate that heavy metal fans' perceptions of social reality would incorporate a higher incidence of sexual, violent, occult, drug-related, and antisocial behaviors than the perceptions of nonfans. We anticipate punk rock fans, relative to nonfans,
to envision a social world with high levels of behavior conducted in rejection of traditional authority.

Method

In return for course credit in introductory psychology classes, 102   12
undergraduates completed a five-page questionnaire booklet in small
mixed-sex groups. Data from 6 respondents over age 25 were excluded,
resulting in usable data from 96 respondents (30 males, 66 females) between 18 and 25 years old. The study was described as a survey of "contemporary attitudes and opinions."

Measures

Perceptions of Social Reality.   Respondents estimated the per-   13
centage of young males and females between 15 and 21 years old who
would hold the following attitudes or engage in the following behaviors: (a) believe in satanism, (b) use cocaine or crack, (c) have never had
sex, (d) have ever vandalized something, (e) rarely or never drink alcohol, (f) have ever shoplifted, (g) take their parents' car without permission, (h) own a weapon, (i) smoke marijuana regularly, (j) enjoy going
to school, (k) have ever gotten a traffic ticket, (l) ever go to jail or prison,
(m) have ever been involved in date rape, and (n) have committed a
crime but were not caught. Eleven neutral filler items also were included
to disguise the intent of the measures.

Personality Scales.   Items measuring machismo (Mosher & Sirkin,   14
1984), machiavellianism (Christie, 1968), and acceptance of authority
(Bales & Couch, 1969) were combined into a measure of personal opinions.

Music References and Reported Self-Exposure.   Respondents in-   15
dicated their preferences (like or dislike) for three types of popular music (with prompts): (a) pop rock (e.g., INXS, Steve Winwood), (b) punk

rock (i.e., Suicidal Tendencies, Danzig), and (c) heavy metal (e.g., Kiss, Anthrax). Respondents also indicated the amount of time spent each week listening to each kind of music on (a) records, tapes, or CDs, (b) radio, and television.

Rock Music Preferences and Personality Characteristics

Heavy Metal.   Preference for heavy metal was significantly related   16
to all but one personality measure. Both hypersexuality and respect for women were strongly associated with heavy metal preference. Fans generated higher hypersexuality scores (M = 3.52) and lower respect for women scores (M = 4.54) than nonfans (M = 1.67, 5.57). Heavy metal fans (M = 88.30) were also more machiavellian than nonfans (M = 76.33).

Punk Rock.   Punk rock preference was significantly related to only   17
one personality measure: acceptance of authority. Punk fans (M = 7.61) were much less accepting of authority than nonfans (M = 17.43).

Rock Music Preferences and Perceptions of Social Reality

Estimates made about the behavior and attitudes of the female pop-   18
ulation differed from those made for the male population on 12 of 14 estimates (see Table 1). These effects may be summarized rather simply. There was a consensus that young men in the population are more likely to hold antisocial attitudes and to engage in antisocial behavior than are young women.

Women in the sample tended to have a more exaggerated view of   19
gender differences in society. With the exception of two measures ("rarely or never drink alcohol," "enjoy going to school"), women in the sample saw the male population as more different from the female population than did men. Respondent gender did not interact with either heavy metal or punk preference on any measure, so that data were collapsed across respondent gender.

Heavy Metal.   Heavy metal preferences were significantly associ-   20
ated with responses on six frequency items. Individuals who liked heavy metal generated higher estimates of consensus for the use of both cocaine and marijuana than did nonfans. Heavy metal fans' estimates of consensus for virginity among young people were also lower. At the same time, their estimates of the number of young people who had been involved in date rape were significantly lower than those of subjects who did not like heavy metal.

Table 1: Differences in the Frequency Estimates by Gender, Heavy Metal Fanship, and Punk Rock Fanship

| Measure | Mean Estimates For Population of | | | Mean Estimates by | | | | | |
| | | | | Heavy Metal | | | Punk | | |
	F (1,82)	Men	Women	F (1,82)	Fans (n = 35)	Nonfans (n = 61)	F (1,82)	Fans (n = 28)	Nonfans (n = 68)
Satanism	29.85	20.78	19.69	57.22	39.02	12.19	5.22	17.00	20.86
Cocaine	31.90	38.89	31.88	23.80	51.89	28.92	ns	35.11	35.49
No sex	37.73	30.98	41.33	14.02	25.83	40.20	ns	34.34	39.90
Vandalized	36.97	55.67	39.89	ns	56.44	44.38	11.05	63.71	41.21
No alcohol	35.85	17.80	25.02	ns	22.06	21.16	ns	23.32	20.63
Shoplifted	ns	44.19	46.31	ns	50.30	43.28	35.71	72.36	34.09
Joyride	89.75	46.96	31.59	7.51	52.19	34.22	ns	40.29	38.86
Weapon	86.18	43.19	19.56	ns	31.07	31.49	40.03	51.93	22.91
Marijuana	35.93	44.89	34.19	16.06	55.20	33.41	ns	40.75	39.04
Enjoy school	30.87	39.57	48.84	ns	38.74	46.35	ns	43.07	44.68
Traffic ticket	23.33	69.32	64.50	ns	65.57	64.62	27.41	87.46	55.59
Jail	84.20	34.27	19.91	ns	26.06	27.49	36.47	45.80	19.38
Date rape	ns	28.36	30.32	27.01	14.13	35.30	ns	30.70	28.79
Crime	48.02	55.31	44.46	ns	51.11	49.41	42.69	80.11	37.44

Punk Rock.   Liking for punk rock was significantly related to a   21
number of frequency estimates. Punk fans estimated less consensus for
satanic beliefs than nonfans. However, for vandalism, owning weapons,
going to jail, and committing a crime, individuals who liked punk made
significantly higher estimates of consensus than did individuals who
did not like punk. Punk fans made higher estimates than nonfans for the
prevalence of shoplifting, but the tendency was much stronger among
those who disliked heavy metal than among those who liked heavy
metal. A similar pattern emerged in estimates for getting a traffic ticket.
Punk fans made higher estimates than nonfans for getting a ticket, but
the difference was more substantial among those who disliked heavy
metal than among those who liked heavy metal. On these two estimates,
discrete liking for punk—that is, liking punk but not heavy metal—was
the market of particularly extreme estimates of antisocial behavior.

Media Exposure Time, Personality Attributes, and Perceptions of Social Reality

Thus far, the results have indicated that rock music preferences are   22
associated with both personality attributes and systematic differences in
perception of social reality. We conducted one final set of analyses to test
the association between self-exposure to rock music and the personality attributes and social perceptions. Time spent in contact with both
heavy metal and punk rock in the various media forms were correlated
(partialled for gender) with each personality measure and social judgment. The results are shown in Table 2.

Heavy Metal.   An inspection of the partial correlations of media   23
exposure to heavy metal music with the personality measures and social judgments reveals a pattern easily predicted from the association of
these variables with heavy metal preferences. Notably, greater media
self-exposure to heavy metal music was associated with machiavellianism and sexist thinking. A pattern of associations similar to those found
between music preference and social perceptions also was obtained here
between media exposure and social perceptions. Notably, increased exposure to heavy metal music was related to perceptions of more drug
use, less date rape, a lower incidence of virginity, and a higher incidence
of satanic beliefs. The pattern of associations was quite similar for three
of the four exposure measures: CDs, tapes, and records; radio; and total
time. On the other hand, the association between time spent watching
heavy metal on television was not significantly correlated with several
of the criterion measures, including most of the personality measures.
The most likely explanation for this failure lies in the fact that television

Table 2: Partial Correlations of Media Exposure to Heavy Metal and Punk Rock Music with Personality Dimensions and Social Perceptions

Measure	Minutes of Heavy Metal Exposure				Minutes of Punk Rock Exposure			
	CTR[a]	Radio	Television	Total	CTR	Radio	Television	Total
Machiavellianism	.29	.28	.16	.31	-.02	-.01	-.03	-.02
Acceptance of authority	-.01	-.01	-.02	-.02	-.40	-.29	-.23	-.38
Hypersexuality	.37	.39	.07	.40	-.15	-.08	-.05	-.12
Respect for women	-.32	-.16	-.19	-.26	.02	.07	.15	.07
Satanism	.39	.40	.28	.48	-.10	-.11	-.11	-.12
Cocaine	.27	.31	.13	.30	-.05	-.07	-.10	-.07
Never had sex	-.29	-.30	-.16	-.32	.18	-.08	-.06	-.07
Vandalized	.01	.19	.13	.13	.04	.03	-.06	.02
Never drink alcohol	-.14	-.04	-.05	-.09	.04	-.07	-.07	-.02
Shoplifted	.02	.16	.13	.08	.43	.39	.24	.44
Take parents' car	.16	.20	.09	.18	.09	.09	.03	.09
Weapon	.11	.05	-.02	.05	.40	.23	.15	.33
Marijuana	.31	.29	.01	.29	.01	.01	-.03	.01
Enjoy school	-.07	-.06	-.16	-.11	-.04	-.12	-.02	-.08
Traffic ticket	-.04	-.04	.02	-.05	.35	.34	.24	.37
Jail or prison	-.10	-.08	-.10	-.13	.48	.43	.36	.49
Date rape	-.16	-.22	-.23	-.24	.05	.05	.03	.06
Crime	.03	.03	.02	.02	.37	.33	.23	.37

Note. The number of minutes per week subjects listened/viewed tapes, records, and compact disks, radio, and television. Total represents the sum of their times within each music category.

322

exposure to heavy metal music is reported to be low by all subjects, regardless of their rock music preferences.

Punk Rock. An examination of the associations of exposure to   24
punk rock with the personality measures and social judgments also indicated the pattern expected from the relationships previously found between liking and the criterion measures. Time spent with punk rock was significantly associated with a rejection of authority and the perception of higher rates of antisocial behaviors directed against traditional values of authority. Specifically, increased exposure to punk rock was associated with perceptions that more people shoplift, own weapons, receive traffic tickets, go to jail or prison, and commit crimes. The association of punk rock exposure with these variables was fairly uniform across the individual forms of media—listening to CDs, tapes, and records, listening to the radio, watching television, and total media consumption.

Consumers Shape Media, Media Shape Consumers

The current investigation uncovered a number of intriguing links   25
between rock music preferences and individual differences in both personality attributes and social perceptions. Because these effects represent, in essence, an association between one set of selected variables and another, the causal direction cannot be determined. Among the three theoretical models, interactive socialization and social cognition theories seem to best explain these results.

Regardless of theoretical explanation, the findings to emerge from   26
this investigation are provocative. Individuals who expressed a liking for punk rock appeared characteristically less accepting of authority both in personality and social judgments than nonfans, while heavy metal fans were more machiavellian and sexist than nonfans. These findings indicate that music preferences are meaningful markers of social attitudes and personality characteristics, strongly implying that for punk and heavy metal fans, some categories of potentially negative social information are highly, if not chronically, accessible. More disturbing, there is a theoretical expectation that punk and heavy metal fans will use these highly accessible social information categories when they make social judgments and decide on their own behaviors.

What, then, do we make of popularity trends in the electronic mu-   27
sic environment? Heavy metal music is increasing in popularity, and the boundary between pop and heavy metal music is becoming less distinct. MTV programming is a good reflection of this trend across all electronic music media. Heavy metal groups such as Motley Crue and Guns 'n

Roses are frequently at the top of MTV's popular music charts. Contrary to their earlier programming policy (Denisoff, 1988), MTV now includes heavy metal in their daytime as well as late-nite programming. Does this expansion of the heavy metal niche in the electronic music environment simply reflect the changing taste of young consumers? Or, is the increased prevalence of heavy metal music altering the cognitive environment of its consumers, creating a larger marketplace for heavy metal? If so, will we see an increase in the incidence of sexism, machiavellianism, and acceptance of satanism and drug use? Are youngsters with a low need for cognition being created?

Social cognitive theories imply that the availability of a niche in the electronic environment, such as heavy metal, parallels the accessibility for young consumers of a compatible perspective on social reality. The more pervasive the niche—like heavy metal—or the more exclusively the consumer inhabits that niche, the greater will be the parallel between the social information provided by music content and the consumer's view of social reality. In light of this last point, the allure of popular music for adolescents and young adults—both in terms of its increasing dominance of their commerce with the electronic environment (Larson & Kubey, 1983) and their apparent uses of it as a benchmark for social reality (Sun & Lull, 1986; Trostle, 1986)—gives added importance to findings that music preferences are markers of stable individual differences. 28

References

Avery, R. (1979). Adolescents' use of the mass media. *American Behavioral Scientist, 23,* 53–70.

Bales, R., & Couch, A. (1969). Value profile. *Sociological Inquiry, 39,* 3–17.

Bargh, J. A. (1984). Automatic and conscious processing of social information. In R. S. Wyer Jr. & T. K. Srull (Eds.), *Handbook of social cognition* (Vol. 3, pp. 1–43). Hillsdale, NJ: Erlbaum.

Bargh, J. A., Bond, R. N., Lombardi, W. J., & Tota, M. E. (1986). The additive nature of chronic and temporary sources of construct accessibility. *Journey of Personality and Social Psychology, 50,* 869–878.

Bashe, P. (1985). *Heavy metal thunder.* Garden City, NY: Doubleday.

Bodinger-deUriate, C. (1985). Opposition to hegemony in the music of Devo: A simple matter of remembering. *Journal of Popular Culture, 18*(2), 57–71.

Cacioppo, J. T., & Petty, R. E. (1982). The need for cognition. *Journal of Personality and Social Psychology, 42,* 116–131.

Cacioppo, J. T., Petty, R. E., & Kao, C. F. (1984). The efficient assessment of need for cognition. *Journal of Personality Assessment, 48,* 306–307.

Christie, R. (1968). Machiavellianism. Unpublished manuscript, Columbia University, New York.

Denisoff, R. S. (1988). *Inside MTV.* New Brunswick, NJ: Transaction Books.

Endres, K. L. (1984). Sex role standards in popular music. *Journal of Popular Culture, 17*(1), 9–18.

Gantz, W., Gartenberg, H. M., Pearson, M. L., & Schiller, S. O. (1978). Gratifications and expectations associated with pop music among adolescents. *Popular Music in Society, 6,* 81–89.

Gerbner, G., Gross, L., Morgan, M., & Signorielli, N. (1986). Living with television: The dynamics of the cultivation process. In J. Bryant & D. Zillmann (Eds.), *Perspectives on media effects* (pp. 17–40). Hillsdale, NJ: Erlbaum.

Gold, B. D. (1987). Self-image of punk rock and nonpunk rock juvenile delinquents. *Adolescence, 22,* 535–543.

Gore, T. (1987). *Raising PG kids in an X-rated society.* Nashville, TN: Abingdon Press.

Hansen, C. H. (1989). Priming sex-role stereotypic event schemas with rock music videos: Effects on impression favorability, trait inferences, and recall of a subsequent male-female interaction. *Basic and Applied Social Psychology, 10,* 371–391.

Hansen, R. D. (1980). Commonsense attribution. *Journal of Personality and Social Psychology, 39,* 996–1009.

Hansen, R. D. (1986). Cognitive economy and commonsense attribution processing. In J. H. Harvey & G. Weary (Eds.), *Attribution: Basic issues and applications* (pp. 65–85). Orlando, FL: Academic Press.

Hansen, C. H., & Hansen, R. D. (1988). Priming stereotypic appraisal of social interactions: How rock music videos can change what's seen when boy meets girl. *Sex Roles, 19,* 287–316.

Hansen, C. H., & Hansen, R. D. (in press). Schematic information processing of heavy metal lyrics. *Communication Research.*

Henry, T. (1984). Punk and avant-garde art. *Journal of Popular Culture, 17,* 30–36.

Hastie, R. (1981). Schematic principles in human memory. In E. T. Higgins, C. P. Herman, & M. P. Zanna (Eds.), *Social cognition: The Ontario symposium* (Vol. 1, pp. 39–88). Hillsdale, NJ: Erlbaum.

Higgins, E. T., & King, G. (1981). Accessibility of social constructs: Information processing consequences of individual and contextual variability. In N. Cantor & J. F. Kihlstrom (Eds.), *Personality, cognition, and social interaction* (pp. 69–121). Hillsdale, NJ: Erlbaum.

Larson, R., & Kubey, R. (1983). Television and music: Contrasting media in adolescent life. *Youth and Society, 15,* 13–31.

Lull, J. (1985). On the communicative properties of music. *Communica-tion Research, 12,* 363–372.

Mosher, D. L., & Sirkin, M. (1984). Measuring a macho personality con-stellation. *Journal of Research in Personality, 18,* 150–163.

Ross, M. (1981). Seek, and ye shall find: Testing hypotheses about other people. In E. T. Higgins, C. P. Herman & M. P. Zanna (Eds.), *Social cognition: The Ontario symposium* (Vol. 1, PP. 277–303). Hillsdale, NJ: Erlbaum.

Snyder, M. (1981). Self-centered biases in attributions of responsibility: Antecedents and consequences. In E. T. Higgins, C. P. Herman, & M. P. Zanna (Eds.), *Social cognition: The Ontario symposium* (Vol. 1, pp. 305–321). Hillsdale, NJ: Erlbaum.

Sun, S., & Lull, J. (1986). The adolescent audience for music videos and why they watch. *Journal of Communication, 36*(1), 115–125.

Trostle, L. C. (1986). Nihilistic adolescents, heavy metal rock music, and paranormal beliefs. *Psychological Reports, 59,* 610.

Tversky, A., & Kahneman, D. (1982). Availability: A heuristic for judg-ing frequency and probability. In D. Kahneman, P. Slovic, & A. Tver-sky (Eds.), *Judgment under uncertainty: Heuristics and biases* (pp. 163–178). New York: Cambridge University Press.

Yee, S., Britton, L., & Thompson, W. (1988, April). *The effects of rock mu-sic on adolescents' attitudes and behavior.* Paper presented at the West-ern Psychological Association Convention, Burlingame, CA.

•••••••••••••••••

Examining the Text

1. According to this article, what are the distinct differences between the subcategories of punk rock and heavy metal music, in terms of both musical elements and prevalent themes? Can you add anything to these observations?

2. The authors discuss interactive "cultivation theory" as one possible explanation of musical preference in young people (paragraph 9). How does the article define this theory of socialization, and how does it ex-plain the relationship of heavy metal or punk fans to their prefered mu-sic? Do you think cultivation theory explains your own musical prefer-ences?

3. Using a "common sense" rather than a scientific approach, evaluate the Hansens' methods and their results. Do you tend to accept their work, or can you think of any objections or questions?

For Group Discussion

In group discussion, critique the authors' research methods, based upon your own knowledge of youth culture and popular music. As an in-class project, design your own study, perhaps to reflect more accurately (or at least differently) the interaction between personality and musical taste.

Writing Suggestion

Media preferences "may be related to differences in social perceptions and personality characteristics," (6) according to the authors of this essay. Explain this statement, specifically as it relates to young people's musical choices. Discuss the validity of this statement, drawing upon your own listening tastes and those of your friends.

Punks in LA: It's Kiss or Kill

Jon Lewis

In the mid 1970s, an unprecedented and provocative subculture emerged on the American scene: the punk movement. At that time, bewildered mainstream pop music critics and social observers derided punk music as atonal, arrhythmic noise, and its adherents as mindlessly disruptive—which, in truth, they often were. But that was the point (if so anti-intellectual a movement can be said to have had a point).

Based on his studies of punks in Los Angeles, Jon Lewis, a professor of film and video at Oregon State University, gives us an historical retrospective and sociological analysis of the entire movement, as well as its relationship to rock 'n' roll and other youth subcultures. Marked by a continual threat of violence, riots, and antisocial behavior, the "self-effacing, self-mutilating, self-abusive" punk crowd was at home in clubs in L.A.'s worst neighborhoods. As a "celebration of resignation," the punk movement attracted and produced a subculture of disenfranchised youth drawn to self-destruction as a means of expressing their sense of alienation and desperation. Lewis argues that "disdain for public propriety" was the lifeblood of the punks, accounting for their embrace of drugs, alcohol, violent slamdancing, graffitti, and nipple-piercing—all emblematic of their tendencies toward excess, illegality, and crude obscenity.

Writing not as an outraged, moralizing citizen, but rather as an objective (even sympathetic) cultural theorist, Lewis argues that the punk movement was but one scene in the ongoing drama of pop culture. Following his interest in cultural and revolutionary disruption, Lewis recreates the spectacles of punk music, videos, movies, and art, giving us the chance to live those chaotic and *dangerous times vicariously. **As you read** about the brief existence of the move-ment—and its eventual assimilation into the mainstream of music and fashion culture, consider whether any youth subculture can be truly subversive.*

•••••••••••••••••••••

Punk surfaced in Los Angeles in the late seventies as a curious blend   1
of anarchy and anomie—as one last desperate attempt for white, urban, lower middle class youths to dramatically express their distaste for a so-ciety that had long since expressed its disinterest in them. What follows is a selective description of the movement; an analysis of its ideology and its symbiotic relationship to mainstream rock and roll and an at-tempt to contextualize punk as a unique moment in the history of Amer-ican youth culture.

The LA punk movement began around 1977 and ended in the first   2
few years of the 1980s. For the duration of its brief hold on the disen-franchised youth of urban LA, punk unapologetically paraded a variety of misanthropic and misogynist tendencies: Nazism, fascism, racism and self-hate. No youth movement before or since has hinged so tenu-ously on bizarre and frightening ceremonies of attraction and repulsion and public displays of absolute anti-social behaviour. No youth move-ment before or since has laid so bare the desperation residing at the heart of the now failed urban American dream.

Like the New York or London based punk movements, the LA vari-   3
ation gained definition as an urban performance art form. The chaos and penchant for public obscenity which were punk's stock in trade found a milieu in the Masque, Madame Wong's and the Hong Kong Cafe—punk clubs in the heart of LA's very worst neighborhoods. Imminent danger characterized every venture to a punk club and the media at-tention to the savagery and very real violence integral to every punk performance and experience made it virtually impossible for anyone to "be there" completely by mistake.

From the start punk's droll, black comic and only marginally ironic   4
celebration of urban squalor and senseless violence generated a kind of outsider mystique. Punk performance—here a very broad term in-deed—generally manifested itself in ritual terms; shared acts or activi-ties displaying a ceremonial and privileged significance. Punk attire and behaviour was opposed to convention; which was consistent with the movement's tendency towards celebrating its members' alienation from the mainstream of bourgeois city life. As a rejection of the late seven-ties/early eighties gearing up of the yuppie lifestyle, the LA punk movement paraded a glib and steadfast embrace of the frustrations in-herent to their outsider status, maintaining an essential insider sub-

culture; one which was simply too extreme to court the likes of the urban bourgeoisie as anything more than dumbfounded spectators.

As with so many urban sub-cultures, punk generated its own peculiar performance art scene, headed up by the redoubtable Sergio Premoli. In his most famous performance to date, Premoli, stationed in front of Gucci's status-packed Italian boutique on Beverly Hills' famed Rodeo Drive, hefted a 120-pound wooden American flag up on his back. "To carry something this heavy, it takes a lot of faith to do it," Premoli told spectators, "That's why Christ was so special." Viewing Premoli bearing his cross down the ritziest commercial LA street, the proprietor of ("the intelligent and tasteful mens' store") Madonna Man suggested that Premoli (clad topless, with loose fitting sweatpants over his bottom half) should have worn something more elegant, like a black raincoat by Benedetto (the Blessed One) of New York. Premoli, citing the true gravity of his task was hardly thinking of fashion, even on so auspicious an avenue. When asked how he felt once he secured the flag on his shoulders, Premoli replied, "Eeets a fucking heavy."[1]

Premoli's art is provocation and it is meant to be offensive. By mixing his metaphors to God and country, Premoli complicates matters with his choice of locale (commercial America; the one street on earth most completely associated with conspicuous consumption). That there is an element of social commentary here is not all that unusual for punk. And that the commentary is obscene (in the Henry Miller sense of the word: as not pornographic or titillating, but ugly and revelatory) and to a great extent confusing and confused, is quite consistent with the peculiar artistic oeuvre of the LA punk scene.

The punk predilection for obscenity is similarly exposed in the LA punk literature: godfathered by the now legendary Charles Bukowski, featured in the unique punk fanzines like *Wet, Slash, Contagion, No Mag* and *The Lowest Common Denominator* and publically exhibited on bathroom walls and decaying building edifices in the often misanthropic/ misogynist, existential or absurdist punk graffiti.

Bukowski, like his more famous counterpart William Burroughs in New York, has been credited as the movement's literary avatar, its truly gifted muse. But like Burroughs, whose reputation and income soared due to an identification with the movement, Bukowski's relationship to the punks themselves is peripheral at most. His readership is comprised primarily of those who viewed punk with fascination (but at arms' length). Bukowski's alcohol-soaked prose and anti-heroic, macho, bar-brawling heroes coincide and resonate with punk anti-social behaviour

---

[1] "Eets a Fuckin' Heavy: Christ Comes to Rodeo Drive," WET, May/June 1981, p. 55.

and lifestyle, but aside from his alleged influence on the punk band X, Bukowski and the punks literally live at opposite ends of town; he in Venice by the sea, the punks far east of La Brea in the heat and smog of downtown.

For those on the inside, graffiti was the "pure punk" form, as it is   9
public, obscene, often mis-spelled and ungrammatical, generally reductive and emblematic (rather than symbolic or allusive) and illegal. A familiar mix of crude drawing and aphoristic outrage, punk graffiti effaced already crumbling property, calling attention to (but never asking anyone to change) the dreadful landscape of decaying urban America.

The graffiti look and literary style is clearly evident in the unique   10
and irreverent punk fanzines. These fan magazines, staffed, funded and distributed from within the punk subculture, provided information on the punk bands and featured pseudo-gonzo New Journalism (apeing Hunter Thompson and Terry Southern) replete with anti-social and often paradoxical and paranoid nihilist rants (for example Richard Meltzer's bizarre punk treatise on communism, "Go for the hammer/go for the sickle/you'll be glad you did. . . . Hitler was just a fairy who dug blue-eyed South Bay surfer boys.")[2]

The fanzines all featured a graffiti layout style, literalizing the effect   11
of cutting and pasting. Unlike *Rolling Stone* and the other popular music magazines, the punk fanzines de-emphasized the stardom of the bands. While *Rolling Stone* et al institutionalized the glamour of the industry, the fanzines wallowed in the glamourlessness of punk.

The punk sense of humour exhibited in the fanzines was character-   12
istically irreverent. For example, when Ronald Reagan's Commission on the Eighties found that for the first time in US history more than one-half of the American population lived west of the Mississippi, *Wet* responded to the rising political influence of the conservative southwest with a black-comical mock advertisement for a solar powered electric chair, touting "Organic Executions for the Sunbelt." The ad credits the chair to New York designer James Hong and guarantees that the device "provides effectiveness even on a partly cloudy day." The chair, as advertised, is "slow rotisserie effective," with "capabilities for torture most of us haven't dreamed about since the days of the Protestant Reformation." And with a typical bit of (not really tongue in cheek) punk social theory, the ad concludes: "Just the thing to stamp out those food stamp cheating single mothers."[3]

---

[2] David E. James, "Poetry/Punk/Performance: Some Recent Writing in LA," the *Minnesota Review*, Fall 1984, p. 135.
[3] "Creative Methodologies," *Wet*, May/June 1981, p. 61.

Two films, both by UCLA film school graduates who were in LA in   13
the late seventies, articulate (for audiences outside LA) the essence of
the LA punks: Penelope Spheeris' *The Decline of Western Civilization* and
Alex Cox's cult-hit *Repo Man*, a film that juxtaposes the punk hallmark
anti-commercialism to the crude narratives and visual styles of truly
bad B-films.

The attraction of punk culture to graduate students, to upper mid-   14
dle class, white, well educated men and women (despite the fact that
they were often the target of punk tirades), was a curious phenomenon
in late seventies' LA. For those in search of a youth movement in post-
Vietnam America, punk positioned itself in diametric opposition to the
optimistic and idealistic flower children of the previous decade. In fact,
the punks often railed against the hippies. One punk (sporting a swa-
sticka medallion on his chest) wryly quips (in an interview with Penelope Spheeris in *The Decline of Western Civilization*): "Like I'm not going
to go out and kill some Jew. C'mon—Maybe a hippie." Such blank, emo-
tionless threats of violence abound in Spheeris' film. One punk argues
that fighting is the only thing that makes him feel good. Claude Bessy,
AKA Kickboy Face, *Slash* editor and lead singer of the punk band
Catholic Discipline puts it all in the peculiar punk perspective: "We're
not grooving on the same vibes anymore. We're grooving on different
vibes . . . ugly vibes."

Eugene, a skinhead who opens *The Decline of Western Civilization*   15
with a treatise on how punk has "no stars—no bullshit," expresses his
rationale for rebellion via vague references to buses and poseurs. For
him, as for so many other punks, the city is both subject and object, at
once sacred and profane, a kind of indecipherable, repugnant yet seductive fact of life.

The most obvious performative outlet for this familiar urban frus-   16
tration was the phenomenon of pogo. A dance, done to music executed
at 250 beats a minute (disco for example is performed at half that speed),
pogo (and its offspring, the even less structured slam dance) was pure
and simple the performance of violence. Whereas mainstream rock and
roll sugarcoats an essential misanthropy and misogyny as teenage romance and rebellion, the punks accepted the "teenage wasteland" for
what it is. Punk was the celebration of resignation. It was anomie as
artistic impulse. And in a cult of aggressive egalitarianism (everyone is
worthless/everyone is the same) everyone involved in the punk performance was part of the performance.

To Spheeris' credit (and coincident with her decision to document   17
rather than comment on the LA punk scene), the concert material in *The
Decline of Western Civilization* is almost exclusively shot from the point
of view of the audience. There the camera is obscured, jostled, harassed,

threatened, knocked over, kicked and cursed and abused by the maniacal pogo dancing punks. "Actually there is no difference between dancing and fighting," a bouncer muses as he grabs a security guard by the throat. Shaking his co-worker like a rag doll he adds, "This, for example, is dancing."

Alex Cox's cult-fiction film *Repo Man* purposefully attends to the   18
significance of the city to LA punk culture. The film's focus on the unglamorous East LA city-scape as opposed to the fun, sun and surf allure of Santa Monica, Malibu or Venice (where the majority of mainstream TV and cinema are shot) depicts the city as just one large bad neighborhood.

From the opening credit sequence to the closing scene hovering   19
above the night-lit city in a radioactive automobile, *Repo Man* leaps and lunges from one thing to the next, never effacing (in fact celebrating) the anti-aesthetics of the low budget B movie. Much of the film is comical and ridiculous, banking on postmodern pastiche, kitsch and camp. The film features aliens, a radioactive car and an obscure plot involving repo men battling g-men. The film's truth-teller, Miller, who waxes philosophical while burning garbage under the striking LA smog sunset, talks of the cosmic relevance of "plates of shrimp" and argues that (in of all places LA) "the more you drive the less intelligent you are." His revelations are characteristically off-center which explains why he has such authority in the film.

Repo Man rather blankly wades through hackneyed dialogue remi-   20
niscent of the strained seriousness of 50's B movie teenage melodramas, as evident in the following scene: Duke (dying from a gunshot wound suffered while robbing a 7-11): "I know a life of crime has led me to this sorry fate. And yet I blame society—Society made me what I am." Otto (the punk cum repo man hero of the film played by Emilio Estevez): "That's bullshit. You're a white suburban punk just like me." Duke: "But it still hurts," (and he dies).

The helter skelter pace of the film not only punctuates the searing   21
punk music score, but allows filmic material to simply appear and disappear without much coherence or apparent authorial organization, as if any pretense to order would betray the punk sensibility of the film. But despite its B-movie cliches and scatterbrained narrative, *Repo Man* successfully posits a realistic and depressing view of the city and its youth. When Kevin, Otto's straight friend, mindlessly stacks and prices cans of generic cling peaches in a small city supermarket he sings the 7-Up jingle ("Feeling' 7-Up/I'm feelin' 7-Up"). Later on in the film, Kevin peruses the want ads, "There's room to move as a fry cook," he says, "in two years I'll be assistant manager. It's key." That Otto rejects such acquiescence helps to define his separation and heroism.

There is a progressive argument to be made about *Repo Man*—a crit-   22
ical position seldom staked with regard to punk art and lifestyle. Fred
Pfeil argues that *Repo Man* "reproduces the relation between the bone-
numbing vacuity and circularity of daily life . . ." noting that the film's
"sudden jolts of idiotic violence"[4] offer a profound if parodic (Pfeil
would argue postmodern) critique of "the nowhere city." Pfeil then
comments on "the simultaneous desire and dread of some ultimate, ex-
ternally imposed moment of truth" in *Repo Man;* a moment that "once
and for all would put an end to the endless, senseless repetitions of
which our lives seem to be made."[5]

Repo Man, though deliberately narratologically incoherent, does   23
evince a coherent tract on the effect of the city on its disenfranchised
youth. And though the film has been championed by its primarily postpunk, white urban and suburban youth audience—and I suppose in effect misunderstood by them as a camp teen film comedy, a *Beach Party*
with 80's nudity, bad language and technology—*Repo Man* should not
be disparaged because of its popularity. It is just unfortunate that punk,
as with all other youth movements, has been annexed into mainstream
popular culture, and, as is so often the case, it has re-surfaced as far less
threatening and far less politically important to those too young or too
rich or too suburban to really understand what the movement meant
less than a decade past.

Certainly mainstream rock and roll has had a significant effect on   24
the American teenage population. And apropos to Tipper Gore, the music and the multi-billion dollar consumer culture that accompanies it
stupidly celebrates sex and drugs and anti-social behaviour.

Punk on the other hand offered no escapist merchandising scheme.   25
The self-effacing, self-mutilating, self-abusive tendencies of punk—
shared by its performers and fans to the point of establishing the movement's most significant bond—were dramatically "performed" in ce–
remonies of complete sexual and physical surrender. Punk slam and
pogo dancing guaranteed physical injury. The indiscriminate abuse of
drugs and alcohol common among the punks involved none of the
glamour and pretense to being cool commonly associated with mainstream rock and roll. Rather, substance abuse among the punks was pur-
poseful. It was a ritual of self-destruction; subsuming the self, not to the
commodity (as in conventional rock and roll), but to a senseless, stupid

---

[4] Fred Pfeil, "Makin' Flippy Floppy: Postmodernism and the Baby Boom PMC," in *The Year
Left* (London: Verso Press, 1986), p. 285.
[5] Pfeil, p. 286.

culture revealed in a decaying urban environment where glamour, romance and petty teenage angst are comical and unacceptable.

A sense of desperation is captured in the music. And despite the speed and volume of the songs, the lyrics are audible and (because they are simplistic and repeated several times) comprehensible. In the baiting, the heckling, the fistfights between band members and the crowd, a kind of bizarre kinship is maintained. Club owner Brenden Mullen called punk the folk music of the 1980's; and in the purest sense of the term "folk," he is right. For the appropriately initiated, the ritual nature of punk was far more significant than it has ever been or ever will be for mainstream rock and roll. 26

The cultural importance of popular music since the advent of rock and roll some thirty years ago is the subject of a rather divergent debate. Some culture critics, here most notably the proponents of the Frankfurt School, cite the almost immediate commodification of rock and roll by "the culture industry." Just as "youth culture" surfaced as a critical term, the same 9–14 and 15–24 year olds became the principal media and consumer target groups. Other critics, many of them rock and roll historians like Robert Christgau, Greil Marcus and Dick Hebdige maintain arguments regarding rock and roll's unifying, even emancipatory function. Bernard Gendron summarizes this idealistic approach as follows: ". . . rock and roll's appearance at a particular juncture of class, generational and cultural struggle has given it a preeminent role among mass cultural artifacts as an instrument of opposition and liberation."[6] 27

In "On Popular Music" (first published in 1941) Theodor Adorno juxtaposes mass market, assembly line commodity production with the "Tin Pan Alley culture industry" that "standardizes" popular music. By connecting popular music to factory production Adorno vents his rage against a popular culture industry that stupefies its audience. In punk, Adorno's fears regarding the repetitive and reductive tendencies of popular music are dramatically played out, but to a significantly different ideological effect. 28

Punk music is fast, loud and for the most part simplistic. The songs seldom last more than a scant two minutes and are often indistinguishable from one another. LA punk bands like Black Flag and the Circle Jerks actually highlight the indistinguishability of their songs, allowing one number to run into (or over) another. This standardization, so abhorred by Adorno and so much a part of his critique of the culture industry, is in punk music part of a unifying ceremonial performance. For 29

---

[6] Bernard Gendron, "Theodor Adorno Meets the Cadillacs," in *Studies in Entertainment*, ed. by Tania Modleski (Bloomington and Indianapolis: University of Indiana Press, 1986), p. 19.

punk, musical and lyrical repetition bears a dramatic political and collective ritual import.

Punk music is simple enough and standard enough to consistently   30 incite violence and riot. In the purest sense punk, however politically confused on the surface, realizes the ever so elusive emancipatory popular culture so optimistically envisioned by Walter Benjamin and so skeptically lamented by Adorno, fellow Frankfurt School theorists Max Horkheimer and Herbert Marcuse, C. Wright Mills and Robert Warshow, who argues the following in his landmark study, *The Immediate Experience*: ". . . the chief function of mass culture is to relieve one of the necessity of experiencing one's life directly."[7]

However we view the function and significance of popular culture   31 in America today, the issue of the specific ideological agenda of punk remains a difficult issue. The songs performed by X, Black Flag, the Circle Jerks, the Germs, Catholic Discipline and Fear often feature overtly political lyrics, but given the setting and performance the precise point is often obscure or paradoxical. Black Flag, for example, a band fronted by an Hispanic lead singer who lives in a gutted church, perform "White Minority," a fascist, racist rant made altogether paradoxical by the lead singer's ethnicity. Another of their songs, "Depression," heralds a conventional rock and roll sentiment, teenage angst, but with a clearly more angry and desperate subtext: "Got no friends/No girls want to touch me/I don't need your fucking sympathy."

X, the one LA punk band to achieve commercial success (by neces-   32 sarily abandoning the movement) match high speed rhythms essential for pogo and slam dancing with ironic, black comic lyrics. Their best known song "Nausea," about vomiting blood after drinking too much is a classic rock and roll bar song with a shifted focus (to the morning after) and "Johnny Hit and Run Pauline," which uncritically tells of a violent rape fantasy, takes the mainstream rock and roll penchant for misogyny and sexual violence to graphic extremes. X, who were discovered by former Doors' member Ray Manzarek, also display a more self-conscious and ironic side with songs about Jacqueline Susann, "sex and dying in high society," and landlord tenant relations (in the classic, "We're Desperate," lyrics as follows: We're desperate/Get used to it/ We're desperate/It's kiss or kill.)

Exene, the lead singer of X who met fellow X member John Doe at   33 a poetry workshop in Venice, argues that "the only performance that 'makes it' is the one that achieves total madness." Curiously, Exene's remark is a direct quote from the British New Wave film *Performance*,

---

[7] Robert Warshow, *The Immediate Experience*, (NY: Athenium, 1970), p. 38.

written and directed by Nick Roeg in 1970. In *Performance*, Rolling Stones' lead singer Mick Jagger plays a down and out rock and roll performer who finally decides that suicide is (on so many levels) the ultimate public act.

The LA punk bands all seem to share Exene's fixation with madness. In the late seventies the most interesting bands made their reputation by getting barred from one club or another for inciting riots. Black Flag for example, introduce one of their numbers in *The Decline of Western Civilization* with the following: "This song is for the *L.A.P.D.* We got arrested the other night . . . for playing punk rock music . . . they called it a public nuisance. This song is for them and it's called 'Revenge'."   34

Since musicianship and professionalism are the trappings of commercial rock and roll, many of the LA punk bands made a spectacle out of their own lack of musical talent. (In this too there are the seeds of a true egalitarian, proletarian art, supported by standardization and simplicity.) Here the Germs provide a most telling example. Germs' performances were never organized around songs but "gained meaning" from the bizarre ramblings and completely drug-altered behaviour of their lead singer Darby Crash. As it may not have been evident at the time, Crash's on stage performance was a thinly veiled public suicide ritual. What had its perversely funny moments (crash's habit for forgetting to sing into the microphone, for example) also had its darker side. Every Germs performance ended with Crash hurling himself limp-limbed into the audience. When he'd emerge he'd be effaced with magic marker drawings all over his face and chest, or worse, cut by a knife or piece of glass in the melee on the floor. When Crash died of a drug overdose at the height of his "fame," he became the movement's unlikely martyr, its rebel, its James Dean.   35

Though terms like "star" and "fame" were anathema to the punks, Crash was the movement's best known figure—a kind of scene-maker who precisely because of his lack of true star qualities (charisma, attractiveness, wit, etc.) became a punk legend. His death, a familiar fate to so many punks who similarly abused drugs, seemed appropriate, like Dean's death (which so symbolized living fast and dying young to his teenage fans).   36

The Circle Jerks, whose "hits" include "Red Tape," "Beverly Hills" (beginning with the lyrics: "Beverly Hills/Century City/everything/looks so pretty/all the people/look the same/don't they know they're fucking lame"), "I Just Want Some Skank" and "Back Against the Wall" (featuring the chorus: "You can curse/spit/throw bottles . . . but it all ends with a swift kick in the ass") efface musicality and professional performance by standardizing their songs to lengths under sixty seconds. Every Circle Jerks' song reveals an identical chord pattern. One song   37 simply begins as another ends. There are no refrains, no codas, no hooks and no payoff endings.

Catholic Discipline, a band founded by a charismatic, misplaced   38
Paris aesthete Claude Bessy, takes its name from graffiti found on the men's room wall in the Masque. Bessy's performance features a caustic harangue at the audience, which is typical of punk. "I just want (the audience) to hate me," Bessy says, "It makes me feel good." Bessy, like performance artist Sergio Premoli, fashions himself an artiste and his songs bear out an irreverent penchant for the mixed metaphor. Catholic Discipline's best known compositions are "Barbie Doll Love," chronicling Bessy's habit of fondling the famous doll in his pocket and "Underground Babylon," featuring references to the Bible, DW Griffith's *Intolerance* and Kenneth Anger's *Hollywood Babylon*.

Of all the bands, Fear was the most provocative and charismatic.   39
Once featured on "Saturday Night Live," their performance was so savage and anarchic and their pogo dancing entourage so out of control that NBC executives forced the show's producer, Lorne Michaels, to cut to commercial long before the set was complete. Their front man, Lee Ving (now something of a film star after his role as a sleazy club owner in *Flashdance*), like Bessy, purposefully provoked the audience between numbers. His remarks were characteristically obscene and bitter and his disdain for public propriety was the kind of punk performance that "made it"—that achieved the madness of public outrage and riot.

In response to a heckler in *The Decline of Western Civilization*, Ving   40
shouts: "Next time don't bite so hard when I come." Preceding their final number in the film, Ving attacks the record industry: "If there are any A and R people out there, go die!" Ving is unapologetic and he is not ironic or parodic. When he mocks homosexuals ("We're from Frisco," he says hanging his wrist limply, "We think you're a bunch of queers . . ."), there is no liberal critical distance. When he says "You know why chicks have their holes so close together? . . . so you can carry them around like sixpacks," his disdain for public propriety is the point of his performance; it is the only real rationale for performance.

Fear's live set includes: "Beef Bologna" (revealing Ving's girlfriend's   41
taste with regard to cuts of meat), "Let's Have a War/So You Can Go Die" (Fear's answer to the population explosion), "I Don't Care About You/Fuck You," and the punk anthem "I Love Livin' in the City" (lyrics as follows: "My house smells just like a zoo/It's chock full of shit and puke/cockroaches on my walls/crabs are crawlin' on my balls/oh I'm so clean cut/I just want to fuck some slut/I love livin' in the city . . . suburban scumbags/they don't care/they just get fat/and dye their hair/I love livin' in the city.") Their performance in *The Decline of Western*

Civilization closes with a satire of the national anthem: "O'er the land of the free/and the homos and Jews."

As a cultural artifact—as a cultural phenomenon—the LA punks dramatically raise certain central questions regarding the relative autonomy of youth culture and the liberating potential of popular culture in general and rock and roll in specific. Bernard Gendron, deferring to the Birmingham School of Culture Theory, paraphrases Dick Hebdige when he writes: "One cannot understand the meaning of a rock and roll record without situating it within the youth cultures which typically consume it. In effect . . . the punks rewrite the recorded text . . . by recontextualizing it within their practices and rituals."[8]

Citing such a point of view in conjunction with Roland Barthes' concept of a "readerly text," Gendron posits the following (familiar) ideological conclusion: "If either the artist or the consuming public is the primary creator of . . . meaning, then rock and roll does have the liberatory power so often claimed for it."[9]

David E. James characterizes punk "as the final modernist capitulation to decadence, irrationality and despair," and posits his argument, finally, in ideological (mass cultural), terms: "(Punk is) a recalcitrant stance against the bland conformity of mass society." James goes on to cite punk as "avant garde and populist,"[10] though here his "progressive ideological" approach and desire to affix a method to the madness that so dominated downtown LA in the late seventies gets the better of him. Certainly punk has many of the qualities of an avant garde practice akin to the Dadaists and Surrealists, though it is stretching things to view the LA of the late seventies as a rebirth of the Paris of the 1920's. More obvious and telling are the unsettling parallels to Berlin circa 1925–1933.

By 1981 punk had all but vanished from the LA club scene. X appeared on "American Bandstand" with Dick Clark and accepted a major label record contract. The clubs that had made their reputations on the riots incited by Fear, Black Flag and the other punk bands began showcasing "safer" acts.

Punk's brief hold on a very unhappy segment of the urban LA population testifies to a mass cultural conclusion made by Dana Polan in "'Brief Encounters': Mass Culture and the Evacuation of Sense": ". . . the new mass culture may operate by offering no models whatsoever, preferring instead a situation in which there are no stable values, in which there are no effective roles that one can follow from beginning to end."[11] In such a scenario, all popular culture becomes part of an intertextual

---

[8] Gendron, p. 34.
[9] Gendron, p. 34.
[10] James, p. 131.
[11] Dana Polan, "'Brief Encounters': Mass Culture and the Evacuation of Sense," in *Studies in Entertainment*, p. 182.

spectacle in which punk was (at the very least) a very significant and disturbing scene.

· · · · · · · · · · · · · · · · · · · ·

Examining the Text

1. According to Lewis, why did Sergio Premoli hoist a 120-pound American flag on his back in the poshest shopping area of Beverly Hills (paragraph 5)? How might this artistic gesture be emblematic of the punk "aesthetic"?

2. What was the "literary style" of punk graffiti? By the author's account, how did punk graffiti influence other forms of popular writing, such as magazines? Do you continue to see this influence anywhere?

3. What was Teodor Adorno's primary objection to popular music (28)? How did punk rock support or refute Adorno's ideas about pop music?

For Group Discussion

As a group, make a list of ways in which punk music's influence might be evident in today's popular concerts, dances, and recorded music. Are punk's "contributions" to contemporary pop culture dead, or might they live on in some modified and updated form?

Writing Suggestion

The author contends that the L.A. punk movement reflected the "desperation residing at the heart of the now failed urban American dream" (2). In an essay, first explain how the American dream might be perceived as having "failed," citing economic and cultural examples as support for your thesis. Then, discuss the ways in which popular music, including the punk movement, might reflect this failure, drawing upon your knowledge of various pop-musical forms to support and develop your points.

Grunge & Glory

Jonathan Poneman

Since the sound began to develop in the Seattle area in 1986, grunge music has risen steadily from its disheveled beginnings to claim a national, even international, spotlight. No longer merely an "alternative" sound and lifestyle, grunge has become the central aesthetic for a youth culture that has adopted its fashion sense (or nonsense, depending on your taste) as its own. A revolt against the rigid conventions and aesthetics of the conservative 1980s, grunge fashion is anti-fashion, its "hobo chic" celebrating an ongoing romance with plaid flannel, industrial footwear, and dirty laundry.

In the following, written for Vogue *magazine, pop music mogul Jonathan Poneman charts the rise of grunge from its humble beginnings on the University of Washington radio airwaves to its emergence on the national music scene. With his partner Bruce Pavitt, Poneman began the record company Sub Pop in the mid-eighties; the company launched grunge bands such as Nirvana and Soundgarden to chart-breaking success. This introspective and frequently tongue-in-cheek piece is a light-hearted and humorous account of grunge's popular success. As you read, consider your own responses to the grunge movement. Do you find Poneman's tone appropriate to the subject?*

•••••••••••••••••••••

Throw out your detergent!   1

This is not a call to arms; it's an invitation to dress down and party   2
up! As the fin de siècle draws near, greed has gone to seed. What started
out as a serfs' rebellion against aristocratic glamour has turned into a
fashion revolution that champions "revolting" for its own sake.

It's pop culture through the looking glass; everything old is new,   3
everything modern is passé, and that hideous "glam rock" getup Mom
snuck from her attic to the thrift shop has reappeared in an uptown boutique. It'll cost you a week's wage to get it back. What started out as irreverent trend bucking is now a buck-making trend. Flannels, ratty tour
shirts, boots, and baseball caps have become a uniform for those in the
know, and their legions are growing. But before a wave of Goodwill
truckjackings puts some enterprising black marketer at the forefront of
haute couture, some things need to be explained.

Seattle, Washington, has become the mecca for an insurgent mob of   4
thrill seekers, carpetbaggers, and rock musicians. As an ironically immaculate setting for the capers of a generation spoiled rotten, Seattle is
nirvana. The Bush-whacked economy hasn't stripped this city of its
prosperous glow, hence the almost exotic allure of all things grungy.

Grunge. Like the mold that flourishes in local cellars, *grunge* has be-   5
come the buzzword that defines Seattle youth culture. From the chart-
busting success of regional heroes like Soundgarden, Pearl Jam, Alice in
Chains, and Nirvana to the big-screen mythologizing of the scene (*Singles*), Seattle's grungemania has captivated the short attention span of
today's trendsetters.

Spawned in dilapidated rock clubs and nurtured to health by in-   6
toxicated fans, the grunge phenomenon started as one city's reaction to
the elitist eighties. The aesthetics that govern the moment have roots in

urban bohemianism and in slacker-era schleppiness. Wary of the prissy pretension that reigned unchecked, frustrated students and minimum-wage slaves banded together and created a lifestyle, ever cynical and utilitarian, that more accurately reflected their conditions. The emphasis was on well-worn comfort, cheap beer, and high-volume rock 'n' roll.

In 1986 Seattle was an unlikely setting for a rock renaissance. With   7
the exception of bands like Heart and Queensryche, the city has not produced any artists with national, let alone international, resonance since Jimi Hendrix. With prohibitive "teen dance" laws and an infant alternative-music scene, Seattle seemed doomed to remain a pop cultural backwater.

But without any fanfare, a support system was developing that   8
would catapult the small-but-noisy community from isolated anonymity to regular rotation on MTV. The University of Washington, a rather staid institution but one of the largest universities on the West Coast, was the home of the student-operated radio station KCMU, which played demo tapes by local bands like Soundgarden, Green River, and Bundle of Hiss alongside hits by the Meat Puppets, Black Flag, and the Butthole Surfers. *The Rocket* magazine, a regional rock monthly, kept close tabs on the incubating scene. Independent labels like Sub Pop (the original home of Soundgarden, Mudhoney, and Nirvana) and Popllama (Young Fresh Fellows, the Posies) provided a regular spate of local releases.

I had moved to Washington from Ohio in the late seventies filled   9
with less-than-great notions, a would-be guinea pig for designer antidepressants. Like many of my peers, I chose not to battle the encroaching ennui. Instead, I let it consume my life. The soggy Northwest climate only dampened my ambition, which makes it all the more amazing that I stumbled onto such a mother lode of inspiration.

I was a disc jockey at KCMU during its mid-eighties heyday. The air   10
staff included Mark Arm (of the band Green River, later Mudhoney), Kim Thayil (of Soundgarden), Bruce Fairweather (also a member of Green River, later of Mother Love Bone, currently of Love Battery), Charles Peterson (the scene's defining photographer), and my soon-to-be partner, Bruce Pavitt. As a "shift whore," I took every opportunity to get on the air. This included taking over *Audioasis*, a rather unpopular local music program that exposed me to the embryonic grunge underground. At the time, local musicians and tastemakers were becoming defiantly resentful of not being taken seriously. Not that it was a serious pursuit. The emphasis was on tumult and partying. And with a cavalcade of self-anointed rock gurus shoving half-baked pop philosophy down your throat, a cold beer to wash it all down provided welcome relief. As the outside world of rock became increasingly safe and

bloodless, the gnarly insularity of the Seattle-bred stuff came into sharper focus. And just as grunge will someday be washed aside by the fresh outpourings of a leaner, hungrier horde, the local crew swaggered in with a whole lot to gain and nothing to lose.

The first band I saw that really turned up the heavy was Soundgar-   11
den. They were playing for about fifty people who sat mesmerized as the singer, Chris Cornell, growled, moaned, and writhed with unpolished abandon. They were as out of control as a wayward truncheon. Because of that show I decided to put my own less-than-blazing musical career to sleep. At the time I was part of a rather timid art-pop band. Our singer had a fake British accent. Not cool. Bruce Pavitt, who was then making a name for himself as a rock critic, had just started Sub Pop records. In a display of selfless devotion, I hustled and conned friends and family members into lending me the money to put out the debut Soundgarden EP, *Screaming Life*. I then joined forces with the terminally underfinanced Pavitt. Together, Bruce and I, as Sub Pop moguls, have bulldozed our way through more local sludge than even the heartiest grunge fan would normally be able to tolerate. It's amazing how a lack of anything better to do can strengthen one's resolve.

Of course, the citizens of the Emerald City did not invent low-rent   12
fast living. There are plenty of rock clubs, two-bit combos, and pierced body parts to go around. Long before any of today's Seattle groups landed major record deals, America's turnpikes were bumper-to-bumper with unwashed poop stars-in-waiting. Getting to the next show on the previous night's earnings was top priority. Food and refreshments were a less pressing concern. Laundry was an expendable luxury.

But in Seattle they've managed to update it quite nicely, and all and   13
all, it adds up to an identifiable style for the repentant nineties. When nobody wants to look like they have money, what better champions of hobo chic than the upwardly spiraling grunge rock elite?

"It [grunge style] didn't start off as a 'look', but it's certainly ended   14
up becoming one," says Linda Derschang, proprietor of the popular Seattle clothing emporium Basic. "With the enormous attention paid to local bands who, generally speaking, dress alike, it was inevitable that their style would be copied to some degree." Under the glare of media-induced scrutiny, sales are up, but the stylistic innovations may already have peaked. "Seattle used to have a unique fashion sense," adds Derschang. "Now there's more conformity out there. . . ." If conformity is the by-product of popularity, we can look forward to boulevards cluttered with shredded cardigans, ratty tour shirts, and thrift-store trousers. Converse and Doc Martens are the requisite footwear.

Anybody who attended the Lollapalooza festival last summer saw   15
the emulation in full effect. Lollapalooza, a touring arts and music spec-

tacle designed to outrage, enlighten, and ultimately entertain, made its way across North America like a hip Barnum and Bailey's circus. Along with a host of other rock superstars, Soundgarden and Pearl Jam were featured. Thus the predominant Seattle fashion sense got linked to a greater event, which, despite its enormous hype, still had a humble heart. Given the origins of grunge, it couldn't be any other way.

The dynamic of the scene first started to change in 1988, when   16
Soundgarden signed with A&M Records, Mudhoney toured Europe to frothing critical praise, and Sub Pop became a full-time job. There was no brilliant marketing strategy, it all just happened . . . one big happy accident; the big bang, if you will.

It's because of the suddenness of the ascendancy of this area's pop   17
hierarchy that it has so far remained an organic phenomenon. Even now, the titans of grunge still look like they've been riding around in a cramped van for months—which is part of the style. And though they're making decent livings doling out the grunge, the primal directness remains undiluted.

But who knows for how long? I must say, I never thought that I'd   18
see a tattoo parlor in a suburban shopping mall. After a few years of the good life, today's nouveau pop idols might start touring the nostalgia circuit with hard-won paunches and remnants of yesterday's glory.

Maybe they'll have a clean wardrobe as well.   19

·················

Examining the Text

1. What point is Poneman making when he writes, "As an ironically immaculate setting for the capers of a generation spoiled rotten, Seattle is nirvana" (paragraph 4)? How does his irony here influence your reading of the rest of the article?

2. Why, according to Poneman, has grunge music had an "exotic allure" for young people in the late 1980s and 1990s (4)? What do you see as the main reasons for its popularity?

3. How did the Lollapalooza touring music festival inadvertently promote grunge as a national fashion phenomenon? By Poneman's account, what is the relationship between pop music and fashion in modern society? Can you give further examples of this relationship?

For Group Discussion

In this article's first sentence, "Throw out your detergent!", Poneman establishes a tone he maintains throughout the piece. As a group, make a list of adjectives to describe Poneman's tone. As a class discuss the ways this kind of writing differs from most academic writing. Why might Poneman's language be appropriate for this kind of article but not for an expository essay?

Writing Suggestion

Write an essay in which you discuss the ways in which popular musical movements such as grunge are "constructed" by the televised media—especially MTV. Drawing upon the readings in this chapter about grunge, rap, and so on, show how media vehicles such as MTV not only reflect the musical tastes of young America, but also create those tastes.

Dreaming America

Danyel Smith

*T*he following essay by Danyel Smith focuses on popular music as the embodiment of the urban experience in contemporary America. Smith creates a fictional character, "Ms. Hip Hop," a street-wise, fast-moving, musically attuned young woman who is more at home among the run-down buildings, the exhaust fumes and cutthroat characters of New York City than in the "big country town" of California. For Smith, Ms. Hip Hop—and by association, contemporary urban music—represents all that is compelling about the city. Using this character, Smith is able to contrast various aspects of modern life—the differences between city and country life, between Eastern and Western cities, between various ethnic groups, between cities past and present.

This piece first appeared in Spin magazine, a non-academic journal devoted to current trends in popular music. For that reason, Smith's article doesn't develop in the way that academic essays do. You will notice that it lacks a focused and coherent thesis statement; it doesn't proceed logically with each abstract point developed with evidence and examples, followed by the next, nor does it conclude with a neat thematic summation. Nevertheless, the article certainly does have a thesis, and it uses rich language to get that point across. *As you read* this piece, then, attempt to discover the creative ways in which Smith uses descriptions of Ms. Hip Hop to suggest meanings about the inner-city experience of New York City specifically and modern-day America more generally.

• • • • • • • • • • • • • • • • • • • •

The music is my life.

Is New York, New York, really the birthplace of hip hop? Is this ultimate city—the preferred setting for most modern-day film fables—the place where the seed took hold? Where the rhymes first flowed and a culture took form? This compressed, dirty place, this mainstream cultural stronghold, is the steamy-hot/snowy region where a generation found an identity, where all the shit went down?

It's where DJ Scott LaRock died and Slick Rick went to prison. Where Run found Christ and Griff got dismissed. Where sneakers became the rule and not the exception: where Latifah grew Treach, and where the Guru *squoze* hip hop out of Bird's horn.

And here she is, Ms. Hip Hop, generic girl-fan. In that place. The city. Looking around for the elusive ticket, the line, the string that tied it all together and turned the music into a thing, a movement—a music.

She is a native Californian in New York for the third time. She never stays long. She always flies back West, over the mountains and the lakes, relieved when she sees Lake Tahoe, ecstatic when she spots the Golden Gate Bridge, its yawning red span as welcoming as a familiar mouth upturned in a smile. Then she knows she is in California, a subdivision of the U.S.A. as long and thin as she would like to be—a huge state broken up into sprawling counties, the seductively warm state she calls her home. California has its glories, and it holds on tight to its trophies—the Eagles, Sly and the Family Stone, Jefferson Airplane, Tower of Power. But as grand and forthright as Cali hip hop is circa 1993—the Coup, Snoop Dogg, Souls of Mischief—in the East lay the lungs and heart of hip hop and so the West holds court in its long shadow.

Tommy Boy president Monica Lynch asked, "Has New York fallen the fuck off?" a long time ago, like maybe it would jar East Coast B-boys and -girls into action. But to no avail. The cast pumps hip hop blood, but out West are the sinewy appendages, out West is where folks are waking and talking it.

New York beckons, though, like an old buddy with gossip, like a preacher who just might know the Truth. The buildings are older, the street fumes stronger, every other car is a taxi. The periodicals seem vital, seem to have more than a tenuous connection to the city. The trains hiss and moan and chug. The place is cutthroat, envious, and mean. Pleasantries are hoarded like money and doled out without enthusiasm. California is one big country town compared with Manhattan and the surrounding boroughs. California piles on big-city makeup in L.A. and Oakland, San Diego and San Francisco—but really, the place is spread out like a big cabbage farm, like the far-flung desert it is.

But cabbage farm or no, in urban southern California, even a mostly middle-class Catholic schoolgirl like Ms. Hip Hop knows which neighborhood is blue and which is red. She knows when to hit the asphalt in the parking lot of Shakey's or Astro Burger because boys are shooting bullets in the air or at certain cars because their varsity hoop squad lost. Or because they won.

She remembers when "urban" didn't have a negative connotation, when urban meant of or having to do with a city or a metropolis. She remembers when "city" didn't mean dank and dark and poor. She vaguely recalls when black people weren't automatically associated with cities and urbanity. She's read about it, about when African-Americans lived mostly on farms and in the "country" and in the South. Arrested Development's Speech reminisces about that era in "Tennessee." Making myth of the post-sharecropping era and country life, he talks convincingly, painfully about climbing the trees his forefathers hung from. It sounds so cleansing and sad and fine. Just as American black people are automatically associated with cities and all of their ills, Speech wants the old life, the old values, the old ways—back to the earth. To being "natural." As if that state—"naturalness"—is an option at this point in Western civilization.

The Catholic schoolgirl, the smart hip hop girl—she is ever anxious 9 for peace for her people and her own state of mind. She wildly reaches for this "oldness," this better way of being. But even as a mindset, while she stands on the streets of New York or West Los Angeles or Fresno or Kettleman of Napa, California—it doesn't work. Images of wooden porches and backyard cornstalks, or roosters pecking and kente cloth flowing, the brightly painted pictures in her desperate imagination fade like a mirage in an old cartoon: quickly and completely in its place are frowns and guns, televisions and straightened hair, housing projects and stucco single-family homes. Fast cars and loud music. Hip hop MC Breed and Too Short. Onyx and Ice Cube.

Still she looks for hip hop's heart in New York City, believing she 10 can find it, thinking naively that if she sees it, she could define it and the definition would make a difference in all that she sees, in all that her mind conjures and remembers. So she presses on.

• • • • • • • • • • • • • • • • • • • •

Examining the Text

1. Smith describes New York City as the place "where sneakers became the rule and not the exception; where Latifah grew Treach, and where the Guru *squoze* hip hop out of Bird's horn" (paragraph 2). Explain the references to sneakers, Latifah, the word *squoze*, and Bird.

2. When Smith says "out West are the sinewy appendages, out West is where folks are walking and talking it" (5), what does she mean by "it"? What does this statement suggest about the shift in geographic influence in the current hip-hop world?

3. What is the significance of the statement "even a mostly middle-class Catholic schoolgirl like Ms. Hip Hop knows which neighborhood is blue and which is red" (7)? What is the point of this image of the "Catholic schoolgirl" in the rest of the essay?

For Group Discussion

As a group, describe Ms. Hip Hop as she is portrayed by Smith, listing as many descriptive words and phrases as you can. Having described this character at some length, discuss as a class the function this character serves for Smith as she develops her ideas about hip hop.

Writing Suggestion

Smith says that California is "spread out like a big cabbage farm, like the far-flung desert it is" (6), a fact which is reflected in the music that comes out of that area. Write an essay that describes a geographical area, ideally one with which you are quite familiar, focusing on locally-popular music as a central feature in your description.

5

Sports

The United States seems to be a nation obsessed with sports, an obsession nowhere more evident than in some fans' virtual addiction to sports statistics. Somewhere there's probably a statistics maven who knows the number of foot faults in the final 1956 Davis Cup match or the most triples by a left-handed batter during Tuesday afternoon World Series games. Fans crave statistics, no matter how minute, as a way of measuring the achievements of their favorite athletes and teams—and perhaps also as a way of holding the memory of never-to-be-repeated athletic performances.

It's not difficult to find further evidence of America's preoccupation with sports. Most daily newspapers allocate an entire section to sports reports and statistics; a number of national weekly and monthly publications concentrate exclusively on sports. Special sporting events such as the Super Bowl are consistently among the most highly rated TV broadcasts, and several cable networks are devoted solely to sports twenty-four hours a day. Americans play sports trivia games, call sports telephone hotlines, and participate in a multi-billion dollar sports gaming industry; they display team logos on T-shirts, sweatshirts, baseball caps, and countless other articles of clothing. Many colleges and universities capitalize on the prominence of their sports programs to increase enrollments and donations.

Sports can affect fans in surprisingly intense ways. We all probably know people whose moods fluctuate with the fortunes of their favorite team, who might "bleed Dodger blue," as they say. Indeed, entire cities rejoice when their team brings home a championship, and our national mood lifts when an American underdog takes a medal at the Olympics or when the "Dream Team" squashes an opponent. Given this obsession, it's no wonder that professional athletes are among our most revered—and highly paid—citizens.

How can we explain the popularity of professional sports? The essays in the first part of this chapter offer views about the role of sports in American life in general, including television commentator Dick Schaap's lament for the days when sportsmanship was more important to professional athletes than their next contract, and reporter Kate Rounds' analysis of the negligible status of women's athletics in a male-dominated sports culture. The essays in the second part focus on four specific sports (baseball, basketball, football, and boxing), and, by implication, the factors—physical ability, the influence of family and friends, climate and environment, even race and gender—that govern an individual's choice to participate in or follow a particular sport.

Obviously, sports can influence the way we speak and the way we feel, our notions of teamwork and individuality, success and failure, and male and female roles. From sports we learn how to deal with pressure, adversity, and physical pain and discover models of grace, skill, and style. As you read the essays in this chapter, think of the sports you play and watch, of the athletes you admire, of the role sports play (or have played) in your life.

THE ROLE OF SPORTS IN AMERICA

So Much of the Joy Is Gone

Dick Schaap

We begin this chapter with a sobering critique of professional sports by a long-time observer. Best-known as a television sports commentator, Dick Schaap has also written extensively about sports from the position of an insider; among other publications, he co-authored football great Bo Jackson's autobiography.

In this essay, originally published in Forbes, *a magazine aimed at business executives and investors, Schaap observes that although professional athletes today are "taller, heavier, faster, stronger, smarter" than their predecessors, the joy in watching them perform is gone. According to Schaap, money and greed are at the heart of the problem. Fun, camaraderie, team loyalty, even racial equality suffer when players and owners are motivated primarily by how much they can earn, when "sports preaches green above all else."*

And, Schaap says, fans suffer, too. While there may be individual amateur and professional athletes who still lift our spirits and serve as role models, Schaap sees sports' overall influence on its fans as increasingly harmful.

As you read, *consider the merits of Schaap's argument. To what extent do you think greed affects sports and athletes? Has the influence of sports become mostly negative? If so, would society be better off without the influence of professional sports?*

••••••••••••••••••

Athletes are better than ever. They are taller, heavier, faster, stronger, smarter. In every sport in which achievement can be measured objectively, their progress is stunning. 1

A girl barely into her teens swims more swiftly than Johnny Weismuller swam in the Olympics, or in his loincloth. 2

A high school boy jumps farther and sprints faster than Jesse Owens jumped and sprinted in front of Adolf Hitler. 3

A 30-year-old married woman surpasses Jim Thorpe's best marks in a variety of track and field events. 4

Even a man over 40 runs a mile faster than Paavo Nurmi ran in his prime. 5

The performances are so much better. But so much of the joy is gone. 6

Sports has too often been called a microcosm of society, yet its present state certainly reflects the uneasy prosperity of the times, the suspicion that, despite encouraging facts and heartening figures, something 7 is fundamentally wrong. The cheers may be louder than ever, but they ring a little hollow.

It is almost impossible to overstate the pervasiveness of sports in   8
American society, the breadth and strength of its special appeal, to bricklayers and novelists, accountants and comedians. "Have you met Mr. Nixon yet?" the future President's press secretary once asked me. "You'll like him. He reads the sports pages first."

Then when I did meet Richard Nixon, he phrased his political   9
thoughts in sports terms, spoke of hitting home runs and getting to first base and striking out. Sports is a language and a diversion and some-times an obsession, and more than ever, it is a business.

The stakes are so high now. The *average* major league baseball player   10
earns more than a million dollars a year. Losing pitchers and feeble hit-ters, men with stunningly modest statistics, demand much more. Steve Greenberg, the deputy commissioner of baseball, used to be an agent, negotiating players' contracts. He once told his father, Hank Greenberg, the Hall of Famer, who was the first ballplayer to earn $100,000 in a sea-son, that he was representing a certain player. "What should I ask for?" Steve said. "He hit .238."

"Ask for a uniform," Hank said.   11

Steve shook his head. "Dad," he said, "you just don't understand   12
baseball any more."

Nobody understands baseball any more. No one relates to the   13
salaries. Not even the players themselves. They earn so much more than they ever dreamed of.

They also throw pitches Cy Young never dreamed of. (Ever see Cy   14
Young's glove? Small. Very small. Now they have big hands, hands that can wrap around a ball and deliver a palmball.) They swing bats with muscles Babe Ruth never dreamed of. They sprint from home to first, or first to third, with incredible speed. That's the biggest difference, the way they run these days. They fly.

But they don't know how to bunt. They don't know how to hit and   15
run. They don't know which base to throw to. They didn't spend child-hoods in cornfields playing baseball 10 or 12 hours a day, absorbing the nuances of the game. They may have developed terrific hand-eye coor-dination playing video games, but that didn't teach them how to hit the cutoff man.

Baseball players earn up to $7 million a season. So do basketball   16
players. Football players are embarrassed. Their ceiling is a few million dollars lower. Golfers and tennis players only go up to a million or two a year in prize money, but they can quadruple their income by wearing the right clothes, wielding the right clubs, advertising the right corpo-rate logos on their visors and their sleeves.

Even athletes who are officially amateurs, runners and skaters and　17
skiers, earn hundreds of thousands of dollars a year. How can anyone
afford to have fun?

Once there was a camaraderie among athletes. They competed on　18
the field, but afterward they were friends, sharing a common experience, a common attitude, bonded by their love for their game. Tennis
players, for instance, traveled together, roomed together, partied together, exchanged advice and rackets. Now each has a coach, and an
agent, and a father or brother, and a fistful of sponsors, walling them off,
separating them. Then can face each other across the net for years and
never get to know each other.

Even in team sports, team spirit is, for the most part, gone, rekin-　19
dled only occasionally by victory. "We are family," in sports terms,
means: "We won." It doesn't mean we worry about each other, bolster
each other, counsel each other.

How can fans relate to these athletes? How can they embrace heroes　20
who have so much money and so little loyalty? Players change teams
now as casually as they change jockstraps. Once you could fall in love
with a lineup, commit it to your heart and your memory, and not have
to learn more than one or two new names a year.

"The names, just to say the names, you could sing them," the play-　21
wright Herb Gardner once wrote, lamenting the Dodgers' move to Los
Angeles. "Sandy Amoros, Jim Gilliam, Hodges, Newcombe, Campa-
nella, Erskine, Furillo, Podres, gone, gone . . . even the sound is gone.
What's left? A cap, I got a cap, Dodgers, '55, and sometimes on the wind
I hear a gull, and Red Barber's voice. . . ."

Now the Dodger lineup changes every day, millionaires come and　22
go, succumbing to minor injuries, whining about imagined slights, and
even the manager, Tom Lasorda, who loves the team so much he says
he bleeds Dodger blue, can't call all his players by name.

Once Dodgers were Dodgers for decades, and Cardinals Cardinals,　23
and Red Sox Red Sox, but now they're L.A. Kings for a day, or maybe a
month or a season, and if an athlete puts in a full career with one team,
in one city, he isn't a hero, he's a monument.

It's easy to fault the players for earning so much money, for dis-　24
playing so little loyalty, but it isn't fair. They didn't invent greed, or in-
gratitude. They learned from their mentors, the owners. The baseball
players of the 1950s, the football players of the 1960s, had little idea of
how underpaid they were. Soon after the salaries started to soar, a baseball player named Ken Singleton told me, "The owners screwed the
players for one hundred years. We've been screwing them for five.
We've got ninety-five more years coming."

The owners came up with the idea of moving for the money, too.   25
The Braves went from Boston to Milwaukee to Atlanta, strip-mining sta-
dia along the way. The Dodgers and the Giants traveled west hand in
hand, with the other hands, of course, thrust out. They left shattered fans
behind.

"They went, and the city went with them," Herb Gardner wrote.   26
"The heart went with them, and the city started to die. Look what you
got now, look what you got without no heart. What's to root for? Duke
Snider! He went away! How many years in the stands hollering? A life-
time in the afternoon hollering, 'I'm witcha, Duke, I'm witcha,' never
dreaming for a moment that he wasn't with *me!*"

Teams, and owners, and athletes, have disappointed us in so many   27
ways. The disappointment goes beyond the greed, beyond the selfishness. How can you put athletes up on a pedestal who flaunt fast cars at
illegal speeds, who succumb to the lures of social drugs and perfor-
mance-enhancing drugs, who maltreat women as spoils, who lose gambling fortunes that would change most people's lives? How can you
pick a hero any more and count on him?

Sports has let us down.   28

Half a century ago, when Jackie Robinson became a Brooklyn Dodger   29
and Joe Louis was the greatest fighter in the world, sports held out so
much hope, so much promise. Equality, that elusive gift bestowed on all
Americans by the Declaration of Independence, was going to be won
and secured, finally, on the playing fields.

Of course. On the playing fields, every competitor was equal. The   30
scoreboard knew no race, no religion, no nationality. Sports offered the
ultimate democracy, where a man or a woman's success derived purely
from his or her ability.

But, as brave as Jackie Robinson was, as good as Jimmy Brown was,   31
and Henry Aaron and Bob Gibson and O.J. Simpson and Ernie Davis
and Wilt Chamberlain and Bill Russell and Althea Gibson and Arthur
Ashe and Rod Carew and Bill White and Julius Erving and Muhammad
Ali and Sugar Ray Leonard and Magic Johnson and Oscar Robertson
and Willie Davis and Lawrence Taylor and Alan Page and Jerry Rice and
Walter Payton and so many more, the brotherhood of man has flourished no more on the playing fields than in the streets.

Thanks to sports, there are many more black millionaires now than   32
there were a few decades ago, but there is not equality, not the kind of
equality that not so long ago seemed possible, or even likely. Black players still tend to sit with black players on team buses and at training tables, and white players cluster together, and so do the black wives of
black players.

For every Bill Bradley or Jack Kemp, who learned from the sports   33
experience, who gained some insight into the dreams and fears of teammates of different color, who has sought to translate those into political
action, dozens of athletes slip back into prejudice as soon as black teammates are out of sight, or out of hearing. They use privately the same
cruel words that Jackie Robinson heard publicly.

Corporate America is no better, only more polite. Michael Jordan and   34
David Robinson and O.J. Simpson and Bo Jackson, men so much larger
than life, have been able to transcend color and earn millions for endorsements, but below the superstar level, white athletes have an unmistak-
able edge, have first call on commercials and appearances and exposure.

It is ludicrous, the infinitesimally low percentage of black managers   35
and coaches and executives in professional and collegiate sports. They
don't have "the necessities," Alex Campanis, a Los Angeles Dodgers executive, once blurted out on network television, clumsily sharing "a
truth," as he, and many other management people in sports, perceived
it. What necessities? Yogi Berra's IQ? Whitey Herzog's charm? They
both managed first-place teams in both big leagues; so much for necessities. There are plenty of black Berras and black Whiteys, and smarter
and more charming blacks—I thought Willie Davis, the former Green
Bay Packer, a Hall of Fame defensive end, an enormously successful
businessman and civic leader, a warm and thoughtful man, would have
been a perfect commissioner of the National Football League; he got
only token consideration—but they are so often overlooked, and more
often snubbed.

I share the guilt. When I was editor of a sports magazine, I was fre-   36
quently scolded by my employer for putting too many black athletes
on the cover. I was told that white athletes sell more magazines, and I
cycled and recycled Joe Namath and Tom Seaver and Dave DeBusschere and Pete Rose. ("I've been on the cover of *Sport* three times,"
Rose once cracked at a luncheon I hosted. "That's not bad for a white
guy.") I've collaborated on books with many athletes—Namath, Seaver,
DeBusschere, Bill Freehan, Frank Beard, Jerry Kramer and Bo Jackson—
and only one was black. I accepted the publishing belief, nourished by
an Ali autobiography that was a commercial disaster, that blacks did not
buy books. When the Bo Jackson book became the best-selling sports autobiography ever, far outgrossing all my other works, that belief was
sternly tested. Still, when I write and narrate feature stories for television, I realize, with a twinge, that I lean heavily upon white athletes as
subjects and as interviewees. They certainly take up a larger portion of
the screen than they do of the playing field.

Fans can be as harsh as they ever were. Once, I was on a plane to   37
Birmingham, Ala., to visit Bo Jackson's home, and a passenger across the

aisle, watching me flip through Jackson clippings, leaned over and said, "You know why they call him 'Bo?'" Before I could answer, he said, "'Cause they didn't know how to spell 'Bob.'"

I don't know why I was stunned.   38

Sports could be forgiven its flaws, at least some of them, if it had   39
compensating strengths, if it taught the heroic lessons that Homer once
sang of, if it emphasized positive values, if it truly rewarded persever-
ance and teamwork and similar virtues.

But these days sports preaches greed above all else. Bad enough that   40
the status of all professional athletes is determined, to a considerable extent, by their income; in golf, pretense is stripped away and the players
are ranked, officially, by their earnings. Worse, the sports world also
glamorizes hypocrisy and deception and corruption.

Big-time college athletic programs are a disgrace. In almost all of the   41
major schools, the question isn't: Do the athletic departments cheat? It's:
How badly do they cheat? Even the squeaky clean programs, the Dukes
and the Stanfords and the Notre Dames, the schools that offer prestige
and power and tradition instead of cash and cars (low monthly payments? would you believe zero?), do not treat the so-called student athletes the way they treat student nonathletes. And the Ivy League, which
preaches purity, does not always practice it. Any good Ivy League football player, and there are more than a few every year, who does not have
a summer job on Wall Street paying an inflated salary is either remarkably passive or independently wealthy.

Colleges with winning big-time football and basketball programs   42
are making millions of dollars a year, and their coaches, with their
camps and their clinics and their TV shows, are earning hundreds of
thousands of dollars—all of that money dependent on the skills and
moods of agile and powerful teenagers. To keep all those dollars coming in, virtually all colleges and coaches to some extent are willing to lie
or distort or bribe or glorify, to stretch rules and ignore academic deficiencies, to pamper the more gifted athletes beyond belief. (Paul Hor-
nung, after whom the Golden Dome at Notre Dame, his alma mater,
may have been named, once said his own epitaph should be: "He went
through life on scholarship.")

Too many college football and basketball players are treated, to use   43
the title of a book one of them wrote, like "meat on the hoof," but surely
black athletes are the most abused, fed visions of professional sports
careers that will never materialize, steered away from academic courses
that might challenge or inspire them, presented with scholarships to
nowhere, free room, free board, free tuition, but not free thought. A few
years ago I visited a very talented college football player, a likable young
man, whose dormitory room was outfitted with the latest in stereo

equipment and Nike posters. There wasn't a book in his student-athlete room, not one. He was lucky. He made it to the National Football League. He was one of the rare ones.

In all this gloom there are glimmers of hope. In high schools and colleges and even in international competition, not all sports corrupt and demean. A pure amateur may be as rare as a whooping crane, but in such college sports as lacrosse (Princeton, of all schools, upset Syracuse for the national championship a few months ago) and field hockey (a dominion dominated by Old Dominion), to name two, sports which hold out little promise of fame or financial reward, men and women still can have fun, still can build character and self-confidence. In the Olympics, I love to wander among the winter biathletes, who couple such contradictory disciplines as shooting and skiing, and the summer pentathletes, who blend riding, shooting, fencing, swimming and running, the pursuits of an ancient courier. Their names are unknown outside the smallest circles, and their per diems are minimal, but their interests often seem to be as varied as their skills. "Our worlds are not confined by ski wax," as a biathlete once told me.   44

I still find individual athletes who lift my spirits: Bonny Warner, America's best female luger in the 1980s, a graduate of Stanford, a reformed sportscaster, now a United Airlines pilot; Jim Abbott, one of the few baseball players ever to leap straight from college to the major leagues, a man who expects neither sympathy nor attention for the fact that he was born with only one hand, yet a man who quietly offers time and hope and encouragement to children with physical differences; Mike Reid, first an All-American football player, then an All-Pro tackle, from Altoona, Pa., a town in which it is easy to play football but takes courage to play piano, now a Grammy Award–winning songwriter and singer of sensitive ballads.   45

In all sports, I find stars with the ultimate saving grace, the ability to laugh at themselves; stars who rose to great wealth from the meanest streets without forgetting their roots; stars whose intellect contradicts athletic stereotypes; stars whose values are the decent traditional ones that start with family and loyalty. "When I was growing up," Bo Jackson recalled, "my mom cleaned people's houses during the day and cleaned a motel at night. She also raised ten children by herself. And people try to tell me that playing two sports is hard." Bo Jackson's wife is a counseling psychologist; their three children are his most prized trophies.   46

Some athletes are better than ever.   47

Even off the field.   48

When I was a graduate student at Columbia, the school had a very good basketball team.   49

The best player on the team became a degenerate gambler, a con- 50
victed criminal.

The second-best player became president of the Ford Foundation. 51

I still see both of them, on infrequent occasion, and they remind me 52
of the potential of sports, and the peril. Sports can inspire greatness, but,
too often these days, it inspires only greed.

••••••••••••••••••••

Examining the Text

1. In what ways does Schaap think sports has let fans down? What does
he say fans should expect from sports? Do you share his sense that
"something is fundamentally wrong" (paragraph 7) when players "have
so much money and so little loyalty" (20)?

2. Schaap spends some time describing race-related problems in sports
(29–40). Summarize this section of the essay. Whom does Schaap blame
for racism still existing in sports? Does your own experience as a player,
spectator, or reader confirm his observations?

3. In the last section of the essay, Schaap offers some positive examples
of athletes he respects. What qualities do these athletes share, and why
does Schaap praise them? Do you find that these qualities correspond
to those you and people you know admire in professional athletes? Why
or why not?

For Group Discussion

Schaap identifies a number of problems with contemporary sports,
but he doesn't suggest specific solutions. As a group, make a list of recommendations Schaap and those who agree with him might offer for
improving professional sports. As you construct your list, consider how
easy or how difficult it might be to implement these recommendations.
As a class, discuss those that are most feasible. Does everyone agree that
the resulting changes would actually improve professional sports? Why
or why not?

Writing Suggestion

Imagine that you own a professional sports team. Write a letter to
Forbes magazine responding to Schaap's assertion that owners are driven
by greed and are disappointing the fans. Alternatively, write a letter
to *Forbes* in which you express your own responses to Schaap's argument.

Sport and the American Dream

Jeffrey Schrank

In the previous selection, Dick Schaap suggests that professional sports play a large role in the lives of many Americans. In the following essay, Jeffrey Schrank, a social commentator who often examines the interaction between the media and society, expands Schaap's analysis of sports to see how it reflects the American character and our wishes, values, and beliefs.

In detailing how sports mirrors American culture, Schrank suggests that different sports appeal to Americans for different reasons and reveal different aspects of the American character. His underlying premise is that a country can trace its national preoccupations, attitudes, and aspirations in its popular sports. For example, football, in which the goal is to gain territory against an opponent, may more accurately reflect contemporary American values than does baseball, a game in which "aggression is subservient to finesse."

If, as Schrank suggests, sports serve as "ritualistic enactments of the American Dream," consider what the currently popular pastimes tell us about the state of this American Dream. As you read, think about how your own favorite sports might provide some insight into your own character, attitudes, and approach to life.

• • • • • • • • • • • • • • • • • •

Sports is a ritual, an acting out of a myth or series of myths. A sport that can be considered a national pastime can be expected to reflect national values and wishes. Sports that capture the national fancy are ritualistic enactments of the American Dream. Baseball is still called our national pastime but is rapidly being replaced by American football. That football should become our "national pastime" is understandable to those who can see sports as reflections of national character.

American football is passionately concerned with the gain and loss of land, of territory. The football field is measured and marked with all the care of a surveyor and the ball's progress noted to the nearest inch. Football is a precise game and its players are often trained like a military unit on a mission to gain territory for the mother country. The players are the popular heroes but the coaches and owners run the game, using the players to carry out their plans—there is comparatively little room for individual initiative. A score comes as the result of a strategic series of well-executed maneuvers and is bought on the installment plan, yard by yard.

The regulation and almost military precision of American football is a reflection of national psychology. Even the words we use to describe the game include throwing the bomb, marching downfield, game plan (which has become nearly a national phrase for any field, from selling toothpaste to covering up political scandals), guards, executions, blitz, zone, platoon, squad, drills, attack, drives, marching bands for entertainment, stars on helmets, lines that can be blasted through and even war paint. Much of the verbal similarity comes from the fact that war was originally the ultimate game played within the confines of certain rules agreed upon by both "teams."

Football, more than any other sport, is a game for spectators to watch   4
superhuman, mythical heroes. Football is a sport that more people watch than play. The game requires too many people, too much space and is simply too dangerous for the weekend athlete. The size and speed of professional players and their uniforms make them into heroic figures capable of feats that invite admiration but not imitation. The football spectator is in awe of the armored monsters. The viewer of a golf match or even baseball or tennis dreams of going out the next day and doing likewise, but football is played only by the gods who can run the 100-yard dash in ten seconds, stand six feet three and weight 260 pounds.

The demise of baseball as our national pastime reflects a change in   5
national character. The change does not mean the disappearance of baseball, merely its relocation to a position as just another game rather than *the* game. Professor John Finlay of the University of Manitoba, writing in *Queen's Quarterlay,* compares baseball to an acting out of the robber baron stage of capitalism, whereas football more clearly reflects a more mature capitalism into which we are now moving. Hence, the rise in popularity of football and apparent decline in baseball. He notes that Japan, still in the early stages of capitalism, has taken avidly to baseball but not to football. It is not a question of Japanese physique serving as a determinant since rugby has a large Asian following. He predicts that when their capitalism moves into a higher stage, the Japanese will move on to football as have Americans.

Baseball is a game of a quieter age when less action was needed to   6
hold interest, when going to the park was enjoyable (baseball is still played in ball parks while football is played in stadiums), when aggression was subservient to finesse. Baseball players did not need exposure as college players to succeed as football players do; they play a relatively calm game almost daily instead of a bruising gladiatorial contest weekly. Baseball has room for unique and colorful characters, while football stresses the more anonymous but effective team member. Baseball is a game in which any team can win at any given contest and there are no favorites; only football has real "upsets." Football's careful concern with time adds a tension to the game that is lacking in the more leisurely world of baseball.

Football has replaced baseball as the favorite American spectator   7
sport largely because of television. A comparison between a telecast of
a football game on one channel and a baseball game on another could
reveal baseball as a game with people standing around seemingly with
little to do but watch two men play catch. Football would appear as
twenty-two men engaged in almost constant, frenzied action. To watch
baseball requires identification with the home team; to watch football
requires only a need for action or a week of few thrills and the need for
a touch of vicarious excitement.

Baseball is a pastoral game, timeless and highly ritualized; its ap-   8
peal is to nostalgia and so might enjoy periods of revitalization in comparison to football. But for now, the myth of football suits the nation
better.

According to a 1974 Harris survey, baseball has already been statis-   9
tically dethroned. In a sports survey a cross section of nearly fourteen
hundred fans was asked, "Which of these sports do you follow?"

The decision to play or "follow" a certain sport is also the decision   10
to live a certain myth. The team violence of football, the craftiness of basketball, the mechanistic precision of bowling, the auto racer's devotion
to machinery are all subworlds within the universe of sport.

Golf, for example, is a unique subworld, one of the few left as a sport   11
(unlike hunting, which does not involve scoring or teams) in which the
game is played between man and nature. The winner of a match is one
who has beaten the opponent, but the game itself is a person versus the
environment. To understand the appeal of golf it is again necessary to
consider the game as a ritual reenactment of an appealing myth.

Golf, perhaps more than any other sport, has to be played to be ap-   12
preciated. Millions who never played football can enjoy the game on TV,
but only a dedicated participant can sit through two hours of televised
golf. Golf is growing in participation but still has the stigma of an upper-
class game. Eighty percent of the nation's golfers must play on 20 percent of the nation's courses that are open to the public. The ratio of public to private facilities hurts public participation in the game but mirrors
the inequities of society and provides a convenient status symbol for
those who can afford club membership. Its TV audience is not the largest
of any sport but it is the most well heeled.

Golf is a reenactment of the pioneer spirit. It is man versus a hostile   13
environment in search of an oasis. The goal is a series of lush "greens,"
each protected by natural hazards such as water, sand and unmanage-
ably long grass. The hazards are no threat to physical life but they are to
the achievement of success. Golf is a journey game with a constantly
changing field. Golfers start the eighteen-hole journey, can rest at a

halfway point and then resume until they return to near the point of origination.

The winner of the match is one who has fallen victim to the fewest   14
hazards and overcome the terrain. Many golf courses have Indian names as if to remind the golfer of the frontier ethos. A local course called Indian Lakes invites golfers to use either one of two courses—the Iroquois trail or the Sioux trail.

Golf, like baseball, is a pastoral sport—with a high degree of ten-   15
sions and drama but relatively little action. It is a game in which players are constantly in awe of the magic flight of the golf ball. To hit any kind of ball 100 or 200 or more yards with accuracy or to hit a small target from 150 yards is an amazing feat to be appreciated only by those who have at least tried the game. Golf is very likely the most difficult game to master, yet one in which the average player occasionally hits a shot as good as the best of any professional. It is this dream of magic results that keeps the golfer on course.

••••••••••••••••••••

Examining the Text

1. Think about the significance of Schrank's title. What is the "American Dream," and what role does Schrank give sports in defining this Dream? Do you find his observations persuasive, or do you think he makes too much of the role of sports?

2. What do you think is Schrank's purpose in writing this essay? What recommendations, if any, do you think he would make about the sports Americans should choose to play or watch? Do you believe your own favorite sports reveal anything about your values and wishes?

3. Schrank wrote this essay in 1977. Some people would suggest that in the interim basketball has overtaken football as America's national pastime. What do you think the current popularity of basketball says about the American national character, and how might this shift fit Schrank's analysis of changing American preferences for certain sports?

For Group Discussion

Schrank states that "the decision to play or 'follow' a certain sport is also the decision to live a certain myth" (10). Reread the section on golf (11–15) and choose another "minor," but familiar sport. As a group, list some of the reasons this sport is appealing. What myths—about the environment, about teamwork and individuality, about winning and losing, for example—does this sport promote? How might it influence participants' beliefs, attitudes, or values? As a class, discuss the similarities and differences among each group's choice.

Writing Suggestion

Schrank's basic premise is that "a sport that can be considered a national pastime can be expected to reflect national values and wishes" (1). Look up information on a sport that is the national pastime of another country, such as hockey in Canada, cricket or rugby in England, or soccer in many European and South American countries. After learning about how the sport is played, and how fans respond, what conclusions can you draw about the "values and wishes" of the players and spectators? In an essay, explain the extent to which the sport reflects the national character of those who play it.

Jockpop: Popular Sports and Politics
James Combs

The following essay is excerpted from James Combs' book Polpop, *a study of the ways in which popular culture affects our political ideas and images. In "Jockpop," Combs looks at how playing and watching sports shapes our thoughts and actions in the realm of politics. Like Schaap and Schrank, Combs' basic premise is that "the 'lessons of sports' help orient us to the world." He argues that we are drawn to sports in large part because they teach us about "competition, teamwork, risk-taking, aggression and defense, winning and losing"; and voters and politicians alike apply these lessons to the world of politics.*

Combs identifies a number of ways in which sports and politics are interrelated. Sporting events provide a setting for political rituals and symbols, such as raising the American flag, singing the national anthem, and other expressions of patriotism. Sports provide metaphors and images politicians use in appealing to voters, explaining their policies, and promoting themselves and their programs. Sporting events, particularly international ones, may in addition take on political and national significance; Combs cites the victory of the American ice hockey team over the Soviet Union in the 1984 Olympics as an example of how a simple game can take on dramatic political overtones.

As you read, *note that Combs uses specific examples to support his general theory about the influence of sports on politics. Try to identify some of the* *ways in which your political views and the American political system in general would be different without the influence of sports.*

•••••••••••••••••••••

Sports and Learning

In the famous opening sequence of the movie *Patton*, General Patton (George C. Scott) delivered a speech to an audience of soldiers. He said in part:

> Men, all this stuff you've heard about America not wanting to fight, wanting to stay out of the war, is a lot of horsedung. Americans traditionally love to fight. All real Americans love the sting of battle. When you were kids you all admired the champion marble shooter, the fastest runner, the big league ballplayers, the toughest boxers. Americans play to win all the time. I wouldn't give a hoot in hell for a man who lost and laughed. That's why Americans have never lost, and will never lose a war, because the very thought of losing is hateful to Americans.

Let us reflect a moment, as General Patton urges, on growing up. When we were kids, we all quickly learned the importance of sports. Playing was fun, and indeed gave us a chance to prove ourselves. We discovered that organized sports at school and the Little League gave us an opportunity to play. We discovered that some could play better than others, that winning was valued, that there was a huge adult interest in sports. We found that there was a big world of sports in which adult athletes played before gigantic audiences for large amounts of money and glory. We adopted heroes among athletes in high school, or more remotely in the pro leagues. We attempted to bat, or dribble, or pass like them, even to act like them. If we hung around locker rooms or played, we heard the slogans: "Quitters never win, and winners never quit." Some of us experienced the "thrill of victory and the agony of defeat." We heard the speeches at sports banquets. We won letters, were cheerleaders and pompom girls, went to the school games. We talked about sports, followed college and pro sports, maybe even dreamed dreams of athletic glory.

And what effect did it all have on us? Specifically here, what impact does the play-world of sports have on politics? Like the other areas of the American play-world, popular sports is not "just a game." Rather, we learn much about the world from sports. Whether consciously or not, the "lessons of sports" help to orient us to the world. It is not an idle metaphor when we speak of the "game of life." For games, and what we are told about games, gives us much learning about life, and even politics. Sports is a form of play which we early on learn is important, come to value, and link to "real life."

Sports and Drama

The root of this may well be in the fact that sports are dramatic. 4
Games are an organized play-area, in which dramatic struggle (*agon*) occurs. The game becomes a public arena for the enactment of the more interesting aspects of human life—competition, teamwork, risk-taking, aggression and defense, winning and losing. Because sports dramatize in microcosm both eternal human truths and specific cultural truths, we are drawn in the same way we are drawn to drama. The drama "represents" life, lets us look at a heightened reality which dramatizes in the story what we want to know about life. Popular drama like soap operas dramatizes exemplary situations with which we can identify. Similarly, sports interest us because they possess such dramatic qualities. We learn from the "story" of a game because we can relate it to our lives. . . .

Sports and Politics

The dramatization of the American Dream in sports suggests that 5
sports has important meanings for us. It is likely that we "read into" sports a variety of messages, including political ones. So we should expect that sports would have political meanings and realize that these meanings have not been lost on politicians and observers of politics. Sometimes the sports-politics connection is obvious, sometimes subtle, but it is nevertheless there. For if sports is a key part of our cultural mythology, and is a play-setting for the dramatization of American myths, then its relevance for the world of politics and government exists. Therefore, we can explore some of the political meanings and uses of sports: sports as a setting for political *ritual;* as a metaphor for political *rhetoric;* as a dramatic microcosm of political *conflicts;* and as a political *resource.* We will consider these in turn.

Sports as a Setting for Political Ritual

Remember that we have stressed the ways that popular culture is a 6
political teacher. We learn things about ourselves as political beings from the social messages that a popular play-form communicates. An

important part of our political socialization was through patriotic ritual at school—saluting the flag, saying the Pledge of Allegiance, school spirit assemblies. But this is not the only setting for such symbolic dramas. We all remember the patriotic rituals attached to sporting events— the national anthem, raising the flag, color guards, and so forth. We would feel uneasy if a high school or college football game did not include such patriotic rituals.

These generalized rituals are more or less universal. Indeed, we 7 commonly expect sporting events to be clothed in not only political symbolism, but also religious symbolism as well. We all recall the invocations given before games, the players all praying in the huddle, and singing "God Bless America." Patriotic and religious symbols are, of course, closely linked in sports ritual. The presence of such ritual underscores that the event is not merely a game, but a play-event conducted with proper deference by participants and audience to transcendent values. The appeal is very largely to the moral community, as when the invocation prays that the players conduct the game with respect to moral values. Thus, the folk drama of sports comes to be imbued with patriotic rituals which remind us not only in what country the game is being played, but that the game occurs in the context of national values.

Now when a political crisis ensues, such patriotic ritual takes on a 8 more intensely felt meaning. During the Iranian crisis, it was common for football game rituals to recognize the hostages through moments of silence immediately before the national anthem was played, a dramatic reminder with political significance. Immediately after the release of the hostages, the 1981 Super Bowl became a festive setting for the ritual recognition of that celebrated event—everyone there wore yellow ribbons, and even the Superdome had a massive yellow ribbon on the outside.

But when the country is divided over some political issue, political 9 rituals at sports events can become controversial and excessive. During the height of the Vietnam War, there was a clear increase in the number of college football halftime shows that involved patriotic themes and pageantry. Indeed, in 1970 ABC refused to televise a halftime show planned by the University of Buffalo band which dramatized antiwar, antiracist, and antipollution themes through music and skits on the grounds that it would be a "political demonstration." But later that season ABC did televise a halftime show at the Army-Navy game which honored Green Berets who had just conducted an unsuccessful raid on a prisoner of war camp in North Vietnam, including statements by military officers critical of antiwar activity at home. So it depends upon whose moralistic myth is to be ritualized! Such incidents do remind us that sports involve the affirmation of cultural myths, since sports "participate" in the social order. Thus, "negative" rituals which celebrate a counter-myth conflict with the traditional patriotic function that sporting rituals have served.

In the past, political rituals which celebrated the symbols of government seemed especially appropriate for sporting events, since major sports seemed to embody so nicely aspects of the American Dream. If myths of the State come to be disbelieved or doubted, then such rituals may ring hollow for many people. One may wonder what sorts of feelings playing the national anthem before a game conjures up in our breasts. But whether we still believe or not, the fact remains that sports is a major stage for the dramatization of political symbols.   10

Sports as a Metaphor for Political Rhetoric

Politicians like to draw upon familiar symbols to illustrate some political point, and sports offer familiar and widely used metaphors. The language of the locker room permeates politics. Sports is a major repository of American mythology, so politicians can utilize the analogy safely assuming wide familiarity with the "lessons" of sports. Since politics has many game-like aspects, reference to the dynamics of sporting games as similar to "the game of politics" is natural. Both coaches and political figures seem to believe in the necessity of inspiration, which is the most common political use of sports analogies, allegories, parables, and so on.   11

The "values" of sports can also be for a variety of political uses. In particular, sports can illustrate the "truth" of either moralistic or materialistic myths. The American sports creed includes many tenets, most of which can be used to support or illustrate different political messages. Even though there is wide popular consensus that sports makes us "better citizens," what that means is subject to interpretation. For instance, Americans repeatedly agree on the positive lessons of sports: e.g., sports are worthwhile because they teach us "self-discipline"; sports are good because they promote "fair play"; and sports are positive because they teach "respect for authority and good citizenship." However, such virtues can be variously interpreted.   12

Let us illustrate this by reference to two often competing aspects of the sports creed: sportsmanship and winning. The ideal of sportsmanship has persisted in political rhetoric as a norm by which the game is supposed to be played, i.e., that one plays fair, enjoys the contest, and accepts victory with magnanimity and defeat with grace. Being a "good sport" was a trait admirable in all areas of life. The "truth" of sports was   13 not whether one won or lost, but how you played the game. A "sports-man" was a gentleman committed to excellence, but within ethical bounds and without cheap tactics. Such an image smacks of the "Ivy League" pop books of an earlier age about sports heroes such as Frank Merriwell.

This venerable notion has been applied to democratic politics again   14
and again. In a classic book about democracy, we learn that sportsman-ship, on the field or in politics, consists of such attitudes as tolerating and honoring the opposition; being a gracious winner and loser; and playing "the game of politics" within the bounds of rules and fair play.

This motif is complicated by a conflicting norm: winning. Winning   15
isn't everything, goes Lombardi's Law, it's the only thing. Nice guys, Durocher's Dictum has it, finish last. The winning motif is related to the idea of sports as war, in which winning takes precedence over gentle-manly traits, and indeed where sportsmanship is a hindrance to victory. The implicit locker room message is often that since winning is para-mount, any means, including bending or breaking the rules, unfair play, and intimidation, are justified. At the extreme, this can justify the virtue of sheer winning in politics. Indeed, the Nixon Administration's fond-ness for sports metaphors was thought to have contributed to the "Wa-tergate mentality," i.e., that the political world is a game of winners and losers locked in relentless strife, and since the "other side" are rogues and will do anything to win, we are justified in being just as nasty as them in order to win. The famous "Plumbers" office in the basement of the Nixon White House, consisting of those assigned to conduct break-ins, dirty tricks, and the like, had a sign that paraphrased Lombardi: "Winning in politics isn't everything, it's the only thing."

The sportsmanship theme is explicitly stated in political rhetoric,   16
but the winning theme, by emphasis, implicitly suggests to us the ne-cessity of aggressiveness, cunning, and even violence. In areas such as business and politics, the sports metaphor reflects the tension we feel about these two values. In business, for example, we believe that pur-suit of material goals all should be bound by the competitive rules of capitalism and moral rules derived from, say, religion; but we also rec-ognize and even admire the business sharpie who makes lots of money by circumventing the rules, participating in underhanded and even il-legal deals, and perhaps even using intimidation and violence. Our fas-cination with the superrich, instant millionaires, and gangsters stems in part from the popular belief that one cannot make it without being a scoundrel. Similarly, it has been widely believed since Machiavelli that one cannot acquire and use power unless you are not bound by moral rules. Since politics, like sports, is a mean and competitive world, the winners have to be equal to the task. Getting the "material" of power

and prestige in politics requires violating morality. Like the Godfather, you have to make people offers they can't refuse.

In American culture, our attitudes toward the conflicting values 17 have roots in the world-view termed social Darwinism. As a metaphor drawn from the theory of evolution, the Social Darwinists argued that business and politics were hard struggles in which the fittest survived and dominated. For this viewpoint, sports offers evidence that life is like that, and thus politics is by necessity that way. Therefore, we want people in charge who use power less bound by moral restraints. But if we take the more "civilized" view of this sportsmanship motif, business and politics, like sports, should be tamed and made fair. For the political rhetorician, sports offers analogies of both motifs, although the "winning" ethic is usually not blatantly said. In any case, it is an indication of a tension in our attitude toward American politics as to which sports metaphor we think most applicable to politics.

Sports as a Dramatic Microcosm of Political Conflicts

The old saw has it that sports reflect society. If sports is a mirror of 18 our conflicts, certainly when our divisions are politicized, sports become a dramatic microcosm of political conflicts. If groups experience material or moral lapses, they may be dramatized on the playing field. We have already mentioned how the post–World War II civil rights revolution was reflected in sports. Many other domestic conflicts work their way into sports. For example, it is nowadays popularly thought that America is a society of litigants eternally suing each other. Certainly this is reflected in sports which involves a great deal of liti-gation over the status of players, franchises, fans, the media, and so on. If Americans think that as a people we spend a great deal of time in court, they certainly are reinforced in that view by reading the sports page.

Perhaps the most spectacular way in which sports come to be in- 19 fested with politics involves international political conflicts. It is no secret that international sports—the Olympics, international track and field meets, even professional sports—often become embroiled in political controversies between nations.

The quadrennial Olympic games are the most important dramatic 20 forum with political overtones. Nations are interested in "proving" the superiority of their political values by success at the Olympic games. The Nazis tried to prove the superiority of the "Aryan race" at the 1936 Olympics, but the dramatic scenario backfired somewhat by the success of American black runners. Communist countries such as the Soviet Union and East Germany invest great resources into Olympic success, since this dramatizes the alleged superiority of "socialist man." Terrorists are attracted to such games to dramatize their cause, as was the case with the Palestinian group that kidnapped the Israeli athletes at the Munich Olympics of 1972.

But the most memorable recent incident involving the United States   21
occurred at the 1980 Winter Olympics. In late 1979, in an already volatile Middle East following the Iranian Revolution and the hostage crisis, the Soviet Union invaded Afghanistan. This was the culmination of a complex series of political events that signified the crisis of "detente" between the United States and the Soviet Union, and brought the world into one of those periods of international tension. Further, it was an election year in the United States, which made the role of American public opinion all the more crucial in the crisis. It became politically important for President Carter to respond to these developments, given the chauvinistic and retributive mood of the country. So he dispatched the fleet, agitated for Persian Gulf resistance to Soviet expansion, and cut off the shipment of some trade materials to the Russians.

But he did something else too: he called for a boycott of the 1980   22
Summer Olympic games in Moscow. He sent boxer Muhammad Ali to Africa to enlist support for the boycott. He advocated and arranged "alternative" games to be held somewhere other than Russia. He pressured NBC to not televise the Soviet Olympics, and stopped American companies from Olympic-related shipments to the Soviets. He sought the support of the athletes themselves, and of the international sports community. The political purpose, of course, was to symbolically (and in some measure, tangibly) "punish" the Soviets for the Afghanistan intervention.

In the midst of the new tension, a dramatic sports event occurred   23
which demonstrated how play can have political significance. At the Winter Olympics in Lake Placid, New York, the American hockey team unexpectedly upset the Soviets, 4–3. This triumph, and then later when the Americans won the gold medal by defeating the Finns, brought an outpouring of rejoicing and national pride. This outburst, which included many people who knew absolutely nothing about hockey, was clearly related to the new international tensions with the Soviets. The defeat of the Soviet hockey team was not "just a game." Boycotting the Olympic games for political reasons dramatized the importance accorded international sporting matches. Inviting the triumphant U.S. Winter Olympic team to the White House, including the cowboy-hatted hockey team, became the focus for national congratulations, and gave a dramatic role to a President up for re-election.

An international sporting event conducted in the midst of a political   24
crisis, then, can take on an intensely patriotic flavor, and, if victorious,

people can feel as if through play they have "won" some sort of political victory. It focuses political emotion onto the drama of the game, and thus gives us deep patriotic pride. Politicians and the news media recognized the political significance of the event, and gave it great play. The triumph gave occasion for political ritual at the White House, associating the event formally with patriotic symbols and offering ritual thanks to the athletes. The drama did nothing to undo Soviet political intentions, but it did help people to deal with their anxieties about international tensions and their own country's worth. The Olympic triumph signaled a new patriotic fervor in the United States, and helped to revive the moralistic myth about our "mission" in the world and national superiority. The hockey match and the national outburst it caused was a dramatic microcosm of a political crisis.

Sports as a Political Resource

Since sports are valued popular play-activities, it is common for 25
politicians to use sports and sports figures for a wide variety of political purposes. Like religion and show business, sports offer the politician association with something non-political that large numbers of people are attracted to. Not only do politicians use the rhetoric of sports for political purposes, they also express their interest in sports to dramatize their commonality. Candidates campaigning for office attend sporting events, mention the local team, and seek the endorsement of famous athletes. Endorsement-seeking illustrates how politics seeks out popular culture. The endorsement of a famous athlete somehow gives the aspiring politician a kind of popular status and humanity he might not earn otherwise. The athlete is an embodiment of both material and moral success on the playing-field, and the politician seems to think that with the association some of the heroic magic might rub off. All this is nothing new: both Al Smith and Herbert Hoover sought the endorsement of Babe Ruth in 1928! But it doesn't always work. Gerald Ford had an endless list of athletes who endorsed him in 1976, but he lost the election anyway. Ford and other politicians have been accused of being "jocksniffers," zealously exploiting their relationship to athletes and athletics, but the transfer of magic is not guaranteed.

President Carter did not appear to be a jocksniffer, but he was aware 26
of the political uses of participation in sports. He cultivated his Southern regional tie, including hunting, fishing, and wading in hipboots for bait. He reigned over slow-pitch softball games between the White House staff and the press. He became the First Jogger, and was pho-

tographed jogging in long distance races with troops in Korea. President Reagan liked to ride, and professed himself a sports fan. (Many older Americans associated him with sports through his depiction of "The Gipper," since he played Notre Dame's famous George Gipp in *Knute Rockne of Notre Dame* as well as baseball pitcher Grover Cleveland Alexander in *The Winning Team*.) It is always difficult to tell the extent to which sports participation by politicians stems from their desire to stay healthy and enjoy strenuous activity, or from their awareness that such activities are popular, and by participating they communicate to the public their common human interest. In any case, most recent Presidents have cultivated some form of popular leisure activity—golf, touch football, sailing, etc. However, if some of the recent revelations about President John Kennedy's "favorite leisure activity" are true, then it must be said that although golf and jogging have their virtues as sports, so does his, although the former type is most politically acceptable and performable in public.

Since sports figures do become popular embodiments of heroic success, the celebrity status they enjoy can become a resource for successful political recruitment. Having played college football or even some professional sport seems to have helped a wide variety of political figures, ranging from Ford to Supreme Court Justice Byron "Whizzer" White (a former All-American) and former baseball pitcher and House member Wilmer "Vinegar Bend" Mizell. Former NBA star Bill Bradley became Senator from New Jersey at least partially on his sports celebrity. Congressman Jack Kemp of New York ran for Congress in the city he was an NFL quarterback, stressed how quarterbacking gave him leadership qualities, and used the rhetoric of football for political purposes. It may be the case in the future that more politicians will be drawn from the ranks of well-known sports figures.   27

Conclusion

We have not exhausted the complex relationships between popular sports and political culture, but the above should give the reader the idea of some of the major linkages. As long as Americans are sports-crazy, we should expect that sports will have political relevance, and that "the game of politics" will be conducted in a culture that includes sports as a value.   28

••••••••••••••••••••

Examining the Text

1. What are some of the "eternal human truths" and "specific cultural truths" (paragraph 4) that Combs says we learn from sports? Can you think of others? Would everyone agree that these are "truths"?

2. Combs divides the main part of his essay (6–27) into four sections, each dealing with a different way in which sports is connected to politics. In your opinion, which of these four seems the *most* influential? Think of examples, other than those mentioned by Combs, to support your opinion.

3. Apply Combs' idea that we learn values and truths through sports to an area in our culture other than politics. For example, how does sports affect our notions of religion, education, or work? You might want to use Combs' four categories (for example, *as a setting for religious ritual, as a metaphor for religious rhetoric,* and so forth).

For Group Discussion

Imagine that your group is assigned to write a speech for a political candidate. Come up with a list of metaphors and images drawn from the world of sports that your candidate could use to appeal to voters. You can refer to Combs' essay, as well as other readings in this chapter, for ideas. As a class, consider the effect of such metaphors on the American political process.

Writing Suggestion

Combs gives an *objective* description of the influence of sports on politics; he doesn't take sides or make recommendations. Using his writing as a resource, write an essay in which you argue either that sports should have (a) less influence on politics, or (b) greater influence on politics. To do this, you'll need to consider both the problems and the benefits of sports' role in the political world.

Why Men Fear Women's Teams

Kate Rounds

Kate Rounds is a freelance writer and a contributor to Ms. *magazine, where this essay originally appeared. She argues here that female athletes have very few opportunities in the world of professional sports, and that women's team sports in particular are faced with what amounts to complete neglect in the media. Since professional sports are big business, if women's sports don't draw the fans and the money, then there's little hope that their professional leagues will last. College sports are similarly male-dominated, although Title IX requires colleges to devote equivalent resources to men's and women's athletic programs. Rounds' essay reminds us that when we discuss popular professional and collegiate sports, we're almost always referring to men's sports, and that sexual bias and gender stereotypes are still strong.*

Rounds contrasts the failure of a number of professional women's leagues (basketball, volleyball, and baseball) in the United States with the success of such enterprises in Europe, Japan, and elsewhere. The question, then, is why Americans fail to support talented female athletes in all but a few sports. Rounds ultimately concludes that the failure of women's professional sports reveals a "deep-rooted sexual bias and homophobia" in our culture, and that we haven't yet fully accepted a notion of femininity that incorporates power, athletic skill, and female camaraderie.

***Before you read,** think back to the essays earlier in this chapter. To what extent do the ideas of Schaap, Schrank, and Combs hold true for professional women's sports? And how might these authors account for gender discrimination in professional sports?*

•••••••••••••••••••

Picture this. You're flipping through the channels one night, and   1
you land on a local network, let's say ABC. And there on the screen is a basketball game. The players are sinking three-pointers, slam-dunking, and doing the usual things basketball players do. They're high-fiving each other, patting one another on the butt, and then sauntering to the locker room to talk about long-term contracts.

Now imagine that the players aren't men. They're women, big   2
sweaty ones, wearing uniforms and doing their version of what guys thrive on—bonding. So far, this scene is a fantasy and will remain so until women's professional team sports get corporate sponsors, television exposure, arenas, fan support, and a critical mass of well-trained players.

While not enough fans are willing to watch women play traditional   3
team sports, they love to watch women slugging it out on roller-derby rinks and in mud-wrestling arenas. Currently popular is a bizarre television spectacle called *American Gladiators,* in which women stand on pastel pedestals, wearing Lycra tights and brandishing weapons that look like huge Q-Tips. The attraction obviously has something to do with the "uniforms."

The importance of what women athletes wear can't be underesti-   4
mated. Beach volleyball, which is played in the sand by bikini-clad women, rates network coverage while traditional court volleyball can't

marshal any of the forces that would make a women's pro league succeed.

It took a while, but women were able to break through sexist barri- 5 ers in golf and tennis. Part of their success stemmed from the sports themselves—high-end individual sports that were born in the British Isles and flourished in country clubs across the U.S. The women wore skirts, makeup, and jewelry along with their wristbands and warm-up jackets. The corporate sponsors were hackers themselves, and the fan— even men—could identify with these women; a guy thought that if he hit the ball enough times against the barn door, he too could play like Martina. And women's purses were equaling men's. In fact, number-one-ranked Steffi Graf's prize money for 1989 was $1,963,905 and number-one-ranked Stefan Edberg's was $1,661,491.

By contrast, women's professional team sports have failed spectacu- 6 larly. Since the mid-seventies, every professional league—softball, basketball, and volleyball—has gone belly-up. In 1981, after a four-year struggle, the Women's Basketball League (WBL), backed by sports promoter Bill Byrne, folded. The league was drawing fans in a number of cities, but the sponsors weren't there. TV wasn't there, and nobody seemed to miss the spectacle of a few good women fighting for a basketball.

Or a volleyball, for that matter. Despite the success of bikini volley- 7 ball, an organization called MLV (Major League Volleyball) bit the dust in March of 1989 after nearly three years of struggling for sponsorship, fan support, and television exposure. As with pro basketball, there was a man behind women's professional volleyball, real estate investor Robert (Bat) Batinovich. Batinovich admits that, unlike court volleyball, beach volleyball has a lot of "visual T&A mixed into it."

What court volleyball does have, according to former MLV execu- 8 tive director Lindy Vivas, is strong women athletes. Vivas is assistant volleyball coach at San Jose State University. "The United States in general," she says, "has problems dealing with women athletes and strong, aggressive females. The perception is you have to be more aggressive in team sports than in golf and tennis, which aren't contact sports. Women athletes are looked at as masculine and get the stigma of being gay."

One former women's basketball promoter, who insists on remain- 9 ing anonymous, goes further. "You know what killed women's sports?" he says. "Lesbians. This cost us in women's basketball. But I know there are not as many lesbians now unless I'm really blinded. We discourage it, you know. We put it under wraps."

People in women's sports spend a lot of time dancing around the 10 "L" word, and the word "image" pops up in a way it never does in men's sports. Men can spit tobacco juice, smoke, and even scratch their testicles on national television and get away with it.

Bill Byrne, former WBL promoter, knows there isn't a whole lot   11
women can get away with while they're beating each other out for a basketball. "In the old league," he says, "my partner, Mike Connors, from
Mannix—his wife said, 'Let's do makeup on these kids.' And I knew that
the uniforms could be more attractive. We could tailor them so the
women don't look like they're dragging a pair of boxer shorts down the
floor."

The response from the athletes to this boy talk is not always outrage.   12
"Girls in women's basketball now are so pretty," says Nancy Lieberman-Cline. "They're image-conscious." The former Old Dominion star,
who made headlines as Martina's trainer, played with the men's U.S.
Basketball League, the Harlem Globe Trotters Tour (where she met husband Tim Cline), and with the Dallas Diamonds of the old WBL. "Everyone used to have short hair," she says. "Winning and playing was everything. I wouldn't think of using a curling iron. Now there are beautiful
girls out there playing basketball."

Lieberman-Cline says she doesn't mind making the concession.   13
"It's all part of the process," she says. "You can't be defensive about
everything."

Bill Byrne is so certain that women's professional basketball can   14
work that he's organized a new league, the Women's Pro Basketball
League, Inc. (WPBL), set to open its first season shortly. Byrne talks fast
and tough, and thinks things have changed for the better since 1981
when the old league went under. "Exposure is the bottom word," he
says. "If you get plenty of TV exposure, you'll create household names,
and you'll fill arenas. It takes the tube. But I'll get the tube this time because the game of TV has changed. You have cable now. You have to
televise home games to show people a product."

There's no doubt that many athletes in the women's sports estab-   15
lishment are leery of fast-talking guys who try to make a buck off wom-
en's pro sports, especially when the women themselves don't profit
from those ventures. In the old league, finances were so shaky that some
players claim they were never paid.

"We weren't getting the gate receipts," says Lieberman-Cline.   16
"They'd expect 2,000, get only 400, and then they'd have to decide to
pay the arena or pay the girls, and the girls were the last choice. There
was a lot of mismanagement in the WBL, though the intent was good."
She also has her doubts about the new league: "There are not enough
things in place to make it happen, not enough owners, arenas, TV coverage, or players. It's going to take more than optimism to make it
work."

Given the track record of women's professional team sports in this   17
country, it's not surprising that the national pastime is faring no better.

When Little League was opened to girls by court order in 1974, one might have thought that professional women's baseball could not be far behind. Baseball is a natural for women. It's not a contact sport, it doesn't require excessive size or strength—even little guys like Phil Rizzuto and Jose Lind can play it—and it's actually an individual sport masquerading as a team sport. Still, in recent years, no one's taken a serious stab at organizing a women's professional league.

In 1984, there was an attempt to field a women's minor-league team. 18 Though the Sun Sox had the support of baseball great Hank Aaron, it was denied admission to the Class A Florida State League. The team was the brainchild of a former Atlanta Braves vice president of marketing, Bob Hope. "A lot of the general managers and owners of big-league clubs were mortified," Hope says, "and some players said they wouldn't compete against women. It was male ego or something."

Or something, says softball hall-of-famer Donna Lopiano. "When 19 girls suffer harassment in Little League, that's not exactly opening up opportunities for women," she says. "Girls don't have the access to coaching and weight training that boys have. Sports is a place where physiological advantages give men power, and they're afraid of losing it. Sports is the last great bastion of male chauvinism. In the last eight years, we've gone backward, not only on gender equity but on civil rights."

Women of color still face barriers that European American women 20 don't, particularly in the areas of coaching and refereeing. But being a woman athlete is sometimes a bond that transcends race. "We're all at a handicap," says Ruth Lawanson, an African American who played volleyball with MLV. "It doesn't matter whether you're Asian, Mexican, black or white."

Historically, baseball and softball diamonds have not been very 21 hospitable to black men and any women. Despite the fact that even men's softball is not a crowd pleaser, back in 1976, Billie Jean King and golfer Jane Blalock teamed up with ace amateur softball pitcher Joan Joyce to form the International Women's Professional Softball Association (IWPSA). Five years later, without sponsorship, money, or television, the league was history.

Billie Jean King has her own special attachment to the team concept. 22 As a girl, she wanted to be a baseball player, but her father gave her a tennis racket, knowing that there wasn't much of a future for a girl in baseball. The story is especially touching since Billie Jean's brother, Randy Moffitt, went on to become a pitcher with the San Francisco Giants. But even as a tennis player, Billie Jean clung to the team idea. She was the force behind World TeamTennis, which folded in 1978, and is currently the chief executive officer of TeamTennis, now entering its eleventh season with corporate sponsorship.

On the face of it, TeamTennis is a bizarre notion because it takes   23
what is a bred-in-the-bones individual sport and tries to squeeze it into a team concept. It has the further handicap of not really being necessary when strong women's and men's professional tours are already in place.

In the TeamTennis format, all players play doubles as well as sin-   24
gles. Billie Jean loves doubles, she says, because she enjoys "sharing the victory." What also distinguishes TeamTennis from the women's and men's pro tours is fan interaction. Fans are encouraged to behave as if watching a baseball or basketball game rather than constantly being told to shut up and sit down as they are at pro tour events like the U.S. Open. The sense of team spirit among the players—the fact that they get to root for one another—is also attracting some big names. Both Martina Navratilova and Jimmy Connors have signed on to play TeamTennis during its tiny five-week season, which begins after Wimbledon and ends just before the U.S. Open.

But you have to go back almost 50 years to find a women's profes-   25
sional sports team that was somewhat successful—though the conditions for that success were rather unusual. During World War II, when half the population was otherwise engaged, women were making their mark in the formerly male strongholds of welding, riveting—and baseball. The All-American Girls Professional Baseball League (AAGPBL) fielded such teams as the Lassies, the Belles, and the Chicks on the assumption that it was better to have "girls" playing than to let the national pastime languish. The league lasted a whopping 12 years after its inception in 1943.

The success of this sandlot venture, plagued as it was by the sim-   26
ple-hearted sexism of the forties (the women went to charm school at night), must raise nagging doubts in the mind of the woman team player of the nineties. Can she triumph only in the absence of men?

It may be true that she can triumph only in the absence of competi-   27
tion from the fiercely popular men's pro leagues, which gobble up sponsorship. U.S. network television, and the hearts and minds of male fanatics. The lack of male competition outside the United States may be partly responsible for the success of women's professional team sports in Europe, Japan, South America, and Australasia. Lieberman-Cline acknowledges that Europe provides a more hospitable climate for women's pro basketball. "Over there, they don't have as many options," she says. "We have Broadway plays, movies, you name it. We're overindulged with options."

Bruce Levy is a 230-pound bespectacled accountant who escaped 28
from the Arthur Andersen accounting firm 11 years ago to market women's basketball. "It's pretty simple," he says. "People overseas are more realistic and enlightened. Women's basketball is not viewed as a weak version of men's. If Americans could appreciate a less powerful, more scientific, team-oriented game, we'd be two-thirds of the way toward having a league succeed."

Levy, who represents many women playing pro basketball abroad, 29
says 120 U.S. women are playing overseas and making up to $70,000 in a seven-month season. They include star players like Teresa Edwards, Katrina McClain, and Lynette Woodward. "A player like Teresa Weatherspoon, everybody recognizes her in Italy," he says. "No one in the U.S. knows her. If there were a pro league over here, I wouldn't be spending all day on the phone speaking bad Italian and making sure the women's beds are long enough. I'd just be negotiating contracts."

Levy claims that U.S. businesswomen aren't supporting women's 30
team sports. "In Europe," he says, "the best-run and most publicized teams are run by women who own small businesses and put their money where their mouth is." Joy Burns, president of Sportswomen of Colorado, Inc., pleads no contest. "Businesswomen here are too conservative and don't stick their necks out," she says. MLV's Bat Batinovich, who says he's "disappointed" in U.S. businesswomen for not supporting women's team sports, figures an investor in MLV should have been willing to lose $200,000 a year for five years. Would Burns have done it? "If I'm making good financial investments, why should I?"

The prospects for women's professional team sports don't look 31
bright. The reasons for the lack of financial support go beyond simple economics and enter the realm of deep-rooted sexual bias and homophobia. San Jose State's Lindy Vivas says men who feel intimidated by physically strong women have to put the women down. "There's always a guy in the crowd who challenges the women when he wouldn't think of going one-on-one with Magic Johnson or challenging Nolan Ryan to a pitching contest."

Softball's Donna Lopiano calls it little-boy stuff: "Men don't want 32
to have a collegial, even-steven relationship with women. It's like dealing with cavemen."

....

Examining the Text

1. How do you respond to the title of this essay? According to Rounds, why do men fear women's teams? What do you think of her reasoning?

2. Rounds points out that individual sports (like tennis and golf) give female athletes more exposure and opportunities for success than team sports. How does she explain this difference? Why do you think women's professional team sports are not popular in the United States? Have you had many opportunities to watch female teams play? How do you think this affects your answer?

3. Summarize the role of television and business in the promotion of professional women's sports. How do mass media and business alter women's sports, according to Rounds? To what extent do they also alter men's sports?

For Group Discussion

Softball player Donna Lopiano is quoted as saying that "sports is the last bastion of male chauvinism." Discuss your group's reactions to Lopiano's statement. List some possible reasons that women today might have greater opportunities in other traditionally male-dominated professions than in sports. Also list any evidence that contradicts Lopiano's claim. As a class, consider whether women's situation in professional sports is likely to change.

Writing Suggestion

Assuming that Rounds' assertion that women have few opportunities in the world of professional sports is correct, do you think this is a significant problem? Determine some of the specific benefits that women miss because of gender discrimination in sports. In an essay express your opinions about what (if anything) should be done to offer women greater access to these benefits.

ANALYZING SPORTS

The Greatest Game

Stefan Kanfer

In the following selection, which originally appeared in Time *in 1973, Stefan Kanfer talks about why professional baseball has such an enduring appeal. Kanfer is a long-time observer of American culture, who writes in popular periodicals such as* Time *and* Life.

Like Jeffrey Schrank in "Sport and the American Dream" Kanfer sees sports as a reflection of the national character and finds football, basketball, and hockey probably closer to the "Zeitgeist," or spirit of the times. However, Kanfer maintains that baseball still has a "hold on the national imagination." In addition to its seasonal association and its intellectual complexity, baseball has a certain timelessness that appeals to us. Kanfer points out that baseball records seem to last longer than other sports' records, and that during the game itself time functions differently than in, say, football or basketball. Kanfer also argues that baseball, despite some changes, has remained basically intact, and so draws us back to an earlier era in our nation's history.

Since Kanfer wrote his essay in 1973, test his statements against the current state of baseball as you read. Has the sport changed significantly in the past twenty years or so, or does the appeal Kanfer describes still hold true?

• • • • • • • • • • • • • • • • • • • •

Slow? Players have been know to sleep *during* a game. Unfocused? 1
It begins when the hockey rinks are frozen and ends when footballs are tossed in snow flurries.

Archaic? Its greatest heroes are locked in the mythic past, an epoch 2
located roughly between the Jurassic era and World War II.

Unfashionable? Of all major team sports, it is the only one that is not 3
played against a clock.

By all rational standards, baseball should have gone the way of the 4
bison and the convertible by now. But there are no rational standards in love. Besieged by Masters tournaments, Olympics, track meets and Super Bowls, the fans have kept baseball incredibly popular. In a recent Harris poll, they were asked which championship event they would prefer to attend. Results:

1. World Series: 23%
2. Super Bowl: 20%

3. Kentucky Derby: 10%

4. Indianapolis 500: 10%

5. College bowl game: 8%

Why should baseball, with its sluggish metabolism and lack of   5
crunch, retain its hold on the national imagination? The answer lies
partly in its seasonal associations. No one is immune to the vernal equi-
nox. The same jump of the blood occurs on ghetto streets and Little
League diamonds, in bleachers and in front of the TV screen. Baseball
implies an earthly benignity: clear skies, vacations and, above all, no
school.

Secondly, there is the peculiarly intellectual quality of the game,   6
with its geometric layout and its deep well of tradition. Philip Roth,
whose new book *The Great American Novel* concerns the fortunes of a
homeless baseball team, recalls: "Not until I got to college and was introduced to literature did I find anything with a comparable emotional
atmosphere and as strong an esthetic appeal . . . baseball, with its lon-
geurs and thrills, its spaciousness . . . its peculiarly hypnotic tedium, its
heroics, its nuances, its `characters,' its language, and its mythic sense
of itself, was the literature of my boyhood."

Almost from the beginning, novelists have gone to bat for the game.   7
Ring Lardner saw baseball as the great American comedy—look through
the knothole and you found uniformed counterparts of Huck Finn and
Charlie Chaplin.

The magic works for spectators as well as novelists. In *The Summer*   8
Game, Roger Angell celebrates a field that never was: the Interior Stadium. "Baseball in the mind . . . is a game of recollections, recapturing
and visions . . . anyone can play this private game, extending it to extraordinary varieties and possibilities in his mind. Ruth bats against
Sandy Koufax or Sam McDowell . . . Hubbell pitches to Ted Williams.
Baseball, I must conclude, is intensely remembered because only baseball is so intensely watched."

No other sport *can* be so intensely watched. There is no jumbled   9
scrimmage that must be clarified with instant replay. The ball may approach home plate at 100 m.p.h. or crawl down the third-base line like
a crab. A 400-ft. fly ball may fall foul by two inches. As in chess, power
radiates from stationary figures. Yet on a given pitch, ten men may be
moving. Clearly, this is a game to be scrutinized.

With all the intensity, there is something more. Baseball's deepest   10
fascination lies in twin aspects of the game: records and time. In other
sports, the past is a laugh. Teen-age girls are breaking Johnny Weismuller's old Olympic marks. The four-minute mile has been shattered beyond repair. Pole vaulters, broad jumpers, skiers, quarterbacks, golfers,

chess players—they have all rewritten the record books until yesterday's hero is exposed as a man with feat of clay. Only baseball has re-
tained so many of its idols. No one has come close to Joe DiMaggio's 56-
game hitting streak of 1941. The Ted Williams of 1941 was the game's
last .400 hitter. Pitcher Cy Young's record of 511 victories has held for
two generations. This permanence extends to the game's oddballs, men
like Casey Stengel, who once tipped his hat to the crowd and released a
bird that was nesting in his hair; Bobo Holloman, who pitched only one
complete game in the majors—and that one a no-hitter. There are players whose names alone would render them immortal: Eli Grba, Fenton
Mole, Eppa Rixey, Wally Pipp, Napoleon Lajoie. All these men, the im-
mortals and the "flakes," exist like the game beyond the erosions of style
and time.

Down on the playing field, another version of time exists, Einstein-　11
ian in its complexity. Other sportsmen keep an eye on the minute hand,
hoping to "kill" the clock. In baseball, time is subservient to circum-
stance. An inning may last six pitches or 80 minutes. Official games have
gone 4½innings, and 26. That timelessness is at once the game's curse
and its glory. At the conclusion of his disastrous World Series with the
Mets, Baltimore Manager Earl Weaver philosophized, "You can't sit on
a lead and run a few plays into the line and just kill the clock. You've got
to throw the ball over the goddam plate and give the other man his
chance." Then he paused and concluded: "That's why baseball is the
greatest game of them all."

Or is it? Surely football is closer to the *Zeitgeist,* with its chatter of　12
"long bombs" and marches downfield. Surely basketball with its constant scoring, or hockey with its eruptions of violence, is America's ideal
spectator sport. The conservative, hidebound sport of baseball can offer
no such qualities; scoring is rare, violence a matter of tempers, not policy. The game is an echo of a vanished pre-TV, prewar America, a by-
gone place of leisure and tranquility.

Baseball was doomed when the Black Sox scandal revealed that the　13
World Series of 1919 was fixed by gamblers. It was finished when it refused to admit black players—gifted men who were forced to play in
brilliant, threadbare leagues where only the ball was white. It was dead
when attendance wavered and franchises fled hysterically to Seattle,
Kansas City, Atlanta, Oakland.

The game survived it all. How? Is it because of the inexhaustible　14
promotional gimmicks, the bat and ball and senior citizens days; the
all-weather artificial turf; the dazzling uniforms? Is it the metaphysics
and momentum that still continue from the zenith of the '30s and '40s?
Or is it that this supposedly stolid, permanent game has impercep-
tibly accommodated change—that in each era it has accepted phys-

ical, textual and social alterations that a decade before had seemed impossibly revolutionary? Is it that, in the end, no other sport is so accurate a reflection of the supposedly stolid, permanent—and ultimately changeable—country that surrounds the interior and exterior stadiums?

••••••••••••••••••••

Examining the Text

1. What is Kanfer's strategy for opening his essay (paragraphs 1–3)? Why might he have chosen to do this? Do you find the strategy effective? Why or why not?

2. List some of the reasons Kanfer gives for baseball's continuing popularity. Which seem most persuasive to you, and why? How do you respond to Kanfer's comments about football, basketball, and hockey in paragraph 12?

3. In paragraph 11 Kanfer suggests that in baseball "another version of time exists, Einsteinian in its complexity." What do you think he means? Why does he say that "timelessness is at once the game's curse and its glory?"

For Group Discussion

Suppose that you have been charged with designing an advertising campaign to promote major league baseball. Which of Kanfer's ideas would you use? How would you convert his ideas into an advertisement for baseball? With your group, develop a specific proposal for such a campaign—including who you would target and the media you would use to reach that audience. Draw on Kanfer's essay and your own thoughts about baseball.

Writing Suggestion

Referring to Kanfer's comments on time in baseball, as well as to other essays in this chapter and your own experience as a player or spectator, extend the comparison of the role that time plays in several different sports. You might begin by listing four or five sports and noting the similarities and differences among them. Does time serve as a constraint in the game, do teams or individuals play against a clock, or is the time factor basically insignificant? To what extent does time enter into spectators' enjoyment and their general level of excitement? Use your comparison to write an essay which analyzes the similarities and differences among several sports in terms of time.

The Black and White Truth about Basketball

Jeff Greenfield

Jeff Greenfield, a political and media analyst for ABC News and a syndicated newspaper columnist, has written extensively about contemporary American culture, focusing on politics, sports, and the media. Originally published in 1975, the essay which follows has been widely anthologized since then and was updated by the author in 1988.

Greenfield's thesis is that there are two different styles—a "black style" and a "white style"—of playing basketball and that these result from differences in the environments the players grow up in. So, although his analysis of basketball focuses on the game and how it's played, Greenfield also looks closely at broader cultural influences. This essay is notable both for its controversial thesis and for its rhetorical technique: this is an excellent example of an essay of comparison and contrast, in which "black" and "white" basketball are carefully contrasted in terms of their style, how they evolved, and how different players embody each style.

As you read, *notice the form of Greenfield's essay, as well as its content. What organizational and descriptive techniques does he use to convey his ideas clearly and persuasively? Do you find yourself agreeing with his points? Why or why not?*

....

The dominance of black athletes over professional basketball is beyond dispute. Two-thirds of the players are black, and the number would be greater were it not for the continuing practice of picking white bench warmers for the sake of balance. Over the last two decades, no more than three white players have been among the ten starting players on the National Basketball Association's All-Star team, and in the last quarter century, only two white players—Dave Cowens and Larry Bird of the Boston Celtics—have ever been chosen as the NBA's Most Valuable Player. 1

And at a time when a baseball executive could lose his job for asserting that blacks lacked "the necessities" to become pro sports executives and when the National Football League still has not hired a single black head coach, the NBA stands as a pro sports league that hired its first black head coach in 1968 (Bill Russell) and its first black general manager in the early 1970s (Wayne Embry of the Milwaukee Bucks). What discrimination remains—lack of equal opportunity for speaking engagements and product endorsements—has more to do with society than with basketball. 2

This dominance reflects a natural inheritance: Basketball is a pas-   3
time of the urban poor. The current generation of black athletes are heirs
to a tradition more than half a century old. In a neighborhood without
the money for bats, gloves, hockey sticks and ice skates, or shoulder
pads, basketball is an eminently accessible sport. "Once it was the game
of the Irish and Italian Catholics in Rockaway and the Jews on Fordham
Road in the Bronx," writes David Wolf in his brilliant book, *Foul!* "It
was recreation, status, and a way out." But now the ethnic names have
been changed: Instead of the Red Holzinans, Red Auerbachs, and the
McGuire brothers, there are Julius Ervings and Michael Jordans, Ralph
Sampsons and Kareem Abdul-Jabbars. And professional basketball is a
sport with national television exposure and million-dollar salaries.

But the mark on basketball of today's players can be measured by   4
more than money or visibility. It is a question of style. For there is a clear
difference between "black" and "white" styles of play that is as clear as
the difference between 155th Street at Eighth Avenue and Crystal City,
Missouri. Most simply (remembering we are talking about culture, not
chromosomes), "black" basketball is the use of superb athletic skill to
adapt to the limits of space imposed by the game. "White" ball is the
pulverization of that space by sheer intensity.[1]

It takes a conscious effort to realize how constricted the space is on   5
a basketball court. Place a regulation court (ninety-four by fifty feet) on
a football field, and it will reach from the back of the end zone to the
twenty-one-yard line; its width will cover less than a third of the field.
On a baseball diamond, a basketball court will reach from home plate to
first base. Compared to its principal indoor rival, ice hockey, basketball
covers about one-fourth the playing area. Moreover, during the normal
flow of the game, most of the action takes place on the third of the court
nearest the basket. It is in this dollhouse space that ten men, each of them
half a foot taller than the average man, come together to battle each
other.

There is, thus, no room; basketball is a struggle for the edge: the half   6
step with which to cut around the defender for a lay-up, the half second
of freedom with which to release a jump shot, the instant a head turns
allowing a pass to a teammate breaking for the basket. It is an arena for
the subtlest of skills: the head fake, the shoulder fake, the shift of body
weight to the right and the sudden cut to the left. Deception is crucial to

---

[1] This distinction has nothing to do with the question of whether whites can play as "well"
as blacks. In 1987, the Detroit Piston's Isaiah Thomas quipped that the Celtics' Larry Bird was
"a pretty good player," but would be much less celebrated and wealthy if he were black. As
Thomas later said, Bird is one of the greatest pro players in history. Nor is this distinction
about "smart," although the Los Angeles Lakers' Magic Johnson is right in saying that too
many journalists ascribe brilliant strategy by black players to be solely due to "innate" ability.

success; and to young men who have learned early and painfully that life is a battle for survival, basketball is one of the few pursuits in which the weapon of deception is a legitimate tactic rather than the source of trouble.

If there is, then, the need to compete in a crowd, to battle for the   7
edge, then the surest strategy is to develop the *unexpected:* to develop a shot that is simply and fundamentally different from the usual methods of putting the ball in the basket. Drive to the hoop, but go under it and come up the other side; hold the ball at waist level and shoot from there instead of bringing the ball up to eye level; leap into the air, but fall away from the basket instead of toward it. All these tactics, which a fan can see embodied in the astonishing play of the Chicago Bulls' Michael Jordan, take maximum advantage of the crowding on the court. They also stamp uniqueness on young men who may feel it nowhere else.

"For many young men in the slums," David Wolf writes, "the school   8
yard is the only place they can feel true pride in what they do, where they can move free of inhibitions and where they can, by being spectacular, rise for the moment against the drabness and anonymity of their lives. Thus, when a player develops extraordinary 'school yard' moves and shots . . . [they] become his measure as a man."

So the moves that begin as tactics for scoring soon become calling   9
cards. You don't just lay the ball in for an uncontested basket; you take the ball in both hands, leap as high as you can, and slam the ball through the hoop. When you jump in the air, fake a shot, bring the ball back to your body, and throw up a shot, all without coming back down, you have proven your worth in uncontestable fashion.

This liquid grace is an integral part of "black" ball, almost exclu-   10
sively the province of the playground player. Some white stars like Bob Cousy, Billy Cunningham, and Doug Collins had it, and the Celtics' Kevin McHale has it now: the body control, the moves to the basket, the free-ranging mobility. Most of them also possessed the surface ease that is integral to the "black" style; an incorporation of the ethic of mean streets—to "make it" is not just to have wealth but to have it without strain. Whatever the muscles and organs are doing, the face of the "black" star almost never shows it. Magic Johnson of the Lakers can bring the ball down court with two men on him, whip a pass through an invisible opening, cut to the basket, take a return pass, and hit the shot all with no more emotion than a quick smile. So stoic was San Antonio Spurs' great George Gervin that he earned the nickname "Ice Man." (Interestingly, a black coach like Boston's K. C. Jones exhibits far less emotion on the bench than a white counterpart like Dick Motta or Jack Ramsey.)

If there is a single trait that characterizes "black" ball it is leaping   11
ability. Bob Cousy, ex-Celtic great and former pro coach, says that
"when coaches get together, one is sure to say, 'I've got the one black kid
in the country who can't jump.' When coaches see a white boy who can
jump or who moves with extraordinary quickness, they say, 'He should
have been born black, he's that good.'"

Don Nelson, now a top executive with the Golden State Warriors,   12
recalls that back in 1970, Dave Cowens, then a relatively unknown graduate of Florida State, prepared for his rookie pro season by playing the
Rucker League, an outdoor competition in Harlem playgrounds that
pits pros against college kids and playground stars. So ferocious was
Cowens' leaping ability, Nelson says, that "when the summer was over,
everyone wanted to know who the white son of a bitch was who could
jump so high." That's another way to overcome a crowd around the basket—just go over it.

Speed, mobility, quickness, acceleration, "the moves"—all of these   13
are catch-phrases that surround the "black" playground athlete, the
style of play. So does the most racially tinged of attributes, "rhythm."
Yet rhythm is what the black stars themselves talk about: feeling the flow
of the game, finding the tempo of the dribble, the step, the shot. It is an
instinctive quality (although it stems from hundreds of hours of practice), and it is one that has led to difficulty between system-oriented
coaches and free-form players.

"Cats from the street have their own rhythm when they play," said   14
college dropout Bill Spivey, onetime New York high school star. "It's not
a matter of somebody setting you up and you shooting. You *feel* the shot.
When a coach holds you back, you lose the feel and it isn't fun anymore."

When legendary Brooklyn playground star Connie Hawkins was   15
winding up his NBA career under Laker coach Bill Sharman, he chafed
under the methodical style of play. "He's systematic to the point where
it begins to be a little too much. It's such an action-reaction type of game
that when you have to do everything the same way, I think you lose
something."

There is another kind of basketball that has grown up in America.   16
It is not played on asphalt playgrounds with a crowd of kids competing
for the court; it is played on macadam driveways by one boy with a
ball and a backboard nailed over the garage; it is played in gyms in the
frigid winter of the rural Midwest and on Southern dirt courts. It is
a mechanical, precise development of skills (when Don Nelson was
an Iowa farm boy, his incentive to make his shots was that an errant
rebound would land in the middle of chicken droppings). It is a
game without frills, without flow, but with effectiveness. It is "white"

basketball: jagged, sweaty, stumbling, intense. Where a "black" player overcomes an obstacle with finesse and body control, a "white" player reacts by outrunning or overpowering the obstacle.

By this definition, the Boston Celtics are a classically "white" team. 17 They rarely suit up a player with dazzling moves; indeed such a player would probably make Red Auerbach swallow his cigar. Instead, the Celtics wear you down with execution, with constant running, with the same play run again and again and again. The rebound by Robert Parrish triggers the fast break, as everyone races downcourt; the ball goes to Larry Bird, who pulls up and takes the shot or who drives and then finds Danny Ainge or Kevin McHale free for an easy basket.

Perhaps the most definitively "white" position is that of the quick 18 forward, one without great moves to the basket, without highly developed hosts, without the height and mobility for rebounding effectiveness. So what does he do?

He runs. He runs from the opening jump to the final buzzer. He runs 19 up and down the court, from base line to base line, back and forth under the basket, looking for the opening, the pass, the chance to take a quick step, the high percentage shot. To watch San Antonio's Mark Olberding or Detroit's Bill Lambeer, players without speed or obvious moves, is to wonder what they are doing in the NBA—until you see them swing free and throw up a shot that, without demanding any apparent skill, somehow goes in the basket more frequently than the shots of many of their more skilled teammates. And to have watched the New York Knicks' (now U.S. Senator) Bill Bradley, or the Celtics' John Havlicek, is to have watched "white" ball at its best.

Havlicek or Lambeer, or the Laker's Kurt Rambis, stand in dramatic 20 contrast to Michael Jordan or to the Philadelphia 76ers' legend, Julius Erving. Erving had the capacity to make legends come true, leaping from the foul line and slam-dunking the ball on his way down; going up for a lay-up, pulling the ball to his body, and driving under and up the other side of the rim, defying gravity and probability with impossible moves and jumps. Michael Jordan of the Chicago Bulls has been seen by thousands spinning a full 360 degrees in midair before slamming the ball through the hoop.

When John Havlicek played, by contrast, he was the living embodi- 21 ment of his small-town Ohio background. He would bring the ball downcourt, weaving left, then right, looking for a path. He would swing the ball to a teammate, cut behind the pick, take the pass, and release the shot in a flicker of time. It looked plain, unvarnished. But it was a blend of skills that not more than half a dozen other players in the league possessed.

To former pro Jim McMillian, a black who played quick forward 22 with "white" attributes, "it's a matter of environment." Julius Erving grew up in a different environment from Havlicek. John came from a very small town in Ohio. There everything was done the easy way, the shortest distance between two points. It's nothing fancy; very few times will he go one-on-one. He hits the lay-up, hits the jump shot, makes the free throw, and after the game you look up and say, 'How did he hurt us that much?'"

"White" ball, then, is the basketball of patience, method and some-   23
times brute strength. "Black" ball is the basketball of electric self-expression. One player has all the time in the world to perfect his skills, the other a need to prove himself. These are slippery categories, because a poor boy who is black can play "white" and a white boy of middle-class parents can play "black." Bill Cartwright of the New York Knicks and Steve Alford of the Dallas Mavericks are athletes who seem to defy these categories.

And what makes basketball the most intriguing of sports is how   24
these styles do not necessarily clash; how the punishing intensity of "white" players and the dazzling moves of the "blacks" can fit together, a fusion of cultures that seems more and more difficult in the world beyond the out-of-bounds line.

••••••••••••••••••••

Examining the Text

1. What reasons does Greenfield give for the predominance of African-Americans in professional basketball? Are his reasons related primarily to race, class, environment, or to a combination of all three?

2. How does the "white style" of basketball differ from the "black style," as Greenfield describes them? How does he account for these differences? Why do you think Greenfield uses quotation marks around "black" and "white" throughout his essay?

3. When this essay was first published in *Esquire* in 1975, it sparked some controversy. Do you find anything controversial or potentially offensive in Greenfield's analysis? Do you think he wanted to cause controversy? If so, why? In determining your answer, consider the author's final paragraph as well as the comparisons he makes with other professional sports in paragraph 2.

For Group Discussion

Apply Greenfield's thesis about the different styles of playing basketball to another sport. (You need not focus on "black" and "white" styles, but rather look at "male" and "female" styles or at different styles embodied by individual players.) As a group, list two or more different, yet complementary, styles in the sport you choose. Describe the styles and how they complement each other, and consider reasons these differences might exist. Report your group's analysis to the class.

Writing Suggestion

In defining "black" and "white" styles of playing basketball, Greenfield vividly describes specific moves, shots, and plays made by players in general and by especially notable individuals. Using Greenfield's descriptions as a model, write your own detailed description of moves and plays in another sport. After your descriptions, try to draw some conclusions about why the sport is enjoyable for players and spectators alike.

Seven Points on the Game of Football

Arthur Asa Berger

*I*n *this chapter from his book* Media Analysis Techniques, *Arthur Asa Berger analyzes football from several different perspectives, treating it—he notes in his final paragraph—as "a creative effort . . . and a work of art that has performance aspects, aesthetic elements, and more."*

First he looks as a semiologist at the signs *in and around a football game: the arena in which it is played; the clothing of players, officials, and fans; the sometimes deceptive signals players send to one another. From these and other signs, Berger suggests we can see some of the different meanings football holds for our culture, as athletic activity, entertainment, even sexual display. (You might want to reread Berger's semiological analysis of the television comedy* Cheers *in Chapter 3.)*

Berger goes on to discuss football from a sociological perspective, noting that it teaches fans "how to get along in society, what roles to play, what life is all about. . . ." He suggests that football "reflects our contemporary social situation," and, from an anthropological perspective, that in many ways it serves as a contemporary alternative to religion, an arena of collective and passionate interest, ritual, mystery, and heroism. Berger also offers a brief interpretation of football from marxist and psychoanalytic perspectives.

As you read, *note Berger's "seven points" about football. Which points do you find particularly insightful, and how might you apply those insights to sports other than football?*

• • • • • • • • • • • • • • • • • • • •

Football Is a Game of Signs

Football is a very interesting subject for the semiologist because the   1
game is, at once, full of signs and also a signifier of some importance. The
stadium is itself one huge sign—a sacred space where enthusiasts (and
sometimes fanatics) gather to watch a highly organized, ritualized contest that many have suggested functions as an alternative to war. It is not
unusual for 60,000 people or more to gather together for a game, and
with television coverage sometimes millions of people watch a game,
which means that the entire country "becomes" a football stadium.

Where one sits in the stadium—on the fifty-yard line or way up be-   2
hind a goalpost—is a signifier of one's wealth or power or status. The
field itself is a huge grid, a one-hundred-yard rectangle of white lines
against brilliant green grass (or Astroturf). The intensity of the colors
adds considerably to the excitement of the event and must not be underestimated. On this field are to be seen people in all kinds of different
uniforms: the officials in their zebra strips, the players with their helmets and pads, matching bands, cheerleaders in sweaters and mini-
skirts, pom-pom girls, coaches with their earphones and electronic paraphernalia, drum majors and majorettes, and many other people. All of
these uniforms and trappings are signifiers of the wide variety of skills,
activities, and functions taking place at a game: rule enforcement, athletic activity, musical diversion, sexual display, planning and rationality, and so on. Thus a football game is not merely an athletic event but
part of a much larger system of events that are connected to the game
but which enlarge its significance greatly.

(I have not said anything about the people who attend the games   3
and who frequently wear the colors or emblems of their teams. Sometimes they carry signs. Frequently there are "sign sections" in stadiums
and various messages are flashed during halftime, when the bands play
and there are various entertainments.)

The game itself is based on signs. Signals are called in the huddles   4
announcing offensive plays. These signals are analogous to what we call
"codes," and indicate a precise series of activities that are to be followed
at a given point in time. Defensive players learn to watch their opponents for indications that a pass is to be thrown or a certain play is to be
run. And a good deal of the game is based on *deception*—that is, giving
opponents false signifiers so they will make mistakes. It is the capacity
of signs to lie, to give false information, that creates much of the complexity in the game.

The officials also use signs—a variety of gestures that indicate the   5
various penalties to be assessed for violations of the rules. These signals
are actually nonverbal, visual metaphors, which enable the officials to

indicate to everyone in the stadium the nature of a given transgression. The sign that is most important, the one in which an official stretches both hands over his head to indicate a score, is a signifier with two signifieds: triumph or success for the offensive team and failure for the defensive team, and at the sign, thousands and thousands of people in the stadium (and in the television audience) cheer madly or groan.

While the game progresses there is much activity on the sidelines.   6
In college games bands play rousing songs at certain times to encourage their teams, and cheerleaders lead cheers, jump up and down (displaying their breasts and legs), and carry on, often in rather mechanical dancing and movement displays. Many professional football teams have groups of young and attractive women who "wiggle and jiggle" on the sidelines, indicating that there is a sexual dimension to the game or, more precisely, to the spectacle in which the game is embedded.

Instant Replay and the Modern Sensibility

As the various subsystems that are part of the spectacle of football   7
work themselves out, there is one sign that is crucial to the understanding of what football means—in its televised form, in particular—and that is the huge scoreboard clock. Time is of the essence in football, but, unlike in baseball and other sports, in football time can be manipulated. And it is this manipulation of time in tightly fought games that leads to the incredible tension generated by the sport.

In a one-sided game there is little tension, and the game often turns   8
into an exhibition of power and competence for the winning team and a study in humiliation for the losing one. But in close games, time is everyone's enemy. The winning team fights to hold on to its advantage and the losing one tries to use what time it has left to best advantage and to score. Many football games are decided in the last minutes and often even in the last seconds of the game. A minute of playing time, because of the rules of the game, can take many minutes of real time.

What further complicates matters, especially in televised games, is   9
the invention of the instant replay, which can show a given play from a variety of different perspectives and which suggests, ultimately, that time doesn't pass the way it does in real life. We keep seeing the past (a given play) over and again from a variety of angles, so that our sense of continuity and perspective are rendered problematic. Time doesn't pass the way we thought it did and our perspective on the world isn't the only one.

Televised football has become an incredibly sophisticated art form   10
and now closely resembles avant-garde films in that both now simulate

stream-of-consciousness thought, which moves backward and forward in time, jumping around almost incoherently at times. Instant replay is vaguely equivalent to the flashback in film, and the invention of instant replay has dramatically altered the nature of televised football (and now other sports as well) in particular, and the modern American sensibility, in general. In Super Bowl XVI, between the San Francisco 49ers and the Cincinnati Bengals, CBS used 16 cameras on the field to televise the game and another 7 for locker room shows and other activities. It had 14 videotape machines for instant replays, which meant that an incredible number of perspectives was possible on every play. Can anyone doubt that a new sensibility arises out of seeing such programming? Or, at least, that a new sensibility is made possible because of the development of such a remarkable kind of program?

Football Socializes Us

Football does more than just entertain us. The word "entertain" is   11
like the word "interesting"—neither tells us very much. The questions we should ask about football are those such as: Why do we find football so entertaining? What do we get out of the game? What does it do *for* us (that is, what gratifications does it offer)? What might it be doing *to* us? What does it tell about society?

One very important aspect of football is the way it socializes and en-   12
culturates us. It teaches us how to get along in society, what roles to play, what rules to follow, what life is all about, and so on. We are not aware that this is going on most of the time, which means that we are all the more susceptible to the influence of what the game suggests, teaches, and implies. Here we are looking at the game as a signifier of values, attitudes, and beliefs and attempting to ascertain what these signifieds are and what effects they may have upon people (admittedly, a speculative activity).

One thing we learn from examining football is that we live in a   13
highly complex society in which time is critical and communication is important. A good deal of the game involves communication between the coaching staff and the players. Signals are called on both sides for every play. Nothing is done that has not been planned, rehearsed, and prepared over and over again in practice sessions. It is only the fact that people make mistakes, or do things that cannot be anticipated, that messes up the plans of coaches.

In addition, we come to learn that society is highly specialized, and   14
that this specialization functions within group situations. Teams are now made up of offensive and defensive specialists, each with particular

talents and abilities. Football teams function as "models" for modern society and we learn, from watching football, that we must be specialists who will work in some highly structured organization, controlled from above (the coaches), and that we must pursue our specialization for the good of the group, first and foremost, and then for ourselves. That's what it means to be a "team player." We learn from football, without being aware of it, that we must prepare ourselves to function in a highly bureaucratic society—most likely within a large corporate entity. Football is "training" for working in the corporate world, and the violence in football becomes transformed into sales campaigns that will "smash" the public or one's competitors or both.

We also learn that specialization and ability constitute a means for   15
upward mobility, especially in professional football, where farm boys, Blacks from working-class families, and others often earn huge salaries. Many youngsters identify very strongly with these football stars, whose heroics on the football field are, at times, quite incredible.

In a sense football is really about containment and breaking free,   16
about order and randomness—though it is always within the context of the game (which is highly structured and rule-dominated). These moments of freedom are exciting and highly exhilarating, but they are fleeting and quite unpredictable. It is not too much of an oversimplification to say that much of football is routine and boring and that what makes the game so exciting is that there are moments when remarkable things happen. Since we can never know when one of these great plays will happen we must pay attention all the time, lest we miss something.

Why Baseball Is Boring

The reason we find football so exciting is that it closely approxi-   17
mates and reflects our contemporary social situation. Football is a twentieth-century sport for people who live in a world in which time is precious (time is money), communication is important (we live in an "information" society), and bureaucratic entities are dominant (corporations, universities, families, and so on). Baseball, on the other hand, is a nineteenth-century pastoral sport in which time is irrelevant, specialization is not crucial, and there is much less reliance on plays and communication. The following list, which contrasts the two sports, is taken from my book *The TV-Guided American*:

Football	Baseball
urban	pastoral
educated players	country boys

time precious	time not important
specialized	general
body contact important	body contact minimal
team effort	individualistic
upsets critical	no upsets
vicarious excitement	relaxation
weekly	daily
spectacle	austere
four quarters with intermission	nine innings, uninterrupted flow
calculation, planning	little strategy
body a weapon	bat as a weapon
small area	large playing area
twentieth century	nineteenth century
territorial	not territorial
team on offense	one player at time on offense

This list offers a set of polar oppositions that reflect the differences 18 between the two sports and their relationship to our character and culture. Baseball is essentially a nineteenth-century sport that is no longer congruent with contemporary American cultural dynamics and thus *seems* terribly slow or "boring" to many people. Baseball games are now events at which to drink beer and relax, and the ambience at baseball games is considerably different from what one finds at football games—especially at crucial games, where ancient antagonisms or a bowl bid hang in the balance.

Our boredom with baseball is a signifier that as a society we have 19 become "hopped up" and thus baseball seems much slower and boring than it used to, years ago. Baseball doesn't offer the gratifications it once did, or, to put it somewhat differently, the gratifications baseball offers don't mean very much to most people any more. Its heroes aren't as important to us as the heroes in football are, it doesn't provide models to imitate or help us gain an appropriate identity the way football does, and it certainly doesn't have the sexual elements in the spectacle surrounding the game that football does.

Baseball still has its attractions and provides many gratifications 20 to people. Some people argue that it is a subtler game than football, which, if true, may be part of the problem. But, for a variety of reasons, it doesn't have the cultural force or resonance that football does, and thus has taken on, inadvertently I would argue, a different role from that of football.

Football as an Alternative to Religion

I have suggested in my discussion of socialization in football that if   21
football's manifest function is to entertain us, its latent function is to so-
cialize us and offer us models to imitate and notions that will help us fit
into the contemporary bureaucratic corporate world. I would like to
turn now to another aspect of functionalist thought, namely, the notion
that some phenomena function as alternatives for other phenomena. My
thesis here is that football functions for many people as an *alternative* to
religion or, perhaps, that it has a religious or sacred dimension to it that
we seldom recognize.

The passionate feelings people have about football (and their teams)   22
and the intensity of our collective interest in the game leads me to think
that football has a dimension far beyond that of simply being a sport.
Indeed, Michael R. Real in *Mass-Mediated Culture* has written convincingly about the Super Bowl as a mythic spectacle and suggested how, in
secular societies, sports "fill the vacuum" left by religions. I would like
to suggest here that football—and I will focus on professional football—
is in many ways analogous to religion. The following list points out
some interesting parallels between the two seemingly different phenomena.

Professional Football	*Religion*
superstars	saints
Sunday game	Sunday service
ticket	offering
great merger	ecumenical movement
complex plays	theology
players on the way to the Super Bowl	knights in search of the Holy Grail
coaches	clergy
stadium	church
fans	congregations

Curiously enough, as religions (especially liberal religions) become   23
more rational and continue to *demythologize* themselves, football becomes more arcane and mysterious, with incredibly complex plays and
tactics that function much the way theology does for religion. People
seem to have a need for myth, ritual, mystery, and heroism, and football, perhaps more than religion in contemporary societies, is helping
people satisfy these needs.

Whether the messages we get from football are as valuable and pos-   24
itive as those we get from sermons and other aspects of religion is another matter, and one that bears thinking about. Has football become

"the opiate of the people"? There are some who hold that belief, and it is to their interpretation that we now turn.

The Marxist Perspective

Football games, held in huge stadiums, with bands, cheerleaders, halftime shows, and so on, are spectacles par excellence. The function of these spectacles (that is, the latent function), it may be argued, is to divert people's attention from their real social situation, to drain them of their emotional energy (which might have been expended on political and social issues), and, ultimately, to convince them of the justness of the political order. A political system that can provide good football is worth keeping. And since football also trains us for our place in the modern, corporate, capitalist world, it is doubly valuable. 25

The great gatherings of people in America are not (generally) for political purposes, though at times this does happen. Instead we gather together to watch spectacles—of which football is of exemplary importance. It isn't hard to see a parallel between the old Roman principle of bread and circuses—to divert the mobs from their misery—and what goes on in America on Fridays (in high schools), Saturdays (in colleges), and Sundays (in the professional games), as well as Monday nights on television. 26

Is the intensity of our interest in football a measure of the alienation we feel in our everyday lives—lives in which we sense a radical separation from our possibilities, in which we feel hemmed in by huge bureaucratic structures that dominate our work lives and by the competitiveness that characterizes our social order? The less satisfying our lives, the more bothered we are by the "rat race," the more we turn to vicarious satisfactions like football and, curiously, the less psychic nourishment we get from them. For, ironically, football is itself essentially routine and boring and teaches us, though we generally are not aware of this, that we must learn how to accommodate ourselves to the society in which we live. 27

Football, especially professional football, is a huge business that exists for one purpose—to make money. It treats players as commodities—objects to be sold and traded, almost at whim (though unionization has modified this a good deal). Players have little sense of loyalty, also. They see the huge profits the owners make and now obtain huge salaries—all that the market can bear. The ultimate irony is that it is television that benefits most from the existence of football, and television uses football for its main purpose—as filler between commercials. Television, as it exists in America, is a business that makes money by selling 28 commercial time. Football attracts large audiences and costs relatively little to produce (compared, say, to a crime show or documentary) so it is very cost-effective.

Thus we have a situation in which everyone is exploiting or trying   29
to exploit everyone else, and the result of all this is that spectacles are produced that are used by people to obtain vicarious excitement and pleasure and that have the hidden functions of teaching people to accept the status quo and to accommodate themselves to corporations and the political order.

The potential for revolutionary violence in the masses is siphoned   30
off as they watch linemen battle one another "in the trenches" and defensive players "hit" halfbacks and cornerbacks. After a weekend of football, the heavy viewer will have participated vicariously in enough violence to fuel a dozen revolutions.

A look at the rosters of football teams shows that Blacks are heavily   31
and disproportionately represented. This is an indication of the fact that Black people suffer more from our economic system that Whites do and thus need football (as well as boxing and other sports) as an instrument of social mobility. For poor Black kids, football is a means of escaping from poverty and achieving middle-class—at least for a while. To be successful, however, one must learn to fit in—to adopt essentially bourgeois values such as being a team player, not causing trouble, doing what one is told, and so on. A player, no matter how talented, who causes "problems" and doesn't follow the rules will not prosper in college or professional football. Thus, there is a price to be paid by players—namely, "accommodation," which leads the way to "co-optation."

Football and the Psyche

I have suggested that football functions as a means of socializing   32
people and of diverting them from paying attention to their real concerns. I would also like to suggest that football is vitally connected with various unconscious processes, which explain, in part, the powerful hold football has on people. If large numbers of people read the comics or watch football or do anything, quite likely it is because there are important psychic gratifications to be obtained, even though people may not be aware of them.

For one thing, there is the matter of violence in football. It is a kind   33
of controlled violence that may satisfy two contradictory desires we have: to be violent and, at the same time, to be controlled so our violence doesn't overwhelm us. This violence is integral to the game, in which there are "blocks," "hits," "tackles," or the like on every play. It stems

from a number of sources, such as the fact that we must restrain ourselves from impulsive behavior, and the fact that we are all involved
(unconsciously) in Oedipal problems, sibling rivalries, and so on. Quite
likely the matter of sexual repression is of primary importance, and the
violence becomes a kind of substitute gratification. (There is a connection, also, between violence and eroticism that must be kept in mind.
There is a sexual dimension to violence just as there is an aggressive and
violent dimension to sexuality.)

The violence in football may also help men with the matter of ob-   34
taining masculine identity. We live in an information society, in which
processing data and communicating account for a dominant part of the
gross national product. In such a society men find it hard to develop a
male identity, especially since American male identity has historically
been connected to our nineteenth-century lifestyle—cutting wood, herding cattle, doing hard physical labor. Watching violence on the football
field becomes one of the few ways in which American men can help
themselves form a male identity, even if this violence is vicarious and
potentially destructive.

Football lends itself to a number of interpretations of a psychoana-   35
lytic nature. For example, we can interpret the game as mirroring the
battle between id, ego, and superego forces in the human psyche:

Id	Ego	Superego
offensive team	officials	defensive team
drives	rules	prevention

In this situation, the offensive team wants to have long "drives" and to
score: the defensive team wants to stop these drives and get control of
the ball; and the officials function as an ego, to keep the game going.

Arnold J. Mandell, a psychiatrist who spent some time with the San   36
Diego Chargers, categorized professional football players as follows:

Position	Personality Traits
offensive linemen	ambitious, tenacious, precise, attentive to detail
wide receivers	narcissistic, vain, loners
quarterbacks	self-confident, courageous
defensive linemen	restless, peevish, irritable, intolerant of detail, uninhibited, wild
linebackers	controlled, brutal, internally conflicted

These personality traits are the ones required for people to be able to play
their positions, Mandell found. The offensive players, he discovered,

keep their lockers neat and orderly, but the lockers of defensive players are invariably messy.

> It became clear that offensive football players like structure and discipline. They want to maintain the status quo. They tend to be conservative as people, and as football players they take comfort in repetitious practice of well-planned and well-executed plays. The defensive players, just as clearly, can't stand structure; their attitudes, their behavior and their lifestyles bear this out.

All of this is important because more than anything else, Mandell reports, "the game is in the mind," which is probably true of all games.

Concluding Remarks

Football, though it might seem to be only a simple entertainment, is   37
actually a matter of some consequence from a number of points of view. We use language from football in our political discourse, it creates the lamentable "football widow" every fall, it is played by children, adolescents, college students, and grown men, it is an industry, it has a long history—I could go on and on, endlessly. It is a subject that attracts great attention from the general public and one that deserves attention from the media analyst.

But there is something else to be said here that every media analyst   38
must remember. When we deal with the programs carried by the media—whether we focus on the football, soap operas, news, or any other genre—we must never forget that we are dealing with art forms. And art forms are extremely complicated phenomena. We must be careful that we do not reduce a program to nothing but a system of signs, nothing but a socializing agent, nothing but a means of manipulating people's consciousness, nothing but a subject in which drives, Oedipal problems, and the like are manifested. We must find a way, somehow, to analyze a program from a number of different points of view but also to respect it as a creative effort (perhaps not a very successful one) and a work of art that has performance aspects, aesthetic elements, and more. To be a media analyst one must know all kinds of things and, in a sense, everything at the same time.

• • • • • • • • • • • • • • • • • • • •

Examining the Text
1. Berger claims that football socializes us, in part by providing an instructive model of the bureaucratic corporate world (paragraphs 11–15).

What are some of the characteristics of that model, as Berger describes it? Can you think of others? Are there ways in which football offers models for rebelling *against* corporate culture?

2. Why does Berger claim that football plays a religious role in society (paragraphs 21–24)? Do you think he is exaggerating, or do you know people for whom football is a "religion"? How might other sports serve a similar function?

3. How does Berger explain the appeal of football's violence (33–35)? What do you think of his explanation?

4. Berger offers several interpretations of football: semiological ("a game of signs"), aesthetic ("an incredibly sophisticated art form"), sociological (it "socializes us"), comparative ("baseball is boring"), anthropological ("an alternative to religion"), marxist ("the opiate of the people"), and psychoanalytic ("vitally connected with various unconscious processes"). Do you find any of these interpretations more persuasive or revealing than others? Why do you think Berger offers several interpretations rather than just one?

For Group Discussion

Choose a sport other than football and list the signs involved in that sport, using Berger's discussion of football signs as a model. Do signs function in other sports as they do in football? As a class, discuss the meanings of various signs in other sports.

Writing Suggestion

Choose one of Berger's seven interpretative perspectives or combine several of them and write an essay in which you similarly analyze another sport.

Champion of the World

Maya Angelou

*M*aya Angelou is a well-known poet, novelist, and performer. Born in 1928 and raised in the segregated South, Angelou persevered through countless hardships to become one of the country's most revered authors and cultural leaders. Angelou read her poem, "On the Pulse of Morning," at the 1993 inauguration of President Bill Clinton.

The selection which follows is from Angelou's first volume of autobiography, I Know Why the Caged Bird Sings *(1969). She relates an important recollection from childhood about the night in the 1930s when world heavy-weight champion Joe Louis, nicknamed the "Brown Bomber," defended his box-ing title against a white contender. Much of Angelou's narrative is made up of the words and feelings of the local black community gathered in her Uncle Willie's store to listen to the broadcast of that highly publicized match. Angelou shows how her neighbors' hopes and fears and their image of themselves as a people were intimately connected to the fortunes of Louis, one of a very few black heros of the day. Her narrative reveals that a "simple" sporting event can be of intense significance for a group of people who see it as a symbol of personal vic-tory or defeat.*

Before you read, recall any experience you've had or heard about in which a sporting event took on an emotional power and significance far greater than the event itself would seem to warrant. Whether this event is one that you par-ticipated in, watched, or read about, think about how and why sports can have such an intense influence on people's lives.

....

The last inch of space was filled, yet people continued to wedge themselves along the walls of the Store. Uncle Willie had turned the ra-dio up to its last notch so that youngsters on the porch wouldn't miss a word. Women sat on kitchen chairs, dining-room chairs, stools, and up-turned wooden boxes. Small children and babies perched on every lap available and men leaned on the shelves or on each other.   1

The apprehensive mood was shot through with shafts of gaiety, as a black sky is streaked with lightning.   2

"I ain't worried 'bout this fight. Joe's gonna whip that cracker like it's open season."   3

"He gone whip him till that white boy call him Momma."   4

At last the talking finished and the string-along songs about razor blades were over and the fight began.   5

"A quick jab to the head." In the Store the crowd grunted. "A left to the head and a right and another left." One of the listeners cackled like a hen and was quieted.   6

"They're in a clinch, Louis is trying to fight his way out."   7

Some bitter comedian on the porch said, "That white man don't mind hugging that niggah now, I betcha."   8

"The referee is moving in to break them up, but Louis finally pushed the contender away and it's an uppercut to the chin. The contender is hanging on, now he's backing away. Louis catches him with a short left to the jaw."   9

A tide of murmuring assent poured out the door and into the yard.   10

"Another left and another left. Louis is saving that mighty right . . ."   11

The mutter in the Store had grown into a baby roar and it was pierced by the clang of a bell and the announcer's "That's the bell for round three, ladies and gentlemen."

As I pushed my way into the Store I wondered if the announcer gave 12
any thought to the fact that he was addressing as "ladies and gentlemen" all the Negroes around the world who sat sweating and praying, glued to their "Master's voice."

There were only a few calls for RC Colas, Dr Peppers, and Hires root 13
beer. The real festivities would begin after the fight. Then even the old Christian ladies who taught their children and tried themselves to practice turning the other cheek would buy soft drinks, and if the Brown Bomber's victory was a particularly bloody one they would order peanut patties and Baby Ruths also.

Bailey and I laid coins on top of the cash register. Uncle Willie 14
didn't allow us to ring up sales during a fight. It was too noisy and might shake up the atmosphere. When the gong rang for the next round we pushed through the near-sacred quiet to the herd of children outside.

"He's got Louis against the ropes and now it's a left to the body and 15
a right to the ribs. Another right to the body, it looks like it was low . . . Yes, ladies and gentlemen, the referee is signaling but the contender keeps raining the blows on Louis. It's another to the body, and it looks like Louis is going down."

My race groaned. It was our people falling. It was another lynching, 16
yet another Black man hanging on a tree. One more woman ambushed and raped. A Black boy whipped and maimed. It was hounds on the trail of a man running through slimy swamps. It was a white woman slapping her maid for being forgetful.

The men in the Store stood away from the walls and at attention. 17
Women greedily clutched the babes on their laps while on the porch the shufflings and smiles, flirtings and pinching of a few minutes before were gone. This might be the end of the world. If Joe lost we were back in slavery and beyond help. It would all be true, the accusations that we were lower types of human beings. Only a little higher than apes. True that we were stupid and ugly and lazy and dirty and, unlucky and worst of all, that God Himself hated us and ordained us to be hewers of wood and drawers of water, forever and ever, world without end.

We didn't breathe. We didn't hope. We waited. 18

"He's off the ropes, ladies and gentlemen. He's moving towards the 19
center of the ring." There was not time to be relieved. The worst might still happen.

"And now it looks like Joe is mad. He's caught Carnera with a left 20
hook to the head and a right to the head. It's a left jab to the body and another left to the head. There's a left cross and a right to the head. The

contender's right eye is bleeding and he can't seem to keep his block up. Louis is penetrating every block. The referee is moving in, but Louis sends a left to the body and it's an uppercut to the chin and the contender is dropping. He's on the canvas, ladies and gentlemen."

Babies slid to the floor as women stood up and men leaned toward the radio.   21

"Here's the referee. He's counting. One, two, three, four, five, six, seven . . . Is the contender trying to get up again?"   22

All the men in the store shouted, "NO."   23

"—eight, nine, ten." There were a few sounds from the audience, but they seemed to be holding themselves in against tremendous pressure.   24

"The fight is all over, ladies and gentlemen. Let's get the microphone over to the referee . . . Here he is. He's got the Brown Bomber's hand, he's holding it up . . . Here he is . . ."   25

Then the voice, husky and familiar, came to wash over us—"The winnah, and still heavyweight champeen of the world . . . Joe Louis."   26

Champion of the world. A Black boy. Some Black mother's son.   27

He was the strongest man in the world. People drank Coca-Colas like ambrosia and ate candy bars like Christmas. Some of the men went behind the Store and poured white lightning in their soft-drink bottles, and a few of the bigger boys followed them. Those who were not chased away came back blowing their breath in front of themselves like proud smokers.   28

It would take an hour or more before people would leave the Store and head home. Those who lived too far had made arrangements to stay in town. It wouldn't do for a Black man and his family to be caught on a lonely country road on a night when Joe Louis had proved that we were the strongest people in the world.   29

• •

Examining the Text

1. Unlike the other selections in this chapter which offer fairly objective analyses of sport, Angelou relates a personal recollection. What conclusions about the influence of sports on culture, and specifically on African-American culture in the 1930s, can you draw from her story? Has that influence changed significantly over the last sixty years?

2. In paragraphs 16 and 17 Angelou describes her own thoughts about the prospect of Louis losing the match. After rereading these paragraphs, what do you think they contribute to the overall meaning and drama of the story? How are they connected to the final paragraph?

3. What is the effect of the concluding paragraph in the story? How would Angelou's message be different if she had not ended it this way?

For Group Discussion

Angelou's recollection demonstrates in vivid detail how a sporting event can take on much larger significance, how people can invest a great deal of emotion in the performance of an athlete or team. In your group, list some other specific examples of sporting contests that have taken on intense emotional significance and meaning for an individual or a group of fans. As a class, discuss the advantages and disadvantages of the strong influence sports has on its fans.

Writing Suggestion

In her narrative, Angelou describes how Joe Louis was an inspiration and sign of hope for African-Americans in the 1930s. Choose another athlete who you think has similarly been an inspiration to his or her fans or has served as a role model. In an essay discuss the qualities that make that person a particularly good model. At the same time, if you think that athlete has negative qualities, you may cite these as well in analyzing how he or she has influenced fans.

ADDITIONAL SUGGESTIONS
FOR WRITING ABOUT SPORTS

1. Using Maya Angelou's "Champion of the World" as a model, write a narrative in which you tell of a past experience with sports, either as a spectator or as a participant, that had a significant effect on your life. Perhaps this experience revealed something about yourself that you didn't realize, helped you to better understand someone else, taught you an important lesson, or corrected a misconception that you had. Or perhaps you're not certain what effect the experience had, and can use this assignment to speculate on its significance. As you write, be sure to consider what the other writers in this chapter have to say.

2. Attend a local sporting event, and bring a notebook and, if possible, a tape recorder or videocamera. Observe and take notes about how the people around you behave, what they do and say, what they wear, how they relate to one another, what interests or bores them, when they seem satisfied or disappointed. Note also how their behavior is different from what it would likely be in other contexts. Try to be an impartial observer, simply recording what you see in as much detail as possible.

From your notes, write an extended description of one or several typical spectators, and then draw some conclusions about why people enjoy watching sports. You may also want to discuss the psychological benefits and/or harm that being a spectator might cause.

3. Choose a sport with which you're very familiar, either because you play it or watch it regularly. Reflect on your experience playing or watching this sport, and write down some of your recollections. Think about what you've learned from this sport, and how it has affected other areas of your life.

Then write an essay in which you show how this particular sport has influenced your beliefs, attitudes and values. Be as specific as possible and try to show precisely how and why the sport has influenced you.

4. Many of the writers in this chapter discuss the impact of professional sports on individuals and on society as a whole. Referring to essays in this chapter, construct your own argument about the influence of professional sports. As a prewriting exercise, make lists of the beneficial and the detrimental influences of professional sports on our society. Try to come up with specific examples to illustrate each of the items on your lists. Then working from those lists, develop a persuasive argument about the influence of sports on our society.

5. Professional athletes are often role models in our society. As a prewriting exercise for this assignment, list some of the reasons why this is so, especially for young people. Also list the ways in which athletes might make good role models, as well as some of the reasons other professionals (for example, teachers or government leaders) might actually be better role models.

Then choose a professional athlete who is either a good or a bad role model in your opinion. Do some library research on this athlete, looking up interviews and articles about him or her, as well as information on his or her activities outside of sports. From this information, write a brief biography of the athlete, focusing on the kind of role model he or she is.

6
Journalism

"This is your ninety-nine-per-cent-news-free six-o'clock news."

Drawing by Dana Fradon; © 1992 The New Yorker Magazine, Inc.

Deservedly or not, journalists in recent years have increasingly acquired a reputation for being "bottom feeders." Like certain fish that subsist on the sediment and garbage at the bottom of lakes, certain types of journalists make their living reporting trashy stories and sordid exposés, covering such "news" as sex scandals, rumors about local satanic cults, and Elvis sightings. Sometimes it seems as if "junk journalism" has become the norm rather than the exception. And indeed, with the number of tabloids, "entertainment news" shows, and twenty-four hour cable news networks competing with the mainstream press for the attention (and dollars) of the reading and viewing public, it's no wonder that reporters are tempted to turn to sensationalist, "sexy" stories to grab the headlines.

Journalism also has a more noble image, of course, and, for much of the last century, journalists have been counted among the country's most trusted public figures. (It may not be a coincidence that Superman's mild-mannered alter-ego, Clark Kent, is a newspaper reporter!) Journalists bring us information that connects us to others in our local community, across the country, and beyond our national borders, sometimes risking their lives to do so. When important events occur—from earthquakes and fires to national elections—the news media activate a vast array of technological and human resources to keep people informed. We rely on newspapers, magazines, television, and radio to present us with clear, honest, and objective accounts of the facts. The news also educates us about significant and ethically challenging issues we face as individuals and as a society.

Thus, whatever the reputation of journalists, they are consistently important in our lives. The local newspaper helps define us as members of a geographical community with common allegiances to sports teams, a shared cultural life, and particular lifestyles. National networks give us the broader picture, informing us of events, trends, and problems of concern to the entire nation, linking residents of dissimilar regions with a similar agenda, a similar set of concerns. Clearly, the media are a crucial component of popular culture.

The first half of this chapter considers the role of the news media in contemporary society, offers some critical viewpoints on the responsibilities of journalists, and suggests ways the media could better serve the public. In the second half of the chapter, a series of essays ask us to go beyond our accustomed role as unthinking consumers of the news to look at the information carefully and analytically, aware of the inevitable distortions and biases inherent in any reporting and particularly problematic in TV news.

As you read the essays in this chapter, keep in mind the news sources with which you are familiar. Try to clarify your own image of journalism, and identify its role in informing, influencing, and educating you.

THE ROLE OF JOURNALISM

Journalism and the Larger Truth

Roger Rosenblatt

This chapter opens with an essay that takes issue with the increasingly common view that journalists should not only provide us with accurate factual information but should also synthesize that information into a larger represen-tation of the "truth" about the world in which we live. Roger Rosenblatt—a prominent journalist, frequent commentator on TV news shows, and author of numerous books, articles, and essays—discounts that view, arguing that jour-nalism's only function is to "present facts accurately," to cover events objec-tively. People who believe they are getting some "larger truth" from the news, Rosenblatt suggests, are simply mistaken; for the larger truths, we need to look to ourselves and our surroundings, and to "history, poetry, art, nature, educa-tion, conversation."

Moreover, if journalists try to offer the "larger truth" to their audiences, they run the dangerous risk of distorting the "facts" to fit that truth. Journal-ists are hard-pressed simply to tell us what's going on in the world, much less why our world is as it is and what can be done to improve it. As consumers of journalism, we need to do our part, Rosenblatt suggests, by becoming more ac-tive supplying the interpretation and larger context necessary to make the events reported meaningful in our lives.

Before you read, ask yourself what you expect when you turn on the nightly television news or open a newspaper. What sort of information or knowledge are you looking for from these sources?

••••••••••••••••••••

When journalists hear journalists claim a "larger truth," they really   1
ought to go for their pistols. *The New Yorker's* Alastair Reid said the
holy words last week: "A reporter might take liberties with the factual
circumstances to make the larger truth clear." O large, large truth.
Apparently Mr. Reid believes that imposing a truth is the same as arriving at one. Illogically, he also seems to think that truths may be
disclosed through lies. But his error is more fundamental still in assuming that large truth is the province of journalism in the first place.
The business of journalism is to present facts accurately—Mr. Reid

notwithstanding. Those seeking something larger are advised to look elsewhere.

For one thing, journalism rarely sees the larger truth of a story be- 2 cause reporters are usually chasing quite small elements of information. A story, like a fern, only reveals its final shocking shape in stages. Journalism also reduces most of the stories it deals with to political consid- erations. Matters are defined in terms of where power lies, who opposes whom or what, where the special interests are. As a result, the larger truth of a story is often missed or ignored. By its nature, political thought lim- its speculative thought. Political realities themselves cannot be grasped by an exclusively political way of looking at things.

Then, too, journalism necessarily deals with discontinuities. One 3 has never heard of the Falkland Islands. Suddenly the Falklands are the center of the universe; one knows all there is to know about "kelpers" and Port Stanley; sheep jokes abound. In the end, as at the beginning, no one really knows anything about the Falkland Islands other than the war that gave it momentary celebrity—nothing about the people in the aftermath of the war, their concerns, isolation, or their true relationship to Argentina and Britain. Discontinuities are valuable because they point up the world's variety as well as the special force of its isolated parts. But to rely on them for truth is to lose one's grip on what is con- tinuous and whole.

Journalism looks to where the ball is, and not where it is not. A col- 4 lege basketball coach, trying to improve the performance of one of his backcourt men, asked the player what he did when he practiced on his own. "Dribble and shoot," came the reply. The coach then asked the player to add up the total time he dribbled and shot during a scrimmage game, how many minutes he had hold of the ball. "Three minutes in all," came the reply. "That means," said the coach, "that you practice what you do in three minutes out of 40 in a game." Which means in turn that for every player, roughly 37 out of a possible 40 minutes are played away from the ball.

Journalism tends to focus on the poor when the poor make news, 5 usually dramatic news like a tenement fire or a march on Washington. But the poor are poor all the time. It is not journalism's ordinary busi- ness to deal with the unstartling normalities of life. Reporters need a *story,* something shapely and elegant. Poverty is disorderly, anticlimac- tic and endless. If one wants truth about the poor, one must look where the ball is not.

Similarly, journalism inevitably imposes forms of order on both the 6 facts in a story and on the arrangement of stories itself. The structures of magazines and newspapers impose one kind of order; radio and television another, usually sequential. But every form journalism takes is designed to draw the public's attention to what the editors deem most important in a day's or week's events. This naturally violates the larger truth of a chaotic universe. Oddly, the public often contributes its own hierarchical arrangements by dismissing editors' discriminations and dwelling on the story about the puppy on page 45 instead of the bank collapse on Page One. The "truth" of a day's events is tugged at from all sides.

Finally, journalism often misses the truth by unconsciously eroding one's sympathy with life. A seasoned correspondent in Evelyn Waugh's maliciously funny novel *Scoop* lectures a green reporter. "You know," he says, "you've got a lot to learn about journalism. Look at it this way. News is what a chap who doesn't care much about anything wants to read." The matter is not a laughing one. A superabundance of news has the benumbing effect of mob rule on the senses. Every problem in the world begins to look unreachable, unimprovable. What could one lone person possibly accomplish against a constant and violent storm of events that on any day include a rebellion of Sikhs, a tornado in Wisconsin, parents pleading for a healthy heart for their child? Sensibilities, overwhelmed, eventually grow cold; and therein monsters lie. Nobody wants to be part of a civilization that reads the news and does not care about it. Certainly no journalist wants that.   7

If one asks, then, where the larger truth is to be sought, the answer is where it has always been: in history, poetry, art, nature, education, conversation; in the tunnels of one's own mind. People may have come to expect too much of journalism. Not of journalism at its worst; when one is confronted with lies, cruelty and tastelessness, it is hardly too much to expect better. But that is not a serious problem because lies, cruelty and tastelessness are the freaks of the trade, not the pillars. The trouble is that people have also come to expect too much of journalism at its best, because they have invested too much power in it, and in so doing have neglected or forfeited other sources of power in their lives. Journalists appear to give answers, but essentially they ask a question: What shall we make of this? A culture that would rely on the news for truth could not answer that question because it already would have lost the qualities of mind that make the news worth knowing.   8

If people cannot rely on the news for facts, however, then journalism has no reason for being. Alastair Reid may have forgotten that the principal reason journalists exist in society is that people have a need to be informed of and comprehend the details of experience. "The right to know and the right to be are one," wrote Wallace Stevens in a poem about Ulysses. The need is basic, biological. In that sense, everyone is   9 a journalist, seeking the knowledge of the times in order to grasp the character of the world, to survive in the world, perhaps to move it. Archimedes said he could move the world as long as he had a long enough lever. He pointed out, too, that he needed a ground to stand on.

······················

Examining the Text

1. According to Rosenblatt, why shouldn't journalism seek a "larger truth"? What should it seek instead?

2. What points does Rosenblatt make about the limitations of journalism? Which of his points do you find most persuasive, and why?

3. What does Rosenblatt mean in his central metaphor: "Journalism looks to where the ball is, and not where it is not. . . . If one wants the truth . . . , one must look where the ball is not" (paragraphs 4–5). In what ways does his metaphor describe journalism's strengths and weaknesses?

4. What do you think Rosenblatt means in the last two sentences of this essay? How does his reference to Archimedes apply to journalism?

For Group Discussion

Look back at paragraph 5 where Rosenblatt suggests that one cannot get the "truth about the poor" from journalism. As a group, brainstorm a list of other subjects about which journalism is unlikely to provide the "truth" because journalists are not concerned with "the unstartling normalities of life," but only with the unusual, the "newsworthy." As a class, discuss how—or whether—the public *can* get the "truth" about the poor and the other subjects your groups have discussed.

Writing Suggestion

Rosenblatt suggests that, in searching for a larger truth, we should look to "history, poetry, art, nature, education, conversation; in the tunnels of one's own mind." Choose a current issue in the news, and in an essay consider how its "larger truth" might be illuminated by any of the means Rosenblatt suggests. What other places might you look for the larger truth about this issue?

A Flood of Pseudo-Events

Daniel Boorstin

You might not have heard of a "pseudo-event," but most likely you've been exposed to thousands of them. According to Daniel Boorstin, "pseudo-events"—press conferences, "news-maker" interviews, political debates, and public relations stunts—dominate mainstream journalism. Their widespread acceptance reflects a shift in attitude toward news and toward the world around us.

Boorstin is former Librarian of Congress and Professor of History at the University of Chicago, and author of many books, including The Americans, a prize-winning trilogy covering American history. In this essay, taken from his 1987 collection, Hidden History, Boorstin takes a broadly historical view of the rise of pseudo-events in American journalism, showing how our concept of "news" has changed over the years. He argues that we now expect journalists to make or manufacture news, rather than simply report it. And he connects this attitude to a larger cultural change: "Demanding more than the world can give us," Boorstin notes, "we require that something be fabricated to make up for the world's deficiencies."

Boorstin argues that pseudo-events are more interesting and appealing to us than real events and, staged, planned, and promoted as they are, are more manageable for journalists to cover. The fact that the pseudo-event has become a fixture in the news media raises important questions for journalists and consumers alike. If the task of journalism is to report facts, then what are we to make of "synthetic facts" and "made-for-TV" events?

As you read, consider Boorstin's questions. Should reporters cover such pseudo-events? And what kind of attention should we give them?

• • • • • • • • • • • • • • • • • • • •

The simplest of our extravagant expectations concerns the amount 1
of novelty in the world. There was a time when the reader of an unexciting newspaper would remark, "How dull is the world today!" Nowadays he says, "What a dull newspaper!" When the first American newspaper, Benjamin Harris' *Publick Occurrences Both Forreign and Domestick,* appeared in Boston on September 25, 1690, it promised to furnish news regularly once a month. But, the editor explained, it might appear oftener "if any Glut of Occurrences happen." The responsibility for making news was entirely God's—or the Devil's. The newsman's task was only to give "an Account of such considerable things as have arrived unto our Notice."

Although the theology behind this way of looking at events soon   2
dissolved, this view of the news lasted longer. "The skilled and faithful
journalist," James Parton observed in 1866, "recording with exactness
and power the thing that has come to pass, is Providence addressing
men." The story is told of a Southern Baptist clergyman before the Civil
War who used to say, when a newspaper was brought in the room, "Be
kind enough to let me have it a few minutes, till I see how the Supreme
Being is governing the world." Charles A. Dana, one of the great American editors of the nineteenth century, once defended his extensive reporting of crime in the New York *Sun* by saying, "I have always felt that
whatever the Divine Providence permitted to occur I was not too proud
to report."

Of course, this is now a very old-fashioned way of thinking. Our   3
current point of view is better expressed in the definition by Arthur
MacEwen, whom William Randolph Hearst made his first editor of the
San Francisco *Examiner:* "News is anything that makes a reader say, 'Gee
whiz!'" Or, put more soberly, "News is whatever a good editor chooses
to print."

We need not be theologians to see that we have shifted responsibil-   4
ity for making the world interesting from God to the newspaperman.
We used to believe there were only so many "events" in the world. If
there were not many intriguing or startling occurrences, it was no fault
of the reporter. He could not be expected to report what did not exist.

Within the last hundred years, however, and especially in the twen-   5
tieth century, all this has changed. We expect the papers to be full of
news. If there is no news visible to the naked eye, or to the average citizen, we still expect it to be there for the enterprising newsman. The successful reporter is one who can find a story, even if there is no earthquake or assassination or civil war. If he cannot find a story, then he
must make one—by the questions he asks of public figures, by the surprising human interest he unfolds from some commonplace event, or by
"the news behind the news." If all this fails, then he must give us a
"think piece"—an embroidering of well-known facts, or a speculation
about startling things to come.

This change in our attitude toward "news" is not merely a basic fact   6
about the history of American newspapers. It is a symptom of a revolutionary change in our attitude toward what happens in the world, how
much of it is new and surprising and important. Toward how life can
be enlivened, toward our power and the power of those who inform
and educate and guide us, to provide synthetic happenings to make up
for the lack of spontaneous events. Demanding more than the world
can give us, we require that something be fabricated to make up for

the world's deficiency. This is only one example of our demand for illusions.

Many historical forces help explain how we have come to our pre- 7 sent immoderate hopes. But there can be no doubt about what we now expect, nor that it is immoderate. Every American knows the anticipation with which he picks up his morning newspaper at breakfast or opens his evening paper before dinner, or listens to the newscasts every hour on the hour as he drives across country, or watches his favorite commentator on television interpret the events of the day. Many enterprising Americans are now at work to help us satisfy these expectations. Many might be put out of work if we should suddenly moderate our expectations. But it is we who keep them in business and demand that they fill our consciousness with novelties, that they play God for us.

The new kind of synthetic novelty which has flooded our experi- 8 ence I will call "pseudo-events." The common prefix "pseudo" comes from the Greek word meaning false, or intended to deceive. Before I recall the historical forces which have made these pseudo-events possible, have increased the supply of them and the demand for them, I will give a commonplace example.

The owners of a hotel, in an illustration offered by Edward L. Ber- 9 nays in his pioneer *Crystallizing Public Opinion* (1923), consult a public relations counsel. They ask how to increase their hotel's prestige and so improve their business. In less sophisticated times, the answer might have been to hire a new chef, to improve the plumbing, to paint the rooms, or to install a crystal chandelier in the lobby. The public relations counsel's technique is more indirect. He proposes that the management stage a celebration of the hotel's thirtieth anniversary. A committee is formed, including a prominent banker, a leading society matron, a well-known lawyer, an influential preacher, and an "event" is planned (say a banquet) to call attention to the distinguished service the hotel has been rendering the community. The celebration is held, photographs are taken, the occasion is widely reported, and the object is accomplished. Now this occasion is a pseudo-event, and will illustrate all the essential features of pseudo-events.

This celebration, we can see at the outset, is somewhat—but not en- 10 tirely—misleading. Presumably the public relations counsel would not have been able to form his committee of prominent citizens if the hotel had not actually been rendering service to the community. On the other hand, if the hotel's services had been all that important, instigation by a public relations counsel might not have been necessary. Once the celebration has been held, the celebration itself becomes evidence that the hotel really is a distinguished institution. The occasion actually gives the hotel the prestige to which it is pretending.

It is obvious, too, that the value of such a celebration to the owners   11
depends on its being photographed and reported in newspapers, magazines, on radio, and over television. It is the report that gives the event
its force in the minds of potential customers. The power to make a re-
portable event is thus the power to make experience. One is reminded
of Napoleon's apocryphal reply to his general, who objected that circumstances were unfavorable to a proposed campaign: "Bah, I make circumstances!" The modern public relations counsel—and he is, of course,
only one of many twentieth-century creators of pseudo-events—has
come close to fulfilling Napoleon's idle boast. "The counsel on public
relations," Mr. Bernays explains, "not only knows what news value is,
but knowing it, he is in a position to *make news happen*. He is a creator of
events."

The intriguing feature of the modern situation, however, comes pre-   12
cisely from the fact that the modern news makers are not God. The news
they make happen, the events they create, are somehow not quite real.
There remains a tantalizing difference between man-made and God-
made events.

A pseudo-event, then, is a happening that possesses the following   13
characteristics:

1. It is not spontaneous, but comes about because someone has   14
planned, planted, or incited it. Typically, it is not a train wreck or an
earthquake, but an interview.

2. It is planted primarily (not always exclusively) for the immedi-   15
ate purpose of being reported or reproduced. Therefore, its occurrence
is arranged for the convenience of the reporting or reproducing media.
Its success is measured by how widely it is reported. Time relations in
it are commonly fictitious or factitious; the announcement is given out
in advance "for future release" and written as if the event had occurred
in the past. The question, "Is it real?" is less important than, "Is it newsworthy?"

3. Its relation to the underlying reality of the situation is am-   16
biguous. Its interest arises largely from this very ambiguity. Concerning a pseudo-event the question, "What does it mean?" has a new
dimension. While the news interest in a train wreck is in *what* happened and in the real consequences, the interest in an interview is
always, in a sense, in *whether* it really happened and in what might
have been the motives. Did the statement really mean what it said?
Without some of this ambiguity a pseudo-event cannot be very
interesting.

4. Usually it is intended to be a self-fulfilling prophecy. The hotel's   17
thirtieth-anniversary celebration, by saying that the hotel is a distinguished institution, actually helps make it one.

In the last half century a larger and larger proportion of our expe-   18
rience, of what we read and see and hear, has come to consist of pseudo-
events. We expect more of them and we are given more of them. They
flood our consciousness. Their multiplication has gone on in the United
States at a faster rate than elsewhere. Even the rate of increase is increasing every day. This is true of the world of education, of consumption, and of personal relations. It is especially true of the world of public affairs. . . .

In many subtle ways, the rise of pseudo-events has mixed up our   19
roles as actors and as audience—or, the philosophers would say, as "object" and as "subject." Now we can oscillate between the two roles. "The
movies are the only business," Will Rogers once remarked, "where you
can go out front and applaud yourself." Nowadays one need not be a
professional actor to have this satisfaction. We can appear in the mob
scene and then go home and see ourselves on the television screen. No
wonder we become confused about what is spontaneous, about what is
really going on out there! . . . The citizen can hardly be expected to assess the reality when the participants themselves are so often unsure
who is doing the deed and who is making the report of it. Who is the
history, and who is the historian?

An admirable example of this new intertwinement of subject and   20
object, of the history and the historian, of the actor and the reporter, is
the so-called news leak. By now the leak has become an important and
well-established institution in American politics. It is, in fact, one of the
main vehicles for communicating important information from officials
to the public.

A clue to the new unreality of the citizen's world is the perverse new   21
meaning now given to the word "leak." To leak, according to the dictionary, is to "let a fluid substance out or in accidentally: as, the ship
leaks." But nowadays a news leak is one of the most elaborately planned
ways of emitting information. It is, of course, a way in which a government official, with some clearly defined purpose, makes an announcement, asks a question, or puts a suggestion. A leak, even more than a
direct announcement, is apt to have some definite devious purpose behind it. It might more accurately be called a "sub rosa announcement,"
an "indirect statement," or "cloaked news."

The news leak is a pseudo-event par excellence. But with the elabo-   22
ration of news-gathering facilities in Washington—of regular, planned
press conferences, of prepared statements for future release, and of
countless other practices—the news protocol has hardened. Both government officials and reporters have felt the need for more flexible and
more ambiguous modes of communication between them. The origins
of the Presidential press conference itself can be traced to a kind of news

leak when President Theodore Roosevelt allowed Lincoln Steffens to interview him as he was being shaved. Other Presidents gave favored correspondents an interview from time to time or dropped hints to friendly journalists. Similarly, the present institution of the news leak began in the irregular practice of a government official's helping a particular correspondent by confidentially giving him information not yet generally released. But today the leak is almost as well organized and as rigidly ruled by protocol as a formal press conference. Being fuller of ambiguity, with a welcome atmosphere of confidence and intrigue, it is more appealing to all concerned. The institutionalized leak puts a greater burden of contrivance and pretense on both government officials and reporters.

In Washington these days, and elsewhere on a smaller scale, the custom has grown up among important members of the government of arranging to dine with select representatives of the news corps. Such dinners are usually preceded by drinks, and beforehand there is a certain amount of restrained conviviality. Everyone knows the rules. The occasion is private, and any information given out afterward must be communicated according to rule and in the technically proper vocabulary. After dinner the undersecretary, the general, or the admiral allows himself to be questioned. He may recount "facts" behind past news, state plans, or declare policy. The reporters have confidence, if not in the ingenuousness of the official, at least in their colleagues' respect of the protocol. Everybody understands the degree of attribution permissible for every statement made: what, if anything, can be directly quoted, what is "background," what is "deep background," what must be ascribed to "a spokesman," to "an informed source," to speculation, to rumor, or to remote possibility.

Such occasions and the reports flowing from them are loaded with ambiguity. The reporter himself often is not clear whether he is being told a simple fact, a newly settled policy, an administrative hope, or whether perhaps untruths are being deliberately diffused to allay public fears that the true facts are really true. The government official himself, who is sometimes no more than a spokesman, may not be clear. The reporter's task is to find a way of weaving these threads of unreality into a fabric that the reader will not recognize as entirely unreal. Some people have criticized the institutionalized leak as a form of domestic counterintelligence inappropriate in a republic. It has become more and more important and is the source of many of the most influential reports of current politics.

One example will be enough. On March 26, 1966, the *New York Times* carried a three-column headline on the front page: "U.S. Expects Chinese Reds to Attack Isles in April; Weighs All-Out Defense." Three days later a contradictory headline in the same place read: "Eisenhower Sees No War Now Over Chinese Isles." Under each of these headlines appeared a lengthy story. Neither story named any person as a source of the ostensible facts. The then-undisclosed story (months later recorded by Douglass Cater) was this. In the first instance, Admiral Robert B. Carney, Chief of Naval Operations, had an off-the-record "background" dinner for a few reporters. There the admiral gave reporters what they and their readers took to be facts. Since the story was "not for attribution," reporters were not free to mention some very relevant facts— such as that this was the opinion only of Admiral Carney, that this was the same Admiral Carney who had long been saying that war in Asia was inevitable, and that many in Washington, even in the Joint Chiefs of Staff, did not agree with him. Under the ground rules the first story could appear in the papers only by being given an impersonal authority, an atmosphere of official unanimity which it did not merit. The second, and contradictory, statement was in fact made not by the President himself, but by the President's press secretary, James Hagerty, who, having been alarmed by what he saw in the papers, quickly called a second "background" meeting to deny the stories that had sprouted from the first. What, if anything, did it all mean? Was there any real news here at all—except that there was disagreement between Admiral Carney and James Hagerty? Yet this was the fact newsmen were not free to print.

Pseudo-events spawn other pseudo-events in geometric progression. This is partly because every kind of pseudo-event (being planned) tends to become ritualized, with a protocol and a rigidity all its own. As each type of pseudo-event acquires this rigidity, pressures arise to produce other, derivative, forms of pseudo-event which are more fluid, more tantalizing, and more interestingly ambiguous. Thus, as the press conference, itself a pseudo-event, became formalized, there grew up the institutionalized leak. As the leak becomes formalized, still other devices will appear. Of course the shrewd politician or the enterprising newsman knows this and knows how to take advantage of it. Seldom for outright deception, more often simply to make more "news," to provide more "information," or to "improve communication." . . .   26

At first it may seem strange that the rise of pseudo-events has coincided with the growth of the professional ethic which obliges newsmen to omit editorializing and personal judgments from their news accounts. But now it is in the making of pseudo-events that newsmen find ample scope for their individuality and creative imagination.   27

In a democratic society like ours—and more especially in a highly literate, wealthy, competitive, and technologically advanced society— the people can be flooded by pseudo-events. For us, freedom of speech   28 and of the press and of broadcasting includes freedom to create pseudo-events. Competing politicians, competing newsmen, and competing news media contest in this creation. They vie with one another in offering attractive, "informative" accounts and images of the world. They are free to speculate on the facts, to bring new facts into being, to demand answers to their own contrived questions. Our "free marketplace of ideas" is a place where people are confronted by competing pseudo-events and are allowed to judge among them. When we speak of "informing" the people, this is what we really mean.

Until recently we have been justified in believing Abraham Lincoln's familiar maxim: "You may fool all the people some of the time; you can even fool some of the people all the time; but you can't fool all of the people all the time." This has been the foundation belief of American democracy. Lincoln's appealing slogan rests on two elementary assumptions. First, that there is a clear and visible distinction between sham and reality, between the lies a demagogue would have us believe and the truths which are there all the time. Second, that the people tend to prefer reality to sham, that if offered a choice between a simple truth and a contrived image, they will prefer the truth. 29

Neither of these any longer fits the facts. Not because people are less intelligent or more dishonest. Rather because great unforeseen changes—the forward strides of American civilization—have blurred the edges of reality. The pseudo-events which flood our consciousness are neither true nor false in the old familiar senses. The very same advances which have made them possible have also made the images—however planned, contrived, or distorted—more vivid, more attractive, more impressive, and more persuasive than reality itself. 30

We cannot say that we are being fooled. It is not entirely inaccurate to say that we are being "informed." This world of ambiguity is created by those who believe they are instructing us, by our best public servants, and with our own collaboration. Our problem is the harder to solve because it is created by people working honestly and industriously at respectable jobs. It is not created by demagogues or crooks, by conspiracy or evil purpose. The efficient mass production of pseudo-events—in all kinds of packages, in words, on film, on the television screen, and in a thousand other forms—is the work of the whole machinery of our society. It is the daily product of men of goodwill. The media must be fed! The people must be informed! Most pleas for "more information" are therefore misguided. So long as we define information as a knowledge of pseudo-events, "more information" will simply multiply the symptoms without curing the disease. 31

The American citizen thus lives in a world where fantasy is more real than reality, where the image has more dignity than its original. We 32 hardly dare face our bewilderment, because our ambiguous experience is so pleasantly iridescent, and the solace of belief in contrived reality is so thoroughly real. We have become eager accessories to the great hoaxes of the age. These are the hoaxes we play on ourselves.

Pseudo-events from their very nature tend to be more interesting 33 and more attractive than spontaneous events. Therefore in American public life today pseudo-events tend to drive all other kinds of events out of our consciousness, or at least to overshadow them. Earnest, well-informed citizens seldom notice that their experience of spontaneous events is buried by pseudo-events. Yet nowadays, the more industriously they work at "informing" themselves the more this tends to be true. . . .

Here are some characteristics of pseudo-events which make them 34 overshadow spontaneous events:

1. Pseudo-events are more dramatic. A television debate between 35 candidates can be planned to be more suspenseful (for example, by reserving questions which are then popped suddenly) than a casual encounter or consecutive formal speeches planned by each candidate separately.

2. Pseudo-events, being planned for dissemination, are easier to 36 disseminate and to make vivid. Participants are selected for their newsworthy and dramatic interest.

3. Pseudo-events can be repeated at will, and thus their impression 37 can be reinforced.

4. Pseudo-events cost more money to create; hence somebody has 38 an interest in disseminating, magnifying, advertising, and extolling them as events worth watching or worth believing. They are therefore advertised in advance, and rerun in order to get money's worth.

5. Pseudo-events, being planned for intelligibility, are more intelli- 39 gible and hence more reassuring. Even if we cannot discuss intelligently the qualifications of the candidates or the complicated issues, we can at least judge the effectiveness of a television performance. How comforting to have some political matter we can grasp!

6. Pseudo-events are more sociable, more conversable, and more 40 convenient to witness. Their occurrence is planned for our convenience. The Sunday newspaper appears when we have a lazy morning for it. Television programs appear when we are ready with our glass of beer. In the office the next morning, any star performer's regular late-night show at the usual hour will overshadow in conversation a casual event that suddenly came up and had to find its way into the news.

7. Knowledge of pseudo-events—of what has been reported, or 41 what has been staged, and how—becomes the test of being "informed." News magazines provide us regularly with quiz questions concerning

not what has happened but concerning "names in the news"—what has been reported in the news magazines. Pseudo-events begin to provide that "common discourse" which some of my friends have hoped to find in the Great Books.

8. Finally, pseudo-events spawn other pseudo-events in geometric 42 progression. They dominate our consciousness simply because there are more of them, and ever more.

By this new Gresham's Law of American public life, counterfeit 43 happenings tend to drive spontaneous happenings out of circulation. The rise in the power and prestige of the Presidency is due not only to the broadening powers of the office and the need for quick decisions, but also to the rise of centralized news gathering and broadcasting, and the increase of the Washington press corps. The President has an ever more ready, more frequent, and more centralized access to the world of pseudo-events. A similar explanation helps account for the rising prominence in recent years of the Congressional investigating committees. In many cases these committees have virtually no legislative impulse, and sometimes no intelligible legislative assignment. But they do have an almost unprecedented power, possessed now by no one else in the Federal government except the President, to make news. Newsmen support the committees because the committees feed the newsmen and they live together in happy symbiosis. The battle for power among Washington agencies becomes a contest to dominate the citizen's information of the government. This can most easily be done by fabricating pseudo-events.

A perfect example of how pseudo-events can dominate is the pop- 44 ularity of the quiz show format. Its original appeal came less from the fact that such shows were tests of intelligence (or of dissimulation) than from the fact that the situations were elaborately contrived—with isolation booths, armed bank guards, and all the rest—and they purported to inform the public.

The application of the quiz show format to the first so-called Great 45 Debates between Presidential candidates, in the election of 1960, is only another example. These four campaign programs, pompously and self-righteously advertised by the broadcasting networks, were remarkably successful in reducing great national issues to trivial dimensions. With appropriate vulgarity, they might have been called the $400,000 Question (Prize: a $100,000-a-year job for four years). They were a clinical example of the pseudo-event, of how it is made, why it appeals, and of its consequences for democracy in America.

In origin the Great Debates were confusedly collaborative between 46 politicians and news makers. Public interest centered around the pseudo-event itself: the lighting, makeup, ground rules, whether notes would be allowed, etc. Far more interest was shown in the performance than in what was said. The pseudo-events spawned in turn by the Great Debates were numberless. People who had seen the shows read about them the more avidly, and listened eagerly for interpretations by news commentators. Representatives of both parties made "statements" on the probable effects of the debates. Numerous interviews and discussion programs were broadcast exploring their meaning. Opinion polls kept us informed on the nuances of our own and other people's reactions. Topics of speculation multiplied. Even the question whether there should be a fifth debate became for a while a lively "issue."

The drama of the situation was mostly specious, or at least had an   47
extremely ambiguous relevance to the main (but forgotten) issue: which participant was better qualified for the Presidency. Of course, a man's ability, while standing under klieg lights, without notes, to answer in two and a half minutes a question kept secret until that moment, had only the most dubious relevance—if any at all—to his real qualifications to make deliberate Presidential decisions on longstanding public questions after being instructed by a corps of advisers. The great Presidents in our history, with the possible exception of FDR, would have done miserably; but our most notorious demagogues would have shone. . . .

The television medium shapes this new kind of political quiz-show   48
spectacular in many crucial ways. Theodore H. White proved this with copious detail in his *The Making of the President: 1960* (1961). All the circumstances of this particular competition for votes were far more novel than the old word "debate" and the comparisons with the Lincoln-Douglas Debates suggested. Kennedy's great strength in the critical first debate, according to White, was that he was in fact not "debating" at all, but was seizing the opportunity to address the whole nation; while Nixon stuck close to the issues raised by his opponent, rebutting them one by one. Nixon, moreover, suffered a handicap that was serious only on television. He has a light, naturally transparent skin. On an ordinary camera that takes pictures by optical projection, this skin photographs well. But a television camera projects electronically, by an "image-orthicon tube" which has an x-ray effect. This camera penetrates Nixon's transparent skin and brings out (even just after a shave) the tiniest hair growing in the follicles beneath the surface. For the decisive first program Nixon wore a makeup called Lazy Shave which was ineffective under these conditions. He therefore looked haggard and heavy-bearded by contrast to Kennedy, who looked pert and clean-cut.

This greatest opportunity in American history to educate the voters   49
by debating the large issues of the campaign failed. The main reason, as White points out, was the compulsions of the medium. "The nature of both TV and radio is that they abhor silence and 'dead time.' All TV and

radio discussion programs are compelled to snap question and answer back and forth as if the contestants were adversaries in an intellectual tennis match. Although every experienced newspaperman and inquirer knows that the most thoughtful and responsive answers to any difficult question come after long pause, and that the longer the pause the more illuminating the thought that follows it, nonetheless the electronic media cannot bear to suffer a pause of more than five seconds; a pause of thirty seconds of dead time on air seems interminable. Thus, snapping their two-and-a-half-minute answers back and forth, both candidates could only react for the cameras and the people, they could not think." Whenever either candidate found himself touching a thought too large for two-minute exploration, he quickly retreated. Finally, the television-watching voter was left to judge, not on issues explored by thoughtful men, but on the relative capacity of the two candidates to perform under television stress.

Pseudo-events thus lead to emphasis on pseudo-qualifications. 50 Again the self-fulfilling prophecy. If we test Presidential candidates by their talents on TV quiz performances, we will, of course, choose Presidents for precisely these qualifications. In a democracy, reality tends to conform to the pseudo-event. Nature imitates art.

We are frustrated by our very efforts publicly to unmask the pseudo- 51 event. Whenever we describe the lighting, the makeup, the studio setting, the rehearsals, etc., we simply arouse more interest. One newsman's interpretation makes us more eager to hear another's. One commentator's speculation that the debates may have little significance makes us curious to hear whether another commentator disagrees.

Pseudo-events do, of course, increase our illusion of grasp on the 52 world, what some have called the American illusion of omnipotence. Perhaps, we come to think, the world's problems can really be settled by "statements," by "Summit" meetings, by a competition of "prestige," by overshadowing images.

Once we have tasted the charm of pseudo-events, we are tempted 53 to believe they are the only important events. Our progress poisons the sources of our experience. And the poison tastes so sweet that it spoils our appetite for plain fact. Our seeming ability to satisfy our exaggerated expectations makes us forget that they are exaggerated.

•••••••••••••••••••••

Examining the Text
1. According to Boorstin, how has the relationship between journalism and theology shifted over the last 300 years (paragraphs 1–6)? In what ways does he see this as a symptom of a larger shift in our attitude

toward what happens in the world? How have the gatherers and consumers of news been affected?

2. What recent "pseudo-events" can you think of? How do these differ from "real events"? Do you agree with Boorstin that pseudo-events blur the distinction between illusion and reality?

3. Boorstin suggests that the 1960 Presidential debates between Kennedy and Nixon were a pseudo-event measuring only "pseudo-qualifications" (44–49). Do you find this example persuasive? Since then, televised debates between candidates have become a staple of Presidential and other political races. Do you agree with Boorstin, or do you think such debates provide "real" information?

4. What do you think is Boorstin's purpose in writing this essay? What recommendations would he make for improving the role of journalism?

For Group Discussion

Boorstin claims that we prefer pseudo-events to real events, and he gives eight reasons to support his claim (33–41). As a group, choose a recent pseudo-event that you have all read about or seen reported on TV. Discuss whether this pseudo-event coincides with Boorstin's eight reasons. Does it differ in any way? As a class, contrast pseudo-events with "real" news stories. Which are more interesting, and why?

Writing Suggestion

Test Boorstin's hypothesis that pseudo-events have become more and more frequent in American media by watching news broadcasts and reading several newspapers for a few days or a week. In a notebook keep track of the number of events that seem to fit Boorstin's category. In an essay, discuss your opinion about what makes each a pseudo-event. What conclusions can you draw from your observations?

Rock, Rap, and Movies Bring You the News

Jon Katz

I magine turning on the nightly news and, instead of seeing Dan Rather or Peter Jennings, discovering Murphy Brown at the anchor desk. Murphy Brown introduces Bruce Springsteen with an update on the economy, filmmaker Oliver Stone covering the latest Washington scandal, and rapper Ice Cube reporting from a beat in the inner city. During the broadcast, a host of celebrities—TV stars, movie directors and actors, rockers and rappers—report on domestic and international issues. As unlikely as it might sound, this is precisely the scenario Jon Katz evokes in the following essay. What's more, in Katz's view, it is from these sources that our information about the world increasingly comes.

Katz, a novelist and media critic for Rolling Stone, *speaks of the "New News"—from movies, from television comedies, dramas, and talk shows, from recordings and MTV, from entertainment and lifestyle publications—replacing the "Old News" for many younger Americans. Pushing aside daily newspapers, weekly news magazines, and television news broadcasts, this New News is "seizing the functions of mainstream journalism, sparking conversations and setting the country's social and political agenda."*

The New News, Katz says, appeals in several ways, perhaps most importantly through communicators who "speak to states of mind, to anger at real issues like poverty and hopelessness, to disenchantment with jingoistic institutions." More and more, he suggests, young Americans are frustrated by the inability of the conventional news media to describe and explain the reality of their experiences. The New News also blurs the boundaries between journalism and entertainment, with pop culture now taking on such crucial social problems as racism, sexism, crime, and poverty. As Katz puts it, "Pop culture— America's most remarkable invention since the car—[has] spawned a new information culture."

As you read, *consider the extent to which your knowledge of current events and issues comes from the New News sources Katz describes.*

••••••••••••••••••••

It's a shame Oliver Stone wasn't running one of the networks when   1
the Bush administration decided journalists couldn't cover the Gulf
War. Nobody denied that conspiracy. Stone would have surely gone
berserk, storming past the blue cabanas, over the berms, and into the
desert with his own camera-armed legions to bring back riveting pictures and shocking notions, like war is hell.

It's a shame, too, that Sinéad O'Connor wasn't providing network   2
commentary in place of one more former general touting new weapons.
When she refused to have the national anthem played at her concerts,
she went further out on a limb than any of the major news organizations
did on behalf of their silenced correspondents.

Too bad, as well, that instead of one of those evening-news suits,   3
Bruce Springsteen isn't reporting on the economy. Springsteen seemed
to know years ago that the jobs weren't coming back. The networks are
still waiting for confirmation from the White House.

Straight news—the Old News—is pooped, confused, and broke.   4
Each Nielsen survey, each circulation report, each quarterly statement,

reveals the cultural Darwinism ravaging the news industry. The people watching and reading are aging and dying, and the young no longer take their place. Virtually no major city daily has gained in circulation in recent years (the *Washington Post* is one of the few exceptions). In the last decade, network news has lost nearly half its audience. Advertising revenues are drying up.

In place of the Old News, something dramatic is evolving, a new 5 culture of information, a hybrid New News—dazzling, adolescent, ir-responsible, fearless, frightening, and powerful. The New News is a heady concoction, part Hollywood film and TV movie, part pop music and pop art, mixed with popular culture and celebrity magazines, tabloid telecasts, cable, and home video.

Increasingly, the New News is seizing the functions of mainstream 6 journalism, sparking conversations and setting the country's social and political agenda. It is revolutionizing the way information reaches peo-ple and moves among them. It is changing the way Americans evaluate politicians and, shortly, elect them.

Think of Walter Cronkite or Ted Koppel if you want to get an image 7 of the Old News. The voice is grave, resonant with the burden of trans-mitting serious matters—White House communications strategies, leaks from State Department sources, leading economic indicators. The sto-ries are remote (from Yugoslavia, Nairobi, Beijing) or from institutions that feel as remote (Congress, Wall Street, the Supreme Court). The re-porters of the Old News cluster there, talking to one another, mired in an agenda that seems increasingly obtuse and irrelevant.

In January 1992, the New News is absorbed with a different agenda: 8 on the eve of Martin Luther King's birthday, Public Enemy focuses the country's attention on his broken dream through its furious new video, an imagined enactment of the killing of Arizona state-government offi-cials. In New York City, inner-city parents are taking their children to see *Juice* to educate them about the consequences of street violence. *JFK*—assaulted for weeks by the Old News as reckless and irresponsi-ble—has prompted the chairman of a congressional committee that in-vestigated the assassination to ask for the release of all government doc-uments on the slaying. The kids on *Beverly Hills, 90210*—"The only show on TV that portrays teen life as it really is," says the editorial director of *16* magazine—are struggling with divorce, sex, and AIDS.

Meanwhile, the remnants of the Old News slowly begin to gather 9 in the bleak towns of New Hampshire for another presidential cam-paign. Only a few years ago, the three networks virtually hosted the presidential campaigns. Great media encampments took over entire motels in New Hampshire, with producers and technicians stuffed into trailers like a circus come to town. But ABC, CBS, and NBC have already announced there will be no vast encampments on the primary trail or at the conventions this year. Day-to-day coverage will be left to cable. One network that has said it will offer more campaign coverage than it did in 1988 is MTV.

Once, the borders were clear and inviolate: newspapers, newscasts, 10 and newsmagazines covered serious events; pop culture entertained us. But in the past generation, the culture sparked by rock and roll, then fused with TV and mutated by Hollywood, ran riot over the traditional boundaries between straight journalism and entertainment.

Now the list of issues addressed by the New News—far from the 11 front pages and evening newscasts—is growing steadily. We're exposed to gender conflict in *Thelma and Louise;* money blues, sexual conflicts, and working-class stress on *Roseanne;* motherhood, corporate takeovers, and journalistic ethics on *Murphy Brown.*

Bart Simpson's critique of society is more trenchant than that of 12 most newspaper columnists. Movies like *Boyz n the Hood* and *Straight Out of Brooklyn* and rappers like Public Enemy and Ice Cube deal with race more squarely than *Nightline.* No wonder Chuck D calls rap the CNN of black America.

In the same way that middle-class blacks rarely appear in the tradi- 13 tional media, disaffected working-class whites don't seem to exist in the world Old News covers. Analysts looking for clues to David Duke's popularity would do better to listen to Guns n' Roses and Skid Row songs than to scan newscasts and newspapers for the source of white resentment.

The country's ascendant magazine is not a newsmagazine but a 14 New News magazine. *Entertainment Weekly* focuses on what editors used to call the back of the book—the arts and culture material once ghettoized behind the important stuff. But today, the back of the book, is the book. In its January 17 cover story, "JFK: The Film and the Furor, What's Behind the Backlash," *EW* dramatically illustrated how popular culture and major stories have steadily converged on one another over the past three decades, redefining what news is and who gets to cover it.

It didn't happen overnight—more like thirty years. Bob Dylan's vi- 15 sion of rock and roll helped mainstream music move from entertainment to political expression, an op-ed page for millions of kids who would never have dreamed of reading—or agreeing with—a newspaper editorial. Following in the tradition of shows like *All in the Family,* TV producers and writers broke free of the censors and produced broadcasts like *Hill Street Blues, St. Elsewhere,* and *L.A. Law,* presenting life more and more as viewers experienced it, not as the networks wanted it seen.

So did tabloid telecasts and made-for-TV movies, which drama-   16
tized, reenacted, and reinterpreted issues like sexism, child abuse, alcoholism, and homosexuality. Hollywood helped define Vietnam in *Apoc-
alypse Now,* racial hatred in *Do the Right Thing,* the takeover culture in
Wall Street. Emerging cable technology gave viewers and programmers
vastly more choices, breaking open the New News. Pop culture—America's most remarkable invention since the car—had spawned a new information culture.

The modern news media—the Old News—was formed in the years   17
after World War II. Major newspapers and instantly powerful network-
news divisions chose Washington and New York as their headquarters,
and presidential politics, the economy, and foreign affairs—the cold
war, mostly—as their preeminent beats. In his heyday, the Old News
showed us the murder of John Kennedy, took us to the moon, then
helped drive a president from office and end a war.

Other stories—the sexual revolution, the role of race, dramatic   18
changes in the relationship between people and their jobs, the evolution
of pop culture, a rebirth of spiritualism—were covered sporadically and
incompletely by the Old News. They often sprang up away from well-
staffed bureaus in a handful of major cities, thus making them harder
for Old News to cover. They were a sideline, never the main event.

But for the New News—and for much of America—they were *the*   19
event. Women, blacks, Hispanics, gays, and Asians had launched an ongoing political and cultural revolution against middle-class white males,
who continue to dominate most institutions, including the news media.
In some countries, revolutions are violent, bloody affairs settled in the
streets. In America, they are slugged out in music videos, movies, and
cable shows.

In the resulting turmoil, the Old News and the new have taken off   20
in opposite directions, diverging more and more dramatically in content, packaging, and audience. Although Americans can watch, in living color, a war or the description of an alleged rape, almost no major
daily deigns to use color photographs, and most anchors are still white
and male.

As Old News habits have ossified, its audience has evaporated.   21
Newspaper readership has been declining for thirty years. According to
a *Times Mirror* study, 71 percent of people between the ages of seventy
and seventy-nine read a daily newspaper, but only 40 percent of people
between the ages of eighteen and twenty-nine do. Of people under
thirty who are married with children, only 30 percent read a paper daily.

The median age of the *New York Times* subscriber is forty-two, *Time*   22
magazine's is thirty-eight. In contrast, *Entertainment Weekly*'s is thirty-

one, *Rolling Stone*'s is twenty-six. Among shows that teenagers watch most often, *The Simpsons* and *Beverly Hills, 90210* rank at the top; *60 Minutes* ranks 110th.

The Old News seems bewildered and paralyzed by the dazzling   23
new technologies competing for its audience, clucking like a cross old lady chasing noisy kids away from her window. Editors and producers prefer "serious topics" to the New News culture. In the same way they once fussed over rock & roll, most newspapers and news shows were too busy attacking Nintendo addiction to notice that more than 50 million entertainment systems had taken up residence in American homes, literally redefining what a TV set was and what it did. In 1991, the Nintendo hot line got 2 million calls from players needing help in ascending yet another level of Tetris or Super Mario Bros. 3.

All the while, news organizations puzzled about why kids were   24
leaving in droves. Interactive video-jukebox systems and sports channels, round-the-clock local-news channels, video shopping and scores of movie and entertainment channels helped to create a new video culture for the young, a profound change in leisure time that the Old News kissed off as a teen fad.

Stung by the mounting evidence that Americans' passions and con-   25
cerns increasingly lie elsewhere, Old News institutions do appear unnerved. They've launched promotional campaigns, experimented disdainfully with color, commissioned marketing studies. ("Perhaps we should start a kids' page?") But it's mostly fussing. Every time real change is broached—two years ago, CBS tried reenactments on *Saturday Night With Connie Chung*—the guardian crows of the old order shriek the innovators into submission.

The networks sneered as CNN haltingly began to construct the most   26
efficient and responsive electronic news-video-gathering machine in history. The newspaper industry's most dramatic response to the New News—*USA Today*—was greeted by the business with the same enthusiasm with which the human body greets a foreign invader. It was dubbed McPaper and dismissed as insubstantial, shallow and, worst of all, TV-like.

Its owner, Gannett, which owns eighty-one newspapers and admits   27
to being alarmed about newspapers' shrinking and aging circulation, recently published a handbook for its editors. It says with shocking bluntness that papers have failed to recognize "key topics that shape readers' lives" and are filled with "dull, formula-based writing" and that newsrooms are "isolationist, elitist and afraid of change."

All the facts add up to a story that, Gannett's urgings notwith-   28
standing, journalism doesn't want to hear. The Old News has clung desperately to the view that the New News culture, like pornography, is

nothing but trash and will eventually go away. Yet journalistically, the New News is often superior to the old at spotting major stories and putting them into context.

All last summer, men and women were talking about men and 29
women. Movies like *Thelma & Louise* and made-for-TV dramas like CBS's *Rape of Dr. Willis* clearly reflected the outrage that coalesced around the Anita Hill–Clarence Thomas confrontation. The view of men as insensitive, frequently hateful creatures who don't get it was also advanced in movies like *The Doctor*, in which a surgeon has to get cancer before he learns how to be compassionate, and *Regarding Henry*, whose hero learns the meaning of life only after he gets shot in the head. *Beauty and the Beast* might be the timeliest animated film ever made: The heroine is courageous and brainy; the two major male characters are a prince who's turned into a beast so that he can learn how to love and a macho man who is a beast, period.

If the white men in the U.S. Senate had spent more time at the 30
movies and less watching Old News Sunday-morning talk shows, they might have heard the sound of thousands of women cheering when Thelma and Louise blew up that tanker truck. They might not have been so shocked when women all over the country exploded in fury at the Judiciary Committee's failure to explore Anita Hill's charges.

One of the most interesting scoops in the Thomas affair—an exclu- 31
sive interview with the justice's wife—was secured by *People*. And just three weeks after the hearings, the characters on *Designing Women* spent an episode watching footage of the hearings and vigorously arguing both sides. For millions of Americans, it was a more relevant hashing of the matter than they would get on any Sunday-morning gasathon.

Other news stories have been foreshadowed by the New News. The 32
FBI was so alarmed by the rap group N.W.A.'s "Fuck Tha Police" that it cautioned local police departments against N.W.A.'s performing in their cities. Yet just two years later, in a stunning example of the new video culture's news-gathering potential, a bystander videotaped the brutal beating of Rodney King by the Los Angeles Police Department, the very force N.W.A. was warning its listeners about.

There is, in fact, almost no story Old News has struggled to come to 33
grips with more dramatically and unsuccessfully than race. America seems continually stunned by episodic explosions of racial hatred—by the murder of Yusuf Hawkins in New York, the violent black-Hasidic confrontations in Brooklyn last summer, the chord struck by David Duke.

Still overwhelmingly owned, staffed and run by whites, and white 34
males in particular, the media are stymied and discomfitted by racial issues. After decades of ignoring brutal racism, they seem to have lurched

from one extreme to the other. Now they're so desperate to avoid the appearance of racism that they seem frozen by the subject.

The members of the media are able to quote demagogues and activists, but they're unable to advance the country's understanding of ghetto fury, to portray and represent the view of the black middle class or to explore white anger and confusion. Few issues in American life generate so much mythology, yet the intrigues of the White House chief of staff are covered in far greater detail. Spike Lee is far ahead of his mainstream journalistic competitors on racial issues. So is Ice Cube: "They have the authority / To Kill a minority / Fucking with me cause I'm a teenager / With a little bit of gold and a pager."

Police advocates don't make many albums, but there's plenty of white backlash to racial tensions evident in white rock, as well as worry about bleak economic futures. Perhaps the leading white working-class New News columnists at the moment are the members of Guns n' Roses, whose "Right Next Door to Hell," from *Use Your Illusion I,* is a national anthem for working-class anger:

> When your innocence dies
> You'll find the blues
> Seems all our heroes were born to lose
> Just walkin' through time
> You believe this heat
> Another empty house another dead-end street

Skid Row sounds like John Chancellor in comparison. From the album and song *Slave to the Grind:* "You got me forced to crack my lids in two / I'm still stuck inside the rubber room / I gotta punch the clock that leads the blind / I'm just another gear in the assembly line."

Rap and rock—music listened to by the same kids the Old News is fretting about losing—are describing a different world than the one reflected on evening newscasts and in daily papers. Washington journalists were abuzz for months in anticipation of the *Washington Post*'s seven-part series on Vice President Dan Quayle, reported and written by Old News royalty David Broder and Bob Woodward. But the tens of thousands of words lavished on Quayle told us more about the remote agenda of the Old News than it did about the vice president.

The most explosive assault the New News has made on the Old is Oliver Stone's *JFK.* Its release has sparked less a free-for-all discussion of a recent historical event than a modern-day heresy trial. Stone set out to upend conventional wisdom, centering his film on Jim Garrison's largely discredited theories. It is unclear why so many Americans remain skeptical about the Warren Commission's findings—only

19 percent believe in the lone-gunman theory, according to polls—yet clearly they do. Whatever the accuracy of his theory, Stone—whose *Platoon, Wall Street* and *Born on the Fourth of July* were dramatically journalistic in their efforts to reflect different cultures at crucial times—has tapped into this dark strain in American life.

The Old News condemns Stone as irresponsible because he is advancing disproved theories and crackpot speculation as truth. The Old News is crying foul, incensed that someone has crossed over into their turf.   40

Yet it is Stone's movie, not years of columnizing by the Old News, that is likely to force the release of Kennedy-assassination documents the government is keeping under wraps. The license Stone took—and the risk—in reinventing a seminal story in the country's history illustrates why the New News is gaining so dramatically on the old: it is wiling to heed and explore the passionate and sometimes frightening undercurrents in American life.   41

The United States is an odd country, a lot stranger than the stilted language or narrow conventions of the Old News can explain. Remember the fascination with *Twin Peaks?* Americans seem to know—though surely not from reading it or seeing it in most journalism—that their country is violent, troubled, and brooding, in almost desperate need of mythological symbols like those advanced by the cultural historian Joseph Campbell.   42

Elvis Presley's death and afterlife so boosted supermarket-tabloid sales that they have become a permanent part of the New News. As Greil Marcus shows in his new book *Dead Elvis,* Americans are as obsessed with Presley's death as they are with Kennedy's assassination.   43

We don't really know why, and how could we? Both stories fall just this side of prostitution to most of the reporters assigned to cover, say, the White House. Stone's assassination theories may or may not have been correct, but his journalistic instinct was sure. He hit one of the rawest nerves in American history, demonstrating at the very least that to many Americans the Kennedy assassination is far from a settled matter.   44

In their anger at Stone, the guardians of journalistic and cultural propriety are saying that Americans aren't capable of drawing their own conclusions, that only journalists operating in conventional ways and within conventional boundaries can be entrusted with weighty or controversial issues. The anger of the Old News demonstrates anew one of its most self-destructive streaks—a patronizing contempt for the young. Much of the criticism leveled at Stone suggests that Americans who weren't alive when Kennedy was shot are too ignorant or impressionable to see beyond Kevin Costner's earnest face, as though people under thirty can't grasp that a Hollywood film is one person's vision, not the provable truth.   45

A youthful audience is no guarantee that a New News product is   46
journalistically superior; what is significant is that younger viewers and
readers find conventional journalism of no particular use in their daily
lives. In fact, given that the media make so much out of fairness and objectivity, it's a puzzle why so few people of any age trust it or its conclusions.

Mainstream journalism frequently checkmates itself. In worshiping   47
balance over truth, objectivity over point of view, moderation over diversity, and credibility over creativity, the Old News gives consumers
a clear choice. Consumers can have a balanced discussion, with every
side of an issue neutralizing the other, or they can turn to singers, producers, and film-makers offering colorful, distinctive, often flawed but
frequently powerful visions of their truth. More and more, Americans
are making it clear which they prefer.

Younger audiences raised on New News traditions of outspoken-   48
ness and hyperbole appear to understand that Public Enemy and Oliver
Stone are not always to be taken literally. These New News communicators speak to states of mind, to anger at real issues like poverty and
hopelessness, to disenchantment with jingoistic institutions, and to a
common perception that mainstream news organizations don't tell the
whole truth or at least don't much reflect their truth.

Stone's *JFK* will have to stand the ultimate capitalist media test, the   49
same one every newspaper, TV station, magazine, and Nintendo dealer
faces: people will buy it, watch it, read it, believe it. Or not. At least Stone
has made it clear where he stands.

It's simply not possible to know yet whether the rise of the New   50
News is good or bad, healthy or menacing. How about all of the above?

The final form the Old News will take is unclear, and New News
technology and content are still rapidly evolving.

This year Time Warner will unleash another Godzilla on the Old   51
News—in New York, a twenty-four hour local cable news channel will
begin broadcasting. For the first time, *truly* local news—fires, high-
school sports, board-of-education hearings on condom distribution—
will be on TV. Advertisers like pharmacies, copy shops, and bridal sa-
lons will have an affordable electronic medium to advertise on.

Another billion-dollar shoe waiting to drop, ferociously opposed by   52
its competitors, will come from the Baby Bells. Now that the federal
courts have given the regional phone companies permission to enter the
information market, they'll use computers and existing and future
transmission technology to offer new kinds of electronic travel, shopping, banking, and commercial services, including news.

In the new world of twenty-four-hour electronic news, can print or   53
commercial broadcasting remain in the breaking-news business, as both

so stubbornly insist on doing? Will newspapers ever stop running ban-
ner headlines over black-and-white photos that appeared live on TV
twenty-four hours earlier? It seems they'd rather die.

The best vantage point from which to watch the dramatic collision   54
of the competing news cultures will be living rooms across the country,
as the Old News struggles to come to grips with its quadrennial Super
Bowl-cum-Olympics—the presidential election. If the Old News is right,
and only it can be trusted to capture and shape major events, then the
country is heading straight for a civics nightmare in which challengers
can't get coverage and issues can't be raised, because Americans, wired
into their personal entertainment complexes, are too busy to think about
who should occupy the White House.

This time around, CNN and C-SPAN will be on all the time, for   55
politicians desperate to communicate with their peers and for political
junkies who want to see crucial votes or speeches. But fewer regular
prime-time programs will be preempted. Except for the Democratic convention in New York, a cab ride across town, the anchors will be watching most of the campaign on studio monitors. A few troops—Sawyer,
Chung—will be running around with their Star Trek earphones, but it
will be a pathetic echo of the glory days for the Old News.

Maybe there's a better way. Maybe the New News should field a   56
team of its own this year. Don Henley could coanchor the convention
coverage with Murphy Brown, prime-time TV's toughest news interviewer, not from a booth, but down on the convention floor, laying bare
a process that would even consider reelecting a president who didn't
know until December 17 that the recession wasn't over. Sinéad O'Connor, the Geto Boys, and Roseanne Arnold will do nightly commentary,
maybe from the floor with working-stiff delegates. Spike Lee will air a
series of documentaries on how race is being manipulated to win still
another election, alternating with reports on how whites are getting
screwed by the system, courtesy of Axl Rose, or perhaps an investigative special by Oliver Stone on how Ronald Reagan's election was the
result of a conspiracy between the media, Hollywood filmmakers, and
jet-aircraft contractors.

....

Examining the Text

1. Katz begins his article with three examples (paragraphs 1–3). What
point is he making? How do the examples lead into his opening observations about the New News and the Old News (4–6)? Do you think
these examples are an effective opening strategy?

2. What does Katz mean when he says that "cultural Darwinism" is causing a shift from Old to New News? Do your observations and experience support Katz's contentions—that is, that Americans in their teens and twenties prefer non-traditional news sources? If so, do you think this will continue as they grow older? Why or why not?

3. How would you define Katz's purpose and tone in his final paragraph?

For Group Discussion

Katz comments that "younger viewers and readers find conventional journalism of no particular use in their daily lives." To what extent does this observation apply to you and others in your group? Poll the group to determine how frequently each of you watches conventional news broadcasts and reads newspapers and news magazines. What are your main sources of information about the world? Does New News have a stronger influence on most of you than traditional news? If there are major differences within your group, how would you explain them? As a class, discuss any such differences and how they support or contradict Katz's views.

Writing Suggestion

Katz describes Old News as "pooped, confused, and broke" and New News as "dazzling, adolescent, irresponsible, fearless, frightening, and powerful." What do you find to be the most significant differences between Old News and New News? In an essay explore the relative advantages and disadvantages of each.

What Readers Want: A Vote for a Very Different Model

Arthur Charity

Jon Katz argues that conventional journalism is on the verge of self-destruction. Arthur Charity's diagnosis in the following essay is not quite as extreme, but he does acknowledge that mainstream news organizations are doing a poor job of meeting some of the public's most basic needs.

A former editor of The Ottawa Citizen *and now a freelance writer, Charity claims that journalists underestimate the seriousness and intelligence of the American public. Rather than "talking down" or "sugar-coating" the news with visually appealing layouts and sensationalistic stories, news organizations have the potential to be one of today's few remaining venues for civil public discourse about important social issues. In an increasingly fragmented society, where else, Charity asks, can Americans meet and talk about education, poverty, crime, unemployment, foreign policy—about the issues and events that shape their lives? Pointing to innovative programs initiated by several local newspapers to bring diverse readers together and facilitate an exchange of ideas, Charity argues that this "very different model" is precisely what the American public wants from the news media: not objective reportage, but a forum in which to satisfy our desire to participate and contribute.*

As you read, recall Roger Rosenblatt's argument for the importance of objectivity in journalism. How does Charity's essay address Rosenblatt's claim that journalism shouldn't pursue a "larger truth"? What sort of "truth" does Charity's model of journalism aim for? Would Charity's model address any of Jon Katz's criticisms of traditional journalism?

• • • • • • • • • • • • • • • • • • • •

I've always had a queasy feeling that we journalists respect the 1
American people less than we think we do. We paste democratic slogans on our mastheads (like "That the people shall know," the motto of Columbia University's Graduate School of Journalism), but invariably act amazed when our readers display seriousness and intelligence. Witness the myriad columns that followed last year's second presidential debate, trumpeting as if it were breaking news the fact that ordinary people had asked smart questions. Many of us seem to think readers aren't as serious as we are about finding the truth; for proof, just look at the assumption underlying much of our "reader-centered" journalism: Americans can be lured into learning about their own public affairs only by clever writing, dramatic visuals, and more readable type.

I think there's a case to be made, however, that ordinary Americans, 2
far from needing lessons from us in serious journalism, understand what it can and ought to be much better than most reporters and editors do. They are not as blinkered as we are by the traditions of Pulitzer, Murrow, Woodstein, and *60 Minutes;* nor are they distracted, like our consultants with their focus groups, by trying to come up with a sugar coating that will somehow transform news that bores people into news that doesn't.

Having in their private lives bought cars, hired employees, and reached consensus at P.T.A. meetings, they know what kinds of facts and discussion people need in order to make smart decisions, and they want us to supply them. It seems a simple thing to ask, and they don't understand why they can't get the information—unless it's because we're too incompetent, biased, or arrogant to do the job right.

Imagine for a moment that you are trying to learn about NAFTA— the Canada-U.S.-Mexico free-trade accord—without the benefit of database, Rolodex, or a publisher paying you to do your homework. Now imagine that NAFTA is a car: you could get its specifications and those of alternatives simply by phoning a few local dealers and asking for brochures; you could get educated opinions on its strengths and weaknesses by asking your neighbors and friends, or reading what the experts thought, presented cogently and fairly, in *Consumer Reports*, say, or a reputable auto magazine.

Since NAFTA is a public choice, not a private one, and since it is too big and complicated for neighbors and brochures, you would have to rely totally on the press. What would you find there? A welter of fragmentary opinions and facts, mixed up with thousands of details that don't help you at all. And as for educated opinions on national TV, you would get, not cogency and fairness, but the quirky sort of talk that passes for discussion. There are, at one extreme, shows like CNN's *Crossfire,* where in a recent discussion of NAFTA Michael Kinsley, Pat Buchanan, and their guests spent five and three quarters of their fifteen minutes all talking at once (sample exchange: "Michael, don't be a simpleton"; Kinsley: *"You're* the simpleton"). There are, at the other extreme, "thoughtful" programs like *MacNeil/Lehrer,* where for twenty minutes gray suits talked about econometric studies (after agreeing at the outset that they were too inexact to be of much value), then for fifteen minutes blue suits discussed how the president could best "sell" the deal (much like watching a convention of GM dealers brainstorm over how to lure in the suckers.)

In the end, you might simply give up.

But Americans don't give up; instead, they try to pick up coherent information and discourse wherever they can find it, including sources that look suspect to us. No wonder that, in the absence of any balanced, comprehensive, and serious journalist's book about NAFTA, Americans are making Ross Perot's unbalanced but informative *Save Your Job, Save Our Country* a paperback bestseller. No wonder they turn to talk shows where, with greater civility than Buchanan or Kinsley, diverse people talk freely in terms of morality, hopes, fears, and life lessons—the many elements of true public discussion that are missing in *MacNeil/Lehrer.* This is intelligence and seriousness at work.

We journalists see as clearly as the public does that our work is full of holes, that it's piecemeal and incomplete, sometimes stupid and shrill. Yet we don't lose sleep over it—or expect the public to—because we rationalize that even if we're not providing all the facts and civil debate necessary to American democracy, at least we're serving up a basic minimum. If people are really serious, we reason, they can find the missing pieces at work and at home, at community meetings, or at their local church, mosque, or temple.

This just shows how little we comprehend the direness of their predicament.

In his fascinating 1988 book on what's known as zip-code marketing, *The Clustering of America,* Michael Weiss tells the story of a computer wizard named Jonathan Robbin, who in the mid-1970s hit on the idea of dividing the United States population into forty disparate groups, each spread in seemingly random pockets across the country but unified by life-style. His zip-code-based taxonomy became one of the most lucrative ideas in marketing. "Tell me someone's zip code," Robbin boasted, "and I can predict what they eat, drink, drive—even think."

Weiss then goes on to prove Robbin right: statistics show that people who live in those zip codes colorfully dubbed "the Urban Gold Coast"—whether they're on the Upper East Side of Manhattan or in Chicago's Fort Dearborn—are apartment-rich and well-educated, ride trains and read *The Atlantic,* eat rye bread and avoid pork sausage with remarkable regularity. Those who live in the "Shotguns & Pickups" zips of, say, Jewett, West Virginia, or Molalla, Oregon, on the other hand, vote conservative and drive domestics. The two groups are alike in hardly anything but this: when they move to a new place, they gravitate toward their own kind.

My own experience illustrates the point. I used to credit myself with being very broadminded, having grown up in a blue-collar suburb of Los Angles and gone to a snooty urban college back East; seen thirty-two states mostly by car; and worked in soup kitchens, theme parks, and summer camps. But when I tallied up all the clusters I've seen in my thirty-three years, I found they represent barely two-fifths of America. When I focused on just the places I knew intimately enough to comprehend, say, the local arguments over abortion or affirmative action, the total plummeted to one-seventh.

Since we no longer fight together in Eisenhower's army or read *The Saturday Evening Post, Look,* and *Life* every week from sea to shining sea; since we find it difficult to even see each other in our daily lives and travels, we Americans really have no place to meet except on television or in the newspapers. Whatever sense of each other we don't get there, we won't have; and if the media can't connect all the clusters in civil discourse, there will be no civil discourse. A shortfall is as good as a failure.

Our isolation may even exceed Weiss's pessimistic picture; harried work schedules, the decline of church-going and social clubs, fault-lines of race and gender, professional jargon and loyalty may make us islands even without our own homes. But that doesn't mean we want to be. When the Minneapolis–St. Paul *Star Tribune* started posing issues-of-the-month a year ago, encouraging readers to form civic roundtables to discuss them, one executive assumed they would just draw the same activist 5 percent who go to school board and city council meetings anyway. Instead, most had never been involved in the community. Coordinator Jeremy Iggers concluded, "I think we take it for granted that these conversations happen casually all the time. My feeling now is, they don't. I think people are hungry for the chance to talk like grown-ups about the things that are happening in their society."

Iggers was further surprised when, in January, the paper named racism the issue of the month and people from the suburbs started busing themselves to meeting places deep inside the city, breaking out of their zip-code clusters. According to Iggers, they were saying, "I don't want to sit around discussing this with a bunch of white guys." And instead of being satisfied to meet once and be done with it, as they had with earlier topics like welfare reform and health, several groups met three and four times, over several weeks. Clearly a passion had been tapped that many of the *Star*'s readers probably didn't even know they had—a passion for contact.   13

It's a source of enthusiasm other journalists have tapped as well. In Columbus, Georgia, the *Ledger-Enquirer*, a particularly imaginative daily, has managed to turn a 1987 survey of public malaise into an ongoing civic movement. It used problem areas identified in a Knight-Ridder phone poll as a starting point for six months of intensive research into ways of improving Columbus: using polling, interviews with community leaders and ordinary citizens, ideas from other small cities and considerable in-house pondering, the editors came up with a twenty-five-page supplement, "Columbus Beyond 2000." Like a more famous twenty-five-page supplement that turned into something big—*The Philadelphia Inquirer*'s analysis of the U.S. economy, "America: What Went Wrong?"—this appeal to intelligence fairly quickly hit a nerve. Businesspeople and citizens appreciated the thoroughness of the work. Town meetings were organized, and a task force was formed that has continued to function (albeit shakily) even after the paper dropped its sponsorship.   14

In Washington, D.C., author/mediator John Marks and his organization, Search for Common Ground, found another way to spark constructive dialogue: they produced a series (shown on PBS stations) of videotaped discussions on divisive public issues. For instance, "What's the Common Ground on Abortion?" brought a pro-life and a pro-choice activist together, not to engage in flashy invective or to restate their irreconcilable differences (the staple of normal discussion-TV), but to identify areas on the periphery of the controversy on which they might   15 agree and work together. They managed to find five. Their discussion prompted the Buffalo, New York, Council of Churches to take the dialogue into its community; having been troubled by Operation Rescue's march through town, the Council used Marks's approach to create the Buffalo Coalition for Common Ground.

Perhaps *The Wichita Eagle* has gone broadest and deepest in actively 16
promoting public discussion. Its seminal Voter Project was profiled in the July 1992 *Columbia Journalism Review,* but since then its work has gotten more ambitious. Its current People Project selects such usually wearying perennial issues as crime and education, then acts as a coordination point for a network of intelligent thought and discussion, via staff-written backgrounds, interviews, and profiles of programs that work; phone calls, faxes, and written proposals from its readers; directories of local organizations active on the issue; television and radio talk-show tie-ins; and town meetings.

The project is the antithesis of fastidious traditional journalism; dis- 17
cussion is guided away from the headline disagreements that normally paralyze public talk ("Should schools teach liberal arts or not?") to the conflicting core values that lie beneath them ("Is education there to make well-rounded citizens, or is it there to produce people who can fill jobs?"). As the paper has moved from just-the-facts journalism to a sort of collective soul-searching, reader satisfaction has increased.

These odd, intrusive forms of journalism may make professionals 18
wince. But everywhere you look there's evidence that intelligence, thoroughness, and a sense of participating in a real exchange of ideas, not some vaguely defined and unsatisfying "objectivity," are just what people want: more people watch C-Span, an average of five hours a week, than watch all three flashy, sound-bite-laden network news shows combined. Americans have bought 625,000 copies of *America: What Went Wrong?* making that newspaper-series-turned book one of last year's most profitable publications.

In the end, the hunger to meet other Americans, so we can deliberate 19
intelligently as citizens here in our common nation, can only be satisfied by mass media. I'm convinced that people have steadily retreated from newspapers and networks until now because what they found there was shrill and shallow. We will not survive if they continue to feel unsatisfied. Our ideals and our bottom lines both point to the same fact—that we stand to gain quite a lot from a little reckless faith in the American people.

• •

Examining the Text

1. Charity claims that ordinary Americans understand what journalism "can and ought to be much better than most reporters and editors do" (paragraph 2). How does he support this claim? What do you think of his reasons? What do you think journalism "can and ought to be"?

2. What is Charity's point about Michael Weiss's zip-code-based categorization of the American populace (8–12)? Does your experience confirm Charity's observation that "Americans really have no place to meet except on television or in the newspapers"?

3. Charity concludes with several examples of the "very different model" of journalism that he advocates. What characteristics do these examples share? What, according to Charity, makes them the kind of journalism most readers want and need? How do you think Roger Rosenblatt and Jon Katz would respond to Charity's models?

For Group Discussion

Charity and the writers earlier in this chapter offer models or ideals for the news media. As a group, list those qualities and goals that you think are most important for effective journalism. As a class, consider the extent to which existing institutions could be modified to reflect these ideals.

Writing Suggestion

Charity points out that when news reporting moves from "just-the-facts journalism to a sort of collective soul-searching, reader satisfaction increases." In this sense, Charity's "very different model" of journalism lies somewhere between the objective model described by Roger Rosenblatt and the "New News" model described by Jon Katz. After reviewing the selections by Rosenblatt and Katz, explore in an essay the comparative benefits of each of these models of journalism, decide which you prefer, and explain why.

A Magazine for the Dead

Jose Antonio Burciaga

*N*ewsstands are overflowing with magazines on news, sports, fashion, nature, science, technology, and many, many other topics. But how about a magazine about death? That's Jose Antonio Burciaga's tongue-in-cheek proposal.

Burciaga—a Resident Fellow, artist, and writer at Stanford University— is a Chicano cultural activist and founding member of the comedy group Culture Clash. In the following essay from his collection Drink Cultura: Chicanismo *(1993), Burciaga expands the potential functions of journalism described in previous selections, suggesting that in glorifying* life *the mainstream media ignore the clearly universal and thus potentially lucrative subject of* death. *To make his point, Burciaga outlines the possible contents of a magazine devoted to death, from the feature articles and classifieds to advertisements, even recipes.*

How large the potential readership of such a magazine would be, we'll leave for you to decide, but it's clear that Burciaga has some serious observations to make about journalism and the broader culture. He notes, for example, that advertisements for the alcohol, tobacco, and weapons industries would find a highly receptive audience in a magazine devoted to the topic of death. He also suggests that compared to other cultures—specifically Indo-Hispanic culture—mainstream America has a lot to learn about death.

Before you read, *think about how the U.S. media generally deal with death. What have you learned about death from watching and reading the news?*

•••••••••••••••••••

Life has to be the most popular magazine of all time in this country. 1
Through vibrant photographs in living color and dramatic black and white, it celebrates life in this country. But to some extent, all magazines are filled with life and the present time, beginning with *Time, Newsweek,* and *People.* There are magazines for all occasions—from walking to war to collecting hangnails. But there is no magazine for the Dead.

And so I would like to propose a national magazine about death. 2
Death is big business in this country. Everybody has to die sometime, some way, somehow, but it's such a hush-hush subject. Why should morticians, embalmers, cemeteries, casket-makers, grave-diggers, cremators and flower shops monopolize the industry? Death is not a dead-end road. There is a lot of money in death.

Some people would consider such a publication in bad taste. But 3
I've never seen bad taste stop anyone from making money in this country. Look at the fast food business.

Moral, social, psychological and economic causes would be well 4
served by such a periodical. It has gotten so expensive to die that many people hesitate to do it because of the expense alone.

Death is constantly hidden from us. There is a daily list of obituaries, 5
but it is usually hidden just before the classified section or in the second-to-the-last page of some obscure section. Unless you are *somebody,* obituaries contain very little information. Only if the person was famous will their death make headlines.

At least one national or international celebrity dies every week. 6
There should be a cover story on not only her or his contributions but also their lifestyle and type of death. Obituary readers are often left wondering if the person smoked, died from drugs, cholesterol or boredom.

Some corporations would find it appropriate to advertise in such a   7
magazine, especially the alcohol, tobacco, automobile, chemical, and
weapons industry. The Marines, Army and Navy could advertise: "Join
up and see the other world? Be all that you can be?" or "We need a few
good dead men!" The profits to be reaped from these grim reapers have
not been totally tapped. A classified section could list other little-known
deaths around the country to help people look for long-lost relatives, in-
heritors or inheritances.

There are many people who experience death and remember hov-   8
ering over their own bodies, speeding down a tunnel, seeing the light at
the end and reaching the clouded dunes of heaven only to be turned
back like a bad dream, like picking a monopoly game card that says, "Go
back to earth. You owe the hospital $10,000."

A classified section could carry requests from living donors looking   9
for body parts or rare blood types. Article ideas are endless: how to have
the perfect funeral; ten tips for frugal funerals; choosing the perfect cas-
ket; color caskets to match your personality; what to put on your tombstone; prevent getting ripped off when a loved one dies; and a horoscope
for the dead.

There could be a recipe section: Ten easy recipes for the grieving and   10
bereaved. *Pan de muerto*, bread of the dead, is a delicious Mexican pas-
try. Mexican candy skulls made from sugar are also very popular during Mexico's Day of the Dead.

Mexico is a gold mine of information about death. If the United   11
States has a fascination with life, so does Mexico—but it is balanced by
a fascination or obsession with death.

Our next-door neighbor has been honoring the faithful dead since   12
before the conquest. Their holiday, *El Día de los Muertos,* sounds just as
scary in English if uttered in a soft guttural voice, "The Day of the
Dead!" The Aztecs celebrated a whole month for the dead and by coincidence ended on All Souls Day. The Spanish conquerors tried to do
away with the month-long celebration by celebrating All Souls day, but
the dead seem to be winning over the saints.

There have been several magazines about death in Mexico but they   13
have been one-time educational or humorous publications without the
capitalist ideas suggested here. Each year for the Day of the Dead, Mexican newspapers publish epitaphs and obituaries for still-living politicians, business people and other well-known personas. Half in jest, on
that day alone, journalists and artists can rake their favorite or least-
favorite *politico* over red-hot coals in rhyme and with or without reason.

Awareness and celebration of El Día de los Muertos in this country   14
is greater each year not only with the Indo-Hispanic population but with
the mainstream popular culture.

Should you be interested in starting up such a magazine, remember   15
where you read it. I have the copyright, 1992.

· · · · · · · · · · · · · · · · · · · ·

Examining the Text

1. What do you think is Burciaga's purpose in writing this piece? To
what extent do you think he intends for us to take his proposal seriously?

2. At the beginning Burciaga ironically contrasts his "magazine for the
Dead" with *Life*, "the most popular magazine of all time in this country." Point out some other passages that are similarly ironic.

3. Why do you think Burciaga refers as extensively as he does to the
"fascination or obsession with death" in Mexican culture (paragraphs
10–14)? How do these paragraphs relate to his overall point?

For Group Discussion

Burciaga points out two interestingly contradictory facts about the
United States: "Death is big business in this country" (2), and "Death is
constantly hidden from us" (5). As a group, list some specific examples
of how death is represented in the various forms of popular culture—
TV, music, movies, the news—and how realistic these representations
are. Consider also the extent to which the idea of death is ignored or suppressed in popular culture. As a class, discuss the influence these representations—and lack of them—have on how Americans deal with
death and dying.

Writing Suggestion

In his proposal, Burciaga adapts typical magazine format—advertisements, articles, classifieds, and recipes—to an unlikely topic. Think
of another unlikely or unusual subject for a magazine, and write a proposal, similar to Burciaga's, describing the sections you might have and
each section's content.

INTERPRETING THE NEWS

An Outsider in My Own World

Jeffrey Schmalz

*T*he following essay challenges the traditional view that contemporary
journalists should be completely "objective" and not let their stories be influ-
enced by personal opinions and allegiances. Jeffrey Schmalz, a long-time re-
porter for The New York Times, *describes how, for twenty years, he played*
by the rules as a "by-the-book Timesman, no personal involvement." And then
he was diagnosed with AIDS and began to see the world "through the prism
of AIDS." It fundamentally changed his approach to his job. Schmalz asked
specifically to cover AIDS stories because he felt "an obligation to those with
AIDS to write about it and an obligation to the newspaper to write what just
about no other reporter in America can cover in quite the same way."

While Schmalz sees this kind of reporting as "the cutting edge of journal-
ism," other journalists disagree. One is John Lee, who, in a 1993 article in U.S.
News & World Report, *criticized Schmalz's subjective and highly emotional*
coverage of AIDS for violating "just about every rule of conventional report-
ing". To Lee, "it's wrong for reporters to bring their allegiances and travails
into their stories." Reporters who feel an allegiance to both journalistic in-
tegrity and to the groups or issues which they cover should, according to Lee,
write for editorial or opinion pages. On the other hand, essays later in the chap-
ter question whether journalistic "objectivity" is even possible.

Jeffrey Schmalz died in 1993 of a brain infection brought about by AIDS,
but he has left us enduring and important questions about how journalists can
best serve society.

Before you read, *consider how mainstream journalism has contributed to*
your understanding of AIDS.

·····················

It will be three years ago Christmas week that I collapsed at my desk   1
in the newsroom of *The New York Times,* writhed on the floor in a seizure
and entered the world of AIDS.

I had been, as far as I knew, absolutely healthy, and it took the doc-   2
tors a few weeks to reach their diagnosis: full-blown AIDS, with a brain
infection often fatal within four months.

That I have lived these two and a half years is a miracle. How long   3
my luck will hold, no one knows. But for now, I am back working, a reporter with AIDS who covers AIDS.

I've thought a lot about my dual identity since the death this past   4
December of Ricky Ray. I wrote about him and his family in 1988, about
their new life in Sarasota, Florida. It was a year after their home was destroyed by arson in Arcadia, Florida, a town where many people hated
Ricky and his two younger brothers because they were infected with
HIV, a town where pickup trucks bore the bumper sticker. "This vehicle protected by a pit bull with AIDS."

I recall my late-summer evening with the Rays vividly: Three bare-   5
foot boys in jeans and T-shirts, scrambling on the floor with their ham-
ster. A sooty Garfield the Cat, himself a survivor of the fire, looking
down from the china cabinet, "I'm only human," Garfield said when his
string was pulled, and the Ray boys would turn giggly.

How proud I was of myself. How noble of me to write about these   6
people nobody wanted to touch. How smug I was that I, a gay man, had
escaped AIDS. (I know now that I was already infected. But I had not
been tested; I felt great.) And how ambivalent I was about the Rays,
these people who had parlayed personal tragedy into celebrity—they
seemed just a little too available for interviews—and who talked so
glibly of death.

Now, four years later, at the age of 39, it is I who talk matter-of-factly   7
of life and death and who have used my affliction to advantage, to obtain interviews and force intimacy. Does that make me feel guilty? You
bet. But to have AIDS is to live with guilt and shame.

So many tensions are at work on those of us with AIDS that it's hard   8
to chronicle them. My mother, seemingly healthy, died last year at 73, a
few months after my sister told her of my AIDS. A coronary? A stroke?
Who knows? In my mind, it will always be a broken heart.

I make sure everyone with AIDS whom I interview knows that I   9
have it, too. To be sure, that is an interview ploy; I'm hoping the camaraderie will open them up. But there is more to it than that: I want them
to take a good look at me, to see that someone with full-blown AIDS can
carry on for a while, can even function as a reporter. Much of the time,
it works. Their faces light up. There is hope.

"You'll Be Here Soon"

But sometimes it fails, and I am the one changed by our chat, over-   10
come by guilt that I have lived these extra years when so many of
my friends and hospital roommates and people I've interviewed have
died. At times, I think my fellow AIDS sufferers are laughing at me,

looking up from their beds with eyes that say, "You'll be here soon enough."

Endlessly, I fret about my interviews. I know the buttons to push   11
with people with AIDS, and I push them well. Do I cross the line, pressing too hard for the sake of a good quote?

"I wish it wasn't true," Bob Hattoy said of having AIDS just before   12
he addressed the Democratic National Convention. "But it isn't overwhelming me. Really. I don't know why."

I knew from my own experience the nightmares of waking up in a   13
coffin, of wondering whether every cold was the big one that would do me in. I challenged him for not being honest, and he broke down. I wanted to hold him. I wanted to apologize. Then he hit me as hard as I had hit him.

"I think I will probably die of AIDS," he blurted out. "Won't you?"   14

Yes, I expect so. In my gut, I know it. Yet in the back of my mind, I   15
just can't believe it: Maybe, just maybe, I'll live to see a treatment breakthrough.

How different these AIDS interviews now are from the one four   16
years ago with the Rays, when all was well, and I was just a spectator to the train wreck, not riding in one of the cars. It was simple then: A quick good-bye. A shake of the hand. A perfunctory wish for the future. Then off into the night. Now, it's embraces and tears and whispers from me and for me: "Stay well," "Don't give up," "God bless." And always there is that one futile question: Have you found the magic cure?

To have AIDS is to be alone, no matter the number of friends and fam-   17
ily members around. Then, to be with someone who has HIV—be it interviewer or interviewee—is to find kinship. "I'm so glad they picked you to do this," Mary Fisher said in an interview just before she spoke at the Republican National Convention as a woman with HIV. With her, as with Magic Johnson and Bob Hattoy and Larry Kramer and Elizabeth Glaser, who spoke at the Democratic convention, the talk was the same: of anger and courage and politics. We talked of that deep nausea in the pit of your stomach when even cancer patients pity you and when a doctor, who should know better, puts on latex gloves just to shake your hand.

There are time-outs in each of the interviews for both of us to get tis-   18
sues, for both to pop our AZT, for both to laugh and always to hug. "I will see you again," Magic Johnson said pointedly, in what was not a social nicety but an affirmation of life between two people with HIV. Like each of the other interviews, ours was therapy for him. It was therapy for me.

"Who are you?" a TV reporter asked me at a funeral march in Green-   19
wich Village for an Act-Up leader dead of AIDS. The reporter knew full well who I was: the guy from *The Times* with AIDS.

The lid of the coffin had been removed, the open box carried on   20
shoulders in the rain, led in the dusk by mourners with torches, the
dirge of a single drumbeat setting the pace of this, a funeral turned
protest against the governments handling of AIDS.

"Are you here as a reporter or as a gay man with AIDS?" the TV cor-   21
respondent persisted, shoving a microphone in my face. His camera
spotlight went on.

I didn't respond. People in the crowd moved closer; they wanted to   22
know the answer. I wanted to know it, too. Finally, it came out: "Reporter." Some shook their heads in disgust, all but shouting "Uncle Tom!"
They wanted an advocate, not a reporter. So there I stood, a gay man with
AIDS out of place at an AIDS funeral, an outsider in my own world.

I walked back to the office in the rain, thinking along the 30 blocks   23
about how tough it must be for blacks to report about blacks, for women
to report about women. Yet that kind of reporting is the cutting edge of
journalism. Some people think it is the journalism that suffers, that objectivity is abandoned. But they are wrong. If the reporters have any integrity at all, it is they who suffer, caught between two allegiances.

Don't misunderstand; it was I, not my editors, who pressed for me   24
to write about AIDS. For 20 years, I had been a by-the-book Timesman,
no personal involvement allowed. But now I see the world through the
prism of AIDS. I feel an obligation to those with AIDS to write about it
and an obligation to the newspaper to write what just about no other reporter in American can cover in quite the same way. And I feel an obligation to myself. This is the place—reporting—where I am at home. This
is the place where I must come to terms with AIDS.

I didn't write an article about the funeral march, judging it worth   25
only a picture and a caption. I passed the journalism test that afternoon
in the rain by failing the activism test. To turn activist would mean that
AIDS, not reporting, would define me. It would be to surrender totally
to the disease.

But no matter how neatly it works out in the mind, that doesn't   26
make it any easier, even when I'm reporting on issues besides AIDS.

Traveling the country to interview voters about the Presidential   27
election, I dropped by an Iowa cafe where, as a reporter from New York,
I was hailed as a mini-celebrity. Asked to say a few words at a breakfast
of 30 leading citizens, I wanted to tell them I had AIDS, to watch the
stunned look on their faces. But I didn't. That would have crossed the
line between reporter and activist.

Yet I do tell some politicians I interview. In my mind, that's okay. I   28
can't explain why. I left the breakfast in Iowa feeling hypocritical, a dis-
ciple who professes to carry the message of AIDS but who is most comfortable preaching to the converted.

"Why are you here with me?" Jerry Brown asked when, while I was   29
covering his Presidential campaign for a few days, the conversation
turned to AIDS and I told him that I had it. "I'm here," I said, "Because
it is what I do."

He leaned closer to me, asking quietly, "Don't you want to be off   30
getting in touch with your spirituality?"

Religion. How I have wrestled with that one. I had wanted to stop   31
in church the day before brain surgery. But to me it would have been the
height of hypocrisy to turn to God in desperation after years of turning
away.

Yet I have become more spiritual. I think often of the dozen friends   32
who have died of AIDS, and I feel them with me. It's not that I am writing editorials, avenging their deaths. It's that I feel their strength, their
soothing me on. They are my conscience, their shadows with me everywhere: in the torchlight of the march. Over my shoulder. By my desk. In
my sleep.

It's Still News

On its surface, life is much the same as before: I walk into the news-   33
room, sit at my desk, work the phone. But it is a through-the-looking-
class world. Sitting in my doctor's office, listening to the latest update,
I can't help thinking, "This is a good story."

An interview with then-candidate Bill Clinton on gay issues   34
and AIDS was the oddest I've ever had. He had been briefed that I
had the virus, but we never discussed it. It seemed self-centered for me
to bring it up, and I guess he thought it rude for him to do so. So there
we were, talking about AIDS. I knew that he knew that I knew that he
knew.

Before me on the desk are the letters—a hundred of them this year,   35
some from people who read that I had AIDS, others from people who
figured it out between the lines of my pieces. Those are the ones that I
am proudest of. "Consider this letter a giant hug," wrote a man from
Philadelphia. I have killed the message on my phone tape from a man
dying of AIDS who had called begging me to save his life, to give him
some nugget of information that would keep him alive. "Please!" he
cried. I called him back to say there was nothing I could do except recommend doctors. I kept that tape for weeks, playing it over and over.
"Please!" I wonder if he is dead now.

Oh, I have come to understand the Rays—those people who seemed   36
so glib. I see now that they are like all of us with AIDS, trying to go on
about their lives but caught up in this nightmare. They do what they

have to do. We all do. I think about them. I am one with them. And I think about Ricky, the newest shadow looking over my shoulder.

My editors keep an eye on me, I am sure, to make certain that AIDS 37 has not yet weakened my reporting. But I suspect I will be the first to say when it is time to call it quits. As write this, I feel tired but sharp. The AZT is holding for now. The brain infection, though diminished, is still present, making the fingers of my right hand stiff and clumsy on the keyboard. I use a tape recorder; my short-term memory isn't what it was.

I hold a different job—one that is supposed to be less stressful. But 38 I am sitting in my old spot in the newsroom to finish this, the same spot where I suffered the seizure. As I look up, I can see the wall clock clearly. I couldn't that Dec. 21 when failing vision was the first sign of trouble. Now, more than two years later, I see things more clearly than ever. And I am alive.

•••••••••••••••••••••

Examining the Text

1. Schmalz reflects in this essay on "how tough it must be for blacks to report about blacks, for women to report about women," and for a man like himself to report on AIDS. Yet he clearly believes that a reporter with AIDS can cover certain stories and conduct certain interviews better than one who doesn't. What does he mean when he says reporters in such situations are "caught between two allegiances" (paragraph 22)? How do you respond to his overall argument? To what extent do you think it applies to areas such as race and gender? Is objectivity likely to be sacrificed to sympathy, and, if so, do you see this as a loss?

2. Schmalz says that he made sure the people with AIDS he interviewed knew about his disease. He called this "an interview ploy" he hoped would "open them up" (8). He knew "the buttons to push with people with AIDS" and pushed them "well" (10). What point is he making about how reporters regard interviews? How do you respond to this view of their job?

3. How would you describe the tone of this essay? What kind of response do you think Schmalz is trying to elicit from readers? What makes you think so?

For Group Discussion

Suppose you were preparing to interview several people with AIDS for a newspaper story about the disease in your community. As a group, list ten or so questions to ask and discuss your lists with your class, trying to decide what kind of story would develop from the interview. Consider how the questions and story might be different if they were developed by a reporter with AIDS.

Writing Suggestion

Schmalz titled his essay "An Outsider in My Own World," but he in fact describes himself as both an outsider and an insider. Write an essay in which you describe several times when your perspective was that of an "outsider" looking in and several times when your perspective was that of an "insider." For a reporter, what might be the advantages and disadvantages of each perspective? Is it possible for an insider to be objective or for an outsider to be fully understanding?

Drug Abuse, Race Relations, and the Prime Time News Program

James Schwoch, Mimi White, Susan Reilly, and Ronald B. Scott

James Schwoch and Mimi White are professors of Radio/TV/Film at Northwestern University; Susan Reilly and Ronald B. Scott are professors at Miami University in Ohio. In the following chapter from their book Media Knowledge, *these four academics present a detailed analysis of a 1989 prime-time news special,* The Koppel Report—D.C./Divided City. *This program, together with a "town meeting" hosted by Ted Koppel on his* Nightline *show later that same evening, looked at drug abuse and racial tension in Washington, D.C.*

The authors' analysis of D.C./Divided City highlights certain contradictions between the words and images presented, the message the show apparently "intended" to send and the message that actually came across. Viewers, the authors note, were simultaneously presented "with an intellectual argument to end racism" and "an emotional argument that justifies the safety of separation." Their analysis reveals the importance of what they call "critical viewership," examining and questioning the information presented by the media. It is urgent, the authors argue, that audiences be engaged and empowered and familiar with "the grammar of media literacy."

As you read, consider carefully the highly detailed and critical analysis the authors offer of D.C./Divided City. Do you find such a thorough analysis illuminating?

••••••••••••••••••••

Drug abuse is continuously presented as the latest blight on the   1
American horizon, both in news and special reports. Due to a lack of historical context, reporting on the drug story often seems to give the impression that the plague of drugs has reached such epic proportions that
at any moment the entire country will either be forced to live in a violent society created by dealers and addicts or become the subjects of an
amoral foreign drug cartel that is uncontrollably forcing its products
upon an innocent American citizenry. Drug abuse has bridged the gap
between American domestic problems and American foreign policy,
most recently in the invasion of Panama by American troops ostensibly
to remove a major international figure in the world of drug abuse
(Manuel Noriega) from a position of power. The reportage surrounding
the drug abuse story has taken on the trappings of an ever-widening
narrative encompassing nightly gang wars, million dollar transactions,
manhunts, glamorous lifestyles, and zombie-like users. Such narrative
elements within the reportage increasingly lead to conclusions that
mandatory testing, profile stops on interstate highways, embargoes and
invasions of other nations, segregation and isolation of users and pushers, and "zero-tolerance" seizures of property might be the most reasonable—indeed, the only—options for controlling the drug problem.
Viewers are presented with the dilemma of trading constitutional rights
for the promise of security. The trade value of the proposed exchange is
potentially skewed by the presentations of the drug problem, presentations that often favor drama over comprehensiveness and strictly defined, immediate law-enforcement solutions in favor of evolving, long-
term social and cultural solutions.

A complicating factor in the drug abuse story has been the inter-   2
twining of race with the drug story. Specifically, the urban black male
has become a leading character in the drug narrative. Serving simultaneously as both villain and victim, the urban black male is often represented as the predator of domestic drug abuse, the go-between for the
foreign supplier and the user, adding drugs to his criminal litany
and/or gang activities. Yet the urban black male is also represented as
the prey, the target, metaphorically trapped in an environment where
confrontation and eventual submission to his criminal counterpart/
blood brother is narratively inevitable. Adding to the tragedy is the fact
that the narrative dichotomy begins at a very early age, in grammar
school and on the playgrounds, working its way up through the rest of
inner city life.

In fact, the image of the black male as drug abuser has its roots in   3
the years just after the American Civil War. David Musto contends in
The American Disease that postwar violence against recently freed blacks
escalated in the South coinciding with the advancement of an argument

by whites that access to narcotics by blacks might embolden blacks and escalate racial confrontations by giving blacks the courage to "fight back." The unfounded speculation about a drug-induced black rebellion served as a rationale for suppression of blacks by whites. Cocaine became the tonic most often feared as having the potential to set off a black revolt. One contemporary myth even suggested cocaine gave black men the power to stop bullets. Thus the notion of the drug abuser became tied to the black community as a way of enforcing racial hierarchies and promoting separation. Troy Duster suggests that in the latter half of the 1800s drug addiction was approximately eight times more prevalent among urban populations (and primarily an activity of middle and upper class whites) than was the case in the 1960s. Addiction was not considered the social anathema it is today, and narcotics often made up some of the ingredients in a variety of over-the-counter medications, soft drinks, and other consumer products. In the early 1900s this relaxed moral attitude toward drugs began to shift toward prohibition.

The recurring conflation of the drug abuse narrative with the mediated image of the black urban male is particularly alarming in that it tends to cast the domestic causes of the drug problem at the feet of racial minorities. This negative aspect of media portrayal—that racial minorities are largely to blame for their own problems—can be traced in television journalism back to the reporting surrounding the American civil rights movement of the 1960s, particularly when the black consciousness movement migrated out of the rural south into the urban areas of the entire nation. The wholesale laying of responsibilities upon racial minorities for the current-day drug problem leads to a melding of issues, a kind of social fusion where the drug problem is only the latest manifestation of the race problem, the "uncontrollable" blacks. 4

It is supremely ironic and paradoxical that the civil rights movement of the 1960s now receives a new kind of historical respect and validation through such respected PBS documentary series as *Eyes on the Prize* while television evening news reports and specials repeatedly construct a narrative surrounding the contemporary drug problem that portrays the urban black male as a major perpetrator of the drug plague. The drug problem in the life of the contemporary urban black male— and it is indeed a problem—is not reported as the latest of obstacles tied to a rich history of black achievement over seemingly insurmountable problems. Instead, the problem remains ahistoricized, a rationale for mistrust and the loss of personal rights and freedoms. These tensions, interactions, and contradictions are visible in an analysis of *The Koppel Report—D.C./Divided City.* 5

On the night of April 27, 1989, ABC aired a prime time news documentary titled *D.C./Divided City.* The host of this one hour program was 6 veteran television journalist Ted Koppel. *D.C./Divided City* was later followed by a special town meeting on the late evening ABC news show *Nightline*. As the title of the show implied, the show would focus on the nation's capital, Washington, D.C., and an array of problems that have divided the city into two discrete populations along racial lines. The report began by suggesting that the entire nation experienced similar problems to those found in the nation's capital, and that Washington, D.C., was an effective microcosm for understanding the various problems of drugs and racism that confront the nation. The rationale of the capital as microcosm was narratively compelling. If the problems of drugs cannot effectively be addressed in the nation's seat of power, then by extension what element of American society could lay claim to be effectively dealing with the problems? As the national center for such federal drug enforcement organizations as the Federal Bureau of Investigation, the Drug Enforcement Agency, and the Bureau of Alcohol, Tobacco, and Firearms, as well as the headquarters for the newly appointed drug czar William Bennett, the program's geographic location carried significant weight for national viewers. The major narrative motivating force, set up early in the program, was that the one element dividing the city, and by implication dividing the nation, was the widespread use, abuse, and sale of drugs.

While drugs alone may be enough to divide any community, *D.C.:* 7 *Divided City* went one step further by introducing the issue of racism as another major dividing factor in the capital district. The choice of Washington as a typical example of the problems confronting the U.S., and especially its black population, appeared well-reasoned. If, despite the resources and talent in the district and its place as the heart of the nation's government and judicial systems, problems of race could still not be transcended, could any other city or region in the nation hope to transcend its own particular manifestations of problematic race relations? Yet the result of introducing the race issue is an implicit bonding of the problems of drug abuse and the problem of race relations. An examination of the program reveals that the linking of these two issues in some ways leads to an implicit conclusion that argues for the continued, if not enhanced, division of the nation—a conclusion markedly at odds with the ostensible aims and goals of the program.

In the program's opening scenes, shots of a black tour guide point- 8 ing out the sites to a busload of white tourists are intercut with shots of a black police officer. This police officer symbolically serves as Koppel's—and by extension the audience's—tour guide. The officer directs attention to various drug havens and discusses the influx of drugs into his own patrol beat. After a sequence of cutaways and narrative bits that depict this drug-infested area, Koppel returns to the screen, shown standing on a street corner, to deliver this message:

> Only blocks from the Capital eleven-year-old boys stand watch for fifteen-year-old drug dealers who are guarded by seventeen-year-old enforcers who kill on behalf of a twenty-four-year-old drug king pin. The year is not yet four months old and already more than 150 people have died in drug-related violence. Almost all of them were black. This is *D.C.: Divided City.*

With this narration, the notion of drug abuse being a problem in which all of us participate begins to shift. Now it is a problem which "concerns" us all—but at least in the visual imagery of this program—a problem in which blacks and blacks alone are the overwhelming participants. To add to the impression that the active participation in drug abuse activity is confined to one segment of the population, additional images of the black community and a series of sound bites that all relate to drugs, violence, or police intervention follow Koppel's opening narration. Koppel then suggests that if one were to place a grid over the district, most of the violence would be confined to the predominantly black neighborhoods. Koppel returns onscreen to conclude this opening sequence with:

> Good evening. Much of what you'll see has to do with drugs, violence, money, and young people . . . threads lead back to the Kerner Commission Report twenty-one years ago that . . . white society is deeply implicated in the ghetto. White institutions created it. White institutions maintain it and white society condones it . . . . What we are about to see may appear to be just a black problem: it is not.

On the one hand, the script does hint that racism is a factor leading   9
to division of the district and by extension the nation, and suggests that the implication of white institutions in the living conditions of urban blacks means that the drug problem is at least indirectly tied to the white community. However, the images of this opening sequence tend to suggest to viewers that the violence, the crime, and the deepest tragedies of drug abuse are contained within the black community, thereby raising the specter of de facto segregation as a sort of picket fence containing the spread of the drug problem. This may undercut the initial idea that "dividedness" is itself a problem. Instead it may lead to the conclusion that dividedness may be socially undesirable but nevertheless serves a practical function of containment and safety for the (white) majority in the face of the (black) drug issue. One is left to wonder whether Koppel's verbal insistence that the program is not only about black problems is sufficient to counter the visual imagery of this opening sequence.

The contradiction of the opening sequence contains the problems   10
that pervade the entire program and, by extension, the failure of the
drug abuse story across the landscape of television news. It fails to
clearly demonstrate that the relation of the drug problem to the African-
American community is in many ways only a symptom, only the latest
manifestation, of the larger historical problem of race relations. The
drug problem is not presented as one of the most recent of a legacy of
seemingly insurmountable obstacles that blacks have faced in the history of American social relations. Instead, drugs *are* the isolated, decon-
textualized problem and if they could only be eliminated from the
ghetto, somehow the district and the nation would automatically become a more unified place. The relative absence of white victims, users,
and pushers on the screen tends to identify the drug problem as a black
problem. By extension, intentionally or not, it also suggests that white
avoidance of the black community is tantamount to protecting whites
from drug abuse. The result is a new sense of dividedness, an unspoken
assumption that the district is divided between black users, pushers,
and victims against white nonusers whose larger social system is threatened by this racially marked drug problem.

Following this introduction, *D.C./Divided City* consists of two sec-   11
tions. The first half focuses on the effects of drug-related violence and
drug addiction on a black neighborhood. This section also includes attempts by local residents to cope with the drug problem. During the second half of the program, the topic shifts more directly to issues of race
relations.

Through three vignettes, the first half explores drug problems in the   12
Anacostia neighborhood of Washington. The first vignette opens with a
scene of a young man lying dead on the street while his mother, restrained by the police, cries hysterically. Certain shots of this scene had
been previously shown in the opening sequence. In a voiceover Koppel
tells the audience that similar scenes of death and despair are being
acted out all over the nation. As the young man's story unfolds, Koppel
interviews his mother. Koppel talks of her son's involvement in the drug
business and identifies the murderer as an employee of the Edmunds
family. The mother appears not to know what he is talking about.
Whether she is simply naive or unwilling to acknowledge the depth of
her son's activities remains unclear.

The Edmunds family is described as a successful drug organization   13
headed by another young black man. Each member of the family is identified for viewers through a wedding photograph. As each person's role
in the organization is described, cutaways show the result of their enterprise—more young black men either dead on the street or under arrest. It is revealed that the Edmunds family paid for luxury autos,

houses, vacations, and other desirable commodities with drug profits and provided these items as perks for faithful employees. Koppel mentions that some members of the Georgetown University basketball team socialized with Edmunds. As another cutaway shows young blacks dancing at a nightclub, a voiceover describes the club as a frequent gathering spot for black college students, basketball players, and drug dealers. Georgetown basketball coach John Thompson is also interviewed. Thompson explains that upon learning of his players' association with a supposed drug dealer, the coach arranged a meeting with Edmunds to voice his concern for the safety of his players. The vignette concludes with a scene of the arrest of the Edmunds family in a recent drug bust carried out by Washington district police, the FBI, and the DEA.

The second vignette explores the worlds of two young black women   14
who are drug addicts. The first woman is interviewed as she leaves her children with her sister and enters a drug treatment program. As she describes her foray into prostitution as a way to get money for drugs, her sister comments how the children had been left to wander the streets alone at night. The doctor in the treatment program identifies her as a second generation drug user, a multiple substance abuser, a high school dropout, and an unwed mother. The second woman, whose whereabouts are unknown, has left her children with her mother who now cares for them. The youngest child has tested HIV positive, increasing the likelihood that the child will eventually contract AIDS. First Lady Barbara Bush is shown holding this child at the special home where he must be kept, and the grandmother praises the efforts of Mrs. Bush in dealing with this problem.

The last vignette is about two community volunteers, middle-aged   15
black men nicknamed Uncle Skeezy and Peter Bug. These men are shown talking with elementary school children, trying to convince them to avoid drugs, get a good education, and become gainfully employed. The men and Koppel agree about the need to reach children and instill good values before "it's too late." They express concern that children may become addicted to making money and that may, in their own minds, justify their becoming involved in the drug business.

During the second half of the program, the focus shifts more cen-   16
trally to race relations. Black churchgoers hear a sermon about "American-style apartheid" as an opening to this segment. In a voiceover, Koppel discusses the high infant mortality rates among black children and high homicide rates among black adults while viewers see shots of hospitalized children and the bodies of murdered young black males. A series of interviews with successful black professionals and businesspeople reveals their concern about de facto segregation in housing, the corporate world, and recreational facilities in Washington. They speak

of an unfulfilled American Dream. The white chairman of a large bank struggles to explain why his firm has no black vice presidents. This segment eventually returns to the streets of Anacostia, where a resident explains that the drug business is one of the few ways for young blacks to become entrepreneurs and assume controlling interest in their own enterprises.

Finally, Koppel introduces a videotape produced by three black   17
high school students. The students have tried to demonstrate how whites are fearful of young black men. In the video, the students stop whites on the street and ask for directions to the Corcoran Museum. Typical reactions of avoidance or inattention are shown. The students report on a sense of fear in many whites whenever they approached. *D.C./Divided City* concludes with Ralph Ellison's poem *The Invisible Man*—a poem also included in the student videotape.

The ways of reading *D.C./Divided City* are somewhat contradictory.   18
On the one hand, viewers see how racial divisions are partially to blame for the current social condition of the community. Yet at the same time, not so much in its soundtrack but in its visual images, many of the shots and scenes seem to reinforce the perception of danger that surrounds blacks and their communities and the perception of safety through white avoidance. The introduction of a typology of familiar black media representational schemas—the dysfunctional black family, dangerous and irresponsible young black men, immoral young black women, enduring black mothers, and good-hearted but simplistic black uncles—becomes a weird kind of mediated historical legacy, reappearing as the contemporary reincarnations of ghosts from media culture past.

Anacostia is represented as a neighborhood of chaos and confusion   19
rather than stability and order. A mother is unaware of her murdered son's involvement in the drug business. A "fixture" of the community is a ruthless criminal family. The chaos reaches out beyond Anacostia, touching a basketball team and a nightclub. Despite the fact that black employment in Washington surpasses eighty percent of the adult male population (a figure that nevertheless could certainly stand improvement), the drug business is presented as the major substitute for business achievement by black males. Conversely, the fact that less than twenty percent of drug users nationwide are black goes by with scarcely a mention, and the equivalent visual representation of drug use in white neighborhoods and the suburbs is remarkable only through its structured absence.

In the latter half of *D.C./Divided City*, as the focus shifts more   20
squarely to race relations, the implicit message behind the interviews with successful blacks is that white society is desirable because it is—compared with Anacostia—drug and crime free. Anacostia, and by

extension any urban black neighborhood, fails to become a challenge for all, white and black, to enter and transform. The finale with the student videotape brings the guilt and blame for a divided city to all community citizens regardless of color. Yet an effective argument for an end to racism cannot and should not primarily be based on white guilt and a plea to middle and upper class citizens for magnanimity. Like so much of the contemporary reportage of drug abuse and race relations, *D.C./Divided City* ultimately fails to show any significant positive value to be gained from an integrated culture or show compelling positive aspects of the current and historical American black experience.

ABC followed *D.C./Divided City* that evening with a special edition   21
of its late-night news show *Nightline*, billed as a live town meeting of the air. The town meeting expanded the local examination of drug abuse and race relations in Washington to urban areas across the nation, including stories from Los Angeles, Denver, Chicago, Atlanta, and New York. Reports from these cities underlie the national, even international, scope of the drug problem. However, the reports had little, if anything, to say about race relations, further isolating the Anacostia experience and implicitly denying any national or international scope to problems of drug abuse, or race relations. The strongest link made in this opening segment was an implication that any large black urban population exacerbates our national drug problem.

The expanded coverage of the drug story began with local angles   22
from Los Angeles, Denver, Atlanta, and New York. The first clip was from Los Angeles, where correspondent Ken Kashiwahara informed viewers that Los Angeles is "a city that has become the major distribution center for more than half the nation's cocaine." James Walker, reporting from Denver, added that the drug problem in Denver was largely attributable to imports of crack by drug gangs from Los Angeles. Having established the West Coast distribution center, the focus shifted to Atlanta, which Jackie Judd described as "a major stopping point along the cocaine corridor . . . vast supplies come up from Miami." Jeff Greenfield reported that in New York the major problem was the "sheer size" of demand for illicit drugs. These segments work toward reinforcing the national nature of the drug problem, with Koppel later adding that the town meeting is held not only "to talk only about drugs and violence in Washington. . . . The problem is a national one, Washington has merely become the symbol."

Paradoxically, questions of race relations are left out of these   23
various correspondent reports, despite their foregrounding in the Washington-based examination. Nothing in the four news reports reminded viewers of the evening's expressed dual purpose of exploring issues along with drug abuse that divide cities. Implicit, however, is the

linkage between the urban inner city and the core of the national drug problem, again sidestepping suburban and rural drug abuse and suggesting the bonds between illegal drug behavior and urban black society. A bit later in this segment, Chicago correspondent Judd Rose, in response to a question by Koppel, goes so far as to assert that the Chicago drug problem has whites only tangentially involved in drug trafficking, with blacks and Hispanics controlling most of the trade. The overall impact is to suggest to the viewer that drugs are exclusively in the control of blacks and other minorities, and therefore it is those minorities who are responsible for the spread of drugs and accompanying violence. Blacks become the veiled yet real "threat" to the security of American whites.

The national town meeting segment, done live from Washington, immediately followed this series of reports from urban centers around the nation. The location of the town meeting was a church in the Anacostia neighborhood with several hundred people in attendance, ranging from local neighborhood residents to a number of representatives of the Washington black community—educators, police personnel, corrections officials, DEA agents, members of the Nation of Islam, National Guard officers, members of Alcoholics Anonymous, directors of various drug treatment programs, community organizers, and local as well as national politicians. Ted Koppel, serving as host and moderator, occupied a central location on an elevated platform with guests and the audience around him. Koppel proved to be less a facilitator of open discussion than a motivator for rapid action and immediate, brief dialogue. For example, in discussion with Washington Mayor Marion Barry, Koppel asks "Who is to blame for the drug problem?" When Barry responds theoretically that all of us are to blame, Koppel replies there is no "time for generalities," asking the mayor to "point to one, two, three segments of society that are to blame." 24

This tendency to direct rather than facilitate dialogue was evident in a number of instances. When audience criticism turned to *D.C./Divided City,* with a high school principal expressing concern over the visual imagery of young black people destroying the neighborhood and by implication the entire district, Koppel replies she has "got it backward" in reference to her interpretation of the program. Koppel also exhorted the audience to strictly adhere to the demands of commercial television, reminding speakers to "make it quick, we have about forty-five seconds before the commercial break." 25

After a thirty minute pause for local news broadcasts by ABC owned-and-operated stations and ABC affiliates, Koppel and *Nightline* returned with Secretary of Housing and Urban Affairs Jack Kemp and drug czar William Bennett as town meeting guests. After instructing the church attenders to use the half-hour with Kemp and Bennett produc- 26 tively, he then turned to Kemp and Bennett for opening comments by both men. When Bennett criticized *D.C./Divided City* for its somewhat negative portrayal of the black community, reminding Koppel that the majority of black people in Anacostia and Washington are law abiding citizens who work hard for a living, Koppel told Bennett he "missed the point . . . (we are) not representing a profile of the city of Washington (but) a profile of drug violence in the city of Washington." In his role as active interventionist and moderator, Koppel also pushed for a passive viewer with a singular, narrow, "correct" reading of *D.C./Divided City* rather than an active and critical viewer with broad, multiple readings— even when that viewer might be William Bennett.

When Kemp and Bennett finished, Koppel selected audience mem- 27 bers to stand up and speak. If a person raised their voice and began to speak in a cadence familiarly associated with black religious rhetoric, Koppel interrupted and insisted that they be brief and ask a question of Bennett or Kemp. During the course of this segment, Koppel controlled the discussion with phrases like:

> Sir, if everyone gets up and gives a speech here, maybe five people will have a chance to speak . . . you're not asking a question . . . forgive me, but I want to take advantage of the time these gentlemen are giving us. . . . I think there's a question mark at the end of that . . . we are going to have chaos here if we don't establish some kind of order. . . . I'm going to give you a chance to raise your questions, if possible, but we still have to take commercial breaks. That's one of the imperatives of television. . . . If it's just going to be the people with the loudest lungs, then I've got the mike, OK? . . . Folks, don't be naive about it, that's how commercial television works.

Ostensibly, Koppel is being a tough but fair moderator, controlling a potentially unpredictable and unruly audience and forcing them to abide by the structure of commercial television. But the subtext presumes that the audience will be unruly and that only a certain kind of rhetorical behavior is appropriate. The insistence on questions to Kemp and Bennett tends to effectively force speakers to constantly yield the floor in favor of government officials who correct the audience's supposed misconceptions and refocus attention on official government policy. Statements of personal belief or attempts by others to move beyond questions into statements and positions of their own rhetorical strategies are repeatedly construed as bad manners, a lack of respect to authority, or a feeble understanding of the inviolability of the paradigms of commercial television programming. Despite the location of the town meeting in a black neighborhood, in a black church, in the midst of black citizens and community workers, the rules of rhetoric are brought in from the outside.

Here, at the town meeting, the representational system is the in- 28
verse of sound and image in *D.C./Divided City*. Formerly, the image track
depicted the violence and despair of the black urban experience while
the soundtrack suggested that this was a problem in part fostered by the
white community. Yet in the town meeting, the visual track shows the
earnestness, the sincerity, the urgency sensed by the black community
as they truly attempt to engage this problem in a sensible manner based
on their own rhetorical culture and experiences, while the soundtrack,
in part through the interventionism of Koppel, presents the meeting as
teetering on the edge of chaos. The strict preservation of order and the
efficient management of time take precedence over the emancipation of
black voices to national audiences.

Throughout the rest of the evening, voices grew in emotion and 29
questions concerning race, class, and even genocide became more common. Koppel and ABC news producers continued to rein in the action
in favor of order and time management. This was done through Koppel
himself (when asked why ABC showed one hour of blacks killing
blacks, Koppel replied "you must have been watching another program"), commercial breaks, cutaways to correspondent reports in other
cities, and finally a return of the student video from *D.C./Divided City*.
At the end of the town meeting, a woman is called on who identifies herself as a former drug addict and ex-convict. She says her oldest son was
recently killed in a drug-related incident. Declaring the problem is "on
the inside, not the outside," she goes on to describe her attempts to be a
productive member of society, saying she does not need welfare, just to
believe in herself. Allowed to go beyond the usual thirty to forty-five
seconds of most other speakers, she speaks emotionally on the power of
self-improvement as cutaways to women in the audience show several
of them wiping tears from their eyes and cheeks. As she finished her so-
liloquy, Koppel concluded the town meeting with:

> Folks, do me a favor and sit down. There is one thing I've learned in
> twenty-six years in the business. Every once in a while somebody says
> it like it is. There is not much point in saying any more. This lady has
> wrapped it up.

With this wrap-up, Koppel wipes away the earlier accusations of genocide and race/class struggle, as well as the implication of government
and social institutions in maintaining racial inequities. The victim is left
to assume the blame for the drug problem and the victim's self-thera-
peutic ability is offered as the only solution. This may have been a convenient, entertaining, even compelling, exit for a television program.
The audience was left to wonder if it was a fitting conclusion to the examination of a significant social problem.

Our analysis of *D.C./Divided City* and subsequent programming by 30
ABC is not some attempt on our part to denigrate the news division
at ABC, Ted Koppel, or other participants in program creation. Indeed,
ABC deserves support for tackling this thorny issue. However, our
analysis does reveal in detail how the ideological biases and exigencies
of American commercial television operate to produce a representation
of reality that tends to reinforce and reestablish existing social and political structures of inequality, even in cases when the ostensible intentions of program creators and news personnel are to question and perhaps even undermine those unequal structures. In the case of *D.C./
Divided City*, viewers are presented with an intellectual argument to end
racism but simultaneously with an emotional argument that justifies the
safety of separation. The viewer can hold an intellectual affinity to the
elimination of racial oppression and injustice while simultaneously reinforcing, in large part through visual imagery, perceptions of the security derived from racial separation. The end result is stasis.

Understanding and analyzing how television news reinforces and 31
reestablishes existing social and political structures of inequality can
lead to pessimistic judgments of the social value of television news.
However, a critical citizenship and active engagement with media culture and the viewing process implies a lifelong process of active questioning as a vital component of social change. Critical citizenship at its
best does not end with pessimistic judgments, but rather moves beyond those judgments in hopes of stimulating the process of change. In
the area of television news, critical citizenship on the part of viewers must be centrally occupied with the kind of active engagement
and questioning demonstrated . . . in the above analysis of *D.C./Divided
City.*

A part of critical citizenship in relation to media culture also means 32
a viewership that regularly includes alternatives to network television
news. As an example that can serve as an alternative to *D.C./Divided
City*, early in 1990 the cable network Black Entertainment Television
(BET) aired a two-hour prime time special titled *Black Agenda 2000*.
Structured with a moderator, a number of panelists, and a participatory
audience, *Black Agenda 2000* opened with an exploration of the representation of blacks in the media, from news and non-dramatic programming to sitcoms and feature films. This initial premise instigated
over two hours of discussion that often wandered from the original
topic, yet returned to the question of black representation over and over
again after rhetorical forays into questions concerning education, par-
enthood, economics, and the drug problem. At times the discussion
grew somewhat chaotic; at times one or two commercial breaks were
ignored; at times voices were raised as debates became heated; yet

overall, this program showed a workable commercial alternative to the tight structure considered sacrosanct in ABC's town meeting.

Other such programs, often found on the cable rather than broad- 33 cast networks, also give evidence of alternatives to the network news structure for the critical viewer. An increasing utilization of toll-free "800" telephone numbers are allowing more viewers to call in and voice opinions on topics or to ask social and government leaders questions of concern. Cable channels such as C-SPAN are not only showing Congressional activities but also the proceedings of a number of conferences and meetings, providing access to in-depth discussions on a wide range of topics, with opinions of participants covering the political spectrum. Just as critical readership in twentieth century American culture has often meant reading beyond the large daily newspapers and into the contents of a number of books and magazines of divergent political and social opinion, so too the critical viewer at the end of the twentieth century will probably move beyond the networks more and more regularly in search of alternative and partisan news and nondramatic programming.

•••••••••••••••••••

Examining the Text

1. The structure and tone of this essay are influenced by the fact that the authors' intended audience is academic. Describe this structure and tone, giving specific examples from the text. How and why would a review of *D.C./Divided City* written for a newspaper or a popular magazine differ from this essay?

2. Briefly restate the authors' observations about the contradictions between the visual imagery and the verbal script of *D.C./Divided City*. According to the authors, how do these contradictions help to create a sharper sense of the division between whites and blacks? How do you respond to their argument?

3. For what reasons do the authors criticize Ted Koppel's performance in the "town meeting" segment of the *Nightline* program? What do you think of their assessment? Can similar criticisms be leveled against television moderators in general?

4. The authors conclude that "the ideological biases and exigencies of American commercial television operate to produce a representation of reality that tends to reinforce and reestablish existing social and political structures of inequality" (paragraph 29). What do they mean here? Does their analysis support their conclusions? Do you agree that this detailed analysis of *D.C./Divided City* demonstrates that viewers must actively question television news?

For Group Discussion

At the end of the essay, the authors offer several alternatives to the network news format: special-interest cable network programs, audience call-in shows, and audience contributions to news shows. As a group, list some of the characteristics of each of these alternatives, and consider their relative advantages and disadvantages. As a class, discuss which you think could be most effective in creating the "critical viewership" that the authors describe.

Writing Suggestion

Do some research to find out how the broadcast of *D.C./Divided City* on April 27, 1989, was originally received by television reviewers in newspapers and magazines. Compare these responses to those of Schwoch and his co-authors. Which do you find most persuasive, and why?

The Bias of Language, The Bias of Pictures

Neil Postman and Steve Powers

*I*n *this essay from their book,* How to Watch TV News *(1992), cultural critics Neil Postman and Steve Powers offer a mini-handbook for those who want to be active, engaged, and insightful viewers of nightly news broadcasts. They first caution that "the words spoken on a television news show" are never "exactly what happened, . . . the absolute truth," but rather a verbal re-creation of the event which will differ from reporter to reporter. They then offer detailed advice for reading and seeing "between the lines" of TV journalism, such as attending to the specific words reporters use and how they reveal subtle biases, and to the visual content of the shows, shaped to a large extent, they say, by what video is available.*

Rather than accepting broadcasts as a purely objective reporting of facts, Postman and Powers interpret news programs as they would stories or film. They suggest, for example, that the opening music, the stage set, and the background activity create an image that we must see beyond if we are to look at the news critically.

Before you read, think about how you regard the news on television. Do you tend to accept everything the anchors and reporters say as "the absolute truth"? To what extent are you influenced by the image of authority that news broadcasts attempt to create?

•••••••••••••••••••

When a television news show distorts the truth by altering or man-   1
ufacturing facts (through re-creations), a television viewer is defenseless
even if a re-creation is properly labeled. Viewers are still vulnerable to
misinformation since they will not know (at least in the case of docu-
dramas) what parts are fiction and what parts are not. But the problems
of verisimilitude posed by re-creations pale to insignificance when compared to the problem viewers face when encountering a straight (no-
monkey-business) show. All news shows, in a sense, are re-creations in
that what we hear and see on them are attempts to represent actual
events, and are not the events themselves. Perhaps, to avoid ambiguity,
we might call all news shows "re-presentations" instead of "re-creations." These re-presentations come to us in two forms: language and
pictures. The question then arises: what do viewers have to know about
language and pictures in order to be properly armed to defend themselves against the seductions of eloquence (to use Bertrand Russell's apt
phrase)?

Let us take language first. Below are three principles that, in our   2
opinion, are an essential part of the analytical equipment a viewer must
bring to any encounter with a news show.

Whatever Anyone Says Something Is, It Isn't.

This sounds more complex—and maybe more pretentious—than it   3
actually is. What it means is that there is a difference between the world
of events and the world of words about events. The job of an honest reporter is to try to find words and the appropriate tone in presenting
them that will come as close to evoking the event as possible. But since
no two people will use exactly the same words to describe an event, we
must acknowledge that for every verbal description of an event, there
are multiple possible alternatives. You may demonstrate this to your
own satisfaction by writing a two-paragraph description of a dinner you
had with at least two other people, then asking the others who were present if each of them would also write, independently, a two-paragraph
description of the "same" dinner. We should be very surprised if all of
the descriptions include the same words, in the same order, emphasize
the same things, and express the same feelings. In other words, "the
dinner itself" is largely a nonverbal event. The words people use
to describe this event are not the event itself and are only abstracted representations of the event. What does this mean for a television viewer?
It means that the viewer must never assume that the words spoken on
a television news show are exactly what happened. Since there are so
many alternative ways of describing what happened, the viewer must

be on guard against assuming that he or she has heard "the absolute truth."

Language Operates at Various Levels of Abstraction.

This means that there is a level of language whose purpose is to *de-* 4
scribe an event. There is also a level of language whose purpose is to *evaluate* an event. Even more, there is a level of language whose purpose is to *infer* what is unknown on the basis of what is known. The usual way to make these distinctions clear is through sentences such as the following three:

Manny Freebus is 5'8" and weighs 235 pounds.
Manny Freebus is grossly fat.
Manny Freebus eats too much.

The first sentence may be said to be language as pure description. It 5
involves no judgments and no inferences. The second sentence is a description of sorts, but is mainly a judgment that the speaker makes of the "event" known as Manny Freebus. The third sentence is an inference based on observations the speaker has made. It is, in fact, a statement about the unknown based on the known. As it happens, we know Manny Freebus and can tell you that he eats no more than the average person but suffers from a glandular condition which keeps him overweight. Therefore, anyone who concluded from observing Manny's shape that he eats too much has made a false inference. A good guess, but false nonetheless.

You can watch television news programs from now until doomsday 6
and never come across any statement about Manny Freebus. But you will constantly come across the three kinds of statements we have been discussing—descriptions, judgments, and inferences. And it is important for a viewer to distinguish among them. For example, you might hear an anchor introduce a story by saying: "Today Congress ordered an investigation of the explosive issue of whether Ronald Reagan's presidential campaign made a deal with Iran in 1980 to delay the release of American hostages until after the election." This statement is, of course, largely descriptive, but includes the judgmental word "explosive" as part of the report. We need hardly point out that what is explosive to one person may seem trivial to another. We do not say that the news writer has no business to include his or her judgment of this investigation. We do say that the viewer has to be aware that a judgment has been made. In fact, even the phrase "made a deal" (why not "arranged with Iran"?) has a somewhat sleazy connotation that implies a judgment of

sorts. If, in the same news report, we are told that the evidence for such a secret deal is weak and that only an investigation with subpoena power can establish the truth, we must know that we have left the arena of factual language and have moved into the land of inference. An investigation with subpoena power may be a good idea but whether or not it can establish the truth is a guess on the journalist's part, and a viewer ought to know that.

Almost All Words Have Connotative Meanings.

This suggests that even when attempting to use purely descriptive language, a journalist cannot avoid expressing an attitude about what he or she is saying. For example, here is the opening sentence of an anchor's report about national examinations: "For the first time in the nation's history, high-level education policymakers have designed the elements for a national examination system similar to the one advocated by President Bush." This sentence certainly looks like it is pure description although it is filled with ambiguities. Is this the first time in our history that this has been done? Or only the first time that high-level education policymakers have done it? Or is it the first time something has been designed that is similar to what the President has advocated? But let us put those questions aside. (After all, there are limits to how analytical one ought to be.) Instead, we might concentrate on such words as "high-level," "policymakers," and "designed." Speaking for ourselves, we are by no means sure that we know what a "high-level policymaker" is, although it sounds awfully impressive. It is certainly better than a "low-level policymaker," although how one would distinguish between the two is a bit of a mystery. Come to think of it, a low-level "policymaker" must be pretty good, too, since anyone who makes policy must be important. It comes as no surprise, therefore, that what was done was "designed." To design something usually implies careful thought, preparation, organization, and coherence. People design buildings, bridges, and furniture. If your experience has been anything like ours, you will know that reports are almost never designed; they are usually "thrown together," and it is quite a compliment to say that a report was designed. The journalist who paid this compliment was certainly entitled to do it even though he may not have been aware of what he was doing. He probably thought he had made a simple description, avoiding any words that would imply favor or disfavor. But if so, he was defeated in his effort because language tends to be emotion-laden. Because it is people who do the talking, the talk almost always includes a feeling, an attitude, a judgment. In a sense, every language contains the history of a people's feelings about the world. Our words are baskets of emotion. Smart journalists, of course, know this. And so do smart audiences. Smart audiences don't blame anyone for this state of affairs. They are, however, prepared for it.

It is not our intention to provide here a mini-course in semantics. Even if we could, we are well aware that no viewer could apply analytic principles all the time or even much of the time. Anchors and reporters talk too fast and too continuously for any of us to monitor most of their sentences. Besides, who would want to do that for most of the stories on a news show? If you have a sense of what is important, you will probably judge most news stories to be fluff, or nonsense, or irrelevancies, not worthy of your analytic weaponry. But there are times when stories appear that are of major significance from your point of view. These are the times when your level of attention will reach a peak and you must call upon your best powers of interpretation. In those moments, you need to draw on whatever you know about the relationship between language and reality; about the distinctions among statements of fact, judgment, and inference; about the connotative meanings of words. When this is done properly, viewers are no longer passive consumers of news but active participants in a kind of dialogue between a news show and themselves. A viewer may even find that he or she is "talking back to the television set" (which is the title of a book by former FCC commissioner Nicholas Johnson). In our view, nothing could be healthier for the sanity and well-being of our nation than to have ninety million viewers talking back to their television news shows every night and twice on Sunday.

Now we must turn to the problem of pictures. It is often said that a picture is worth a thousand words. Maybe so. But it is probably equally true that one word is worth a thousand pictures, at least sometimes—for example, when it comes to understanding the world we live in. Indeed, the whole problem with news on television comes down to this: all the words uttered in an hour of news coverage could be printed on one page of a newspaper. And the world cannot be understood in one page. Of course, there is a compensation: television offers pictures, and the pictures move. Moving pictures are a kind of language in themselves, but the language of pictures differs radically from oral and written language, and the differences are crucial for understanding television news.

To begin with, pictures, especially single pictures, speak only in particularities. Their vocabulary is limited to concrete representation. Unlike words and sentences, a picture does not present to us an idea or concept about the world, except as we use language itself to convert the image to idea. By itself, a picture cannot deal with the unseen, the remote, the internal, the abstract. It does not speak of "man," only of *a* man; not of "tree," only of *a* tree. You cannot produce an image of "nature," any more than an image of "the sea." You can only show a particular fragment of the here-and-now—a cliff of a certain terrain, in a certain condition of light; a wave at a moment in time, from a particular point of view. And just as "nature" and "the sea" cannot be photographed, such larger abstractions as truth, honor, love, and falsehood cannot be talked about in the lexicon of individual pictures. For "showing of" and "talking about" are two very different kinds of processes: individual pictures give us the world as object; language, the world as idea. There is no such thing in nature as "man" or "tree." The universe offers no such categories or simplifications; only flux and infinite variety. The picture documents and celebrates the particularities of the universe's infinite variety. Language makes them comprehensible.

Of course, moving pictures, video with sound, may bridge the gap   11
by juxtaposing images, symbols, sound, and music. Such images can present emotions and rudimentary ideas. They can suggest the panorama of nature and the joys and miseries of humankind.

Picture—smoke pouring from the window, cut to people coughing,   12
an ambulance racing to a hospital, a tombstone in a cemetery.

Picture—jet planes firing rockets, explosions, lines of foreign sol-   13
diers surrendering, the American flag waving in the wind.

Nonetheless, keep in mind that when terrorists want to prove to the   14
world that their kidnap victims are still alive, they photograph them holding a copy of a recent newspaper. The dateline on the newspaper provides the proof that the photograph was taken on or after that date. Without the help of the written word, film and videotape cannot portray temporal dimensions with any precision. Consider a film clip showing an aircraft carrier at sea. One might be able to identify the ship as Soviet or American, but there would be no way of telling where in the world the carrier was, where it was headed, or when the pictures were taken. It is only through language—words spoken over the pictures or reproduced in them—that the image of the aircraft carrier takes on specific meaning.

Still, it is possible to enjoy the image of the carrier for its own sake.   15
One might find the hugeness of the vessel interesting; it signifies military power on the move. There is a certain drama in watching the planes come in at high speeds and skid to a stop on the deck. Suppose the ship were burning: that would be even more interesting. This leads to an important point about the language of pictures. Moving pictures favor images that change. That is why violence and dynamic destruction find their way onto television so often. When something is destroyed violently it is altered in a highly visible way; hence the entrancing power

of fire. Fire gives visual form to the ideas of consumption, disappearance, death—the thing that burned is actually taken away by fire. It is at this very basic level that fires make a good subject for television news. Something was here, now it's gone, and the change is recorded on film.

Earthquakes and typhoons have the same power. Before the viewer's eyes the world is taken apart. If a television viewer has relatives in Mexico City and an earthquake occurs there, then he or she may take a special interest in the images of destruction as a report from a specific place and time; that is, one may look at television pictures for information about an important event. But film of an earthquake can be interesting even if the viewer cares nothing about the event itself. Which is only to say, as we noted earlier, that there is another way of participating in the news—as a spectator who desires to be entertained. Actually to see buildings topple is exciting, no matter where the buildings are. The world turns to dust before our eyes.

Those who produce television news in America know that their medium favors images that move. That is why they are wary of "talking heads," people who simply appear in front of a camera and speak. When talking heads appear on television, there is nothing to record or document, no change in process. In the cinema the situation is somewhat different. On a movie screen, close-ups of a good actor speaking dramatically can sometimes be interesting to watch. When Clint Eastwood narrows his eyes and challenges his rival to shoot first, the spectator sees the cool rage of the Eastwood character take visual form, and the narrowing of the eyes is dramatic. But much of the effect of this small movement depends on the size of the movie screen and the darkness of the theater, which make Eastwood and his every action "larger than life."

The television screen is smaller than life. It occupies about 15 percent of the viewer's visual field (compared to about 70 percent for the movie screen). It is not set in a darkened theater closed off from the world but in the viewer's ordinary living space. This means that visual changes must be more extreme and more dramatic to be interesting on television. A narrowing of the eyes will not do. A car crash, an earthquake, a burning factory are much better.

With these principles in mind, let us examine more closely the structure of a typical newscast, and here we will include in the discussion not only the pictures but all the nonlinguistic symbols that make up a television news show. For example, in America, almost all news shows begin with music, the tone of which suggests important events about to unfold. The music is very important, for it equates the news with various forms of drama and ritual—the opera, for example, or a wedding procession—in which musical themes underscore the meaning of the

16

17

18

19

event. Music takes us immediately into the realm of the symbolic, a world that is not to be taken literally. After all, when events unfold in the real world, they do so without musical accompaniment. More symbolism follows. The sound of teletype machines can be heard in the studio, not because it is impossible to screen this noise out, but because the sound is a kind of music in itself. It tells us that data are pouring in from all corners of the globe, a sensation reinforced by the world map in the background (or clocks noting the time on different continents). The fact is that teletype machines are rarely used in TV news rooms, having been replaced by silent computer terminals. When seen, they have only a symbolic function.

Already, then, before a single news item is introduced, a great deal 20 has been communicated. We know that we are in the presence of a symbolic event, a form of theater in which the day's events are to be dramatized. This theater takes the entire globe as its subject, although it may look at the world from the perspective of a single nation. A certain tension is present, like the atmosphere in a theater just before the curtain goes up. The tension is represented by the music, the staccato beat of the teletype machines, and often the sight of news workers scurrying around typing reports and answering phones. As a technical matter, it would be no problem to build a set in which the newsroom staff remained off camera, invisible to the viewer, but an important theatrical effect would be lost. By being busy on camera, the workers help communicate urgency about the events at hand, which suggests that situations are changing so rapidly that constant revision of the news is necessary.

The staff in the background also helps signal the importance of the 21 person in the center, the anchor, "in command" of both the staff and the news. The anchor plays the role of host. He or she welcomes us to the newscast and welcomes us back from the different locations we visit during the filmed reports.

Many features of the newscast help the anchor to establish the im- 22 pression of control. These are usually equated with production values in broadcasting. They include such things as graphics that tell the viewer what is being shown, or maps and charts that suddenly appear on the screen and disappear on cue, or the orderly progression from story to story. They also include the absence of gaps, or "dead time," during the broadcast, even the simple fact that the news starts and ends at a certain hour. These common features are thought of as purely technical matters, which a professional crew handles as a matter of course. But they are also symbols of a dominant theme of television news: the imposition of an orderly world—called "the news"—upon the disorderly flow of events.

While the form of a news broadcast emphasizes tidiness and con-   23
trol, its content can best be described as fragmented. Because time is so
precious on television, because the nature of the medium favors dynamic visual images, and because the pressures of a commercial structure require the news to hold its audience above all else, there is rarely
any attempt to explain issues in depth or place events in their proper
context. The news moves nervously from a warehouse fire to a court decision, from a guerrilla war to a World Cup match, the quality of the film
most often determining the length of the story. Certain stories show up
only because they offer dramatic pictures. Bleachers collapse in South
America: hundreds of people are crushed—a perfect television news
story, for the cameras can record the face of disaster in all its anguish.
Back in Washington, a new budget is approved by Congress. Here there
is nothing to photograph because a budget is not a physical event; it is
a document full of language and numbers. So the producers of the news
will show a photo of the document itself, focusing on the cover where
it says "Budget of the United States of America." Or sometimes they will
send a camera crew to the government printing plant where copies of
the budget are produced. That evening, while the contents of the budget are summarized by a voice-over, the viewer sees stacks of documents being loaded into boxes at the government printing plant. Then
a few of the budget's more important provisions will be flashed on the
screen in written form, but this is such a time-consuming process—using television as a printed page—that the producers keep it to a minimum. In short, the budget is not televisable, and for that reason its time
on the news must be brief. The bleacher collapse will get more time that
evening.

While appearing somewhat chaotic, these disparate stories are not   24
just dropped in the news program helter-skelter. The appearance of a
scattershot story order is really orchestrated to draw the audience from
one story to the next—from one section to the next—through the commercial breaks to the end of the show. The story order is constructed to
hold and build the viewership rather than place events in context or explain issues in depth.

Of course, it is a tendency of journalism in general to concentrate on   25
the surface of events rather than underlying conditions; this is as true
for the newspaper as it is for the newscast. But several features of television undermine whatever efforts journalists may make to give sense
to the world. One is that a television broadcast is a series of events that
occur in sequence, and the sequence is the same for all viewers. This is
not true for a newspaper page, which displays many items simultaneously, allowing readers to choose the order in which they read them.
If newspaper readers want only a summary of the latest tax bill, they

can read the headline and the first paragraph of an article, and if they want more, they can keep reading. In a sense, then, everyone reads a different newspaper, for no two readers will read (or ignore) the same items.

But all television viewers see the same broadcast. They have no   26
choices. A report is either in the broadcast or out, which means that anything which is of narrow interest is unlikely to be included. As NBC News executive Reuven Frank once explained:

> A newspaper, for example, can easily afford to print an item of conceivable interest to only a fraction of its readers. A television news program must be put together with the assumption that each item will be of some interest to everyone that watches. Every time a newspaper includes a feature which will attract a specialized group it can assume it is adding at least a little bit to its circulation. To the degree a television news program includes an item of this sort . . . it must assume that its audience will diminish.

The need to "include everyone," an identifying feature of commer-   27
cial television in all its forms, prevents journalists from offering lengthy or complex explanations, or from tracing the sequence of events leading up to today's headlines. One of the ironies of political life in modern democracies is that many problems which concern the "general welfare" are of interest only to specialized groups. Arms control, for example, is an issue that literally concerns everyone in the world, and yet the language of arms control and the complexity of the subject are so daunting that only a minority of people can actually follow the issue from week to week and month to month. If it wants to act responsibly, a newspaper can at least make available more information about arms control than most people want. Commercial television cannot afford to do so.

But even if commercial television could afford to do so, it wouldn't.   28
The fact that television news is principally made up of moving pictures prevents it from offering lengthy, coherent explanations of events. A television news show reveals the world as a series of unrelated, fragmentary moments. It does not—and cannot be expected to—offer a sense of coherence or meaning. What does this suggest to a TV viewer? That the viewer must come with a prepared mind—information, opinions, a sense of proportion, an articulate value system. To the TV viewer lacking such mental equipment, a news program is only a kind of rousing light show. Here a falling building, there a five-alarm fire, everywhere the world as an object, much without meaning, connections, or continuity.

....

Examining the Text

1. Why do Postman and Powers say it would be healthy "for the sanity and well-being of our nation . . . to have ninety million viewers talking back to their television news shows every night . . ." (paragraph 8)? What kind of "talking back" do you think they mean?

2. What do the authors see as some of the important differences between words and pictures in television news? How do words and pictures affect us differently, and what sorts of different messages do they convey? Do the authors' observations correspond to your own experience?

3. What, according to Postman and Powers, are the important similarities and differences between TV and print journalism? Do you think it is easier to spot bias in one or the other?

For Group Discussion

Powers and Postman suggest that television news presents the unprepared viewer with "the world as a series of unrelated, fragmentary moments . . . as an object, much without meaning, connections, or continuity" (28). As a group, come up with some specific proposals to improve the quality of TV news, based on Postman and Powers's ideas. As a class, discuss the obstacles each of your proposals would face.

Writing Suggestion

Choose a newspaper article of at least six paragraphs, and read it critically, applying the principles about language discussed by Postman and Powers. Note language that is purely descriptive and language that is evaluative; look for inferences; think about the connotations of the words the reporter has used. In a critical essay, explain how the reporter's choice of language has influenced the meaning of the story.

Tales from the Cutting Room Floor

Debra Seagal

T he following article focuses on a fairly recent genre of television program that blurs the edge between "documentary journalism" and "entertainment." The so-called "reality-based" cop show—Fox Network's Cops *is probably the most popular—presents videotapes of actual law-enforcement officers "live," as they respond to drunk and disorderly complaints, carry out drug raids, and deal with domestic disturbances. The popularity of these shows, with their voyeuristic images of an urban landscape filled with violence and despair, raises some troubling questions not only about the mood of popular culture in America today but also about the whole concept of documentary journalism.*

Originally published in Harper's Magazine, *freelance writer Debra Seagal's diary-like account of her work on the now-defunct* American Detective *provides an insider's view of how these shows are put together. As a "story analyst" or "logger," Seagal's job was, in her words, to reduce "fifty or sixty hours of mundane and compromising video into short, action-packed segments of tantalizing, crack-filled, dope-dealing, junkie-busting cop culture." Seagal describes what she saw in the raw footage—including the "reality" that didn't make it to the TV screen. She describes the disturbing effect her job had on her personally, and speculates about the effect these shows have on the TV-viewing public.*

As you read, note that Seagal has structured her essay as a series of diary entries over the course of several months. What effect does the format have on you as you read?

· · · · · · · · · · · · · · · · · · · ·

May 6, 1992

Yesterday I applied for a job as a "story analyst" at *American Detective,* a prime-time "reality-based" cop show on ABC that I've never seen. The interview took place in Malibu at the program's production office, in a plain building next door to a bodybuilding gym. I walked past rows of bronzed people working out on Nautilus equipment and into a dingy array of padded dark rooms crowded with people peering into television screens. Busy people ran up and down the halls. I was greeted by the "story department" manager, who explained that every day the show has camera crews in four different cities trailing detectives as they break into every type of home and location to search, confiscate, interrogate, and arrest. (The crews have the right to do this, he told me, because they have been "deputized" by the local police department. What exactly this means I was not told.) They shoot huge amounts of videotape and it arrives every day, rushed to Malibu by Federal Express. Assistants tag and time-code each video before turning it over to the story department.

After talking about the job, the story-department manager sat me in front of a monitor and gave me two hours to "analyze" a video. I watched the camera pan through a dilapidated trailer while a detective searched for incriminating evidence. He found money in a small yellow suitcase, discovered a knife under a sofa, and plucked a tiny, twisted marijuana butt from a swan-shaped ashtray. I typed each act into a computer. It took me forty-five minutes to make what seemed a meaningless record. When I got home this afternoon there was a message on my phone machine from the story-department manager congratulating me on a job well done and welcoming me to *American Detective.* I am pleased.

May 18, 1992

Although we're officially called story analysts, in-house we're referred to as "the loggers." Each of us has a computer/VCR/print monitor/TV screen/headphone console looming in front of us like a colossal dashboard. Settling into my chair is like squeezing into a small cockpit. The camera crews seem to go everywhere: Detroit, New York, Miami, Las Vegas, Pittsburgh, Phoenix, Portland, Santa Cruz, Indianapolis, San Jose. They join up with local police teams and apparently get access to everything the cops do. They even wear blue jackets with POLICE in yellow letters on the back. The loggers scrutinize each hour-long tape second by second, and make a running log of every visual and auditory element that can be used to "create" a story. On an average day the other three loggers and I look at twenty to forty tapes, and in any given week we analyze from 6,000 to 12,000 minutes—or up to 720,000 seconds of film.

The footage comes from handheld "main" and "secondary" cameras as well as tiny, wirelike "lock-down" cameras taped to anything that might provide a view of the scene: car doors, window visors, and even on one occasion—in order to record drug deals inside an undercover vehicle—a gear-shift handle. Once a videotape is viewed, the logger creates a highlight reel—a fifteen-minute distillation of the overall "bust" or "case." The tapes and scripts are then handed over to the supervising producer, who in turn works with technical editors to create an episode of the show, each of which begins with this message on the screen: "What you are about to see is real. There are no re-creations. Everything was filmed while it actually happened."

There are, I've learned, quite a few of these reality and "fact-based" shows now, with names like *Cops, Top Cops,* and *FBI: The Untold Stories.* Why the national obsession with this sort of voyeuristic entertainment? Perhaps we want to believe the cops are still in control. The preponderance of these shows is also related to the bottom line: they are extremely inexpensive to produce. After all, why create an elaborate car-chase sequence costing tens of thousands of dollars a minute when a crew with a couple of video cameras can ride around with the cops and get the "real" thing? Why engage a group of talented writers and producers to make intelligent and exciting TV when it's more profitable to dip into the endless pool of human grief?

I've just participated in my first "story meeting" with the supervis-   6
ing producer. He occupies a dark little room filled with prerecorded sounds of police banter, queer voice-over loops, segments of the *American Detective* theme song, and sound bites of angry drug-busting screams ("Stop! Police! Put your hands up, you motherfucker!"). A perpetual cold wind blows from a faulty air duct above his desk. He is tall, lanky, in his fifties; his ambition once was to be a serious actor. His job is to determine what images will be resurrected as prime-time, Monday-night entertainment. He doesn't look miserable but I suspect he is.

There are six of us in the story meeting, the producer, four loggers,   7
and the story-department manager. Each logger plays highlight reels and pitches stories, most of which are rejected by the producer for being "not hot enough," "not sexy." Occasionally, I learned today, a highlight reel is made of a case that is still in progress, such as a stakeout. Our cameramen then call us on-site from their cellular phones during our story meeting and update us on what has been filmed that day, sometimes that very hour. The footage arrives the next morning and then is built into the evolving story. This process continues in a flurry of calls and Federal Express deliveries while the real drama unfolds elsewhere—Pittsburgh or San Jose or wherever. We are to hope for a naturally dramatic climax. But if it doesn't happen, I understand, we'll "work one out."

May 26, 1992

I'm learning the job. Among other tasks, we're responsible for com-   8
piling stock-footage books—volumes of miscellaneous images containing every conceivable example of guns, drugs, money, scenics, street signs, appliances, and interior house shots. This compendium is used to embellish stories when certain images or sounds have not been picked up by a main or secondary camera: a close-up of a suspect's tightly cuffed wrists missed in a rush, a scream muffled by background traffic noise. Or, most frequently, the shouts of the cops on a raid ("POLICE! Open the door! Now!") in an otherwise unexciting ramrod affair. Evidently the "reality" of a given episode is subject to enhancement.

Today the story-department manager gave me several videotapes   9
from secondary and lock-down cameras at an undercover mission in Indianapolis. I've never been to Indianapolis, and I figured that, if nothing else, I'd get to see the city.

I was wrong. What I saw and heard was a procession of close-up   10
crotch shots, nose-picking, and farting in surveillance vans where a few

detectives waited, perspiring under the weight of nylon-mesh raid gear and semiautomatic rifles. Searching for the scraps of usable footage was like combing a beach for a lost contact lens. The actual bust—a sad affair that featured an accountant getting arrested for buying pot in an empty shoe-store parking lot—was perhaps 1 percent of everything I looked at. In the logic of the story department, we are to deplore these small-time drug busts not because we are concerned that the big drugs are still on the street but because a small bust means an uninteresting show. A dud.

Just before going home today, I noticed a little list that someone   11
tacked up on our bulletin boards to remind us what we are looking for:

DEATH
STAB
SHOOT
STRANGULATION
CLUB
SUICIDE

June 3, 1992

Today was the first day I got to log Lieutenant Bunnell, which is con-   12
sidered a great honor in the office. Lieutenant Bunnell is the show's mascot, the venerated spokesperson. Only two years ago he was an ordinary narcotics detective in Oregon. Today he has a six-figure income, an agent, fans all over the country, and the best voice coach in Hollywood. He's so famous now that he's even stalked by his fans, such as the strange woman who walked into our office a few days ago wearing hole-pocked spandex tights, worn-down spike-heeled backless pumps, and a see-through purse. She'd been on his trail from Florida to California and wanted his home phone number. She was quietly escorted out the door to her dilapidated pickup truck.

At the beginning of each episode, Lieutenant Bunnell sets the scene   13
for the viewer (much like Jack Webb on *Dragnet*), painting a picture of the crime at hand and describing the challenges the detectives face. He also participates in many of these raids, since he is, after all, still a police lieutenant. The standard fare: Act I, Bunnell's suspenseful introduction; Act II, Bunnell leads his team on a raid; Act III, Bunnell captures the bad suspect and throws him in the squad car, etc. The format of each drama must fit into an eleven-minute segment. So it is that although *American Detective* and its competitors seem a long way from *Dragnet, The Mod Squad, The Rookies*, et al.—all the famous old cop

shows—they follow the same formula, the same dramatic arc, because this is what the viewers and advertisers have come to expect.

June 10, 1992

The producers are pleased with my work and have assigned me my 14 own beat to log—Santa Cruz in northern California. Having spent several summers there as a teenager, I remember its forests, its eucalyptus and apple orchards. But today, two decades later, I strap on earphones, flip on the equipment, and meet three detectives on the Santa Cruz County Narcotic Enforcement Team. Dressed in full SWAT-team regalia, they are Brooks, an overweight commander; Gravitt, his shark-faced colleague; and Cooper, a detective underling. The first image is an intersection in Santa Cruz's commercial district. While an undercover pal negotiates with a drug dealer across the street, the three detectives survey an unsuspecting woman from behind their van's tinted windows. It begins like this:

> [*Interior of van. Mid-range shot of Commander Brooks, Special Agent Gravitt, and Detective Cooper*]
>
> COOPER: Check out those volumptuous [*sic*] breasts and that volumptuous [*sic*] ass.
>
> BROOKS: Think she takes it in the butt?
>
> COOPER: Yep. It sticks out just enough so you can pull the cheeks apart and really plummet it. [*Long pause*] I believe that she's not beyond fellatio either.
>
> [*Zoom to close-up of Cooper*]
>
> COOPER: You don't have true domination over a woman until you spit on 'em and they don't say nothing.
>
> [*Zoom to close up of Gravitt*]
>
> GRAVITT: I know a hooker who will let you spit on her for twenty bucks . . . [*Direct appeal to camera*] Can one of you guys edit this thing and make a big lump in my pants for me?
>
> [*Zoom to close-up of Gravitt's crotch, walkie-talkie between his legs*]

June 15, 1992

I'm developing a perverse fascination with the magic exercised in 15 our TV production sweatshop. Once our supervising producer has picked the cases that might work for the show, the "stories" are turned over to an editor. Within a few weeks the finished videos emerge from the editing room with "problems" fixed, chronologies reshuffled, and, when necessary, images and sound bites clipped and replaced by old filler footage from unrelated cases.

By the time our 9 million viewers flip on their tubes, we've reduced   16
fifty or sixty hours of mundane and compromising video into short, action-packed segments of tantalizing, crack-filled, dope-dealing, junkie-
busting cop culture. How easily we downplay the pathos of the suspect;
how cleverly we breeze past the complexities that cast doubt on the very
system that has produced the criminal activity in the first place. How ef-
fortlessly we smooth out the indiscretions of the lumpen detectives and
casually make them appear as pistol-flailing heroes rushing across the
screen. Watching a finished episode of *American Detective,* one easily forgets that the detectives are, for the most part, men whose lives are over-
burdened with formalities and paperwork. They ambush one downtrodden suspect after another in search of marijuana, and then, after a
long Sisyphean day, retire into red-vinyl bars where they guzzle down
beers among a clientele that, to no small degree, resembles the very people they have just ambushed.

June 23, 1992

The executive producer is a tiny man with excessively coiffed,   17
shoulder-length blond hair. He is given to wearing stone-washed jeans,
a buttoned-to-the-collar shirt, and enormous cowboy boots; he also frequently wears a police badge on his belt loop. As I log away, I see his
face on the screen flashing in the background like a subliminal advertisement for a new line of L.A.P.D. fashion coordinates. He sits in on in-
terrogations, preens the detectives' hair, prompts them to "say something pithy for the camera." He gets phone calls in surveillance vans and
in detective briefing rooms. With a cellular phone flat against his ear, he
even has conversations with his L.A. entourage—Lorimar executives,
ABC executives, other producers—while he runs in his police jacket behind the cops through ghettos and barrios.

I am beginning to wonder how he has gained access to hundreds of   18
cop cars from California to New Jersey. Clearly the cops don't fear they
will be compromised; I see the bonding that takes place between them
and the executive producer, who, after a successful raid, presents them
with *American Detective* plagues that feature their own faces. Their camaraderie is picked up continuously by the cameras. One of my colleagues has a photograph of our executive producer and Lieutenant
Bunnell with their arms around a topless go-go dancer somewhere in
Las Vegas; underneath it is a handwritten caption that reads, "The Unbearable Lightness of Being a Cop."

June 25, 1992

Today I logged in several hours of one detective sitting behind a   19
steering wheel doing absolutely nothing. How a man could remain

practically immobile for so long is beyond my comprehension. He sat and stared out the window, forgetting that the tiny lock-down camera under his window visor was rolling. After an hour, it seemed as though *I* had become the surveillance camera, receiving his every twitch and breath through the intravenous-like circuitry that connects me to my machine and my machine to his image. There was, finally, a moment when he shifted and looked directly at the camera. For a second our eyes met, and, flustered, I averted my gaze.

June 26, 1992

20

Today would have been inconsequential had not the supervising producer emerged from his air-conditioned nightmare and leaned over my desk. "We'll have a crew covering Detroit over the weekend," he said. "Maybe we'll get a good homicide for you to work on." I was speechless. I've never seen a homicide, and I have no interest in seeing one. But I'm working in a place where a grisly homicide is actually welcomed. I am supposed to look forward to this. After work, I prayed for benevolence, goodwill, and peace in Detroit.

June 29, 1992

21

My prayers have worked—no Detroit homicide case came in today. That doesn't mean, however, that I'm any less complicit in what is clearly a sordid enterprise. This afternoon I analyzed a tape that features detectives busting a motley assortment of small-time pot dealers and getting them to "flip" on their connections. The freshly cuffed "crook" then becomes a C.I. (confidential informant). Rigged with hidden wires and cameras, the C.I. works for the detectives by setting up his friends in drug busts that lead up the ladder. In exchange for this, the C.I. is promised a more lenient sentence when his day comes up in court. Some of the C.I.'s have been busted so many times before that they are essentially professional informants. Ironically, some have actually learned how the game is played by watching reality-based cop shows. This is the case with a nervous teenage first-time pot seller who gets set up and busted in a bar for selling half an ounce of pot. When the undercover cop flashes his badge and whips out his cuff, a look of thrilled recognition brightens the suspect's face. "Hey, I know you!" he gasps. "You're what's-his-name on *American Detective*, aren't you? I watch your show every week! I know exactly what you want me to do!"

22

The cops are flattered by the recognition, even if it comes from a teenage crook caught selling pot. They seem to become pals with the C.I.'s. Sometimes, however, they have to muscle the guy. The tape I saw today involves a soft-spoken, thirtysomething white male named

Michael who gets busted for selling pot out of his ramshackle abode in the Santa Cruz mountains. He's been set up by a friend who himself was originally resistant to cooperating with the detectives. Michael has never been arrested and doesn't understand the mechanics of becoming a C.I. He has only one request: to see a lawyer. By law, after such a request the detectives are required to stop any form of interrogation immediately and make a lawyer available. In this case, however, Commander Brooks knows that if he can get Michael to flip, they'll be able to keep busting up the ladder and, of course, we'll be able to crank out a good show.

So what happens? Hunched in front of my equipment in the office 23 of Malibu, this is what I see, in minute after minute of raw footage:

> [*Michael is pulled out of bed after midnight. Two of our cameras are rolling and a group of cops surround him. He is entirely confused when Brooks explains how to work with them and become a confidential informant.*]
>
> MICHAEL: Can I have a lawyer? . . . I don't know what's going on. I'd really rather talk to a lawyer. This is not my expertise at all, as it is yours. I feel way outnumbered. I don't know what's going on. . . .
>
> BROOKS: Here's where we're at. You've got a lot of marijuana. Marijuana's still a felony in the state of California, despite whatever you may think about it.
>
> MICHAEL: I understand.
>
> BROOKS: The amount of marijuana you have here is gonna send you to state prison. . . . That's our job, to try to put you in state prison, quite frankly, unless you do something to help yourself. Unless you do something to assist us. . . .
>
> MICHAEL: I'm innocent until proven guilty, correct?
>
> BROOKS: I'm telling you the way it is in the real world. . . . What we're asking you to do is cooperate . . . to act as our agent and help us buy larger amounts of marijuana. Tell us where you get your marijuana. . . .
>
> MICHAEL: I don't understand. You know, you guys could have me do something and I could get in even more trouble.
>
> BROOKS: Obviously, if you're acting as our agent, you can't get in trouble. . . .
>
> MICHAEL: I'm taking your word for that? . . .
>
> BROOKS: Here's what I'm telling you. If you don't want to cooperate, you're going to prison.
>
> MICHAEL: Sir, I do want to cooperate—
>
> BROOKS: Now, I'm saying if you don't cooperate right today, now, here, this minute, you're going to prison. We're gonna asset-seize your property. We're gonna asset-seize your vehicles. We're gonna asset-seize your money. We're gonna send your girlfriend to prison and we're gonna send your kid to the Child Protective Services. That's what I'm saying.

MICHAEL: If I get a lawyer, all that stuff happens to me?

BROOKS: If you get a lawyer, we're not in a position to wanna co-operate with you tomorrow. We're in a position to cooperate with you right now. Today. Right now. Today. . . .

MICHAEL: I'm under too much stress to make a decision like that. I want to talk to a lawyer. I really do. That's the bottom line.

[*Commander Brooks continues to push Michael but doesn't get far.*]

MICHAEL: I'm just getting more confused. I've got ten guys stand-ing around me. . . .

BROOKS: We're not holding a gun to you.

MICHAEL: Every one of you guys has a gun.

BROOKS: How old is your child?

MICHAEL: She'll be three on Tuesday.

BROOKS: Well, children need a father at home. You can't be much of a father when you're in jail.

MICHAEL: Sir!

BROOKS: That's not a scare tactic, that's reality.

MICHAEL: That is a scare tactic.

BROOKS: No, it isn't. That's reality. . . . And the reality is, I'm send-ing you to prison unless you do something to help yourself out. . . .

MICHAEL: Well, ain't I also innocent until proven guilty in a court of law? . . . You know what, guys? I really just want to talk to a lawyer. That's really all I want to do.

BROOKS: How much money did you put down on this prop-erty? . . . Do you own that truck over there?

MICHAEL: Buddy, does all this need to be done to get arrested? . . .

BROOKS: Yeah. I'm curious—do you own that truck there?

MICHAEL: You guys know all that.

BROOKS: I hope so, 'cause I'd look good in that truck.

MICHAEL: Is this Mexico?

BROOKS: No. I'll just take it. Asset-seizure. And you know what? The county would look good taking the equity out of this house.

MICHAEL: Lots of luck.

[*Commander Brooks continues to work on Michael for several minutes.*]

MICHAEL: I feel like you're poking at me.

BROOKS: I *am* poking at you.

MICHAEL: So now I really want to talk to a lawyer now.

BROOKS: That's fine. We're done.

[*Brooks huffs off, mission unaccomplished. He walks over to his pals and shakes his head.*]

BROOKS: That's the first white guy I ever felt like beating the fuck-ing shit out of.

If Michael's case becomes an episode of the show, Michael will be   24
made a part of a criminal element that stalks backyards and threatens
children. Commander Brooks will become a gentle, persuasive cop
who's keeping our streets safe at night.

July 1, 1992

Today I got a video to analyze that involves a car chase. It includes   25
the three Santa Cruz cops and a few other officers following two Hispanic suspects at top speed through a brussels-sprout field in the Central
Valley. Our cameramen, wearing police jackets, are in one of their undercover vans during the pursuit. (One of them has his camera in one
hand and a pistol held high in the other. The police don't seem to care
about his blurred role.) When the suspects stop their car and emerge with
their arms held high, the detectives bound out of their vans screaming in
a shrill chorus ("Get on the ground, cocksucker!" "I'll blow your moth-
erfucking head off."). I watch. Within seconds, the suspects are pinned
to the ground and held immobile while cops kick them in the stomach
and the face. Cooper is particularly angry because his van has bounced
into a ditch during the pursuit. He looks down at one of the suspects.
"You bashed my car," he complains. "I just got it painted, you motherfucker." With that he kicks the suspect in the head. Our main cameraman focuses on the detectives ambling around their fallen prey like
hunters after a wild-game safari; a lot of vainglorious, congratulatory
backslapping ensues. Our secondary cameraman holds a long, extreme
close-up of a suspect while his mouth bleeds into the dirt. "I feel like I'm
dying," he wheezes, and turns his head away from the camera. I watch.

This afternoon, in the office, the video drew a crowd. One producer   26
shook his head at the violence. "Too bad," he said. "Too bad we can't
use that footage." This was clearly a case of too much reality for reality-
based TV. I couldn't help but wonder what the producers would do if
these two suspects were beaten so badly that they later died. Would they
have jeopardized their own livelihoods by turning over the video to the
"authorities"?

September 21, 1992

I'm losing interest in the footage of detectives; now it is the "little   27
people" who interest me, the people whose stories never make it past a
highlight reel. I am strangely devoted to them. There is "the steak-knife
lady" who waves her rusty weapon in front of a housing project in Detroit. I replay her over and over again. There is something about her: her

hysteria, her insistence on her right to privacy, and her flagrant indignation at the cameras ("Get those cameras outta my face, you assholes!"); the way she flails her broken knife in self-defense at a drunk neighbor while her gigantic curlers unravel; the way she consoles her children, who watch with gaping mouths. This woman is *pissed*. She is *real*. Little does she know I'm going to be watching her in Malibu, California, while I sip my morning cappuccino, manipulating her image . ›r my highlight reel. I feel like I'm in the old Sixties movie *Jason and th › Argonauts*, in which Zeus and Hera survey the little humans below them through a heavenly pool of water that looks, oddly enough, like a TV screen.

And there is a skinny, mentally disturbed redhead who took in a 28
boyfriend because she was lonely and friendless. Unknown to her, he is selling heroin out of her apartment. But in the eyes of the law she is considered an accomplice. When the cops interrogate her, all she can say about her boyfriend is, "I love him. I took him in because I love him. He's a little bit retarded or something. I took him in." Later she breaks down sobbing. She is terrified that her father will throw her into a mental institution. "I need love. Can't you understand that?" she cries to the policeman who is trying to explain to her why they are arresting her boyfriend. "I need love. That's all I need, sir."

There are, too, the hapless Hispanic families living in poverty, stash- 29
ing marijuana behind tapestries of the Virgin Mary and selling it to some of the same white middle-class couch potatoes who watch reality-based cop shows. There are the emotionally disturbed, unemployed Vietnam veterans selling liquid morphine because their SSI checks aren't enough to cover the rent. And there are AIDS patients who get busted, their dwellings ransacked, for smoking small quantities of pot to alleviate the side effects of their medication.

In our office the stories of people like these collect dust on shelves 30
stacked with *Hollywood Reporters,* cast aside because they are too dark, too much like real life. I feel overwhelmed by my ability to freeze-frame their images in time-coded close-ups. I can peer into their private lives with the precision of a lab technician, replaying painful and sordid moments. I am troubled that something of their humanity is stored indefinitely in our supervising producers' refrigerated video asylum. Some of their faces have even entered my dreamworld. This afternoon when I suggested that such unfortunates might be the real stars of our show, my boss snapped, "You empathize with the wrong people."

September 28, 1992

This morning I realized that watching hour after hour of vice has 31
begun to affect me. After a raid, when the detectives begin to search for

drugs, money, and weapons while our cameras keep rolling, I find my-self watching with the intensity of a child foraging through a grassy backyard for an exquisitely luminous Easter egg. The camera moves through rooms of the unknown suspect as the detectives poke through bedrooms with overturned mattresses and rumpled, stained sheets, through underwear drawers and soiled hampers; into the dewy, tiled grottoes of bathrooms, past soap-streaked shower doors and odd hairs stuck to bathtub walls, clattering through rows of bottles, creams, tubes, and toothbrushes, their bristles splayed with wear. The exploration con-tinues in kitchens, past half-eaten meals, where forks were dropped in surprise moments earlier, past grime-laden refrigerators and grease-pitted ovens, past cats hunched frozen in shock, and onward, sometimes past the body of a dog that has recently been shot by the police, now stiffening in the first moments of rigor mortis.

In the midst of this disarray the police sometimes find what they are   32
so frantically looking for: abundant stacks of $100 bills stuffed in boots, behind secret panels and trap doors; heroin vials sealed in jars of corn-meal stashed in the dank corners of ant-infested cupboards; white pow-ders in plastic Baggies concealed behind moldy bookshelves; discarded hypodermic needles in empty, economy-size laundry-detergent boxes; and thin, spindly marijuana plants blooming in tomato gardens and poppy fields. And, finally, on a lucky day, the guns: the magnums, au-tomatics, shotguns, machine guns, and, in one case, assault rifles leaned against walls, their barrels pointed upward.

I feel as though my brain is lined with a stratum of images of hu-   33
man debris. Sitting at home in my small bungalow, I have begun to won-der what lurks behind the goodwill of my neighbors' gestures, what they are doing behind their porches and patios.

September 30, 1992

Today was stock-footage day. I spent ten hours finding, cutting, and   34
filing still-shots of semiautomatic rifles and hypodermic needles. I am starting to notice signs that I am dispirited and restless. I spend long mo-ments mulling over camera shots of unknown faces. Today I took my lunch break on the Malibu pier, where I sat transfixed by the glassy swells, the kelp beds, and minnows under the jetty. I know I can't go on much longer, but I need to pay the rent.

October 1, 1992

I've just worked through a series of videos of the Las Vegas vice squad   35
as they go on a prostitute rampage with our cameramen and producers.

Pulling down all-nighters in cheesy motel rooms, the detectives go undercover as our camera crew, our producers, and some of the detectives sit in an adjacent room, watching the live action through a hidden camera. It is, essentially, a voyeur's paradise, and definitely X-rated. The undercover cops' trick is to get the call girls into a position where they are clearly about to accept money for sexual acts. The scam goes something like this: "Hi, I'm John. Me and my buddies here are passing through town. Thought you gals might be able to show us a good time . . ."

"What did you have in mind?" they ask. The detectives respond 36
with the usual requests for blow jobs. Maybe the undercover cops ask the girls to do a little dancing before getting down to real business. They sit back and enjoy the show. Sometimes they even strip, get into the motel's vibrating, king-size bed, and wait for just the right incriminating moment before the closet door bursts open and the unsuspecting woman is overwhelmed by a swarm of detectives and cameramen.

"He's my boyfriend?" many insist as they hysterically scramble for 37
their clothes.

"What's his name?" the cops respond while they snap on the cuffs. 38
"Bill. Bob. Uh, John . . ." 39

It doesn't matter. The police get their suspect. The camera crew gets 40
its footage. The cameras keep on rolling. And what I see, what the viewer will never see, is the women—disheveled, shocked, their clothes still scattered on musty hotel carpets—telling their stories to the amused officers and producers. Some of them sob uncontrollably. Three kids at home. An ex who hasn't paid child support in five years. Welfare. Food stamps. Some are so entrenched in the world of poverty and pimps that they are completely numb, fearing only the retribution they'll suffer if their pimps get busted as a result of their cooperation with the cops. Others work a nine-to-five job during the day that barely pays the rent and then become prostitutes at night to put food on the table. Though their faces are fatigued, they still manage a certain dignity. They look, in fact, very much like the girl next door.

I can't help but see how each piece of the drama fits neatly into the 41
other: one woman's misery is another man's pleasure; one man's pleasure is another man's crime; one man's crime is another man's beat; one man's beat is another man's TV show. And all of these pieces of the drama become one big paycheck for the executive producer.

October 5, 1992

Today the executive producer—in the flesh, not on tape—walked 42
into the office and smiled at me. I smiled back. But I was thinking: one false move and I'll blow your head off.

October 9, 1992

It would seem that there could not be any further strangeness to everything that I've seen, but, in fact, there is: almost all of the suspects we film, including the prostitutes, sign releases permitting us to put them on TV. Why would they actually want to be on TV even when they've been, literally, caught with their pants down? Could it be because of TV's ability to seemingly give a nobody a certain fleeting, cheap celebrity? Or is it that only by participating in the non-reality of TV can these people feel *more* real, more alive? I asked around to understand how the release process happens. 43

Usually a production coordinator—an aspiring TV producer fresh out of college—is assigned the task of pushing the legal release into the faces of overwhelmed and tightly cuffed suspects who are often at such peak stress levels that some can't recognize their own faces on their driver's licenses. "We'll show your side of the story," the production coordinator might say. Sometimes it is the police themselves who ask people to sign, suggesting that the cameras are part of a training film and that signing the form is the least of their present concerns. And to anyone in such a situation this seems plausible, since the entire camera crew is outfitted with police jackets, including the executive producer, who, with his "belt badge," could easily be mistaken for a cop in civilian attire. And, clearly, many of those arrested feel that signing anything will help them in court. In the rare event that a suspect is reluctant to sign the release, especially when his or her case might make for a good show, the *American Detective* officials offer money; but more frequently, it seems, the suspect signing the release form simply doesn't adequately read or speak English. Whatever the underlying motive, almost all of the arrested "criminals" willingly sign their releases, and thus are poised—consciously or not—to participate in their own degradation before the American viewing public. 44

October 16, 1992

Today I saw something that convinced me I may be lost in this netherworld of videotape; I did, finally, get a homicide. The victim lived in Oregon and planned to save up to attend Reed College. She was a stripper who dabbled in prostitution to make ends meet. On the tape the cops find her on her bed clutching a stuffed animal, her skull bludgeoned open with a baseball bat. A stream of blood stains the wall in a red arc, marking her descent just three hours earlier. 45

The guy who killed her was a neighbor—blond, blue-eyed, wore a baseball cap, the kind of guy you'd imagine as the head of a Little 46

League team, or a swim coach. He has that particularly American blend of affability, eagerness, and naiveté. When the cops ask him why he bludgeoned her repeatedly after clubbing her unconscious with the first stroke, he replies, "I don't know. I don't really know."

She was Asian, but you would never have known it from what was 47 left of her. What one sees on the tape is that bloody red stain on the wall. We never know why he killed her. We never really know who she was. But it doesn't really matter. She is "just another prostitute." And she will be very good for the show's ratings.

October 19, 1992

This morning I explained my feelings to my boss. I said I "didn't feel 48 good" about the work and had decided to quit. He understood, he said, for he'd once had certain ideals but had eventually resigned himself to the job.

Before departing, I asked a colleague if he was affected by the grief 49 and vice on our monitors. "They're only characters to me," he replied. I noted this quietly to myself, and, with barely a good-bye to my other co-conspirators, I slipped out of the *American Detective* offices into the noon blaze of the California sun, hoping to recover what it is I've lost.

·····················

Examining the Text

1. Seagal's essay is in the form of a series of diary-like entries which chart the gradual evolution of her thoughts and feelings about her job. Why do you think Seagal organized her essay in this way? How might it serve to underline her central point?

2. In an early entry, Seagal speculates on possible reasons for "the national obsession with this sort of voyeuristic entertainment" (paragraph 5). Do you agree with her reasoning? Can you think of other reasons? How do Seagal's views change during the course of her work on the show?

3. Throughout the essay Seagal comments on how the job affects her, and at the end she says she left "hoping to recover what it is I've lost." What do you think Seagal lost? How did the job affect her? Has her account influenced your view of shows like *Cops* and *American Detective?* How?

For Group Discussion

As Seagal explains, "reality-based" cop shows like *American Detective* combine entertainment and law enforcement in a "documentary"-

style presentation. As a group, list how these shows are similar to and different from other types of documentary and news programs. As a class, consider what these similarities and differences suggest about mainstream television journalism, the stories it tells, and the way it tells them.

Writing Suggestion

With Seagal's essay as an example, write a series of diary entries describing, interpreting, and speculating about your own encounters with the various news media over the course of several days or a week. Based on the reading and thinking you have done in this chapter and on the specific news stories you read or programs you watch over the next few days, use this as an opportunity to consolidate and expand your thinking about the functions of the media in our culture.

ADDITIONAL SUGGESTIONS
FOR WRITING ABOUT JOURNALISM

1. As Jon Katz points out in "Rock, Rap, and Movies Bring You the News," quite a lot of our information about important social and political issues comes from the "New News"—movies, television series, recordings and music videos, celebrity interviews and talk shows, advertising, stand-up comics' routines, and other forms of popular culture. In an essay, examine how the "New News" represents one important social issue or problem, such as teenage pregnancy, or the problems of the inner city, or the debate over multiculturalism.

2. Write an essay modeled after "Drug Abuse, Race Relations, and the Prime Time News Program," by Schwoch, White, Reilly and Scott, in which you construct a detailed analysis of one segment of a prime-time news program such as *Nightline* or *60 Minutes*. In order to do this, you should videotape the segment and view it carefully several times. In your analysis, try to pinpoint any political or social biases implicit in the images presented, the language used, the questions asked (and not asked), and so forth.

3. Imagine that you've just recently arrived in the U.S. and pick up a local newspaper to try to learn about your new community. Based on one edition of your local paper, write a description of the interests, attitudes, lifestyles, and customs of the people in this community. Try to include information gathered from every section, and make sure that each element of your description is supported by some article, advertisement, or other bit of information taken from the paper. You might conclude with a separate brief analysis that compares your "naive" description with a more knowledgeable view, considering the extent to which the newspaper presents a distorted view of the community and why.

4. Write an essay in which you discuss the relative advantages and disadvantages of the three primary sources of news: TV, radio, and newspapers. Which of the three do you think keeps us informed most effectively, and why? What are the strengths and weaknesses of each mode? To develop your thinking, you might monitor the coverage of particular news stories in all three media over several days.

5. Based on what you have read in this chapter, how would you define the role journalism can best play in our culture? Be realistic in developing your definition, keeping in mind the requirements of the marketplace, the limits of objective reporting, and other issues raised.

6. Investigative journalists occupy an unusual position in our society. On the one hand, they are held in esteem as committed professionals who diligently dig out information crucial to "truth, justice, and the

American way." On the other hand, they are vilified as scandal-mongers with no respect for individual privacy who blow stories out of proportion for their own ego-gratification. Use several recent news stories to analyze these conflicting roles. Give examples of when, in your opinion, journalists fulfill their mission and when they go too far in reporting on public figures.

7

Movies

It's Friday night. You park in an exhaust-filled subterranean garage or a vast asphalt lot surrounding a mall. You make your way into the neon-lit mega-eight-plex, where you and a companion or two pay half a day's salary for tickets, a tub of artery-clogging popcorn, and a couple of ten-gallon sodas. You wind your way through a maze of corridors to the theater of your choice, where a psychedelic montage filling the screen is soon replaced by the first of an interminable series of quick-cutting, MTV-style previews, as you bathe in rolling quadraphonic surroundsound. You sink into your space-age plastic seat and kick back, surrendering to the waves of sound and images. . . .

Such is moviegoing of the '90s. Gone are the nickel matinee and the discount double-feature, newsreels, cartoons, and comic short subjects, and the drive-in, where many a pair of teenagers learned human anatomy in the back seat of a Chevy.

The external trappings of the moviegoing experience may have changed, but the reasons people go are still pretty much the same: to get out of the house and escape the routine of their daily lives; to be part of a communal group sharing an experience; to find a romantic setting where conversation is at a minimum; to indulge, for one night, in an orgy of junk food; and, above all, to be entertained and, perhaps, touched emotionally. So strong is the draw of motion pictures that Americans fork over billions of dollars a year on domestic movies alone.

As there are many reasons for going to the movies, so there are many ways of explaining their popularity and studying their influence within the fabric of contemporary culture. From a sociological perspective, movies can reflect, define, or even redefine social norms, and—in the work of politically-focused filmmakers like Spike Lee—depict urgent social problems within the relative safety of the big screen. From a psychological perspective, viewers identify with the character and project their own feelings into the action, giving them a deep emotional connection to a protagonist along with feelings of tension and, ultimately release. From a literary perspective, movies can be interpreted in terms of genres—horror movies, or crime dramas or menaced-female stories—or in terms of plot, characterization, imagery, and so forth. From an economic perspective, movies may be seen primarily as a consumable product, defined solely by the marketplace. To the cultural critic, this economic influence might seem to be negative, reducing a potentially powerful artistic form to the lowest common denominator. The capitalist observer might see such forces as positive, however, because they encourage the worldwide spread of American cultural values. Finally, from a semiological perspective, movies are ripe with symbolic imagery, from the multiple associations possible in a character's name to the way images are juxtaposed in the editing.

This chapter introduces film criticism arising from several of these views. The first readings focus on the art and business of moviemaking and criticism, ending with an overview of the major critical schools. The second part looks specifically at the genre of the horror movie, interpreting horror heroes such as Frankenstein, Freddy Kreuger, and Dracula from a variety of critical perspectives. As you think and write about film and the film industry, you may find that you want to pick and choose among these various approaches, incorporating parts of any number of them into your own theoretical analyses.

MOVIEMAKING AND CRITICISM

The Way We Are

Sydney Pollack

If anyone knows American moviemaking, it's Sidney Pollack. A director of more than sixteen films—including The Way We Were, Tootsie, Out of Africa, *and* The Firm—*and an occasional actor (Dustin Hoffman's agent in* Tootsie*), Pollack has had an unparalleled opportunity to observe the changing tastes of the American viewing public and the movie industry's response to those changes. In the following article, a transcript of an address Pollack delivered at a conference about the influence of the popular media on American values, Pollack suggests that changes in the moral fabric of our society are responsible for the kinds of movies we see today, not vice versa.*

When he looks at contemporary America, Pollack finds a conspicuous lack of the "kind of scrupulous ethical concern for the sanctity of life" that prevailed in past decades and was reflected in motion pictures of the time, when there were less frequent and less graphic scenes of violence, when characters were esteemed for their humility and personal integrity, and when explicit sexuality was found only in "stag" films, not in mainstream theaters. Many people today, Pollack notes, are nostalgic for the "old values" and believe that movies should encourage the return of these values rather than reflecting current values. Pollack disagrees, however, pointing out that, although screenwriters and directors may want their movies to reflect some moral content, the economics of the industry require first and foremost that movies be entertaining, and therefore, they must appeal to a buying audience whose values may be very different from those of the reformers.

As you read, consider whether you agree with Pollack's notions of artistic integrity, especially his assertions that a filmmaker's prime goal should be to entertain an audience and that movies simply reflect the surrounding society. Is it possible that, in responding to their audience's changing tastes, filmmakers also "construct" public attitudes towards violence, sexuality, and so forth by pushing their explicitness further and further?

· · · · · · · · · · · · · · · · · · ·

Six weeks ago, I thought I was going to be happy to be a part of this   1
conference, which shows you how naive I am. The agenda—for me at least—is a mine field. Normally, I spend my time worrying about specific problems and not reflecting, as many of you on these panels do. So

I've really thought about this, and I've talked to anyone who would listen. My colleagues are sick and tired of it, my wife has left for the country, and even my agents—and these are people I pay—don't return my phone calls. By turns, I have felt myself stupid, unethical, a philistine, unpatriotic, a panderer, a cultural polluter, and stupid. And I've completely failed to solve your problems, except in one small way. You have delayed by at least six weeks the possibility of my contributing further to the problems you see.

I know your concerns have to do with American values and 2 whether those values are being upheld or assaulted by American entertainment—by what I and others like me do. But which values exactly?

In the thirties, forties, and fifties, six men in the Valley, immigrants 3 really, ran the movie industry. Our society was vastly different. The language of the movies was a language of shared values. If you put forward a virtuousness on the part of your hero, everybody responded to it.

When Sergeant York, played by Gary Cooper, refused to endorse a 4 breakfast cereal, knowing he'd been asked because he'd won the Medal of Honor, he said: "I ain't proud of what I've done. You don't make money off of killing people. That there is wrong." We expected him to behave that way.

But society's values have changed. That kind of scrupulous, ethical 5 concern for the sanctity of human life doesn't exist in the same way, and that fact is reflected in the movies. There's a nostalgia now for some of the old values, but so many people embrace other expressions of values that it's hard to say these other expressions aren't reality.

Their idea of love, for example, is a different idea of love. It's a much 6 less chaste, much less idealized love than was depicted in the earlier films. We are seeing some sort of return to the ideal of marriage. There was a decade or two when marriage really lost its popularity, and while young people are swinging toward it again, I don't believe one could say that values have not changed significantly since the thirties, forties, and fifties.

Morality, the definitions of virtue, justice, and injustice, the sanctity 7 of the individual, have been fairly fluid for American audiences in terms of what they choose to embrace or not embrace.

Take a picture like *Dances With Wolves*. You could not have made it 8 in the thirties or forties. It calls into question every value that existed in traditional Westerns. It may not reflect what everybody thinks now, but it expresses a lot of guilty re-evaluation of what happened in the West, the very things shown in the old Westerns that celebrated the frontier.

If we got the movies to assert or talk about better values, would that 9 fix our society? Well, let me quote Sam Goldwyn. When he was told by his staff how poorly his studio's new—and very expensive—film was doing, Sam thought a minute, shrugged, and said, "Listen, if they don't want to come, you can't stop them."

Now that's as close to a first principle of Hollywood as I can come.   10
It informs everything that we're here to discuss and it controls every solution that we may propose.

Out of Hollywood

Before they can be anything else, American movies are a product.   11
This is not good or bad, this is what we've got. A very few may become art, but all of them, whatever their ambitions, are first financed as commodities. They're the work of craftsmen and artists, but they're soon offered for sale.

Whether we say that we're "creating a film" or merely "making a   12
movie," the enterprise itself is sufficiently expensive and risky that it cannot be, and it will not be, undertaken without the hope of reward. We have no Medicis here. It takes two distinct entities, the financiers and the makers, to produce movies, and there is a tension between them. Their goals are sometimes similar, but they do different things. Financiers are not in the business of philanthropy. They've got to answer to stockholders.

Of course, the controlling influence in filmmaking hasn't changed   13
in 50 years: it still belongs to the consumer. That's the dilemma and, in my view, what we're finally talking about. What do you do about culture in a society that celebrates the common man but doesn't always like his taste?

If you operate in a democracy and you're market-supported and   14
-driven, the spectrum of what you will get is going to be very wide indeed. It will range from trash to gems. There are 53,000 books published in this country every year. How many of them are really good? Tired as I may be of fast-food-recipe, conscienceless, simple-minded books, films, TV, and music, the question remains, Who is to be society's moral policeman?

Over the course of their first 30 or 40 years, the movies were a cot-   15
tage industry, and the morality that was reflected in them was the morality of the early film pioneers. Now, film studios are tiny divisions of multinational corporations, and they feel the pressure for profits that happens in any other repeatable-product business. They look for a formula. Say you get the recipe for a soft drink and perfect it; once customers like it, you just repeat it and it will sell. More fortunes have been lost than made in the movie business pursuing such a formula, but unfortunately today, more junk than anything else is being made pursuing it. And film companies are folding like crazy.

Since we are in the democracy business, we can't tell people what 16
they should or shouldn't hear, or support, or see, so they make their
choices. The market tries to cater to those choices, and we have what we
have.

Making Films

Are American films bad? A lot of them surely are, and so are a lot 17
of everybody else's, the way a lot of anything produced is bad—breakfast cereals, music, most chairs, architecture, mail-order shirts. There
probably hasn't been a really beautiful rake since the Shakers stopped
making farm implements. But that is no excuse.

I realize that I am a prime suspect here, but I'm not sure that you re- 18
ally understand how odd and unpredictable a business the making of
films actually is. It just doesn't conform to the logic or rules of any other
business. It's always been an uneasy merger of two antithetical things:
some form of art and sheer commerce.

If the people who make films get the money that is invested in them 19
back to the people who finance them, then they'll get to make more. We
know that the business of films is to reach as many people as possible.
That works two ways; it's not just a market discipline. You have to remember that most of us who are doing this got into it for the romance,
the glory, the applause, the chance to tell stories, even to learn, but rarely
for the money. The more people you reach, the greater your sense of success. Given the choice, I'd rather make the whole world cry than 17 intellectuals in a classroom.

But, paradoxically, if you are the actual maker of the film—not the 20
financier—you can't make films and worry about whether they'll reach
a large audience or make money, first, because nobody really knows a
formula for what will make money. If they did, I promise you we would
have heard about it, and studios would not be going broke. Second, and
much more practically, if you spent your time while you were making
the film consciously thinking about what was commercial, then the real
mechanism of choice—the mechanism that is your own unconscious,
your own taste and imagination, your fantasy—would be replaced by
constant reference to this formula that we know doesn't work.

So the only practical approach a filmmaker can take is to make a film 21
that he or she would want to see. This sounds arrogant, but you try to
make a movie for yourself, and you hope that as many people as possible will like it too. If that happens, it's because you've done something
in the telling of the story that makes people care. One of the things that
makes a film distinct from other American business products is this

emotional involvement of the maker. A producer of auto parts can become pretty emotional about a sales slump, but it isn't the same thing. His product hasn't come from his history; it isn't somehow in the image of his life; and it lacks mystery. It is entirely measurable and concrete, which is certainly appropriate in the manufacture of auto parts. I wouldn't want to buy a carburetor from a neurotic, mixed-up auto manufacturer.

Fortunately for those of us in film, no such standards apply. Quite   22
the contrary, in fact. No matter what his conscious intentions are, the best part of what the filmmaker does—the part, when it works, that makes you want to see the film—doesn't come from a rational, consciously controllable process. It comes from somewhere inside the filmmaker's unconscious. It comes from making unlikely connections seem inevitable, from a kind of free association that jumps to odd or surprising places, conclusions that cause delights, something that creates goose pimples or awe.

This conference has suggested a question: While you're actually   23
making the movie, do you think about whether or not it will be doing the world any good? I can't answer it for filmmakers in general. For myself, candidly, no, I don't.

I try to discover and tell the truth and not be dull about it. In that   24
sense, the question has no significance for me. I assume that trying to discover the truth is in itself a good and virtuous aim. By truth I don't mean some grand, pretentious axiom to live by; I just mean the truth of a character from moment to moment. I try to discover and describe things like the motives that are hidden in day-to-day life. And the truth is rarely dull. If I can find it, I will have fulfilled my primary obligation as a filmmaker, which is not to bore the pants off you.

Most of us in this business have enormous sympathy for Scehehera-   25
zade—we're terrified we're going to be murdered if we're boring. So our first obligation is to not bore people; it isn't to teach.

Most of the time, high-mindedness just leads to pretentious or well-   26
meaning, often very bad, films. Most of the Russian films made under communism were of high quality in terms of craft, but they were soporific because their intent to do good as it was perceived by the state or an all-knowing party committee was too transparent.

I'm sure that you think the person in whose hands the process ac-   27
tually rests, the filmmaker, could exert an enormous amount of control over the film's final worthiness. The question usually goes like this: Should filmmakers pander to the public, or should they try to elevate public taste to something that many at this conference would find more acceptable? Is the job of an American filmmaker to give the

public what it wants or what the filmmaker thinks the public should have? This doesn't leave much doubt as to what you think is the right answer.

But framing your question this way not only betrays a misunder-   28
standing of how the filmmaking process works but also is just plain wishful thinking about how to improve society. I share your nostalgia for some of those lost traditional values, but attempting to reinstill them by arbitrarily putting them into movies when they don't exist in every-day life will not get people to go to the movies or put those values back into life. I wish it were that simple.

Engaging an Audience

This conference is concerned with something called popular culture   29
and its effect on society, but I am concerned with one film at a time and its effect. You are debating whether movies corrupt our souls or elevate them, and I'm debating whether a film will touch a soul. As a filmmaker, I never set out to create popular culture, and I don't know a single other filmmaker who does.

Maybe it's tempting to think of Hollywood as some collective be-   30
hemoth grinding out the same stories and pushing the same values, but it's not that simple. Hollywood, whatever that means, is Oliver Stone castigating war in *Born on the Fourth of July* and John Milius celebrating it in *The Wind and the Lion*. It's Walt Disney and Martin Scorsese. It's Steven Spielberg and Milos Foreman. It's *Amadeus* and *Terminator* and hundreds of choices in between.

I don't want to defend Hollywood, because I don't represent Hol-   31
lywood—I can't, any more than one particular writer can represent lit-erature or one painter art. For the most part, the impulse toward all art, entertainment, culture, pop culture, comes from the same place within the makers of it. The level of talent and the soul, if you'll forgive the word again, is what finally limits it.

At the risk of telling you more than you need to know about my own   32
work, I make the movies I make because there is in each film some ar-gument that fascinates me, an issue I want to work through. I call this a spine or an armature because it functions for me like an armature in sculpture—something I can cover up and it will support the whole structure. I can test the scenes against it. For me, the film, when prop-erly dramatized, adds up to this idea, this argument.

But there are lots of other ways to go about making a film, and lots   33
of other filmmakers who do it differently. Some filmmakers begin

knowing exactly what they want to say and then craft a vehicle that contains that statement. Some are interested in pure escape. Here's the catch. The effectiveness and the success of all our films is determined by exactly the same standards—unfortunately, not by the particular validity of their message but by their ability to engage the concentration and emotions of the audience.

Citizen Kane is an attack on acquisition, but that's not why people go 34 to see it. I don't have any idea if the audience that saw *Tootsie* thought at any conscious level that it could be about a guy who became a better man for having been a woman; or that *The Way We Were*, a film I made 20 years ago, may have been about the tension between passion, often of the moment, and wisdom, often part of a longer view; or that *Out of Africa* might be about the inability to possess another individual and even the inability of one country to possess another. That's intellectual and stuffy. I just hope the audiences were entertained.

I may choose the movies I make because there's an issue I want to 35 explore, but the how—the framing of that issue, the process of finding the best way to explore it—is a much more mysterious, elusive, and messy process. I can't tell you that I understand it; if I did, I would have a pep talk with myself and go out and make a terrific movie every time.

I would not make a film that ethically, or morally, or politically 36 trashed what I believe is fair. But by the same token, I feel an obligation—and this is more complicated and personal—to do films about arguments. I try hard to give each side a strong argument—not because I'm a fair guy but because I believe it's more interesting. Both things are going on.

I do the same thing on every movie I make. I find an argument, a 37 couple of characters I would like to have dinner with, and try to find the most fascinating way to explore it. I work as hard as I can to tell the story in the way I'd like to have it told to me.

What is really good is also entertaining and interesting because it's 38 closer to a newer way to look at the truth. You can't do that consciously. You can't start out by saying, "I am now going to make a great film."

The virtue in making a film, if there is any, is in making it well. If 39 there's any morality that's going to come out, it will develop as you begin to construct, at every moment you have a choice to make. You can do it the honest way or you can bend it, and the collection of those moments of choice is what makes the work good or not good and is what reveals morality or the lack of it.

I've made 16 films. I've had some enormous successes and I've had 40 some colossal failures, but I can't tell you what the difference is in terms of what I did.

An American Aesthetic?

In some circles, American films suffer by comparison with Euro-   41
pean films precisely because a lot of our movies seem to be the product
of little deliberation and much instinct. It's been said of European
movies that essence precedes existence, which is just a fancy way of saying that European movies exist in order to say something. Certainly one
never doubts with a European film that it's saying something, and often it just comes right out and says it.

American films work by indirection; they work by action and move-   42
ment, either internal or external, but almost always movement. Our
films are more narratively driven than others, which has a lot to do with
the American character and the way we look at our lives. We see ourselves and our lives as being part of a story.

Most of our movies have been pro the underdog, concerned with in-   43
justice, relatively anti-authority. There's usually a system—or a bureau-
cracy—to triumph over.

More often than not, American movies have been affirmative and   44
hopeful about destiny. They're usually about individuals who control
their own lives and their fate. In Europe, the system was so class-bound
and steeped in tradition that there was no democratization of that
process.

There's no prior education required to assimilate American movies   45
or American culture. American culture is general, as opposed to the
specificity of Japanese or Indian culture. America has the most easily di-
gestible culture.

Our movies seem artless. The best of them keep us interested with-   46
out seeming to engage our minds. The very thing that makes movies so
popular here and abroad is one of the primary things that drives their
critics to apoplexy, but seeming artlessness isn't necessarily mindless-
ness. There's a deliberate kind of artlessness in American movies that
has come from a discipline or aesthetic long ago imposed by the marketplace. Our movies began as immigrants' dreams that would appeal
to the dreams of other immigrants, and this aesthetic has led American
films to transcend languages and cultures and communicate to every
country in the world.

The Filmmaker's Responsibility

It has been suggested to some extent in this conference that I ought   47
to study my own and American filmmakers' responsibilities to the public and to the world. I realize I have responsibilities as a filmmaker, but

I don't believe that they are as a moralist, a preacher, or a purveyor of values. I know it's tempting to use filmmaking as such, but utility is a poor standard to use in art. It's a standard that has been and is still used by every totalitarian state in the world.

My responsibility is to try to make good films, but "good" is a sub- 48 jective word. To me at any rate, "good" doesn't necessarily mean "good for us" in the narrow sense that they must elevate our spirits and send us out of the theater singing, or even that they must promote only those values that some think are worth promoting.

Good movies challenge us, they provoke us, they make us angry 49 sometimes. They present points of view we don't agree with. They force us to clarify our positions in opposition to them, and they do this best when they provide us with an experience and not a polemic.

Somebody gave the okay to pay for *One Flew Over the Cuckoo's Nest,* 50 *Driving Miss Daisy, Stand By Me, Moonstruck, Terms of Endearment,* and *Amadeus,* and despite conventional wisdom that said those films could not be successful, those decisions paid off handsomely because there are no rules. Studio executives and other financiers do exceed themselves. They take chances. They have to, and we have to hope that they'll do it more often.

What we see in movie theaters today is not a simple reflection of to- 51 day's economics or politics in this country but is a sense of the people who make the movies, and they vary as individuals vary. So what we really want is for this very privileged process to be in the best hands possible, but I know of no force that can regulate this except the moral climate and appetites of our society.

What we're exporting now is largely a youth culture. It's full of ado- 52 lescent values; it's full of adolescent rage, love, rebelliousness, and a desire to shock. If you're unhappy with their taste—and this is a free market—then an appetite has to be created for something better. How do we do that? Well, we're back to square one: the supplier or the consumer, the chicken or the egg? Let's not even ask the question; the answer is both.

Of course filmmakers ought to be encouraged toward excellence, and audiences ought to be encouraged to demand it. How? That's for 53 thinkers and social scientists to figure out. I have no idea. But if I had to play this scene out as an imaginary dialogue, I might say that you must educate the consumer first, and the best places to start are at school and at home. And then you would say that that is my job, that popular entertainment must participate in this education. And I would say, ideally, perhaps, but I do not think that will happen within a system that operates so fundamentally from an economic point of view. On an individual basis, yes, one filmmaker at a time; as an industry, no. An appetite or market will have to exist first.

That's not as bad as it sounds, because in the best of all possible   54
worlds, we do try to satisfy both needs: entertain people and be reasonably intelligent about it. It can be done, and it is done more often than
you might think. It's just very difficult.

It's like the two Oxford dons who were sitting at the Boarshead.   55
They were playwrights, grousing because neither one of them could get
produced, neither one could get performed. One turned to the other and
said, "Oh, the hell with it. Let's just do what Shakespeare did—give
them entertainment."

••••••••••••••••••••

Examining the Text

1. What is Pollack's point in paragraph 8? How does *Dances With Wolves*
"call into question every value that existed in traditional Westerns," and
how does it reflect a change in society's values? Is *Dances With Wolves* a
good example of the kind of movie that critics would say contributes to
the decline in American values? Why do you think Pollack mentions it
so early in his speech?

2. Pollack says there "probably hasn't been a really beautiful rake since
the Shakers stopped making farm implements" (paragraph 17). What
does his point say in terms of questioning whether American films are
"bad"? Do you find his analogy persuasive?

3. When Pollack asserts that he'd "rather make the whole world cry
than 17 intellectuals in a classroom" (19), what is he implying about
his—and other filmmakers'—motivations? Do you think most creative
people feel this way?

4. Pollack describes his interest in making "films about arguments" and
giving "each side a strong argument" (36). What does he mean? Do you
think movies that balance two sides of an "argument" are "more interesting" than those with clear-cut "good guys" and "bad guys"?

For Group Discussion

Pollack himself does not make the kinds of graphically violent
movies that critics claim have a negative influence on American society.
Nonetheless, he argues that "scrupulous, ethical concern for the sanctity of human life doesn't exist in the same way [it did in the past], and
that fact is reflected in the movies." As a group, list examples from current events and recent films that demonstrate this lack of concern for human life. As a class, consider whether, based on these examples, you

agree with Pollack that movies only reflect the values of society and do not contribute to their creation.

Writing Suggestion

Rent and watch one or more of Pollack's films (titles in addition to those mentioned in the headnote include *They Shoot Horses, Don't They?*, *Three Days of the Condor,* and *The Electric Horseman*). In an essay analyze Pollack's work as a reflection of contemporary American life. What themes or messages do you discover beyond his aim to tell a good story? Does he succeed in his stated goal of presenting an "argument"?

Do the Right Thing Production Notes
Spike Lee

*S*pike Lee—*film writer, director, producer, and actor—believes he has a social responsibility beyond merely making films that entertain audiences. His movies, such as* Do The Right Thing *and* X, *a biographical treatment of black leader Malcolm X, frequently embody Lee's strong convictions about race relations in America—and, more specifically, about the problems facing black people in this country. Lee's commitment to social responsibility does not end with the content of his films, however; it also extends to their actual production. In the following production notes made during the filming of* Do The Right Thing, *Lee offers some unique behind-the-scenes perspectives on movie-making and illuminates some difficult issues facing minority and female film professionals.*

If you haven't already seen Do The Right Thing, *you might want to rent it. The movie is a vivid and highly controversial comedy-drama that takes place during the course of one steamy summer day in a Brooklyn ghetto. Lee himself plays Mookie, one of the neighborhood residents, and Danny Aiello and John Turturro play the Italian-American owner of Sal's Pizzeria and his racist son. The movie explores the sometimes uneasy relationship between a white business owner and his customers in a black neighborhood, culminating in a riot during which the pizzeria is torched and the neighborhood left in shambles.*

As you read this piece, consider your own ideas about minority representation in the filmmaking industry, both as actors and as production personnel. Do you agree with the methods Lee used to achieve a more equitable racial balance in making Do The Right Thing? *Do you think such efforts are important?*

· · · · · · · · · · · · · · · · · · · ·

Do The Right Thing was my first union film. To keep our costs down, Universal suggested that we shoot the film with a nonunion crew someplace outside of New York, like Philadelphia or Baltimore. I'm sorry, Philly and Baltimore are great cities, but they just aren't Brooklyn. This film had to be shot in Brooklyn, if it was to be done at all. However, there was no way we could shoot a $6.5 million film in New York City without giving the film unions a piece of the action.

On every film, I try to use as many Black people behind the camera as possible. A major concern I had about shooting with an all-union crew was whether this would prevent me from hiring as many Blacks as I wanted. There are few minorities in the film unions, and, historically, film unions have done little to encourage Blacks and women to join their ranks.

Originally we planned to sign a contract with the International Alliance of Theatrical State Employees (IATSE, or IA) because they have more Black members. They proved to be too expensive, so we entered into negotiations with the National Association of Broadcast Employees and Technicians (NABET). The negotiations with NABET lasted a month, but we were able to win some important concessions.

One concession was that NABET allowed us to hire a number of Blacks to work on the film who were not members of the union, including Larry Cherry, our hairstylist, my brother David Lee, the still photographer, and Darnell Martin, the second assistant cameraperson. (At the time, there were no Blacks in these union categories.) In addition, we were able to hire some nonunion people as trainees in the grip and electric departments. NABET agreed to consider granting union membership to these people if their work on the film proved satisfactory. Eventually they were admitted to the union.

We cut a similar deal with the Teamsters union, which is responsible for all the vehicles driven on a union shoot. The Teamsters have the right to determine how many drivers are assigned to a union production. At $1,500 to $2,000 per week per driver, this can eat a hole in your budget. The Teamsters allowed us to hire a small number of union drivers and use nonunion production assistants to supplement this group. Out of the five union drivers they assigned to the production, two were Black.

I wanted to film *Do The Right Thing* entirely on one block. Our location scout combed the streets of Brooklyn for two weeks and came back with a book of photos. One Saturday, Wynn Thomas, the production designer, and I visited all the locations suggested by our scout. It turned out the block that we chose was the first one he had looked at— Stuyvesant Street between Lexington and Quincy Avenues, in the heart of the Bedford-Stuyvesant section of Brooklyn.

The block had everything that we needed: brownstones which   7
weren't too upscale or too dilapidated. And, most importantly, it had
two empty lots that faced each other, where we could build sets for the
Korean market and Sal's Famous Pizzeria. Once we decided on the
block, Wynn went to work designing the sets and supervising construction.

I think it was Monty Ross's idea to hire the Fruit of Islam, the secu-   8
rity force of the Nation of Islam, the Black Muslim organization, to patrol the set. Cops really have no respect in Black communities in New
York, especially not in Bed-Stuy, where cops have been convicted in the
past on drug trafficking charges. We knew we couldn't bring in a white
security force, it had to be Black. And Black people who were respected
in the community. All this led us to the Fruit of Islam.

It was obvious that crack was being sold on the block. One of the   9
first things we did was let the crack dealers know they weren't welcome.
We boarded up an abandoned building that was being used as a crack
house and turned another into a location site. We managed to move the
dealers off the block, but we weren't able to put them out of business.
They just closed up shop and moved around the corner.

During preproduction, Universal asked me to recommend a film-   10
maker to do the electronic press kit that the studio would use to promote
the film. I recommended the veteran documentary filmmaker St. Clair
Bourne. When I met with St. Clair to discuss the press kit, I asked him
to consider directing a film about the making of *Do The Right Thing*. We
were shooting in Bed-Stuy. We were taking over an entire city block for
eight weeks. And we had hired the Fruit of Islam—Farrakhan's private
security force—to patrol the set and to close two crack houses. Certainly,
this needed to be documented. St. Clair got to work on the project immediately.

Casting for *Do The Right Thing* was on a much smaller scale than   11
School Daze. Most of the major roles I had decided upon even before I
completed the script. We held auditions in New York only, whereas for
School Daze, we saw actors in Los Angeles, Atlanta, and New York. I
wanted to cast white actors who feel comfortable around Black people.
A white actor nervous about setting foot in Bed-Stuy wasn't gonna work
for this film. The fact that Danny Aiello grew up in the South Bronx, and
John Turturro in a Black neighborhood in Queens, made them ideal
choices.

The first day of rehearsal the full cast met to read through the script,   12
then I opened up the floor for discussion and suggestions. Paul Benjamin, who plays ML, one of the Corner Men, is a veteran actor who I've
wanted to work with for a long time. Paul was the first actor to raise
a question about script. He was worried that it showed nothing but

lazy, shiftless Black people. It seemed to Paul that no one in the film had a job, and that his character and the other Corner Men just hung out all day.

It was Rosie Perez (Tina), who had never acted before in her life, 13 who answered Paul's question. Rosie grew up in Bed-Stuy and stayed with relatives there during the shoot. She went off on a ten-minute tirade about how people like the Corner Men actually exist and that Paul and everyone else should go to Bed-Stuy and take a look.

I told Paul that *Do The Right Thing* was not about Black people in 14 three-piece suits going to work, it was about Black underclass in Bed-Stuy, a community that has some of the highest unemployment, infant mortality, and drug-related homicide rates in New York City. We're talking about people who live in the bowels of the social-economic system, but still live with dignity and humor. Paul and I talked about it the next day and he understood.

We spent the rest of the rehearsal week meeting in small groups to 15 talk about characters. When the Corner Men met for their group rehearsal, they were having trouble getting their characters to mesh. I decided that we should take a trip to the location and read the dialogue there. We drove out to Stuyvesant Street and set up some chairs in the same spot where the Corner Men's scenes would be shot. Being on the set, in the community, made all the difference.

The fact this film takes on one single day was a challenge for every- 16 one involved. Continuity was a motherfucker. Especially for Ernest, who had to make two months worth of footage to look like it was shot on one day. For the most part, he had to rely on available light, since we spent most of our time outdoors.

Though this film is about young Black people in Brooklyn, Ruthe 17 Carter, the costume designer, and I wanted to downplay the gold fad. Besides the gold teeth that Mookie and Buggin' Out wear, and Radio Raheem's knuckle rings (which are really brass), you don't see much gold in this film. I think it's crazy for young Black kids to spend money they don't have on gold jewelry. The kids pick it up from the rappers. I mean no disrespect to L.L. Cool J and Eric B. & Rakim, but this gold-chains-by-the-ton shit is ridiculous.

I knew I wanted my character Mookie to wear tight bicycle shorts 18 underneath a pair of loose-fitting shorts. I got this from basketball players. Instead of wearing jock straps now, many are wearing bicycle pants beneath their uniforms. I like the look because of the contrast. So I had an idea for the bottom of my costume, but I was stumped on what to wear on top.

Cecil Holmes, one of the bigwigs in Black music at CBS Records, 19 knows I'm a baseball fan and once gave me a Jackie Robinson jersey. The night before we started shooting, I was still undecided about my costume, then I remembered the jersey.

The jersey was a good choice. I don't think Jackie Robinson has gotten his due from Black people. There are young people today, even Black athletes, who don't know what Jackie Robinson did. They might know he was the first Black Major Leaguer, but they don't know what he had to bear to make it easier for those who came after him. 20

When you're directing a film, it takes over your life completely. You get up at the crack of dawn, shoot for twelve to fourteen hours (if you're lucky), watch dailies, grab something to eat before you go to bed, then you're up again at the crack of dawn. 21

The first week of production went well. I felt we could have been better organized in terms of communication between the assistant directors and other departments, but by the end of the week it all came together. 22

It rained on and off for three of the days of the first week, and we were forced to shoot an interior scene, one of our precious few cover sets. There was concern about using up our cover sets so early in the shoot, since we had less than five to last us the entire shoot. But there was nothing we could do about that except pray for good weather. Depending on the size of the scene, overcast days were potential problems for us as well. Creating the effect of sunshine on a cloudy day over an area the size of a city block was something our budget didn't allow for. 23

We had a budget for extras on *Do The Right Thing*, which was a first for me. With no money to pay extras on *School Daze*, we could never predict if we'd get the number needed for a given scene. But if you look at the film, I think we did a good job disguising how few extras we actually had. 24

We had two open calls for extras, one for members of the Screen Actors Guild, and one for nonunion actors. We also held a community open call at a church near the location, Antioch Baptist, which graciously served as our meal hall during the shoot. 25

We cast a core group of extras to play block residents and they worked the entire shoot. Additional extras were brought on for the big scenes. The first week of shooting we had a time coming up with a system of documenting the extras and background action scene by scene. We had to establish which core extras would be placed on various sides of the block, how long they would remain there, and how many new extras we should see in each scene. I didn't want to look at this film a year later and see the same two extras crossing through every shot. Again, this was a task made complicated by the fact that the film takes place in a 24-hour period, but was shot out of sequence. 26

One sequence that took forever to shoot was the johnny pump sequence, where Charlie (played by Frank Vincent) and his white con- 27 vertible get drenched by the kids. We allotted two days to shoot it, but we should have been more generous because it ended up taking five.

The car had to be specially rigged to withstand all the water, and 28 dried off between takes. And each time Frank got wet, he needed a wardrobe change. We used two cameras to film the kids playing in the hydrant. One was encased in underwater housing, and we used that camera to shoot the closeups of the hydrant. The camera department had a lot fun with it. It was orange and looked like an old diver's mask.

It's a compliment to Wynn Thomas's design work that people off 29 the street were constantly wandering into Sal's Famous Pizzeria and the Korean Market, unaware they were sets. We spent almost a straight week shooting inside Sal's Famous Pizzeria. With the heat from the lights, and the crew and actors packed into one room, it really got hot in there. As soon as a take was over, people rushed to turn on the air conditioner. During lunch break, crew members used the booths as beds and caught some shut-eye.

Despite the heat, we were able to get through these interior scenes 30 pretty quickly. John Turturro exploded one day over the prop pizza. The property master didn't have enough pies on set for John and Richard Edson to actually cut them into slices. They were told to fake it. John went off. He refused to fake it because it suspended all his belief in the scene. He was right. We saw dailies the next night and had to reshoot all the fake cutting.

I was pleased with the way we staged the conversation about "nig- 31 gers" vs. "Blacks" that Mookie and Pino have in the pizzeria. As it reads in the script, the scene could have been a yelling match. It works just as well as a simple conversation, and it manages to keep the same intensity. There is enough yelling and screaming in this movie as it is.

Pino and Mookie's scene sets up the racial-slur sequence. Jump-cut 32 sequences featuring a group of characters speaking toward the camera have been a staple of each of my films so far. *She's Gotta Have It* has the Dogs, *School Daze* has Half-Pint's unsuccessful attempt to pick up girls, and *Do The Right Thing* has representatives of different ethnic groups slurring each other.

In the first two films, the camera remains static while the subjects 33 talk. I wanted to vary this formula a bit in *Do The Right Thing*, so I had the camera move in quickly to the person speaking. It was Ernest's idea to have the final actor in the sequence, Mister Señor Love Daddy, come toward camera. We hooked up Love Daddy's chair to a trick wire so it looks like he's being propelled by magic.

The racial-slur sequence was meant to rouse emotions. It's funny the 34 way people react to it. They laugh at every slur except the one directed at their ethnic group. While we were watching the dailies of Pino's slur of Blacks, a woman in the Kraft Services department started hissing at John. She couldn't separate John from his character and was less than courteous to him for the rest of the shoot.

Some of the best acting in the film happens in the scene where Pino   35 asks his father to sell the pizzeria. Danny, John, and I tinkered with the dialogue while the crew was setting up for the shot. We finally got it down, but we still didn't have a clincher to end the scene. I was always on the lookout for ways to work Smiley into the film, since for the most part, he wasn't scripted. It hit me that we could end the scene by having Smiley knock on the pizzeria window and interrupt Danny and John's conversation.

Danny and John are sitting at a table in front of the pizzeria window.   36 What makes that scene so great to me is that as Danny tells John about the neighborhood and why he has chosen to remain there, through the window you can see activity on the block. It lends visual support to Danny's speech.

Even if principal actors didn't have dialogue in a scene, we often   37 used them in the background, walking down the street or hanging out, to give a sense that their characters really lived on the block. Most of the deals we made with our principals were for eight weeks of work—the entire shoot—so we could have them on standby for that very reason.

The climactic fight in the pizzeria was just as I envisioned it—a   38 messy street fight, complete with choking and biting. It starts inside the pizzeria and ends up outside on the pavement. After Sal demolishes Radio Raheem's box with his baseball bat, we wanted to do a shot where Raheem would grab Sal by the neck, slam his face into the counter, and drag him the length of the counter.

Danny refused to do the shot. He felt it was slapstick and had been   39 done a million times. Some cast members felt that Danny's refusal was a question of ego, of not wanting to be wasted that bad on screen. I sat down with Eddie Smith, the stunt coordinator, Danny, Danny Jr., Aiello's son and stunt double, and Bill Nunn, to hear the opinions of all involved. I decided that Bill should pull Danny over the counter instead of giving him a "facial." Danny was still not totally satisfied, but we proceeded anyway.

The cast was spurred on by Danny's reluctance to cooperate with   40 what we had planned for the fight scene. As if to compensate for Danny's lapse of team spirit, they worked extra hard to make the scene realistic. Everyone suffered their share of bruises, including Martin Lawrence (Cee) who took a nasty shot in the eye.

Good things come out of adversity. I think the compromise we came   41 up with made for a better shot, and I'm grateful to Danny for standing his ground. There was no tension on my part because of our disagreement. I think Danny felt isolated from the cast for a while. But I noticed that in no time he was back to his usual habit of hugging on everyone. Conflicts are bound to crop up on a film shoot. There are always differences of interpretation.

The riot scene was more involved than anything I've done on film   42
before. Just the sheer numbers of people and vehicles involved—from extras to special-effects coordinators, from cop cars and paddy wagons to fire trucks—made it a big deal.

In order to capture all the action in the scene, we had to burn the   43
pizzeria in stages, starting with the interior and moving outside. A big concern was how many days the pizzeria would hold up under the fire. If the fire got out of hand or the set caved in before we finished shooting the riot, we'd be up shit's creek with no paddle. But things worked out and we were able to get all the shots we wanted without losing the pizzeria.

My most pressured moment as an actor on this film was definitely   44
when I had to throw the garbage can through the pizzeria window. No one thought about this beforehand, but the window glass was almost one-quarter inch thick. Breaking glass that thick is no easy feat. I was throwing hard, but it took four or five takes before I could get the garbage can through the window. On one take it even bounced off like a rubber ball. I was on the spot: We were filming with a special crane that had to be sent back to the rental house the next day, and the sun was coming up. Finally we got the shot.

The first night we shot the firemen turning their hoses on the crowd,   45
the water pressure wasn't forceful enough. The stuntmen were overacting to compensate for it. The whole effect was fake, so we redid the shot the following evening.

The script called for a number of stunts involving characters getting   46
swept away by the force of the water. Ruby Dee and my sister Joie were to get hit by a blast of water and go flying down the street. I decided the scene was powerful enough without these stunts. I cut them and came up with a different way to end the scene. Ruby Dee is in the middle of the street screaming hysterically because of all the chaos around her. Da Mayor comforts her with a hug.

Sam Jackson pointed out to me that he had the honor of acting in the   47
first scene we shot of *School Daze* (he played one of the local yokels), and in the last scene we shot of *Do The Right Thing* (Mister Señor Love Daddy wakes up the Block). I hope this means luck for both of us.

Most wrap days are joyous occasions, unless your film is a real   48
bomb. I felt I had a lot to be thankful for when we wrapped *Do The Right Thing*. We had a relaxed, practically hassle-free shoot. We had shot an

entire film for eight and a half weeks at one location. (What could be easier?) The block residents and the community of Bed-Stuy had given us full cooperation. And the dailies looked good.

A couple of hours before wrap, a bet was waged on the exact time, 49 down to the minute, that we would complete our last shot. One of the drivers won the bet and a pool of forty-five dollars. We broke out the champagne. And after listening to the movie unit cops grumble about permissions, we laid a plaque in front of We Love Radio Station that states that the film was shot on the block. We even put up a street sign renaming Stuyvesant Street "Do The Right Thing Avenue," but the wind blew it down, so it stays in my office now.

· · · · · · · · · · · · · · · · · · · ·

Examining the Text

1. Look again at veteran actor Paul Benjamin's original objections to the script of *Do the Right Thing* and at the arguments in its favor offered by Rosie Perez and Spike Lee (paragraphs 12–14). Do you think that the filmmaker's responsibility is to present positive images or to present life as it "actually exists"?

2. Why did Lee choose to "play down the gold fad" (17)? How does this decision square with the arguments he made to Paul Benjamin about showing the reality of the "Black underclass in Bed-Stuy" (14)? What other examples can you find where Lee bases his artistic decisions on his political convictions? What do you think of what he did?

3. Lee notes that during the "racial-slur sequence" of *Do the Right Thing* viewers "laugh at every slur except the one directed at their ethnic group" (34). Based on this observation, why do you suppose Lee's included the sequence in his film? If you saw the movie, how did you react to this sequence?

For Group Discussion

Lee says his goal was to use "as many Black people behind the camera as possible." Other minority and female directors have expressed similar commitments to include greater numbers of under-represented groups in their production crews. In debating this issue, have half of your group take Lee's perspective, and the other half the perspective of a leader of a predominantly white male union. Then as a class, try to reach consensus about what is "fair."

Writing Suggestion

One of the criticisms of *Do The Right Thing* is that it perpetuates racial stereotypes—Asians, police, Italians, Black militants, stutterers, Puerto Ricans, miscellaneous white bicyclists and bystanders—and ironically uses those stereotypes to condemn racism. After viewing the film, write an essay in which you agree or disagree with this criticism. Does Lee's portrayal of his secondary characters rely on stereotypes, or does he make a conscious effort to portray individuals as real people with complex personalities and motivations?

As the World Turns
David Denby

*E*ven *as American movies are charged with being "big-budget" and mindless, the United States continues to be a major supplier of movies to the rest of the world. In fact, in many countries, American films are more popular (and more profitable) than locally produced movies. What effect does this barrage of American pop imagery have on the world's cultures?*

In the following piece—ostensibly a review of the American movies Back to the Future Part II *and* Harlem Nights, *film critic David Denby considers some of these effects and reports on measures foreign governments take to limit the availability and influence of American films.*

Denby credits western mass culture with having a role in revolutionary changes which saw communist governments in Central Europe topple and the Soviet Union dissolve. Pop is fun and "can be good for the soul," he says, while communist regimes are "dryly bureaucratic." Capitalist culture, as depicted in American movies, looked more appealing than the drab, regimented world under communism.

Yet Denby is not entirely comfortable with the influence the American film industry has on the world. Although he doesn't support the imposition of quotas, he doesn't want to see foreign filmmakers abandon their own cultural heritage to produce "American-style spectaculars." He would also like to see a stronger American market for foreign films, and American "indifference and self-protecting chauvinism . . . vanish."

As you read, notice that Denby digresses widely from his original task of reviewing Back to the Future Part II *and* Harlem Nights, *and ask yourself how well he relates those films to his broader thesis about the pervasive influence of American movies on world markets.*

•••••••••••••••••••

As I was out buying a quart of milk the other day, the leadership of   1
Czechoslovakia's Communist Party fell from power. The revolution
sweeping Central Europe has come deliriously hard and fast, so fast
that staying interested in new movies like *Back to the Future Part II*
and *Harlem Nights* has been a little tough. Whole governments collapse
between chase scenes. The possibility of a future in which America is
irrelevant teases us, haunting our lockjawed president, a man fright-
ened not only of events but of words. De Tocqueville correctly predicted 150 years ago that Russia and America would someday hold sway.
But a united Europe may dominate the next century, which will
change the way Americans think of themselves. It may even change the
movies.

At the moment, America is supplying movies to the entire world.   2
Many Europeans resent the popularity of our films in their own markets. When people flock to American movies, less money flows back to
local film industries. As a result, some countries have established quotas—restricting American movies to, say, 50 percent of the theaters.
These quotas may be reinforced or expanded when the European Community becomes a single market in 1992. At the same time, many Europeans, surrounded and overwhelmed by American pop, fear the corruption of their own cultures.

I have contradictory, unresolvable feelings about this. On the one   3
hand, American mass culture is a liberator. German students threw
themselves a party on top of the Berlin Wall a few weeks ago—and what
were they singing? Ray Parker Jr.'s theme from *Ghostbusters.* Bopping
on the wall, they zapped the Communist phantoms. Pow, you're dead!
Pop is an important element in the seduction of the East by the West, the
seduction of Communism by capitalism. It's easy pleasure, quick satisfaction; it's one of the things that Communists are not very good at. For
years, the longing of Eastern-bloc youth for American and British rock
has amounted to a de facto aesthetic rejection of drably bureaucratic
regimes. Governments trying to persuade people to give up good times
in return for a future Utopia have lost their credibility. Western mass culture helped do them in.

At the same time, many educated Europeans fight American movies.   4
In 1978, I showed George Lucas's *American Graffiti* to some very serious
students at the Polish state film school in Lodz, and they roared with
laughter from beginning to end. But afterward, they told me that the
movie was trash, completely without value. Europeans can sound awfully priggish when putting down American movies (the students
weren't amused when I accused them of hypocrisy). Of course, this was
a state school, and someone from the Party may have been listening. The
students—all of whom would move into the government-sanctioned

film apparatus if they behaved—may have been priggish out of necessity. I trust their first, spontaneous reactions.

Pop can be good for the soul. As for quotas, I'm instinctively against 5 them, since they amount to a form of censorship. People should be able to watch what they want. On the other hand, I'm also repelled by the idea of American junk playing every small town in France and Germany—and soon, presumably, every town in Hungary and Poland too. The habit of easy, violent pleasures could discourage more thoughtful kinds of local filmmaking. Some people say it already has. As a counterforce, the new European pride—the reemergent sense of Europe as the rightful center of Western civilization—may well lead to increased demands for cultural protectionism; the resistance to American pop may stiffen, which might not be such a bad idea. Americans could resist their own mass culture a little more.

Another reason the Europeans are sore is that their movies have 6 barely kept a toehold in the American market, the biggest in the world. In 1989, domestic box office (i.e., American and Canadian) may reach a record $5 billion. Yet the share of tickets sold for foreign-language films amounts to about $50 million, or one percent. As far as the United States is concerned, the German and Italian cinemas might as well not exist; the number of French films opening here has been declining, too, from 48 in 1968 to 24 last year.

The French keep trying, though. A few weeks ago, at the first Sara- 7 sota French Film Festival, a group of high-powered French movie-industry types, including producers, directors, and actors, met with American film importers and a few critics to show off some of the new French movies. . . . My guess is that five of the thirteen new movies shown at the festival will receive American distribution, not a bad ratio at all.

At a panel of American critics, there was general agreement that French films had recently fallen off in quality (this took no courage to say—the French had already flown back to Paris); everyone also agreed that the merely good French films were finding it harder to attract an audience here. If the French, as part of the new Europe, are able to amass large amounts of capital for film production, they could, of course, make American-style spectaculars and begin to claim a larger share of the world market. But then we would miss what we've always valued most in French movies—intimacy. It's not so much that French movies need to change as that American indifference and self-protecting chauvinism have to vanish. Perhaps our impending reduced standing in the world will have an effect on our moviegoing habits.

Intimacy is certainly not a quality anyone could find in Rob___ ___meckis's *Back to the Future Part II*. In the original, Michael J. Fox___ ___gle to bring his parents together so they could mate and prod___ had a wrenching force. And with that wild man Crispin Glover giving a painfully expressive performance as the wimpy father, the comedy veered recklessly into pathos and back. But the sequel is just noise and frenzied activity. Fox and Christopher Lloyd, as the mad doctor, fly forward and then backward in time, running into other versions of themselves from the first movie's trip back in time. We get plot complexity without any point—a desperate attempt to double and redouble the central gimmick so it will explode like the grand finale of a fireworks display. The wild-eyed Lloyd, shouting gibberish, is desperately unfunny, and Fox is little more than a shuttlecock with mussed feathers. I don't care how much money it makes; the movie is a brutal setback for Zemeckis's career. As for Eddie Murphy's *Harlem Nights,* this promisingly swank fantasy of black club owners and white gangsters in thirties Harlem falls into racial and sexual taunting of frightening crudity. Eddie Murphy the mass-entertainment genius seems to be turning into Eddie Murphy the pop demagogue.

....

Examining the Text

1. Why, according to Denby, do many Europeans resent the popularity of American films in their own countries, and what measures have governments taken to counteract this popularity? Why does Denby say that his feelings about this are "contradictory" and "unresolvable" (paragraph 3)? What are your own feelings?

2. What does Denby mean when he claims that pop culture is an "important element in the seduction of the East by the West" (3)? What does he mean by "pop can be good for the soul" (5)? Can you give other examples of redeeming qualities of American-style pop culture?

3. How does Denby explain the poor reception for foreign films in the United States? What does he have to say about this issue? Why do you think Americans are so "chauvinistic" when it comes to foreign films?

4. How does Denby relate his central argument to his dismissive comments about *Back to the Future Part II* and *Harlem Nights?* Do you find his strategy effective?

For Group Discussion

As a group, compare several current popular American-made films with any foreign films you have seen recently, and make a list of important similarities and differences. (If no one in your group has seen a foreign film recently, you can list some reasons for that.) Then, as a class, consider what qualities a foreign film must have to succeed with American audiences. Why do American audiences tend to shun foreign films?

Writing Suggestion

Generally a fan of popular culture, Denby nonetheless contends that "Americans could resist their own mass culture a little more" (5). In an essay explain his comment and evaluate his view, drawing on specific examples from your own experience with American movies, television, and advertising.

Film Criticism

Mark J. Schaefermeyer

There's much more to criticizing a film than just deciding whether one likes it or not. This is the central point of the following essay by Mark J. Schaefermeyer. A film critic and professor of communications studies at Virginia Polytechnic Institute, Schaefermeyer begins by drawing a crucial distinction between reviewing movies and film criticism. Movie reviews, he says, are directed toward the general public, primarily to help people decide what movies to see. By contrast, film criticism is written primarily by university academics and other scholars to be published in specialized journals and read by academics and professional filmmakers.

Schaefermeyer outlines some of the main theoretical approaches critics currently use to analyze films. He breaks film criticism down into three broad subcategories—semiotic, structuralist, and contextual—and explains the premises and specific methodologies of each. Semiotic studies, as you have learned from earlier readings in this text (see especially Jack Solomon's "Masters of Desire" in Chapter 2 and Arthur Asa Berger's semiological analysis of Cheers in Chapter 3), analyze symbolic structures and relationships. Structuralist methodology attempts "to impose its own orientation or structure"—for instance mythic, or political, or sociological—on a film. Finally, contextual critics look at a movie within a specific context, such as its directorial style, its narrative type, or its historical position.

As you read this survey of film criticism, think about which approach most closely resembles your own way of interpreting film. Are you a budding semiotician, finding symbolic meanings in Lauren Bacall's cigarette or Arnold Schwarzenegger's big gun? Are you a political structuralist, finding social and economic implications in a film's plot and characterization? Are you a contextualist, looking for the hallmarks of a director's style or for the ways the conventions

*of a genre are met or broken? Or are you satisfied just to "know what you like,"
without approaching film from a more academically critical position?*

. . . .

The place occupied by movie critics in the popular media is perhaps   1
stronger today that it ever has been. The success of Gene Siskel and
Roger Ebert in moving from PBS to syndication with their self-described
movie review program is evidence that the medium is not without those
who are paid to pass judgment on it. Paperback books that describe and
rate all the films available on television abound; local news programs
often have a critic of their own or regularly utilize a video version of
the syndicated columnist. Major news magazines and large city dailies
regularly review films; even the smallest of newspapers offers a column
discussing the film industry's latest releases. In some cases, movies
are reviewed a second time when they are released in videocassette
format.

And yet these instances of criticism are only part of the effort that   2
goes into analyzing film. This reading puts into perspective the act of
film criticism while providing an overview of the critical approaches
currently being used. The bulk of this essay will focus on academic criticism versus the more popular media forms. The general public is aware
of and utilizes criticism that is more aptly termed *movie reviewing.* Movie
reviews are meant to recommend or not recommend particular films to
the potential viewing public. In one sense, the popular media critic is a
consumer watchdog keeping a wary eye on the film industry's attempts
to obtain the viewers' dollars.

Distinguishing the popular media form of criticism from academic   3
or scholarly criticism is not to suggest that the former is unscholarly or
a poor cousin to the latter. Movie reviews are meant for a specific audience, and they perform a specific function: to assist consumers in choosing what films to see. For the most part, movie reviewers rely on such
categories as plot, characterization, or strength of the actors' performances to arrive at their assessment of the film (this is probably a
holdover from the early beginnings of such criticism when reviewers of
this new medium generally were drama critics taking on additional duties). In most cases today, reviewers' closest comments regarding purely
filmic qualities are related to a director's use of particular techniques.

In contrast, academic critical pursuits are directed toward publica-   4
tions intended for fellow academicians and/or filmmakers. Their purpose is to foster a better understanding of film as a medium and as an
art form. Hence scholarly criticism of film invariably touches the medium's history, functions, practitioners, techniques, or aesthetics. In most

cases, such criticism attempts to answer questions about the film's history and other issues in order to further our knowledge about art, ourselves, and the world.

Sidney Pollack (1986), director of the critically acclaimed and successful films *Out of Africa* and *Tootsie,* has stated that each film is a revelation of the director's perceptions about how the world operates. Each film is thus a communication of the director's overall vision of the world. Those who seek to understand a film implicitly seek understanding of what the director has communicated. In many cases, what is communicated is not always obvious to the viewer or the critic. Close analysis is necessary to reveal, interpret, or merely aid the viewer's understanding.

There are a variety of methods and critical models imposed on films, all of which propose to answer specific questions about those works of art. Indeed, the question of what the filmmaker "meant" is not an appropriate query (many critical theorists have long ago abandoned the quest for artist's intent). Rather, the meaning of a film is just that: what the film (or work of art) communicates. The film's meaning, then, depends on how it is perceived, by whom, and with what particular perspective(s).

This situation appears to indicate that film meanings vary and therefore criticism as a method for arriving at that meaning must be fruitless pursuit. Quite the contrary is true. Works of art will often hold different meanings for people because of their varied experiences and backgrounds. Hence, each viewer approaches a film with different sets of expectations and prejudices, as well as a distinct worldview and knowledge base. The variety of critical perspectives allows each individual to explore the perspective most meaningful to that person. More important, for those of us studying the mass media, an additional gain from the variety of critical perspectives used to analyze film is the differences that are highlighted and what those differences tell us about ourselves, others, and the human condition in general.

The remainder of this reading will . . . review the various types of film criticism, with examples for each type of criticism. Although no particular perspective should be viewed as more useful or proper than any other, no doubt each reader will find one or two of those discussed to be more functional than the others. The key is that no perspective should be dismissed out of hand; each has its own merits as well as faults. Like the cinematic works of art they attempt to analyze, some critical methods work for us, and others do not. To aid us in our understanding of film as a mass medium and as an art form, it is necessary to be acquainted with the basic theory and the tools utilized by critics of film.

Critical Methods in Film Criticism

Each of the critical approaches to film discussed here falls within   9
one of three categories:

Semiotic: realist, formalist, rhetorical, mise-en-scène.
Structuralist: mythic, political, feminist, psychoanalytic, sociologi-
    cal, phenomenological
Contextual: auteur, genre, historical.

Grouped within the *semiotic* category are methods that tend to focus on
the meaning of the filmic signs (shots and shot transitions), the relationship of these signs to other filmic signs, or the effect of the signs on
the film viewer. Methods that fall under the *structuralist* category seek
to define and understand the structures into which individual films
and/or from where they are derived. Those under the *contextual* heading focus on aspects of film in the context of other aspects of film.

Semiotic Studies

The most logical place to start in the review of critical approaches   10
with a semiotic impetus is with both the *realist* and *formalist traditions*
within film theory. The *realist* tradition focuses on the use of film to represent reality based on the power of photography's ability to render
the real world objectively (Bazin 1967). Bazin argues that long takes,
depth of focus, location shooting, sunlight, and the use of nonprofes-
sional actors all contribute to a film's realist aesthetic. In his analysis of
Visconti's *La Terra Trema* (1971), Bazin discusses how the film is "real"
by virtue of the manner in which the narrative is presented: without the
trappings of montage (where reality is fragmented through such techniques as close-up shots and excessive editing). "If a fisherman rolls a
cigarette, he [Visconti] spares us nothing: we see the whole operation; it
will not be reduced to its dramatic or symbolic meaning, as is usual with
montage" (Bazin 1971, p. 43). In a review of De Sica's *Bicycle Thief*, Bazin
praises the realist use of location shooting (nothing has been filmed in
the studio) and actors without any previous experience in theater or film
(Bazin 1971, p. 52).

Analyses using the *formalist* approach have a different focus. Be-   11
cause of his influence on the early history of filmmaking, the Russian
filmmaker and theorist Sergei Eisenstein is most often linked (above
other theorists) to film's *formalist* tradition. Eisenstein's theory of di-
alectical montage is influenced by the Japanese hieroglyph, as a pictor-
ial representation of language symbols, and by Hegel's dialectic. First,
Eisenstein believes that the Japanese language was built on the princi-

ple of montage. For example, the picture symbol for a *dog* plus the symbol for *mouth* means "to bark" (1949, p. 30). The combination of "two hieroglyphs of the simplest series is to be regarded not as their sum, but as their product, i.e., as a value of another dimension, another degree; each, separately, corresponds to an *object*, to a fact, but their combination corresponds to a *concept*. From separate hieroglyphs has been fused— the ideogram" (Eisenstein 1949, pp. 29–30).

Eisenstein theorizes that film relied on the same process: a shot combined in the editing process with another shot created a new concept. Paralleling this approach is the influence of Hegel's dialectic. *Thesis* and *antithesis* combine to form a *synthesis*—a new concept that is no longer reducible to those ideas that in combination make up the editing (as well as any other art form). Montage is the collision of independent shots (shots that are opposite to one another) (Eisenstein 1949, p. 49). Meaning in film, then, evolves from the juxtaposition of film shots that manifest conflict. The differences might be in lighting, shot composition, shot length, conflict of volumes, lines, movement of objects, or something else. Excluding Eisenstein's philosophical and political (or Marxist) orientation, the basis of his theory is film construction: shot plus shot plus shot . . . Hence, any critic interested in how the shots of a film are combined to "mean" would essentially be conducting formalist criticism.   12

Ted Perry's essay (1970) on Michaelangelo Antonioni's film *L'Eclisse* argues that the meaning of the film depends on certain cues given within the film. In distinguishing between what he calls *fact context* and *value context*, the author argues that the film's meaning is born of the formative forces within the film (p. 79). Perry's analysis relies heavily on the notion of combination. The value context (the attitudes, impressions, and values by which the film frames the fact context) influences the viewer's reading of the fact context (the elements that represent the actions, objects, and events of the physical world depicted in the motion picture images). This analysis reflects the formalist tradition in its focus on meaning that is built upon the combination of shots.   13

A third type of analysis within the semiotic orientation is *rhetorical* in focus. This type of criticism examines the film as a rhetorical artifact that exhibits intentional meaning and structure. It is an approach based on traditional notions of rhetoric as a means to persuasion. Often relying on critical models from other disciplines, the rhetorical criticism of film deals with the communicative potential of film.   14

In "Image and Ambiguity: A Rhetorical Approach to *The Exorcist*," Martin Medhurst (1978) examines the key images in six of the film's episodes in order to define the film's central stance: a rhetoric of choice. The author argues that certain recurring images combine in clusters to   15 foster the contention that people have choices to make: "Humans must choose between the forces of good and the legions of evil. . . . They must consciously will the good and then by a step of faith act on that choice. This is exactly what Damien Karras does in the climax of the film. He consciously chooses to assert that Regan will not die and then proceeds to ace on the basis of that assertion" (Medhurst 1978, pp. 90–91).

Medhurst (1982) has also analyzed Alain Resnais' *Hiroshima, Mon*   16 *Amour* as a film about the problem of knowing reality. In essence, Medhurst's analysis is traditionally rhetorical in his focus on the filmmaker's "cinematic statement": "Resnais has built into the film the very paradox which forms its thesis. . . . Resnais has been able to take his thesis and transform it into a cinematic resource. . . . To know reality, Resnais seems to be saying, is no easy task" (Medhurst 1982, p. 370). Clearly in evidence is the rhetorical quest concerning what the filmmaker means. Both of the Medhurst essays ostensibly rely on examining and interpreting the filmmaker's message.

The final type of semiotic-oriented criticism relys on *mise-en-scène*—   17 the environment of the film, which is created by its lighting, sets, costumes, movement, and any other features that comprise the scene as photographed by the camera. Film analysis that focuses on these elements and on the expressive function of the individual shots is the basis of mise-en-scène criticism (Stromgren and Norden 1984, p. 265). Mise-en-scène criticism lies in the boundary zone between formalism and realism; it is "largely concerned with stylistic or expressive qualities of the single shot . . . in contrast to Bazin's perception of the long take as a transparent realism . . . and in sharp distinction to Eisenstein's herding of all expressive categories under the single umbrella of montage" (Nichols 1976, p. 311).

One notable example of mise-en-scène criticism is Place and Peter-   18 son's "Some Visual Motifs of *Film Noir*" (1974). Here, the authors define visual style by utilizing the technical terminology of Hollywood. Their analysis reveals a style reliant on low-key lighting, night-for-night photography (versus day-for-night where the scene, shot in the bright sunlight of day, is manipulated to create an illusion of night), depth of field (the entire shot is in focus), and antitraditional camera setups and angles: "The 'dark mirror' of *film noir* creates a visually unstable environment in which no character has a firm moral base from which he can confidently operate. All attempts to find safety or security are undercut by the antitraditional cinematography and *mise-en-scène*" (Place and Peterson, p. 338).

All of these types of criticism have semiotic underpinnings: each at-   19 tempts to understand and/or interpret the meaning of cinematic signs, the relationship of cinematic signs to each other, and their meaning to the viewer. There are not always clear-cut boundaries between the vary-ing elements. However, the distinctive features of the type are clear: The primary focus is on cinematic features and the use of film theory. This is contrary to the structuralist studies, which utilize literary-cultural fea-tures. They are, in effect, extracinematic (outside of cinema).

Structuralist Studies

There are several types of structuralist methodology. Each method   20
attempts to impose its own orientation or structure on the film; each ar-gues that the film exhibits particular features of the society within which it is produced.

The *mythic* approach asserts the presence of one or more specific   21
myths that, by virtue of their preeminence, are found (or likely to be found) in a society's aesthetic artifacts. Dale Williams's essay (1984) on the religious nature of Stanley Kubrick's *2001: A Space Odyssey* is an ex-ample of criticism that uncovers the meaning of the film by defining its mythic overtones. Using the theories of Kenneth Burke (1969), Williams argues that *2001* revolves around the concepts of order and redemption, sacrifice and rebirth, self-denial, and communion with God (Williams 1984, p. 321). Similarly, Martha Solomon (1983) argues that British-made *Chariots of Fire* was successful in the United States because it reflects two contradictory facets of the American dream—what Fisher (1973) calls the materialistic myth and the moralistic myth. The film's success, in part, is due to its reaffirmation of both competing myths for an audience likely to follow, individually, one or the other. *Chariots,* according to Solomon, functions both mythically and metaphorically in its depiction of a series of successful, archetypal quests by the film's mythic hero characters (p. 275).

The *political* approach to criticism is likely to focus on films and their   22
relationship to the areas of history, ideology, economics, and social crit-icism. Jeffrey Richards's essay (1970) on Frank Capra illustrates how the films of a single director can contain political undertones. In this case, Capra's films reflect ideals of the populist party: self-help and individ-ualism versus political machines and big government. Richards finds the presence of Capra's emphasis of populism in the motifs of anti-intellectualism, wealth, pursuit of happiness, and the quintessential good neighbor. Capra's films in the postwar era cast aside these themes because the world had progressed, and the forces of organization had won out.

The *feminist* perspective in criticism has gained sufficient status as   23
a category, though it could be argued that its impetus is political in na-ture. Most of the feminist critics analyze films' treatment of women as

they support or negate the role of women in contemporary society. For example, Diane Giddis (1973) explores a woman's dilemma (the fear that love represents loss of autonomy) in her analysis of *Klute*. Giddis finds that the film reflects woman's need to love and make a deep emotional commitment—a commitment unnecessary, to the same degree, for men. Constance Penley (1973) analyzes Ingmar Bergman's *Cries and Whispers* in the perspective of Bergman's other films. Penley's analysis runs counter to the majority of the film's reviews; she sees *Cries* as another example of Bergman's excessive portrayal of woman as victim, temptress, evil incarnate, and earth mother.

Psychoanalytic and *sociological* criticisms are likely to use models of   24
analysis from accepted theorists or contemporary social concerns. Rushing and Frentz (1980), for example, derive their analysis of *The Deer Hunter* from the psychological theories of Carl Jung. In a sociological critique, the critic uses sociological concepts, such as class, status, interaction, organization and culture, to analyze a film. They may also use the perspective and language of social movements.

Finally, the *phenomenological* approach to criticism is concerned with   25
the manner in which viewers perceive the film and/or its images (always, however, in relation to the whole) (see Andrew 1978). An example of this type is Janice Schuetz's analysis (1975) of *The Exorcist*. Schuetz utilizes the symbols of yin and yang from the *I Ching* as a paradigm for explaining the viewer's perceptions of the film. She argues that the film "presents reality in an organismic way, showing goodness and evil, doubt and faith, despair and hope, secular and sacred . . . as realistic representations of an integrated reality" (pp. 100–101). In addition, the images are sufficiently ambiguous to permit viewers to attribute meaning based on their own frame of reference (p. 101).

Contextual Studies

The three types included here—auteur, genre, and historical—have   26
in common the study of film(s) within a specific context: directorial style (in its broadest sense), narrative type, and impact on or development of the film industry and/or the film as art form. Examples of each type are readily available in single texts, film periodicals, and collections of essays.

The most controversial of the three types is *auteur* criticism. Auteur   27
theory assumes a certain amount of directorial autonomy in film production regardless of the fact that film is a product of producers, screenwriters, cinematographers, actors, musicians, film editors, and others. The film's creation and the stylistic choices made are assumed to be those of a single person—the director. Auteur criticism, then, focuses on

film directors and the style manifested in two or more of their films. Directors such as Alfred Hitchcock, Charles Chaplin, John Ford, Howard Hawks, and Orson Welles have indirectly generated numerous auteur studies. No doubt, and not far off, there will be studies of George Lucas and Steven Spielberg.

Andrew Sarris (1968) uses auteur theory to rank various directors. 28 Relying on three criteria—technical competence, stylistic identity, and communicability of worldview—he estimates their worth as directors. John Simon's analysis of Ingmar Bergman (1972) is an auteur study that looks at four films that Simon thinks represent Bergman's best work up to the early 1970s. Ian Cameron's two-part essay on Hitchcock (1972a) is another example of auteur criticism. It analyzes a specific feature of the director's overall style, his ability to create suspense in his films:

> Having arrived at such a disturbing view [everything is a potential threat], Hitchcock paradoxically relishes it and loves more than anything to torture his audiences by making them find the most innocuous thing alarming so that he can surprise and terrify them when the real threat is revealed. (Cameron 1972b, p. 34).

By examining a single film, *The Man Who Knew Too Much,* Cameron 29 validates his auteur assumptions about Hitchcock's style. Another typical example of auteur criticism is Michael Budd's essay (1976) on visual imagery in John Ford's Westerns.

Genre criticism focuses on the narrative structures common to film: 30 Westerns, war films, musicals, gangster films, and so on. This type of criticism also categorizes films according to specific characteristics. Thus, to be able to classify an object, to know where it fits, is a means toward understanding it better. We are then able to analyze a certain film based on how well it fits a particular genre and "how the director of that work used the elements of the genre—its *conventions*—to make a statement unique to that film" (Stromgren and Norden 1984). (For additional comments on genre criticism, see Kaminsky 1974; see also the extensive bibliography of genre studies in Cook 1981, pp. 691–692.)

Finally, *historical* studies inevitably analyze the entire scope of the 31 film's development. Cook (1981), Ellis (1985), Giannetti and Eyman (1986), and Mast (1986) are fine representatives of historical criticism. In addition, studies of particular studios (Buscombe 1975; Gomery 1976) analyze the film industry from economic, political, or corporate perspectives or the impact of new technology. A relatively new annual series edited by Bruce A. Austin, "Current Research in Film: Audiences, Economics, and Law," publishes original essays on corporate structure, film financing, legal issues, marketing and promotion strategies, and others in an attempt to provide a place for those critics whose interests and work lie outside of the scope addressed by existing film journals.

Conclusion

There is a danger in establishing category systems. Inevitably ex- 32 amples of criticism exhibit features appropriate for more than one type of critical method. Judgment as to the correct placement of each of the examples here is left up to the reader. However, no apology is made for the classification contained within; what these essays accomplish is typical of the category they exemplify. Nor are they to be considered examples of superior criticism. In some cases, they create as many questions as they answer.

There will continue to be a need to analyze the best, worst, and av- 33 erage output of the film industry. Although the ultimate arbiter for judging a film's success may be its box office receipts, those with expertise should continue to analyze film with the express purpose of better understanding it as a mass media art form. Critics of both kinds, public and scholarly, can always hope that filmmakers, and ultimately audiences, will benefit from their efforts.

From the opposite viewpoint, those who practice film criticism have 34 no monopoly on perfection. Critics must continue to read other critical analyses of film in order to improve their own craft. Like the student in a public speaking course, critics benefit from witnessing the successes and blunders of other critics. New methods are tried and either validated or rejected. In a rapidly progressing world, there is comfort in the thought that our critical stance and methods also continue to progress.

References

Andrew, Dudley. 1978. "The Neglected Tradition of Phenomenology in Film Theory." *Wide Angle* 2:44–49.

Bazin, André. 1967. *What Is Cinema?* Vol. 1. Translated and edited by Hugh Gray. Berkeley: University of California Press.

———. 1971. *What Is Cinema?* Vol. 2. Translated and edited by Hugh Gray. Berkeley: University of California Press.

Budd, Michael. 1976. "A Home in the Wilderness: Visual Imagery in John Ford's Westerns." *Cinema Journal* 16:62–75.

Burke, Kenneth. 1969. *A Rhetoric of Motives.* Berkeley: University of California Press.

Buscombe, Edward. 1975. "Notes on Columbia Pictures Corporation, 1926–1941." *Screen* 16. Reprinted in Nichols 1985:92–108.

Cameron, Ian. 1972a. "Hitchcock and the Mechanics of Suspense." *Movie Reader.* New York: Frederick A. Praeger.

———. 1972b. "Hitchcock 2: Suspense and Meaning." *Movie Reader.* New York: Praeger.

Cook, David A. 1981. *A History of Narrative Film.* New York: W. W. Norton.

Eisenstein, Sergei. 1947. *The Film Sense.* New York: Harcourt Brace Jovanovich.

———. 1949. *Film Form: Essays in Film Theory.* Translated and edited by Jay Leyda. New York: Harcourt, Brace and World.

Ellis, Jack C. 1985. *A History of Film.* 2d ed. Englewood Cliffs, N.J.: Prentice-Hall.

Fisher, Walter. 1973. "Reaffirmation and Subversion of the American Dream." *Quarterly Journal of Speech* 59:160–167.

Giannetti, Louis, and Scott Eyman. 1986. *Flashback: A Brief History of Film.* Englewood Cliffs, N.J.: Prentice-Hall.

Giddis, Diane. 1973. "The Divided Woman: Bree Daniels in *Klute.*" *Women and Film,* nos. 3–4. Reprinted in Nichols 1976:194–201.

Gomery, Douglas. 1976. "Writing the History of the American Film Industry: Warner Brothers and Sound." *Screen* 17. Reprinted in Nichols 1985:109–119.

••••••••••••••••••••

Examining the Text

1. Why do you think Schaefermeyer begins by distinguishing between movie reviewing and movie criticism? In what ways does he suggest that the reviewer and the critic both perform important functions? Based on his examples, do you agree with his evaluation of the critic's role?

2. Briefly summarize in your own words each of the three basic critical approaches Schaefermeyer describes. How do they differ from one another? Which would you find most interesting and illuminating?

3. Schaefermeyer concludes that "the ultimate arbiter for judging a film's success may be its box office receipts" (32). Do you think he is being entirely serious? What other ways are there to judge a film's "success"? Is any of these a better criterion than earnings?

For Group Discussion

Choose a film that each member of your group has seen and discuss how it could be analyzed using each of the three critical approaches described by Schaefermeyer. Come up with several specific examples from the film to illustrate one or more of the methods within each approach. As a class, discuss which approaches work best with which kinds of films.

Writing Suggestion

Critically analyze a specific film (or several films of the same genre, such as horror, science fiction, or romantic comedy), restricting your thematic focus to one of the structuralist approaches described by Schaefermeyer. For instance, if you consider yourself a feminist, point out instances of sexism or the objectification of women; if you're a political conservative, you might write from the perspective of a Rush Limbaugh, pointing out examples of liberal excess and misguidedness; if you are a student of mythology, you might take that approach. If possible, see the movie or movies you are writing about again, preferably on video, so that your examination can be a close one.

THE HORROR MOVIE

Why We Crave Horror Movies

Stephen King

A hotel with ghosts as its guests, a downtrodden teenager whose teleke-
netic powers wreak havoc at her prom, a giant dog from hell, a satanic antique
store owner . . . all are products of the fertile (and some would say twisted)
imagination of Stephen King, whose books are so widely read—and the movies
made from them so popularly viewed—that his creations may well have become
part of the American collective consciousness. In the following article, King
takes a break from story-telling to reflect on the genre that has brought him
worldwide recognition.

King begins by stating a bold and not entirely tongue-in-cheek premise: "I
think that we are all mentally ill." Underneath a frequently thin veneer of civilization, he suggests, we all have fears, homicidal rages, and sexual desires—
baser urges which he calls "anticivilization emotions"—and the function of
horror movies is to appeal to those dark elements of our selves and therefore reduce their psychic energy. Thus purged of our negative impulses, we can go on
to engage in positive feelings of love, friendship, loyalty and kindness. According to King, then, horror movies serve an important regulating function, defusing people's destructive urges and helping to maintain a society's psychic
equilibrium.

Before you read this article, consider your own feelings about portrayals
of the macabre, especially in films. If you enjoy horror movies, are you drawn
to them for the reasons Stephen King suggests—that is, do you have deep-seated
fears, angry urges, or inappropriate sexual drives that need defusing—or are
there other factors involved which King has not considered? More to the point,
how do you respond to King's basic premise: that everyone is in some sense mentally ill.

• • • • • • • • • • • • • • • • • • •

I think that we're all mentally ill; those of us outside the asylums   1
only hide it a little better—and maybe not all that much better, after all.
We've all known people who talk to themselves, people who sometimes
squinch their faces into horrible grimaces when they believe no one is
watching, people who have some hysterical fear—of snakes, the dark,
the tight place, the long drop . . . and, of course, those final worms and
grubs that are waiting so patiently underground.

When we pay our four or five bucks and seat ourselves at tenth-row center in a theater showing a horror movie, we are daring the nightmare. 2

Why? Some of the reasons are simple and obvious. To show that we can, that we are not afraid, that we can ride this roller coaster. Which is not to say that a really good horror movie may not surprise a scream out of us at some point, the way we may scream when the roller coaster twists through a complete 360 or plows through a lake at the bottom of the drop. And horror movies, like roller coasters, have always been the special province of the young; by the time one turns 40 or 50, one's appetite for double twists or 360-degree loops may be considerably depleted. 3

We also go to re-establish our feelings of essential normality; the horror movie is innately conservative, even reactionary. Freda Jackson as the horrible melting woman in *Die, Monster, Die!* confirms for us that no matter how far we may be removed from the beauty of a Robert Redford or a Diana Ross, we are still light-years from true ugliness. 4

And we go to have fun. 5

Ah, but this is where the ground starts to slope away, isn't it? Because this is a very peculiar sort of fun indeed. The fun comes from seeing others menaced—sometimes killed. One critic has suggested that if pro football has become the voyeur's version of combat, then the horror film has become the modern version of the public lynching. 6

It is true that the mythic, "fairytale" horror film intends to take away the shades of gray. . . . It urges us to put away our more civilized and adult penchant for analysis and to become children again, seeing things in pure blacks and whites. It may be that horror movies provide psychic relief on this level because this invitation to lapse into simplicity, irrationality and even outright madness is extended so rarely. We are told we may allow our emotions a free rein . . . or no rein at all. 7

If we are all insane, then sanity becomes a matter of degree. If your insanity leads you to carve up women like Jack the Ripper or the Cleveland Torso Murderer, we clap you away in the funny farm (but neither of those two amateur-night surgeons was ever caught, heh-heh-heh); if, on the other hand your insanity leads you only to talk to yourself when you're under stress or to pick your nose on the morning bus, then you are left alone to go about your business . . . though it is doubtful that you will ever be invited to the best parties. 8

The potential lyncher is in almost all of us (excluding saints, past and present; but then, most saints have been crazy in their own ways), and every now and then, he has to be let loose to scream and roll around in the grass. Our emotions and our fears form their own body, and we 9 recognize that it demands its own exercise to maintain proper muscle tone. Certain of these emotional muscles are accepted—even exalted—in civilized society; they are, of course, the emotions that tend to maintain the status quo of civilization itself. Love, friendship, loyalty, kindness—these are all the emotions that we applaud, emotions that have been immortalized in the couplets of Hallmark cards and in the verses (I don't dare call it poetry) of Leonard Nimoy.

When we exhibit these emotions, society showers us with positive   10
reinforcement; we learn this even before we get out of diapers. When, as children, we hug our rotten little puke of a sister and give her a kiss, all the aunts and uncles smile and twit and cry, "Isn't he the sweetest little thing?" Such coveted treats as chocolate-covered graham crackers often follow. But if we deliberately slam the rotten little puke of a sister's fingers in the door, sanctions follow—angry remonstrance from parents, aunts and uncles; instead of a chocolate-covered graham cracker, a spanking.

But anticivilization emotions don't go away, and they demand pe-   11
riodic exercise. We have such "sick" jokes as, "What's the difference between a truckload of bowling balls and a truckload of dead babies? (You can't unload a truckload of bowling balls with a pitchfork . . . a joke, by the way, that I heard originally from a ten-year-old.) Such a joke may surprise a laugh or a grin out of us even as we recoil, a possibility that confirms the thesis: If we share a brotherhood of man, then we also share an insanity of man. None of which is intended as a defense of either the sick joke or insanity but merely as an explanation of why the best horror films, like the best fairy tales, manage to be reactionary, anarchistic, and revolutionary all at the same time.

The mythic horror movie, like the sick joke, has a dirty job to do. It   12
deliberately appeals to all that is worst in us. It is morbidity unchained, our most base instincts let free, our nastiest fantasies realized . . . and it all happens, fittingly enough, in the dark. For those reasons, good liberals often shy away from horror films. For myself, I like to see the most aggressive of them—*Dawn of the Dead*, for instance—as lifting a trap door in the civilized forebrain and throwing a basket of raw meat to the hungry alligators swimming around in that subterranean river beneath.

Why bother? Because it keeps them from getting out, man. It keeps   13
them down there and me up here. It was Lennon and McCartney who said that all you need is love, and I would agree with that.

As long as you keep the gators fed.   14

• • • • • • • • • • • • • • • • • • • •

Examining the Text

1. How seriously do you think King expects readers to take his opening statement? What evidence does he offer to support his assertion? Does disagreeing with him here mean that you must automatically reject the rest of his argument about the appeal of horror movies?

2. King states that the horror movie is "innately conservative, even reactionary" (paragraph 4). Is he using these terms politically or in another sense? In what ways can horror movies be seen as "reactionary, anarchisitic, and revolutionary all at the same time" (11)?

3. King basically offers three reasons for the popularity of horror movies (3, 4, and 5–14); obviously the third is his main thesis. Summarize King's three reasons. Which do you find most persuasive, and why? Can you offer any other reasons?

4. King's tone throughout this essay is quite informal (it was originally published, by the way, in *Playboy* magazine). Find several examples that illustrate his informality and describe the overall effect.

For Group Discussion

For the sake of discussion, accept King's premise that we all have "anticivilization emotions" (11). List as a group some other things besides horror movies and "sick" jokes that we use to purge these emotions and "keep the gators fed." As a class, consider the extent to which these examples are products of contemporary society and what this suggests about how our psychic lives differ from those of people who lived a century or more ago.

Writing Suggestion

Consider several of your favorite horror movies. In an essay analyze these in light of King's theories about the horror genre's appeal. Do your examples support or disprove King's point about the daredevil, normative, and psychological functions of horror movies?

Monster Movies: A Sexual Theory

Walter Evans

*I*n an essay earlier in this chapter, Mark J. Schaefermeyer breaks film criticism down into three categories: semiotic critics look for signs and relationships among images in films; contextual critics examine movies in a specific context, focusing, for example, on a director's style or on a movie as a representative of a particular genre; and structuralists look at films from the per-

spective of a certain theory or belief system, whether mythic, political, psycho-
logical, or historical. Walter Evans, the author of the following essay, belongs
to the last of these camps. In "Monster Movies: A Sexual Theory," he relies on
a psychological approach to human sexual development to explain why mon-
ster movies are especially appealing to adolescents. Compared to Stephen King's
explanation, Evans's is both more limited and more detailed.

Evans's central thesis is that monster movies embody many of the power-
ful—and sometimes socially unacceptable—impulses that preoccupy teenagers
as they begin to mature, to experience unprecedented physical changes, and to
be pulled by unfamiliar drives and urges. "The key to monster movies and the
adolescents which understandably dote upon them," says Evans, "is the theme
of horrible and mysterious psychological and physical change; the most impor-
tant of these is the monstrous transformation . . . directly associated with sec-
ondary sexual characteristics and with the onset of aggressive erotic behavior."
Since most of those aggressive, animalistic impulses cannot be acted upon in
"civilized" society, Evans believes that monster movies serve as an outlet
through which teenagers can ritually act out those drives.

Evans relates each of the various aspects of the movie monster's aggressive
behavior to a specific adolescent erotic impulse or physical change—the onset
of menstruation, the impulse to masturbate, the drive to marry and to create
life. He then examines two specific film "monsters," Frankenstein and Drac-
ula, from this perspective. The former, he says, must "give up dangerous pri-
vate experiments on the human body" and learn to "deal safely and normally
with the 'secret of life,'" just as adolescents must move from secretive mastur-
batory practices to more socially acceptable forms of sexuality: marriage and child-
rearing. Similarly, Dracula is like an adolescent, thrust into "a world he does
not understand, torturing him with desires he cannot satisfy or even admit."

As you read these interpretations, consider your own intellectual re-
sponse to them: do you believe that Evans makes some valid points in using ado-
lescent developmental psychology to explain the attraction of monster movies,
or is he forcing his belief system on the genre?

• • • • • • • • • • • • • • • • • •

The key to monster movies and the adolescents which understand-   1
ably dote upon them is the theme of horrible and mysterious psychological and physical change; the most important of these is the monstrous
transformation which is directly associated with secondary sexual
characteristics and with the onset of aggressive erotic behavior.[1] The

---

[1] Though many critics focus on adult themes in monster movies, I believe that adolescents
provide the bulk of the audience for such films, particularly the classic films shown on late
night television all across America. Adolescents, of course, may be of any age.

Wolfman, for example, sprouts a heavy coat of hair, can hardly be contained within his clothing, and when wholly a wolf is, of course, wholly naked. Comparatively innocent and asexual females become, after contact with a vampire (his kiss redly marked on their necks) or werewolf (as in *Cry of the Werewolf*), quite sexy, aggressive, seductive—literally female "vamps" and "wolves."[2]

As adolescence is defined as "developing from childhood to maturity"[3] so the transformation is cinematically defined as movement from a state of innocence and purity associated with whiteness and clarity to darkness and obscurity associated with evil and threatening physical aggression. In the words of *The Wolfman's* gypsy:

> Even a man who is pure at heart
> And says his prayers by night
> May become a wolf when the wolfbane blooms
> And the moon is full and bright

The monsters are generally sympathetic, in large part because they themselves suffer the change as unwilling victims, all peace destroyed by the horrible physical and psychological alterations thrust upon them. Even Dracula, in a rare moment of self-revelation, is driven to comment: "To die, to be really dead. That must be glorious. . . . There are far worse things awaiting man, than death." Much suffering arises from the monster's overwhelming sense of alienation; totally an outcast, he painfully embodies the adolescent's nightmare of being hated and hunted by the society which he so desperately wishes to join.

Various aspects of the monster's attack are clearly sexual. The monster invariably prefers to attack individuals of the opposite sex, to attack them at night, and to attack them in their beds. The attack itself is specifically physical; Dracula, for instance, must be in immediate bodily contact with his victim to effect his perverted kiss; Frankenstein, the Wolfman, the Mummy, King Kong, have no weapons but their bodies. The aspect of the attack most disturbing to the monster, and perhaps most clearly sexual, is the choice of victim: "The werewolf instinctively seeks to kill the thing it loves best" (Dr. Yogami in *The Werewolf of London*).

---

[2] The transformation is less obvious, and perhaps for this reason more powerful, in *King Kong* (1933). Kong himself is safe while hidden deep in the prehistoric depths of Skull Island, but an unappeasable sexual desire (made explicit in the cuts restored in the film's most recent release) turns him into an enemy of civilization until, trapped on the world's hugest phallic symbol, he is destroyed. The psychological transformation of Ann Darrow (Fay Wray) is much more subtle. While alone immediately after exchanging vows of love with a tough sailor she closes her eyes and, as in a dream vision, above her appears the hideously savage face of a black native who takes possession of her in preparation for the riotous wedding to the great hairy ape. Significantly, only when civilization destroys the fearful, grossly physical beast is she finally able to marry the newly tuxedoed sailor.

[3] *Webster's New World Dictionary of the American Language*, 2nd College Edition (Englewood Cliffs, N.J.: Prentice-Hall, 1970). Interesting, in view of the fiery death of Frankenstein's monster and others, is one of the earlier meanings of the root word: "be kindled, burn."

Dracula's Mina Seward must attack her fiance, John. The Mummy must physically possess the body of the woman in whom his spiritual bride has been reincarnated. Even more disturbing are the random threats to children scattered throughout the formula, more disturbing largely because the attacks are so perversely sexual and addressed to beings themselves soon destined for adolescence.

The effects of the attack may be directly related to adolescent sexual 5 experimentation. The aggressor is riddled with shame, guilt, and anguish; the victim, once initiated, is generally transformed into another aggressor.[4] Regaining innocence before death seems, in the best films, almost as inconceivable as retrieving virginity.

Many formulaic elements of the monster movies have affinities with 6 two central features of adolescent sexuality, masturbation and menstruation. From time immemorial underground lore has asserted that masturbation leads to feeblemindedness or mental derangement; the monster's transformation is generally associated with madness; scientists are generally secretive recluses whose private experiments on the human body have driven them mad. Masturbation is also widely (and, of course, fallaciously) associated with "weakness of the spine," a fact which helps explain not only Fritz of *Frankenstein* but the army of feebleminded hunchbacks which pervades the formula. The Wolfmen, and sometimes Dracula, are identifiable (as, according to underground lore, masturbating boys may be identified) by hairy palms.

Ernest Jones explains the vampire myth largely in terms of a mys- 7 terious physical and psychological development which startles many adolescents, nocturnal emissions: "A nightly visit from a beautiful or frightful being, who first exhausts the sleeper with passionate embraces and then withdraws from him a vital fluid: all this can point only to a natural and common process, namely to nocturnal emissions accompanied with dreams of a more or less erotic nature. In the unconscious mind blood is commonly an equivalent for semen. . . ."[5] The vampire's bloodletting of women who suddenly enter full sexuality, the werewolf's bloody attacks—which occur regularly every month—are certainly related to the menstrual cycle which suddenly and mysteriously commands the body of every adolescent girl.

Monster movies characteristically involve another highly significant 8 feature which may initially seem irrelevant to the theme of sexual change: the faintly philosophical struggle between reason and the darker emotional truths. Gypsies, superstitious peasants, and others associated

---

[4] It is interesting, and perhaps significant that the taint of vampirism and lycanthropy have an aura of sin and shame not unlike that of VD. The good doctor who traces the taint, communicable only through direct physical contact, back to the original carrier is not unlike a physician fighting VD.

[5] See Ernest Jones, "On the Nightmare of Bloodsucking" in *Focus on the Horror Film*, 59.

with the imagination eternally triumph over smugly conventional rationalists who ignorantly deny the possible existence of walking mummies, stalking vampires, and bloodthirsty werewolves. The audience clearly sympathizes with those who realize the limits of reason, of convention, of security; for the adolescent's experiences with irrational desires, fears, urges which are incomprehensible yet clearly stronger than the barriers erected by reason or by society, are deeper and more painful than adults are likely to realize. Stubborn reason vainly struggles to deny the adolescent's most private experiences, mysterious and dynamic conflicts between normal and abnormal, good and evil, known and unknown.

Two of the most important features normally associated with monster movies are the closely related searches for the "secret of life" and "that which man was not meant to know." Monster movies unconsciously exploit the fact that most adolescents already know the "secret of life" which is, indeed, the "forbidden knowledge" of sex. The driving need to master the "forbidden knowledge" of "the secret of life," a need which seems to increase in importance as the wedding day approaches, is closely related to a major theme of monster movies: marriage.   9

For the adolescent audience the marriage which looms just beyond the last reel of the finer monster movies is much more than a mindless cliche wrap-up. As the monster's death necessarily precedes marriage and a happy ending, so the adolescent realizes that a kind of peace is to be obtained only with a second transformation. Only marriage can free Henry Frankenstein from his perverted compulsion for private experimentation on the human body; only marriage can save Mina Harker after her dalliance with the count. Only upon the death of adolescence, the mysterious madness which has possessed them, can they enter into a mature state where sexuality is tamed and sanctified by marriage.[6] The marriage theme, and the complex interrelationship of vari-   10

---

[6] In "The Child and the Book," *Only Connect,* Sheila Egoff, ed., G.T. Stubbs, and L.F. Ashley (New York: Oxford UP, 1969) noted psychiatrist Anthony Storr has discussed a precursor of monster movies, fairy tales, in a similar context.

Why is it that the stories which children enjoy are so often full of horror? We know that from the very beginning of life the child possesses an inner world of fantasy and the fantasies of the child mind are by no means the pretty stories with which the prolific Miss Blyton regales us. They are both richer and more primitive, and the driving forces behind them are those of sexuality and the aggressive urge to power: the forces which ultimately determine the emergence of the individual as a separate entity. For, in the long process of development, the child has two main tasks to preform if he is to reach maturity. He has to prove his strength, and he has to win a mate; and in order to do this he has to overcome the obstacles of his infantile dependency upon, and his infantile erotic attachment to, his parents. . . . The typical fairy story ends with the winning of the princess just as the typical Victorian novel ends with the marriage. It is only at this point that adult sexuality begins. . . . It is not surprising that fairy stories should be both erotic and violent, or that they should appeal so powerfully to children. For the archetyal themes with which they deal mirror the contents of the childish psyche; and the same unconscious source gives origin to both the fairy tale and the fantasy life of the child." (93–4)

ous other formulaic elements, may perhaps be best approached through a close analysis of two seminal classics, *Frankenstein* and *Dracula*.

Two events dominate the movie *Frankenstein* (1931), creation of the monster and celebration of the marriage of Henry Frankenstein and his fiancee Elizabeth. The fact that the first endangers the second provides for most of the conflict throughout the movie, conflict much richer and more powerful, perhaps even profound, when the key thematic relationship between the two is made clear: creation of life. As Frankenstein's perverse nightly experiments on the monstrous body hidden beneath the sheets are centered on the creation of life, so is the marriage, as the old Baron twice makes clear in a toast (once immediately after the monster struggles out of the old mill and begins wandering toward an incredible meeting with Henry's fiancee Elizabeth; again, after the monster is destroyed, in the last speech of the film): "Here's to a son to the House of Frankenstein!"[7]

Frankenstein's fatuous father, whose naive declarations are frequently frighteningly prescient (he predicts the dancing peasants will soon be fighting; on seeing a torch in the old mill he asks if Henry is trying to burn it down), declares, when hearing of the extent to which his son's experiments are taking precedence over his fiancee: "I understand perfectly well. Must be another woman. Pretty sort of experiments they must be." Later, after receiving the burgomaster's beaming report on the village's preparations for celebration of the marriage, he again associates his son's experiments with forbidden sexuality: "There is another woman. And I'm going to find her."

There is, of course, no other woman. The movie's horror is fundamentally based on the fact that the monster's life has come without benefit of a mother's womb. At one point Frankenstein madly and pointedly gloats over his solitary, specifically manual, achievements: "the brain of a dead man, ready to live again in a body I made with my hands, my own hands!"

Significantly, a troubled search for the "secret of life" is what keeps Henry Frankenstein separated from his fiancee; it literally proves impossible for Henry to provide for "a son to the House of Frankenstein" before he has discovered the "secret of life." Having discovered the "secret of life," he ironically discovers that its embodiment is a frightening monster horrible enough to threaten "normal" relations between himself and Elizabeth. Henry's attempt to lock the monster deep in the mill's nether regions are finally thwarted, and, in a wholly irrational and dramatically inexplicable (yet psychologically apt and profound) scene, the monster—a grotesque embodiment of Frankenstein's newly discovered

11

12

13

14

---

[7] The dialogue is followed by a close-up of a painfully embarrassed Henry Frankenstein.

sexuality—begins to move threateningly toward the innocent bride who is bedecked in the purest of white, then quite as irrationally, it withdraws. On his return Henry promises his wildly distracted fiancee that there will be no wedding "while this horrible creation of mine is still alive."

The monster is, of course, finally, pitilessly, destroyed,[8] and Henry is only ready for marriage when his own body is horribly battered and weakened, when he is transformed from the vigorous, courageous, inspired hero he represented early in the film to an enervated figure approaching the impotent fatuity of his father and grandfather (there is plenty of fine wine for the wedding feast, Frankenstein's grandmother would never allow grandfather to drink any), prepared to renounce abnormal life as potent as the monster in favor of creating a more normal "son to the House of Frankenstein."   15

The message is clear. In order to lead a normal, healthy life, Henry Frankenstein must—and can—give up dangerous private experiments on the human body in dark rooms hidden away from family and friends. He must learn to deal safely and normally with the "secret of life," however revolting, however evil, however it might seem to frighten and actually threaten pure, virgin womanhood; only then, in the enervated bosom of normality, is it possible to marry and to produce an acceptable "son to the House of Frankenstein."   16

Dracula's much more mature approach to womankind is clearly aimed at psyches which have overcome Henry Frankenstein's debilitating problem. *Dracula* (1931), obviously enough, is a seduction fantasy vitally concerned with the conditions and consequences of premarital indulgence in forbidden physical relations with attractive members of the opposite sex.   17

Of all the movie monsters Dracula seems to be the most attractive to women, and his appeal is not difficult to understand, for he embodies the chief characteristics of the standard Gothic hero: tall, dark, hand-   18

---

[8] Significantly, the monster himself is pitifully sympathetic, suffering as adolescents believe only they can suffer, from unattractive physical appearance, bodies they don't understand, repulsed attempts at love, general misunderstanding. Though endowed by his single antagonistic parent with a "criminal brain," the monster is clearly guilty of little but ugliness and ignorance, and is by any terms less culpable than the normal human beings surrounding him. He does not so much murder Fritz as attempt to defend himself against completely unwarranted torchings and beatings; he kills Dr. Valdeman only after that worthy believes he has "painlessly destroyed" the monster (a euphemism for murder), and as the doctor is preparing to dissect him; the homicide which propels his destruction, the drowning of the little girl, is certainly the result of clumsiness and ignorance. She had taught him to sail flowers on the lake and, flowers failing, in a visual metaphor worthy of an Elizabethan courtier, the monster in his ignorant joy had certainly meant only for the girl, the only being who had ever shown him not only love, but even affection, to sail on the lake as had the flowers. His joyful lurch toward her after having sailed his flower is, beyond all doubt, the most pathetic and poignant lurch in the history of film.

some, titled, wealthy, cultured, attentive, mannered, with an air of command, an aura of sin and secret suffering; perhaps most important of all he is invariably impeccably dressed. With such a seductive and eligible male around it is certainly no wonder that somewhere in the translation from fiction to film Dr. Seward has become Mina's father and thus leaves Lucy, who also lost the two other suitors Bram Stoker allowed her, free to accept the Count's attentions. Certainly any woman can sympathize with Lucy's swift infatuation ("Laugh all you like, I think he's fascinating.") and Mina's easy acceptance of Dracula as her friend's suitor ("Countess, I'll leave you to your count, and your ruined abbey.").

Having left three wives behind in Transylvania, Dracula is obviously not one to be sated with his second English conquest (the first was an innocent flower girl, ravaged immediately before he meets Lucy and Mina), and he proceeds to seduce Mina, working a change in her which does not go unnoticed, or unappreciated, by her innocent fiance: "Mina, you're so—like a changed girl. So wonderful—." Mina agrees that indeed she is changed, and, on the romantic terrace, alone with her fiance beneath the moon and stars, begins, one is certain, the first physical aggression of their courtship. John is suitably impressed. "I'm so glad to see you like this!" Discovered and exposed by Professor Van Helsing, Mina can only admit that (having had relations with Dracula and thus become a Vamp) she has, indeed, suffered the proverbial fate worse than death, and shamefully alerts her innocent, naive fiance: "John, you must go away from me."   19

Only when John and his older, respected helpmate foil the horrible mock elopement—Dracula and Mina are rushing to the abbey preparing to "sleep," he even carries her limp body across the abbey's threshold—only when the castrating stake destroys the seducer and with him the maid's dishonor, is Mina free to return to the honest, innocent, suitor who will accept her past, marry her in the public light of day, and make an honest woman of her.   20

Lucy, who has no selfless suitor to forgive her, marry her, and make an honest woman of her, is much less successful. When last seen she has become a child molester, a woman of the night who exchanges chocolate for horrible initiations.   21

The thematic importance of such innocent victims turned monster as Lucy and Mina, Dr. Frankenstein's creation, King Kong, the Wolfman and others points directly to one of the most commonly observed and perhaps least understood phenomena of monster movies, one which has been repeatedly noted in this paper. In those classics which are best loved and closest to true art the audience clearly identifies with the monster. Child, adult or adolescent, in disembodied sympathetic fascination, we all watch the first Karloff Frankenstein who stumbles with   22 adolescent clumsiness, who suffers the savage misunderstanding and rejection of both society and the creator whose name he bears, and whose fumbling and innocent attempts at love with the little girl by the lakeside turn to terrible, bitter, and mysterious tragedy.

Clearly the monster offers the sexually confused adolescent a sympathetic, and at best a tragic, imitation of his life by representing a mysterious and irreversible change which forever isolates him from what he identifies as normality, security, and goodness, a change thrusting him into a world he does not understand, torturing him with desires he cannot satisfy or even admit, a world in which dark psychological and strange physical changes seem to conspire with society to destroy him.   23

••••••••••••••••••••

Examining the Text

1. In his first footnote, Evans states his belief that "adolescents provide the bulk of the audience" for monster movies. Do you think this is so? Why, according to Evans, are adolescents especially drawn to monster movies? In what ways do movie monsters reflect adolescent problems and concerns? Do you find Evans's evidence convincing?

2. Evans wrote this essay in 1975, drawing all his examples from classic monster movies of the 1930s and 1940s: the Wolfman, Frankenstein, Dracula, the Mummy, King Kong. What do these have in common, and what do they represent for Evans? Is his thesis generally supported by more contemporary movie monsters—Jason, Freddy Krueger, Chuckie, and others? Or might they suggest some evolution in adolescent sexuality since Evans's generation?

3. One of Evans's main points is that in classic monster movies, which, he says "are best loved and the closest to true art, the audience clearly identifies with the monster" (paragraph 22). Do you agree? Does this hold true for contemporary movie monsters? Why or why not?

For Group Discussion

Taking into account Stephen King's ideas about the appeal of horror movies as well as Evans's connection of monster movies to adolescent sexuality, broaden your scope to include both classic and contemporary examples and then, as a group, explain why adolescents seem to be particularly attracted to monster/horror movies. Bring your own knowledge of such movies and first-hand experience and observation of adolescent behavior into the discussion. As a class, see if you can agree on a ranking of your reasons.

Writing Suggestion
    Apply a psychological critical model to another genre of film with which you are familiar, such as futuristic action pictures, *Airplane-* or *Naked Gun*-style satires, menaced-female thrillers, bratty-kid comedies, *Rambo*-esque revenge stories, and so on. In an essay, account for that genre's popularity by discussing its specific appeals to an audience's basic emotional needs. Like Evans, you may want to focus on a specific audience with which your genre seems most popular.

Nightmare on Elm Street: A Review and a Cultural Analysis

*A*s Mark J. Schaefermeyer suggested in an essay earlier in this chapter, *movie reviewing and film criticism are not the same thing. Film criticism, such as the pieces in this chapter by Walter Evans and Richard Dyer, generally appears in scholarly journals whose readers are primarily academics at universities, along with serious filmmakers. Movie reviews appear in popular magazines, newspapers, and broadcast media and are aimed at the general public, with the purpose of entertaining people and letting them know whether they'd enjoy a movie. Popular periodicals also may offer articles that attempt to put movies in a social or cultural context.*

The first of the following newspaper pieces is a review by Stephen Hunter of the Baltimore Sun *of A* Nightmare on Elm Street 5: The Dream Child, *which discusses its plot twists, set designs, and gory sequences in an amusing, ironic way. As his central thesis, Hunter states, "I'm proud to report that as a professional moviegoer of many years standing, I have no idea what was going on in the movie"—and he means this as a compliment. In the second article, Douglas Heuck of the* Pittsburgh Press *goes beyond a simple review of the* Nightmare on Elm Street *films to make some serious points about their influence on the broader popular culture: Freddy Krueger—the wise-cracking, child-murdering monster in these films—has become a cult figure, and several real crimes have been "inspired" by Krueger (although Heuck is careful to avoid suggesting that the* Nightmare on Elm Street *films "caused" these crimes).*

*Heuck's article leads necessarily to a question: Do contemporary pop-cultural artifacts, especially those that receive wide media dissemination, influence people's behavior to the point that they will actually commit antisocial acts? **Before you read,** consider your own position with regard to this question. Do you believe, for example, that Jeffrey Dahmer was inspired to commit his gruesome mass murders because he saw too many "Nightmare on Elm Street" films, or do believe he would have committed those crimes without Freddy's influence?*

• • • • • • • • • • • • • • • • • • • •

Review of *Nightmare on Elm Street 5*
Stephen Hunter

It turns out that all along, all you've had to do to stop Freddy 1
Krueger, the razor-digited, pizza-complexioned, fedora-crowned mad-
man of the "Nightmare on Elm Street" series, is what you do to any bad
boy. You tell his mother.

That's the gist of *A Nightmare on Elm Street 5: The Dream Child*, 2
which opened Friday on about a zillion screens. And gist is all you're
going to get out of me, friends. If the Freddies of the past have been
dense in their narrative lines, this one is so packed it's close to critical
mass. The plot may go nuclear at any second. I'm proud to report that
as a professional moviegoer of many years standing, I have no idea what
was going on in the movie.

That's by design, actually. What has propelled the "Elm Street" 3
movies and made them consistently the most watchable—the only
watchable—entrants in the various serial slaughterfests that seem to so
beguile American teen-agers has been their high level of visual ingenu-
ity, their willingness to punch through the membrane of the literal and
to take up space in the crazed precincts of the completely surrealistic.

"The Dream Child" certainly hews to the line. It's not a story so 4
much as a pageant, a dark tapestry of horrific—but always fascinating—
murders. What the Freddy films have done is restored abstract beauty
to movie mayhem, rescuing it from the utter banality into which it had
fallen in such routine atrocities as the "Fridays the 13th" and "Hal-
loweens"—but at the expense of coherence. The set pieces in the film are
like murder videos.

As "The Dream Child" has it, Freddy (Robert Englund) is back for 5
still a fifth time to haunt the kids of Elm Street, this time selecting the
nubile Alice (Lisa Wilcox) as his main squeeze in that he continually
uses her as bait to draw her friends closer so that he can dispatch them
in spectacular ways.

But at the same time, she's flashing back (somehow) to his past and 6
origins, and comes to realize that he's the son of a nun raped by a thousand maniacs in an asylum one very long evening, and that the nun may
still be alive in the deserted ruins of the joint, which look more or less
like the Spanish city of Seville in the year 1456.

To everybody's perpetual confusion, it now seems that Freddy can 7
kill outside of dreams as well as in them; so you never know whether
you're in dreamland or on Elm Street or at some weird fusing of both or
neither. I don't even think the director, Stephen Hopkins, knew; but I
don't think he cared much, either.

What's left is operatic mayhem, much of it spectacular. The main in- 8
fluence on director Hopkins appears to have been M. C. Escher, the
Dutch genius of geometrical paradox and oxymoron, for Hopkins' best
tricks are to warp perspective in mind-bending ways, creating a world
where gravity is the most treacherous illusion of all. In the best of the sequences, a teen-age boy who's a comic artist is somehow sucked into the
world of his own comic books, becomes a two-dimensional picture in
black and white, and is set upon and destroyed by a two-dimensional
Freddy. In another, a motorcycle becomes some poisoned nightbloom
that actually penetrates the body of its rider and becomes one with
him.

As Alice's friends keep dying, she struggles to understand the rid- 9
dle, and then to enlist Mother Freddy in the quest to end Freddy and the
movie. I couldn't begin to make sense of the climax; it was like watching an Italian opera directed by an evil 12-year-old genius who had
nothing but contempt for his audience and an unlimited budget. But I'll
tell you this: If this sucker pulled in more than $8 million this weekend,
he'll be ba-ack.

Freddy Krueger: Twisted Role Model?

Douglas Heuck

'Freddy' Debate Lives On: Pop Icon or Twisted Role Model?

Long, long ago, in a place called Hollywood, a relatively unknown 1
actor named Robert Englund won a role in a low-budget slasher film. To
prepare for the role of bogyman Freddy Krueger, Englund came up with
this vision of his character:

"Lee Harvey Oswald smoking a cigarette, saying 'Want some candy, 2
little girl?'" he told a reporter. "Freddy has a cocky, arrogant, sexual way
of moving."

From that image of distortion, who could have guessed that Freddy 3
would become the star of six movies, have his own TV show, gross about
$460 million, and—trick-or-treat—receive civic honors?

It all happened, though, even the last part. Los Angeles Mayor Tom 4
Bradley last month declared Freddy Krueger Day, an honor reserved for
entities that "benefit the people of Los Angeles or deserve praise," Bradley's press secretary said.

From mere script character to wisecracking child-murderer to Amer- 5
ican cult hero—Freddy has come a long way.

There's the Freddy board game and Nintendo video game. There 6
have been two Freddy rap songs and a couple of Freddy books. And
Freddy T-shirts, mini caskets, buttons, towels, fedoras, sweaters,
sheets—you name it.

And there is the 30-minute MTV special released last month, "Slash 7
and Burn: The Freddy Krueger Story."

Including the last film, "Freddy's Dead, The Final Nightmare," 8
which opened last month, the series has had such actors as Dick Cavett,
Zsa Zsa Gabor, Johnny Depp and Roseanne Barr. And aside from having teen fans across the world, the dream stalker also included Malcolm
Forbes among his admirers.

Many people think the whole fascination with a murdering mad- 9
man is sick. Many others feel it's just harmless fun.

But now that the Sultan of Slash and his switchblade fingers are 10
gone, killed off for good, we're told, in the final movie, what will be the
legacy of Freddy?

Part of it will be clear when children throughout Western Pennsyl- 11
vania set out for Halloween this week, wearing $14.99 Freddy knife-
gloves and $29.99 masks.

Other parts are a matter of debate. Although Freddy attacks through 12
dreams and is clearly a fantasy character, some fans have committed real
crimes since the first Freddy movie, "Nightmare on Elm Street" debuted:

- In 1989 in Pittsburgh, a fast-food worker with an obsession with
  Krueger stabbed and bludgeoned to death Dr. Jeffrey Farkas, a
  promising pediatric intern.
- In 1988, a 15-year-old North Carolina boy who was obsessed with
  Freddy was convicted for killing his father with multiple shotgun
  blasts. He was wearing a Freddy costume when he was arrested.
- In 1989, a 19-year-old man from San Pedro, Calif., who dressed up
  as Freddy while committing crimes was convicted of murder.
- The same year, an ax-wielding man in Cedar Rapids, Iowa, shouted
  he was Freddy Krueger and charged two police officers, who shot
  him.
- Also in 1989, a Virginia girl who said she loves what Freddy
  Krueger does attempted to strangle a 13-year-old boy. It was the
  third time she attempted to strangle small boys. She said it was fun.
- And finally, People magazine reported in August that alleged
  Milwaukee mass murderer Jeffrey Dahmer was "fascinated" by
  "Nightmare on Elm Street."

The effects of television and film violence are greatly debated. 13
Groups like the National Coalition on Television Violence see a cause
and effect relationship.

Others dispute that claim. Among them are Michael DeLuca, 26-   14
year-old vice president for New Line Cinemas, which made Freddy.

"I think most of the people making those claims have either never   15
seen the Elm Street films, or they've seen them and not understood
them," said DeLuca, who wrote the script for the final movie.

"None of the films are gratuitous in their depiction of violence. Most   16
of it is fantasy-oriented—you're in a dream universe."

DeLuca said he had never heard of cases where Freddy fans com-   17
mitted crimes. When he was made aware of a few, though, he said, "If
it wasn't Freddy, they'd dress up as something else."

"It's much easier to blame a movie or TV show than to accept the   18
blame that through child abuse or whatever, parents created this creature."

Research contradicts DeLuca, according to Dr. Joseph Strayhorn, as-   19
sociate professor of child psychiatry at the Medical College of Pennsylvania and director of the early childhood clinic at Allegheny General
Hospital.

"The research evidence is very convincing to me that there is a cause   20
and effect relationship between exposure to violence in the media and
actual violent behavior in human beings," said Strayhorn, who is a member of NCTV.

Strayhorn called DeLuca's claim that there is no gratuitous violence   21
in the "Nightmare on Elm Street" movies "absurd."

"The whole point of the movie is gratuitous violence, at least that   22
was it in the one I saw," he said.

"And lots of younger children see them. Once movies like this are   23
on videotapes, 2½-year-old children are very capable of running videotape machines themselves. Once the video revolution occurred, the concept of an 'intended audience' went out the window."

The issue is not as clear-cut for Larry Cohn, motion picture editor at   24
Variety magazine in New York.

"It's a tough question. I'm not a great believer in cause and effect of   25
this stuff. I do think popular culture is important, but more as a backdrop, as an ether in which we live.

"People want to turn on TV and have that immediate gratification   26
of seeing someone's head blown off. That's a shame, but you can't go
back. That's sensationalism. People like that, and that's a problem."

Laying the blame at the feet of Freddy Krueger, however, ignores   27
his precursors, Cohn said.

Before the 1970s, horror movies were generally the domain of the   28
horror fan, said Cohn.

"But 15 years later, everybody's into it. Horror became in some   29
way embraced and acceptable in the same way that pornography is

acceptable. Horror became in the mainstream," he said, citing such other movies as "When a Stranger Calls," "Halloween" and "Friday the 13th."

By 1984, when the first "Nightmare on Elm Street" came out, the   30
horror boom was mostly over, and, as Cohn said, "since then only the strong have survived. Freddy is the last survivor."

The reason Freddy survived was quality, according to Anthony Tim-   31
pone, editor of the horror magazine Fangoria. "It's the first horror film in a long time to introduce a memorable horror figure. It's one of the most original horror films, with the dreams and nightmares."

For whatever reason, Freddy is indisputably large in the line of hor-   32
ror creatures.

"Traditionally, you had the literary horror figures, like Dracula and   33
Frankenstein," Cohn said. "Freddy is the closest to joining that group in years, since, perhaps 'Psycho.'"

Freddy has been more successful than Jason of "Friday the 13th"   35
and Michael Meyers of "Halloween" because he's a more full-bodied and personal character.

"And he's more sadistic because he's more personal" Cohn said.   36

"To me, the sadism is the key to all this. The whole idea of people   37
identifying with sadists is a new phenomenon. In earlier horror, people would identify with the woman. For instance, in 'The Phantom of the Opera,' people—including myself—would identify with the woman when he takes his mask off. This was the old way."

James Bond, Clint Eastwood and Charles Bronson were the three   38
main breakthrough figures in making sadism in the movies more acceptable, Cohn said, because the good guys were the sadists.

"Bond was the first acceptable sadistic character" because he could   39
kill someone, or at least beat up someone, and throw in a wisecrack while doing it. Freddy also is a master of the one-liner.

"Freddy is the spiritual heir to that. And that's sadistic, making fun   40
of the killing. Freddy is the bad guy, but he's not if people idolize him and make him into a cultural figure."

However, to Cohn, whether Freddy Krueger has become an icon is   41
not very significant.

"These movies are a product of planned obsolescence. Their pur-   42
pose is to be consumed and to get out of the way of the next one. The horror film is almost an endangered species now. It's burned itself out."

Beverly Hills–based script consultant and media psychiatrist Dr.   43
Carole Lieberman has a different view.

"It's a sorry commentary on the state of youth and young adults in   44
America that more of them know Freddy Krueger than some of the presidents.

"The fact that we have raised a figure like Freddy Krueger to become   45
an icon of society and have that be reflected in his best-selling Halloween costumes is an indication of how our society has come to worship violence."

Dr. Lieberman said high school youths particularly like the films be-   46
cause high school youths are the ones who get killed—especially the
more popular and attractive students.

"To dress up like Freddy Krueger makes them feel powerful, as if   47
they could destroy their objects of envy."

Dr. Lieberman believes more Freddy movies will be made.   48

"But even if they don't make anymore movies, he's not going to dis-   49
appear. There are always videotapes."

Just think of the blend: Nintendo, MTV, Roseanne Barr, rap mu   50
sic, Malcolm Forbes, TV, the movies and Freddy Krueger—a distinctly
American "Nightmare."

· · · · · · · · · · · · · · · · · · · ·

Examining the Text

1. Stephen Hunter suggests that *Nightmare on Elm Street 5: The Dream Child* is virtually incomprehensible, but goes on to say that the "dense narrative line" of the movie is a quality that sets the *Nightmare* movies apart from other "serial slaughterfests" (paragraph 3). What is Hunter praising about these movies? If you have seen any of them, do you find his comments justified? If you haven't, does his review make you want to? Why or why not?

2. Like any good reporter, Douglas Heuck balances his article by including different viewpoints regarding the relationship between violent films like *Nightmare on Elm Street* and actual crime in our society. Identify each of these. Which do you find most convincing? Why?

3. Specifically, how do these two newspaper articles define the appeal of Freddy Krueger? If you are familiar with the *Nightmare on Elm Street* movies—or have friends or children who are fans—how would you explain the movies' appeal, and how do your ideas compare with Hunter's and Heuck's?

For Group Discussion

Based on your reading of Stephen King, Walter Evans, and the two previous articles and your own viewing experiences, work together to develop a "treatment" for the first in a series of successful new horror/monster movies. Define the prime audience for the movie; devise one or more monsters of villains and describe him/her/it/them in detail; create a cast of non-monster characters; decide on a setting; and roughly outline a plot. Have a recorder present your "treatment" to the rest of the class. Be prepared to justify your choices by discussing the assumptions you made about your movie's audience.

Writing Suggestion

Choose a new film that you have seen recently or that you can see soon, and write a newspaper-style article about it. You may review it as Hunter does *Nightmare on Elm Street* (focusing directly on the merits of the film itself as you work to entertain and be witty as well as informative), or you may write a discursive article, like Heuck's, that focuses more broadly on responses to the film and its potential influences.

Dracula and Desire

Richard Dyer

Ever since Bram Stoker's classic novel, Dracula, *appeared in 1897, the image of that archetypal, bloodsucking anti-hero has haunted the public consciousness. Stage and film versions have reached a wide audience. There were the early silents, the original talkie with Bela Lugosi, numerous low-budget Hollywood sequels, a series of over-produced British variations by the Hammer studios in the 1960s, and, most recently, Francis Ford Coppola's 1992* Bram Stoker's Dracula, *which Richard Dyer reviews in the following article.*

Dyer offers a variety of ways to interpret the Dracula story in general and Coppola's film in particular. One possibility is "the attraction and terror of sexuality," including the spectre of AIDS; another is in terms of "the vampire as the old world, old Europe, Eastern Europe, leeching off modern, industrialising Western Europe (and North America)." The story may also be viewed in terms of gender roles, Christian iconography, and/or how we are distanced from and yet identify with the vampire.

It is this last mode of interpretation that ultimately leads Dyer to his own judgment of Coppola's film. Approaching vampire stories specifically from a gay perspective, Dyer's critical stance arises from "a queer reading of vampirism;" from this perspective, Bram Stoker's Dracula *fails. Coppola's "dominant image of the vampire, so commandingly virile, so unerringly straight" is, he says, "not what I want from vampires." What he admires, rather, are vampire movies such as* Kiss of the Vampire *(1965) and* Daughters of Darkness *(1970) because those vampires have a "marginalised, sexualised identity . . . despicable as well as defiant, shameful as well as unashamed."*

As you read, consider the extent to which your gender and sexuality influence your response to and analysis of films and other products of popular cul-

ture. Do you think an author should be expected to make these personal perspectives explicit when commenting on popular culture?

•••••••••••••••••••

The cinema was packed. Tom and I took the first two seats together 1
we could find and I didn't take notice of whom I was sitting next to. We
were in any case too engrossed in unguarded conversation to be bothered. It was freezing outside, but hot in the cinema, so we had to take
off successive layers of clothing. I was just starting to struggle out of a
pullover when the person sitting next to me gave my knee a sharp
knock. I turned in surprise and he hissed, "There's no need to keep rubbing your leg against mine." I was so startled by this sudden eruption
of homophobia that I immediately went into politeness overdrive. I was
sorry. I really hadn't realised. And throughout the film I kept my body
tensed away from him, lest my relaxed knee inadvertently touch his
dreary thigh. Perhaps it was only this that made me feel alienated from
the new *Dracula,* but I suspect also that Coppola's Stoker's vampires are
not my vampires, not by any means queer.

There is no doubt that Bram Stoker's *Dracula,* which the new film 2
follows so fully, is the literary *locus classicus* of the vampire. Huge
though the corpus of vampire tales is, the character of Dracula dominates. His is probably the only vampire's name most people know: it
sells holiday tours and images of dictatorship in Romania, it is used in
the titles of films in which he does not appear (such as *Dracula's Daughter* and *Brides of Dracula*). Dracula is the vampire *par excellence.* Yet, admirable and fascinating as much of Stoker's novel is, I prefer Sheridan
LeFanu's "Carmilla," or Richard Matheson's *I Am Legend,* or above all
Anne Rice's *Interview with the Vampire* and its sequels. Similarly in films,
I prefer non-Draculas like the aforementioned *Daughter, Kiss of the Vampire, Daughters of Darkness,* or *Near Dark,* or those that only take Stoker's
Dracula as a point of departure (Murnau's *Nosferatu,* Bela Lugosi's incarnations, Peter Sasdy's *Taste the Blood of Dracula*). The new *Dracula* is
not of these.

Francis Ford Coppola and scriptwriter James V. Hart have, as the 3
credit that opens the film, "Bram Stoker's *Dracula*" suggests, indeed
gone back to Stoker. In terms of inclusion of incidents and characters,
there is more left of the novel here than in any previous film version,
with the possible exception of the 1970 Spanish *El Conde Dracula* (Jesús
Franco). To the now well-trod lines of Jonathan Harker's visit to Transylvania and Dracula's coming to England to wreak havoc on Harker's
friends and relatives are added elements that have only occasionally
appeared in previous versions (the character of the Texan, Quincy P.

Morris; the pursuit of Dracula back to Transylvania finally to ensnare him). The one substantial new element added to this, a prologue explaining how Vlad the Impaler became Dracula, gives a particular inflection to the story, but remains true to the project: it is well known that Vlad was an inspiration to Stoker.

The manner of telling also owes more than usual to Stoker. The use 4 of multiple narrative strands (Jonathan and Mina, Lucy and her beaux, the asylum, Van Helsing) is sustained in the novel, until two-thirds of the way through, when it is ironed out into a linear, much less engrossing stalk-and-kill climax. The film also makes a stab at retaining the novel's multiple points of view, with sequences inaugurated by voiceovers, captions and visuals that link the subsequent events to a particular character's perspective. Care is even taken with the novel's emphasis on different ways of telling, both formal modes (diaries, letters, news stories) and media (handwriting, typing, cylinder recording). To the latter is added reference to the cinematograph, not as a source of the story we are seeing, but as something that Dracula himself has recourse to in his seduction of Mina.

Coppola's *Dracula* flings itself at all this narrative material, emerg- 5 ing like a music video directed by Dario Argento. As in a video, narrativity comes at you in snatches, more a suggestion of connected incidents across a welter of vivid imagery than a fully presented plot. As in Argento's *Suspiria,* say, or some other post-60s horror movies like Sam Raimi's *The Evil Dead,* narrative, and with it the pleasures of tease and suspense, are unimportant; it's the maelstrom of sensation that matters. This means that the story may be hard to follow if you either haven't read Stoker's *Dracula* or have a less than total recall of it (I remembered who Renfield and Quincy were, but it goes so fast that I had a hard time figuring out how and why at the end Mina gets to Transylvania before her menfolk). With *Suspiria* or *The Evil Dead,* this doesn't matter too much since there's so little plot anyway, and it may not matter with this *Dracula* either. The point, perhaps, was not to do Stoker in full-blooded re-creation, but simply to allude to as much as possible of the book while getting on with the business of creating a particular feeling and exploring the connotations of the Dracula idea.

As to the feeling, Coppola has certainly achieved something dis- 6 tinctive. Always one of cinema's great colourists, he has here come up with a symphony in engulfing red and black. The prologue is shot in near-silhouette, black on red, setting the colour key signature for the film. Early sequences in Victorian England are anaemically coloured, gradually to be swallowed by red and black, vermilion and pitch, blood and the night. I am not the first to have reached for 'engorgement' as a word to describe the film. It's not just the redness of blood swelling the film's climaxes, but the fullness of the image, bursting to the edge of the frame with thick colour and dense visual texture. Most remarkably, it's in the vampires' costuming, most voluminous when they are most needy. They look bloated with lust, and yet move then with greatest speed and ease, gliding not walking, as if motored by the desperate urgency of desire. When Lucy has become a vampire, she is dressed entirely in white, with bridal lace and fold upon fold of silk, and her face too is pale as death; yet her shrouded body rears up turgidly, the lace ruffs round her neck are puffed like a monstrous lizard, even her cheeks seem fuller. Even without the red, she is the embodiment of engorgement.

To this stunning—and wearying—feeling, Coppola adds many of the connotations of vampirism. The vampire motif always has something to do with the idea of a being, or way of being, that literally lives off another. It was born (in the early nineteenth century) of a society increasingly conscious of interdependency, while losing that firm sense of fixed, rightful, social hierarchy that had concealed dependency; in short, it was born of industrial capitalist democracy. The vampire idea deals in the terror of recognising, challenging or being challenged by dependency, and always registers this through the body; the dependencies of its needs and drives, especially, but not exclusively, sexuality. Like all long-lived popular cultural ideas, innumerable variations can be played on this basic concept, its vivid iconography and compelling narrative patterns. Folklorists stress the fear of the living that the dead are not well and truly dead, a fear that may also conceal a hope; Marxists liked to compare capitalists to vampires, feeding off the labour of the working class. In *Ganja and Hess* (1971), Bill Gunn used the vampire idea to explore the dependencies of race and colonialism; the British short, *The Mask of Lilith* (1986), similarly explored vampirism as a metaphor for gender, sexual and racial oppression and resistance.

The possibilities are endless, and Coppola and Hart know a good few of them. You want the attraction and terror of sexuality? Here it is, in Dracula's metamorphosis from glowering bearded prince to cadaverous old goat to *fin-de-siècle* dandy, and in the wolf/ape thing that takes Lucy in the night. You want, more specifically, male fears of female sexuality? Here is the engorged, uncontrollable libidinous preference of Lucy and Mina for Gary Oldman's dandy Dracula over Keanu Reeves' sensitive but proper Jonathan. Or AIDS is a possibility, flung in here in a few lines ominously connecting sex, blood and disease. There's even a vegetarian reading, in a cut that has the audience groaning as at a bad pun and which is borrowed from *The Hunger*, where Van Helsing's dismemberment of Lucy's head is followed straight on by him carving with relish into a side of rare beef.

Or how about the vampire as the old world, old Europe, Eastern Europe, leeching off modern, industrialising, Western Europe (and North America)? This has in recent years been seen as one of the novel's most interesting themes, stressed not only in the references to modern means of communication (typewriters, cylinders), but in the characters of the Texan (the new rich of the New World) and Jack Seward, the lunatic-asylum director with new, rational and humane ideas about madness and its treatment. This is all there in Coppola's *Dracula*, given new inflection by a sequence at the cinematograph and by rendering parts of the final stalk-and-kill to look like a Western, the genre that encapsulates the conquering destiny of ethnically European expansion. The film is even aware of a gendered dimension to modernity, not so much, as in the book, through Mina, associated through typing with the New Woman's skill with technology and the possibility of an independent career, but in the way female nudes are interpolated into the endlessly repeated film shown in the sideshow booth where Dracula seduces Mina, a recognition of the simultaneous historical production of woman and cinema as spectacle.

The film seems to know about all the above; such themes are there not just by virtue of the completeness of its use of the novel's incidents and characters. Yet none of them is really developed or compelling. It's post-modern allusionism, a welter of things to make reference to without any of them mattering much. The most interesting and, surprisingly enough, original, is a Christian interpretation. Christianity has, of course, always been part of the vampire tale, but often in a rather perfunctory way. Holy water and a cross held up in the vampire's face might put him or her off for a while, but so did a bunch of garlic; real destruction could only come about by a stake through the heart, vaguely Christian perhaps, but pretty pagan too. The Christian possibilities seem not to have survived the riposte of the character in Roman Polanski's *Dance of the Vampire* (1967), who waives aside a proffered crucifix with the information that he's Jewish. There are few vampire films (or pieces of writing) since in which Christianity has any force, yet it is the one theme that gets some development in the new film.

The potential for a fuller Christian reading of the vampire idea is obvious. The central sacrament of Christianity is wine drunk as blood (in the Catholic doctrine of transubstantiation, this is at the spiritual level no mere symbol, it is the actual blood of Christ); the most important icon of Christianity is a dead man who has eternal life. Most writers and filmmakers have failed to exploit this, either because they depict vampires as the enemy of Christianity, or because they are not interested enough in Christianity to bother. In Coppola's *Dracula*, by contrast, Dracula is strongly associated with Christ.

The opening section depicts Vlad as the Defender of the Faith against   12
the Turks, in other words, against Islam, though the film perhaps pru-
dently plays that down); when he discovers that his beloved Princess
Elizabeth has killed herself, thinking him dead, he believes God has deserted him (as, on the cross did Christ); blood gushes from the crucifix
at the altar and Vlad, soaking and drinking it up, while railing against
God, becomes a vampire, Dracula. When Dracula seduces Mina (a reincarnation of Elizabeth), he makes a cut in his breast for her to suck at;
such a cut is familiar iconography in medieval and later Christian art,
and the connection is insisted on by cross-cutting with Mina marrying
Jonathan and taking communion with him, drinking wine/blood as a
sign of transcendent union. When Dracula is finally impaled, his face
metamorphoses from hideous white slug to long-haired dandy via a
bearded incarnation that is Vlad but also looks like countless images of
Christ. In short, though the theme disappears from view from time to
time, Dracula here is an anti-Christ, not so much in the sense of being
an enemy of Christ as in being an inversion of the Christ idea. Drinking
Christ's blood while cursing God damns him to eternal life, dependent
forever on human blood, having gorged on and rejected divine blood.
He offers his eternal life by the same token as Christ offered his, the
drinking of his blood.

But what do we feel about all this? Christ-like or anti-Christ, what   13
is our relation to him? Worship or identification, pity or revulsion? The
long life of the vampire idea resides in just such various possibilities. If
the image started out as one seen from the outside, there was always the
possibility that it could be seen and felt from within; if the vampire is an
Other, he or she was also always a figure in whom one could find oneself. The image allowed that from the start of its appearance in modern
western culture (if indeed it had any life before in folk cultures, as many
modern western writers like to claim). The narrative devices used ostensibly keep the vampire at a distance; the tale is often presented as one
told to the narrator by another narrator who sometimes themselves
have only heard it told; even when a direct first-person narrative is used,
the vampire is not the narrator. Yet he or she is always the most interesting, memorable and even attractive figure in the tale. If the narrator
and all around so easily fall prey to the vampire's magnetism, nay
charm, the latter must have something; the narrator often tells us little
about him or her self, and other characters, for all the vampire needs
their blood, seem anaemic by comparison. The vampire was always a
figure to be desired as well as feared, to be identified with as well as distanced from. One of the magical things about *Interview with the Vampire*
is the device of presenting the tale as a transcript of a taperecording of
the hero telling his story to a journalist; not only does this give the word

to the vampire himself, it also draws attention to the fact of doing so. Jody Scott's polymorphous lesbian science-fiction variant carries this breakthrough triumphantly forward in its very title, *I, Vampire.*

In film, there is no such grammar to tell you with whom you are   14
supposed to identify. Without voiceover or relentless subjective camera, it's much less clear who is 'telling' a film. But like vampires in literature, film sets up distance only to have it converted to identification.

The device of the journey, taken from Stoker, often serves to put the   15
vampire at a distance: there is a strong sense of a movement away from what the western, urban-minded audience would find familiar and towards the strangeness of foreignness. Honeymooners, the next step for the young unmarried heterosexual couples supposedly making up the bulk of the audience, might especially seem ideal identification figures to lead the viewer into the realm of the vampire other. Yet this device is even less insistently (if resistibly) distancing than the narrational devices of written fiction. It is true that few vampire films make the vampire a clear central figure whom we stay with throughout—I can only think of movies such as *Graveyard Shift, Nick Knight* or *To Die For,* plus films about real-life "vampire" Peter Kürten (*Le Vampire de Dusseldorf* and *The Tenderness of Wolves*) and George A. Romero's *Martin.* (The film of *Interview with the Vampire,* supposedly under contract, has not yet seen the light of day.) Yet the journey motif has led in some interesting directions, often inviting involvement more than encouraging distance.

In *Kiss of the Vampire* (Don Sharp, 1965) the lacklustre honeymoon-   16
ing couple cannot hold a candle to the vampires who prey on them. With the wife in their thrall, their leader says to the husband, "Now that your wife has tasted one of life's rarer pleasures, do you think she will want to return to you?" Who cannot see that he is right? Who would not rather spend time with the sister and brother, she bursting voluptuously out of her gown, he gazing with intense, melancholy eyes at you as he plays intense, melancholy music at the piano? And who would not prefer that delirious costume ball to sitting at home with this stodgy British hubby? Similarly in *Daughters of Darkness* (Harry Kumel, 1970) a pasty pair of newlyweds wind up on a wintry night in a deserted hotel on the Belgian coast. In the circumstances, who would want to keep to the straight and narrow when you could feel queer with the only other guests, Delphine Seyrig and companion? Well, of course, many people would, including the man sitting next to me. There's undoubtedly a queer way of reading vampirism, and my neighbour knew that's what I was hoping for.

I want "queer" here to carry as many meanings as possible. Cer-   17
tainly I don't just mean lesbian and gay, but any apparently marginalised, sexualised identity (which includes many perceptions of women

and non-white, even non-Anglo ethnic groups). But I do mean to include the old as well as the new connotations of queer, the despicable as well as the defiant, the shameful as well as the unashamed, the loathing of oddness as well as pride in it. The vampire has played every variation on such queerness. The 1922 Nosferatu is a hideous outsider, driven on by his lust, eyes falling out of his head at the sight of Thomas' sturdy frame and unable to resist Mina's deadly allure; to identify with him, as one still might, is to identify with loneliness, self-hatred and loathsome desire. To identify with Bela Lugosi's Count is still to identify with isolated outsiderdom, but already with someone more refined and fascinating than the dullards ranged against him. *Taste the Blood of Dracula* (1969) is one of the most enjoyable exposés of Victorian values in all cinema, with respectable bourgeois fathers secretly randy for the sensation that only Dracula can bring their jaded palates and their daughters, killing them off with glee under Dracula's tutelage; Christopher Lee's Count is as straight (and English) as can be, but how deliciously he provokes normal society against itself. And with *Kiss of the Vampire, Daughters of Darkness* or *Near Dark*, the vampires become the thing to be, infinitely preferable to the world they feed off.

Coppola's Dracula, like Stoker's, like Christopher Lee's, does not   18
belong with these vampires. He's not a pervert. He might occasionally turn to male flesh (between the scenes in the film as between the chapters in the book) and have on hand female vampires mutually pleasuring each other, but there is none of the delighted and sustained homoeroticism of "Carmilla" and *Interview with the Vampire*, or *Daughters of Darkness, The Velvet Vampire, The Hunger*, Barbara Steele in *Danza Macabra* and, a rare male example, the Dutch *Blood Relations*. He may in the end be destroyed for his disruptive desire, but it's really business as usual in terms of the representation of heterosexual male sexuality. Dracula—Stoker's, Lee's and Coppola's—is rampant, driven, rearing sexuality, uncontainable by modern, domestic, feminised society. It is ugly—beneath the dandy veneer lurks slug-like, leech-like desire; but it's what women want, even in its ugliness: Lucy is ecstatic beneath the half-ape, half-wolf that takes her in the garden and Mina does not flinch, even when her dandy slits his chest open for her. And like Stoker's dripping prose and Hammer's thickly coloured textures and solid *mise en scène*, only more so, Coppola's film is full of blood, stiff with desire, a hymn to engorgement.

Yet Dracula is an outsider, without being socially marginal. One ver-   19
sion of the vampire idea precisely presents normal male sexuality as outside of society. If "society" resides in moral order, in marriage, in the unemotional, unerotic workplace, then it has no place for driving randiness and uncontrollable priapism, themselves conceived as the nature

of male sexuality. Normal male sexuality in this perspective accords straight men, too, the glamorous badge of outsiderdom. No matter that they also have unequal power over women and children, no matter the vastness of the heterosexual sex industries, no matter the ubiquity of sexual tension at work—at the level of representation, male sexuality is seen as profoundly unsocialised and unsocialisable. Thus Stoker's, Lee's and Coppola's Dracula, thus the dominant image of the vampire, so commandingly virile, so unerringly straight, also expresses the profound contradictoriness of the cultural construction of heterosexual masculinity, at once dominant and disgusting, natural and horrible, mainstream and beyond the pale.

But that's not what *I* want from vampires. For all its incidental plea- 20
sures (some of the costumes, the US stars doing English accents, picking up the allusions as a genre aficionado is bound to, the new *Dracula* was not addressed to me. Just as I held myself off from the man in the seat next to me, so I held myself off from the film. Just as he perhaps believed that all gay men are after all straight men, so the only place for me in relation to this *Dracula* would have been as alienated assistant at the spectacle of straight male engorgement. In a way, the man next to me was right: I had no place there. But with so many other vampires to feast with, I can manage without this one.

• • • • • • • • • • • • • • • • • • • •

Examining the Text

1. In his first paragraph, Dyer describes an "eruption of homophobia" from the man sitting next to him in the cinema before the screening of *Bram Stoker's Dracula*. He mentions this man again in paragraph 16 and in his closing paragraph. What is his point in highlighting this incident in this critical essay? How is it related to his larger evaluation?

2. According to Dyer, Coppola's version of the Dracula story is unusually true to the style and content of Stoker's original novel. In what ways? Coppola's "one substantial new element" is the prologue featuring Vlad the Impaler (paragraph 3), which, in turn, contributes to the film's other original feature, its "Christian interpretation" (10–13). How does Dyer view both Coppola's adherence to the novel and these additions? How do they affect his interpretation?

3. In paragraphs 16–17, Dyer uses the word "queer" to describe his critical perspective and says he wants the term "to carry as many meanings as possible." (Often used derogatorily, the term has recently been adopted as the "label of choice" by many young homosexuals.) How does Dyer define the term, and how does he apply it to vampire stories and movies? Why, in Dyer's view, is Coppola's Dracula not "queer" in the way that some other vampire representations have been, but rather "business as usual in terms of the representation of heterosexual male sexuality" (18)?

For Group Discussion

Consider the ways that gender and sexuality influence the perspective of someone who is interpreting a film. Do you expect that men and women, straight people and gay people, are more likely to have different reactions or similar reactions to a film? Are there other factors that may well be more responsible for producing differing reactions? Discuss these questions as a group and see if you can come to some mutually agreed-upon conclusion.

Writing Suggestion

Rent *Bram Stoker's Dracula* as well as another vampire movie, if possible one that Dyer praises, such as *Dracula's Daughter, Daughters of Darkness, Kiss of the Vampire, Near Dark,* or *The Hunger.* In an essay, evaluate the two movies based on your own critical perspective, whether one that is described in this chapter, or one that you have consciously developed for yourself. Which, for you, is the better movie? Why? Be sure to use specific examples from each movie's plot, dialogue, set and costume design, cinematography, and performance to provide substance for your evaluation.

ADDITIONAL SUGGESTIONS
FOR WRITING ABOUT MOVIES

1. Find several reviews of a movie that interests you, either one that you've seen recently or one you can see before doing this assignment. The movie need not be one that you like; it could just as well be one that you didn't like at all, even though it was popular. Then write your own review of the movie, responding to, arguing with, or simply drawing from the published reviews. In your review, be sure to summarize the movie, identify its major themes or conflicts, evaluate its relative success, offer specific reasons for your assessment, and give advice to potential moviegoers. Support your opinions with examples from the movie.

2. In an interpretative essay, compare and contrast several movies dealing with similar themes or issues. For instance, you might compare several about the Vietnam War, or about the lives of the current generation of "twenty-somethings," or about inner city gangs, or about parent-child relationships. Choose movies that interest you and, ideally, that you can see again.

You might want to structure your essay as an argument aimed at convincing your readers that one movie is in some way "better" than the others. Or you might use your comparison of the movies to draw some larger point about popular culture and the images it presents to us.

3. In a researched essay, consider the complex relationship between film and social morality. Do you think films can cause people to act in anti-social ways, as do some of the critics of *Nightmare on Elm Street* quoted by Douglas Heuck? What do other experts say? Can you find specific current events that support your arguments?

4. Based on your reading of the essays by Mark J. Schaefermeyer, Walter Evans, and Richard Dyer and other essays you find by academic film critics, evaluate this kind of intellectual criticism. In your own essay, use examples which, in your opinion, show such criticism to be valid and enlightening, illustrate when it is difficult to follow, and indicate when a critic has gone too far in imposing a particular theoretical framework on a film.

5. Just as Stephen King looks at "Why We Crave Horror Movies," in an essay of your own, explore why we crave another popular genre of movies—futuristic techno-thrillers, movies based on television sitcoms and cartoons, chase movies, menaced-female dramas, psychotic killer stories, romantic comedies, supernatural comedies, and so forth.

Choose a type of movie familiar to you so that you can offer as many specific examples as possible.

Try to answer some of the same questions King does: What is the "fun" of seeing this type of movie? What sort of "psychic relief" does it deliver? Are there specific types of people who are likely to enjoy the genre more than others? Does the genre serve any function for society? In what ways do movies in this genre affect us, changing our thoughts or feelings after we've seen them?

6. In an essay, describe what you think might be done to improve the American film industry. Be sure to read the pieces by Sydney Pollack, Spike Lee, and David Denby in this chapter; those by Douglas Heuck and Richard Dyer might also be useful resources.

7. Compare and contrast the experience of seeing a movie in a theater and seeing one at home on a VCR. You might organize your essay as an argument, advocating for one way of movie-viewing over the other.

8. Choose an important recent movie and subject it to the kind of thorough critical analysis demonstrated by Richard Dyer's analysis of *Bram Stoker's Dracula*. In doing so, rely on your own set of critical standards and on a theoretical perspective for analyzing movies that you've developed for yourself based on your reading and your own interests, beliefs, and values.

8

LEISURE

Prehistoric humans spent only 40 percent of their waking hours on the necessities of life, such as food and shelter, according to anthropologists. That left 60 percent for "leisure" pursuits—napping, grooming, story telling, painting pictograms on cave walls, and dreaming up the wheel, the knife, and, who knows, maybe the Veg-O-Matic. Despite the proliferation of "labor-saving" devices ranging from microwave ovens to drip-irrigation systems, modern humans seem to have less leisure time than their long-lost ancestors. Visions of a twenty-hour work week, a noble idea proposed by philosopher Bertrand Russell in the 1930s, have never come to pass. In fact, as the global and domestic economy sags, many people find themselves working fifty and sixty hours a week just to get by.

In this culture, our sense of identity and even self-worth is measured largely by the work that we do, rather than by what we do with our spare time. In fact, the very adjective "spare" suggests that any time left over from work is of lesser importance. Paradoxically, however, what we do in our spare time more often defines our personalities than what we do nine to five. Certainly for some people, their professional career is congruent with personal satisfaction, but for many, work is the way to pay the bills, while leisure is an opportunity to pursue activities that truly nurture them. Juliet Schor, in her essay "Exiting the Squirrel Cage," takes this argument a step further. Drawing a distinction between "unpaid-work" and "true leisure," she argues that much of what we do in our "non-working" hours, mundane activities such as house cleaning and trimming our toenails, is actually *work*. Therefore, when we add this unpaid work time to forty-odd hours per week on the job, we're left with almost no "true leisure" time. Yet ironically, it is this tiny fraction of "true leisure" time that plays what some would argue is the most important role in defining us as unique individuals. As Witold Rybczynski suggests, our attitude toward leisure and our leisure pursuits also serve to define us as a culture.

With so little "true leisure," the pressure to have fun and fill that time with satisfying activities becomes greater. Our weekends should be filled with great parties, hot dates, productive creativity, and meaningful spiritual activity, or we feel as though we've failed in some way. Although we look forward to the parts of our lives away from work, the pressure to occupy free time with stimulating activity can actually become as oppressive as work itself. Walt Schafer, Professor of Sociology and Social Work at Chico State University in California, calls this sense of the burden of leisure "the lifestyle trap." When the stress of work flows over into non-working hours, then leisure becomes hectic, action-packed and anything but relaxing.

The readings in the first section of this chapter consider leisure in general: what leisure is; why our free time has declined; whether the pressure to have fun on weekends actually makes our "off" hours more stressful than working hours; and what we can do to get more meaningful, satisfying leisure in our lives. In response to the latter, Schor makes several recommendations, such as getting off the "consumption track" by redefining our values so that making money becomes less important than cultivating our talents.

The second part of the chapter focuses on specific leisure pursuits, such as playing video games, visiting amusement parks, shopping, and eating. These essays approach the phenomenon of leisure from different points of view. James Gorman, for example, provides an account of his obsession with a video game, while Russell Nye analyzes amusement parks from several theoretical perspectives. Still, all the essays consider questions central to leisure activity in the modern world. Why, for example, do certain activities like rollerblading or bungee-jumping suddenly become appealing to the public en masse? What satisfactions do activities like these offer to participants? Finally, what do *your* leisure activities, whether passive, like sunbathing and watching television, or active, like zipping across sand dunes in an all-terrain vehicle and performing gravity-defying skateboard tricks, reveal about you as a person and, more broadly, about the unique and sometimes quirky preoccupations of modern Americans?

THEORIES OF LEISURE

The Cult of Busyness

Barbara Ehrenreich

*I*n this essay from her collection The Worst Years of Our Lives *(1990),
Barbara Ehrenreich describes "the cult of conspicuous busyness" that she sees
around her, particularly among professional women on the road to success.
Ehrenreich, a well-known commentator on contemporary culture and author of
many books and articles (including another in Chapter 3), observes that "busyness has become an important insignia of upper-middle-class status." Accord
ing to Ehrenreich, it is now fashionable to be too busy for leisure activities,
whether hobbies, conversation with friends, or inner contemplation. Indeed, the
contemporary mass media's idea of success is embodied in the image of the high-
powered professional simultaneously reading the* Wall Street Journal, *closing
a deal via one cellular phone channel and instructing his or her broker on another, all the while driving an expensive car down a busy freeway.*

*The paradox, according to Ehrenreich, is that busyness doesn't necessarily
lead to happiness or success; in fact, "The secret of the truly successful . . . is
that they learned very early in life how* not *to be busy." Though her essay focuses on busyness, Ehrenreich implicitly suggests that free time is more crucial
even than success. "If it is true that success leads to more busyness and less
time for worthwhile activities . . . then who needs it?" she asks.*

*Ehrenreich's essay introduces some crucial concepts that are explored
throughout this chapter: leisure, busyness, success, happiness, work, recreation.*

***Before you read,** consider how these concepts are defined, in your own life
and in the lives of those around you.*

. . . .

Not too long ago a former friend and soon-to-be acquaintance called   1
me up to tell me how busy she was. A major report, upon which her professional future depended, was due in three days; her secretary was on
strike; her housekeeper had fallen into the hands of the Immigration Department; she had two hours to prepare a dinner party for eight; and she
was late for her time-management class. Stress was taking its toll, she
told me: her children resented the fact that she sometimes got their
names mixed up, and she had taken to abusing white wine.

All this put me at a distinct disadvantage, since the only thing I was   2
doing at the time was holding the phone with one hand and attempting to touch the opposite toe with the other hand, a pastime that I had

perfected during previous telephone monologues. Not that I'm not busy too: as I listened to her, I was on the alert for the moment the dryer would shut itself off and I would have to rush to fold the clothes before they settled into a mass of incorrigible wrinkles. But if I mentioned this little deadline of mine, she might think I wasn't busy enough to need a housekeeper, so I kept on patiently saying "Hmm" until she got to her parting line: "Look, this isn't a good time for me to talk, I've got to go now."

I don't know when the cult of conspicuous busyness began, but it   3
has swept up almost all the upwardly mobile, professional women I know. Already, it is getting hard to recall the days when, for example "Let's have lunch" meant something other than "I've got more important things to do than talk to you right now." There was even a time when people used to get together without the excuse of needing something to eat—when, in fact, it was considered rude to talk with your mouth full. In the old days, hardly anybody had an appointment book, and when people wanted to know what the day held in store for them, they consulted a horoscope.

It's not only women, of course; for both sexes, busyness has become   4
an important insignia of upper-middle-class status. Nobody, these days, admits to having a hobby, although two or more careers—say, neurosurgery and an art dealership—is not uncommon, and I am sure we will soon be hearing more about the tribulations of the four-paycheck couple. Even those who can manage only one occupation at a time would be embarrassed to be caught doing only one *thing* at a time. Those young men who jog with their headsets on are not, as you might innocently guess, rocking out, but are absorbing the principles of international finance law or a lecture on one-minute management. Even eating, I read recently, is giving way to "grazing"—the conscious ingestion of unidentified foods while drafting a legal brief, cajoling a client on the phone, and, in ambitious cases, doing calf-toning exercises under the desk.

But for women, there's more at stake than conforming to another   5
upscale standard. If you want to attract men, for example, it no longer helps to be a bimbo with time on your hands. Upscale young men seem to go for the kind of woman who plays with a full deck of credit cards, who won't cry when she's knocked to the ground while trying to board the six o'clock Eastern shuttle, and whose schedule doesn't allow for a sexual encounter lasting more than twelve minutes. Then there is the economic reality: any woman who doesn't want to wind up a case study in the feminization of poverty has to be successful at something more demanding than fingernail maintenance or come-hither looks. Hence all the bustle, my busy friends would explain—they want to succeed.

But if success is the goal, it seems clear to me that the fast track is   6
headed the wrong way. Think of the people who are genuinely successful—path-breaking scientists, best-selling novelists, and designers
of major new software. They are not, on the whole, the kind of people who keep glancing shiftily at their watches or making small lists
entitled "To Do." On the contrary, many of these people appear to be in
a daze, like the distinguished professor I once had who, in the middle of
a lecture on electron spin, became so fascinated by the dispersion properties of chalk dust that he could not go on. These truly successful people are childlike, easily distractable, fey sorts, whose usual demeanor resembles that of a recently fed hobo on a warm summer evening.

The secret of the truly successful, I believe, is that they learned very   7
early in life how *not* to be busy. They saw through that adage, repeated
to me so often in childhood, that anything worth doing is worth doing
well. The truth is, many things are worth doing only in the most slov-
enly, halfhearted fashion possible, and many other things are not worth
doing at all. Balancing a checkbook, for example. For some reason, in
our culture, this dreary exercise is regarded as the supreme test of personal maturity, business acumen, and the ability to cope with math anxiety. Yet it is a form of busyness which is exceeded in futility only by going to the additional trouble of computerizing one's checking
account—and that, in turn, is only slightly less silly than taking the time
to discuss, with anyone, what brand of personal computer one owns, or
is thinking of buying, or has heard of others using.

If the truly successful manage never to be busy, it is also true that   8
many of the busiest people will never be successful. I know this first-
hand from my experience, many years ago, as a waitress. Any executive
who thinks the ultimate in busyness consists of having two important
phone calls on hold and a major deadline in twenty minutes, should try
facing six tablefuls of clients simultaneously demanding that you give
them their checks, fresh coffee, a baby seat, and a warm, spontaneous
smile. Even when she's not busy, a waitress has to look busy—refilling
the salt shakers and polishing all the chrome in sight—but the only
reward is the minimum wage and any change that gets left on the
tables. Much the same is true of other high-stress jobs, like working as
a telephone operator, or doing data entry on one of the new machines
that monitors your speed as you work: "success" means surviving the
shift.

Although busyness does not lead to success, I am willing to believe   9
that success—especially when visited on the unprepared—can cause
busyness. Anyone who has invented a better mousetrap, or the contemporary equivalent, can expect to be harassed by strangers demanding

that you read their unpublished manuscripts or undergo the humiliation of public speaking, usually on remote Midwestern campuses. But if it is true that success leads to more busyness and less time for worthwhile activities—like talking (and listening) to friends, reading novels, or putting in some volunteer time for a good cause—then who needs it? It would be sad to have come so far—or at least to have run so hard—only to lose each other.

•••••••••••••••••••••

Examining the Text
1. Why do you think Ehrenreich begins with the anecdote about the friend who calls to say she's too busy to talk? Do you think the story is true? What do you think of this as an opening strategy?

2. What does the term "cult" imply? Why do you think Ehrenreich refers to the obsession with busyness as a "cult" (paragraph 3)? Is this a valid characterization?

3. In paragraph 8, Ehrenreich says that "many of the busiest people will never be successful." Who, according to her, are the "busiest" people, and how are they different from the participants in the "cult" of busyness? What is Ehrenreich suggesting in making this distinction?

For Group Discussion
Ehrenreich focuses on professional people in the working world. How well do her ideas apply to college students? Is there a similar "cult of conpicuous busyness" among any of your fellow students? Is busyness ever a status symbol or is the opposite more often the case? As a group, determine what most students think about the kind of busyness Ehrenreich describes. Then as a class discuss some reasons underlying the students' attitudes.

Writing Suggestion
At the end of the essay, Ehrenreich lists some activities that are more "worthwhile" than busyness. What are the differences between these activities and the "busyness" that Ehrenreich criticizes? In an essay consider your own daily activities in terms of Ehrenreich's definitions. How many of these are "worthwhile" in her sense, how many may be seen as part of your own "cult of busyness," and how many are simply "surviving the shift" (8)?

Exercising the Brain

Jim Spring

*T*he following essay offers an interesting twist on Ehrenreich's notion
of the "cult of busyness." Jim Spring proposes that people aren't actually as
busy as they claim to be, or rather, that the things that keep them busy are
more often passive, "no-brainer" activities than active, challenging leisure
pursuits.

Spring's results are based on surveys conducted by Leisure Trends, a firm
which gathers information about the leisure habits of Americans and provides
it to businesses seeking customers. Thus, the purpose of this essay (which originally appeared in American Demographics) is to offer companies advice
about consumer attitudes and behaviors. However, we can also read Spring's
essay as a fairly objective report on American leisure activities, and, perhaps,
see ourselves reflected in the observation that "most Americans normally end
up doing the things that are easiest to do and not necessarily the things they
claim to enjoy the most." For instance, as Spring points out, people who say
they are skiers may actually opt to spend most of their free time watching TV
or reading.

Before you read, think of the three or four activities that you say you enjoy most and ask yourself how often in the past several months you have actually done them. If your answer is a few times or not at all, what has kept you
from pursuing them? How have you actually spent most of your leisure time?

·····················

Norma Puzzle invited Charlie to a concert a month away, and Char-   1
lie said he "really wanted to go." Norma considered it a date. But when
she showed up to take him, Charlie wasn't home. "Just because I said I
wanted to go didn't mean we had a date," he said later. "I want to do
lots of things I never do."

Norma wasn't happy. Aside from the costly tickets, she believed he   2
had made a commitment. But Charlie is a typical American, according
to Leisure Trends' surveys of leisure activities. Most Americans normally end up doing the things that are easiest to do and not necessarily
the things they claim to enjoy the most. The result is a wide gap between
the number of people who say they enjoy an activity and the much
smaller number who actually do the activity regularly.

To understand this phenomenon, it helps to separate leisure activi-   3
ties into three categories; No-Brainers, Brainers, and Puzzlers. No-Brainer
activities are habitual, easy to do, require a low level of decision-making,

have few entry barriers, and tend to entertain. Watching television is the best example of a No-Brainer.

Brainer activities are less habitual, may involve other people, are 4 more complex because they require some interaction with a person or thing, and have moderate logistical barriers. Hobbies, movie-going, and socializing at home or on the telephone are good examples of Brainers.

Puzzlers tend to break away from habits entirely and include the 5 most difficult activities. The barriers to entry are higher, and the decision-making process is more complex. Puzzlers inspire questions such as "Do I really like Amy?" or "Can I afford it?" Most sports activities, parties, going to the theater, or taking a weekend in the country are examples of Puzzlers. These activities involve thinking and taking inventory. To do them, people must make complex decisions. Before a party, for example, many people wrestle with the following puzzler: "Do I have the right clothes, or should I go shopping first?"

No-Brainers and Puzzlers

The difference between what people say and what they do shows 6 up clearly in eight activities that fall into the three categories described above. This article compares what people aged 16 or older did the previous day with what they say they "enjoy doing the most."

It's no surprise that the most frequent activity reported is the ulti- 7 mate No-Brainer—watching television. It is simple and can be done alone. While it eats up lots of time and 77 percent of respondents did it the day before the survey, only 14 percent say they enjoy it the most.

Television viewing is such a perfect No-Brainer that many people 8 don't remember doing it at all. When asked the open-ended question, "What did you do yesterday in your leisure time?" just 31 percent of respondents spontaneously mention television. We uncovered that 77 percent of the total population actually watched television only by asking this followup question: "Did you watch television yesterday?" In this context, the small proportion of Americans who admit that television is their favorite activity starts to look suspicious. Perhaps we don't want to admit we enjoy what is offered on the tube. Or perhaps people don't count the time they spend reading, cooking, or conversing while one eye is on the television. But in any case, the gap between watching, enjoyment, and memorability is so great as to suggest that TV is a low-key form of fun.

Brainer activities such as socializing and going to the movies are 9 done less frequently than No-Brainers. But people claim to enjoy them more, so the gap between saying and doing for Brainers is smaller than for No-Brainers. Shopping for fun and do-it-yourself activities are different. People say they like these activities, and they participate in them frequently. It seems they are sufficiently motivated to overcome the barriers in getting to the store and buying materials. At the other extreme are Puzzler activities such as fishing. People claim to enjoy them greatly, but don't do them very often.

Attitude clearly does not always predict behavior, and the data offer evidence that most Americans operate on both levels. We are a combination of what we do and what we think, and the two do not necessarily go together. Which form of consumer information best predicts participation or consumption will depend on the product or service being consumed.   10

Behavioral data are more dependable, because past and present behavior is often the best indicator of future behavior. Yet attitudinal data can indicate new opportunities. Marketers whose products and services fall into the No-Brainer category know that people don't need a great deal of encouragement to participate in them, and that those who do it today will probably do it tomorrow. They can concentrate on broadening their market by enhancing existing products and finding new niches.   11

For example, snack foods are often consumed during No-Brainer activities such as watching television. Mass media advertising is appropriate for these products. On the other hand, businesses with links to Brainer or Puzzler activities may have to resort to stronger inducements. For activities people say they enjoy but don't do often, marketers can offer incentives such as discount coupons to movies or free transportation to ski areas.   12

Coaxing Armchair Athletes

The problem with predicting participation in Puzzler and Brainer activities is the large difference between expectation and reality. In a two-part study for the alpine ski industry, we measured the differences between people's intentions to ski and their actual behavior. Over a span of three years, we discovered that in any given year, as few as 65 percent of self-defined skiers actually go skiing.   13

Many people who consider themselves skiers have not skied at all in the last four to five years. One self-proclaimed skier had not skied since 1947! Yet virtually all self-defined skiers who had not skied in the last several years say they plan to ski again.   14

Here is a strong positive attitude that defies the facts. Anyone who estimates a market's potential based on intention in this sport will be   15 in for a rude shock. If you're selling a skiing magazine, attitude is as important as behavior. But if you're selling lift tickets, you need a real skier.

Skiing qualifies as a true Puzzler activity because it involves special 16 equipment, can be quite costly, depends on the weather, and requires special locations and physical skill. Fishing falls into the same category for most of the same reasons. The rule of thumb is that the more difficult something is, the more important behavioral data are in measuring trends in participation.

On the other hand, attitudinal information provides clues about 17 potential markets, because changes in attitudes can signal a potential change in behavior. To understand how attitudes may predict behavior, it is important to understand why people don't do things. People often cite a lack of time or money as the reasons they don't pursue a Puzzler activity. For some, however, excuses disguise the true reason, which is a lack of brain power or energy. People find plenty of time for No-Brainer activities, perhaps because they provide low-energy relaxation. After a long day at work or with the kids, many people don't want to keep coordinating and planning. To the time-pressured adult, thinking about a weekend at a local ski area may seem like too much work.

Some people who say they enjoy an activity like skiing are perpet- 18 ual "wannabes." Even given the chance, they will not hit the slopes. But others who say they would enjoy doing something really mean it. To encourage these people, businesses that sell Brainer and Puzzler activities should make it easy for people to translate their positive attitude into behavior. Family ski packages that include bus transportation, rental equipment, lift tickets, and lessons for the children could persuade even weary souls to brave the slopes. For those whose biggest barrier is cost, something as simple as a free trial lift ticket could change a positive attitude into long-term purchasing behavior.

Each Sport Is Different

Changes in attitudes and behavior do not always run parallel to 19 each other, so it is important to track both of them. A comparison of attitudes in 1990 and 1992 shows that interest in reading has increased, for example, while interest in watching television and socializing has declined slightly. A look at behavior shows that reading and socializing have increased—but that television viewing has not changed much.

Demographic trends in leisure can be surprising. Reading may be a 20 highly intellectual activity, for example. Yet this study classifies it as a

No-Brainer because it is easy to do anywhere and is almost always done alone. More women than men read, and more women consider it their favorite leisure activity. Reported reading is increasing sharply among 16-to-24-year-olds and those aged 45 and older. The attitude of 25-to-34-year-olds toward reading is increasingly positive, but their behavior has not changed much. Adults aged 35 to 44 are showing a decrease in interest in reading, but are reading slightly more.

Movies in theaters, which fall into the Brainer category, are becoming more appealing to men, according to the 1990 and 1992 surveys. Men are also watching them more often. Americans under age 35 went to more movies in 1992 than they did in 1990, and a greater share considered them a favorite activity.   21

Do-it-yourself activities are Puzzlers with a twist. In particular, women are more likely to participate in do-it-yourself activities than to say they enjoy them. But as the share of female do-it-yourselfers rises, so does their enjoyment level. Perhaps practice does make perfect, as tasks done repeatedly become easier and more fun. It may also be that people are discovering that do-it-yourself activities are stress reducers. Baking bread and other activities were once necessities, but now they are usually done as a way to relax.   22

Another way to find clues about future trends in leisure behavior is to study the attitudes of people who have just begun a new activity. In the 1990 interviews, the proportion of people who said they had gardened, camped, hiked, or backpacked for the first time had increased noticeably over 1988. Two years later, the share of regular participants in these activities had increased. Similarly, changes in attitudes often precede changes in behavior. The share of people who enjoy doing home improvement and yard work grew between 1988 and 1990, and the share who do these things grew between 1990 and 1992.   23

What's the leisure forecast for the 1990s? The surveys show that people may be doing more shopping for fun, traveling, walking for exercise, and outside recreational activities such as camping, hiking, and alpine skiing. Organized religion also seems poised for a comeback, and interest in working on the home and yard continues to grow.   24

It is worth noting that all upward trends in attitudes fall into the Puzzler category. Aging baby boomers may be less willing to spend time on passive activities, but only time will tell if they are ready for more challenging leisure. By the way, Norma left Charlie's house and stopped by Lance's house on the way to the concert, and he agreed to go with her. Two months later, they got married. Now they have a small Puzzle to ponder, and they don't go to concerts anymore.   25

• • • • • • • • • • • • • • • • • • • •

Examining the Text

1. What are the differences between No-Brainer, Brainer, and Puzzler activities? Which favorite activities do you have in each of these categories? Based on the likelihood of your participating in each of these favorites, do Spring's observations hold true?

2. According to Spring, what is the relationship between what people say they do during their leisure time and what they actually do? From your own experience, do you think Spring's findings are correct?

3. How does the purpose of Spring's article—to inform leisure-related businesses on how to attract customers—influence your response to his ideas?

For Group Discussion

Imagine that your group is asked to promote a specific Puzzler activity, such as mountain-biking, wine-tasting, or doing volunteer work. After choosing an activity, use Spring's article for ideas on how to best structure your promotional campaign and the incentives you could offer to get people to participate. Once you've developed your campaign, discuss the specific strategies with the rest of your class.

Writing Suggestion

Using the pattern of the Leisure Trends research, informally survey twenty people you know. Ask them about their leisure activities of the day before and what their three favorite leisure activities are. You might also follow up about specific interests not mentioned and about time that has elapsed since they participated in a favorite activity. In an essay, describe how your informal research corresponds to the Leisure Trends' findings.

Exiting the Squirrel Cage

Juliet Schor

*T*he following essay considers ways to increase the quantity and quality *of our leisure time. Taken from her* The Overworked American, *a 1991 study of work and leisure in contemporary American culture, this essay by Juliet Schor argues for "a right to free time" that we need to protect actively for our own sake and for our families and our culture in general. For Schor, the problem of decreasing duration and quality of leisure time begins with the capitalist equation, time equals money. As she says, "The more time substitutes for* *money, the more difficult it is to establish an* independent *measure of time's value." Thus the more likely we are to spend our time in pursuit of money, even when we already have more than enough to live comfortably.*

Schor suggests how both employers and employees can make a number of changes to increase time for relaxation, contemplation, conversation, family outings, hobbies, and volunteer activities. Once we regain leisure hours, Schor advises, we'll need to learn (or relearn) how to spend those hours wisely: "If we veer too much toward work, our 'leisure skills' will atrophy."

Before you read, *consider your own attitudes toward work and leisure. Schor argues that psychological (as well as social and economic) changes will be required if we are to take full advantage of leisure. What sorts of changes do you think you personally would need to make to enjoy your free time more fully?*

· · · · · · · · · · · · · · · · · · · ·

It is often said that an economist is a person who knows the price of 1 everything and the value of nothing. On the question of time, we may all have become economists. We are keenly aware of the price of time— the extra income earned with a second job, the wage and a half for an hour of overtime. In the process, we may have forgotten the real worth of time.

The origins of modern time consciousness lie in the development of 2 a capitalist economy. Precapitalist Europe was largely "timeless"—or, in historian Jacques Le Goff's words, "free of haste and careless of exactitude." As capitalism raised the "price" of time, people began to think of time as a scarce resource. Indeed, the ideology of the emerging market economy was filled with metaphors of time: saving time, using time wisely, admonitions against "passing" time. The work ethic itself was in some sense a time ethic. When Benjamin Franklin preached that time is money, he meant that time should be used productively. Eventually capitalism did more than make time valuable. Time and money began to substitute for each other. Franklin's aphorism took on new meaning, not only as prescription, but as an actual description. Money buys time, and time buys money. *Time itself had become a commodity.*

Moneylending was the first example of the sale of time, its nature 3 revealed in the colloquial "to buy on time." Then the sale of time developed in the labor market, and became, for most people, the area where the impact has been greatest. Today the principle of sale of labor time is thoroughly accepted. But this is the result of a long and contentious process. As the British historian Edward Thompson has argued, workers struggled at first from a traditional ideology of "timelessness" against the very idea of time. They resented employers' attempts to impose time and time discipline. As decades passed, they struggled over the ownership of time—how much was theirs, how much the boss's. And today, many fight for *over*time—the right to sell as much time as they can.

The unencumbered sale of time for money is now a reigning value,   4 its legitimacy so entrenched that it is no longer fully voluntary: most employees can be forced to put in overtime. The monetary equivalence to time has expanded far beyond the labor market. Patients have begun to charge doctors when they are kept waiting. The government pays jurors for each day they spend in court. The legal value of a human life is based on the future sale of working time. Every hour has a price.

The virtues of the sale of time and the equation of time and money   5 are well known: putting a price tag on each hour allows a person (or a society) to use time efficiently. But there are also vices, which are less well recognized. Many aspects of the value of time are difficult to incorporate into a purely market exchange—such as the effects of individuals' use of time on the quality of social life, or the concept of a basic human right to free time. Every society has a culture of time. Has ours perhaps gone too far in the direction of collapsing time into money?

The more time substitutes for money, the more difficult it is to es-   6 tablish an *independent* measure of time's value. And our diminishing ability to make this judgment contributes to long hours. If the market recognizes only the measure of money, then arguing that a job requires "too many hours" makes no sense: it is tantamount to saying that it pays "too much money." The inflated working hours of the Wall Street financier or the corporate lawyer are a fair trade for their inflated salaries. If low-wage employees in the nursing home industry have two full-time jobs, it is because they value money over time. In a culture where time is merely money, we risk perverse effects such as occurred after 1938 with legislation to regulate overtime. This policy was designed to install a forty-hour week, but its disincentive to companies (time and a half) turned into a powerful incentive for workers to work as many hours as they could. In the end, the legislation contracted both leisure and employment, the two things it was designed to expand.

Where time is money, it's hard to protect time for those who—such   7 as low-wage workers, children, aged parents, or community organizations—can't pay for it. And it's hard to protect time for ourselves, for relaxation, hobbies, or sleep. The pressures toward long working hours have become too powerful. But common sense tells us that working hours *can* be too long. Excessive hours are unhealthy and antisocial, and ultimately erode the quality of life.

The commensurability of time and money has other detrimental so-   8 cial effects. It transforms a resource that is equally distributed (time) into

one that is distinctly unequal (money). Both wealth and income are un-
equally distributed. But everyone is born with twenty-four hours in a
day. And while money does skew the distribution of time to some extent (higher-income people live longer), "ownership" of time is still far
more equally allocated. The sale of time undermines its egalitarianism.
As time outside work becomes more precious, those with money can
economize on it. And this appears to be happening. Fast-track careerists
are hiring people to cook their meals, watch their children, even wait in
line for them. Small companies have sprouted up, offering services from
grocery shopping to changing light bulbs. The people whose time is being sold are those less economically well situated—as happened earlier,
of course, in the nineteenth century when the growth of the middle class
spawned a huge demand for servants. Today's scarcity of time puts us
in jeopardy of producing a new servant class and undermining the egalitarianism of time.

Establishing a right to free time may sound utopian—but the prin-   9
ciple of limiting exchange has already been established. It is not legal to
sell oneself into slavery. It is not legal to sell one's vote. It is not legal to
sell children. Even the principle of limiting the exchange of time is well
established. The state has regulated working hours since the colonial period. The right to free time has been legislated in some forms, such as legal holidays. Most important of all is the social security system, which
assumes that workers have a right to leisure for a period at the end of
their lives. What I am arguing for is the extension of this right—so that
everyone can enjoy free time while they are still young and throughout
their lives. . . .

Overcoming Consumerism

Economic feasibility is an important condition for gaining leisure.   10
So is breaking the automatic translation of productivity into income. But
for many Americans escaping the trap of overwork will also entail stepping off the consumer treadmill, which requires altering a way of life
and a way of thinking. The transformation must be not only economic
and social but cultural and psychological.

The first step is practical—to put oneself in a financial position   11
where a fixed or smaller income is sufficient. For example, one California environmental planner spent three years preparing to cut back his
work hours. He had to "grind down the charge cards," pay off his car,
and convince his partner that life with less money would be okay:
"There are two ways to get through. You either have to make the money

which will buy you the kind of life that you think you have to have, or you can change those expectations and you don't need the money anymore. And that's what I've done."

Being able to change expectations depends on understanding the 12 psychological and cultural functions that material goods fulfill. They can be the means to an identity or a way to create self-esteem. Things fill up empty spaces in our lives. Many couples concentrate on owning a house or filling it with nice furnishings, when what they really crave is an emotional construction—home. Some women turn to fashion to create a fantasy self that compensates for what they are consciously or unconsciously missing. Materialism can even be an altruistic vice. Men pursue the pot of gold to give it to their wives or children—to provide the "best that life can offer" or "what I never had." But in the process everyone is cheated: "I thought I was doing the right thing making money at work all the time. But I was never home." Realization often comes too late: "Now that I'm older, I can see . . . what I was missing."

Involuntary reductions in income caused by a company shutdown 13 or an inability to work can be painful, often devastating. But those who willingly reject the quest for affluence can find themselves perfectly satisfied. One public employee, currently on a four-fifths schedule, swears that only a financial disaster could get her back to full-time: "The extra twenty percent just isn't worth it." Even at the California company where employees were forced to take a ten-percent reduction in pay and hours, reactions were positive: only 22 percent of the workforce rated the program negatively, and half were positive about it.

For many, opting out of the rat race has transformed their lives: "In 14 the last four years, I went from upper middle class to poor, but I am a lot richer than most people, and I'm happier too." A divorced father raising three young children rejected the long hours, high-income route. He's at home with his children in the evenings, and has learned that "less is more." A career woman gave up her job, and along with it designer clothes, hair and nail appointments, lunching out and a second car: "I adopted a whole new set of values and put aside pride, envy, competitiveness and the need for recognition."

The Value of Leisure Time

Some people are skeptical of Americans' need for leisure time. Work 15 may be bad, but perhaps leisure isn't all it's cracked up to be either. According to economist Gary Burtless, "Most Americans who complain they enjoy too little leisure are struggling to find a few extra minutes to watch Oprah Winfrey and 'L.A. Law.'" Will free time be "wasted," in front of the tube or at the mall? What will we do with all that leisure? Won't people just acquire second jobs? These are serious questions, embodying two main assumptions. The first is that people prefer work or, if they don't, they should. The second is that leisure time is wasted time that is neither valued nor valuable.

One possibility is that work is irrepressible. The Akron rubber   16
workers immediately come to mind. After they won the six-hour day, many of the men who worked at Firestone started driving cabs, cutting hair, and selling insurance. While no one knows exactly what percentage of the workers took on extra jobs, during the 1950s it was thought to be between one in five and one in seven. Some observers concluded from this experience that American workers do not want, or cannot handle, leisure time. If they are right, so be it. My aim is not to force leisure on an unwilling population but to provide the possibility of a real choice. If the chance to work shorter hours—when fairly presented—is not appealing, then people will not take it. But before we take the Akron experience as definitive, let's ask a few more questions.

Why did so many take a second job? The male rubber workers were   17
reasonably well paid by the blue-collar standards of the day, and many of their wives worked. They did not labor out of sheer economic necessity. I suspect that their behavior was dictated more by a cultural imperative . . . that says that men with leisure are lazy. It is significant that women rubber workers did not seek a second paycheck.

Today there are signs that this cultural imperative is becoming less   18
compelling. Perhaps most important is the transformation of sex roles. Women have taken up responsibility for breadwinning. And men are more at home around the house. Increasing numbers of fathers want to parent. In a recent poll of men between the ages of eighteen and twenty-four, nearly half said they would like to stay home and raise their children. The ethos of "male sacrifice" is disappearing: a declining portion of the population believes that being a "real man" entails self-denial and being the family provider.

The traditional work ethic is also undergoing transformation. Com-   19
mitment to hard work retains its grip on the American psyche. But young people are moving away from "the frenzied work ethic of the 1980s to more traditional values." In addition, ideas of what work is and what it is for are being altered. The late 1960s and 1970s witnessed the rise of what some have called "post-materialist values"—desires for personal fulfillment, self-expression, and meaning. Throughout the industrialized world, a culture shift occurred as young people especially

began demanding satisfying work. Although there was a burst of old-style materialism during the 1980s, it did not permanently dislodge what now looks more and more like a long-term trend. People are expecting more from work than a paycheck and more from life than what 1950s culture offered.

People *will* work on their time off. They will work hard and long in   20
what is formally designated as leisure time. But where the Akron example leads us astray is the quest for the second paycheck. Americans need time for unpaid work, for work they call their own. They need the time to give to others. Much of what will be done was the regular routine in the days when married women were full-time housewives. And it is largely caring work—caring for children, caring for sick relatives and friends, caring for the house. Today many haven't got the time to care. If we could carve the time out from our jobs, we could prevent the current squeeze on caring labor. And this time around, the men should share the load. The likelihood is good that unpaid work would occupy a significant fraction of any "leisure" gained in the market. At the California company that gave its employees two days off a month, nearly as much time was devoted to household and volunteer work as to leisure itself. Predictably, women did more of this labor. But times are changing.

Other productive activities would take up uncommitted time as   21
well. Many people would like to devote more time to their churches, get involved in their children's schools, coach a sports team, or help out at a soup kitchen. But the time squeeze has taken a toll on volunteer activities, which have fallen considerably since the rise in hours began. Time out of work would also be used for schooling. Education remains a primary factor in economic success. And continual training and retraining are projected to be increasingly important in the economy of the twenty-first century, as job skills become obsolete more rapidly. A survey at two large Boston corporations found that over 20 percent of full-time employees were also enrolled in school.

The unpaid work—at home and in the community—that will fill   22
free time is vital to us as individuals and as a society—as should be clear from the mounting social problems attendant upon its decline. Still, if we were to gain free time only to fill it up again with work, the battle will be only half won. There is also a pressing need for more true leisure. For the first time in fifteen years, people have cited leisure time as the "more important" thing in their lives than work. The nation needs to slow down, unwind, and recover from its ordeal of labor. But can we handle leisure time?

The skeptics, who cite heavy television viewing or excessive shop-   23
ping, have a point. It may be, however, that work itself has been erod-

ing the ability to benefit from leisure time. Perhaps people are just too tired after work to engage in active leisure. Evidence from the Gallup Poll suggests this may be the case. Today, the most popular ways to spend an evening are all low-energy choices: television, resting, relaxing, and reading. Although it certainly isn't proof, it is suggestive that the globe's only other rich, industrialized country with longer hours than the United Sates—namely, Japan—is also the only nation to watch more television.

The issue goes beyond the physical capacity to use free time. It is 24 also true that the ability to use leisure is not a "natural" talent, but one that must be cultivated. If we veer too much toward work, our "leisure skills" will atrophy. At the extremes are workaholics like Sheila Mohammed. After sixteen-hour days—two full-time shifts—as a drug rehabilitation counselor, Sheila finds herself adrift outside the job: "I'm so used to . . . working and then when I have the time off, what do I do, where do I go?" But even those with moderate working habits are subject to a milder version of this syndrome. Many potentially satisfying leisure activities are off limits because they take too much time: participating in community theater, seriously taking up a sport or a musical instrument, getting involved with a church or community organization. In the leisure time available to us, there's less of interest to do. To derive the full benefits of free time, we just may need more of it.

A final impediment to using leisure is the growing connection be- 25 tween free time and spending money. Private corporations have dominated the leisure "market," encouraging us to think of free time as a consumption opportunity. Vacations, hobbies, popular entertainment, eating out, and shopping itself are all costly forms of leisure. How many of us, if asked to describe an ideal weekend, would choose activities that cost nothing? How resourceful are we about doing things without spending money? A successful movement to enhance free time will have to address this dynamic head on. Governments and communities will need to subsidize more affordable leisure activities, from the arts to parks to adult education. We need a conscious effort to reverse "the commodification of leisure."

Whatever the potential problems associated with increasing leisure 26 time, I do not think they are insurmountable. A significant reduction in working hours will by itself alleviate some of the difficulties. And if we can take positive steps to enhance the value of leisure time, we will be well rewarded. The experience of the Kellogg workers calls for optimism: "The visitor sees . . . a lot of gardening and community beautification . . . athletics and hobbies were booming . . . libraries well patronized . . .

and the mental background of these fortunate workers . . . becoming richer."

· · · · · · · · · · · · · · · · · · · ·

Examining the Text

1. What is Schor's basic point about the relationship between time and money? (Note, by the way, the pervasiveness of the metaphor that "time is money": we "spend" time, "save" time, "waste" time, and so forth.) How and why has the development of a capitalist economy influenced this relationship, according to Schor? What does she mean by "the real worth of time" (paragraph 1)?

2. Schor argues that equating time and money has several negative social effects. List them. Which do you think are the most serious and detrimental to society? Do you think Schor exaggerates any of these effects?

3. What is a "cultural imperative"? How does this concept explain why workers might take on a second job? Do you accept Schor's contention that this imperative is becoming "less compelling"?

4. What social and personal benefits does Schor argue would come from decreasing work time and increasing leisure time? Which benefits do you think are the most important?

For Group Discussion

Schor refers to "the rise of what some have called 'post-materialist values'—desires for personal fulfillment, self-expression, and meaning" (19). Which values do you think are most prevalent in contemporary society, "materialist" or "post-materialist"? As a group, debate this question briefly, and then consider whether there is a difference in the way the mass media depicts contemporary values and the way people you know actually live their lives.

Writing Suggestion

Those who are critical of creating a greater amount of leisure time say that people will just spend it watching television, shopping, and taking part in other "No-Brainer" activities, to use Spring's term. However, Schor counters that people would use the opportunity to pursue activities that are currently "off limits because they take too much time" (24).

Considering yourself and people you know, which view do you think is closer to the truth?

The Problem of Leisure

Witold Rybczynski

*V*irtually all of us recognize the saying "TGIF." "Thank God It's Friday" means the weekend approaches, releasing us from our weekday schedules of work and school. We look forward to sleeping late, catching up on chores, socializing with family and friends, enjoying our favorite recreational activities.

But as Witold Rybczynski points out in the following chapter from his book Waiting for the Weekend (1991), weekends present us with the interesting, sometimes anxiety-provoking question of how best to fill our free time. In his words, "The freedom to do something has become the obligation to do something. . . . [and] the obligation to do it well"—to excel at whatever we take on. "For many," he says, "weekend free time has become not a chance to escape work but a chance to create work that is more meaningful," "leisure work" that offers personal satisfaction no longer found in the workplace.

The "problem of leisure" is compounded by the decline of free time in a culture filled with fax machines, pagers, cellular phones, and portable computers that mean the work day no longer ends once we leave the office. Women may be in the work force in record numbers but are still responsible for most housework. Economic conditions force many of us to trade leisure time for money, to work overtime or take on a second job to make ends meet. Leisure hours decrease, weekends shrink, and our decisions about how to spend our "free time" become ever more problematic: "We want leisure, but we are afraid of it too."

One of Rybczynski's interesting points is that one person's leisure activity may be a burden or even a form of work for another. Consider your own favorite leisure activities. Would everyone take pleasure in these activities? Can you think of things other people do for enjoyment that are simply chores from your perspective?

••••••••••••••••••

In 1919 the Hungarian psychiatrist Sándor Ferenczi published a short paper entitled "Sunday Neuroses." He recounted that in his medical practice he had encountered several neurotics whose symptoms recurred on a regular basis. Although it's common for a repressed memory to return at the same time of year as the original experience, the symptoms he described appeared every week. Even more novel, they appeared most frequently on one day: Sunday. Having eliminated possible physical factors associated with Sunday, such as sleeping in, special holiday foods, and overeating, he decided that his patients' hysterical symptoms were caused by the holiday character of the day. This hypothesis seemed to be borne out by one particular case, that of a Jewish boy whose symptoms appeared on Friday evening, the commencement of the Sabbath. Ferenczi speculated that the headaches and vomiting of these holiday neurotics were a reaction to the freedom that the weekly day of rest offered. Since Sunday allowed all sorts of relaxed behavior (noisy family games, playful picnics, casual dress), Ferenczi reasoned that people who were neurotically disposed might feel uncomfortable "venting their holiday wantonness," either because they had dangerous impulses to control or because they felt guilty about letting go their inhibitions.

Ferenczi described the Sunday holiday as a day when "we are our   2
own masters and feel ourselves free from all the fetters that the duties and compulsions of circumstances impose on us; there occurs in us— parallel with this—a kind of inner liberation also." Although "Sunday neurosis" was a clinical term, the concept of a liberation of repressed instincts coupled with a greater availability of free time raised the menacing image of a whole society running amok. Throughout the 1920s there were dozens of articles and books of a more general nature, published by psychiatrists, psychologists, and social scientists in both Europe and America, on the perils of what was often called the New Leisure. There was a widespread feeling that the working class would not really know what to do with all this extra free time.

The underlying theme was an old one: less work meant more   3
leisure, more leisure led to idleness, and idle hands, as everyone knew, were ripe for Satan's mischief. This was precisely the argument advanced by the supporters of Prohibition, who maintained that shorter hours provided workers with more free time which they would only squander on drink. Whatever the merits of this argument—and undoubtedly drinking was popular—one senses that this and other such "concerns" really masked an unwillingness to accept the personal freedom that was implicit in leisure. The pessimism of social reformers— and many intellectuals—about the abilities of ordinary people to amuse themselves has always been profound, and never more so than when popular amusements do not accord with established notions of what constitutes a good time.

In *Work Without End,* Benjamin K. Hunnicutt describes how such   4
thinking had an important effect on reinforcing employers' opposition to the Saturday holiday in pre-Depression America. The shorter workday had eventually, and often reluctantly, been accepted by manage-

ment; one reason was that studies had shown how production increased when workers had longer daily breaks and were less tired. The same did not apply, however, to the weekend. "Having Saturdays off," Hunnicutt observes, "was seen to offer the worker leisure—the opportunity to become increasingly free from the job to do other things." And if these "other things" were not good for him, then it was only proper that he should be kept in the workplace, and out of trouble.

The Depression saw this paternalistic resistance set aside, or at least   5
modified. Although both employers and Roosevelt's administration opposed the thirty-hour week (which effectively meant a two- or three-day weekend) proposed by labor as a work-sharing measure, the Thirty-Hour Bill was passed by Congress in 1933. The law had a two-year trial period, and was watered down by the National Industrial Recovery Act, but the pressure for some sort of work sharing was too great to ignore. Many industries adopted a shorter day and reduced the length of the workweek from six days to five.

There were different views as to what people should do with this   6
newfound freedom. Some economists hoped the extra free time would spur consumption of leisure goods and stimulate the stagnant economy. Middle-class social reformers saw an opportunity for a program of national physical and intellectual self-improvement. That was the message of a book called *A Guide to Civilized Loafing*, written by H. A. Overstreet in 1934. Despite the title, which in later editions was changed to the more seemly *A Guide to Civilized Leisure*, the author's view was that free time was an opportunity, and the book described a daunting array of free-time activities, from amateur drama to volunteer work. Overstreet was prescient in some of his recommendations, like bicycling and hiking, although other of his enthusiasms—playing the gong, for example—have yet to catch on. If his suggestions for "loafing" seem at times obsessive, it is because there were now so many free hours to fill. Overstreet, like earlier reformers, had a narrow idea of leisure—he neglected, for example, to list two favorite American pastimes, hunting and fishing, and, despite the repeal of Prohibition, he did not mention social drinking.

The two goals of filling leisure time—one economic and one   7
cultural—appeared to many to be incompatible. Walter Lippmann's 1930 article in *Woman's Home Companion* entitled "Free Time and Extra Money" articulated "the problem of leisure." He warned that leisure offered the individual difficult choices, choices for which a work-oriented society such as America had not prepared him.* Lippmann was

---

* More than a quarter century later, in *The Human Condition*, Hannah Arendt echoed this view: "What we are confronted with is the prospect of a society of laborers without labor, that is, without the only activity left to them. Surely, nothing could be worse."

concerned that if people didn't make creative use of their free time, it would be squandered on mass entertainments and commercial amusements. His view spawned many books and articles of popular sociology with titles such as *The Challenge of Leisure, The Threat of Leisure,* and even *The Menace of Leisure.*

Much of this concern was based on the widespread assumption that   8
the amount of available free time was greater than ever, and that the "problem of leisure" was without precedent. Before the Depression, an American working a forty-hour week spent less than half his 5,840 waking hours each year on the job—the rest was free time. By comparison, a hundred years earlier, work had accounted for as much as two thirds of one's waking hours. But as Hannah Arendt observed, this reduction is misleading, since the modern period was inevitably measured against the Industrial Revolution, which represented an all-time low as far as the number of working hours was concerned. A comparison with earlier periods of history leads to a different conclusion. The fourth-century Roman, for example, with 175 annual public holidays, spent fewer than a third of his waking hours at work; in medieval Europe, religious festivals reduced the work year to well below the modern level of two thousand hours. Indeed, until the eighteenth century, Europeans and Americans enjoyed *more* free time than they do today. The American worker of the 1930s was just catching up.

Most critics however, preferred to look to the future. What they saw   9
was further mechanization, as well as technological innovations such as automation, which promised continued gains in efficiency and productivity in the workplace. "The old world of oppressive toil is passing, and we enter now upon new freedom for ourselves . . . in an age of plenty, we can look forward to an increasing amount of time that is our own." Overstreet wrote this the year after the Thirty-Hour Bill was passed, and to him, as to many others, it appeared that the shortening of the working day was a trend that would continue for some time. "It would be a rash prophet who denies the possibility that this generation may live to see a two-hour day," wrote another observer.

How wrong they turned out to be. Working hours bottomed out   10
during the Depression, and then started to rise again. Job creation, not work sharing, became the goal of the New Deal. By 1938 the Thirty-Hour Bill had expired and the Fair Labor Standards Act provided for a workweek of not thirty but forty hours. As Hunnicutt observes, this marked the end of a century-long trend. On the strength of the evidence of the last fifty years, it would appear that the trend has not only stopped but reversed. In 1948, thirteen percent of Americans with full-time jobs worked more than forty-nine hours a week; by 1979 the figure had crept up to eighteen percent. Ten years later, the Bureau of Labor Statistics es-

timated that of 88 million Americans with full-time jobs, fully twenty-four percent worked more than forty-nine hours a week.

Ask anyone how long they spend at work and they can tell you ex-   11
actly; it is more difficult to keep track of leisure. For one thing, it is irregular; for another, it varies from person to person. For some, cutting the
lawn is a burden; for others it is a pleasurable pastime. Going to the mall
can be a casual Saturday outing, or it can be a chore. Most would count
watching television as leisure, but what about Sunday brunch? Sometimes the same activity—walking the dog—can be a pleasure, sometimes
not, depending on the weather. Finally, whether an activity is part of our
leisure depends as much on our frame of mind as anything else.

Surveys of leisure habits often show diverging results. Two recent   12
surveys, by the University of Maryland and by Michigan's Survey Research Center, both suggest that most Americans enjoy about thirty-nine
hours of leisure time weekly. On the other hand, a 1988 survey conducted by the National Research Center of the Arts came to a very different conclusion and found that "Americans report a median 16.6
hours of leisure time each week." The truth is probably somewhere in
between.

Less surprising, given the number of people working more than   13
forty-nine hours a week, was the National Research Center's conclusion
that most Americans have suffered a decline in weekly leisure time of
9.6 hours over the last fifteen years. The nineteenth-century activists
who struggled so hard for a shorter workweek and more free time
would have been taken aback by this statistic—what had happened to
the "Eight Hours for What We Will"?

There are undoubtedly people who work longer hours out of per-   14
sonal ambition, to escape problems at home, of from compulsion. The
term "workaholic" (a postwar Americanism) is recent, but addiction to
work is not—Thomas Jefferson, for example, was a compulsive worker,
as was G. K. Chesterton—and there is no evidence that there are more
such people today than in the past. Of course, for many, longer hours
are not voluntary—they are obliged to work more merely to make ends
meet. This has been particularly true since the 1970s, when poverty in
America began to increase, but since the shrinking of leisure time began
during the prosperous 1960s, economic need isn't the only explanation.

Twenty years ago Staffan Linder, a Swedish sociologist, wrote a   15
book about the paradox of increasing affluence and decreasing leisure
time in the United States. Following in Lippmann's steps, Linder observed that in a prosperous consumer society there was a conflict between the market's promotion of luxury goods and the individual's
leisure time. When work hours were first shortened, there were few

luxury items available to the general public, and the extra free time was generally devoted to leisure. With the growth of the so-called "leisure industry," people were offered a choice: more free time or more spending? Only the wealthy could have both. If the average person wanted to indulge in expensive recreations such as skiing or sailing, or to buy expensive entertainment devices, it would be necessary to work more— to trade his or her free time for overtime or a second job. Whether because of the effectiveness of advertising or from simple acquisitiveness, most people chose spending over more free time.

Linder's thesis was that economic growth caused an increasing   16
scarcity of time, and that statistics showing an increase in personal incomes were not necessarily a sign of growing prosperity. People were earning more because they were working more. A large percentage of free time was being converted into what he called "consumption time," and mirrored a shift from "time-intensive" to "goods-intensive" leisure. According to *U.S. News & World Report,* Americans now spend more than $13 billion annually on sports clothing; put another way, about 1.3 billion hours of potential leisure time are exchanged for leisure wear— for increasingly elaborate running shoes, certified hiking shorts, and monogrammed warm-up suits. In 1989, to pay for these indulgences, more workers than ever before—6.2 percent—held a second, part-time job; in factories, overtime work increased to an average of four hours a week, the highest number in nearly twenty years.

Probably the most dramatic change is the large-scale entry of   17
women into the labor force. In 1950 only thirty percent of American women worked outside the home, and this primarily out of economic necessity. Beginning in the 1960s middle-class women, dissatisfied with their suburban isolation and willing to trade at least some of their leisure time for purchasing power, started to look for paid employment. By 1986 more than half of all adult women—including married women with children—worked outside the home. Nor are these trends slowing down; between 1980 and 1988, the number of families with two or more wage earners rose from 19 to 21 million.

"Working outside the home" is the correct way to describe the situ-   18
ation, for housework (three or four hours a day) still needs to be done. Whether it is shared, or, more commonly, falls on the shoulders of women as part of their "second shift," leisure time for one or both partners is drastically reduced. Moreover, homes are larger than at any time in the postwar period, and bigger houses also mean more time spent in cleaning, upkeep, and repairs.*

---

* The average size of a new American home in the 1950s was less than 1,000 square feet; by 1983 it had increased to 1,710 square feet, and in 1986 had expanded another 115 square feet.

Even if one chooses to consume less and stay at home, there are 19 other things that cut into free time. Commuting to and from work takes longer than it used to. So does shopping—the weekly trip to the mall consumes more time than a stroll to the neighborhood corner store. Decentralized suburban life, which is to say American life, is based on the automobile. Parents become chauffeurs, ferrying their children back and forth to dance classes, hockey games, and the community pool. At home, telephone answering machines have to be played back, the household budget entered into the personal computer, the lawn mower dropped off at the repair shop, the car—or cars—serviced. All these convenient labor-saving devices relentlessly eat into our discretionary time. For many executives, administrators, and managers, the reduction of leisure time is also the result of office technology that brings work to the home. Fax machines, paging devices, and portable computers mean that taking work home at night is no longer difficult or voluntary. Even the contemplative quiet of the morning automobile commute is now disrupted by the presence of the cellular telephone.

There is no contradiction between the surveys that indicate a re- 20 versing trend, resulting in less free time, and the claim that the weekend dominates our leisure. Longer work hours and more overtime cut mainly into weekday leisure. So do longer commuting, driving the kids, and Friday-night shopping. The weekend—or what's left of it, after Saturday household chores—is when we have time to relax.

But the weekend has imposed a rigid schedule on our free time, 21 which can result in a sense of urgency ("soon it will be Monday") that is at odds with relaxation. The weekly rush to the cottage is hardly leisurely, nor is the compression of various recreational activities into the two-day break. The freedom to do something has become the obligation to do something, just as Chesterton foretold, and the list of dutiful recreations includes strenuous disciplines intended for self-improvement (fitness exercises, jogging, bicycling), competitive sports (tennis, golf), and skill-testing pastimes (sailing, skiing).

Recreations such as tennis or sailing are hardly new, but before the 22 arrival of the weekend, for most people, they were chiefly seasonal activities. Once a year, when vacation time came around, tennis racquets were removed from the back of the cupboard, swimwear was taken out of mothballs, skis were dusted off. The accent was less on technique than on having a good time. It was like playing Scrabble at the summer cottage: no one remembers all the rules, but everyone can still enjoy the game. Now the availability of free time every weekend has changed this casual attitude. The very frequency of weekend recreations allows continual participation and continual improvement, which encourage the development of proficiency and skill.

Skill is necessary since difficulty characterizes modern recreations.   23 Many nineteenth-century amusements, such as rowing, were not particularly involved and required little instruction; mastering windsurfing, on the other hand, takes considerable practice and dexterity—which is part of the attraction. Even relatively simple games are complicated by the need to excel. Hence the emphasis on professionalism, which is expressed by the need to have the proper equipment and the correct costume (especially the right shoes). The desire for mastery isn't limited to outdoor recreations; it also includes complicated hobbies such as woodworking, electronics, and automobile restoration. All this suggests that the modern weekend is characterized by not only the sense of obligation to do something but the obligation to do it *well*.

The desire to do something well, whether it is sailing a boat—or   24 building a boat—reflects a need that was previously met in the workplace. Competence was shown on the job—holidays were for messing around. Nowadays the situation is reversed. Technology has removed craft from most occupations. This is true in assembly-line jobs, where almost no training or experience, hence no skill, is required, as well as in most service positions (store clerks, fast-food attendants) where the only talent required is to learn how to smile and say "have a good day." But it's also increasingly true in such skill-dependent work as house construction, where the majority of parts come ready-made from the factory and the carpenter merely assembles them, or automobile repair, which consists largely in replacing one throwaway part with another. Nor is the reduction of skills limited to manual work. Memory, once the prerequisite skill of the white-collar worker, has been rendered superfluous by computers; teachers, who once needed dramatic skills, now depend on mechanical aids such as slide projectors and video machines; in politics, oratory has been killed by the thirty-second sound bite.

Hence an unexpected development in the history of leisure. For   25 many, weekend free time has become not a chance to escape work but a chance to create work that is more meaningful—to work at recreation—in order to realize the personal satisfactions that the workplace no longer offers.

"Leisure" is the most misunderstood word in our vocabulary. We   26 often use the words "recreation" and "leisure" interchangeably—recreation room, rest and recreation, leisure suit, leisure industry—but they really embody two different ideas. Recreation carries with it a sense of necessity and purpose. However pleasurable this antidote to work may be, it's a form of active employment, engaged in with a specific end in mind—a refreshment of the spirit, or the body, or both. Implicit in this idea of renewal—usually organized renewal—is the notion that recreation is both a consequence of work and a preparation for more of it.

Leisure is different. That was what Lippmann was getting at when   27
he contrasted commercial recreation with individual leisure. Leisure is not tied to work the way that recreation is—leisure is self-contained. The root of the word is the Latin *licere* which means "to be permitted," suggesting that leisure is about freedom. But freedom for what? According to Chesterton's cheerful view, leisure was above all an opportunity to do nothing. When he said "doing nothing," however, he was describing not emptiness but an occasion for reflection and contemplation, a chance to look inward rather than outward. A chance to tend one's garden, as Voltaire put it. That is why Chesterton called this kind of leisure "the most precious, the most consoling, the most pure and holy."

Bertrand Russell placed leisure into a larger historical context in his   28
essay "In Praise of Idleness." "Leisure is essential to civilization," he wrote, "and in former times leisure for the few was only rendered possible by the labours of the many. But their labours were valuable, not because work is good, but because leisure is good." Russell, a member of the aristocracy, pointed out that it had been precisely the leisure classes, not the laborers, who had written the books, invented the philosophies, produced the sciences, and cultivated the arts. But he was not arguing for a continuation of the class system; on the contrary, he proposed extending the leisure that had previously been reserved for the few to the many. This was an explicit attack on the work ethic, which he considered a device to trick people into accepting a life without leisure. In his view, the trick hadn't succeeded; working men and women had no illusions about work—they understood it was merely a necessary means to a livelihood.

Russell's underlying argument was that we should free ourselves   29
from the guilt about leisure that modern society has imposed on us. Hence the use of terms such as "idleness" and "doing nothing," which were intended as a provocation to a society that placed the highest value on "keeping busy." Both Russell and Chesterton agreed with Aristotle, who considered leisure the aim of life. "We work," he wrote, "to have leisure."

"In Praise of Idleness" was written in 1932, at the height of the De-   30
pression, and Russell's proposal of a four-hour workday now appears hopelessly utopian. But the weekend's later and sudden new popularity in so many societies suggests that leisure is beginning to make a comeback, although not as fully as Russell desired, nor in so relaxed a way as Chesterton would have wished. I cannot shake the suspicion that

something more than mere functionality accounts for the widespread popularity of the weekend. Can its universal appeal be explained by a resonance with some ancient inclination, buried deep in the human psyche? Given the mythological roots of the planetary week, and the devotional nature of Sunday and the Sabbath, the answer is likely to be found in early religious attitudes.

Mircea Eliade, a historian of religion, characterized traditional pre-   31
modern societies as experiencing the world in two distinct ways corresponding to two discontinuous modes of being: the sacred and the profane. According to Eliade, the sacred manifested itself in various ways—how physical space was perceived, for example. The profane, chaotic world, full of menace, was given structure and purpose by the existence of fixed, meaningful sacred places. Sacred places could occur in the landscape, beside holy trees or on certain mountains, but they could also be man-made. Hence the elaborate rituals practiced by all ancient people when they founded settlements and erected buildings, rituals not only to protect the future town or building but to delineate a sacred space.

The prime sacred space was the home, for houses were not merely   32
shelters but consecrated places that incorporated cosmic symbolism into their very construction. The Navajo Indians, for example, affirmed that their homes—hogans—were based on a divine prototype. The conical shape of the hogan resembled a mountain in New Mexico that the Navajo called "the heart of the Earth." They believed that God had created the first forked-stick hogan using posts made of white shell, turquoise, abalone, and obsidian. When a new hogan was built, pieces of these four minerals were buried beneath the four main posts, which also corresponded to the four points of the compass. In this way the builder interrupted the continuity of the everyday world by creating a separate magical space.

A person stepping out of the desert sun into the dark, cool interior   33
of a hogan was entering a space that was a part of the ancient past, and thus he was entering not only a sacred space but a sacred time. According to Eliade, profane time was ordinary temporal duration, but sacred time, which was also the time of festivals and holy days, was primordial and mythical, and stood apart from everyday life. During sacred time, the clock not only stopped, it was turned back. The purpose of religious rites was precisely to reintegrate this past into the present. In this way, sacred time became part of a separate, repetitive continuum, "an eternal mythical present."

Eliade characterized modern Western society as "nonreligious," in   34
the sense that it had desacralized and demythologized the world. For nonreligious man there could be only profane space and profane time. But, he pointed out, since the roots of this society lay in a religious past,

it could never divest itself completely of ancient beliefs; remnants of these remained, although in camouflaged form: for example, movies employing mythical motifs, such as the struggle between hero and monster, descent into an underworld, or the cleansing ordeal. Even in our homes, which no longer incorporate cosmic symbolism in the comprehensive way of the Navajo hogan, rituals have not altogether disappeared. Giving a housewarming party, carrying the bride over the threshold, receiving important guests at the front door instead of at the back door, decorating the exterior at festal times of year—these are all reminders that although we treat our houses as commodities, the home is still a special space, standing apart from the practical world.

Is it fanciful to propose that the repetitive cycle of week and weekend is a modern paraphrase of the ancient opposition of profane and sacred time? Obviously the weekend is not a historical remnant in any literal sense, since it didn't even exist until the nineteenth century, and its emergence was in response to specific social and economic conditions. Nor am I suggesting that the secular weekend is a substitute for religious festivals, although it is obviously linked to religious observance. But there are several striking parallels.　35

Weekday time, like profane time, is linear. It represents an irreversible progression of days, Monday to Friday, year after year. Past weekday time is lost time. Schooldays are followed by workdays, the first job by the second and the third. I can never be a schoolboy again, or a college student, or a young architect anxiously waiting to meet my first client.* Not only is weekday time linear, but, like profane time, it encompasses the unpredictable. During the week, unforeseen things happen. People get promoted and fired. Stock markets soar or crash. Politicians are elected or voted out of office. One has the impression that history occurs on weekdays.†　36

The weekend, on the other hand, is, in Plato's words, a time to take a breather. It's a time apart from the world of mundane problems and mundane concerns, from the world of making a living. On weekends time stands still, and not only because we take off our watches. Just as holidays at the beach are an opportunity to re-create our childhood, to build sand castles with the kids, to paddle in the surf, to lie on the sand and get a sunburn, many of the things we do on weekends correspond to the things we did on weekends past. Weekend time shares this sense　37

---

* Several years ago I attended a high-school class reunion, which could be described as an attempt to recover weekday time. Revealingly, the subject of conversation was sports and extracurricular activities, not what we had done in the classroom.

† The notable exception is war, which often begins on the weekend, when it is least expected. The German blitzkrieg of 1940 was launched on a Saturday morning; the Japanese attack on Pearl Harbor occurred on a Sunday; the Egyptians started the Yom Kippur War on the Sabbath.

of reenactment with sacred time, and just as sacred time was characterized by ritual, the weekend, despite being an opportunity for personal
freedom, is governed by convention: raking leaves, grilling steaks on the
barbecue, going to the movies, Saturday night out, reading the Sunday
paper, brunch, the afternoon opera broadcast, weekend drives, garage
sales, weekend visits. The predictability of the weekend is one of its
comforts.

Although Eliade described examples of sacred time from different 38
societies and periods of history, the specific rites and rituals varied. An
event could be holy in one culture and have no meaning in another; a
festival could be a taboo time because the day was considered unlucky,
while elsewhere it was observed for exactly the opposite reason. The
myths of their sacred histories differentiated societies.

The conventions of weekend leisure, too, vary from place to place. In 39
Europe, for example, northerners read more books than southerners,
Germans and Danes spend more than others on musical instruments, the
British are the greatest gamblers, the Italians the greatest moviegoers,
and every one favors tennis except the French. Canada and the United
States, which have many similarities, differ in their attitude to leisure,
and surveys have consistently shown that Americans believe more
strongly in the work ethic than Canadians do. Probably for that reason,
Canadians give personal leisure a higher importance and have been
much slower to accept commercial intrusions such as Sunday shopping.

The differences in national attitudes toward leisure are arresting be- 40
cause we live in a world where the character of work is increasingly international. Around the world, in different countries, what happens between nine and five during the week is becoming standardized. Because
of international competition and transnational ownership of companies,
the transfer of technology from one country to another is almost in-
stantaneous. All offices contain the same telephones, photocopiers,
word processors, computers, and fax machines. The Japanese build automobile plants in the United States and Canada, the Americans build
factories in Eastern Europe, the Europeans in South America. Industries
are increasingly dominated by a diminishing number of extremely large
and similar corporations. The reorganization of the workplace in Communist and formerly Communist countries, along more capitalist lines,
is one more step in the standardization of work. And as work becomes
more standardized, and international, one can expect that leisure, by
contrast, will be even more national, more regional, more different.

Leisure has always been partly a refuge from labor. The weekend, 41
too, is a retreat from work, but in a different way: a retreat from the abstract and the universal to the local and the particular. In that sense,
leisure is likely to continue to be, as Pieper claimed, the basis of culture.

Every culture chooses a different structure for its work and leisure, and in doing so it makes a profound statement about itself. It invents, adapts, and recombines old models, hence the long list of leisure days: public festivals, family celebrations, market days, taboo days, evil days, holy days, feasts, Saint Mondays and Saint Tuesdays, commemorative holidays, summer vacations—and weekends.

The weekend is our own contribution, another way of dealing with   42
the ancient duality. The institution of the weekend reflects the many unresolved contradictions in modern attitudes toward leisure. We want to have our cake, and eat it too. We want the freedom to be leisurely, but we want it regularly, every week, like clockwork. The attraction of Saint Monday was that one could "go fishing" when one willed; the regularity of the weekend—every five days—is at odds with the ideas of personal freedom and spontaneity. There is something mechanical about this oscillation, which creates a sense of obligation that interferes with leisure. Like sacred time, the weekend is comfortingly repetitive, but the conventionality of weekend free time, which must exist side by side with private pastimes and idiosyncratic hobbies, often appears restrictive. "What did you do on the weekend?" "The usual," we answer, mixing dismay with relief.

We have invented the weekend, but the dark cloud of old taboos still   43
hangs over the holiday, and the combination of the secular with the holy leaves us uneasy. This tension only compounds the guilt that many of us continue to feel about not working, and leads to the nagging feeling that our free time should be used for some purpose higher than having fun. We want leisure, but we are afraid of it too.

Do we work to have leisure, or the other way around? Unsure of the   44
answer, we have decided to keep the two separate. If C. P. Snow had not already used the term in another context, it would be tempting to speak of Two Cultures. We pass weekly from one to the other—from the mundane, communal, increasingly impersonal, increasingly demanding, increasingly bureaucratic world of work to the reflective, private, controllable, consoling world of leisure. The weekend; our own, and not our own, it is what we wait for all week long.

· · · · · · · · · · · · · · · · · · · ·

Examining the Text

1. What is a "Sunday neurosis" (paragraphs 1–2)? Have you ever suffered any of its symptoms? Why does Rybczynski begin by describing this "clinical term"?

2. In paragraphs 2–10 and 26–29 Rybczynski traces early twentieth century theorizing about leisure time. Why was leisure the subject of so much speculation during these years? For example, why was Walter Lippmann concerned that "free time . . . would be squandered on mass entertainments and commercial amusements" (7)? What does Rybczynski's survey of these ideas contribute to his own argument about the tension we feel about the weekend?

3. Rybczynski uses historian Mircea Eliade's notion of sacred and profane time to characterize the difference between weekends and weekdays (31–38). Summarize what Rybczynski names as the characteristics of weekdays that make them "profane" and the characteristics of weekends that make them "sacred". Do you find his analyses persuasive? What can you add to this discussion?

4. Rybczynski's central point is that "We want leisure, but we are afraid of it too" (43). What reasons does he offer for our fear of leisure? Does he convince you?

For Group Discussion

Reread paragraphs 11–13. Determine how many hours a week you spend on leisure activities and what those activities are. Compare your results with other members of your group. Are there interesting divergences in the estimated amounts of leisure time; that is, do some group members suggest they have much less free time than others? If so, discuss the reasons for such differences. If not, is there also general agreement on what constitutes a "leisure activity"?

Writing Suggestion

Rybczynski asserts that "Every culture chooses a different structure for its work and leisure, and in doing so it makes a profound statement about itself" (41). Focus on some of the most popular leisure activities in the United States today and in an essay explore any "profound statements" these activities make about American culture. If you're familiar with life in another culture, you might draw some comparisons between that culture's structures of work and leisure and those in the U.S.

LEISURE ACTIVITIES

The Inside Story of a Video Game You Can Get Inside

James Gorman

*V*ideo games are one of the most popular leisure pursuits among today's children and young adults. Almost every community has crowded video arcades; family rooms offer home versions on television sets and computer screens; portable devices allow players to zap obstacles and collect "power-ups" virtually anywhere. Sociologists and psychologists study the effects of the violence in some games on children, but we ask even broader questions about this particular leisure pursuit: why do the games appeal to us and how do they influence—and reflect—our character and culture?

The following essay gives us a chance to ponder these questions. In it, James Gorman describes his experiences as a "video-junkie," more specifically as a player of "Planet Photon." While influenced by video games, Photon is a "real-life" game played on a 10,000-square-foot indoor field that includes hazards, hiding places, and goals. Participants don helmets and score points by firing "phasers" at opponents and capturing their goals. Gorman, author of The Man With No Endorphins *and articles in* Audubon, New Yorker, *and* The New York Times, *makes compelling points about his youthful infatuation with video games as well as his infatuation, as an adult, with Photon.*

Before you read, *think about your own experience with video games. What do you enjoy about playing them? Even if you've never played a game, why would you imagine they are so addictive, particularly to children and adolescents?*

••••••••••••••••••••

OZ and I—OZ is his code name, mine is GOR—are considerably older than most of the other Photon Warriors. We're standing by our base goal, listening to a disembodied woman's voice tell us about our mission. The voice is husky, and either menacing or seductive (I always get those two confused). Most of the time I can't understand what the voice is saying but I don't think that's supposed to be part of the game.

With our phasers at the ready, OZ and I discuss strategy. We've been getting murdered. We keep getting an awful "Buzz!" in our helmets that means we've been shot (−10 points). Usually we don't even see who's shooting us. We run, hide, spin, shoot, and what we get is more buzzes. 2

Other people, like CD DISK, are scoring 600 or 700. We've been getting scores like 140 and −90. Not this time. This time we have a plan. At the end of the countdown we sprint to the sniper's nest. We hunker down, picking off the red team players (10 points per hit) when they come out of hiding. Sometimes we get picked off too. As the game wanes, we rush their goal (200 points if you hit it three times in a row). OZ tears down a ramp into a corridor, flattens himself against a wall, jumps out into the open, spins, shoots, gets shot. I make my dash to a tunnel, where I start getting buzzes from an invisible enemy. I look for cover. Crouched in the dark, hiding, I ask myself: Is this any way for a grown man to spend Friday night? And what's my score?

Incredibly, our strategy doesn't pay off. After the game, on the big   3
TV screen in the lobby, many lines below CD DISK, are GOR 180, and OZ 40. If you think I'm depressed, you should see OZ.

Back in the old days, before Photon, before you could get *inside* a   4
video game, there was Asteroids, and Space Invaders, and what, for my money (and I spent enough on it), was, and still is, the greatest video game of them all—Missile Command. I can't say I was a great player. At the Times Square arcade where I spent my lunch breaks, I was just a hacker. Of course, the competition was tough. Times Square is to video games what Times Square is to crime—and it's the same people who are good at both. However, once, on a trip to Brattleboro, Vt., I played Missile Command at a little arcade, a spot of bright urban blight beeping and flashing in the midst of the health food stores. I got the highest score the machine had ever seen, and left singing "You don't tug on a Superman's cape, you don't spit into the wind, you don't pull the mask off the old Lone Ranger, and you don't mess around with Jim." At least not in Brattleboro.

I was deeply involved in video games. I still think there's no music   5
as sweet as the noise of the Playland arcade at 48th and Broadway with all the games going at once. It's like being in an electronic rain forest. And there's nothing like seeing that the top three scores on a game are 999,999 (as high as the counter goes), and that three players who beat the game are GEE, MAX, and GOD. When you see that you say to yourself, "This is the place."

I myself never noticed any negative effects of video games. Some-   6
times, after a three-hour, $15 Missile Command lunch I would feel cheap and used—not if I had a good score, though. I did stop playing, only because I started working at home, far from the good arcades. Then, finally, I moved out of Manhattan, bought a house, and had children. I mowed the lawn. I learned how to use a screwdriver. And I took up tennis. Now that's a game that can really make you feel cheap and used.

So, when Planet Photon was born I was ripe for recruitment. Cer- 7
tain things were missing from my life, like sound effects. And I wasn't
yet prepared to see myself as others (my neighbors) saw me: round-
shouldered and beleaguered, pushing a double stroller with two kids in
it, dragging along two untrained, ungroomed dogs in a circus parade of
domestic confusion—in other words, as the exact opposite of Arnold
Schwarzenegger. I wanted to see myself differently, as a guy in a helmet, with a phaser in his hand, zapping the Klingons. As soon as I heard
about the game, I started practicing my moves.

Planet Photon was invented by George A. Carter III, the man who 8
also invented, and I quote his news release "the world's first motorized
surfboard." Remember the motorized surfboard? No? Well, as Carter III
himself has admitted, he "anticipated the market a little too soon." Ah,
but then he thought of Photon, a cross between a science fiction movie
and a very large video game. The promotional literature on the game
mentions the movie *Tron,* a fantasy in which people enter a video game.
According to Carter, with Photon, the fantasy is now reality.

Photon is played on an indoor field of 10,000 square feet. The basic 9
field (three of the nine existing Photons have the more complex Omega
field) is high-ceilinged, carpeted, and has two levels. There are ramps,
tunnels, some tacky lighting, music, hidey holes, walls, base goals—
pretty much anything you might want in a planet. There's also one
slightly grotesque touch, a gallery, or walkway over the field, from
which spectators may watch the game, or, for a dollar, use one of the
gallery's phaser stations. From these stations you take target practice.
You can shoot the players. But they can't shoot you.

The players must shoot each other. To this end, they're issued hel- 10
mets, battery belts, chest pods, and phasers, and allowed to sign on with
any code name they like, "Ace" or "Ed Norton" (who was very good)
or "Fooltron" (who wasn't). There are referees to explain and enforce the
rules. You're not allowed to stick your phaser through grates or around
corners, run at 90 miles an hour down the ramps, or get within five feet
of another player. (I'm sure full-contact Photon will evolve in the near
future.) Unlike tennis, Photon has sound effects. Helmet speakers ring
with zings, zaps, and buzzes when you hit or miss opponents, or get
shot yourself.

Naturally, computers are involved. The scorekeeping and sound ef- 11
fects are managed by two IBM PCs. I suppose that, depending on your
point of view and how good a shot you are, you might look on Photon
as part of the humanization of technology or as just another form of electronic leprosy. I'd say that Photon is a positive contribution to human
life, but not that positive. I would compare it in value to the introduction of the three-point shot in professional basketball. The difference, of

course, is in the infrared light (this is what the phasers shoot, not laser beams) and the little computer chips in each player's chest pod, which register hits and communicate, by means of radio waves, with the PCs. Larry Bird, as we know, doesn't wear a chest pod, although I'm not entirely convinced that Kevin McHale isn't at least partly electronic.

I've now played Photon in Dallas, by myself, and in Kenilworth, N.J., 12 with OZ. (The shooters in New Jersey are tougher, although I can't say why or Don Corleone will send somebody to break my legs.) And I'm sorry to say that Photon is nothing at all like being in a video game. The two experiences are physically, and metaphysically, opposite. At its peak, video game play is an "out of body" experience. What happens is that after an hour or two the brain reaches a state of deep relaxation, a technologically induced trance. The mind enters the game. Like Zen archers who can hit the target blindfolded because they *are* the arrow (at least that's my idea of how they do it) you *are* the missile, or the ray, or the blip. The self disappears, along with the self's quarters. Action occurs without the usual physical limits. Maybe your fingers are limited by the speed of light, maybe not. Maybe they're your fingers, maybe not. Until you run out of change. That's when the self re-emerges and drags the fingers kicking and screaming out into the harsh and sobering light of Broadway.

Photon isn't like this. For one thing, it costs more than a quarter to 13 play. It's $3 or more per six-and-a-half-minute game, depending on where you play, and $4.50 or more for the membership fee. More important, Photon is a decidedly in-body experience, and in my body this isn't such a great thing. If they had rented me Ivan Lendl's body (or Martina Navratilova's—what the hell, as long as it's a Czech) my scores might have been higher. But the game isn't that advanced yet. They only provide helmets and phasers. It's BYOB (bring your own body). And you never know, until you try it, what popping up and down from behind good cover and sprinting through tunnels in a modified duck walk will do to your thighs.

Thigh pain isn't the stuff of fantasy, at least not my fantasies. In Pho- 14 ton it's impossible to believe, for more than 90 seconds, that you're anybody other than yourself, and I can get that at home for free. It's not just the limits of your own body that serve as reminders of dull reality. There are other bodies in this game too. In particular, there are a lot of junior high school kids who sign in with names like Psychopath or Gaddafi (this kid wasn't well received in Dallas) or Lord Corwin (from a series of science fiction novels), and then wander around, chubby and befuddled, getting riddled with light beams by 18-year-old ne'er-do-wells who are presumably taking a break from substance abuse. Of course, the advantage to having little kids in the game is that everybody gets to shoot them. OZ, who teaches junior high school, found this particularly gratifying. And it was in the game with the kids that we both got our highest scores.

As to the effect of Photon on the kids themselves, I don't think it will rot their brains. Drugs and television will rot their brains. Infra-red light is no big deal. Besides, Photon will keep them in good enough physical condition so that when they're my age they can play tennis. And I don't believe, as I'm sure somebody does, that Photon is part of the Rambo-ization of America. I suspect that pinging people with toy phasers is far less inducive to violence than watching one of Stallone's ketchup classics. The sad truth (for those of us who like the occasional evening on another planet) is that although there's a little shooting going on, the big difference between Photon and Capture the Flag is that Photon uses more electricity.

Nonetheless, the game seems to be a success. According to Carter III's office, 147 franchises have been sold, including the licensing of 20 playing fields in Japan. Everybody I've talked to agrees that the Japanese will love the game. Most people think it's the electronic gadgetry that will attract them. I think it's also the code names. A friend who just returned from Japan with a huge hangover told me that businessmen there, when they go drinking, use special names (not their own) so that they won't be ashamed of what they do and say. Such names are ready-made for Photon. And once the game takes off in Japan I think we can rely on the Japanese to take it a step further and produce a street and subway version. In this game each player will carry a completely self-contained, miniaturized apparatus about the size of a portable tape player. It will be called, naturally, the Sony Hit Man.

• • • • • • • • • • • • • • • • • • • •

Examining the Text

1. How would you describe Gorman's attitude toward his subject and toward himself in this essay? Find specific passages that illustrate his attitude. Why do you think he adopts this stance?

2. What features of Photon appeal to Gorman? In what ways is the game similar to and different from video games? What do these comparisons suggest about the appeal and the limitations of video games and of Photon?

3. What does Gorman mean when he comments that "you might look on Photon as part of the humanization of technology or as just another form of electronic leprosy" (paragraph 11)? What are the implications of these two alternate views? Based on Gorman's description of the game, which do you find more accurate?

4. What are the implications of the phrase "the Ramboization of America" (15)? Do you agree with Gorman that Photon doesn't contribute to this "Ramboization" or promote violence? What about other video games?

For Group Discussion

Imagine that you're designing an advertising campaign to promote a local Photon franchise. What audience would you target? What information would you draw from Gorman's article to induce people to give Photon a try? What would be the top four or five selling points that you would focus on to promote Photon?

Writing Suggestion

Gorman suggests that video games produce an "out of body" experience, a "technologically induced trance." Recall your own experiences with video games and interview friends or family members about their experiences; perhaps even visit a video arcade to observe and talk with players. What do you find are the most popular games, and why do players like them? In an essay evaluate Gorman's statements and speculate on why video games have become such a popular way to spend leisure time in our country.

Eight Ways of Looking at
an Amusement Park
Russell B. Nye

*W*hether *we pose for pictures with Mickey Mouse, scream in (mock?) terror hurtling around a 350-degree loop on a roller coaster, or pitch baseballs at milk bottles for a stuffed animal, we go to amusement parks for any number of reasons. In the following article based on extensive research, Russell B. Nye offers eight possibilities to explain people's enjoyment of amusement parks.*

Beginning with an overview of how the modern park developed, Nye suggests that its basic functions have remained very much the same over time: to provide excitement, adventure, and a spectacular alternative world in which to transcend inhibitions and conventional behavior, enjoy the "vicarious terror" of "riskless risks," and simply play. *Moving from the parks of centuries past to World's Fairs to today's Six Flags adventurelands and Disney extravaganzas, Nye attempts to distill the amusement park's essential qualities and define our relationship to it.*

Nye's essay was originally published in the Journal of Popular Culture *in 1981.* **As you read,** *test his ideas against the amusement parks you have vis-*

ited recently. Do his eight categories describe the experience of an amusement park in the 1990s?

• •

The park is an urban phenomenon, a reaction to the crowded cities 1
of the eighteenth century. Historically it is tied to the Romantic era, which saw nature as a curative, educational force—"God's visible smile," to quote William Cullen Bryant, on mankind. It was no accident that William Penn chose to call his colony "Penn-sylvania," with all the connotations of natural peace and beauty that the Latin word brought from the pastroal tradition.[1]

In 1812 Philadelphia landscaped five acres of the east bank of the 2
Schuylkill River to create the beginnings of Fairmont Park, the birthplace of the American park system. Other city parks were founded over the next few decades in response to the demands of an emergent, prosperous middle class for access to those natural surroundings and open spaces previously available only on the estates of the rich. A third factor in the rise of the public park, particularly during the phenomenal burst of urban population in mid-century, was the desire of reformers to counteract what they believed were the dangerous social effects of city life.

The crowded city afforded no chance to be alone with nature or 3
one's self, to ponder questions of life and identity, to learn from God's plants and flowers. Cities bred suspicion, selfishness, isolation; public parks could provide an effective antidote. Thus Central Park was designed by Frederick L. Olmsted and Calvert Vaux in 1858 to furnish New Yorkers a "harmonizing influence" and to "cultivate among the community loftier and more refined desires." It was to be a passive place, without "boisterous fun and rough sports," a contrast to as well as escape from the city. Central Park would provide a pattern for many subsequent city parks and was indeed a precursor of the philosophy that underlay the national park system.[2]

The exposition or "world's fair," a coincidental nineteenth-century 4
development, introduced another set of factors. Instead of an escape

---

[1] Penn in his Philadelphia plan of 1682 in fact set aside five squares as parks, four of which still exist. John Maass, *The Glorious Enterprise: The Centennial Exposition of 1876* (Watkins Glen, N.Y.: Association Press, 1915), pp. 16–18.

[2] See the discussion in John F. Kasson, *Amusing the Million* (New York: Hill and Wang, 1978), pp. 11–16. Kasson's study of Coney Island is the best treatment of an American amusement park in its socio-cultural context. One of the most handsomely designed and illustrated studies of a single park is L. Bush, E. Chukayne, R. Hehr, and R. Hersey, eds., *Euclid Beach Park is Closed for the Season* (Mentor, Ohio: Amusement Park Books, 1978).

from the city, the exposition was intended to take advantage of the urban environment for educational, cultural and especially commercial purposes, reaching as wide an audience as possible. World's Fairs at London (1851, 1862), Paris (1855, 1867, 1878, 1900) and Vienna (1873) served as models for the first major American fair, Philadelphia's Exhibition of 1876, which not only commemorated the nation's Centennial but also exhibited "the arts, manufactures, and products of soil and mine" to the country and the world. Its purposes, concluded a writer in 1812, were to[3]

> teach knowledge of the markets . . . , form taste and judgment . . . , offer instructive insights into creative spheres . . . , and to extend the great civilizing task of educating man to be a world citizen.

Its themes were enlightenment, national pride and most of all progress. The planners of Chicago's Columbia Exposition of 1893 built their project on Philadelphia's success; chief architect Daniel Burnham envisioned a "White City" of monumental grandeur to serve as the ideal pattern of what the modern city could be. The Chicago Fair, unlike Central Park, was not an escape from the city but an idealization of it— a meeting place for art, uplift, education, social participation, the good life.[4]

Whatever Burnham's intentions, a substantial part of the Fair's success derived not from its magnificent architecture and hundreds of educational and artistic exhibits, but from the Midway Plaisance, a mile-long corridor of privately operated concessions, shops, shows, and games that the Fair's planners included with—but kept quite separate from—the rest of the exposition. The Midway, as a contemporary account put it, was "a sideshow pure and simple of halls of entertainment, pavilions, and gardens." It featured girls—an International Beauty Show of "forty gaily dressed beauties from forty lands"; Algerian Dancers in their famous Love Dance ("the coarse animal passions of the East"); "sleek odalisques" from the Persian Palace of Eros; three lovely Samoan damsels named Lola, Mela and Feteia—in company with jugglers, sword swallowers, a Chinese joss house, the Hagenbeck Circus, glass blowers, a replica of Kilauea in eruption, and of course the huge wheel designed by George W. Ferris looming over it all.[5] Without denigrating the cultural and educational contributions of the Columbia Ex-

5

---

[3] See Maass, *op. cit.* pp. 26–72, 93. The Exhibition contained 249 buildings, 5½ miles of railroad, 153 acres of lawn and flower beds, 20,000 trees and shrubs, and three telegraph systems. It "dazzled and astounded" Ralph Waldo Emerson but depressed Henry Adams.

[4] See the discussion in Kasson, pp. 17–20.

[5] For excellent photographs and descriptions see volume IV of *The Portfolio of Photos of the World's Fair* (Chicago: Household Art Press, 1898).

position, it is not unreasonable to say that the two sights which remained most vividly in the American imagination were the "hootchy kootchy" dance of Fatima in the Turkish Village and the profile of the great Ferris wheel which dominated the landscape.[6] The Midway was energetic, amusing, titillating and plain fun. After that no world's fair could afford to omit a "midway," though it might be called (as in St. Louis) The Pike or (in San Francisco) The Joy Zone. There, in Chicago, lay the germ of the modern amusement park.[7]

Another kind of public entertainment, the county or state fair, also contributed to the creation of the amusement park, although its original purpose was commercial and educational. The first agricultural fair was probably held at Georgetown, D.C., in 1809, followed by an increasing number scattered throughout the East, particularly in New York State and New England. By the close of the century, the fair was an autumn fixture everywhere, a place to display farm machinery and farm products and to serve as an annual gathering place for the rural and small town population. Though exhibits were undoubtedly of first interest at fairs, those who attended expected entertainment—animal shows, acrobats, lectures, slide shows (later movies), horse and automobile races, and rigidly-controlled acts and games. There was almost always a section set aside for merry-go-rounds, rides and concessions that was, in effect, a pleasure park in embryo.

But most certainly the Chicago Fair showed that there was a huge waiting urban market for more Midways, a clientele both available and mobile via railway, streetcar and automobile. There were literally millions of Americans eager to pay for this kind of recreation, people with leisure and money to spend on dancehalls, vaudeville, professional sports, movies, theaters, circuses, carnivals and much else.[8] There were also shrewd men ready to take advantage of them. One, George C. Tilyou, bought and transformed New York's Coney Island in 1895, setting off a wave of similar parks in New York and other urban areas— Sea Lion Park, Steeplechase Park, Luna Park (made out of Sea Lion) and Dreamland. Parks sprang up across the land, promoted by railroads, inter-urbans, breweries and local entrepreneurs. The years 1900 to 1910,

6

7

---

[6] Chicago's Century of Progress Midway in 1933 featured Sally Rand and her famous fan dance and the Skyride, two 628-foot towers with a rocket car ride at the 200-foot level.

[7] This is not to say that the amusement park is uniquely American. European "pleasure parks" on city outskirts date certainly from the sixteenth century; London's Vauxhall Gardens (1661) and Ranelagh Gardens (1690), Paris' Ruggieri and Tivoli Gardens (later moved to Denmark) date from the eighteenth century. However, none seems to have had direct major influence on the American version.

[8] Dana Tatlin, "Amusing America's Millions," *World's Work* 26 (July 1913), 325–40 is an interesting and insightful survey of the exploding market for public recreation in the period. See also Richard Henry Edwards, *Popular Amusements* (New York: Association Press, 1915).

in the words of a contemporary, saw "a hysteria of parks followed by panic." Fortunes were made and lost, parks opened and closed, new rides and concessions tried and abandoned. In 1907 the national capitalization of amusement parks was calculated at over $100,000,000, with predictions of double the sum within the decade.[9]

Alert managers and designers knew what the publc wanted and gave it to them. The park was "pleasure to the multitude." It should never be serious, but entertaining; it must be "different from ordinary experience"; it must have "life, action, motion, sensation, surprise, shock, swiftness, or else comedy." Those who paid to get in wanted innocent fun, not morality or education—as Frederic Thompson said, they wanted "elaborated child's play." The amusement park, he continued, should be "frankly devoted to fun, the fantastic, the gay, the grotesque."[10]

The modern American amusement park, then, was never a pastoral retreat. It was not a place of quiet self-evaluation but one for participation, noise, jostle, light, color, activity. Tilyou, Thompson and the rest integrated the park into the city by railway, trolley, bus and automobile. It was not a flight from urban life but a journey to an intensified version of it, where one mixed with the same city crowds in a different context, "catching," an observer commented, "the full live sense of humanity." An early visitor described it quite accurately as "essentially a place of merriment . . . , there is no other reason for going there."[11] And by enclosing the park and charging admission, operators immediately established control of who entered and what went on inside—creating an engineered environment, carefully planned to manipulate visitors into having fun but also spending money in an orderly, safe, relaxed atmosphere.

1. Thus our first view of the amusement park—as an alternative world to that of our daily lives. The amusement park provides all who come with a chance to be something other than what they are—workers, bosses, fathers, mothers, sons, daughters, anyone with responsibilities or socio-economic functions. Frederic Thompson put it succinctly: "Everything must be different from ordinary life." The park allows people the chance to operate in a different environment for purposes and rewards quite different from those of the outside workaday world. It is

---

[9] Tatlin, pp. 335–6.

[10] Thompson explained his theories in two remarkable essays, "The Summer Show," *Independent* 62 (June 20, 1907) 1460–62; and "Amusing the Million," *Everybody's Magazine* 19 (Sept. 1908), 395–7. See also Edwin E. Slosson's classic "The Amusement Business," *Independent* 67 (July 21, 1904), pp. 134–38.

[11] Lindsay Denison, "The Biggest Playground in the World," *Munsey's Magazine* 33 (August 1905), pp. 555–61.

a place where each can set his own easily attainable goals in a known, controllable situation. In this world nothing is done for profit, nothing by necessity. We can beat the weight guesser or win the teddy bear, but in the park's insulated environment we don't have to try to do either, nor does success or failure really matter. We can live in Space World, Frontier Village or Safari Land; take chances without real risk on rides, and in games of skill or chance. In a real sense, within the park we can— for the moment—live in a way we cannot outside it, and at relatively small cost.

2. A second way of looking at an amusement park is related to the   11
first, that is, to see it as fantasy, a stage set, a never-never land where one can walk out of his own world into a much more interesting one. This, of course, is one of the oldest attractions of the amusement park and still one of its most powerful. When the visitor arrives at the park's gate, wrote Frederic Thompson,

> His eyes tell him he is in a different world—a dream world, perhaps a nightmare world—where all is bizarre and fantastic—crazier than the craziest part of Paris—gayer and more different from the everyday world. . . . He is prepared to accept all sorts of extravagances—things that elsewhere would be impossible—in perfect faith for the time being.

O. Henry, a constant visitor to Coney Island, loved it for its "breathtaking though safeguarded dip and flight of adventure, the magic carpet that transports you to the realms of fairyland."[12] The park names themselves—Luna, Dreamland, Avalon, and the like—underlined their illusory quality and encouraged the visitor's anticipation. Luna Park gave its customers a wide choice of fantasy worlds, among them a Chinese theater, a Dutch town, a Japanese garden, an Eskimo camp, a tour of Venice and an Indian durbar. The element of fantasy is, of course, still a major element of the modern theme park since Disney pioneered this reemphasis in 1955. Walt Disney World in Florida, for example, forthrightly calls itself "A Magic Kingdom" and offers the public six different lands which (in prose Thompson and his era would have admired)

> capture the spirits of history, fantasy and adventure—with magic. Stroll beneath the soft glow of gaslights in turn-of-the-century Main Street, U.S.A. Sail with a crew of rowdy pirates and explore the tropical rivers of the world in Adventureland. Let a group of zany singing bears entertain you in the Old West atmosphere of Frontierland. Walk along Liberty Square's cobblestone streets and relive America's strug-

---

[12] "The Summer Show," *op. cit.*, 1461. O. Henry set two of his more sentimental stories at Coney Island: "The Greater Coney," in *Sixes and Sevens* and "Brickdust Row" in *The Trimmed Lamp*.

gle for freedom. Greet your favorite childhood storybook characters amidst the happy aura of Fantasyland. And travel to a visionary future of rockets and space journeys in Tomorrowland.

This recent trend in amusement parks, the device of unifying 12 themes, is chiefly the result of the transfer of Hollywood stage-set skills of illusion, developed over a half-century of movie making, to the park locale. Here, out of sight of the world outside, one may cross the boundaries of space and time to the Old West, the African jungle, early America, or nearly any fantasy land he chooses. "Take a step back in time and ride an authentic Iron Horse," advertises one park, "Transport into the future when you take a voyage to another World." Another invites the customer to an "Enchanted Voyage, an animated journey through a world of make believe," and so do dozens more.[13] What Tilyou and Thompson and the Midway promoters knew would work still does. "From the moment you enter King's Island," the Ohio park's folder says, "a whole new world of fantasy unfolds before your eyes," just as it did at Dreamland two generations ago.[14]

The theatrical element of the park, suggested by the stage set, has 13 been powerfully enhanced by the trend toward "happenings," or playlets, acted out at intervals by employees in costume. Disneyland's parade of story-book characters represented an early phase of this; later theme parks elaborated the idea into what were small but full-scale places and times. The attack on the stage coach, for example, soon became standard fare in Western theme parks. Silver Dollar City, an Old West theme park, had one hundred and three "happenings" daily, staged by thirty-three "image characters," among them the town's marshal, doctor, undertaker, mayor, various gunmen, dancehall girls and the like.[15]

The fantasy element of the park is often extended into farce and 14 foolery. Certain games and shows violate our anticipations; they reverse what we expect, take situations and devices out of the normal world and use them absurdly. Things that are harmless and functional in ordinary life take on wild aspects—as in the Hall of Mirrors, the Funhouse, the

---

[13] A very short list of fantasy lands would include at least six Frontier Towns, several Ghost Towns, Storytowns, Space World, Old Town, Rivertown, several Safari Parks or Trails, Gaslite Village, Main Street, U.S.A., Joyland, Oz City, Mother Goose Park, Dogpatch, Silver Dollar City, Octoberfest, Alice-In-Wonderland, Lion Country, and so on. As of 1975 there were 695 amusement parks, almost all with similar fantasy lands and many with more than one. See *U.S. News and World Report*, July 21, 1975; *Seventeen*, July 1973; and *Holiday*, June-July-August 1975, for reports.

[14] Dreamland Park in Nara City, Japan, a Disney-land operation, opened in 1960. The first theme park based on television characters seems to have been Bedrock City, Custer, South Dakota (1960) built about the Hanna-Barbera characters The Flintstones. Other Flintstone-theme parks appeared in Holland and Denmark in the sixties.

[15] *Amusement Business*, January 1, 1962, 9.

Oriental Maze, Krazy Kastle and certain games which have long been part of carnival and park attractions. One of the early rides, for example, called The Haunted Swing, placed the visitor in a room which seemed to turn around and upside down while he did not, leaving him with the sensation of spinning around while standing on his head. The Tilt Room, which does exactly that, is an old-time favorite developed around the turn of the century. And who really wants a kewpie doll, or needs a tasselled whip, or carries (outside the park) a pink parasol or a balloon with a silly device? There is also a strong quality of the absurd in some of the rides; there are little cars that don't steer right, floors that spin, sidewalks that jiggle, gusts that blow off hats, mirrors that turn visitors into freaks, strange noises that challenge sanity. What happens is that something that *should* do something suddenly does something quite different; the pleasure comes from the harmless surprise which is itself an essential component of the fantasy the park evokes. We all suspect, at times, that the world is an absurd place, and an amusement park, for a few hours, confirms this without threatening us.

3. A third way of looking at an amusement park is to view it as spectacle, as a unified, harmonious production meant to be *seen* and *heard*. Park planners have always been aware of the importance of the park as a total visual and aural experience that envelopes the visitor as he enters and enfolds him until he leaves. The impact is more apparent today, perhaps, than ever before because of the movie set influence. People arrive as separate figures; once inside the gates they merge into and become part of the spectacle. Early designers and operators recognized the necessity of maintaining spatial and architectural unity within the park to emphasize this sense of unified spectacle. Thompson, for example, decided to make Luna Oriental, calling up illusions of the mysterious East; he combined towers, turrets, walls, flags, colors, lights and costumes into one big display with such success that remnants of the Oriental theme are still visible in older amusement parks of today—as in The Arcade of Cedar Point, Ohio, for example.[16]

Thus Lindsay Denison, approaching Coney, saw before him "rising to the sky a thousand glittering towers and minarets, the magically realized dream of poet or painter," a great spectacle of color, activity and excitement. Albert Bigelow Paine, Mark Twain's friend, on leaving Coney Island, looked back as its lights went out in the dusk:

> Tall towers that had grown dim suddenly broke forth in electric outlines and gay rosettes of color, as the living sparks of light travelled

---

[16] See Kasson, pp. 66–67, on Luna and Dreamland.

hither and thither, until the place was transformed into an enchanted
garden, of such a sort as Aladdin never dreamed of.[17]

The contrast of this spectacle with, say, the Chicago or St. Louis fair was
deliberate—the exposition style monumental, stately, disciplined; the
amusement park a swirl of forms and colors. White City asked for contemplation, Luna for participation. Shapes, sounds, colors and movement combined in one great prospect that drew people into it—"it simply shouted," said one visitor, of "joyousness."

> In cupolas and minarets, in domes and flaunting finials, in myriads of
> gay bannerets, in the jocund motion of merry-go-rounds, circle swings
> and wondrous sliding follies, in laughter and shrieks, in the blare of
> brazen music and the throbbing of tom-toms—it speaks its various lan-
> guage—joyous forever.[18]

4. A fourth way of looking at an amusement part is to consider it as
a release from conventional behavior, a place where some of the restraints of daily life may be relaxed. As Tilyou said, visitors can "cut
loose from repressions and restrictions, and act pretty much as they feel
like acting—since everyone else is doing the same thing." The amusement park, said one analyst in 1907, "was not founded for the culture of
decorum, it was founded for the culture of hilarity." "The spirit of the
place," he continued, encourages the visitor "to cancel every canon of
conventionality, every rubric of discretion," an overstatement but nonetheless a shrewd comment on a traditional component of the park's popularity. But though ordinary rules of behavior might be modified, they
were never abandoned. The park may be "frisky," wrote Frederic
Thompson, "but it knows where to draw the line."[19]

Still, one could—and can—wear funny hats, weird shirts, carry
stuffed animals and fancy canes, laugh and shout, and indulge in unusual diets of

> crimson sausages, green corn in the ear, retrospective soft-shell crabs,
> (*and*) chrome colored beverages . . . which once had bowing acquain-
> tance with oranges and lemons.[20]

---

[17] Denison, *op. cit.*, pp. 565–6; and Paine, "The New Coney Island," *Scribner's* 68 (August
1904), pp. 535, 538. Chicago's "White City" was the first to capitalize on the new electric light
and other parks were quick to follow. Chicago's 1933 Fair, in memory of 1893, called itself "The
City of a Million Lights." On the importance of lighting, see "Painting With Light," *Amusement
Business*, May 8, 1965, pp. 20–22.
[18] Rollin Lynde Hartt, "The Amusement Park," *Atlantic Monthly*, Vol. XCXIX (May, 1907),
p. 669.
[19] Tilyou is quoted by Kasson, 59. The other observer is Hartt, *op. cit.*, 669. Thompson's statement is in "The Summer Show," p. 1612.
[20] Guy Wetmore Carryl, "Marvelous Coney Island," *Munsey's Magazine* 25 (September 1901),
p. 814.

A variety of games and contests allowed the client to transcend his in-hibitions. A booth that provided baseballs to throw at dishes advertised, "If you can't do it at home, do it here!"[21] While no man in his right mind would dare to impress his girl friend during business hours by striking a post with a maul to ring a bell, he can do it without shame in a park, a fact operators have recognized for generations.

Part of the appeal of the park's unconventionality lay in its pretense   19 of wickedness, its illusion of letting down the bars of propriety, if only a bit. The amusement park postcard, still a standard souvenir, soon be-came a part of this—"Having a H--- of a Time at Lansing Park"; "Don't Bring Your Wife to Pine Point!"; "Look What I Found at Joyland!"—with pictures of girls in bathing suits or men with upraised bottles. Early amusement parks had various devices (and some still do) to blow air jets up women's skirts and rides and games intended to expose legs, thighs and whatever, all within acceptable limits of jocular deviltry. Cer-tain rides were constructed so as to jostle people into physical contact— Love's Journey, Barrel of Fun, The Haunted House, and the traditional Tunnel of Love ("Kiss Her in The Dark!"). The proprietor of one con-cession called the Foolish House attributed its success to the simple fact that "the men like it because it gives them a chance to hug the girls and the girls like it because it gives them a chance to be hugged," an opin-ion no doubt equally fitting today.

In the easy environment of the park, the rules of etiquette tend to   20 loosen. Introductions are often dispensed with; one can be interested in another's activities and strike up a conversation with strangers. Fami-lies meet and share the day; people find common interests that might extend beyond the park, but need not. Like the dancehall, just then gain-ing respectability in the cities, the early amusement park provided a meeting place where the young could meet without embarrassment within the sanctioned conventionality of the midway, at the bandstand, or as part of the camaraderie of the boardwalk. "Many come singly,"[22] wrote an observer,

> each lad with an as yet unidentified pompadour in his heart, each lass cherishing a shy anticipation. But how, you ask, shall these youthful strangers be made acquainted? Leave that to them.

One reason, no doubt, for this sense of "cutting loose" (as Thomp-   21 son called it) lies in the fact that entrance into the amusement park makes the visitor part of the show—he becomes, in effect, both spectator and

---

[21] H. Rhodes, "City Summer," *Harper's* 131 (June 1915), p. 13.
[22] Hartt, p. 676.

performer. Early observers noted how easily people assumed roles without quite realizing it.[23] A woman having her weight guessed or a man at ring-toss is performing and knows it. The group watching is an audience and also knows it; in fact, it may even applaud.

People-watching has long been one of the most obvious participa- 22 tory elements of park activity, and as each day progresses the merger of spectator and performer becomes quite evident. That those who ride the roller-coaster, for example, are playing roles has long been known to operators and observers—the ritual screamer, the front-seat show-off, the marathon rider, the nerveless cynic, and others. People share rides together, eat together, line up together, play games together; one may for the moment be the center of attention by winning (or losing) a prize or performing in some spectacular way. Thus the park visitor becomes, in a real sense, a part of a collective unit, a partner in the day's play; the rules of social separation are gradually relaxed, as at sporting events and traffic accidents.

5. A fifth way of understanding the amusement park is to consider 23 it as an extension of the backyard outing or family picnic. Early promoters, by altering the atmosphere and character of the old park, practically guaranteed a greatly expanded and much more profitable middle class market. They made it attractive to "respectable funseekers with their families . . . with decent shows, honest prices for food and drink, and some semblance of cleanliness and public order."[24] Frederic Thompson, in refurbishing Coney Island, got rid of "the tinhorn gambler, the short-change artist, the gamblers, swindlers, and thugs" to make it, he proudly wrote, "the place where your mother, your sister, and your sweetheart would be comfortable and safe." The change was immediately noticeable and highly profitable. "Everywhere," wrote Paine, "were clean, freshly-clad, well-groomed people and gaily-decked, brightfaced children," an impression borne out by contemporary photographs. Not only was it moral, but also good business. Businessman found[25]

> that decent people have in the aggregate more money to spend than the dissipated even though they spend it more sparingly; that eleven dimes are more than a dollar; and that a show which can take in the whole family pays better than a show to which only one would go.

---

[23] Denison, *op. cit.*, pp. 565–6.

[24] *Ibid.*, p. 558. See especially his contrast of the old and new style parks. Fred F. McClure in 1911 made a survey of commercial recreation in Kansas City, rating each attraction on a "moral worth" scale from 0% to 100%. Kansas City's five amusement parks gained a 71% rating, behind shooting galleries (84% the highest), skating rinks (74%), and theaters (72%). Lowest were "stag shows" (0%), riverboat excursions (7.7%) and dancehalls (23%). Edwards, *Popular Amusements*, pp. 19–20.

[25] "Summer Show," *op. cit.*, 1467; "Amusing the Million," *op. cit.*, 386; *op. cit.*, p. 537; and Slosson, *op. cit.*, 134.

Parks were shrewdly planned to provide something for everybody in the family at every age group; even those who came without family escort were made to feel somehow they were included in this excursion-like holiday venture.

Amusement parks have carefully maintained this family orienta- 24 tion. Walt Disney World advertises "Bring the Whole Family! We have 43 square miles for you and your family to discover, explore, and enjoy!" Cedar Point calls itself "Family Fun Capital of the Midwest . . . , the most exciting innovation in modern family entertainment!" Kings Island, "the perfect one-stop family vacation resort," promises "fun, adventure, and excitement for every member of the family. From the smallest toddler to the oldest grandparent." Such emphasis on family participation is a constant theme in park publicity. "Family," in this context, implies cleanliness, order, landscaping, no liquor or suggestive shows, a wide mix of attractions, cheerful and helpful young staff (like the kids next door), and plenty of free toilets.[26]

The point is to get the whole family into the park and keep it there 25 as long as possible. Operators have been notably successful at this. About one family in five pays from $4.50 to $9.50 each for entrance to the two dozen major parks, not including admission to the smaller operations. The big "superparks" keep customers an average of seven and a half hours, during which time they spend about $4.50 each over the original admission fee. The reason is clear and simple—as *United States News and World Report* summarized its study of amusement parks, it is "wholesome family entertainment at reasonable prices."[27] One might well underline *family*. A survey conducted in 1972 showed that 58% of daily attendance at amusement parks derived from family trade, a figure probably substantially higher today.[28]

6. A sixth way to look at an amusement park is to see it as an adap- 26 tation and extension of construction and transportation technology. As Edwin Slosson perceptively pointed out seventy-five years ago, the park of his day took clever advantage of two recent technological innovations, structural steel and electric lights, and of their application to

---

[26] Walt Disney World has a 24-hour custodial service; Cedar Point boasts that an empty cigaret pack will be picked up in five minutes or less. Disney forbids its staff to wear sunglasses since they give the impression of impersonality. Six Flags emphasizes the importance of the smile—the company song tells employees, "If you see a frown, you gotta turn it upside down." See *Fortune* (December 1977), 171–2 on staff training programs; see also "Housekeeping at Cedar Point," *Amusement Business*, February 27, 1965, 18–20.

[27] July 2, 1975, 38–40. Also *Newsweek*, July 23, 1973, 42.

[28] *Amusement Business*, January 8, 1972. Sanlando Springs Park in Florida, in fact, experimented with year-round family memberships in the style of country clubs or golf clubs. "Funtown Atlanta" was planned on the model of a shopping mall, to make it "an integrated family recreational center." *Ibid.*, July 3, 1961. On the importance of attracting family trade, see "Is It For You?" *Ibid.*, January 8, 1960, pp. 18–20.

bridge building and skyscraper construction. Not only park architecture, but the park rides have always been directly indebted to the kinds of transportation in common use by urban society and industry—the roller coaster and whip (railroad and streetcar); the Ferris Wheel, see-saw, and its various mutations (the elevator); the towers and buildings (bridges and office buildings).[29]

Similarly, the automobile, airplane, motor boat, and space module were quickly adapted to rides in later years—The Dodgem, the Parachute Drop, the Rocket Ride, The Jet Whirl, Ride The Rapids, and the like. What park engineers have done since Slosson's time is simply to transfer—quickly, ingeniously, and with shrewd grasp of crowded psychology—the most recent technological innovations into amusement park equivalents. The famous Switchback Railroad, for example, one of the most popular early roller coasters, was actually a real railroad to an abandoned mine, later run through a tunnel to complete the work-day analogy. The commercial use and social convenience of this technology in daily life is thus transposed to the non-utilitarian purposes of pleasure, excitement, awe, and counterfeit danger. Going to work on a train, auto, elevated car, or bus day after day is deadly dull; riding a big roller coaster (which is simply an exaggerated version of the daily commuter experience) is anything but. Such famous present-day coasters as Cedar Point's Gemini, Six Flags Over Georgia's Great American Scream Machine or Bob-Lo's Skystreak are actually great big trolley-car rides.[30]

In effect, the amusement park pushed technology beyond rational limits toward parody into the realm of the comic. Small wagons go up-hill and downhill at great speed to nowhere; toy autos skitter about and crash without danger or destination; boat-rides down the swirling rapids hardly get the rider wet. The normal technology of transportation and construction in daily life is burlesqued into child's games—sliding on cellar doors, racing coasters down hill, riding bikes no-hands, pumping high on the backyard swing.[31]

7. The illusory or imitative aspect of the amusement park suggests a seventh way of looking at it—as what might be called the riskless risk, a place where one may take chances that are really not chances. The

27

28

29

---

[29] Slosson, *op. cit.*, pp. 135–36.

[30] Gemini, a double-track ride, has a lift height of 125 feet, reaches sixty or more miles per hour, and can handle 52,000 riders per day.

[31] The amusement park ride, in fact, may have developed from the public ice slides of early Russia, adapted by a Frenchman in 1804 to small wagons rolling downhill. The first modern American roller coaster seems to have appeared at Coney Island in 1884. Chicago's Columbian Exposition featured an "Ice Ride" with refrigerated tracks. One may also speculate that some amusement park games and rides may be adaptations of the dollhouse, the treehouse, and the game room.

park's basic appeal has long been to provide a sense of imminent danger and the likelihood of disaster without the culmination of either. Early parks specialized in so-called spectacle shows that re-created famous disasters—the Johnstown Flood, the Fall of Pompeii and San Francisco Earthquake were favorites—with great theatrical verisimilitude, creating the thrill but not the tragedy. Parkgoers thus had "a chance to shudder and a chance to be scared out of their wits."[32] For the same reason many parks have featured lion tamers, balloon drops, auto races, wirewalkers, and so on. Just as simulated earthquakes, floods or train wrecks fascinated earlier patrons, so the auto "thrill show" attracted later generations conscious of the dangers of auto travel and street traffic. The original auto "thrill show" appeared in Toledo in 1923; the demolition derby, its carnival-amusement park descendant, was initiated in 1961 in Islip, New York, an interesting adaptation of changing technology to the park's attractions.[33]

A favorite feature of early amusement parks was the fire show (Coney Island's "Fire and Flame" was a pioneer) in which a building was set afire to be extinguished by park firemen with meticulous realism, including screaming women who jumped to death (into safety nets), clouds of smoke, and frequent explosions. Since fire was a constant threat in the city, particularly in tenement districts, the show touched on very real urban experience. The fact that all the performers were trained acrobats and skilled showmen did not detract from the power of the illusion.[34] While disaster shows are still to be seen in some amusement parks, the movies, of course, caught on very early and did them better. Catastrophe is still big box-office; witness *The Poseidon Adventure, Airport 77, The Towering Inferno,* or the recent hit called simply *Disasters.*

The primary appeal of many park rides, like that of the spectacles, was thus predicated on the same "conspicuous joys . . . of vicarious terror and firsthand hair's-breadth escape." Observers of park attractions from that day to this agree on the delightful feeling of fearful anticipation, the dizzying moments of panic and the flattering sense of bravery at having dared an intimidating ride and won out, even if that risk is sham. Riders, too, often remark on the sudden feeling of camaraderie in the group at the finish at having conquered and survived. The scenic railway at Coney Island, for example, had a wooden beam that looked as if it was about to decapitate the riders but just missed—that beam

---

[32] Denison, *op. cit.,* 340; Hartt, *op. cit.,* pp. 671–72.

[33] *Amusement Business,* July 24, 1961.

[34] See Hartt's vivid account of such a fire show, p. 673ff., and the effect on spectators of this "coquet with death."

seemed to have stuck in many minds for years after.[35] Designers of park rides still play heavily on this appeal. Although the actual risk is statistically quite minimal, it is a sense of danger which is ingeniously built into them. In fact, one reason that the roller-coaster structure is left unsheathed is that the latticework of open girders (usually of wood) gives a false impression of fragility that heightens the prospective rider's apprehensions. Though engineers are quite capable of designing relatively noiseless cars, they know that the sound of the ride is an integral part of it, and that the rattles, squeaks and thunderous roar of the wheels impart a sense of speed and danger that adds immeasurably to the total effect. The imaginative names given to rides also tend to excite trepidation—Wildcat, Cyclone, Tornado, Blue Racer, Silver Streak, Speed Demon, The Beast—and park advertising strongly reinforces it.[36] Rides continue to constitute the amusement park's major attraction, since they seem to elicit some deep psychological response in everyone—a human need for "the delight of danger and the pleasure of peril," as Edwin Slosson called it. As a modern writer put it, in a superb analysis, to find out why we ride them we need to look inside ourselves:

> They go fast. It's like going over the speed limit without the danger and illegality.
>
> They're scary. People like to get scared.
>
> They're fun. They're different, a bit mysterious, almost unnatural.
>
> Some people need coaxing. Others giggle. Some rub their hands in anticipation. The anticipation is half the fun. There's no doubt the anxiety adds to the pleasure, both physical and mental, despite the hand-wringing, the sweaty palms.
>
> At the crest of the hill you open your mouth. It's hard not to. Some people gasp, others scream. You look down. Straight down.
>
> Your body tenses a bit. You look down at your hands and discover someone has painted them white. The car is picking up speed now. Your stomach notes that the bottom of the hill is an awfully long way down.
>
> Then you are up again. A mysterious force wants to lift you off your seat. There are more hills and dips up ahead. More anticipation.
>
> You are screaming. It is a strictly reflex action. Try to hold it in. You can't. Things are flying by awfully fast—track, trees, sky, lights—and your senses have to work overtime to keep up with it all.
>
> When you get out of the car your knees are likely to be weak. Like rubber. Your heart is thumping. Your hands are tingling. Your eyes are

---

[35] Hartt's detailed analysis of the rides and his reactions (674–5) is worth re-reading. He rode the Scenic Railway, The Flying Airship, and a shoot-the-rapids water ride called Hell Gate.

[36] One of the more ingenious public relations tricks was that devised by Crystal Beach Park in Niagara Falls, Canada, which placed a first-aid station and a trained nurse at the unloading platform of its Cyclone roller coaster.

refocusing. You remark that it all happened so fast. You think back on it. The experience is a wild blur of sight, sound, feeling. It's exhilarating. Scary. Fun.[37]

8. The eighth way of looking at an amusement park is to view it as   32
the closest approximation of the *total* play experience. It may be the only place in modern life in which all forms of play are represented in a single controlled environment.[38] All human play, as French social psychologist Roger Caillois sees it, may be grouped in four categories:

Competition: contests, both individual and team.
Chance: poker, lotteries, bingo, roulette, parimutual betting, and the like.
Mimicry: theater, spectacles, movies, television, ceremonies.
Vertigo: swinging, skiing, horseback riding, racing, and other activities which distort sensory stability.[39]

The amusement park, separated by fences and guards from the out-   33
side world, is itself a kind of play field, through whose gates visitors come expecting to be both spectators and participants. It is a place of action, noise, color and confusion which people enter only to play, filled with nothing but devices and situations to help them do so. There are games of competition—all sorts of shooting and throwing games, weight-guessing, strength-testing devices, and whole buildings devoted to pinball and other competitive machines. Games of chance abound—lotteries, spinning fortune wheels, and the ubiquitous bingo hall. Mimicry, of course, is the entire purpose of the theme park. Many parks also hire clowns, actors of book characters and animals and other masked or costumed players to wander the grounds. Vertigo-inducing rides such as whips, Ferris wheels, swings and slides form the backbone of the park's traditional attractions. Roller coasters, in particular, combine real speed, simulated danger and sensory disorder and relief—in two- to three-minute intervals—to produce the most powerful vertiginous

---

[37] Adapted from *The Coaster Enthusiast's Guide to Cedar Point* (Cedar Point, Ohio: Marketing Department, 1978). For an account of the designing and construction of a roller coaster see Jim McHugh, "Anatomy of a Roller Coaster," *Amusement Business,* August 1, 1965, dealing with Riverview Park's Jetstream, built by John Allen of the Philadelphia Toboggan Company.

[38] There are at least six modern theories of play, usefully summarized by Thomas Kando, *Leisure and Popular Culture* (St. Louis: C. V. Mosby Co., 1977), pp. 28–32. The most interesting, however, is that of Roger Caillois, *Man, Play, and Games* (New York: Free Press of Glencoe, 1961), particularly his classification system and his chapter, "Revivals in the Modern World." This portion of the paper is based on his interpretations of fairs, carnivals, parks and circuses.

[39] See Chapter I, "Classification of Games," in Caillois. *Vertigo* is defined as play "designed to distort, mislead, and stimulate confusion, anxiety, nausea, and momentary terror, quickly transformed back into order, at its conclusion." Slosson, *op. cit.*, pp. 136–37, makes precisely the same point, calling it "delightful dizziness."

effect of all. Nowhere else in modern life may one put together in the space of a few hours and with such minor expenditure of money and energy so complete a play experience.

••••••••••••••••••

Examining the Text

1. Which of Nye's eight ways of looking at amusement parks come closest to your own point of view? Why? If you enjoy amusement parks, do you think Nye explains your reasons satisfactorily? Similarly, if you don't enjoy these parks, do any of Nye's ideas explain why not?

2. Nye does not suggest directly that some of his eight explanations should take precedence over others. Do you think that the order he uses for the eight suggests anything about how he might rank them, or does he want readers to treat them as essentially "equal"?

3. What conclusions can be drawn about Americans' interests, desires, and values based on the kinds of parks they build and visit?

For Group Discussion

Using Nye's eight viewpoints as a starting point, decide on eight to ten reasons for the popularity of amusement parks and come to some agreement about their order of importance. As a class, discuss the extent to which the most familiar parks meet these criteria and how they do so. How would you improve the modern amusement park?

Writing Suggestion

Nye essentially lumps all amusement parks together, suggesting they have the same basic appeals. Yet it could be argued that conventional amusement parks like Six Flags and Busch Gardens differ in some significant ways from the Hollywood-inspired parks like Disneyworld and Universal Studios, that these differ from exhibition parks such as Epcot Center and Sea World, and that all these differ from carnivals and fairs. If you have been to several different parks, write an essay comparing and contrasting them in terms of what they offer and the kind of patron to whom they are most likely to appeal.

Shopping and Other Spiritual Adventures
in America Today

Phyllis Rose

"*I* shop therefore I am" declare the bumper stickers, tote bags and sweat-shirts that are the hallmark of one of the country's newest leisure activities. It may be the butt of innumerable jokes and the object of both concern and deri-sion among social commentators, but shopping as a pastime is as popular to-day as watching television, reading, or playing sports.

As Phyllis Rose suggests in the following essay from her collection Never Say Goodbye *(1991), for many people, shopping is much more than just buy-ing something or searching for something to purchase. Shopping in her view is an intellectual and emotional pursuit that satisfies us in both psychological and social terms. Indeed, according to Rose, shopping can be a form of therapy, a way of connecting to others, even a "spiritual adventure"; and the most re-warding shopping experiences can occur when no purchase is made. This ap-proach to shopping is possible, Rose says, because Americans are able to admire and appreciate the variety of goods available to us without feeling the need to own them.*

As you read, *consider the various reasons Rose offers for Americans' in-terest in shopping, in addition to the obvious desire to purchase goods. Do any of your reasons for shopping correspond to the reasons she mentions? What sorts of gratifications or benefits do you get from the experience?*

•••••••••••••••••••••

Last year a new Waldbaum's Food Mart opened in the shopping   1
mall on Route 66. It belongs to the new generation of superduper-mar-kets open twenty-four hours that have computerized checkout. I went to see the place as soon as it opened and I was impressed. There was trail mix in Lucite bins. There was freshly made pasta. There were coffee beans, four kinds of tahini, ten kinds of herb teas, raw shrimp in shells and cooked shelled shrimp, fresh-squeezed orange juice. Every sophis-tication known to the big city, even goat's cheese covered with ash, was now available in Middletown, Conn. People raced from the warehouse aisle to the bagel bin to the coffee beans to the fresh fish market, ex-claiming at all the new things. Many of us felt elevated, graced, compli-mented by the presence of this food palace in our town.

This is the wonderful egalitarianism of American business. Was it   2
Andy Warhol who said that the nice thing about Coke is, no can is any

better or worse than any other? Some people may find it dull to cross the country and find the same chain stores with the same merchandise from coast to coast, but it means that my town is as good as yours, my shopping mall as important as yours, equally filled with wonders.

Imagine what people ate during the winter as little as seventy-five years ago. They ate food that was local, long-lasting, and dull, like acorn squash, turnips, and cabbage. Walk into an American supermarket in February and the world lies before you: grapes, melons, artichokes, fennel, lettuce, peppers, pistachios, dates, even strawberries, to say nothing of ice cream. Have you ever considered what a triumph of civilization it is to be able to buy a pound of chicken livers? If you lived on a farm and had to kill a chicken when you wanted to eat one, you wouldn't ever accumulate a pound of chicken livers.

Another wonder of Middletown is Caldor, the discount department store. Here is man's plenty: tennis racquets, panty hose, luggage, glassware, records, toothpaste, Timex watches, Cadbury's chocolate, corn poppers, hair dryers, warm-up suits, car wax, light bulbs, television sets. All good quality at low prices with exchanges cheerfully made on defective goods. There are worse rules to live by. I feel good about America whenever I walk into this store, which is almost every mid-winter Sunday afternoon, when life elsewhere has closed down. I go to Caldor the way English people go to pubs: out of sociability. To get away from my house. To widen my horizons. For culture's sake, Caldor provides me too with a welcome sense of seasonal change. When the first outdoor grills and lawn furniture appear there, it's as exciting a sign of spring as the first crocus or robin.

Someone told me about a Soviet emigré who practices English by declaiming, at random, sentences that catch his fancy. One of his favorites is, "Fifty percent off all items today only." Refugees from Communist countries appreciate our supermarkets and discount department stores for the wonders they are. An Eastern European scientist visiting Middletown wept when she first saw the meat counter at Waldbaum's. On the other hand, before her year in America was up, her pleasure turned sour. She wanted everything she saw. Her approach to consumer goods was insufficiently abstract, too materialistic. We Americans are beyond a simple, possessive materialism. We're used to abundance and the possibility of possessing things. The things, and the possibility of possessing them, will still be there next week, next year. So today we can walk the aisles calmly.

It is a misunderstanding of the American retail store to think we go there necessarily to buy. Some of us shop. There's a difference. Shopping has many purposes, the least interesting of which is to acquire new articles. We shop to cheer ourselves up. We shop to practice decision-making. We shop to be useful and productive members of our class and society. We shop to remind ourselves how much is available to us. We shop to remind ourselves how much is to be striven for. We shop to assert our superiority to the material objects that spread themselves before us.

Shopping's function as a form of therapy is widely appreciated. You don't really need, let's say, another sweater. You need the feeling of power that comes with buying or not buying it. You need the feeling that someone wants something you have—even if it's just your money. To get the benefit of shopping, you needn't actually purchase the sweater, any more than you have to marry every man you flirt with. In fact, window-shopping, like flirting, can be more rewarding, the same high without the distressing commitment, the material encumbrance. The purest form of shopping is provided by garage sales. A connoisseur goes out with no goal in mind open to whatever may come his or her way, secure that it will cost very little. Minimum expense, maximum experience. Perfect shopping.

I try to think of the opposite, a kind of shopping in which the object is all-important, the pleasure of shopping at a minimum. For example, the purchase of blue jeans. I buy new blue jeans as seldom as possible because the experience is so humiliating. For every pair that looks good on me, fifteen look grotesque. But even shopping for blue jeans at Bob's Surplus on Main Street—no frills, bare-bones shopping—is an event in the life of the spirit. Once again I have to come to terms with the fact that I will never look good in Levi's. Much as I want to be mainstream, I never will be.

In fact, I'm doubly an oddball, neither Misses nor Junior, but Misses Petite. I look in the mirror, I acknowledge the disparity between myself and the ideal. I resign myself to making the best of it: I will buy the Lee's Misses Petite. Shopping is a time of reflection, assessment, spiritual self-discipline.

It is appropriate, I think, that Bob's Surplus has a communal dressing room. I used to shop only in places where I could count on a private dressing room with a mirror inside. My impulse then was to hide my weaknesses. Now I believe in sharing them. There are other women in the dressing room at Bob's Surplus trying on blue jeans who look as bad as I do. We take comfort form one another. Sometimes a woman will ask me which of two items looks better. I always give a definite answer. It's the least I can do. I figure we are all in this together, and I emerge from the dressing room not only with a new pair of jeans but with a renewed sense of belonging to a human community.

When a Solzhenitsyn rants about American materialism, I have to look at my digital Timex and check what year this is. Materialism? Like conformism, a hot moral issue of the fifties, but not now. How to spread the goods, maybe. Whether the goods are the Good, no. Solzhenitsyn, like the visiting scientist who wept at the beauty of Waldbaum's meat counter but came to covet everything she saw, takes American materialism too materialistically. He doesn't see its spiritual side. Caldor, Waldbaum's, Bob's Surplus—these, perhaps, are our cathedrals.

······················

Examining the Text

1. Consider the title of this essay. Why does Rose call shopping a "spiritual adventure"? In what ways does she see it as "spiritual" and how is it an "adventure"? Do you think she is entirely serious?

2. Rose comments on the abundance and variety of products in American stores. In her view, how does this abundance influence American attitudes toward shopping? What is the point of her anecdote about the Soviet scientist (paragraph 5) who "came to covet everything she saw"?

3. Rose refers to shopping as "a form of therapy" (7). In what ways does she say this is the case? Why does she believe that garage sales are "perfect shopping"? Do you agree that most people benefit from this form of therapy?

4. How do you interpret Rose's last sentence in the essay: "Caldor, Waldbaum's, Bob's Surplus—these, perhaps, are our cathedrals"? Is she being sarcastic or is her point a serious one?

For Group Discussion

As a group, discuss your individual habits and preferences as shoppers. What different reasons do you have for shopping? How frequently (or infrequently) do you shop? Where do you spend most of your shopping time? What are your attitudes toward shopping and toward people who shop as a leisure activity? Make a list of the differences exhibited in your group. Then discuss as a class whether these differences can be attributed to factors such as gender, age, ethnic or racial heritage, socio-economic status or regional location.

Writing Suggestion

Rose maintains that shopping has its benefits and that the impulse to shop is a positive aspect of American culture. Yet the kind of shopping she describes—browsing in supermarkets and discount stores, going to garage sales, trying on jeans in a communal fitting room—hardly fits the image we associate with most of the "shop-till-you-drop" types we expect to find in upscale malls and specialized boutiques. In an essay evaluate Rose's argument about shopping by considering the motives and habits of the other kinds of shoppers she seems to ignore.

Big Mac and *Caneton A L'Orange:* Eating, Icons and Rituals

Pamela Malcolm Curry and Robert M. Jiobu

Eating, like shopping, may seem a mundane part of our lives, but Pamela Malcolm Curry and Robert M. Jiobu say there's more to eating than meets the stomach. Eating and its related activities—buying groceries, cooking, cleaning, and socializing—occupy a significant portion of our time. And eating is, Curry and Jiobu suggest, a richly cultural phenomenon, a social institution with its own "norms, folkways, habits and rituals." For example, on special occasions we eat special foods that have acquired widely-recognized symbolic meaning; cranberry sauce and candle-covered cakes symbolize certain events, while hot dogs and snails are at another level of gustatory sophistication. In this sense, food is more than just what we put in our mouths.

Whether we "gobble and go" at a fast food emporium or "dine" at a gourmet restaurant, pig out in front of the TV or sup in the dining room, we follow certain rituals or ceremonies influenced by certain icons or symbols. It's worth taking a closer look at this activity to see what it tells us about ourselves and our culture.

***Before you read,** think about the symbols and rituals associated with different eating situations—fast food places, family-style and gourmet restaurants, cafeterias, and picnics, for example. Are these behaviors "natural"? How did we learn them?*

· · · · · · · · · · · · · · · · · · ·

We eat away an important portion of our lives—for the traditional 1
male, a reasonable estimate might be four out of sixteen waking hours
are involved in dining and related activities; for the traditional housewife as much as eight of the sixteen hours if we count grocery shopping,
cooking and cleaning up. Considering the amount of time devoted to it,
eating obviously involves more than just ingesting a prescribed quantity of nutrients (after all, NASA food bricks would serve that purpose
quite well). Yet, despite the broader implications, few social scientists
have addressed the topic. Perhaps we have tended to ignore our own

eating behavior because it is so commonplace, obvious and banal that it falls below our threshold of interests. Only under unusual circumstances does our eating become salient, and then only ephemerally.

But the human lot requires food; and as with many everyday necessities, eating is surrounded by norms and folkways, many of which are also rituals and habits. This makes life easier since day-to-day decisions, once converted to habit, require less time and effort and once ritualized provoke less anxiety. A pleasant sense of calm comes to prevail. The world appears less chaotic. Life flows more smoothly. Eating behavior, in short, becomes institutionalized.   2

A social institution, by definition, is a collection of norms, folkways, habits and rituals, all of which relate to an important activity—in this case, eating. Peter Berger and Thomas Luckman in a widely read sociological work say this: 3

> An institutional world, then, is experienced as an objective reality. . . .
> It was there before (the individual) was born, and it will be there after
> his death. . . . The institutions are *there*, external to him, persistent in
> their reality, whether he likes it or not. He cannot wish them away.
> They resist his attempt to change or evade them. They have coercive
> power over him, both in themselves, by the sheer force of their factic-
> ity, and through the control mechanism that is usually attached to the
> most important of them.[1]

A scene from Ernest Hemingway's "The Short Happy Life of Francis Macomber" nicely illustrates the point.   4

Wilson, the guide, and Macomber and his wife Margot, are eating lunch served by a porter. That morning Macomber had proved himself a physical coward. He had gut shot a lion, then bolted when it charged.   5

> "That's eland he's offering you," Wilson said.
> "It's very good meat," Macomber said.
> "Did you shoot it, Francis?" she asked.
> "Yes."
> "They're not dangerous, are they?"
> "Only if they fall on you," Wilson told her.
> "I'm so glad."
> "Why not let up on the bitchery just a little Margot," Macomber
> said, cutting the eland steak and putting some mashed potato, gravy
> and carrot on the down-turned form that tined through the pieces of
> meat.

---

[1] Peter L. Berger and Thomas Luckman, *The Social Construction of Reality* (New York: Double-day Anchor books, 1966), p. 60. Our discussion of institutions relies heavily on this work. Sociologists and anthropologists almost always connect ritual to religion in some way. We do not. Our use of the term ritual is simply as a ceremonial act in accordance with custom; it may or may not be religious. George A. Theodorsen and A.G. Theodorsen, *A Modern Dictionary of Sociology* (New York: Thomas Y. Crowell, 1969), p. 351.

"I suppose I could," she said, "since you put it so prettily."
"Tonight we'll have champagne for the lion," Wilson said. "It's a bit too hot at noon."[2]

Macomber's praise of the eland meat, the way he places his food on his fork in the proper English manner, and Wilson's offhand remark on the appropriateness of drinking champagne at noon all exemplify ritualized and habitualized norms and folkways. The characters feel they must somehow play out the rituals—what we learn as etiquette and decorum—no matter how painful it might be. In other words, institutions force us to act in certain ways, yet we are unaware of it. Our behavior is thus compelled, preconscious and predictable. 6

Cultural anthropologist Mary Douglas points out that among the Tikopia (a Polynesian group), many ceremonies and associated rituals had to be cancelled when their crops failed—the necessary symbolic foods were not available.[3] Such behavior might strike us as a bit odd, but our culture is filled with examples not too unlike the Tikopia's. 7

We use a specially decorated cake to symbolize many ceremonial occasions: birthdays, christenings, weddings, anniversaries, and retirements to name a few. It's difficult to imagine a formal wedding without the traditional multitiered, white cake decorated with flowers and rosettes fashioned from sugary icing and topped off with a little plastic bride and groom. And surely the bride must ritualistically cut the cake and stuff a piece into her new husband's mouth. Similarly, a birthday party without cake and candles would seem rather empty or somehow incomplete because there wouldn't be an icon summarizing the event. And how tacky it would be if the guest of honor refused the ritual of blowing out the candles; and how odd if the candles were stuck on a dish rather than a decorated cake. 8

Once we begin to catalog them, other iconic foods and rituals associated with holidays and ceremonies pop into mind: Christmas cookies for carolers; chocolate rabbits and hunting decorated eggs for Easter; turkey and the gathering at Grandmother's for Thanksgiving; and champagne toasts for New Year's Eve. 9

Foods also symbolize life styles, whole gestalts of meanings and ritualistic behaviors. Hamburgers broiled over a charcoal grill in the backyard suggest suburbia. Even sex role behaviors are represented by specific foods: thick T-bone steaks and straight bourbon for virility and masculinity; watercress sandwiches and creme de menthe for daintiness 10

---

[2] Ernest Hemingway, "The Short Happy Life of Francis Macomber."
[3] Mary Douglas, "Account for Taste," *Psychology Today* 13 (July 1979), pp. 44–51. The Tikopia were described by Raymond Firth, *Social Change in Tikopia* (London: Allen and Unwin, 1960).

and femininity. We could go on, but the point is clear: within an institution some (but not all) icons and rituals are linked to one another. An icon might call out a ritual, and a ritual might be meaningless without the associated icon.

Institutions emerge slowly, and in the process enfold symbols and   11
rituals. The development of food icons and rituals can be historically traced: First, diet expanded and diversified as a result of new technology; and second, the rise of name brands, supermarkets, and fast food establishments encouraged even more diversity.

During the early days of the Republic, crude technology necessar-   12
ily limited diet; but with the development of fast transportation, refrigeration and food preservation, the American diet became more varied. The increase in diversity can be indexed in the number of pages in cookbooks:

> . . . it was not until 1796 that the first manual by an American author appeared. This volume bore the imposing title *American Cookery, or the Art of Dressing Viands, Fish, Poultry, and Vegetables, and the Best Modes of Making Pastes, Puffs, Pies, Tarts, Puddings, Custards, and Preserves, and All Kinds of Cakes, from the Imperial Plumb to Plain Cake. Adapted to This Country, and All Grades of Life. By Amelia Simmons: An American Orphan.* . . . (This) first edition was of vest-pocket size and contained only 46 pages. Its meager dimensions help to illustrate the fact that to some people the physical size of cookbooks serves to show the diversification of diet which has taken place during the past century. *The Frugal Housewife* (1829) contained 95 pages. Mrs. Putnam's *Receipt Book and Young Housekeeper's Assistant*, published in 1858, numbered 223. The 1896 edition of the Boston Cook School Cook Book contained 567 and the pages of the 1930 edition of this work numbered 831.[4]

Today, cookbooks of 600 and 700 pages are not uncommon and the   13
traditional ones have sales in the millions.[5] Cookbooks index a huge breadth on the one hand and specialization on the other: from the elaborate inclusive work of the renowned French chef Jaques Pepin[6] to unknowns William Shurtleff and Akiko Aoyagi, authors of a cookbook about an unknown food, *tofu*.[7] There is also great diversity as to how to cook food. There are books on quick methods (micro ranges)[8] as well as on slow methods (crock pots),[9] and everything in between. The interest

---

[4] Richard Osborn Cummings, *The American and His Food* (New York: Arno Press, 1970), p. 42.
[5] In the last 80 years almost 19 million copies of *Better Homes and Gardens Cookbook* were sold, and 13 million copies of *Betty Crocker's Cookbook*.
[6] Jacques Pepin, *La Technique* (New York: Pocket Books, 1976).
[7] William Shurtleff and Akiko Aoyagi, *The Book of Tofu: Food for Mankind* (New York: Ballantine Books, 1979).
[8] For example, Luisa Scott and Jack Denton Scott, *Mastering Microwave Cooking* (New York: Bantam Books, 1976).
[9] For example, Rose Cantrell and Ruth Kershner, *Crockery* (New York: Crown Publishers, Inc., 1979).

goes beyond books. Cooking schools are flourishing and sales of cookware booming.[10] Technology and learning have brought us to a point where we can cook just about anything just about any way.

While technology was changing the American diet, an organizational development occurred that diversified it even more. Because they are so much a part of our everyday lives, we sometimes forget that the supermarket is a relatively new social invention. Before the supermarket, shoppers conveyed their requests to a clerk who would fetch and package the item. Many times the clerk broke bulk: repackaging items from wholesale containers to smaller ones. Specialized stores—butcher shops, produce markets and dry goods—were the rule and shoppers had to visit many different places to complete their market baskets.   14

But smaller, specialized stores gave way to supermarkets which were originally touted as low cost, cut rate operations. In the East they were originally called "cheapies" and were enormously successful from their inception during the Great Depression.[11] While manufacturers had already begun to distinguish their products with visual and verbal symbols, the supermarket accentuated—required in fact—that the product be symbolized. Shopping was no longer done through a clerk. Customers had to be somehow enticed to choose one brand over another as they pushed carts down aisles surrounded by competing brands and products. The role of visual and verbal symbols came into extreme prominence since without direct human contact, what better way was there to attract customers than by icon and jingle?   15

We can easily verify the success of advertising campaigns in creating a dependence on icons. Most adults can't identify Count Chocula, Cap'n Crunch, or Franken Berry—cartoon icons representing different brands of dry cereal. But then most adults haven't been exposed to the Saturday morning cartoon shows that saturate the TV screen with cereal icons.[12] In a supermarket all the adult sees is a shelf filled with a mass of brightly colored cartoon characters. In this situation a great asset is a child who knows the iconic language and can easily pick out those which go with each cereal.   16

Eating patterns have also changed. Caught in the middle of rapid developments, few families can maintain the kind of eating behavior   17

---

[10] "The Kitchen: America's Playroom," *Forbes* 117 (March 15), pp. 24–38; "Food: The New Wave," *Newsweek* (August 11, 1975), pp. 50–57; "In Ohio: Sauteing Together," *Time* 112 (May 21, 1979), not paginated.

[11] Rom J. Markin, *The Supermarket: An Analysis of Growth, Development and Change,* revised edition (Pullman, Washington: Washington State University, Bureau of Economic and Business Research, 1968).

[12] A monitoring of 5 Boston TV stations revealed that 25% of children's advertisements were for cereals. In total, children see about 20,000 TV commercials a year. See *Consumer Reports* 43 (August 1978), p. 432.

found in the early part of this century. According to one account: "We ate at set hours: approximately 7:30, 12:30 and 6. Father sat at one end, Mother at the other; Brother on one side; I on the other. The whole family ate together, and in the dining room."[13] Toady, meals are frequently catch-as-catch-can. Breakfast, if eaten at home, is often self prepared and eaten with no expectation of family interaction. A letter to Amy Vanderbilt complained:

> My husband buries his head in the newspaper at breakfast and doesn't say a word to me throughout. He just hands me the second section. Shouldn't a husband be expected to carry on some conversation with his wife at breakfast?

Amy answered:

> No one *should be expected* to carry on a conversation at breakfast. Many people don't really wake up until later in the day. Enjoy that second section. . . .[14]

The forces that led to the decline of the family-centered meal— urbanization, increased labor force participation of women, increased mobility and diversification of family leisure activities—also created a complex environment that needed to be reduced to some simpler form.[15]   18

From its beginning, the fast food industry recognized and rushed to meet this need. The use of icons to channel behavior along predetermined lines has perhaps evolved to its highest form in the world of fast foods. Ray Kroc, the driving force behind McDonald's, describes the necessity of creating the right icons and the success that can follow: 19

> I like Paul Schrage's approach, because he was a "detail man" in his field, and he was on the same wave length as I was concerning the McDonald's image. For example, a great deal of study has gone into creating the appearance and personality of Ronald McDonald, right down to the colour and texture of his wig. I loved Ronald. So did the kids. Even the sophisticates at *Esquire* magazine loved him. They invited Ronald to their "Party of the Decade" for top newsmakers of the sixties. McDonald's was chosen to cater the party because we had the biggest impact on the eating habits of the Americans in the decade.[16]

---

[13] James H. Bossard and Eleanor S. Boll, *Ritual in Family Living* (Philadelphia: Univ. of Pennsylvania Press, 1950).

[14] Amy Vanderbilt, *Everyday Etiquette* (New York: Bantam Books, 1979), p. 13. (Italics added.)

[15] See, for example, Robert S. Lynd and Helen M. Lynd, *Middletown in Transition: A Study of Cultural Conflicts* (New York: Harcourt Brace Jovanovich, 1937).

[16] Ray Kroc and Robert Anderson, *Grinding it Out: The Making of McDonald's* (Chicago: Henry Regnery Co., 1977), p. 152.

The right icon is important; and an industry's success in develop- 20
ing them is evident in that they can take on a quasi-sacred quality. For
instance, they are immortal or at least never grow older. Colonel
Sanders, as best the eye can tell, is as young (or old) as he ever was; and
freckle faced Wendy is still the same as when introduced to the public.
Even more miraculously, some character symbols become younger as
they grow older. Aunt Jemima used to be mature and matronly but now
is thin and young.

This quasi-sacred quality becomes salient when an icon deviates 21
from its perceived perfection and becomes profane. An extreme example, though not a food symbol, is Marilyn Chambers who could no
longer represent the purity of Ivory Snow after she starred in the porn
film *Behind the Green Door.* A person who played Ronald McDonald was
fired for lending out his clown costume for use at a private houseparty—
clearly outside the quasi-sacred sphere.

Even though food products are meant to be eaten, the character 22
symbols which represent them are never eaten. To do so would symbolically violate the general societal taboo against cannibalism; for the
character symbols are endowed with human qualities. Star Kist constantly rejects Charlie Tuna; he will never appear in our tuna salad on
rye. "Sorry, Charlie," intones the voice-over in the television commercial. The Pillsbury Doughboy supervises the baking of dinner rolls but
never jumps into the oven to be heated and served. Eventually both
product and icon are integrated into the overall value scheme of American culture, largely being imposed on us from above. This is nowhere
more clearly seen than in the commercials sponsored by television's
single largest advertiser: McDonald's. Their workers—who sing and
dance a lot—are industrious, young, bouncy, attractive and smily. They
alleviate any guilt we have about eating out as they sing "We're doing
it all for your," because "you *deserve* a break today."

The symbols, the product, and the activity of eating at these sym- 23
bolic places are thus linked with happiness, success, a job well done, and
hard work. We end up being taught a curious blend of philosophies: a
clown's version of a happy Puritan Ethic.[17]

The constant repetition of the icons and of the corresponding mes- 24
sages cause both to become completely taken for granted as part of
everyday living. They disappear into the ritualistic background and we
come to accept, with little challenge, that fast foods are a way to quickly
eat socially approved, work-a-day meals.

---

[17] For several discussions of McDonald's see Marshall Fishwick (ed.) "Focus on the World of
Ronald McDonald," *Journal of American Culture* 1 (Summer 1978), pp. 336–474.

The result of this acceptance by the larger society has been to po-   25
larize American eating style—schizophrenia characterizes the institution of eating. At one time we will frequent the highly symbolized yet
sterile world of fast food, while at another we will leisurely partake of
the ritualistic world of gourmet eating and formal dinners.

The contrast between gourmet and fast food eating is quite extreme.   26
One is mostly ritualistic, the other is mostly instrumental. If one were
to count the rituals associated with gourmet and fast food eating,
surely a comparison would make the latter seem virtually ritual-less.
Since few rituals exist for fast food dining, few must be learned, and few
are in place to slow down the dining process. The plastic and chrome
environment structures behavior and varies little from one fast food
place to another: self-serve counters, plastic forks, formica tables and
minimal social interaction—no waitresses, no busboys, no tips, no talk.
Fast foods are fast, and dining is basically "gobble and go." So, although
the rituals associated with such a spartan activity do exist, they are
scarcely noticeable and only barely inhibit the flow of traffic in everyday life.

Such is not the case, obviously, when dining in a gourmet or more   27
conventional restaurant. There certain rituals have to be engaged. For
instance, we must first choose the restaurant itself, and this can take
much time: a whole litany of questions and answers, feelings and biases
must be considered in finally choosing which restaurant one will "dine"
in on any certain occasion. Once there, a person must choose a wine
from an elaborate list of brands and types, the names of which we might
hesitate to pronounce in our high school French. And when the waiter
serves the wine, we must examine the cork and, if satisfactory, delicately
try the first sip. But what are we looking for when examining the cork,
and how should the wine taste? That we know the technically correct
answers to the questions is far less important than that we correctly go
through these rituals, and all the other rituals of etiquette and deport-
ment, including how many times and to what extent to be displeased
with the preparation of the food itself, up through eventually knowing
when to tip the person who brings the car around.

None of these rituals (and others) are really "rational." We could eat   28
just as well without them. They do not directly contribute to the taste of
the food. Nevertheless we must learn and observe them if we are to engage in gourmet eating, for stripped of ritual gourmet does not exist.

While the symbols remain relatively fixed over time, one can expect   29
the links with American values and popular culture to modify with the
changing environment.

The American diet is becoming a national political issue. The Sen-   30
ate Select Committee on Nutrition and Human Needs, chaired by

George McGovern, published a report the purpose of which was "to point out that the eating patterns of this century represent as critical a public health concern as any now before us."[18] The report advocates that Americans substantially decrease their consumption of meats, fats, high cholesterol foods, sugar and salt while increasing consumption of fruits, vegetables, whole grains, poultry and fish. A minor brouhaha followed the release of the report. It was condemned for not going far enough—chemical additives were not mentioned. And, to no one's surprise, it was condemned for going too far, notably by the affected food industries.[19]

The condemnation of the American diet may be gaining even more 31 momentum, this loud cry against the fast food industry becoming itself a ritualized litany of the woes that will affect the nation if the trend is not reversed. The Junk Food Hall of Shame recently opened in the nation's capitol city. Its goal is to educate the public to the sorry state of the American diet. While we expect sugared cereals and soft drinks to be center displays, it shocks us to see such stand-bys as Shake 'n Bake, Jello and Dream Whip also nominated to the infamous Hall.

Still, the alarms of the McGovern report, the Hall of Shame, and 32 other media warnings have not significantly altered the American diet. Though several inchoate counter trends can be observed, none seems on the verge of taking off and encompassing the bulk of the population. The fast food rituals are too deep seated to be easily brought to the surface and purged.

People who practice alternative diets—vegetarian, lactovegetarian, 33 ovolactovegetarian, and opponents of chemical additives, for example—must learn a different set of behaviors. At first everything is problematic for them. Only slowly, and by trial and error, do they find their own routines, establish their own rituals and learn a different set of icons.[20]

Under these circumstances, rather than switching diets, it seems 34 more likely that an ever increasing dominance of fast food will lead to a new set of standards and rituals. This may be occurring already in regard to home cooking. Recently a brand of "heat-and-serve" fried chicken was introduced via advertisement on our local television. The mother is harried and tired and obviously "deserves a break today"; but

---

[18] Select Committee on Nutrition and Human Needs, *Dietary Goals for the United States* (Washington, D.C.: U.S. Government Printing Office, 1977), p. v.
[19] "The Pure, the Impure, and the Paranoid," *Psychology Today* 12 (October 1978), pp. 67–77, 123.
[20] See, for example, "A True Believer Who Gave Up the Faith," *Psychology Today*, 12 (October 1978), p. 85.

she feels guilty about eating out again. Her family should have a home cooked meal. What to do? Aha! The solution! Out of the freezer and into the radar range with heat-and-serve fried chicken that the announcer claims is "as good as the kind you go out for!"

The inevitable conclusion? Over time, technological and social 35 changes have slowly brought eating behavior under the firm control of icons and the rituals that go with them. As consumers this works well for us. Our daily lives are rendered more orderly and our decision making more efficient. It also works well for entrepreneurs, helping them to capture specific segments of the commercial market.

Fast food restaurants have made particularly heavy use of icons to 36 attract customers and rituals to keep people buying once they have learned; but at the same time, have divorced their icons from eating rituals. Fast food dining is pretty much instrumental and pragmatic.

By way of contrast, gourmet dining—the highest form of restaurant 37 eating—is virtually all ritual but calls few icons to mind. Indeed a problem that such restaurants have is advertising the notion of gourmet without seeming crass. The announcement of stars, which are symbols of rare quality, is perhaps as iconic as gourmet establishments become.

In a broad sense, social science maintains—doomsday prophecies 38 and changing technology notwithstanding—that we go through our daily lives in a highly structured, unthinking, organized, routinized and ritualized way. Eating as a social institution and as part of popular culture is yet another confirmation of this valid generalization.

· · · · · · · · · · · · · · · · · · · ·

Examining the Text

1. At the beginning of the essay, the authors spend some time defining eating as a "social institution." Briefly summarize their definition to show the ways in which eating is a social institution.

2. Though Curry and Jiobu use the term "icon," they don't specifically define it. Based on what you've read in the essay and on the dictionary definition of "icon," explain what the authors mean by the term and how they see food as "icon."

3. The authors list some of the ways in which technology has changed the American diet (paragraphs 12–19). What other factors can you think of that have led to changes in what, where, when, and how we eat?

For Group Discussion

Individually make a list of the rituals and symbols associated with a particular holiday meal, preferably one in which all members of your group participate. Then share your lists, noting similarities and differences and explaining the source of any individual rituals or symbols associated with the meal. As a class, hypothesize about why such rituals become so widespread. Are they encouraged through the media, or are they primarily passed down through our families?

Writing Suggestion

Curry and Jiobu discuss the "social institution" of eating, but the concept of "social institution" can be applied to other leisure activities discussed in this chapter. In an essay, apply the notion of a social institution (especially Berger and Luckman's definition in paragraph 3) to another leisure activity that you've read about in this chapter, explaining the conventions, icons, and rituals involved in that activity. What new insights do you gain into this leisure activity when you see it as a social institution?

ADDITIONAL SUGGESTIONS
FOR WRITING ABOUT LEISURE

1. For the next seven days, keep track of how you spend your time. Use a "time diary" such as the one on page 637 or some other chart to record the activity, the amount of time you spend on it, and the extent to which you enjoy it.

When you've done this for seven days, look back over your charts to develop conclusions about your own habits of work and leisure. Look for patterns and contrasts in your activities. For example, you might focus on free time versus work time; or on daytime versus evening activities; or on leisure activities which are social versus those which are solitary; or on the kinds of satisfaction you receive from leisure and work activities.

Based on your analysis, write an essay explaining the place of leisure time in your life right now. In developing this essay, draw on some of the readings in this chapter and comment on how keeping track of how you spent your time altered your behavior, if indeed it did.

2. The essays in this chapter were clearly not written with the schedules of college students in mind. Interview some friends and reflect on your own experience to identify the specific characteristics of college students' leisure activities. In what ways are they similar to and different from the leisure activities of nonstudents? After reflecting on these issues, write a definition of leisure that applies specifically to college students. Illustrate your definition with concrete examples drawn from your experiences or observations.

3. For a leisure activity with which you're familiar, offer a detailed analysis modeled after the essay of Gorman, Nye, Rose, or Curry and Jiobu. You might begin by describing the activity, and go on to consider some of the following questions: What satisfactions does this activity bring its participants? What are its drawbacks or detrimental effects? What sort of people are interested in this activity? Are there differences in terms of gender, age, class, ethnicity, or geographical location? How might this activity influence participants? What does it teach them? In what ways does it fit or fail to fit the criteria for leisure?

Considering these and other questions, try to develop a thorough analysis of this leisure pursuit.

4. The table on page 639, taken from *The Futurist*, identifies the number of hours per week that Americans devote to specific leisure activities and provides figures regarding gender differences and changes over a twenty-year period.

Imagine that you're a visitor from another country who has been provided with this list to help introduce you to American culture. Write

What you did from 5 in the afternoon until midnight

Time	What did you do?	Time Began	Time Ended	Where	List Other People With You	Doing Anything Else?	Enjoyment On a Scale of 1–10 Dislike = 1, Like = 10
5 PM →							
6 PM →							
7 PM →							
8 PM →							
9 PM →							
10 PM →							
11 PM →							

an essay explaining the conclusions you can draw about Americans from this list. What values, beliefs and attitudes does this list reveal? Be as specific as possible.

5. One of Witold Rybczynski's more striking observations is that "Americans now spend more that $13 billion dollars annually on sports clothing; put another way, about 1.3 billion hours of potential leisure time are exchanged for leisure wear—for increasingly elaborate running shoes, certified biking shorts, and monogrammed warm-up suits." Judith Schor makes a similar point when she suggests that time is valued only in terms of money and that if we would control our consumerism, we would have more leisure time. In an essay explore the relationships among work, leisure, and consumerism in our society. Use your own experience as the basis for your argument. How much of the money you and your family members make goes to support leisure activities? What about your friends?

Spare Time: hours per week adults aged 18 to 64 spend in leisure activities.

	Total			Men			Women		
	1985	1975	1965	1985	1975	1965	1985	1975	1965
Total	40.1	38.3	34.5	41.1	38.6	34.4	39.6	38.3	34.4
TV	15.1	15.2	10.5	15.7	16.2	11.7	14.5	14.1	9.3
Visiting	4.9	5.5	6.6	5.0	5.1	5.8	4.8	5.7	7.5
Talking	4.3	2.2	2.6	3.5	1.9	1.6	5.1	2.7	3.6
Traveling	3.1	2.6	2.7	3.4	2.8	3.0	3.0	2.4	2.4
Reading	2.8	3.1	3.7	2.7	3.0	4.2	2.9	3.3	3.3
Sports/outdoors	2.2	1.5	0.9	2.9	2.3	1.4	1.5	0.8	0.5
Hobbies	2.2	2.3	2.1	1.9	1.6	1.4	2.6	3.0	2.8
Adult education	1.9	1.6	1.3	2.2	2.1	1.6	1.6	1.3	0.9
Thinking/relaxing	1.0	1.1	0.5	1.2	1.0	0.2	0.9	1.2	0.6
Religion	0.8	1.0	0.9	0.6	0.8	0.7	1.0	1.3	1.0
Cultural events	0.8	0.5	1.1	0.8	0.3	1.3	0.8	0.6	0.9
Clubs/organizations	0.7	1.2	1.0	0.8	0.9	0.9	0.6	1.5	1.2
Radio/recordings	0.3	0.5	0.6	0.4	0.6	0.7	0.3	0.4	0.4

Note: Figures may not total due to rounding.
Source: Americans Use of Time Project. University of Maryland. Reprinted with permission *American Demographics*, November 1990

For Further
Reading:
A Popular Culture
Bibliography

Chapter 2: Advertising

Barthel, Diane. *Putting on Appearances: Gender and Advertising*. Philadelphia: Temple University Press, 1988.
>   Examines the influence of advertising on conceptions of femininity and masculinity and, in particular, on our sense of the importance of appearance and "beauty."

The Best Campaign Commercials, 1992. Washington, DC: *Campaign Magazine*, 1992. Videocassette.
>   A compilation of campaign commercials for presidential candidates Bill Clinton, George Bush, and Ross Perot.

Craig, Steve, ed. *Men, Masculinity, and the Media*. Thousand Oaks, CA: Sage, 1992.
>   Explores the ways in which masculinity is represented in advertising, as well as in commercial television and music videos.

Kilbourne, Jean, Director. *Still Killing Us Softly*. Cambridge, MA: Cambridge Documentary Films, 1992.
>   A documentary that examines images of women in advertising.

Leo, John. "Madison Avenue's Gender Wars." *U.S. News and World Report*, 25 October 1992, 25.
>   Looks critically at the trend toward presenting aggressive, confrontational images of women in recent advertisements.

Mitchell, Arthur. *The Nine American Lifestyles: Who We Are and Where We're Going*. New York: Warner Books, 1983.
>   A detailed explanation of VALS and psychographics.

Stale Roles and Tight Buns. Boston, MA: OASIS, 1991. Videocassette.
>   A documentary examining images of men in advertising.

Sturges, Ingrid. "Black Images in Advertising. *Emerge*" (September 1993): 21-24.
>   Examines the use of African-American images and culture in mainstream television advertising.

Chapter 3: Television

Berger, Arthur Asa. *Television as an Instrument of Terror*. New Brunswick, NJ: Transaction Books, 1980.
>   An engaging semiotic study of television and other forms of popular culture.

Berman, Ronald. *How Television Sees Its Audience*. Thousand Oaks, CA: Sage Publishers, 1987.
   Studies of the presuppositions and influences of various genres of television programming.
Brown, Mary Ellen, ed. *Television and Women's Culture*: The Politics of the Popular. Thousand Oaks, CA: Sage Publishers, 1994.
   An anthology that looks at how televised genres such as game shows, police fiction, and soap operas offer women opportunities for negotiating their own meanings and developing their own artistic appreciation.
Gitlin, Todd. *Inside Prime Time*. New York: Pantheon, 1983.
   Offers an indictment of programming practices from a Marxist perspective.
Grossberger, Lewis. "Reading the Tube." *Mediaweek*, 17 January 1994, 30.
   Suggests that television is so common and pervasive in our cultural life that even without watching TV we can be aware of what is on television.
Mander, Jerry. *Four Arguments for the Elimination of Television*. New York: Morrow, 1978.
   Offers four readable arguments for the harmful influence of television, in terms of both the technology and the content of television programs.
Newcomb, Horace. *Television: The Critical View*. New York: Oxford University Press, 1987.
   A collection of essays on different genres of television, including sections on seeing television, thinking about television, and defining television.
Postman, Neil. *Amusing Ourselves to Death*. New York: Penguin Books, 1985.
   An indictment of television as a force debasing public discourse in America because its claims are made with images rather than language.
Waters, Harry F. "Black Is Bountiful." *Newsweek*, 6 December 1993, 59.
   Discusses six television programs featuring African Americans and examines both sides of the controversy over whether these shows reinforce stereotypes and fail to reflect the diversity of the African-American community.

Chapter 4: Music

Braun, Dennis Duane. *Toward a Theory of Popular Culture*. Ann Arbor, MI: Ann Arbor Publishers, 1969.
   Draws thematic connections between theories of sociology and the history of American popular music and dance.
Chambers, Ian. *Urban Rhythms*. Hampshire, England: Macmillan, 1985.
   Part of a communications and culture series, this volume traces the influence of urban popular music on the broader fabric of popular culture.
Ferguson, Andrew. "Mossback Meets Guns 'n' Roses." *National Review*, 21 October 1991, 56.
   A conservative perspective on the unappealing side of popular culture and rock music, focusing specifically on the Guns 'n' Roses album, *Use Your Illusion II*, which the author calls "stupid."
Frith, Simon. *Facing the Music*. New York: Pantheon Books, 1988.
   A compendium and guide to contemporary music and popular culture.
Goodwin, Andrew. *Dancing in the Distraction Factory*. Minneapolis: University of Minnesota Press, 1992.
   Discusses the influence of music television on American popular culture.
Smith, Danyel. "House of Pain: The Fight Against Gangsta Rap Hits Capitol Hill," *Rolling Stone*, 7 April 1992, 22.
   Discusses several U.S. Senators' attempts (along with Jesse Jackson's) to get Congress to censor rap music that has violent or sexual themes.
Stewart, Andrea. "Lost in the Mix." *New Statesman & Society*, 7 February 1992, 31.
   Examines the complex relationship between ethnicity, Black culture, and contemporary popular music, and suggests that Caucasian popular musicians often have achieved success by liberally borrowing from Black music, thereby robbing Blacks of their identity.

Chapter 5: Sports

Blum, Debra F. "Rumbles on the Court." *Chronicle of Higher Education*, 2 March 1994, A34-35.
    Reports on the aggressive, confrontational behavior of some high-profile college basketball coaches and the effect on players and fans.
Cahn, Susan K. *Coming on Strong: Gender and Sexuality in Twentieth-Century American Sports.* New York: Macmillan, 1994.
    A study of the role and image of the female athlete in American culture from the early twentieth century to the present.
Early, Gerald. *Tuxedo Junction: Essays on American Culture.* New York: Ecco Press, 1989.
    Contains several essays on professional boxing and African-American culture in urban America.
"Game Plan." Editorial in *The Economist*, 19 March 1994, 108.
    Argues that television blurs the distinction between sports and entertainment.
George, Nelson. *Elevating the Game: Black Men and Basketball.* New York: Harper-Collins, 1992.
    Examines the contributions of African-American basketball players in refining the way the game is played.
Oleksak, Michael M., and Mary Adams Oleksak. *Beisbol: Latin Americans and the Grand Old Game.* Grand Rapids, MI: Masters Press, 1991.
    Discusses the contributions of Latin American players and coaches to the "All-American" game of baseball.
Schrof, Joanie M. "A Sporting Chance?" *U.S. News and World Report*, 11 April 1994, 51-53.
    Reports on female athletic programs in American schools and suggests that women athletes are still second-class citizens, twenty-two years after the passage of Title IX, which required equal distribution of resources to men's and women's athletics.
Will, George. *Men at Work.* New York: Macmillan, 1992.
    Examines the careers of four exemplary baseball professionals: manager Tony LaRussa, pitcher Orel Hirshiser, outfielder Tony Gwynn, and shortstop Cal Ripkin, Jr.

Chapter 6: Journalism

Bird, Elizabeth. *For Enquiring Minds: A Cultural Study of Supermarket Tabloids.* Knoxville: University of Tennessee Press, 1992.
    Traces the roots, recurrent themes, and formulas of tabloid journalism and speculates about its influence on and popularity among American readers.
Joachim Maitre, H. "The Tilt of the News." *Current* (March/April 1994):4-9.
    Argues that mainstream news reporting in the United States is seriously flawed by a liberal bias.
Love, Robert, ed. *The Best of the Rolling Stone: Twenty-Five Years of Journalism on the Edge.* New York: Doubleday, 1993.
    A compilation of stories from *Rolling Stone* magazine.
Manoff, Robert Karl, and Michael Schudson, eds. *Reading the News.* New York: Pantheon, 1986.
    A collection of essays on the "who, what, when, where, why, and how" of contemporary journalism.
Parenti, Michael. *Inventing Reality: The Politics of News Media.* New York: St. Martin's Press, 1993.
    Critiques the notion of a free press and examines the ideological and economic conditions under which the American news media operate.
Sabato, Larry J. *Feeding Frenzy: How Attack Journalism Has Transformed American Politics.* New York: Free Press, 1991.
    Studies abuses and excess in news coverage of political scandals.

Squires, James D. *Read All About It!: The Corporate Takeover of America's Newspaper.* New York: Random House, 1993.
> Looks at how conglomeration and the push toward high profit has affected the daily newspaper business.

Wolf, Naomi. "Are Opinions Male?" *New Republic,* 19 November 1993, 20-24.
> Examines the small percentage of women appearing on programs like *Crossfire* and writing for the op-ed pages of major newspapers; asks whether there is a conscious or unconscious bias against women's opinions.

Zoglin, Richard et. al. "Easing the Sleaze." *Time,* 6 December 1993, 72-74.
> Reports on tabloid programs such as *Hardcopy* and the effect of such programs on mainstream television news.

Chapter 7: Movies

Berger, Arthur Asa, ed. *Film in Society.* New Brunswick, NJ: Transaction Books, 1980.
> Semiological critique of movies in contemporary American culture.

Bryan, Stuart, and Elisabeth Weis, eds. *The National Society of Film Critics on Movie Comedy.* New York: Penguin Books, 1977.
> Overview of critical perspectives on comedy in film.

Ehrenreich, Barbara ."Why Don't We Like the Human Body?" *Time,* 1 July 1991, 80.
> Amusing essay that accounts for the current success of slasher movies.

Gates, Henry Louis, Jr. "Niggaz with Latitude." *The New Yorker,* 21 March 1994, 143.
> Discussion of Black directors Allen and Albert Hughes's film "Menace II Society."

MacCann, Richard Dyer. *Film and Society.* New York: Scribner, 1964.
> Part of the Scribner research anthology series, this edition focuses on the relationship between film and culture.

Quart, Leonard, and Albert Auster. *American Film and Society.* New York: Praeger, 1984.
> Historical perspective on American moviemaking since World War II.

Stead, Peter. *Film and the Working Class.* London: Routledge, 1989.
> Part of the series entitled "Cinema and Society"; this volume examines the feature film in British and American society.

Chapter 8: Leisure

Gabriel, Gail. "Games People Play." *Success,* April 1992, 20-1.
> Reports on the popularity of a number of recent computer and board games for adults.

Hall, Trisha. "A Nation of Watchers Forgets How to Play." *New York Times,* 31 March 1993, C1.
> Discusses research that shows Americans are losing the skills necessary to enjoy free time.

Kaplan, Max. *Essays on Leisure: Human and Policy Issues.* Rutherford, NJ: Fairleigh Dickinson University Press, 1991.
> A sociological study of leisure activities and their effects on personal, social, and public policy issues.

Neulinger, John. *The Psychology of Leisure.* Second edition. Springfield, MA: Charles C. Thomas Publishers, 1981
> Examines leisure from a psychological perspective, proposing that leisure is a "state of mind" rather than simply any nonwork-related activity.

Rybczynski, Witold. *Waiting for the Weekend.* New York: Penguin, 1991.
> Studies the profound influences of leisure time from ancient Rome to contemporary America, and looks particularly at the institution of the weekend.

Schor, Juliet B. *The Overworked American: The Unexpected Decline of Leisure.* New York: BasicBooks, 1991.
> Examines the decline in the amount and quality of American's leisure time and of-

fers suggestions on how to break the work-and-spend cycle in order to protect the individual's "right to free time."

Utne Reader. January/February 1994.
Special leisure issue with six essays on the topic, including Deborah Balwin, "As Busy as We Wanna Be"; Charlie Creekmore, "Theory of Leisure Trap"; and Stephan Rechtschaffen, "Why an Empty Hour Scares Us."

Wallace, Bruce. "Hours of Labor." *Mclean's,* 14 March 1994, 38-41.
Reports on proposals for shorter work hours in industries across Europe.

Worshop, Richard. "Gambling Boom." *CQ Researcher,* 18 March 1994, 241-61.
Reports on one of America's fastest-growing leisure pursuits, i.e., gambling.

ACKNOWLEDGMENTS

Text Credits

"Americans Use of Time Project, University of Maryland." Chart from *American Demographics* Magazine, November, 1990. Reprinted by permission of American Demographics, Inc.

Angelou, Maya, "Champion of the World." Reprinted by permission of Random House, Inc. From "I Know Why the Caged Bird Sings" by Maya Angelou. Copyright © 1969 by Maya Angelou.

Barthel, Diane, "A Gentleman and a Consumer." Reprinted by permission of Temple University Press from "Putting on Appearances: Gender and Advertising," by Diane Barthel. Copyright © 1988 by Temple University.

Berger, Arthur Asa, "'He's Everything You're Not. . .': A Semilogical Analysis of "Cheers." Reprinted with permission from Television Studies: Textual Analysis, eds., Gary Burns and Robert Thompson. Praeger Publishers, an imprint of Greenwood Publishing Group, Westport, CT, 1989, pp. 89-101. Copyright © 1989 by Gary Burns and Robert Thompson.

Berger, Arthur Asa, "Seven Points on the Game of Football." Excerpt reprinted by permission of Sage Publications, Inc. From Media Analysis Techniques by Arthur Asa Berger, 1991, (pp. 107-117).

Berman, Ronald, "Soaps Day and Night." Excerpt from "How Television Sees Its Audience." Reprinted by permission of the author.

Bloom, Allan, "Music." Reprinted with permission of Simon & Schuster, Inc. From The Closing of the American Mind by Alan Bloom. Copyright © 1987 by Alan Bloom.

Boorstin, Daniel, "The Republic of Technology and the Limits of Prophecy." Excerpt reprinted by permission of Harper-Collins Publishers, Inc. from The Republic of Technology by Daniel Boorstin. Copyright © 1978 by Daniel Boorstin.

Burciaga, Jose Antonio, "A Magazine for the Dead." From Drink Cultura. Reprinted by permission of Joshua Odel Editions.

Chapkis, Wendy, "Skin Deep." Reprinted by permission of South End Press. From *Beauty Secrets: Women and the Politics of Appearance* by Wendy Chapkis.

Charity, Arthur, "What Readers Want: A Vote for a Very Different Role Model." Reprinted from the Columbia Journalism Review, November/December, 1993. Copyright © 1993. Reprinted with the author's permission.

Combs, James, "Jockpop: Popular Sports and Politics." Reprinted by permission from Popular Press. From Polpop: Politics and Popular Culture in America by James Combs.

Curry, Pamela Malcolm and Jiobu, Robert, M., "Big Mac and 'Caneton A L'Orange': Eating, Icon, and Rituals." Reprinted by permission of Popular Press from Rituals and Ceremonies in Popular Culture, ed., Ray B. Browne.

Denby, David, "As the World Turns." Reprinted by permission of the author. Copyright © 1989 by David Denby.

Dyer, Richard, "Dracula and Desire." Reprinted from Sight & Sound, Vol. 3, January, 1993. Reprinted by permission of Sight & Sound.

Ehrenreich, Barbara, "Spudding Out." Reprinted by permission of Pantheon Books, a division of Random House, Inc. From *The Worst Years of Our Lives* by Barbara Ehrenreich. Copyright © 1990 by Barbara Ehrenreich.

Ehrenreich, Barbara, "The Cult of Busyness." Reprinted by permission of Pantheon Books, a division of Random House, Inc. From The Worst Years of Our Lives by Barbara Ehrenreich. Copyright © 1990 by Barbara Ehrenreich.

Evans, Walter, "Monster Movies." Originally published in *Journal of Popular Film and Television*, Vol. 2, No. 4, Fall, 1973, pp. 353-365. Reprinted by permission of the Journal of Popular Film and Television.

Ewen, Stuart and Elizabeth, "In the Shadow of the Image." Second edition copyright © 1992 by the Regents of the University of Minnesota. Orginally published by McGraw-Hill, 1982. Copyright © 1982 by Stuart and Elizabeth Ewen.

Frith, Simon, "Rock and Sexuality." Reprinted with permission of Constable Publishers from Sound Effects: Youth Leisure and Politics of Rock and Roll by Simon Frith. Copyright © 1981 by Simon Frith. Reprinted by Pantheon Books, a division of Random House, Inc.

Fowles, Jib, "Advertising's Fifteen Basic Appeals." Reprinted from Etc. Vol. 39, No. 3, with permission of the International Society for General Semantics, Concord, California.

Frank, Thomas, "Busy Hip." Reprinted by permission. Copyright © 1992, The Baffler, PO Box 378293, Chicago, IL 60637.

Gates, Henry Louis, Jr., "2 Live Crew Decoded." *New York Times*, June 19, 1990, Section A, p. 23. Copyright © 1980/90 by The New York Times Company. Reprinted by permission.

Gorman, James, "The Inside Story of a Video Game You Can Get Inside." From *Discover Magazine*, August, 1986. Copyright © by James Gorman.

Greenfield, Jeff, "The Black and White Truth about Baseball." Reprinted by permission of Sterling Lord Literistic, Inc. from The Black and White Truth by Jeff Greenfield. Copyright © 1991 by Jeff Greenfield.

Grossberger, Lewis, "Triumph of the Wheel." Reprinted by permission from *Rolling Stone*, December 4, 1986. Straight Arrow Publishers, Inc., 1986. All rights reserved.

Hansen, Christine Hall and Ronald D., "Popular Music and Individual Differences." From *The Journal of Broadcasting and Electronic Media*, Summer, 1991. Reprinted by permission of Broadcast Education Association.

Heuck, Douglas. "Freddy Krueger: Twisted Role Model." October 27, 1991. Reprinted by permission of The Pittsburgh Press.

Hunter, Stephen, "Review of Nightmare on Elm Street." Used courtesy of The Baltimore Sun Company. Copyright © 1989 The Baltimore Sun and Stephen Hunter.

Kaler, Anne K., "*Golden Girls:* Feminine Archetypal Patterns of the Complete Women." From *Journal of Popular Culture*, Vol. 15, No. 1, Summer, 1981. Reprinted with permission.

Kanfer, Stefan, "The Greatest Game." Copyright © 1973 Time Inc. Reprinted by permission.

Katz, Jon, "Rock, Rap and Movies Bring You the News." Reprinted by permission from *Rolling Stone*, March 5, 1992. Straight Arrow Publishers, Inc., 1992. All rights reserved.

King, Stephen, "Why We Crave Horror Movies." Reprinted with permission. Copyright © Stephen King. All rights reserved.

Kottak, Conrad P., "Television and Cultural Behavior." Reprinted by permission of Wadsworth Publishing, Co. From Prime Time Society. Copyright © 1990.

Lee, Spike, "Do the Right Thing Production Notes." Reprinted by permission of Simon and Schuster, Inc. From "Do the Right Thing" by Spike Lee and Lisa Jones. Copyright © 1989 by Spike Lee.

Leo, John, "The Indignation of Barbie." Copyright © October 12, 1992 by U.S. News and World Report. Reprinted by permission.

Lewis, Jon, "Punks in L.A.: It's Kiss or Kill." From *Journal of Popular Culture*, Fall, 1988. Reprinted by permission.

Marsden, Michael T., "Television Viewing as Ritual." Reprinted by permission of Popular Press. An excerpt from Rituals and Ceremonies in Popular Culture, ed. Ray Browne, 1980.

Miller, Mark Crispin, "Family Feud." Reprinted by permission of Northwestern University Press from "Boxed In: The Culture of TV."

Modelski, Tania, "Soap Opera, Melodrama and Women's Anger." Reprinted from "Loving with a Vengeance: Mass-Produced Fantasies for Women" By permission of the publisher, Routledge, New York, 1982.

Moog, Carol, "Media Mirrors." Excerpt (pp. 21-35) from "Are They Selling Her Lips?" by Carol Moog. Copyright © by Carol Moog. Illustrations: Copyright © by permission of William Morrow & Company, Inc.

Motz, Marilyn Ferris, "'Seen Through Rose-Colored Glasses': The Barbie Doll in American Society." Reprinted by permission of the publisher. From *Popular Culture: An Introductory Text*, eds. Jack Nachbar and Kevin Lause (Bowling Green, Ohio: Bowling Green State University Popular Press).

Nye, Russell B., "Eight Ways of Looking at an Amusement Park." Reprinted by permission of Popular Press. From *Journal of Popular Culture*, Vol. 15, No. 1, Summer, 1981.

Pollack, Sydney, "The Way We Are." Copyright © 1992 The American Enterprise. Distributed by The New York Times Special Features/Syndication Sales.

Poneman, Jonathan, "Grunge & Glory." Originally published in "Details." Reprinted from *Vogue*, December, 1992. Reprinted by permission of the author.

Postman, Neil and Powers, Steve, "The Bias of Language, the Bias of Pictures." Used by permission of Viking Penguin, a division of Penguin Books USA, Inc. From How to Watch TV News by Neil Postman and Steve Powers. Copyright © 1992 by Neil Postman and Steve Powers.

Rice, Berkeley, "The Selling of Lifestyles." Reprinted with permission from *Psychology Today* magazine. Copyright © 1988 by Sussex Publishers, Inc.

Rose, Phyllis, "Shopping and Other Spiritual Adventures in America Today." Used by permission of Bantam Doubleday Dell Publishing Group, Inc. From "Never Say Good-bye" by Phyllis Rose. Copyright © 1991 by Phyllis Rose.

Rosenblatt, Roger, "Journalism and the Larger Truth." Copyright © 1984 Time, Inc. Reprinted by permission.

Rounds, Kate, "Why Men Fear Women's Teams." Reprinted by permission of *Ms.* magazine. From *Ms.* magazine, January/February, 1991. Copyright © 1991.

Rybczynski, Witold, "The Problem of Leisure." Used by permission of Viking Penguin, a division of Penguin Books USA, Inc. From "Waiting for the Weekend" by Witold Rybczynski. Copyright © 1991 by Witold Rybczynski.

Samuels, David, "The Rap on Rap." From *The New Republic*, November 11, 1991.

Schaap, Dick, "So Much of the Joy Is Gone." Reprinted by permission of the author. Copyright © 1992 by Dick Schaap.

Schaefermeyer, Mark J., "Film criticism." Reprinted with permission of Lexington Books, an imprint of Macmillan Publishing Company From Mass Media and Society, ed., Alan Wells. Copyright © 1987 by Lexington Books.

Schmalz, Jeffrey, "An Outsider in My World." *New York Times*, December 20, 1992. Copyright © 1992 by The New York Times Company. Reprinted by permission.

Schmalz, Jeffrey, "Covering AIDS and Living It." *New York Times*, December 20, 1992. Copyright © 1992 by The New York Times Company. Reprinted by permission.

Schor, Juliet, "Exiting the Squirrel Cage." Chapter 6 and Notes reprinted by permission of BasicBooks, A Division of HarperCollins Publishers, Inc. From *The Overworked American: The Unexpected Decline of Leisure* by Juliet Schor. Copyright © 1991 by BasicBooks, A Division of HarperCollins Publishers, Inc.

Schrank, Jeffrey, "Sport and the American Dream." Used by permission of Delacorte Press, a division of Bantam Doubleday Dell Publishing Group Inc. From *Snap, Crackle, and Popular Taste: The Illusion . . .* by Jeff Schrank. Copyright © 1977 by Jeffrey Schrank.

Schwoch, James, et al., "Drug Abuse, Race Relations, and the Prime Time News Program." Reprinted by permission of the State University Press. From *Media Knowledge: Readings In Popular Culture, Pedagogy and Critical Citizenship*. Copyright © 1992 by the State University Press Albany. All rights reserved.

Segal, Debra, "Tales from the Cutting Room Floor." Reprinted by special permission from *Harper's* magazine, November, 1993. Copyright © 1993 by *Harper's* magazine.

Smith, Danyel, "Dreaming America." From *Spin*, August, 1993. Reprinted by permission of Spin.

Solomon, Jack, "Masters of Desire." Reprinted by permission of The Putnum Publishing Group/Jeremy P. Tarcher, Inc. from *The Signs of Our Times* by Jack Solomon. Copyright © 1988 Jack Solomon, Ph.D.

Spring, Jim, "Exercising the Brain." From *American Demographics* magazine, October, 1993, pp. 55-56. Copyright © 1993, American Demographics, Inc. Ithaca, NY.

Steinem, Gloria, "Sex, Lies, and Advertising." Reprinted by permission of the author.

Tham, Hilary, "Barbie's Shoes." Copyright © by Hilary Tham. Reprinted by permission of Hilary Tham and Three Continents Press, United States and Canada.

Wallace, Michele, "When Black Feminism Faces the Music and the Music Is Rap." *New York Times*, July 29, 1990. Copyright © The New York Times Company. Reprinted by permission.

Waters, Harry, "Life According to TV." *Newsweek*, December 6, 1982. Copyright © 1982 Newsweek, Inc. All rights reserved. Reprinted by permission.

Wells, Allan, "Popular Music: Emotional Use and Management." From the *Journal of Popular Culture*, Summer, 1988. Reprinted by permission.

Photograph and Illustration Credits

Chapter 1: Photograph courtesy of Mattel Toys.

Chapter 2: Photograph from Benetton Services Corporation.

Chapter 3: Drawing by Glen Baxter. Copyright © 1991 The New Yorker Magazine, Inc.

Chapter 4: Photograph from Lord, Dentsu & Partners/NY. Copyright ©1993 TDK Electronics Corporation

Chapter 5: Photograph by Mimi Forsyth; courtesy of Monkmeyer Press.

Chapter 6: Drawing by Dana Fradon. Copyright © 1992 The New Yorker Magazine, Inc.

Chapter 7: Photograph courtesy of Photofest

Chapter 8: Photograph courtesy of FPG International

INDEX BY RHETORICAL MODE

INDEX BY ACADEMIC DISCIPLINE

INDEX BY AUTHOR AND TITLE